THE

ORIGIN OF PAGAN IDOLATRY

ASCERTAINED FROM

HISTORICAL TESTIMONY

AND

CIRCUMSTANTIAL EVIDENCE.

BY GEORGE STANLEY FABER, B. D.

RECTOR OF LONG-NEWTON.

Every reasonable Hypothesis should be supported on a fact.
WARBURTON's Div. Leg. vol. v. p. 458.

THREE VOLUMES.

VOL. I.

London:

Printed by A. J. Valpy, Tooke's Court, Chancery Lane,

FOR F. AND C. RIVINGTONS;

ST. PAUL's CHURCH YARD.

1816.

PLATE I.

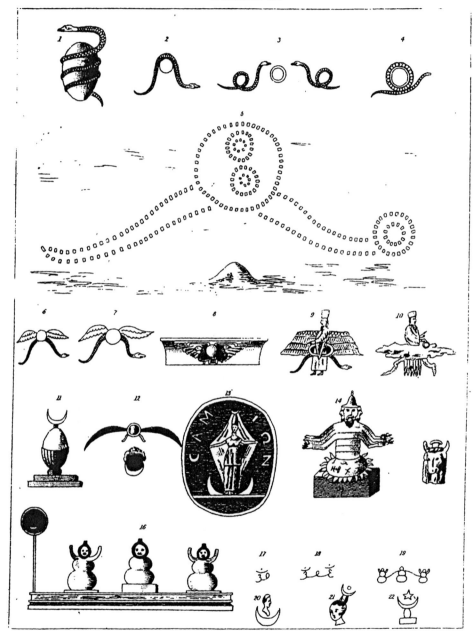

To the Right Hon.ble and Revnd GEORGE, LORD VISCOUNT BARRINGTON,
this Plate is respectfully inscribed by his obliged humble Servant.
THE AUTHOR.

TO THE

HONOURABLE AND RIGHT REVEREND,

SHUTE BARRINGTON, L. L. D.

LORD BISHOP OF DURHAM,

THIS WORK

IS RESPECTFULLY INSCRIBED,

IN ACKNOWLEDGEMENT

OF THE

MANY UNSOLICITED FAVOURS,

WHICH

HE HAS CONFERRED UPON

HIS OBLIGED

AND

DUTIFUL HUMBLE SERVANT

THE AUTHOR.

'I esteem all Thy precepts concerning all things to be right, and I hate every false way'   Ps. 119:128

PREFACE.

THE general argument of the following work is briefly this.

The various systems of Pagan Idolatry in different parts of the world correspond so closely, both in their evident purport and in numerous points of arbitrary resemblance, that they cannot have been struck out independently in the several countries where they have been established, but must have all originated from some common source. But, if they all originated from a common source, then either one nation must have communicated its peculiar theology to every other people in the way of peaceful and voluntary imitation; or that same nation must have communicated it to every other people through the medium of conquest and violence; or lastly all nations must in the infancy of the world have been assembled together in a single region and in a single community, must at that period and in that state of society have agreed to adopt the theology in question, and must thence as from a common centre have carried it to all quarters of the globe.

These are the only three modes, in which the universal accordance of the Gentiles in their religious speculations can possibly be accounted for. But, as the incredibility of the first, and as the equal incredibility and impossibility of the second, may be shewn without much difficulty; the third alone remains to be adopted. Now this third mode both perfectly harmonizes with the general purport of Heathen Idolatry, and minutely accords with an historical fact which is declared to us on the very highest authority. An examination of the theology of the Gentiles forces us to conclude, that all mankind were once assembled together in a single community, and that they afterwards spread themselves in detached bodies over the face of the whole earth: Holy Scripture asserts, that such was actually the fact.

Under these circumstances, I am necessarily led to treat largely of the dispersion from Babel and specially to insist upon an important peculiarity in that dispersion which has hitherto been entirely overlooked. I am also led to discuss certain other subsequent great movements, which stand closely connected with the peculiarity alluded to. In short, the events, which occurred in the plain of Shinar, have stamped a character upon the whole mass of mankind that remains vividly impressed even to modern times. The powerful and martial family, that once obtained a decided preëminence over their brethren, have never down to the present hour, ceased with a strong hand to vindicate their superiority.

March 4, 1815.

ERRATA.

~~~~~

VOLUME I.

CONTENTS.

BOOK I.

CHAPTER I.

CHAPTER III.

CHAPTER IV.

CHAPTER V.

HEATHEN Cosmogonies were not borrowed from that of Moses, though they
  bear a close resemblance to it.   They all originated from a common
  source : and, though the Gentiles delivered them in a corrupt manner,
  yet Moses really declared nothing but what was already for the most
  part well known.   The Pagans however have defaced the truth ; both
  by rejecting the belief in a proper creation, and by mingling their cosmogonies with the history of the deluge.   Of these, the one was the
  natural consequence of the other : for each world was thought to be
  formed out of the wreck of a prior inundated world   -   -   ib.

BOOK II.

CHAPTER I.

Concerning the garden of Paradise and mount Ararat - 281

CHAPTER II.

Respecting pagan transcripts of Paradise and mount Ararat   314

CHAPTER III.

*Respecting the connection of Paradise and Ararat with conse-
crated lakes and islands*   -   -   -   357

CHAPTER IV.

CHAPTER V.

CHAPTER VI.

On the origin and import of the veneration paid to the bull, the lion, and the eagle - - - - 402

CHAPTER VII.

On the origin and import of the worship of the serpent -   -   439

CHAPTER VIII.

On the origin and purport of sacrificial rites - - 465

EXPLANATION OF THE FIGURES IN PLATE I.

Fig.

1. Sacred snake and mundane egg of the Tyrians.
2. Snake and globe from the Isiac table.
3. Two snakes and ring of the Chinese.
4. Snake and globe of the Hindoos from a painting of Vira-Bhadra. Moor's Hind. Panth. pl. 25.
5. Druidical temple of Abury, in the form of a serpent attached to a circle. The sacred high place of Silbury hill appears in the foreground between the head and tail of the serpent.
6. Winged snake and globe from the Isiac table.
7. Winged snake and globe from the ruins of the Persian Naki Rustan.
8. Winged globe with double serpent from the cornice of the Egyptian temple of Essnay.
9. The Persian god Azon or Mithras.
10. The Persian god Azon or Mithras slightly varied.
11. The god Lunus of Heliopolis.
12. The winged globe and serpent hovering over the head of Osiris, which was annually placed in a boat shaped like the Moon, and was thus thought to sail spontaneously to Phœnicia.
13. The Juno of the Samians, standing in the lunette or sacred ship.
14. The triplicated great father of the Japanese.
15. The head of the sacred bull of Osiris with the modius between his horns.
16. Bal-Rama, Subhadra in the centre, and Jagan-Nath.
17. Indian Pranava or name of deity.
18. The same formed into a cypher.
19. Mode, in which the hieroglyphical cypher, and thence the Pranava, has originated.
20. The god Lunus of Carrhæ.
21. The head of Cali from the Courma Avatar of Hindostan.
22. The god Lunus of Carrhæ.

VOLUME II.

BOOK III.

CHAPTER I.

CHAPTER II.

Miscellaneous traditions relative to the period between the creation and the deluge - - - - - 34

CHAPTER III.

On the antediluvian and diluvian history, as exhibited in the Zend-Avesta   58

CHAPTER IV.

Pagan accounts of an universal deluge - - - 107

PAGAN accounts of the deluge have generally some reference to the creation :
a circumstance, which originated from the doctrine of an endless succes-

<hr>

CHAPTER V.

Respecting the sacred books - - - 147

<hr>

I. There was a general notion, that certain sacred books were either composed
   or preserved or recovered from the deluge by the great father - ib.

CHAPTER VI.

Pagan accounts of the deluge, as erroneously confined by local
appropriation to particular regions   -   -   157

THE pagan accounts of partial deluges have in a great measure originated
    from the phraseology of the commemorative Mysteries   -   ib.

BOOK IV.

CHAPTER I.

Concerning the identity and astronomical character of the great gods of the Gentiles - - - -

ALL the gods of the Gentiles resolve themselves into one person, the great universal father - - - - -

CHAPTER II.

*Respecting certain remarkable opinions which the Gentiles enter-
tained of the Sun* - - - - - 215

CHAPTER III.

Respecting the division of the gentile mythologists into two great primeval sects

CHAPTER IV.

*Respecting the human character of the great father, as exhibited
  in the Osiric or Bacchic or Saivic or Brahmenical superstition*   -   -   -   -   -   -   237

CHAPTER V.

Respecting the human character of the great father, as exhibited in the Buddhic or Thothic or Hermetic or Samanèan theology - · · · · · 327

CHAPTER VI.

*Respecting the union of the two great superstitions in the worship
of Jagan-Nath, Saturn, and Baal*

EXPLANATION OF THE FIGURES IN PLATE II.

VOLUME III.

BOOK V.

CHAPTER I.

CHAPTER II.

CHAPTER III.

Respecting the navicular, infernal, and human, character of the great mother - - - - - - 23

CHAPTER IV.

CHAPTER V.

———◆———

━━━━━━━━━━━━━━━━━━

CHAPTER VI.

———◆———

CHAPTER VII.

Concerning the places used by the Pagans for religious worship   193

CHAPTER VIII.

BOOK VI.

CHAPTER I.

Respecting the primeval union of all mankind in a single body politic,
and the building of the tower of Babel - - 359

CHAPTER II.

Respecting the chronological epoch and duration of the primeval Iranian empire, and the peculiar form of its civil polity 377

CHAPTER III.

Respecting the primitive division of the world among the children of
Noah, the triads of the Gentiles, the confusion of languages,
and the mode of the dispersion from Babel - - 446

CHAPTER IV.

Respecting the various settlements and migrations of the unblended part of the military caste - - - 499

CHAPTER V.

Respecting the Shepherd-kings of Egypt, and the various settlements
of the military caste in consequence of their expulsion   -   526

CHAPTER VI.

*Respecting the mode, in which Pagan Idolatry originated; the
resemblance between the Ritual Law of Moses and the
Ritual Ordinances of the Gentiles; and certain peculiarities in the several characters of the
Messiah and the great father.*

EXPLANATION OF THE FIGURES IN PLATE III.

The rise and progress of Temple Architecture.

Fig.

1. THE lunar ship of Osiris, with the oracular navel containing the god in the centre of it. From Pococke.

2. The lunar ship resting on the summit of Ararat, the original mountain of the Moon.

3. The sacred mountain with two natural peaks, viewed as a physical copy, on an immense scale, of the two horns of the lunette or of the stem and stern of the ship.

4. The lunar ship, with the great father supplying to it the place of a mast, resting on the top of the mountain of the Moon.

5. The sacred mountain with three natural peaks, viewed as a physical copy of the two horns and mast of the lunette. This is a supposed form of Meru; and the real form of the sacred mount Olivet, on the three peaks of which were worshipped Astoreth, Chemosh, and Milcom.

6. Japanese temple at Quano, built as a copy of the lunar mountain. From Kæmpfer's Japan. pl. xxxii. fig. 14.

7. Indian pagoda at Tanjore, supporting the hull of a ship. From Maurice's Ind. Ant.

9. Great pagoda at Tanjore, terminating, like the fabled Meru, in three peaks. From Maurice's Ind. Ant.

Fig.

9. Ancient pagoda at Deogur, sustaining the mystic egg and trident; which last is a copy of the lunar ship Argha with its mast. From Maurice's Ind. Ant.

10. Temple of Belus at Babylon, according to Herodotus. This seems to have been the ancient tower of Babel completed by Nebuchadnezzar. It is a supposed form of Meru.

11. An Egyptian pyramid near Sakarra. From Norden.

12. Mexican temple of the Sun and Moon. From Maurice's Ind. Ant.

13. Great pyramid of Cairo.

14. Shoemadoo, the great temple of Buddha at Pegu. From Symes's Embassy to Ava.

15. A holy mountain with a consecrated cavern in its side.

16. Section of the great pyramid of Cairo, exhibiting its dark central chamber or artificial cavern. From Pococke.

17. Holy two-peaked artificial tumulus of New-Grange with Mercurial columns and door of approach to its central chamber. From Ledurch's Ant. of Ireland.

18. The Ark, resting among the crags of Ararat, and exhibiting the semblance of a dark grotto.

19. Rock temple of Jugneth Subha at Ellora, excavated out of the bowels of a mountain in imitation of the Ark. Such places of worship frequently occur in India, Persia, Egypt, Palestine, and the Crimea. From Asiat. Research. vol. vi.

20. Gateway of the Egyptian temple at Edfu, designed to imitate the two-peaked mountain and sacred cavernal door. From Norden.

21. A supposed form of mount Meru, surmounted by the Ida-vratta or sacred mundane ring of hills.

22. A temple of the sort usually called *Druidical,* designed to imitate the Ida-vratta on the top of the lunar mountain.

23. A temple of Buddha in Ceylon, uniting the two forms of the egg and the pyramid. From Asiat. Research. vol. vi.

24. A pyramid at Sakarra, uniting the two forms of the egg and the pyramid. From Norden.

25. A Persian fire-temple, exhibiting the form of the egg. From Hyde.

26. The Pantheon at Rome, exhibiting the form of the egg.

27. Oviform Tolmen in Cornwall, with the sacred door or orifice used in the initiation of aspirants. From Borlase.

28. A holy grove of palms.

29. Portico of an imitative Grecian temple.

Fig.

30. An Egyptian temple at Essnay, exhibiting conjointly the mountain, the cavern, and the grove. The cornice over the portal is decorated with the hieroglyphic of the winged globe and serpent. See Plate I. Fig. 8. From Norden.

31. Kitt's Cotty house in Kent. An artificial cell or cavern of Ceridwen, within which aspirants were wont to be inclosed, and from which they were reputed to be born again. From Borlase.

SUBSCRIBERS.

A

Tʜᴇ Very Rev. the Dean of Ardagh
George Allan, Esq. M. P.
Thomas Athorpe, Esq. Dinnington.   2 copies
Rev. Chris. Anstey, Vicar of Norton
John Arden, Esq. Pepper Hall, Yorkshire

B

The Earl of Bridgewater
Lord Viscount Barrington
Sir David Baird, Bart.
Sir Thomas Baring, Bart.   2 copies
Sir Thomas Bernard, Bart.
Lady Bernard
Joseph Baker, Esq. Wimpole Street
Rev. T. Baker, Rector of Whitburne
Rev. C. Baillie, Archdeacon of Cleveland
Rev. G. Baring, Durstan
John Thomas Batt, Esq.
Rev. James Barmby, Fellow of University College
Rev. W. L. Beaufort, Upton

Mr. John Beart, Yarmouth,   2 copies
Messrs. Beilby and Knott, Birmingham
Rev. J. Berry, Warminster
George Best, Esq.
Rev. Mr. Birkett, Vicar of Kelloe, Durham
Colonel Bosville
Rev. C. Brackenbury, Residency of Hydrabad
Rev. J. Brewster, Rector of Egglecliffe
George Brown, Esq. Stockton
Isaac Hawkins Browne, Esq.
Rev. Dr. Buchanan, Edinburgh
Rev. Dr. Buckeridge
J. M. Buck, Esq. Montagu Place
Rev. G. Burrard, Rector of Middleton Tyas
John Burnet, Esq. Kemnay
Joseph Butterworth, Esq. M. P.

C

His Grace the Archbishop of Canterbury
His Grace the Archbishop of Cashell
The Very Rev. the Dean of Canterbury
The Very Rev. the Dean of Chester
Canterbury Chapter Library
John Carr, Esq. Dunstan House
Rev. W. Carr, Bolton Abbey
John Cator, Esq. Bickenham, near Bromley, Kent
Catherine Hall, Cambridge
Dean and Chapter of Chichester
Dr. Adam Clarke
Messrs. Christopher and Jennett, Stockton
Church Missionary Library
Rev. J. Collinson, Rector of Gateshead
Mrs. C. Comyn, Vicars Hill
William Courtenay, Esq. M. P.
Samuel Coxe, Esq. Foundling Hospital
Thomas Coutts, Esq.
Rev. Dr. Craven, late Master of St. John's, Cambridge
John Cros, Esq. Hull

Miss Currer, Eshton Hall
Rev. D. R. Currer, Gledstone House
William Cunninghame, Esq. Lanshaw
J. C. Curwen, Esq. Workington Hall
Miss M. Cust, Newbiggen Hall, Westmorland

D

The Lord Bishop of Durham,   5 copies
The Lord Bishop of St. David's
Darlington Library
W. Davidson, Esq. Kensington
Rev. Dr. Davidson, Edinburgh
Derby Book Club
Rev. I. Dudley
Dudley Library
Durham Chapter Library
Rev. D. Durell, Prebendary of Durham

E

The Very Rev. the Dean and Chapter of Ely
Sir Robert Johnson Eden, Bart. Windleston
East India Company,   6 copies
Rev. E. Ellerton, Magdalen College, Oxon
G. Scott Elliott, Esq. Hans Place
Rev. Mr. Ellis, Doncaster
Hon. M. Elphinstone, Hydrabad
G. F. Evans, Esq. Laxter Hall, Stamford
Rev. T. Ewbank, Rector of Elton
Exeter College Library

F

Earl Fitzwilliam
Earl of Fife
C. D. Faber, Esq. Swinton
Richard Faber, Esq. M. D.
Rev. T. Faber, Vicar of Calverley
Rev. W. Faber
Rev. C. Fanshaw, Rector of Dungie

J. Fawcett, Esq. Knosthorpe
Benjamin Flounders, Esq. Yarm
Dr. Franck, Temple
Francis Freeling, Esq.
Strickland Freeman, Esq. Oxon

G

The Lord Bishop of Gloucester
The Very Rev. the Dean and Chapter of Gloucester
Rev. J. Gilpin, Vicar of Stockton
Charles Grant, Esq. M. P.
Rev. Dr. Gray, Prebendary of Durham

H

Earl of Harewood
Lady Charlotte Howard
Rev. Dr. Hales, Rector of Killesandra
Miss Hamilton
Right Hon. W. Hastings, Dailesford House
James Hastings, Esq. Rochdale
Richard Heber, Esq.
W. Hervey, Esq. Bradwell Grove
C. Hoare, Esq. Fleet Street
Brown Hodgson, Esq. Nentsbury Hall
John Hogg, Esq. Norton
George Lewis Hollingsworth, Esq.
Rev. N. Hollingsworth, Vicar of Haltwhistle
Simon Horner, Esq. Hull
Rev. R. Hudson, Hipperholme
Rev. C. Hoyle, Vicar of Overton
Rev. R. Humphreys, Leeds
Rev. N. Humphreys, Rector of Thorpe Mandeville
H. Hutchinson, Esq. Stockton
Hull Library
Hull Reading Room

J.

B. Jefferys, Esq. Throgmorton Street

K

Lord Kenyon
Rev. F. F. Knottesford, Stoke, Suffolk
King's College Library, Cambridge

L

Earl of Lonsdale
The Lord Bishop of Lichfield
Sir T. C. Liddell, Bart. Ravensworth Castle
Thomas Lane, Esq. Bramham Park
Rev. T. Lear, Vicar of Downton, Wilts
R. Leeson, Esq. Thurland Hall, Notts
C. H. Lichfield, Esq. Solicitor to the Treasury
Rev. G. H. Liddell, Rector of Boldon
M. Linning, Esq.
W. Little, Esq.
Mr. W. Horton Lloyd, New Ormond Street
J. W. Lubbock, Esq. M. P.

M

His Grace the Duke of Marlborough
The Earl of Macclesfield
Lord Viscount Midleton
Lord Viscount Milton
Lord Macdonald, 2 copies
Sir John Malcolm, Bart.
Sir J. M. Murray, Bart.
Sir Richard Musgrave, Bart.
General Macauley
———— Mangles, Esq. Hurley, Berks
J. M. Marriot, Esq. London
Mr. Marriott, Derby
Rev. Dr. Herbert Marsh, Margaret Professor of Divinity
Rev. E. Mellish, Vicar of Tudenham
Rev. John Mendham, Sutton Coldfield
George Mickle, Esq. Hydrabad
Rev. William Mills, Fellow of Magdalen College, Oxford
Walter Moir, Esq. Edinburgh

Rev. John Morris
Colonel Murray

N

The Lord Bishop of Norwich
Sir Henry Burrard Neale, Bart.
Rev. E. Neale, Taplow, Bucks
William Newnham, Esq. Farnham, Surrey
Norton Book Club

O

Messrs. Ogles, Duncan, and Cochran, London,   2 copies

P

Rev. Dr. Parkinson, Archdeacon of Leicester
E. Parry, Esq. Gower Street
Rev. D. M. Peacock, Rector of Stainton
———— Peacock, Esq. Norton
L. H. Petit, Esq. Lincoln's Inn
Dr. Perceval, M. D. Dublin
E. Protheroe, Esq. M. P. Harley Street
Rev. Dr. Prosser, Prebendary and Archdeacon of Durham
Rev. Dr. Pryce, Prebendary of Durham

Q

Queen's College Library, Cambridge

R

Sir John Reade, Bart.
Mrs. Raikes, Upper Grosvenor Street
John Reade, Esq. Ipsden House
Colonel Reed, Chipchase Castle
James Remington, Esq. Hillsborough, Sheffield
Mrs. Rusher, Melrose Hall, Wandsworth
Charles Russell, Esq. Hydrabad
Henry Russell, Esq. Hydrabad
J. W. Russell, Esq. Hydrabad

S

Earl Spencer
Lord Charles Spencer
Right Rev. Bishop Sandford
Sir John Sinclair, Bart.
Lady O. B. Sparrow
Sir Mark M. Sykes, Bart.
Rev. John Saunderson, Darfield
Salisbury Chapter Library
Rev. G. Sayer, late Rector of Egglescliffe
Jonathan Scott, Esq. Bath
Rev. L. Sharpe
John Albin Slack, Esq.
William Sleigh, Esq. Stockton
Mrs. Smith, Newcastle under Lyne
J. Smyth, Esq. Bowcliffe, Wetherby
H. Stokes, Esq. Brunswick Row
Mrs. Storey, Lockington, near Derby
Stockton Book Club
Rev. M. Surtees, Prebendary of Canterbury
Robert Surtees, Esq. Mainsforth

T

Rev. Dr. Tatham, Rector of Lincoln College, Oxford
Rev. R. Tatham, Fellow of St. John's College, Cambridge
W. Tilson, Esq. Watlington Park
Thomas Thompson, Esq. M. P.
Rev. —— Thomason, Calcutta
Samuel Thornton, Esq. M. P.
—— Thomas, Esq.
Rev. C. Thorpe, Rector of Ryton
Rev. F. Thurston, Caius College
G. Tollet, Esq. Betley Hall, Staffordshire
Provost of Trinity College, Dublin
Trinity College, Dublin, 2 copies
Trinity Hall Library, Cambridge
C. Turner, Esq. Wood Lodge, Kent
Mrs. Turrell, Thorn Hill, near Derby

V

Right Hon. N. Vansittart, Chancellor of the Exchequer
Rev. Ashton Vade, Vicar of Harding-stone
A. J. Valpy, Esq. Tooke's Court
Rev. Dr. Valpy, Reading
Rev. E. Valpy, Norwich
Miss Vansittart
Jasper Vaux, Esq.
W. Vavasour, Esq. Weston Hall

W

Sir Francis Wood, Bart.
Thomas Wainewright, Esq. Dudley
Sir Wathen Waller
Mrs. Walker, Aston Hall, Derby
Major Scott Waring
Edward Scott Waring, Esq. Bundlecund
Mrs. Scott Waring
John Waterhouse, Esq. Halifax
Lewis Way, Esq.
Rev. H. B. Whitfield, Fellow of St. John's College, Cambridge
Rev. T. White, Mary-le-bone
Rev. W. Wheeler, Chaplain to the Royal Military College
William Wilberforce, Esq. M.P.
Robert Wilkinson, Esq. Stockton
Dr. Willis, Belfast
Rev. John Wilson, Lincoln College
Matthew Wilson, Esq. Eshton Hall
Matthew Wilson, Esq. Manor House, Otley
Mr. Wilson, Bookseller, Hull
Wimondley House Library
Rev. F. Wrangham, Rector of Hunmanby

Y

His Grace the Archbishop of York
Right Hon. Charles Yorke, M. P.
York Chapter Library
York Subscription Library

THE ORIGIN

OF

PAGAN IDOLATRY.

BOOK I.

PLATE I.

To the Right Hon.ble and Rev.nd GEORGE, LORD VISCOUNT BARRINGTON,
this Plate is respectfully inscribed by his obliged humble Servant.
                                            THE AUTHOR.

CHAPTER I.

———

General Idea of the Mythology of Paganism.

———

T HE discussion of an intricate topic will always be rendered more easy and perspicuous to the reader, if its general result, as deduced by the person who has conducted it, be first presented to him. Such an arrangement possesses so many obvious advantages, that it is not lightly to be abandoned. In the investigation of mathematical truth, it has by common consent been preferred : and it will be found no less convenient, in prosecuting topics of a very different description. Among these, AN INQUIRY INTO THE ORIGIN OF PAGAN IDOLATRY may justly be specified. Here a variety of important conclusions necessarily depend upon the proof of certain leading positions. But those leading positions cannot all be demonstrated *at the same moment of time :* the establishment of them must be *successive.* Hence the author, as his subject progressively leads him to make remarks and to draw infe-rences, which, so far as their solidity is concerned, depend upon points not yet formally established, is frequently compelled to require, that some degree of credit may be given to his bare assertion. Each point *will* indeed be proved in its due order : but, for a season, it must occasionally be taken for granted. This being the case (nor could the matter be well ordered otherwise), it will be useful to give a brief introductory statement of the general result: how far that result be well founded, the reader must hereafter gradually judge for himself.

I. Holy Scripture, in more than one place, teaches us very unequivocally what were the objects of pagan adoration: and the knowledge, which we may thence collect, perfectly corresponds with the deductions that must inevitably be drawn from the universal system of ancient idolatry.

The inspired writers inform us, that the Gentiles, when they departed from the worship of the one true God, venerated, partly the host of heaven, and partly certain beings, who, in the New Testament, are usually called *Demonia*, and, in the Old, *Baalim* or *Siddim*. The first of these appellations has, in our English version, been unfortunately rendered *devils;* as if the Pagans *literally* and *properly* worshipped evil spirits. That such indeed was the opinion of the Jews, we may collect from their bestowing upon Satan the name of the idol-god Baal-Zebub; and this notion they seem to have transmitted to the Christians, who long and strenuously maintained it: but the word, which our translators (evidently under the influence of the then prevailing idea) have rendered *devils*, does by no means give any countenance to such an hypothesis.[1] In the religious system of the old mythologists, Demons were the same as Hero-gods: and these Hero-gods were acknowledged to be the souls of eminent benefactors to mankind; who, after they had quitted this mortal sphere of existence, were worshipped as deities by a too grateful posterity.[2] Among the philosophic few, they

---

[1] I need scarcely observe, that this notion forms the basis of the machinery employed by Milton in his Paradise Lost.

[2] Hesiod. Oper. et dier. lib. i. ver. 120, 125. Platon. Cratyl. p. 398. de repub. lib. v. p. 468. Some philosophical speculatists maintained, that there were *two* sorts of Demons; the souls of illustrious men separated from their bodies after death, and certain ethereal spirits which had never inhabited any bodies at all. I doubt, however, whether this distinction be not a comparatively modern refinement: for I can find scarcely any traces of it in the system of pagan theology, which was generally established. There, almost universally, the Demons appear as the souls of the mighty dead; though a notion very often prevailed, that they had descended from heaven or from the orb of the Moon, previous to their entering into mortal bodies. Apul. de deo Socrat. p. 690. Plut. de defect. orac. p. 431. See Bp. Newton's Dissert. on the Proph. Vol. ii. p. 417, 418.

seem to have been chiefly considered in the light of potent mediators between man and a supreme divinity: but with the multitude, less influenced by speculation than by sense, they usurped the worship due only to the Most High; and the unseen and all-pure Jehovah was overlooked and forgotten in the midst of a host of Demons, whose symbolical images could be seen and felt, and whose semimortal attributes courted (as it were) a greater familiarity.' Accordingly, both among the Greeks and the Egyptians, the gods are described as having once reigned upon earth: and the principle of deifying illustrious benefactors after their death was openly acknowledged by both those nations as forming the basis of one part at least of their popular theology.

Some of the Christian fathers, notwithstanding the common idea that the pagans worshipped evil spirits, were well aware that the real objects of their adoration were not devils, but the souls of departed mortals. Thus Tertullian informs us, that the Demons of the Gentiles were the shades of the dead: Arnobius asserts, that the heathens venerated dead men as immortal gods, and that their shrines were no better than so many sepulchres: and Clemens Alexandrinus remarks, that the more skilful theologists placed in their temples the coffins of the deceased, called their souls *Demons*, and taught that they ought to be worshipped by men.*

These then are the Demons, mentioned in the New Testament as adored by the pagans: and, agreeably to such an interpretation, Epiphanius understands a remarkable prophecy of St. Paul relative to the great apostasy of the latter times. The apostle had foretold, that certain persons in the Christian Church should depart from the sound doctrine of the Gospel, and should give heed to mythic tales and speculations concerning Demons. On this, Epiphanius, rightly concluding that the word *Demons* was used in its well-known pagan sense, remarks, that the import of the prophecy was, that there should hereafter be worshippers of dead men among apostate

' Platon. Sympos. p. 202, 203. Apul. de deo Socrat. p. 674, 675, 676. apud Newton ibid. p. 415, 416.

* See Mede's Works, b. iii. c. 3, 4, 5; where various authorities are given, and where the subject is discussed at large.

Christians, even as there formerly were among the apostate Israelites.[1] The fathers indeed appear to me to have erred in supposing, that the pretended coffins of the Demon-gods were *truly* the coffins which had contained their corpses, and that their temples were *really* their sepulchres: but they are perfectly right in their opinion, that the Demons of the gentile world were no other than deified men.

How far evil spirits may have influenced the pagan oracles.

1. I mean not however to say, that the writers of the New Testament *always* use the word *Demon* in this sense: they doubtless *sometimes* employ it to describe evil spirits; and from this application we may, I think, gather some awful truths relative to the false religion of Paganism.[2]

Though the Gentiles did not, literally and strictly, worship the prince of hell; their whole theology may well be deemed to have originated from the evil one, and to have been employed by him as an useful instrument to subserve his infernal purposes. In every country and in every age, the leading features of idolatry have been cruelty and obscenity, sacrificial bloodshed and unbridled systematic licentiousness: to adopt the accurate language of our great poet, *lust hard by hate* has sat enthroned wherever the genius of polytheism prevailed.

But Scripture seems to intimate, that idolatry was even yet more immediately the religion of Satan. We read in the Acts of a young female, who was possessed *with a spirit of divination* according to our version, *with a spirit of Python* according to the original Greek. This spirit enabled her to utter certain oracular responses, by which a considerable profit accrued to her masters. Whenever she beheld Paul and his companions, the spirit was compelled to testify through her organs, that they were the servants of the Most High God, and that they showed to men the way of salvation. At length the Apostle, grieved at so deplorable a sight, charged the spirit in the name of Jesus Christ to come out of the girl; and this adjuration he

[1] See Mede's Works, b. iii. c. 6.

[2] It may be observed, that the pagan Greeks also sometimes use the word *Demonia* to express *wicked and malignant demons*, who, according to what Plutarch speaks of as an ancient opinion, envy good men, and strive to hinder them in the pursuit of virtue lest they should at last be partakers of greater happiness than themselves. Plut. in vit. Dion. Such a belief seems to have originated from some tradition of the fallen angels.

was constrained forthwith to obey.' Now, according to the plain unvarnished import of this narrative, the young female was possessed by *an evil spirit*, which impelled her to utter responses of an oracular nature. The spirit was *an intelligent and living agent*, as appears from his conveying to the girl a clear knowledge of the character and office of St. Paul. And he is denominated *a spirit of Python*: which is the precise name of the Delphic serpent, that was slain by Apollo, but which himself originally delivered oracles from a sacred cave in Mount Parnassus.' This fabulous monster, as it is well known, communicated the title of *Pythius* to the god, and of *Pythia* to his oracular priestess; who was supposed to receive the vapour of inspiration from a cleft in the rock.. Putting these matters together, we certainly seem to collect, that there was something more than mere juggling imposture in the responses of the ancient oracles. For, if the spirit of Python, as ejected by St. Paul, was properly *an infernal spirit.;* it appears only reasonable to infer, that the spirit of Python, which was said to influence the Delphic priestess, was likewise *an infernal spirit.* And some, I think, of the old oracular responses (I mean not those which are employed to decorate poetry, but those which are detailed in sober history) warrant such an inference.

Since the devil is termed in Scripture *the prince of the power of the air*, and since the rapidity of a spirit's action must far exceed that which marks the action of a corporeal being; we may infer, that Satan is able to convey intelligence respecting *things present* with inconceivable rapidity from one quarter of the world to another. We may likewise conclude from his native superiority to man, however his faculties may have been debased by his rebellious apostasy, that his knowledge of *things past* is both clear and extensive. But a prophetic view of *things future* is the prerogative of God alone: on this point, without a special inspiration from him, angels whether good or bad are involved in the same profound ignorance as short-sighted man himself. A spirit indeed, who by the subtlety of his nature possesses opportunities of knowing and combining things present which never could be known and combined even by the most consummate statesman, may draw.

Due to their vastly superior intellect they may accurately predict by plotting all the permutations to arrive at an accurate guess. This way outcomes of battles etc have been "prophecied". But all true knowledge of future events are the prerogative of God alone.

' Acts xvi. 16, 17, 18.   ' Hyg. Fab. 140.

more probable inferences and guesses relative to futurity than a statesman could do; just as a statesman, whose means of information are greater, may anticipate an event more clearly than a private person of confined intelligence: but still the united wisdom of hell can do no more than *guess*; God alone knows *with infallible certainty* what is about to come to pass. With these speculations the responses of the pagan oracles remarkably accord. They appear in some instances to declare *things present* with an accuracy, possible to the rapidity of spirit, but utterly impossible to the slowness of man: while, respecting *things future*, which neither spirit nor man can penetrate without divine inspiration, they are indefinite or ambiguous.

The intercourse of Crœsus with the Delphic oracle of the Pythian Apollo excellently illustrates the preceding remarks.

That king, by way of trying the knowledge of the Demon-god previous to consulting him on matters of real importance, directed his ambassadors to inquire, on the hundredth day after their departure from Sardis, what he was himself doing at that precise point of time. The ambassadors faithfully executed their commission; and Crœsus, determining to elude the vigilance of Apollo by the improbability of his employment, devoted the appointed day to the boiling of a lamb and a tortoise in a brazen kettle covered with a brazen lid: but the god, as soon as he was consulted, declared without hesitation, that he perceived the odour of a lamb boiled with a tortoise, while brass was at once beneath it and above it. The accuracy of the reply convinced Crœsus in an evil hour that the oracle might be depended on; and, most unfortunately for himself, he next consulted it relative to the issue of his projected war with Persia. Between this question, however, and his former one, there was a most important difference, to which the king did not sufficiently advert. The first related to *things present*; and, though the Pythia by her *unassisted* intellect obviously could not have solved it, yet there is no difficulty in conceiving, that an evil spirit, who was permitted thus to exercise his natural power, might with the velocity of thought successively hear the proposed question, witness the employment of Crœsus, and declare through the organs of the priestess the nature of that employment: but the second related to *things future*; and therefore did not admit of a solution equally easy: in this case, all that the spirit of divination could do was to veil his ignorance in the specious garb of intentional ambiguity. Accordingly, the second answer differs from the first in a manner perfectly corresponding with the difference between the two questions. The king was informed, that, if he went to war with the Persians, he should overthrow a great empire. Delighted with the prediction, he took it for granted that the fall of the rival monarchy was decreed: but the event proved, that the ruin of Lydia, not of Persia, was intended. Still however, wishing to render himself as secure as possible, he a third time consulted the oracle. The question, which he now put, was, whether his power should ever be diminished. This was coming closely to the point: but the art of the evil spirit (if evil spirit *were* concerned in the transaction) was still an overmatch for the credulous prince. He was advised to consult his safety by a precipitate flight, whenever a mule should acquire the sovereignty of the Medes. Crœsus was now fully convinced of his future success: and it was not till his empire was totally ruined, that he discovered too late the predicted mule in the semi-Persian and semi-Median Cyrus.[1]

The palpable ambiguity of the second response, so different from the unequivocal precision of the first, requires no comment: but the third seems, upon a careless survey of it, to approach very near to the limits of genuine prophecy. Yet it is *only* on a careless survey that any such character can be attributed to it: if strictly examined, it will be found, though in a more refined manner, to equal even the second in point of ambiguity. Crœsus was told, that he should be safe, until a mule became king of Media. This response secured the credit of the oracle, whatever might be the issue of the war: if Crœsus were vanquished, then Cyrus was ready to be adduced as the fatal mule; if he should prove victorious, then the god had familiarly predicted his success by declaring that nothing could endanger his charmed empire save an utter impossibility.[2]

2. But, whatever might be the nature and extent of diabolical influence over the pagan oracles, this at least is certain, that the Gentiles were not

[1] Herod. lib. i. c. 47, 48, 53, 55, 91.

[2] Dr. Hales has some judicious remarks on this curious subject in his Chronol. vol. iii. p. 125—129.

worshippers of evil spirits. Both the acknowledged import of the word *Demon*, and the characters attributed to the heathen divinities, prove with sufficient plainness, that those divinities were once mere mortals; though their worship was inseparably blended with that of the heavenly bodies and the elemental powers of nature. The chief question therefore is, *what mortals were venerated after their death as the hero-gods of pagan antiquity.*

This question is solved in a very remarkable manner by Hesiod: and it will be found hereafter, that his solution perfectly agrees with the human characters sustained by the deified objects of gentile adoration. *When the mortal remains of those who flourished during the golden age were hidden beneath the earth, their souls became beneficent Demons; still hovering over the world which they had once inhabited, and still watching as guardians over the affairs of men. These, clothed in thin air and rapidly flitting through every region of the earth, possess the royal privilege of conferring wealth and of protecting the administration of justice.*[1] The passage is curious; both as accurately pointing out the notions entertained respecting the offices of the Demon-gods, as specifying that they were originally mere men, and as defining the precise race of mortals who obtained such honours after their death. They, who flourished during the golden age, were the persons counted worthy of being venerated as Demons.

3. If then we would know what particular persons those were, we must ascertain the epoch to which this celebrated poetical period ought to be chronologically referred. Here I will venture to affirm, what shall be proved at large in the sequel, that the mythology of the gentiles acknowledges *two* golden ages; the *first* coinciding with the period which immediately followed the creation, the *second* coinciding with the period which immediately succeeded the deluge. Such being the case, since the Demon-gods of Paganism were the mortals who lived during the golden age, and since there was a golden age both immediately after the creation and immediately after the deluge; it will plainly follow, that those Demon-gods were the members of the Adamitic family in the one instance and the members of the Noëtic

[1] Hes. Op. et dier. lib. i. ver. 120—125.

Handwritten margin note (top left): "Howbeit then, when ye knew not God, ye did service unto them which by nature are no gods" Gal 4:8

Handwritten margin note (left): Epoch of the golden age. There were 2 golden ages, the antediluvian and the postdiluvian: and the gods were deified mortals who had flourished during those ages.

Handwritten note (bottom): The Pre- and Post-diluvian origin of Hero-gods

From the destruction of the Adamic world and its renovation as the Noetic world, men formulated the doctrine of Materialism, the eternality of matter.

family in the other. Eminent persons, who flourished subsequently to each golden age, might occasionally be added, and in fact *were* added : but the individuals of these two primeval families may safely be esteemed the original and genuine prototypes of the Demon-gods. Thus the heads of the Sethite generations from Adam to Noah, perhaps also those of the Cainite generations, were remembered with a certain degree of reverence ; thus likewise after the deluge some of the younger patriarchs, particularly those of the line of Ham, were adored as Demons, and even usurped (as it were) the titles and honours of their diluvian fathers : yet, if we examine the legendary histories of the chief deities worshipped by the Gentiles, we shall almost invariably find them replete with allusions to the creation and Paradise on the one hand and to the deluge and the Ark on the other.

4. The reduplication of the golden age originated from a very remarkable opinion prevalent among the pagans, which, so far as I am able to judge, can alone bring us to a satisfactory and consistent elucidation of ancient mythology.

The pagan doctrine of a succession of similar worlds originated from the real succession of 2 similar worlds

It was well known to the Gentiles, that the first world was destroyed by an universal deluge, and that a second world arose by a sort of new creation out of its ruins. But their speculative genius did not rest satisfied with this simple truth. They applied, to an acknowledged and notorious fact, a specious kind of analogical reasoning ; and deduced, from a *single* destruction and renovation of the world, a *series* of similar destructions and renovations.* Nor did they extend this theory *prospectively* alone, they employed it also *retrospectively :* whence they inferred, that, as a new world would hereafter arise out of the wreck of the present world just as the present world arose from the wreck of the antediluvian world ; so the antediluvian world itself was but the successor of a yet prior mundane system. Some fancifully *limited* the number of these worlds ; in which case their favourite sums were *seven* or *fourteen*, in allusion to the seven companions of Noah or to those seven doubled : but others carried the speculation yet further. It began to be doubted whether there was any such thing as *a strictly proper creation*. As the new world after the deluge was but a modification of that which preceded it, and as the antediluvian world was similarly esteemed a modification of a prior world ; the vain curiosity of man proceeded to inquire, whether matter itself was not

The Eternality of the World thought to be implied in the Flood

*Considering that the earth was not created "tohu bohu" we must recognise that the first cataclysm happened between Gen. 1:1 and 2. Thus, the deluge was the 2nd destruction and a surer basis for the supposition that there were, or would later be, more.

eternal, and whether each world through an infinite series could be deemed more than a mere organization of preëxisting substance. The first of these theories produced the doctrine of a limited succession of worlds; the other, that of an unlimited one. Such speculations were of very remote antiquity; and the exordium of the book of Genesis seems to me to have been evidently written in decided opposition to them. We are there taught, that matter is *not* eternal, but that it was *created out of nothing* by the word of God: and we are further taught, that there was no world before that which preceded the deluge; for the Almighty is unequivocally represented as forming the newly created matter into that identical world, which was inhabited by Adam and his posterity.

the purpose of Genesis?

* This is not so.

5. But the speculations of the old mythologists did not stop with either a limited or an everlasting succession of worlds. They were not ignorant of certain singular coincidences, which produced some degree of resemblance between the antediluvian world and that which was reproduced from its ruins.

Points of similarity between the antediluvian and postdiluvian worlds.

The primitive world commenced with a single pair; who may indeed have had other children, but who were chiefly memorable as being the parents of a triad of sons espoused to a triad of daughters. Mankind was originally cradled in the garden and mount of Paradise: here were placed Adam and Eve; and from that lofty region, from that sacred mount of God, all the earth was, as from a centre, replenished with inhabitants. Of the three sons of Adam one was distinguished from his brothers by a spirit more prone to daring wickedness; and the consequence was, that he was driven out from the society of his family labouring under the curse of God. As for Adam himself, we know little of his character and actions, save that he was by occupation a husbandman, and that in point of patriarchal rank he might be esteemed an universal sovereign of that earth which was wholly peopled with his own descendants. We learn however from the very short authentic narrative which we possess of antediluvian matters, that the new world even in its infancy beheld the institution of the rite of sacrifice, certainly no later than the recorded sacrifice of Cain and Abel, most probably (I had almost said assuredly) as early as the fall, after which and in consequence of which Adam seems to have been the first sacrificer.[1] Yet, short as the inspired narration is, we further learn from it, that Adam dwelt fearless and secure in the midst of the brute creation while he continued in a state of innocence; but that, after he transgressed, a gradual deterioration of manners took place, first in the line of Cain and at length in the line of Seth, until God was provoked to destroy the aboriginal world by the waters of an universal deluge.

Now it is a curious circumstance, that in all these particulars the new world, with more or less exactness, resembles the old. *It* also commenced from a single pair, remarkable as having for their offspring a triad of sons espoused to a triad of daughters-in-law. *It* also, as from a centre, was re-peopled from the lofty region of Paradise : for there is sufficient reason to believe, that mount Ararat, where the Ark rested after the flood, coincides, in point of geographical situation, with the mount of Eden ; there is sufficient reason to believe, that the land of Ararat is in fact the very same high country as that where the sacred primeval garden was planted by the hand of God. With regard to the three sons of Noah, one of them seems to have been distinguished from his brothers by a more daring spirit and a greater propensity to violence; characteristics, which have strongly marked his posterity in all ages, however the native fire and high chivalric soul of one great branch may have been happily tempered by the mild genius of Christianity. This son did not indeed fall *himself* under a curse like Cain, nor ought he justly to be compared to the first murderer : but the malediction pronounced upon his offspring

See p. 89ff

---

[1] Such an opinion I collect in the following manner. The sacrifice of the two brothers is indeed *circumstantially recorded ;* but no intimation is given, that the rite itself was *then instituted :* hence we may infer, that its *institution* was *prior.* Now, though we have no specific account of any such institution ; yet we read, that immediately after the fall the man and his wife were clothed by the hand of God himself with the skins of beasts. As yet, however, death was unknown in the world: whence then were the skins of these animals procured ? The only satisfactory answer seems to be ; that the beasts were slain for sacrificial purposes, and that they were thus slain by the express command of God : for it was by the direction of God, not by the contrivance of man, that their skins were used for raiment ; and no grant of animal food was made until after the deluge. If then the beasts were slain for sacrifice, Adam must obviously have been the first sacrificer. See below book ii. c. 8. § 1.

The first animal Sacrifice

Canaan formed a coincidence, imperfect indeed, yet such as could scarcely be overlooked in drawing an extended comparison. Respecting Noah, few historical particulars have come down to us in detail: those few however serve to mark a strong resemblance between him and Adam. Noah was the great universal father of the second race of mankind, as Adam was of the first. He was by occupation a husbandman. He was the general sovereign of that earth, which was afterwards peopled by his posterity. He was the first postdiluvian sacrificer: and, as the primeval victims appear to have been offered up within the precincts of Paradise, for Adam and Eve were clothed with the skins of the slaughtered animals *previous* to their expulsion from the garden; so the earliest victims after the flood were offered up, immediately subsequent to the liberation from the Ark, on the summit of mount Ararat, which, there is reason to believe (as I have already hinted), coincides geographically with Paradise. He dwelt secure in the midst of the brute creation, with which he was shut up in the Ark. His general piety produced, however imperfectly, a sort of second golden age, a renewed image of the Paradisiacal state, a period of decided innocence and holiness compared with the lawless and abandoned times which preceded the flood. But a fresh corruption of manners soon again infected the earth: the floodgates of unrestrained violence and obscenity were once more opened: and similar deeds of rapine, and tyranny, and bloodshed, were reacted by a new race of warlike Nephelim.

Such being the close analogy between the histories of the two worlds, a fresh theoretical refinement was built upon it. The doctrine of a *mere* succession of worlds was heightened to the doctrine of a succession of *similar* worlds. Each mundane system was thought to present an exact resemblance of its predecessor. The same persons re-appeared in new bodies; the same parts were acted by them afresh; the same deeds, whether good or bad, were repeated. The appointed circle being run, the four ages of increasing depravity having reached their termination, again that awful catastrophe takes place; which, resolving the elements into their original chaos and blending in one common destruction the minor hero-gods and their votaries, leaves only the chief of those gods sleeping in the deep silence of perfect solitude. But to destroy is merely to create afresh: a new world springs from the chaotic mass; a new great father appears; a new triad of hero-gods emanates from his substance; and the eternal wheel again rolls forward.

6. The necessary consequence of this theory was the doctrine of the transmigration of souls. Each person was believed to have existed in a prior world: and each person, after his death, was expected, when the appointed term of ages had elapsed, to reappear in a new theatre of action. The Metempsychosis, in lapse of time, experienced certain refinements which shall be noticed in their proper place; but such appears to have been its original and most simple form.

Origin of the doctrine of Metempsychosis and its application to the 2 successive races of hero-gods.

Agreeably to these speculations, while Noah and Adam were each esteemed the great universal father both of gods and men, the former was supposed to be no other than a reappearance of the latter; and, in a similar manner, the divine souls, which once animated the Adamitical triad, were thought to have been again incarnate in the persons of the Noetic triad. Hence we find the two aboriginal Patriarchs of the two worlds perpetually designated by the same appellation, but distinguished from each other as the first and the second or as the elder and the younger: and hence, where the knowledge of such a distinction was lost, we find a sort of mixed character produced, whose history refers him partly to the age of Adam and partly to that of Noah. The remembrance indeed of the flood was imprinted so much more deeply on the minds of the Gentiles, than that of the creation and the antediluvian world; that, in the persons of the Demon-gods, Noah predominates far above Adam, and the Noetic triad above the Adamitical triad: yet the knowledge of events prior to the deluge was by no means lost even in the west, while throughout the east it was preserved in many instances with a remarkable degree of accuracy.

Speculative error however is seldom stationary: the doctrine of the Metempsychosis was soon carried to a greater extent, than even a long succession of similar worlds might seem to warrant. Whenever any eminent character arose in the early ages, he was deemed a reappearance either of the great father or of a person of the sacred triad; though the period, in which he flourished, was not that of the commencement of a new world. Hence the titles of the Demon-gods were bestowed upon him; and hence, instead of only *two* Menus or *two* Buddhas, we find *several* who bore those appella-

Avatars

tions, though we may distinctly observe a Menu and a Buddha placed at the era of the flood and a Menu and a Buddha ascribed to the era of the creation. From this refinement evidently originated the oriental doctrine of Avatars or various successive incarnations of the same Demon-god; a doctrine, which had taken such deep root in the minds of the eastern theologists, to whose airy theories many of the first heresies which infested the Church may easily be traced, that Christ himself was venerated by the ductile faith of more than one Asiatic sect, as an incarnation or Avatar of Buddha or Vishnou, and as the head of a new chronological epoch.

The triads of the Gentiles sprang from the triple offspring of Adam, viewed as reappearing in the triple offspring of Noah.

7. Ancient mythology ever delighted to veil the simplest truths in the language of mysterious allegory; the hierophants rightly judging, from their knowledge of human nature, that the religion which they inculcated would thus be rendered more venerable in the eyes of the abused multitude. From this humour originated the adoption of a tenet, which may be traced with greater or less distinctness in perhaps every system of old mythology.

Adam and Noah were each the father of three sons: and to the persons of the latter of these triads, by whose descendants the new world was repeopled, the whole habitable earth was assigned in a three-fold division. This truth, though it sometimes appears in its naked and undisguised form, was usually wrapped up by the hierophants in the cloak of the most profound mystery. Agreeably to the doctrine of the Metempsychosis, each of the sons of Noah was supposed to be animated by the spirit of his father, as that father was himself animated by the spirit of Adam. Hence, instead of plainly saying that the mortal, who had flourished in the golden age and who was venerated as the universal demon-father both of gods and men, was the parent of three sons; they were wont to declare, that the great father had wonderfully triplicated himself, yet that he still in effect continued but one, inasmuch as each of his three forms was mutually the same both as the other forms and as the primeval sire himself. They taught accordingly, that there was *really* but one original Demon-god and ancestor of mankind; that this deity had indeed triplicated himself by a wonderful multiplication; but that his three forms were only delusion, because, so far as the *general* descent of the human race is concerned, they might be ultimately resolved into one person.

One god supposedly triplicating himself in 3 sons, yet remaining essentially one

Pursuing this vein of mysticism, they industriously contrived to obscure the triple division of the habitable globe among the sons of Noah, just as much as the characters of the three sons themselves. A very ancient notion universally prevailed, that some such triple division had once taken place: and the hierophants, when they had elevated Noah and his three sons to the rank of deity, proceeded to ring a variety of corresponding changes upon that celebrated threefold distribution. Noah was esteemed the universal sovereign of the world; but, when he branched out into three kings, that world was to be divided into three kingdoms or (as they were sometimes styled) three worlds. To one of the three kings therefore was assigned the empire of heaven; to another, the empire of the earth including the nether regions of Tartarus; to a third, the empire of the ocean. Yet the characters of the three kings, as we examine them, mutually melt into each other; until at length we find but one world and one sovereign, who rules with triple sway the three grand mundane divisions.

So again: when Noah became a god, the attributes of deity were inevitably ascribed to him; otherwise, he would plainly have been incapable of supporting his new character: yet, even in the ascription of such attributes, the genuine outlines of his history were never suffered to be wholly forgotten. He had witnessed the destruction of one world, the new creation of another, and the oath of God that he would surely preserve mankind from the repetition of such a calamity as the deluge. Hence, when he was worshipped as a hero-god, he was revered in the triple character of the destroyer, the creator, and the preserver: and, when he was reputed to have multiplied himself into three cognate divinities, the three attributes were divided among them. Thus were produced three gods, different yet fundamentally the same: one, mild though awful as the creator; another, gentle and beneficent as the preserver; a third, sanguinary, ferocious, and implacable, as the destroyer. Agreeably to such notions, we find the same deity, who is elsewhere described as sailing in a ship over the waters of the deluge, and who is dressed out with every historical characteristic that can mark him to be Noah, invocated nevertheless as the potent being that successively consumes and reproduces all things.

8. I am fully aware, that many persons, whose talents I respect, have imagined, that the triads of the Gentiles originated from some perverted tra-

ditions of the doctrine of the Holy Trinity: nor need any one blush to have been drawn into such a theory, since the mighty mind even of a Horsley rested in it as satisfactory. So far as I can judge however, it is not sufficient merely to notice *the frequent recurrence* of a triad in the theology of the pagans, nor even to adduce *the phraseology* which is sometimes employed by them :[1] we must also examine *the mythological history* of the persons who compose those triads, if we wish distinctly and satisfactorily to ascertain whence they originated. Now such an examination seems to me very clearly to prove, that they have no sort of relation whatever to the Christian doctrine of the Trinity, but that they sprang from a totally different source: and, though I think the language employed by Sir William Jones much too severe, I yet cannot refrain from regretting with him that the theory in question has ever been brought forward.[2] As the tenet of the Trinity could not have been proved, in the first instance, to any Christian believer from the triads of the gentile world; so neither can it receive any confirmation from them. It solely rests on the declarations of the inspired volume; nor does it either admit or require any extraneous assistance from the demon-theology of paganism.

Analogy of character between the Earth or greater world and the Ark or smaller world.

9. There was yet however another coincidence to be elicited, in order that the theory of a succession of similar worlds might be rendered complete.

At the period of the creation, the Earth was the great universal mother, from whose fruitful womb both men and animals and vegetables were produced: but, at the period of the renovation after the deluge, it was well

---

[1] This occasionally is very remarkable, and in some instances genuine: in others, as we shall hereafter see, there is great reason to believe, that it has been heightened by the mistaken zeal of some of the early Christian fathers. I particularly allude to the Orphic triad.

[2] *Very respectable natives have assured me, says he, that one or two missionaries have been absurd enough, in their zeal for the conversion of the gentiles, to urge, that the Hindoos were even now almost Christians, because their Brahma, Vishnou, and Mahesa, were no other than the Christian Trinity; a sentence, in which we can only doubt, whether folly, ignorance, or impiety, predominates—The tenet of our Church cannot, without profaneness, be compared with that of the Hindoos, which has only an apparent resemblance to it, but a very different meaning.* Asiat. Res. vol. i. p. 272, 273.

known, that the same part was not again performed by the Earth. A substitute therefore must be found: and the hierophants had only to attend to simple matter of fact, in order to discover precisely such a substitute as their system demanded. When the waters had retired into the central abyss from which they issued, the Ark rested on the summit of mount Ararat, and both men and animals and vegetables were born (as it were) from its womb. Hence the Ark was naturally made the great mother of the postdiluvian world, as the Earth was of the antediluvian world: and, since each successive world was deemed a perfect transcript of its predecessor, and since Adam the first great father was thought to have reappeared in Noah the second great father; the Ark was thence, in a similar manner, closely connected, and in some sort even identified, with the Earth.

The correspondence was strengthened by the notions which the ancients entertained respecting that body both at and after the epoch of the creation. They supposed, that it floated, during the process of formation, in the thick turbid waters of the primeval Chaos; and that afterwards, when the work was completed, it rose above the surface of the circumfluent ocean after the manner of some immense island. In this last particular, so far as the great eastern continent is concerned, they are not mistaken; for it is now well known, that the tract of land, which comprehends Europe, Asia and Africa, is surrounded on every side by the sea: but they probably were alike ignorant of the globosity of the ocean and of the existence of America.

Such were their ideas of the Earth; and correspondent with them was the condition of the Ark during the prevalence of the deluge. It floated in what was esteemed the Chaos of a new world; it was encompassed, like an island, by the ocean; and, when the work of a fresh creation was completed, it brought forth a new great father, a new triad of Demon-gods, a new race of animals, and the seeds of a new succession of vegetables.

Agreeably to these speculations, when the Earth and the Ark were each considered as a great mother, the latter was esteemed a transcript of the former, as the great father Noah was deemed a revival of the great father Adam. The Earth was the Megacosm; the Ark was the Microcosm: and

their attributes, titles, and symbols, were almost invariably interchangeable.

Earth & Ark
interchangeable
Symbols

Thus, while the Earth was thought to resemble in shape an enormous
boat, floating tranquilly on the surface of the ocean stream; the Ark was
conversely compared to, and identified with, the Earth. The one was furnished exactly in the same manner as the other : the sole difference between
them consisted in the scale of magnitude. A vast centrical mountain formed
the mast or boss of the mundane boat: and the great father, rising out of
the sacred umbilicus of the arkite world, supplied to it the place of a mast.
That mountain was the hill of Paradise, the hill also where the ark rested
after the deluge, consequently the hill whence the inhabitants of both worlds
equally derived their origin: *that* great father was properly Noah, ultimately Adam, and consequently the parent whence the inhabitants of both
worlds were equally descended.

Thus again the aquatic Lotos, which has the remarkable property of ever
rising to the surface of the water and never sinking beneath it, was made a
symbol of the Earth. In this case, the calix of the flower represented the
whole mundane boat; the four larger leaves, the four great arbitrary continental divisions, Europe, Siberia, China, and Hindostan ; the eight smaller, the eight supposed principal intervening islands; and the petal springing out of the centre, the sacred diluvian mount of Paradise, from which
flowed in opposite directions the four holy rivers of Eden. Yet the Lotos
was equally a symbol of that ship, in which the great father is said to have
sailed over the ocean during the prevalence of the deluge, and which is
fabled to have been transformed into a dove while the waters were retiring
from off the face of the earth. In this case, the calix represented the body
of the arkite world; and the petal, which had before shadowed out the centrical mountain, now typified the great father, whose favourite haunt, whether
he multiplied himself into a triad of Demon-gods or shone conspicuous in
his eight refulgent forms, was ever allowed to be that hallowed patriarchal
hill.

Thus also the egg is well known to have been universally a symbol of
the Earth: yet it was not more a symbol of the Earth than of the Ark: for
that same being, who is literally declared to have once floated in an ark on

the surface of the Ocean, is also said to have been born from an egg which had long been tossed about at the mercy of the elements; and the three Demon-gods, into whom he was thought to have triplicated himself, are nevertheless similarly pronounced to be egg-born.

Thus likewise a cow was very generally employed to represent the great mother; and that great mother, we are told, was the Earth: yet we find, that the mystic name of that animal was *Theba*, which literally signifies *an ark* and which is the very word employed by Moses to designate the ship of Noah; and we likewise find, that it was thought the most proper hieroglyphic of that ark within which the principal Demon-god is said to have been inclosed during the permitted reign of his enemy the ocean, for the god is indifferently described as having been shut up and set afloat in a wooden ark and in a wooden heifer.

Such being the intercommunion both of character and symbols, we may naturally expect a similar intercommunion of titles: nor shall we be disappointed.

All the goddesses of paganism will be found ultimately to melt together into a single person, who is at once acknowledged to be the great mother and the Earth: yet that person is also declared to have assumed the form of a ship when the mighty waters of the vast deep universally prevailed, to have peculiarly presided over navigation, to have sprung from the sea and yet to have been born from that sacred mountain whence flowed the holy rivers of Paradise, to have contained within her womb all those hero-gods who are literally said to have each sailed in an ark, to have been in some remarkable manner connected with the dove and the rainbow, or to have had a ship for her special representative.

In consequence of this intercommunion, what ought properly to be predicated of the Earth is also predicated of the Ark; and conversely, what ought properly to be predicated of the Ark is also predicated of the Earth.

10. As the Earth and the Ark were each reputed the great universal mother, and as Noah and Adam were each esteemed the great universal father, the hierophants were obviously led to place them in a certain degree of relationship to each other. Here we have much mythological refinement arising from very simple causes. The connection, which most na-

[right margin handwritten notes:]
Cow = the great Mother = the Ark.
THEBA = an ark
Moses uses theba to describe Noah's Ark.

THE NUPTIAL relationship of the great father and the great mother gave rise to the various pagan tales of incestuous union and to the contradictatory genealogies of the hero-gods.

turally might be supposed to subsist between two persons who were reckoned the father and the mother both of gods and men, was the matrimonial one : hence they were considered in the light of husband and wife. But it was at the same time observed, that Noah was himself born out of the womb of the Ark, no less than the triad of younger Demon-gods who were his offspring; as Adam had previously been born from the womb of the all-productive Earth : hence they were considered in the light of a mother and her son. Yet the hierophants could not but remark, that, although Noah was born *from* the Ark, he nevertheless existed *before* it and even *produced* it; they would also observe, that he existed *before* the renovated world, and might thus be allegorically deemed its *parent* : hence they were considered in the directly opposite light of a father and his daughter. These two ancient beings they placed at the head of every renovated world, supposing them to exist before all other creatures and to be themselves produced from Chaos and dark Night : hence they were lastly considered in the light of a brother and a sister.

It is obvious, that such allegorical speculations as these would naturally lead to a variety of wild fables relative to the mystic union of the great father and the great mother. From this source originated therefore all the tales of an incestuous connection, which was thought, in many different modifications, to have subsisted between those two primeval personages. Thus the great father is said to have sometimes espoused his own mother, sometimes his sister, and sometimes his daughter.

Nor did the confusion end here : it produced those singular demon genealogies, which at the first sight appear to involve a direct contradiction. We perpetually find an older god and a younger god associated together and viewed in the light of a father and a son: yet, if we examine their characters, we soon perceive that they are fundamentally but one person; and, if we further inquire into the notions entertained respecting them by the old mythologists, we shall have no occasion to build merely upon our own deductions, for we shall be unequivocally assured that the two *are* in reality but one deity. Sometimes, instead of a father and a son, two brothers are similarly joined together: but still we find, that no more than a single person is intended by both of them. This division of one god into two characters naturally arose out of the different relations which the great father was supposed to bear to the great mother. When he was esteemed the husband of the goddess, and when the goddess was thought to have produced a son; that son was naturally deemed the offspring of her consort likewise, though he was in reality the very same person viewed under a somewhat different aspect. In a similar manner, when the great father was said to be the brother of the goddess, and when the goddess was also feigned to be united in marriage to a husband; her husband and her brother would of course appear in the relation of brethren to each other, though but a single person was truly meant by both of them. The hierophants had also another motive for dividing Noah into two persons, nearly allied to the speculation which we are now considering. That patriarch in an eminent degree sustained a double character. As the mystic parent of the Ark, and as an inhabitant of a former world, he wore the semblance of a venerable old man: as the child of the Ark, and as the first inhabitant of a new world, he seemed as one restored to a state of youthful vigour.

The same division of character, which marks the great father, will be found also to mark the great mother. It originated partly from the desire of establishing a complete analogical resemblance, and partly from the same source as the other. Thus we may continually observe an older goddess and a younger goddess associated together, and viewed in the light of a mother and a daughter: yet their characters will prove upon examination to melt into one person; and the old mythologists, instead of suffering the matter to remain in any doubt, plainly assure us, that the two *are* fundamentally but one. We may trace the origin of this notion just in the same manner as that of the corresponding opinion respecting the great father. The goddess was sometimes said to be the wife, and sometimes the daughter, of the chief Demon-god. When she was esteemed *his* daughter, she was naturally esteemed the daughter also of his *consort:* yet the wife and the daughter were after all but one person, though divided into two characters; whence we are perpetually told, that the wife of the great father was his own daughter.

11. From this diversified relationship arose several curious varieties in the triads of the Gentiles.

HENCE LIKEWISE originated certain variations in the triads.

The genuine triad doubtless consisted of three sons, born from one father and united in marriage with their three sisters : and this was sometimes mystically expressed under the notion of the primeval Demon-god wonderfully triplicating his substance.   But the pagan mythologists introduced many refinements upon the original doctrine, in consequence of their speculations relative to the varied connexion of the great father with the great mother.   Thus we find triads consisting of a god and two goddesses, and again of two gods and one goddess.   Each of these principal varieties had also its subvarieties.   Under the first we have a father, a mother, and a daughter ; a mother, a son, and a daughter ; and a father, a sister, and a daughter : under the second we have a father, a mother, and a son ; a father, a sister, and a son ; or two brothers and a sister.   Yet, whatever variations may have been struck out in allusion to the proper triad of Demon-gods, we shall constantly find the old hierophants confessing, that in reality they have but one god and one goddess, for that all the male divinities may be ultimately resolved into the great father as all the female divinities finally resolve themselves into the great mother.

THE GREAT FATHER and the great mother were viewed as the two principles of fecundity.

12. These two ancient personages, from whom all things were allowed to have been produced, were on that account esteemed the patrons of generation, and were thought to preside over births of every sort and description.   They were reckoned the two principles of fecundity, whether animal or vegetable : and, as the Universe was supposed to have originated from their mystic union, they were in every quarter of the globe represented by two symbols, which were indeed sufficiently expressive of their imagined attributes, but which cannot be specified consistently with a due regard to decorum.   Every where did the degraded wisdom of paganism discover the symbols in question.   If the mundane lotos was contemplated ; they were seen in the calix representing the earth surrounded by the ocean, and in the petal exhibiting that pristine mountain of Ararat whence the inhabitants of both worlds derived their origin.   If the mystic ship, equally typified by the lotos, was viewed ; they were seen in the hull which was the form assumed by the great mother during the prevalence of the deluge, and in the mast which shadowed out the great father during the same period.   As the deities of generation, they were thought to preside over the opening of the

womb; and, since the rudiments of the new world were all born from the door of the Ark when it was first opened on the summit of Ararat, the same divinities, who were the two reputed principles of fecundity, were ever venerated as the gods of the door or as the gods of opening.

Such being the notions entertained respecting their powers, and such being the symbols by which they were represented, it is easy to conceive how much practical licentiousness might be expected to prevail, when refractory and apostate man was once given up by divine justice to follow his own vain imagination. In the corrupt theology of paganism, prostitution was not *incidental*, but *systematic*. It flowed naturally from the doctrines, and formed a constituent part of the ritual. The violation of female chastity was not the mere result of unrestrained licentiousness, but was esteemed the surest mode of propitiating the two great principles of generation, from whose mysterious union was produced the world and all that it contains.

13. But this religion of hell led its deluded votaries into even worse crimes, into even greater abominations.

Prone as the pagans were to polytheistic multiplication, they were equally prone to a strange amalgamation. The union of the great father and the great mother was sometimes thought to be of so intimate a nature, that it was even inseparable. They ceased to be two distinct persons; the one became a component part of the other; and, by a mysterious conjunction or combination perfect as the union of the petal and the calix in one Lotos, a single divine being was produced whose compound person partook of both sexes. This blended hermaphroditic deity was at once the great father, and the great mother; at once the primeval male, and the nymph who by successive renovations could boast the attribute of immortality. This god was the sire of the Universe: yet from his pregnant womb were produced alike the sacred triad of demons and the whole vegetable and material creation.

Now it was the ordinary custom of the priests and priestesses to personate the deity, whom they served. They assumed his titles, imitated his character, ascribed to themselves his attributes, and endeavoured to exhibit to the life the principal circumstances of his mythological history. These no-

tions produced the corruptions of the phallic worship and the solemn prostitution of female virtue, when the great father and the great mother were
considered as two distinct persons severally presiding over the powers of
generation : but, when they were viewed as a single person partaking of
both sexes and alone presiding over both powers, it is easy to conceive what
monstrous enormities were the consequence among a race of theologists,
who deemed it laudable and meritorious to imitate in their own persons the
supposed character and actions of their deity. The priests, while they assumed the titles of their god, studied also to take upon them his imagined
hermaphroditic nature. They wore the dress and copied the manners of
women : they literally, urged to the deed by a frantic enthusiasm, ceased to
be men : and, while they endeavoured in imitation of their deity to partake
of both sexes, they really failed to partake of either. Scripture abounds in
allusions to the practices attendant upon this mode of worship : and, in
order to preserve the Israelites from being contaminated by them, it strikes
at the root of the evil by specially prohibiting men to appear in the garb of
women or women in the garb of men. Suffice it to observe, that the practices in question were such, that the land of Canaan is even said, in the
nervous metaphorical phraseology of Holy Writ, to have vomited out in
very disgust its polluted inhabitants. Nor were such deeds peculiar to
Canaan, nor yet were they merely the result of a depraved appetite : they
prevailed more or less in almost every part of the pagan world from India
even to America, and flowed as an immediate practical consequence
from the religious theory which had been adopted relative to the amalgamation of the two great parents.

14. Yet, however common these speculations might be, the hierophants
seem to have been aware, that the union of the great father and the great
mother was purely allegorical and therefore altogether imaginary. Neither
the Earth nor the Ark produced their mystic offspring, animal and vegetable,
in consequence of any *real* marriage with Adam or Noah : on the contrary,
they each brought forth both the great father himself and the whole race of
their metaphorical children without any coöperation of a husband Demon-
god.

Hence originated a very remarkable opinion, which was occasionally entertained respecting the character of the great mother. She was by some theologists esteemed a virgin, and was thought by her own energy alone to have given birth to the principal hero-deity. At the same time, we are left in no doubt, how we ought to interpret this fable: for it is usually blended inseparably with some legend, which either refers the god thus miraculously produced to the period of the deluge, or describes him as having been once set afloat in an ark on the surface of the ocean.

This speculation, like the two which have been last noticed, was reduced to practice, so far as it was capable of being thus reduced, by one remarkable class of ancient priestesses. In imitation of the supposed virginity of the great mother, colleges of sacred maids under a regular monastic discipline were established ; and, whether in the old continent or in that of America, a breach of their vows of chastity was visited by the most severe and horrible punishment.

15. Upon the imputed characters and imagined relationship of the great father and the great mother was founded the whole machinery of the pagan Mysteries, whether Mithratic, Eleusinian, Isiac, Cabiric, or by whatever other name they might be designated.

FROM THE ALLEGORIZED history of the two great parents originated the Pagan Mysteries

The egress of Noah from the Ark was considered in the light of a new or second birth, by which he was introduced into a state of fresh existence. Hence he was frequently represented as an infant, either exposed on the summit of a mountain in allusion to Ararat, or set adrift on the ocean in a small ark, or floating helplessly in the expanded calix of the mysterious Lotos. Those, who were initiated, sought to imitate this allegorical birth of the god. Accordingly, the epoptæ were invariably supposed to have experienced a certain regeneration, by which they entered upon a new state of existence, and were fantastically deemed to have acquired a great increase of light and knowledge. Hitherto, they were exoteric and profane : now they became esoteric and holy.

The second birth or rebirth of Paganism arises from Noah: it is not in any way a precog of New Birth as in NT.

This regeneration of the Mysteries was effected by sundry different pro_cesses, equally wise and equally edifying. Sometimes the aspirant had to fight his way through fire and water, to endure the most rigid fasts and penances, and to encounter all the horrors of darkness and all the yells of infernal apparitions : at other times, he had to brave the edge of the oppos-

ing sword, or to submit patiently to the strictness of a solitary confinement.
Such however were only the preludes to the initiatory rite; and they were
designed to prove the fortitude of the votaries, as that of Noah was proved
during his awful and perilous seclusion within the Ark. The rite itself consisted, sometimes in the aspirant's being born as it were out of a small covered boat, in which he had been previously committed to the mercy of the
ocean; sometimes in his being produced from the image of a cow, within
which he had been first inclosed; and sometimes in his coming forth through
the door of a dark rocky cavern or artificial stone cell, in which he had
been shut up during the time appointed by the hierophant.

Of these three modes of regeneration, that by the boat sufficiently explains itself. Nor need there much be said respecting that by the cow:
from the earliest times, the Ark was symbolized by that animal; consequently, the birth from the cow meant the very same as the birth from the
boat. But the origin of regeneration by the cavern is not at first sight quite
so obvious: it is capable however of being easily elucidated by certain other
remarkable phrases, employed by the hierophants as synonymous with those
which describe their allegorical new birth.

The principal Demon-god was not only said to have existed in a prior
state as a venerable old man, and then to have returned to infancy and
youth by a second nativity: but he was likewise described as having been
lost and then found, as having died and then experienced a wonderful revival, as having been shut up in a coffin or as having descended into the
infernal regions and then returned in safety to the light of day. Sometimes
also he was represented as having been wrapt in a profound sleep, and
as floating in that condition on the surface of the ocean during the period
which elapsed between the destruction of one world and the formation of
another. At the end of that period, when the new creation at length appears above the water in youthful beauty, the god awakes; and, quitting
the vehicle on which he reposed, whether the mysterious lotos or the sacred
aquatic serpent coiled up so as to exhibit the form of a boat, assumes the
government of the renovated world.[1]. All these different images meant the

----

[1] See Plate II. Fig. 1.

very same thing: and the variety seems to have arisen from the mixed character of the great mother, who was at once the Megacosm and the Microcosm, the Earth and the Ark.   When the doctrine of a succession of similar worlds was adopted, and when the tenet of the Metempsychosis was superadded to it, death was naturally esteemed nothing more than the prelude to a renewed life; and that renewal was indifferently considered in the light of a resurrection from the dead or a new birth from the grave.   Such speculations exactly suited the identification of the Earth and the Ark in the person of one great universal mother.   The entrance of Noah into the Ark corresponded with the entrance of Adam into the Earth   But the entrance of Adam into the Earth was his burial: hence the entrance into the Ark was also deemed a burial, or an inclosure within a coffin, or a descent into the gloomy regions of Hades; and the person, who thus entered, was considered as one that died or was plunged in a deep deathlike sleep.   Adam however, the first great father, was thought to have reappeared in the person of Noah, the second great father: hence the egress of Noah from the Ark was esteemed a revival or a resurrection or a return from the infernal regions.   On the other hand, the inclosure of Noah within the Ark was said to be his inclosure within the womb of the great mother, and consequently his exit to be a birth from that womb: hence the burial of Adam was considered only in the light of a temporary return to the womb of his primeval parent, from which in due time he was destined to be born again at the commencement of another world.   This being the case, the interior of the Earth and the interior of the Ark were, by a mystic intercommunion of terms, indifferently called *the womb of the great mother* and *the infernal regions:* and the same god, who had floated in an ark upon the sea, who had experienced a wonderful second birth, who had been lost and found again, who had died and revived; was constantly either esteemed an infernal deity, or was said to have descended into Hades, or was reputed the president of obsequies and the sovereign lord of departed spirits.   Now, whatever the aspirants scenically represented in the Mysteries, the god himself was believed to have previously undergone.   He was thought to have been slain by the mighty enemy that overwhelmed the primeval world, to have been set afloat when dead in an

ark which was deemed his coffin, and to have afterwards returned to life
and thus to have been born again out of the boat in which he had reposed
on the surface of the mighty deep. He was likewise supposed to have
been shut up in the hollow interior of a wooden cow, which is explained
to be the same as his ark and which accordingly is designated by the appellation of *Theba;* and thus, as he was born again from the ark, to have
been similarly born again from the cow. He was further celebrated, as the
god who was born out of a rock or who sprang from the door of a sacred
rocky cavern, within which he had for a season lain concealed. Now
Porphyry assures us, that the holy grotto was a symbol of the World; and
the whole analogy of paganism proves him to be right in his assertion.
The gloomy interior therefore of the grotto must have represented the
gloomy central cavity of the Earth. But that cavity was the womb of the
great mother: and the great mother was not only the Earth, but likewise
the Ark. Hence the sacred cavern must additionally have represented the
interior of the Ark; and its door, through which both the god and the aspirant were equally supposed to be born again, must have shadowed out
the door of the Ark. Accordingly, the same god and the same imitative
aspirants, who were sometimes said to have been born from a boat or from
a floating machine which bore some resemblance real or imaginary to a
cow, were also thought to have been regenerated by emerging to open day
through the door of a gloomy cavern. But, if the birth of the very same
characters from the ark or the cow was the same as their birth from the cavern; then the ark, the cow, and the cavern, must mean one and the same
thing. And, that this was the case, appears in a very remarkable manner
from there being exactly the same intercommunion of attributes between the
sacred cavern and the ship of the principal hero-god, as there is between the
Earth and the Ark. An ancient opinion prevailed, that the primeval grotto
was situated in the deep recesses of the ocean; that, on every side, it was
encompassed by the raging waves; and that once, in a season of peculiar
danger, the great father concealed within its sheltering womb his children,
who consisted of three sons and three daughters. On the other hand, a
curious legend has come down to us, which teaches, that the ship of the
same great father was once changed to stone in the midst of the sea, by

which metamorphosis it of course became a rocky cavern: and we perpetually find a notion predominating, both that the goddess, whose peculiar form or symbol was a ship, delighted to dwell in a consecrated grotto; and that the god, who was exposed in an ark, was born or nursed in a cave said to be situated on the summit of a lofty mountain the transcript of Ararat.

II. We must now turn our attention to another great branch of ancient mythology, differing essentially in some respects from Demonolatry, yet most curiously and inseparably blended with it: the branch, of which I speak, is Astrolatry or Sabianism; that is to say, the worship of the Sun, the Moon, and the Host of Heaven.

1. The hierophants of old appear to have been very early addicted to the study of astronomy: though unfortunately, instead of pursuing their researches in a legitimate manner, they perverted them to the vain reveries of Magic, and prostituted them to the purposes of idolatry. As they highly venerated the souls of their paradisiacal and arkite ancestors, considering them in the light of Demon-gods who still watched and presided over the affairs of men; it was an easy step in the progress of apostate error to imagine, that they were translated to the heavenly bodies, and that from those lofty stations they ruled and observed all the passing events of this nether world. When such a mode of speculation was once adopted, whatever virtues might afterwards be attributed to the planets, and in whatever manner the stars might be combined into mythological constellations, the first idea, that must obviously have occurred to the astronomical hierophants, would undoubtedly be this: since they perceived the Sun and the Moon to be the two great lights of heaven, and since they worshipped with an especial veneration the great father and the great mother, they would naturally elevate those two personages to the two principal luminaries. Such accordingly was the plan, which they adopted. Those ancient writers, who have treated on the subject of pagan mythology, assure us. that, by what was called *a mystic theocrasia*, all the gods of the Gentiles ultimately resolved themselves into the single character of the great father; and, in a similar manner, all their goddesses into the single character of the great mother: and they further declare, that, as all their gods melt insensibly into one, they are all equally the Sun; and, as all their goddesses no less

Marginalia: SABIANISM UNITED TO DEMONOLATRY The souls of the demon-gods were thought to have passed into the heavenly bodies; particularly the great father into the Sun, and the great Mother into the Moon. Hence the actions of the hero-gods were attributed to the Host of Heaven

melt into one, they are all equally the Moon.   Yet, notwithstanding these avowed and recognized doctrines, the gods of the Gentiles are allowed to have been the souls of their ancestors, and are described as having once acted a conspicuous and sufficiently intelligible part upon earth.   The only conclusion, that can be drawn from these apparently opposite declarations, is; that the Demon-gods were worshipped in the heavenly bodies: and, agreeably to such a conclusion, we are unequivocally told, that the souls of certain deified mortals were believed to have been elevated after their death to the orbs of the Sun, the Moon, the Planets, and the Stars.   Hence originated the notion, that all those celestial bodies, instead of being mere inert matter, were each animated by a divine spirit, were each a wise and holy intelligence.[1]

The consequence of this astronomical refinement was the introduction of the whole history of the Demon-gods into the sphere, and with it perhaps every opinion that was in any way connected with that history.   It is most curious and interesting to trace the matter in its various ramifications.

Exemplification in the SUN

2. As the great father was peculiarly venerated in the Sun, whatever symbol represented the great father represented also the Sun, and whatever was predicated of the great father was likewise predicated of the Sun.   So intimately were they united in the reveries of the ancient hierophants, that their characters are perpetually blended together: and, thence, what can only be properly said of the Sun is said of his human associate the great father, and what can only be properly said of the great father is said of his celestial vehicle the Sun.

Thus we are told, on the one hand, that the Sun was a husbandman; that he was born out of the deluge; that he sailed in a ship over the surface of the ocean; that he was produced, like an infant out of the womb of its

---

[1] This notion was combined with Paganism even to the very last: nay there are not wanting instances of both Jews and Christians being led away by it.   Philo ventured to adopt the pseudo-philosophical speculation, and the learned Origen was seduced to assent to his opinion.   For this he was anathematized by Pope Vigilius: and it would have been well, if the Romish Church had always as carefully guarded herself against the contamination of paganism.   *Siquis dicit, Cælum, et Solem, et Lunam, et Stellas, et Aquas quæ super Cælos sunt, animatas et materiales esse quasdam virtutes, Anathema sit.*

mother, from the calix of the mystic Lotos, while it floated on the bosom of the mighty deep; that he was born from the door of a rocky cavern; that he slept, during the interval between the destruction of one world and the new creation of another, on the folds of a huge water serpent, coiled up in the shape of a boat and thus safely supporting him on the top of the waves; that he once saved himself from the fury of the ocean by taking refuge in a floating island; that he reigned upon earth after the flood, the most ancient sovereign of the postdiluvian world; that he was once actually drowned in the sea; and that the present Sun had been preceded by a succession of others, each of which perished, when the world over which he presided perished. On the other hand, we are told, that the human being, who was saved in an ark when all the rest of mankind were destroyed by the waters of a flood, was either a child of the Sun, or the Sun himself, or an emanation of the Sun, or a being compounded of a man and the Sun; that this same personage is the king, who rises in light and ascends the vaulted sky; that he is the sovereign of heaven, radiant with celestial splendour; that he is the sacred fire, which warms and animates the circle of the Universe.

9. The same observations equally apply to the mythological character of the other chief luminary of heaven. As the great mother was peculiarly venerated in the Moon, whatever symbol represented the great mother represented also the Moon, and whatever was predicated of the great mother was also predicated of the Moon. But the great mother was a compound character, uniting in herself both the Earth and the Ark; hence we find various matters attributed to the Moon, which properly belong not to that body but either to the Earth or to the Ark.

The great mother was symbolized in every quarter of the globe by a cow: yet, while the old mythologists tell us that a cow was the symbol of the Earth, they also tell us that it was equally a symbol of the Moon; and they complete the whole by assuring us, that a cow was mystically denominated *Theba*, which properly signifies not *a cow* but *an ark*. Exactly correspondent with this intercommunion of symbols is the most remarkable action ascribed to the great father. Sometimes he is said to have descended into the infernal regions; sometimes he is said to have been shut up in an ark; sometimes he is said to have been inclosed within a wooden cow; and sometimes he is said to have entered into the Moon. All these different matters were asserted of the Egyptian Osiris : and they all at the bottom meant the same thing ; they meant the two successive entrances of the great father, in his two successive characters of Adam and Noah, into the womb of the great mother, the Grave and the Ark. Hence we are told, that the ark of Osiris was sometimes made to resemble a cow in form, and sometimes the crescent which the Moon exhibits during her first and last quarters. The consecrated living cow, denominated *Theba*, was herself also studiously managed so as to display the same appearance of the Moon. The figure of a crescent was artificially impressed upon her side; and her horns, themselves even naturally exhibiting that figure, were filed and cut and polished, so that they might present it to the beholder with the greatest possible degree of accuracy.

Agreeably to the same astronomico-symbolical speculation, the Moon was represented by the ancient mythologists sailing in a ship : and that very goddess, whose peculiar symbol was a ship, who is said during the period of the deluge to have successively assumed the forms of a ship and of a dove, who is described as being born from the ocean, and whose womb is declared to have once been the common receptacle of all the Demon-gods, is yet asserted to be sidereally the Moon. So again, we find a notion prevalent, that the Moon is of an aqueous nature, that she was born or produced out of the retiring waters of the deluge, that she presides over navigation, and that she might justly bear the title of *the queen of the waves*. All these characteristics are perfectly intelligible, if we suppose, that the Moon is only intended so far as she is the type of the Ark; but they are any thing rather than intelligible, if we imagine the literal Moon in the firmament to have been thus described by the ancient mythologists.

We are not however to forget, that the great mother, whose astronomical symbol was the Moon, was the Earth, no less than the Ark: hence we find, that certain characteristics of the Earth are ascribed to the Moon, as well as those by which the Ark is specially designated. The Moon, though she literally rides high in the heavens, is yet made an infernal goddess. As such, she is sometimes secreted in a gloomy grotto, and sometimes placed in the central cavity of the Earth; where she presides over those mighty waters, which support the ship of the infernal ferryman, and which once burst forth to overwhelm an impious race of giants that were feigned to have contended in arms with the eight primeval Demon-gods. With a similar allusion to her earthly character, the streams of the deluge itself, which retired in every direction from the summit of the arkite mountain by the channels of the four rivers of Paradise, are said to have burst forth in the first instance from her hollow womb. Such opinions require little comment: when the astronomical hierophants chose to place the great mother in the sphere, perhaps they could not have found a type more accurately shadowing out her double character, than that which analogy itself led them to pitch upon. While the circle of the full Moon exhibits the form of the sacred mundane circle: the beautiful crescent of the first and fourth quarters presents the figure of a boat, and thus aptly represents the ship of Noah.

That this idea is not purely imaginary, but that the ancients had really observed the resemblance between a boat and the lunar crescent, is manifest from the shape which they attributed to the ark of Osiris. Both the ark in which the god was inclosed, and the commemorative ark which was borne by the priests in the celebration of the Mysteries, was formed like the kind of ship, which the Latins called *Biprora* and the Greeks *Amphiprymnais*: its figure, in short, was precisely that of the modern life-boat. [1] It might however have been supposed, that the choice of such a form was purely accidental, and consequently that it had no intentional reference to the lunar crescent: but this supposition is effectually prevented by the express declaration, that the ark of Osiris was shaped like the Moon; and by the assertion, that he equally entered into a luniform ark, into a heifer whose horns represented the lunar crescent, and into the Moon herself. Hence it is evident, if we strip off the disguise of a mystic astronomical jargon, that the entrance of the god into the Moon means only his entrance into a boat shaped like the Moon, and that the form of a crescent was given to the boat because the hierophants had observed the general resemblance between a boat and the lunar crescent.

4. Having thus disposed of the two great luminaries in particular, the astronomical mythologists next directed their attention to the solar system in general.

Exemplification of the SOLAR SYSTEM

They observed, according to the imperfect degree of science then possessed,

[1] See Plate III. Fig. 1.

that there were seven planets, over which the Sun appeared to preside as a sovereign and moderator.[1] The number coincided too exactly with their diluvian speculations to be overlooked: for it answered minutely to that of the seven holy persons, who were preserved in an ark with the great father, and who constituted with him at their head the eight primeval Demon-gods of Egypt. Such being the case, as the hierophants had before likened the Earth to a ship, because the character of their great mother was of a mixed nature, and because the antediluvian world like the postdiluvian commenced from an ogdoad; so they now applied the very same comparison astronomically. It is a most curious circumstance, though perfectly according with that system which sought inseparably to blend together Sabianism and Demonolatry, that the ancient mythologists considered the whole frame of the heavens in the light of an enormous ship. In it they placed the Sun, as the fountain of light and heat; and assigned to him, as the acknowledged celestial representative of the great father, the office of pilot. But he was not a solitary mariner in the huge ship of the heavens: seven planetary sailors, who were brethren and who resembled each other by partaking of a common nature, were his eternal companions. With these he performs his never-ending voyage: and thus from year to year exhibits to the eyes of mortals the fortunes of their diluvian ancestors.

It is easy to see, that this astronomical refinement is in a considerable degree built on an extension of the idea affixed to the term *World*. The Ark was a World in miniature: the Earth is a greater World: but the Universe is the greatest, and therefore the only proper, World. Hence they are manifestly analogical to each other: and hence a sort of mystic intercommunion was thought to subsist between them. This eminently appears in the circumstance of both the Earth and the Universe being compared to a ship; but it is not the only circumstance, in which the prevalence of the same notion may be detected. The inclosure of the Ark was called *the circle of the World:* the name of the goddess, to whom that circle was sacred, literally denotes *the World:* and the circle itself was sometimes remarkably denominated *the Ark* or *Ship of the World.* Yet the circle represented not only the inclosure of the Ark and

---

[1] They made up the number of the then known planets to seven, by including the Moon. See Macrob. in somn. Scip. lib. i. c. 6. p. 25.

the ring exhibited by the sensible terrene horizon; it also symbolized that circle in the heavens, in which the Sun revolves during his apparent progress through the signs of the zodiac.

5. As for the Stars, the only use, which the hierophants could conveniently make of *them* in the furtherance of their system, was to arrange them into constellations, and to ascribe to each groupe an imaginary form and character which might best suit their purpose. And this was the precise course, which they followed. The tales of pagan mythology have been transferred to the sphere: and the whole face of heaven has been disguised by the forms of men and women, beasts and birds, monsters and reptiles. Yet these were not without their signification: as the heavens in general were compared to a vast ship manned by eight sidereal mariners; so, without pretending to decypher *every* catasterism, we may at least venture to say, that the Stars, in various different modes, have been employed to relate the history of the deluge.

Since that awful history is thus written in the sphere, and since each Star was thought to be animated by an intelligence whose mortal body had once lived upon earth, we may readily perceive whence all the follies of judicial astrology have originated. Because the events of the deluge were *commemoratively* inscribed on the heavens, it was supposed that every passing event might *literally* and *prophetically* be traced either in the constellations or in the conjunctions of the planets: and, because the Stars were believed to be animated by the souls of the Demon-gods, it was concluded, that these speculators of the heavens, as they have been called by an ancient Phenician mythologist, still overlooked and influenced the affairs of men.[1] Such pagan absurdities continued to prevail long after the introduction of Christianity: and, even at the present day, the race of star-gazing impostors, fed by the silly credulity of the vulgar, is not altogether extinct.[2]

---

[1] That the souls of the hero-gods were thought by the Egyptians to have migrated into the stars, is expressly asserted by Plutarch. Τας δε ψυχας εν ουρανω λαμπειν αστρα. Plut. de Isid. et Osir. p. 354.

[2] Astronomy, thus blended with hero-worship, certainly originated at Babylon; agreeably to the very just remark of Herodotus, that the Egyptians received it from the Babylonians. Herod. Hist. lib. ii. c. 109. This was the primeval centre, whence, with the prevailing system of theology, it was carried to all parts of the world. Accordingly, Mr. Bailli has observed, that several ancient nations, such as the Chaldeans, the Egyptians, the Indians, and

The character of the great father and the great mother is curiously exhibited in the Sun and the Moon. The Metempsychosis of Sabianism.

6. Such and so intimate being the union of Sabianism and Demonolatry, whatever properly belonged only to the latter was transferred with most curious systematical regularity to the former.

The great father was esteemed an hermaphrodite; and the great mother was, in like manner, thought to partake of both sexes: consequently, in this respect, their characters intimately blended together; and each became, in some sort, the same as the other. From the two great parents the idea was extended to their celestial representatives. The Sun was reckoned sometimes male, and sometimes female: and there was a god Moon, no less than a goddess Moon. Helius and Lunus were equally the great father; for we are assured, that the very masculine deity, who was venerated in the Sun, was yet the same as the lunar god: and Helia and Luna were equally the great mother; though the character of the solar goddess occurs much less frequently, than that of the lunar goddess. The only difference, in short, between them was this: each equally represented the same compound character; but in the hermaphroditic Sun we behold the great father presiding over the great mother, while in the hermaphroditic Moon we behold the great mother supporting the great father.

Agreeably to this mixed and united character of each, and still in perfect accordance with the attributes of those earthly personages whom they represented, the Sun was feigned to have mysteriously triplicated himself, and the Moon was also thought to have branched out into three forms or natures. So likewise the Sun was supposed to have been born out of a rocky cavern: and a sacred grotto was deemed the most appropriate temple for the worship of the Moon. A similar correspondence may be observed in almost every other particular. The Sun and the Moon were peculiarly venerated on the tops of mountains and of pyramidal buildings constructed in imitation of mountains: because every such sacred mountain and pyramidal edifice was deemed a copy, as we are unequivocally assured, of the primeval arkite mount of Pa-

the Chinese, though seated at a great distance from each other, possessed astronomical formulæ common to them all. These were handed down to them by tradition from some general course: for they used them, as our workmen use certain mechanical or geometrical rules, without any knowledge of the principles on which they were originally constructed. See Hales's Chronol. vol. i. p. 144. Our present sphere is in the main the same as that of the old Babylonians, Indians, and Egyptians, from whom no doubt the Greeks received it.

radise, that favourite abode of the great father and the great mother. The Sun and the Moon, strange as it may at first appear, were thought to be infernal deities: because the great father and the great mother were reckoned deities of Hades. The Sun and the Moon were each supposed to be furnished with a gate or door; through which, and likewise through the similar doors of the planets, transmigrating souls were feigned to be born during their sidereal progress towards perfection: because there was a door in the side of the Ark, through which the Noëtic family were born into a new state of existence; and because every sacred cavern had a door, by passing through which aspirants were believed to procure the benefits of a mysterious regeneration.

On the same principle, we may account for another curious opinion entertained respecting all the celestial luminaries. They were equally thought to have sprung out of the chaotic fluid, in which the earth floated (as it were) both at the time of the creation and of the deluge: they were supposed to be intelligent animals produced out of unintelligent animals: and they were said to have been all formed alike in the shape of an egg. The notion doubtless originated from the circumstance of an egg being employed to symbolize both the World and the Ark. By the mystic theocrasia, so familiar to the ancient mythologists, each luminary, taken separately, represented the primeval hermaphrodic deity, who united in his own person the blended characters of the great father and the great mother: hence, each was born out of the aqueous fluid; each, from non-intelligence, became endowed with intelligence; and each had attributed to it the form of that egg, out of which the principal Demon-god and the three kings into whose persons he multiplied himself were feigned to have been born by a certain ineffable generation. In exact accordance with this speculation, the hierophants invented a curious legend, which describes the Dioscori or Cabiri as produced from a wonderful egg that fell out of the Moon. Now the Cabiri were evidently the great father and his family; and the egg, out of which they were born, was the acknowledged symbol of the great mother: yet the Moon, for reasons which can now be scarcely misunderstood, is immediately connected with that egg. Thus exact throughout is the correspondence between Sabianism and Demonolatry: each answers to each with the minute accuracy of the parts of a severed indenture.

III. The union of Sabianism and Demonolatry engendered Materialism: but it was a Materialism of such a nature as faithfully to preserve the lineaments of its parents.

1. When all things were supposed to be produced from the conjunction of the great father and the great mother, and when these were elevated to the Sun and Moon or were thought in their different emanations to animate the starry host of heaven; it was an easy step to adopt the opinion, that the various parts of creation were but so many members or (as they were sometimes called) forms of the universal compound hermaphroditic deity. All nature was produced from him, and returned to him: all nature was his body: and his pervading Spirit was the Soul of the World. Yet the name, which was given to this soul, seems not obscurely to point out the character chiefly intended by it.

The import of the Greek *Nous* and of the Sanscrit *Menu* is precisely the same: each denotes *Mind* or *Intelligence;* and to the latter of them the Latin *Mens* is evidently very nearly allied; or, to speak more properly, *Mens* and *Menu,* perhaps also our English *Mind,* are fundamentally one and the same word.[1] Yet I strongly suspect, that the idea of *Intelligence,* which all these terms equally convey, is but a secondary and acquired sense. The question will still recur, why *Intelligence* has been called *Nous* or *Menu* or *Mens* or *Mind.* The names seem to me to have been equally borrowed, in the first instance, from the name of that primeval personage; who, reappearing (as it was supposed agreeably to the transmigratory system) at the commencement of the postdiluvian world, was esteemed, in his character of the great father, the animating Soul of that World his body. *Nous* and *Menu,* so far as their *original* derivation is concerned, are both probably mere variations of the name of *Noah:* the former expressing that name simply; the latter giving it, according to its oriental pronunciation *Nuh,* with the Sanscrit *Men* which denotes *Intelligent* prefixed to it.[2] But, however this may be (and it is a matter of very little moment, whether the conjecture be well or ill founded), both the *Nous* of the

[1] See Sir W. Jones's Preface to the Instit. of Menu. p. 10.

[2] Jones's Pref. to Instit. of Menu. p. x. Asiat. Res. vol. i. p. 239.

The great father + great mother blended in one hermaphroditic unity created all things from their/its womb

Greek philosophers and the *Menu* of the Hindoos, though the import. of each be similarly *Mind* or *Intelligence*, and though in the material system each be the Soul of the World, are alike, in point of personality, the great father: for Menu-Satyavrata was preserved in an ark at the time of the deluge; and Nous himself, together with three younger Noës into whom he was thought to have triplicated himself, was born from the mysterious primeval egg.

2. The writings of the old mythologists strongly maintain the doctrine, which identifies both the great father and the great mother, or those two persons blended into one compound hermaphroditic character, with the whole material creation.

The great father and the great mother jointly, or the compound hermaphroditic god singly, was the Universe.

That primitive double god was esteemed one, and yet all things. From his productive womb was born the Universe: at the end of each successive world, every thing is swallowed up or absorbed by him: and, at the commencement of each new world, every thing is born again from him; for to destroy is still only preparative to creating afresh. Agreeably to these notions, every part of the visible creation was esteemed a member or form of the great hermaphroditic parent: all things were comprehended within himself, and his stupendous body was composed of all things.

This is not taught in the Bible

Yahweh is wholly separate from + transcendent to His creation

Such was the idea, which produced the curious definition of the chief deity of the Egyptians, that occurs in the writings of Hermes Trismegistus: *God is a circle, whose centre is every where, but whose circumference can no where be found.* The circle, or ring, or egg, or globe, was a symbol of the World, under whatever modification it was viewed; whether as the Ark or Microcosm, as the Earth or Megacosm, as the Universe or Megistocosm. In its largest signification, it was deemed, and perhaps actually is, boundless: yet, in the material system, it was esteemed the body of that great father; who was himself born from an egg, who was thought mysteriously to have triplicated himself, and whose soul was reckoned the animating principle of the whole.

Egyptian

An idea, the same in substance, was perfectly familiar to the Hindoo philosophers. At the earnest request of Arjun, the primeval Brahm, who triplicated his substance into the three chief Demon-gods of India, or (in plain English) who begot three sons, disclosed to him his celestial form,

Hindu

beaming with glory a thousand times more vivid than the light of the meridian Sun. *The son of Pandu then beheld, within the body of the deity, standing together, the whole Universe divided forth into its vast variety. He was overwhelmed with wonder, and every hair was raised on end. He bowed down his head before the god.* Here the universe is placed within the womb of the great hermaphrodite; from which at the beginning of every world it was produced, and to which at the end of every world it returned.

Just the same notion prevailed among the hierophants of Greece. *All things, we are told, were framed within the body of Jupiter: the bright expanse of the ethereal heavens, the solid earth, the vast ocean, the central realms of Tartarus, every flowing stream, every god and goddess, every thing that is, and every thing that shall be ; each of these equally proceeded from him, for all were produced together within his capacious womb. Jupiter was alike the beginning and the ending, the head and the middle : Jupiter was at once a male and an immortal nymph. Earth, heaven, air, fire, the sea, the sun, and the moon, were each equally and severally Jupiter. The whole Universe constituted one body; the body of that king, from whom originated all things : and within that body every elemental principle alike revolved; for all things were contained within the vast womb of the god. Heaven was his head : the bright beams of the stars were his radiant locks : the east and the west, those sacred roads of the immortals, were his tauriform horns: the sun and the moon were his eyes : the grosser atmosphere was his back, his breast, and his shoulders, expanding into two wings with which he flies over the face of universal nature : the all-productive earth was his sacred womb: the circling ocean was his belt: the roots of the earth and the nether regions of Tartarus were his feet: his body, the universe, was radiant, immoveable, eternal: and the pure ether was his intellectual soul, the mighty Nous, by which he pervades, animates, preserves, and governs, all things.* This horned universal Jupiter is declared to be the same deity as Pan; the same also as Dionusus, Pluto, Serapis, and Osiris: accordingly, we find the god Pan described in a manner almost exactly similar. The ancient poet, who has left us upon record the preceding mythological character of Jupiter, celebrates Pan, *as being the*

[margin notes:]
Greece

Jupiter the origin of all things to the Greeks.

Jupiter = Pan, Dionusus, Pluto, Serapis + Osiris

Pan

whole of the world, and as uniting in his own person all the elements of nature. Heaven, earth, sea, and fire, are all but members of the god. He is the universal father, the lord of the world, the productive source of every thing. Through his wisdom imperishable nature undergoes a perpetual change; and by his energy the generations of men, throughout the boundless world, follow each other in endless succession.

Exactly similar is the character of the Egyptian Serapis, as exhibited in an oracle said to have been delivered by himself to the Cyprian Prince Nicocreon. *The celestial world is my head: the sea is my womb: the earth supplies to me the place of feet: the pure ether furnishes me with ears: and the bright lustre of the sun is my eye.* Such also in effect is Isis; for that goddess, viewed in her character of an hermaphrodite, identifies herself with the great two-fold father. She is invocated as being one and all things: and she is described as saying, *I am whatever has been, is, or shall be; and no one among mortals has ever taken off my veil: I am nature, the mother of all things, the mistress of the elements, the beginning of ages, the sovereign of the gods, the queen of departed spirits.*

Thus, when the great father and the great mother were blended together into one character, the compound deity thus produced was, in the material system, the Universe animated by what was called the Soul of the World: when they were viewed as two distinct characters, the former became the fructifying principle, the latter the matrix of nature which was rendered fruitful; and this idea was variously expressed. Sometimes it was mind acting upon matter; sometimes it was the sun impregnating the general frame of nature; and sometimes it was the mighty paternal ether descending to embrace his consort the earth.

3. The great father and the great mother being now identified with the Universe, as they had before been astronomically translated to the orbs of the Sun and the Moon, every idea which Sabianism had borrowed from Demonolatry, was yet further extended to Materialism.

Wherever the hierophant turned his eyes, or whenever he pursued his favourite speculations, the notion of death succeeded by a revival or a new-birth, of disappearance succeeded by reappearance, of sepulture succeeded by resurrection, of destruction succeeded by reproduction, perpetually pre-

(margin notes)

SERAPIS

Same claims as Jupiter

ISIS

Same claims as Serapis

All the ideas of Demonolatry were extended to Materialism.

sented itself to his mind in an almost endless variety. Each animal revived·
in its offspring : each seed died, was buried, and rose again, in the form of
a new plant: Each day, after dying into the gloom of night, returned to
life in the succeeding day : each year expired only to live afresh in the new
year. Every winter, the whole vegetable creation appeared to sink into the
torpidity of death : every spring, it seemed to burst forth into fresh· life.
Even the great globe itself, as well as all that inhabit it ; even the yet
greater Universe, in all its parts ; was thought to follow the general analogy of nature. Matter itself indeed was eternal : but, at certain immense
stated periods, the world, which was formed out of it, was resolved into
its original chaos ; and, after the allotted time of repose subsequent to destruction, started afresh from its deathlike condition of ruin and desolation
into new life and beauty and action. Thus accurately did the regeneration of
the great father in his mundane character in general, and in every modification of that character in particular, correspond with his regeneration from
the Ark in his proper human character.

But that ancient personage was not only thought to have been mysteriously born again from the dead ; he was likewise feigned to have triplicated
his substance into three younger and subordinate deities, who might yet be
ultimately resolved into the unity of their parent. Hence, when in the material system he was identified with the Universe which was supposed to
have sprung from his prolific womb, it became necessary, in order to preserve the decorum and concinnity of his character, to discover or invent
some corresponding triplication in the Universe. From this source originated the various material triads of the Gentiles : for, whether they addicted
themselves to Demonolatry, to Sabianism, or to gross Materialism, we still
invariably find the same propensity to the triple division, which was esteemed so peculiarly dear to the god whom they worshipped. Pursuant to such
a speculation, the unity of the whole world, that supposed body of the
great father, was divided into what were called three worlds, though the
three were nevertheless fundamentally but one Universe. Nor was this the
only triad of Materialism. Sometimes the three conditions of light, heat,
and fire, excited the fanatical veneration of the misguided idolater : sometimes he bowed down to the subtle ether, the grosser atmospheric air, and

the all-productive earth : sometimes he worshipped the sun, the air, and the thunder : and sometimes he devoutly adored the elements of earth, fire, and water; applying to these the names of that identical triple divinity, who, in one or other of his persons, was born from the symbolical egg, reposed in a death-like sleep on the surface of the ocean during the period that intervenes between each two succeeding worlds, floated in the calyx of the mysterious lotos on the bosom of the mighty deep, or sailed securely in a divine ship the form of the great mother over the waters of the general deluge.

There was yet another characteristic of the chief Demon-god, which was not to be overlooked. The ancients well knew, that his family at the commencement of both worlds consisted of eight persons. In the astronomical system they had contrived to man the vast ship of the sphere with eight celestial mariners : they had now to devise a similar arrangement for the material system. Nor were they here very anxious to attend to the strict natural propriety of things: they had already procured the number *three;* and, at all hazards, these determined analogical speculatists were resolved to elicit the number *eight* from the reluctant frame of the unbending Universe.

Accordingly, they tell us, that the great father, who once floated in a ship on the surface of the deluge, and who, together with the vessel which carried him, was transformed into a dove while the waters were retiring, shone forth conspicuously in eight forms on the summit of that sacred paradisiacal mountain; where the ark, in which eight holy persons were preserved, rested at the close of a general flood that destroyed a former world. From the whole connexion of this legend, there can be no doubt, I think, that the eight forms of the great father mean the eight persons who were saved in the Ark ; those eight persons, whom the Egyptians adored as their chief gods, and whom they depicted sailing together in a ship over the ocean. Yet, when that same great father is materially identified with the Universe, his eight forms are then expressly pronounced to be the somewhat heterogeneous ogdoad of Water, Fire, Sacrifice, the Sun, the Moon, Ether, Earth, and Air. From this combination I think it sufficiently clear, that eight forms were not ascribed to the great father because the Universe

[margin, handwritten:] The number 8

is capable of a natural division into eight parts ; but that, it being *already* known that the great father as a Demon-god *had* precisely eight forms, the Universe was arbitrarily divided by the number *eight* because that number was requisite to complete the system. The propriety of such a remark will further appear from the circumstance, that the same enumeration of forms was not always adhered to, though the exact number *eight* was duly retained. An ogdoad is said to have been produced from the womb of the hermaphroditic Jupiter, who is described as the great parent identified with the Universe : but, while it is just as heterogeneous in point of composition as the last, its members are by no means coincident, though the sum total in both cases equally produces the number *eight*. This second ogdoad consists of Fire, Water, Earth, Air, Night, Day, Metis, and Eros. Here again, as in the case of the former one, the members are plainly accommodated to the number : the number is not chosen, because by a natural arrangement the members exactly amounted to eight; but eight members are arbitrarily associated together, because the precise number *eight* had been previously selected and the sum total was to be made up whether congruously or incongruously.

As the great demon-father, when materialized, was thus multiplied into eight forms, because in his human character his family comprehended just eight persons : so the great mother, from her hermaphroditic identification with her allegorical consort, was, in the material system, likewise said to have eight forms. These eight forms therefore, by a necessary consequence, were the very same as the eight forms of her consort: and, accordingly, as, in the Orphic theology, Fire, Water, Earth, Air, Night, Day, Metis, and Eros, are the offspring of Jupiter both male and female; so, in the Hindoo theology, Water, Fire, Sacrifice, the Sun, the Moon, Ether, Earth, and Air, are alike and equally the forms of Iswara and Isi, the Osiris and Isis of Egypt. It may be remarked, that, when Iswara and Isi are joined together in one hermaphroditic person, who then bears the name of *Arddha-Nari*, they perfectly answer to the double Jupiter.[1]

4. But the material system did not stop with representing merely the

---

[1] See Plate II. Fig. 8.

larger parts of the Universe as members or forms of the great parent, or with fancifully dividing the immense body of the god by the numbers *three* or *eight*. If the whole world was the varied deity, every thing in that world, though comparatively it might be small in size, would be equally one of his forms or members : he would breathe in every bird, beast, and reptile ; no less than he would diffuse light and fertility from the Sun, or scatter plenty over the earth from each aërial shower. This seems to have occasioned that endless variety of symbols, by which the great parent was wont to be represented ; a variety, amounting almost literally, as the prophet expresses it, to *every form of creeping things and abominable beasts.*[1] Certain symbols indeed, in particular, may have had an additional distinct origin of their own : but the endless multiplication of them certainly appears to have sprung from the source here pointed out.

We may observe a regular system pervading the whole of animal symbolization : by whatever creature the great father was represented, the great mother was invariably typified by the corresponding female. If the one was a man, the other was a woman : if the one was a bull, the other was a cow : if the one was a horse, the other was a mare : if the one was a merman, the other was a mermaid : if the one was a male serpent, the other was a female serpent. By similar pairs of hieroglyphics, the fancy of the ancient materialists ran, consistently enough, almost through the whole circle of creation : and the two great parents were equally discovered in a cock and a hen, a male dove and a female dove, a male fish and a female fish, a male ass and a female ass, a male elephant and a female elephant, a male centaur and a female centaur, a boar and a sow, a dog and a bitch, a ram and an ewe, a bee the sex of which was doubted, a male crocodile and a female crocodile.

A passage, yet extant in an ancient writer, throws much light on this curious subject. *Nothing existed in this world before the production of Mind : this Universe was encircled by Death eager to devour, for death is the devourer. He framed Mind, being desirous of himself becoming endued with a soul.* The commentators here explain Death to be the intel-

[1] Ezek. viii. 10.

[Margin note: system, every part of the Universe was a member of the great parent: hence, in part at least, originated symbolical imagery.]

lectual being, who sprang from the golden mundane egg. I believe them to be perfectly right, not only because they may be supposed to understand best their own theology, but because such an exposition fully accords with the prevailing notions of paganism. The person here called *Death* is doubtless the great father in his character both of an infernal god and a destroyer. Yet he destroys only to regenerate: and both he himself, and the world which is his body, successively die and are born again after the lapse of certain stated periods.

But let us observe the actions of this mysterious being, when he first appears upon the renovated world after his production from the sacred egg and his union with an intelligent soul. *Looking round, he saw nothing but himself; and he said* I am I: *therefore his name was* I; *and thence, even now, when called, a man first answers* It is I, *and then declares any other name which appertains to him. He felt dread; and therefore man fears when alone. But he reflected,* Since nothing exists besides myself, why should I fear? *Thus his terror departed from him: for what should he dread, since fear must be of another? He felt not delight: and therefore man delights not, when alone. He wished the existence of another: and instantly he became such as is man and woman in mutual embrace. He caused this his own self to fall in twain; and thus he became a husband and a wife. Therefore was this body so separated an imperfect moiety of himself. The blank is completed by woman. He approached her; and thence were human beings produced. She reflected doubtingly,* How can he, having produced me from himself, incestuously approach me? I will now assume a disguise. *She became a cow; and the other became a bull, and approached her: and the issue were kine. She was changed into a mare; and he, into a stallion: one was turned into a female ass; and the other, into a male ass. Thus did he again approach her; and the one-hoofed kind was the offspring. She became a female goat; and he, a male one: she was an ewe; and he, a ram. Thus he approached her; and goats and sheep were the progeny. In this manner did he create every existing pair whatsoever, even to the ants and minutest insect.*

The person, it will be observed, who undergoes such a series of transformations, is that regenerative Death, who, having destroyed a former world, is himself, after an appointed interval, born again from a golden egg, and becomes the universal father of a new order of things. Assuming a human shape, he now bears the name of *Viraj*, and is described as being the parent of Menu : but he is evidently the same as Menu himself; for Menu was the first man both of the antediluvian and postdiluvian worlds, and a similar story is told of each Menu having incestuous communication with his daughter Satarupa and Ila, the latter of which appellations denotes *the world:* accordingly, the commentators rightly understand the incestuous marriage of Menu to be alluded to in the preceding legend of Death or Viraj. The person therefore, who in the mythology of the pagans is venerated as the creator of the world, who is esteemed the Soul of the Universe, and of whom every thing material whether great or small is a member or form, is plainly not the Supreme Being, whom by their perverted wisdom they had ceased to know ; but a mere man, who was deemed the head and parent of each successive similar world, who was thought to have produced and still to animate every living creature, and who was worshipped as the chief and oldest of the Demon-gods.

Now, as the Universe in general was the reputed body of this primeval character, and as each element and more conspicuous part of the Universe was one of his forms or members ; so, from his having successively assumed the shape of every animal while employed in the work of creation, every animal became sacred and was entitled to divine worship, every animal was a form or symbol of the great polymorphic deity. Of these innumerable hieroglyphics some indeed came more generally into use than others : but all obtained a certain degree of veneration; inasmuch as all represented by pairs the primeval father and mother, who had successively passed by transmigration through every one of them.

5. This notion gave a new and last form to the doctrine of the Metempsychosis. Its *proper* origin we have traced to the belief, that similar worlds succeeded similar worlds in endless progression, and that the same persons who had appeared in one world reappeared in another, their souls passing from their former corporeal vehicles to the new ones which were prepared for them on each reproduction of the mundane system. We have next observed, when Sabianism was united with Demonolatry, and when each idea proper to

The doctrine of Metempsychosis adapted to Materialism

the latter was transferred to the former, that the Metempsychosis experienced its first corruption by an adaptation to astronomical reveries: as souls were then thought to be born, in some mysterious manner, from the doors of the Sun and the Moon; so they were feigned to pass by a celestial transmigration through the spheres of the different planets, until at length, purified from all their mortal stains, they were absorbed in the divine paternal essence from which they had originally emanated. We are now finally brought to the Metempsychosis of Materialism: for, as that theory closely imitated Demonolatry in its speculations concerning a great father and a great mother, destruction and regeneration, triads and ogdoads; so it likewise copied it in the tenet of a certain transmigration of souls through the different parts of material nature.

It was an axiom in ancient paganism throughout all its branches, that, whatever was done or suffered by the chief Demon-god, should also be mystically done and suffered by the aspirant in his progress to an ideal perfection. Hence, since the various elements were each a form of the deity, since he lived in every vegetable and had tenanted the body of every animal, the aspirant must revolve through a similar circle of perpetual change, ere he had attained a complete likeness to the god whom he venerated. The whole of the curious mythological poem of Ovid is founded upon this extravagant notion: and every river and fountain, every tree and animal, was in the pagan creed endowed by it with a living and intelligent spirit. Agreeably to such an opinion, the transmigrating soul, according to the different degrees of pollution which it had contracted in the flesh, was thought sometimes to flit into the subtle element of air, sometimes to be plunged into the vasty deep, sometimes to be cast into a blazing fire, sometimes to be whirled round and round in Hades or the central cavity of the earth, sometimes to be wedged fast in mineral substances, sometimes to be embodied in trees or low shrubs or gramineous vegetables, and sometimes to pass through a long succession of birds and beasts and reptiles. Hence we find it asserted, that *all animals and vegetables, by reason of past actions, have internal conscience, and are sensible of pleasure and pain; and that all transmigrations, recorded in sacred books, from the state of the chief Demon-god himself to that of plants, happen continually in this tremendous world of beings, a world always tending to decay.* Hence also we find a fanatical hierophant, when detailing the process of his manifold regeneration, describe his progress through various animals, in a manner exactly resembling the progress of the great father himself through the whole bestial creation when engaged in the work of renewing a destroyed world. *A second time was I formed. I have been a blue salmon: I have been a dog: I have been a stag: I have been a roebuck on the mountain: I have been a stock of a tree: I have been a spade: I have been an axe in the hand: I have been a pin in a forceps for a year and a half: I have been a cock, variegated with white, upon hens: I have been a stallion upon a mare: I have been a buck of a yellow hue, in the act of feeding: I have been a grain of the arkites, which vegetated on a hill; and then the reaper placed me in a smoky recess, that I might be compelled freely to yield my corn, when subjected to tribulation. I was received by a hen with red fangs and a divided crest: I remained nine nights an infant in her womb: I have been Aedd,* returning to my former state: I have been an offering before the sovereign:* I have died: I have revived: and, conspicuous with my ivy-branch, I have been a leader, and by my bounty I became poor. Again was I instructed by the cherisher with red fangs. Of what she gave me, scarcely can I utter the great praise that is due.*

In consequence of the great father and the great mother being supposed to have assumed the forms of all animals, they were sometimes expressly called by the names of those animals which were now become their symbols. Thus we find them severally denominated, according to their sexual difference, *a bull, a cow, a dragon, a cock, a hen, a bee,* or *a dog.* And, as their priests or priestesses assumed upon all occasions the titles of the deities whom they served and laboured to exhibit in their own persons each action or suffering which was attributed to them, we also find, that the ministers were designated by the names of those animals, through which both their gods and themselves were feigned to have passed by a mystic transmigration. Thus they were called, similarly allowing for sexual difference, *horses, mares, bees, ravens, doves, lions, dogs,* and *swine.* I think it probable, from some cir-

---

[1] A name of Hades, or Death, or Menu, or the great father, who presides over reciprocal destruction and renovation.

[2] One of the eight forms of the great hermaphroditic parent is said to be Sacrifice.

cumstances, that, in the celebration of the Mysteries, they wore grotesque masks; by means of which they actually appeared, like the sculptured forms of some of their gods, to be human beings deformed by bearing the heads of the sacred animals.   Such was the wisdom of Egypt and of the children of the east! Such were the absurdities, into which men were gradually seduced when they forsook the Lord their God! Perhaps no one can thoroughly appreciate our weight of obligation to the Gospel for extricating us from this thick darkness, unless he has been led to investigate both the theory and the practice of ancient paganism.

6. Some writers of note, while they reasonably enough reject the opinion which once very much prevailed that the heathens actually and literally worshipped the devil, have been led, perhaps incautiously, into the other extreme.   From some remarkable expressions, which have been used by gentile authors in various countries, and which in their legitimate acceptation can only be applied with propriety to the Supreme Being, they have inferred, that the true God was the object of pagan, no less than of Jewish and Christian, veneration, though his attributes were disguised and his worship was debased by much vanity and superstition.   And they have been the rather led to adopt such a conjecture, by finding, that all the gods and goddesses of the pagans, in whatever country they may be adored, melting insensibly into each other, are at length resolved into one essence; who is represented as being the creator of the world, and who is grossly though not unfitly described as uniting in himself the productive energy of both sexes.   Hence those remarkable expressions, and some equally remarkable descriptions, have been brought forward as highly sublime and as indicating the just conceptions which the pagan sages entertained of the nature of God.[1]   And this has been done, not merely by the adversaries of revelation, but by men of high respec-

The pagans did not worship the true God, though they ascribe His attributes to their chief hero-divinity.

---

[1] Thus the description of Arjun beholding the whole Universe within the body of the great god of the Hindoos, which I have noticed above, has been pronounced to be very sublime by a writer both of talent and good religious principle, and the god spoken of has been concluded to mean the true God. The latter position I do not believe: and the propriety of the former is of course a matter of taste.   It *may* be very sublime to put the whole mundane system into the capacious paunch of a gigantic deity: but I must confess, that it rather excites in my own mind an idea bordering on the ludicrous.

tability and attainments; who are themselves fully convinced both of its authenticity and importance; and who have laboured to promote its cause.

It is undoubtedly true, that language is used respecting the chief object of pagan worship, which in strict propriety can only be employed in speaking of the true God; and it is highly probable, that such phraseology, which sometimes bears a strong resemblance to certain scriptural expressions, has been handed down from a period prior to the commencement of apostate idolatry, even from the days of Noah himself.[1] It is reasonable also to believe, as I have already intimated, that the more thinking few of the ancient heathens, partly from tradition not wholly obliterated, and partly from attending even to the light of nature, might be thoroughly convinced, that there must be some intelligent spiritual eternal cause of all things, himself uncaused and existing anterior to the production of every created being and substance. Such a belief forces itself almost irresistibly upon every reflecting mind, even from the mere contemplation of the regularity and order so conspicuous in the disposition of the Universe; though, without revelation, the unassisted inquirer must be greatly in the dark respecting the true nature and attributes of that awful and invisible Being: accordingly, much good reasoning on the necessity of a first cause is to be found in the writings of the pagan philosophers; such writings, for instance, as the treatise of Tully on the nature of the gods. But this, so far as I can judge, is wholly insufficient to establish the hypothesis, that the chief deity of the Gentiles was *truly* and *properly* Jehovah, acknowledged as the creator of the world, though dimly viewed through the mist of polytheistic absurdity. The mere ascription of certain attributes of Jehovah to that deity will not prove their identity; nor can it set aside the apostolic declaration, that by their wisdom the heathens knew

---

[1] The following may serve as a specimen of the language in question. It is addressed by Brahm, whom I cannot agree with Sir W. Jones in believing to be the Supreme Being, to Brahma one of his three emanations or sons. *Even I was even at first, not any other thing; that, which exists unperceived, supreme: afterward, I am that which is; and he, who must remain, am I. Except the first cause, whatever may appear, and may not appear in the mind, know that to be the mind's delusion, as light, as darkness. As the great elements are in various beings, entering, yet not entering (that is, pervading, not destroying), thus am I in them, yet not in them. Even thus far may enquiry be made by him, who seeks to know the principle of mind in union and separation, which must be every where always.* Bhagavat in Asiat. Res. vol. i. p. 245, 8vo. edit.

not God, and that to all intents and purposes they were no better than atheists. [1]   The reason of this is sufficiently obvious.   When a mere mortal was elevated to the rank of deity, the attributes of deity were of course ascribed to him: for, without such an ascription, the concinnity of his new character could not have been preserved; it being plainly impossible to worship a man as a god, and yet give him no one characteristic of the godhead.   The great father therefore being deified by the blind veneration of his posterity, he was thenceforth inevitably addressed and spoken of in corresponding language: that is to say, the very expressions, which have been too hastily thought to imply a worship of the true God, were, by a necessary consequence, employed in describing or in adoring a mere deified mortal.   Such deification having once taken place, the thing could not possibly have been otherwise than it is.   The new divinity usurped the honours of Jehovah: and, what properly belong only to the latter, were blasphemously ascribed to the former.   The creature was worshipped rather than the Creator: and, as the recollection of the proper nature of the fictitious deity was never wholly lost, while the adoration of the true God was discontinued, a system of gross material atheism was sometimes the result; and the apostasy of paganism thus received its final consummation.   Cosmogonies were invented without any first intelligent cause, and a succession of acknowledged semi-human Demon-gods governed that world from which the real Demiurge was excluded, though it was impossible to give any satisfactory account whence they themselves originated.   Such impieties peculiarly marked the Hermetic or Buddhic theology: yet they resulted not unnaturally from the pagan system, compounded as it was of Demonolatry, Sabianism, and Materialism, and substituting as it did the worship of the creature for that of the Creator, when once it was pushed by daring men to its furthest extremity.

7. It being thus shewn, that the mere ascription of divine attributes, even in terms of the greatest sublimity, is in itself no proof whatsoever of the ultimate identity of the true God and the chief deity of the Gentiles; would we know what person is really meant by that chief deity, we must inquire into the historical facts recorded of him, not weary ourselves with abstract reasonings which will leave the matter just as undecided as they found it.

Hero-divinity was Adam reappearing in the person of Noah.

[1] 1 Corinth. i, 21, Rom, i, 21—25, 28. Ephes. ii. 12.

Now we learn, that all the divinities of Paganism do indeed resolve themselves, first into a god and goddess, and at length into one god compounded of those two and distinguished by a participation of both sexes: but we have little reason indeed to believe, that that one god is Jehovah, notwithstanding the creation of the world is ascribed to him. The historical character of the personage in question is briefly, as follows.

Matter being eternal, and there being an endless succession of similar worlds (for to destroy is but to create afresh in another form); he, who appears at the commencement of each world, and who, as a female, produces from his fruitful womb every thing that has life, is, in one respect, eternal also: for it is not a new character, who then makes his appearance; but a primeval personage merely reappears in a new form, who had already appeared in other forms at the beginning of every renovated world. At the end of each world, when its organization is destroyed and when it is resolved into its component eternal matter, this personage sleeps the sleep of death, during the space of a year (sometimes called *a year of the gods*), floating securely on the surface of the ocean, either in the calix of the Lotos, or on a leaf of the betal tree, or on a vast serpent coiled up in an oval form like a boat, or in a huge fish, or in a cow, or in the womb of a goddess whose ribs he had himself fashioned, or lastly and literally in a wonderful ship which was esteemed a type of the Universe. After he has duly slept the appointed intermediate space between two successive worlds, and when the time has now arrived for the creation of a new world out of the material wreck of the former one, he then awakes from his deathlike slumber; and, as he had before exchanged the season of energy for that of repose, he now exchanges the season of repose for that of energy. At this period, though he is declared to be the creator of all things, yet he himself is born out of a golden egg, which had been tossed about by the winds and waves on the surface of the ocean. Thus being reproduced, or born again, or restored to life, or awakened from sleep (for all these various expressions are indifferently used to denote the same thing); he begins, as he had before begun, with causing a woman to be born out of his own substance, he himself having previously assumed the form of a man. Then he triplicates himself, and thus produces three younger gods; as he had already similarly triplicated himself at the com-

mencement of a former world. About the same time, he and his consort
successively assume the forms of all animals: and, as in a human shape they
are the parents of mankind, so in various bestial shapes they become the
parents of the whole brute creation. When the end of this world arrives,
its frame is dissolved like that of its predecessor. Nothing is properly left
but the great father; for his three emanations, each of which is described as
having a wife, are considered, with their respective consorts, as being virtually one with their parent. Again he sleeps, during the limited period of
a year, on the surface of the ocean: again he awakes to a new existence:
again he is born from a wonderful golden egg: again he triplicates himself: again he creates a new world out of the wreck of the former one: and
thus, with an everlasting interchange of destruction and reproduction, rolls
on, through an endless succession of ages, the vast wheel of the material
Universe.

These are the outlines of his eventful history: but various explanatory
particulars are added to it, which throw additional light on the character
of the egg-born creator of the world, who by some has been identified with
Jehovah of hosts.

We find him acknowledged by the commentators on the sacred books to
be fundamentally the same character as one; who, in different countries,
bears the cognate titles of *Menu, Menes, Manes, Mneuis, Menwyd, Mannus, Man,* and *Minos :* for the production of the woman from the egg-
born Viraj or Death or Brahma, who similarly springs from an egg and who
similarly is at first an hermaphrodite, is allowed to be no other than the
production of Satarupa from the side of a former Menu; whence it will
follow, that Menu must be the same as Viraj or Death or Brahma, and
consequently the same as that creator of the world respecting whom those
remarkable expressions are used which have induced the supposition that he
was really the true God. Now this former Menu and his consort, the literal woman that was produced out of his side, with whom a world anterior
to the present commenced, are said to have borne among their other titles
the names of *Adima* and *Iva :* [1] and, in the persons of their three sons, one of

---

[1] Pronounced *Eva*, according to the French mode of sounding the letter *I;* or rather *Eve,*
for in Sanscrit the final short *A* is quiescent like the final *E* of the French.

IV: All the various modifications of Paganism in every quarter of the globe originated from a common source, not from different or independent sources.

THE ORIGIN OF PAGAN IDOLATRY. 57

whom (we are told) slew his unoffending brother at the offering up of a re-markable sacrifice, the three periodical emanations of the great father, which regularly appear at the beginning of every world, became incar-nate.

But there was another younger Menu, with whom this present world com-menced, who was a reappearance of the former Menu, who bore the same name, and in whose triple offspring the three emanations again became in-carnate. This personage, who was esteemed the same as Death or Hades or the god of obsequies or the ferryman of departed spirits, was directed at the close of a prior world to build an ark. He obeyed the command : at the appointed time, that prior world was destroyed by a flood : but he, with seven holy companions and a requisite number of animals and veget-able seeds, was preserved in the ark to repeople and stock afresh a new world.

Here, from the acknowledged identity of Menu and the demiurgic Viraj or Death, we have a literal explanation, which cannot be misunderstood, of the sleep of the chief deity of the Gentiles, during the year which intervenes between two worlds, on the surface of the ocean : and the history of a former Menu at the commencement of a former world is scarcely more equivocal or more unintelligible. Yet to this person, who is plainly Adam fancifully deemed to have transmigrated into the body of Noah, the Gen-tiles ascribed the creation of the world, decked him with the borrowed at-tributes of the true God, and spoke of him in language properly applica-ble only to Jehovah. But the great deity of paganism, whose history I have thus briefly detailed and whose character must be determined solely by his history, is not on *that* account to be confounded with the pure and holy spirit ; who alone *exists unperceived and supreme,* who alone can claim the title of *I am that which is,* who alone is *the first cause,* and who alone *is every where always.*

IV. In this prefatory sketch of pagan superstition I have made no dis-tinction between the mythologies of different nations, but have considered them all together as jointly forming a single well-compacted and regular sys-tem : I am perfectly aware however, that it was at one time very much the humour to view paganism as a thing altogether capricious and irregular.

Adam blended with Noah and worshipped as if Jehovah.

Each nation was thought to have its own ritual and its own set of deities; framed independently of every other nation: and, if any coincidence were occasionally observed, it was deemed the effect of pure accident, not of design. In short, paganism was supposed to have as many different origins, as there were nations which had apostatized from the truth. Men agreed only in equally following the vagaries of their wayward imaginations : and the consequence was, that, as they gradually settled in different parts of the globe, an almost endless variety of discordant and unconnected systems was struck out. Idolaters indeed would generally resemble each other in worshipping the Sun, the Moon, and the Stars: because, when they departed from the knowledge of God, those bright bodies, which are such manifest benefactors to the earth, would first engage their attention and excite their grateful adoration. They would probably also agree in venerating the departed spirits of heroes, who had distinguished themselves above their fellows, and who had rendered essential service to their country : because this superstition, as well as the last, would be obvious and natural. But here the resemblance ceased: each nation had its own arbitrary mode of worship, each nation had its own peculiar speculations. They agreed in what was *obvious* ; they disagreed in what was *circumstantial*. But original correspondence of design can only be proved by *arbitrary circumstantials*: and a coincidence in the worship of the host of heaven or of the souls of departed benefactors can no more demonstrate, that the theological systems of different pagan nations had all one common origin ; than a coincidence in fishing, and hunting, and dwelling in huts, and pointing weapons with the bones or teeth of animals, and filth, and petty warfare, and cruelty, can demonstrate two antipodal clans of barbarians to have sprung in common from some one special primitive tribe. Hence, when the classical writers bestowed, as was their ordinary custom, the names of *Jupiter* or *Bacchus* or *Mercury* on the gods of other nations ; it does not shew, that those other nations really agreed with the Greeks and Romans in worshipping Jupiter or Bacchus or Mercury, neither does it prove, that they closely symbolized with them in those *arbitrary circumstantials* which can alone be allowed to constitute the essence of a regular system : it merely proves, that the writers in question, observing some casual and imperfect resemblance between their own Bacchus (for instance) and a god of some other people; instantly designated that god by the name of *Bacchus* without giving themselves the trouble to make any more accurate inquiries into the matter.[1]

F. I have stated this opinion with all the force, I believe, of which it is capable; and I will readily allow, that, if the premises were well founded, the conclusion would be inevitable: that is to say, if the theological systems of the various pagan nations resembled each other only in what was *obvious* and *natural*, while they totally differed from each other in what was *arbitrary* and *circumstantial* and *artificial*, we might be perfectly sure that they did not originate from any common source, but on the contrary that they were invented severally by each people *after* their settlement in their own particular country. The very reverse however of this will be found to be the case. The Greeks and Romans were not so ignorant of their own system, as to imagine that a trifling resemblance was sufficient to establish an absolute identity of godhead. They knew the arbitrary peculiarities of their own religious creed; and they found those self-same peculiarities in the creeds of other nations: hence, though the deities might bear different names, they reasonably inferred that they were fundamentally one character.

The fact is, that the various theological systems of the Gentiles agree, not only in what is *obvious* and *natural*, but in what is *arbitrary* and *circumstantial.* There is such a singular and minute and regular accordance between them, both in *fanciful speculations*, and in *artificial observances*, that no person, who takes the pains of thoroughly investigating the subject, can avoid being fully persuaded, that they must all have sprung from some common origin. Differences there doubtless are to a certain extent: but, even putting other causes out of the question, they are no more than what might have been reasonably anticipated from the now ancient division of mankind into distinct and often widely separated nations. As the old Teutonic language may be clearly traced through all its dialectic variations of German, English, Swedish, Danish, Norwegian, and Icelandic; while no union of subjects under the same crown, no long-continued intercourse of fellow-citizens, has been able

The position proved from their accordance in arbitrary circumstantials [margin note]

[1] See Bp. Warburton's Div. Leg. book iv. sect. 5. p. 257, 238. and note in loc. p. 429—431.

to effect the least resemblance between that primeval tongue and any modification of the Celtic: so a regularly digested system of apostatic idolatry may be just as distinctly traced through the mythologies of all the pagan nations; while no such universal arbitrary resemblance could possibly have been produced, had each people independently arranged its own creed in the land of its settlement or colonization. It is excellently remarked by Mr. Wilford, that one and the same code both of theology and of fabulous history has been received *through a range or belt about forty degrees broad, across the old continent, in a south-east and north-west direction, from the eastern shores of the Malaya peninsula to the western extremity of the British isles; that, through this immense range, the same original religious notions re-appear in various places, under various modifications, as might be expected; and that there is not a greater difference between the tenets and worship of the Hindoos and the Greeks, than exists between those of the churches of Rome and Geneva.*' Immense as such a territorial range may be, the preceding observation is yet too limited. It applies with equal propriety to the whole habitable globe: for the arbitrary rites and opinions of every pagan nation bear so close a resemblance to each other, that such a coincidence can only have been produced by their having all had a common origin. Barbarism itself has not been able to efface the strong primeval impression. Vestiges of the ancient general system may be traced in the recently discovered islands of the great Pacific Ocean: and, when the American world was first opened to the hardy adventurers of Europe, its inhabitants from north to south venerated, with kindred ceremonies and kindred notions, the gods of Egypt and Hindostan, of Greece and Italy, of Phenicia and Britain.

2. Now, since this remarkable agreement in *arbitrary circumstantials* could never have been produced if each mythological system had been *independently* framed by each people *subsequent* to their territorial settlement as a nation, we may thence safely conclude, that each system could *not* have been thus framed by each people in the land which they colonized. The common arbitrary opinions and observances, which alike prevail in every

There are only three ways in which the origination of the various systems of Paganism can be accounted for

' Asiat. Res. vol. viii. p. 264, 265.

part of the globe, must have had a common origin: and each national system, however some minor differences might distinguish it from other national systems, must have been equally a shoot from a primeval system so vigorous as to extend its ramifications to all countries of the habitable world.

If then every system of pagan theology had a common origin, which is proved by an agreement in arbitrary circumstantials, such a fact, so far as I am able to judge, can only be accounted for in one of the three following ways: either *all nations, after their settlement, agreed by mutual consent to adopt the religious code struck out by some one nation in particular; or all nations, after their settlement, were conquered by the irresistible arms of some powerful and roving tribe, and either compelled or persuaded to adopt the mythology of that tribe; or lastly all nations, while yet in embryo, and during those ages of the infancy of society which immediately followed the deluge, were assembled together in one community, previous to their separation and dispersion over the face of the earth, and in that state of primitive union agreed in the adoption of a system, which, when afterwards broken into tribes the germs of future nations, they equally carried with them into whatever region they might at any subsequent time be induced to colonize.* I know not any fourth mode, by which we can account for the circumstance in question.

(1.) The first of these opinions has had its decided advocates; who have endeavoured to support it with much learning and ingenuity, though they have been by no means unanimous as to the people, whom the rest of the world is supposed to have imitated with so much servility.

Either all nations agreed peaceably to ~~borrow from one.~~

Some have pleaded the cause of Egypt; others, of Phenicia. Others again have imagined, that the idolatry of at least the nations, which bordered upon the land of Canaan or were seated at but a small distance from it, was all borrowed pervertedly from the Israelites. A lively French writer gives the honour of the invention to a very ancient nation; which, far prior to any authentic records that *we* possess, tenanted, in the better days of the world, the warm and delightful regions of the Arctic circle and the north pole. At present, India seems to be the reigning favourite: yet Egypt can still boast some determined advocates, who indignantly behold the almost sacrilegious attempt to pluck her ancient honours from the brow of the venerable matron; and it is still a matter of litigation, whether the Hindoo theology be Egyptian, or the Egyptian theology Hindoo.

On the claims of these various rival systems, which have all emanated from a common fundamental hypothesis, it is no easy matter to decide with impartiality: yet, whenever the decision *is* made, a still harder task remains to be accomplished; we must then proceed to account for the extraordinary circumstance, that all nations upon the face of the earth, whether seated in Europe or in Asia or in Africa or in America, should have been content to borrow, with rare unanimity, the religious system of one single people.

(2.) The second theory, mingled in a degree with the first, has been adopted and managed with wonderful ingenuity and learning by the late venerable analyst of ancient mythology.

He supposes, that, at a certain appointed period after the deluge, all mankind, according to their nations and their families, quietly retired to their destined settlements, with the exception of one contumacious tribe and an indefinite number of turbulent spirits from the other tribes who ranged themselves under a common standard of opposition to the divine purposes. The members of this powerful tribe, thus augmented by an heterogeneous association of kindred souls, were the builders of Babel and the original inventors of the primeval mythologic system. Dispersed miraculously from the seat of their projected empire, they penetrated, in armed bodies, to almost every quarter of the globe. Their superiority in arts and arms over the rest of mankind rendered them uniformly victorious in their enterprizes. Wherever they prevailed, they either compelled or persuaded the conquered to adopt their favourite mode of worship and their peculiar system of opinions. They were alike successful in bending the minds, and in subduing the bodies, of men: and, in the lapse of a few ages, the whole world in a manner, forsaking the pure religion of the righteous Noah, wondered to find itself become altogether Cuthite.

This hypothesis, though recommended by all that talents of the first rate could advance in its favour, bears, even on the first glance, the semblance of an ingenious mythological romance.

Or, all nations, subsequent to their several settlements, were compelled by arms to adopt the superstition of one: a theory which is equally untenable

Allowing for a moment that the children of Cush and a few associated adventurers were alone concerned in the rebellious apostasy of Babel, we find it difficult to conceive, how a single tribe, and that too broken into small fragments by an eminent display of divine vengeance, could manage to subdue and convert all the rest of mankind, who had previously retired in a prosperous and orderly manner to their appointed settlements. It is doubtless true, that a comparatively small body of men, regularly organized and well disciplined, are generally found sufficient both to conquer, and to retain in subjection, much greater numbers than themselves when scattered over the face of a country and pursuing the ordinary occupations of civil life: but still there must be *some* proportion between the assailants and the assailed, otherwise no superiority of military tactics could compensate for an immeasurable disproportion of numbers. But even such a statement as this allows far more than can fairly be conceded. The single tribe of the Cuthites, according to the hypothesis of Mr. Bryant, was not only broken into a variety of small fragments; but each fragment must have left Babel, thoroughly dispirited with a recent awful judgment, and conscious of the weakness necessarily produced by an entire disunion and disorganization of the collected force by which it had been hoped to acquire universal dominion. Under these depressing circumstances, it is hard to believe, that, spreading themselves in all directions, they should venture in small troops to attack regularly settled communities, comparatively small *themselves* as yet, I allow, but still very far exceeding in numbers each fragment of Cuthite assailants: communities moreover, whose spirits in the hour of danger would of course be raised by the very event which would sit heavy on the souls of their enemies; for the miraculous interposition at Babel was not a thing done in a corner, neither could it possibly be concealed from the knowledge of the surrounding nations. Difficult then as it is to believe a general attack, made by the scattered members of a single tribe under such disheartening circumstances; it is obviously still more difficult to believe, that this daring attack should be uniformly crowned with success. Granting every thing that can be desired to the chivalrous intrepidity of the Cuthites, and a braver race of men never existed than they have shewn themselves to be in all ages; still no courage can vanquish what are little less than absolute impossibilities. That every nation should fall beneath their always victorious arms; that none should be found brave enough to offer any effectual resistance to the progress of disjoined handfuls of stragglers, trembling under a recent sense of divine indignation, and precipitately flying in all directions from the scene of their signal humiliation : is a phenomenon so unexampled in history, and gives one such a thoroughly contemptible idea of the manhood of all the other descendants of Noah, that nothing short of evidence the most incontrovertible can effect the belief of it. But the most difficult achievement yet remains to be accomplished. It has ever been found far more easy to conquer men's bodies, than to subjugate their minds. When the hardy Cuthites have in each region attacked and vanquished those tribes, which quietly retired to the fixed places of their settlement, and which, having no hand in the apostasy of Babel, may be presumed to have carried with them the unadulterated religion in the practice of which their great ancestor lived and died; they have next to commence the arduous task of proselytism. The difficulties, which they would have to encounter in their spiritual mission, would partly arise from the rooted dislike which the conquered must inevitably feel towards their ruthless and unprovoked assailants, partly from that uncontroulable humour in man which always makes him resist whatever is forced upon him by the strong arm of capricious tyranny, and partly from the sentiments which these hitherto uncorrupted worshippers of God must have felt towards the new religion now first recommended to them by their insolent and oppressive victors. I will not dwell upon the abstract horror, which they might be supposed to feel at a broad proposition of open apostasy, however veiled in the garb of pretended wisdom; both because unhappily in all ages men have been but too prone to depart from the truth, and because the apostasy in question must plainly have had a beginning at *some* time : but I certainly think, that no period could have been found more inauspicious for the promulgation of idolatry, than that which the Cuthites are represented as having chosen. They themselves must have been not only hated as wanton aggressors, but they must have been abhorred as impious apostates labouring under the manifest wrath of the incensed Deity. And yet, great in eloquence as in arms, they persuade those, whom they had already most deeply injured, to adopt the theological system, which had called down the divine vengeance upon themselves, and which must have been known to their proselytes to *have* thus called it down. We do not meet with occurrences like this in history: still less do we meet with a general agglomeration of such occurrences. There have been instances, in which barbarous victors adopted the religion of a vanquished people more polished than themselves: but rarely indeed has the introduction of a new theology gone hand in hand with the demon of war and desolation. The progress of Mohammedism might indeed be adduced as a striking exception to what has generally happened: but there are many things that will account for this circumstance, which we vainly seek for in the supposed progress of the Cuthic superstition. While men had far departed from the pure faith of the gospel, and were therefore prepared for a yet further departure, the prevalence of Christianity and the dispersion of the Jews had tended greatly through a large tract of country to shake the foundations of Paganism. Of these propitious events Mohammed artfully availed himself, and fabricated his imposture accordingly. He proclaimed open war against the now languishing cause of idolatry: but, professing a high reverence both for Moses and for Christ, he declared himself sent not so much to destroy as to complete. He was the last and greatest of the prophets: he was the divine Paraclete especially promised by the son of Mary. He called upon the worshippers of the one God to attend to his final communication to erring man: and his whole system, chiefly borrowed as it is from the garbled Law and Gospel, may well be esteemed, not so much a novel and unheard-of phenomenon, as a recently excogitated Christian heresy. This very appellation has accordingly been employed to designate its character: and, as Gnosticism and Arianism had each had their day, so Mohammedism only occupied the minds of men ready prepared to receive it. Hence it most flourished in the speculative eastern empire; while, in the western division of the Roman world, recently occupied by the unlettered warriors of the north, it made little progress, and took no permanent root. Even in the east it was not uniformly successful. The Greek church still lives to protest against it, still lives in hope of liberation from its tyranny: and, out of the limits of the Roman empire, though it established itself in Persia, it has never been able wholly to eradicate Magianism; while the stubborn theology of the inflexible Hindoos has hitherto bid defiance to every prose-lyting attempt whether Mohammedan or Christian. Their bodies have in-deed been subdued by the votaries both of the Koran and of the Gospel: but their minds, I speak of them as a nation, have ever been found invin-cible. Yet are the Cuthic warriors, under every disadvantage that can well be imagined, supposed to have been alike successful in the labour of subjugation and in the more arduous work of conversion.

What I have hitherto said is built wholly upon the concession, that the children of Cush with some perturbed spirits from the other Noëtic tribes were *alone* concerned in the apostasy of Babel; while the rest of mankind, previous to the building of the tower, had quietly retired to their appointed settlements : but it still remains to be examined, whether such a theory will accord with the scriptural account of those early transactions, as under-stood in its most plain and obvious acceptation. I must confess, that, al-though I had once assented, not indeed with perfect satisfaction, to the hy-pothesis of Mr. Bryant, a more attentive consideration of the subject has led me to a thorough conviction that it is untenable : there seems to me to be no warrant for believing, that the children of Cush and the accidental adherents to their party were the *sole* agents at Babel, and that they were dispersed from thence over the face of the earth *subsequent* to an orderly settlement of the *other* descendants of Noah; on the contrary, the Mo-saical account plainly intimates, so far as I can judge, that the building of the tower was a joint attempt of *all* mankind, and therefore that there was but *one* dispersion and settlement of the Noëtic tribes subsequent to the deluge which commenced from the land of Shinar in consequence of some preternatural manifestation of divine wrath.

(3.) This brings me to the third opinion, by which we may account for the remarkable uniformity that subsists in the various systems of pagan my-thology. Even independent of other considerations, it certainly has a great advantage above the former two in point of abstract probability. We have seen the difficulty of believing, either that all nations after their settlement became the servile imitators of some one single people, or that they were all conquered and converted by the unassisted power and eloquence of a single

Or all nations were once assembled together in a single place and community where they adopted a corrupt form of religion, which they afterwards carried with them

scattered and disjointed tribe. But no such difficulty occurs in admitting the *into the lands that they colonised; a theory which is adopted as the truth.* third opinion: the adoption of it renders every thing easy, natural, and probable. The theory may be briefly stated in the following manner.

While the world was yet in its infancy, and before the rapidly progressive increase of mankind had rendered their separation etiher necessary or desireable, the rudiments of all future nations would be assembled together in one region and would jointly form one moderately large community. Such a community, during the lives of the first patriarchs, would be greatly influenced by them both in religion and polity: but, when they were removed from this earthly scene, and when no one by mere succession could hope to obtain an equal degree of authority over the daily increasing multitude, a moderate knowledge of human nature will teach us, that ambition would soon begin to agitate the breast of some aspiring individual whose conscious talents raised him above the level of his political equals. Weaker minds have ever been found to bend before the commanding powers of those strong minds which seem born for empire.

Such an individual, as I have supposed, in order to further his project, would naturally *first* communicate it to his immediate brethren and relatives. Prudence would however teach him to suppress all intimation of his own *private* views. The ambition of the tribesmen would be *generally* stimulated by the prospect of their *common* aggrandisement.

The union of a powerful family, and the steady cooperation of its members on all public occasions, would soon insensibly give them a decided superiority over their disjointed associates; who were held together by no particular band, who were led by no regular plan to act in concert, and who had no suspicion of the domination which was about to be established over them. Every hour the various branches of that aspiring family would be more closely linked together, both by a sense of interest, and by the love of newly-tasted empire: while the animating soul, who, with popular manners and with a shew of unobtrusive humility, was the main-spring of each movement, would daily acquire fresh influence over the whole community, and would daily be felt by the members of his own tribe to be more and more necessary to their projects of self-advancement.

As mankind continued to increase, various laws would from time to time be

found necessary.   But laws cannot be enforced without authority: and authority, however it may weigh with the better disposed who acknowledge the benefits of an equal legislation, is held in little reverence by the profligate and the
turbulent. unless it be supported by the strong arm of efficient power.   In
such a state of things, the first magistrates would inevitably be appointed out
of that active paramount tribe, which had now for some years been in the
habit of taking the lead on all public occasions: and these magistrates, thus
invested with authority, would soon speciously point out the necessity of their
being provided with a force sufficient to ensure the due execution of their
sentences.   But who could be deemed more proper persons than themselves,
to select fit coadjutors? The superiority of their mental endowments, naturally
produced by habits of business, would give them a degree of influence, which
few would be either able or willing to oppose. As they had insensibly occupied
the magistracy, they would also nominate the inferior retainers and officers
of justice.   These, it is almost superfluous to observe, would be appointed
out of their own tribe; both because they could best depend upon the steady
coöperation of their immediate brethren, and because such an arrangement
would most effectually further their plans of empire.

The first weapons then would be forged for a regularly organized body of
conservators of the public peace; and the members of this formidable body
would soon become accustomed to act together under the orders of magistra-
tual superiors, who were of their own family.   United among themselves,
and provided with arms, they would feel their power and importance; and
could not but know, that, instead of being the servants of the state, they were
its absolute masters.   Occasions of active interference would soon be either
found or made.   Weak and uncombined resistance would soon be discovered
to be fruitless.   Offenders would speedily be brought to condign punishment.
And, by frequent skirmishes with the refractory, the armed ministers of justice
would daily improve in courage and discipline.   Thus a caste of *warriors*,
jealous in transmitting their high privileges to their own exclusive posterity,
would imperceptibly arise out of the wants of society, even when as yet
there was no foreign enemy in being: while the mass of the community,
over which they ruled, whatever subdivisions might afterwards be developed
by increasing wants or luxury, would, by a progress equally gradual and

equally sure, constitute two subordinate castes of *artizans or tradesmen* and of *peasants or personal cultivators of the ground.*

Meanwhile, can the energetic mind, which has set the whole machine in motion, be supposed to be a supine and unobservant spectator of what is passing? As his tribe would be preëminent among the people, as the armed magistrates would be preëminent in the war-tribe; so would he be preëminent among the magistrates. From his talents and from his influence, he would habitually take the lead on every occasion: his authority would be tacitly felt, and recognized: he would almost insensibly glide into the seat of empire: and a chief, thus supported, differs but in name from a king. The want of a head, to whom all might look up as their superior, who might be the fountain of justice and honour, and who in short might fill the place of the chief of the magistrates, would be felt and owned. The first king would be a soldier chosen out of the war-tribe.

Such a man was Nimrod

. The ambition of the aspiring individual is now crowned with success: henceforth he has only to study, how he may best render his authority firm and perpetual. In a political point of view, however unfavourable such an arrangement is to the display of talent, the division into castes, which the infant society had almost spontaneously undergone, would be singularly useful in the solid establishment of regal power. The system therefore, which the new prince would adopt, is sufficiently obvious even on the very first sight of the question. As the pride and ambition of the soldier would be equally gratified, by assigning to his caste the first rank in the community as it is now constituted, and by ordaining that no one should bear arms but the son of one who had borne arms before him: so would the yoke of servile obedience be most securely rivetted upon the necks of the two inferior castes, so formidable to the warrior in point of numbers should the energy of their minds ever have an opportunity given of displaying itself, by decreeing, under the specious pretext of the public good, that the son should invariably follow the occupation of his father; because, when the grave experience of one generation was thus perpetually handed down to another, agriculture and the mechanical arts would most surely attain the highest possible state of perfection.

Yet, however efficacious this policy might be to a certain extent; how-

ever the loyalty of the soldier might be secured by the proud consciousness
that his sovereign would invariably be his tribesman, and the spirits of the
artizan and the peasant bowed down to unresisting submission by the feeling
of habitual and irremediable inferiority: still such a prince, as I have supposed, could not but be deeply convinced, from his long study of human
nature, that mind can only be permanently governed by the operation of
mind.   He would be aware, that his project of establishing a perpetual universal empire stood in direct opposition to the well-known command, that
the children of Noah should replenish the whole earth, and that for this
purpose they should branch out by their tribes and by their families according as the Most High had divided to each infant nation the appointed lot of
its future inheritance. '   The religion therefore of his people decidedly mili-
tated against his schemes of imperial grandeur: and, since the worship of the
true God was but an indifferent engine of state policy, some other more
flexible system must be invented, and the knowledge of the truth must be
suppressed as much as possible, otherwise his empire will fall to pieces at its
very commencement by the mere emigration of his subjects.   Under such circumstances, the crooked policy of this accomplished statesman would be of a
kind, pretty nearly resembling that of the scripturally proverbial son of Nebat
who made Israel to sin: and unhappily human nature, instead of opposing,
has, from its radical corruption, been ever found ready to facilitate and promote each iniquitous project of the present description.   He would conceive
the idea of introducing a new religion, which, when moulded into a proper
form, would be a most powerful engine of state: for thus would he govern
men by the united influence of armed authority and of appalling superstition.

But to render such a religion efficacious in accomplishing his purpose, it
would be necessary to set apart a regularly organized body of men, who might
assume the sacred character of *the priesthood*, and who, by solely ministering
in misnamed holy things, might acquire an uncontrouled empire over the minds
and consciences of the abused community.   The body, to which so important
a charge was entrusted, would not be lightly chosen.   It must be composed
of men, whose steady coöperation could be depended upon, and whose ta-

---

' Gen. ix. 1, 7. Deut. xxxii. 8.

lents were equal to the task of so plausibly recommending the new system as not too violently to offend old habits and opinions. But where could he look for such coadjutors. except to the faithful and kindred tribe of warriors, whose interests were so closely linked with his own? The project would be communicated to his confidential ministers: proper persons would be selected to arrange and manage the apostasy: and *the sacerdotal caste* would thus emanate from *the military caste.* As the regular and necessary succession of son to father was already established in the three other castes, the same policy would naturally be adopted in regard to the priesthood: but this alone would not be sufficient to give it that degree of spiritual influence over the minds of the governed, which was necessary to bring them effectually into due subjection. The armed magistracy and the sovereign himself must set the example of paying a high veneration to the ministers of religion, otherwise they could hope to carry but little weight with the great mass of the community. To give precedence to those, who were at once their brethren by blood, and who were invested with the high office of serving the god whom they adored, would not shock the pride of a newly rising military nobility: and the prince himself would politically affect to consider it as his highest honour and prerogative to be at once a priest and a king. He would ambitiously on all occasions obey the instructions of the sacerdotal order, as being the special communications of heaven: but he would duly take care, that those instructions should, in the first instance, originate with himself. Thus would he govern by the two-fold engine of force and fraud: the military caste would uphold the priestly caste by force of arms; and the priestly caste, in return, would consecrate each state measure of the military caste by the awful sanctions of religion.

When the community was in such a state, if it suddenly fell asunder either by civil violence, theological dissention, some preternatural interposition of God, or a mixture of all these causes, it is sufficiently easy to perceive what would be the almost inevitable consequence. The bulk of the people, depressed by the two governing castes, and thoroughly inured to passive submission, would have no leaders of *their own* castes or families, under whose guidance they would be disposed to place themselves: hence, though the members of each tribe would naturally set out *conjointly* in quest of new

settlements and would *separate* themselves from all other tribes, and though
such tribes as sprang from some noted common ancestor would be disposed
to keep more in the immediate neighbourhood of one another than of such as
sprang from some *different* common ancestor, still they would almost invariably emigrate under the rule of those whom they had been accustomed to
obey.   Every family, with very few exceptions, would set out under a priesthood and military nobility of an entirely distinct family from themselves.
The governors of course would bear but a very small arithmetical proportion
to the governed : consequently, although the governors would long haughtily
preserve the name of their own peculiar ancestor and would boast of a more
pure and noble genealogy than the governed, each family, as it increased into
a nation, would obviously distinguish itself from all other families by the appellation of him, from whom, as a body, it was descended.

But, though such tribes, as constituted the inferior castes of the original
community, could not emigrate except under the guidance of certain of their
former leaders, sacerdotal and military; the reverse would by no means be
necessarily the case.   From various causes, in such a state of general com-
motion, many members of the two higher castes might be separated from
their brethren; and might be left without any, or at least with a very small
proportion of, retainers.   These, retiring in an unmixed state, would form a
nation in its own opinion peculiarly noble, as consisting almost wholly of
priests and warriors.   Of such a nation the characteristics would infallibly
be a high chivalrous spirit, an ardent thirst after military glory, a propensity to live by rapine rather than by peaceful labour, a habit of invading the
territories of its less warlike neighbours, a roving unsettled humour which
would incline its members far more to personal than to local attachments, an
adoption of the pastoral life as best calculated to gratify at once their love
of idleness and their hatred of repose, [1] an extreme sensibility as to the point
of personal honour, a strong jealousy with regard to their own liberty united
with a proneness to trample on the freedom and privileges of those whom they
might subjugate, a contempt for commerce, and a ready submission to the
ministers of their ancient paternal theology though they would consider

---

[1] *Mira diversitate naturæ,* says a great historian, *cum iidem homines sic ament inertiam, et
oderint quietem.*   Such a diversity naturally arises out of the military and pastoral life.

themselves as degraded by bowing the servile neck to mere secular despotism. Each citizen of a nation like this would consider himself as noble, and would look down with high-souled contempt on a plebeian world. Hence names would probably be invented expressive of a sense of superiority. They, who constituted such a people, remembering the empire possessed by their ancestors, and proud of the uncontaminated purity of their descent, would be apt to style themselves *kings* and to add the epithet of *royal* either to their professional name of *shepherds* or to the gentile name which they inherited from their great forefather: and their actions would be agreeable to their notions; whenever, in consequence of a desolating excursion, they established their sovereignty in regions already occupied by a more peaceful and industrious race, they would reduce the inhabitants to a state of villainage, and by the distribution of the landed property among themselves according to the military rank which they had held they would in the natural course of things distinctly mark out the rudiments of what has been called *the feudal system.* But several years, perhaps centuries, must elapse after the dispersion of mankind by the breaking up of the first community, before these pastoral warriors would be in a condition to undertake any distant enterprizes upon a large scale. Time alone could supply the deficiency in their original numbers: but, when once such a people was set in motion, it is hard to say when they would be stopped. Age after age would witness their destructive conquests; and the fairest parts of the habitable globe would, at different periods, fall a prey to the rapacity of these military adventurers.

Meanwhile it is evident, that, if genuine religion were first debased and corrupted to apostate idolatry when all mankind formed but a single community, the same theological system, making due allowance for sectarial variations, would be carried away from the common centre, and would be established in every quarter of the globe, according as the dispersed tribes might happen to settle themselves. Doubtless the first colonies would be planted in the immediate neighbourhood of the region occupied by the primeval community, the only *real* universal empire that ever subsisted; and many ages must have rolled away, before the whole world was peopled: but the same causes would still produce the same effects: each new tribe, as it

broke off from its parent stock and advanced into empty and unknown regions in quest of an independent settlement, would carry with it the religion
of its fathers ; each would set forth under the guidance of young and enterprizing supernumeraries of the military and sacerdotal castes ; and each,
when it became a nation, would faithfully reflect the features, both religious
and political, of the society whence it sprang.   The same operation, allowing for those smaller changes which time and human fickleness will ever produce, would be repeated again and again, until the earth was replenished to
its utmost extremities.   Circle would be succeeded by circle in the allegorical
waters of many nations, each caused by each, though all ultimately originating from *one* centrical agitation; until further progress was stopped only
by the restraining banks of the mighty lake : but the form of every new un-
dulation would still be an exact, though less distinct, transcript of that, by
which it was occasioned.

This last theory is confirmed by the scriptural history of Nimrod and the tower of Babel.

3. I pretend not to say, that such, in *every* particular, would be the origin
and progress of society and idolatry from the earliest postdiluvian age : but
the great *outlines* at least of this theory seem to me to accord, in a very remarkable manner, with history both sacred and profane.

The striking uniformity, observable throughout the various mythological
systems of paganism as established in countries widely separated from each
other, is *the matter of fact* to be accounted for : and of three different hypotheses, which may be employed for that purpose, that, which supposes all
mankind to have been once united together in a single community, to have
corrupted themselves during the period of their union by adopting a certain
system of apostate theology, and afterwards when they were dispersed to
have equally carried off in their several tribes the same religious speculations
and practices, appears, even as a matter of abstract conjecture, to afford the
most easy and natural solution.

Now, if we proceed to consult the inspired volume, we shall find something very similar to what has been supposed, described as taking place in
the infancy of postdiluvian society.

According to the least constrained and most obvious interpretation of the
language used by Moses, all mankind, with the exception *perhaps* of some
few pious individuals, at the close of the first march, which they had jointly

undertaken from the region where the Ark rested and where they had continued to live for some generations after the flood, find themselves in a large and fertile plain. Here they agree, by common consent, to build a city and a tower, for the express purpose of preventing their dispersion over the face of the earth. Hence it is evident, that they *knew* it to be the intent of heaven, that they *should* be thus dispersed, in order that different nations should arise in every quarter of the globe and that the whole world should be gradually filled with inhabitants by the increasing population of *distinct* and *independent* societies. This determination of Providence however did not suit the project, which had occupied their minds. They were resolved, that they would *not* be dispersed, but that adhering firmly together they would form one single community. In process of time, as they increased in numbers, colonies might be freely allowed to branch off from the parent state: but, for the present, they were bent upon coalition, and were determined not to suffer any diminution either of glory or comfort by what they deemed a premature separation.

The ringleader in this rebellion was Nimrod: for the city, which they engaged in building, was called *Babel* or *Babylon;* and the beginning of Nimrod's kingdom is said to have been *Babel* and three subordinate towns: their city also was built in the land of *Shinar;* and Nimrod's Babel is likewise said to have been situated in the land of *Shinar.*[1] There can be no doubt therefore, that Nimrod's Babel was the identical Babel, which mankind in one great society had begun to erect: whence it will plainly follow, since Babel was the beginning of *Nimrod's* kingdom, that *he* must have been the person who was the author of the rebellion. Nor is this all: the phraseology employed by Moses, and the account which he gives of the character of Nimrod, indisputably prove, that that aspiring character had made himself the sovereign of the assembled multitude, and that he was unwilling to see his empire dissolved at its very commencement by the secession and dispersion of his subjects. If Babel were the beginning of his *kingdom*, then he must necessarily have been *a king;* for the establishment of *a kingdom* involves the idea of *the royalty* of its founder. Accordingly, he is said to

[1] Gen. xi. 2, 9. x. 10.

have been *a mighty one in the earth* and *a mighty hunter before the Lord;* terms, expressive of power on the one hand, and of violence used to uphold that power on the other.[1]

Nimrod was the son of Cush, the son of Ham, the son of Noah: and, as he is mentioned the last of all the children of Cush and in a manner which seems to imply some sort of difference from them, it is probable, that he was the favourite child of his father's old age, born many years after his first-specified brethren, and chronologically coinciding perhaps with the sixth or seventh generation from Noah in some lines though standing himself only in the third place of descent. Such being the genealogy of Nimrod, the family, by whose instrumentality and coöperation he would attain to sovereign power or (in the phraseology of Scripture) become *a mighty hunter in the earth*, would obviously be that of Cush: consequently, the first or rather the only universal empire would be founded by the Cushim or Cuthim under the guidance of Nimrod. These would therefore be the associates of their daring sovereign in the chase, whether literal or figurative: these would constitute the order of his military nobility, when he undertook the project of erecting a kingdom on the necks of the other descendants of Noah.

In the short account, which Moses gives of this early transaction, no direct mention is made of any attempt to introduce a new system of religion; though something of the kind seems to be hinted at in the assertion, that nothing could restrain the roving imagination of this rebellious community: but the Jews have ever supposed, that idolatry commenced at Babel; whence they have a story, that Abraham was cast into a furnace by Nimrod for refusing to worship the sacred fire, which was the symbol of the solar deity.[2] We have however far better authority than Jewish tradition, though I see no reason why we should slight it as altogether nugatory, for asserting, that

---

[1] It is not improbable, that he might literally have trained his military officers of justice in the hardy exercise of hunting wild beasts, which has ever been esteemed a lively image of war. Certain it is, that the descendants of these warriors have always been peculiarly attached to the chase, and have deemed it a prerogative of nobility too valuable to be communicated to plebeians. See Bochart. Phaleg. lib. iv. c. 12. p. 227, 228.

[2] Fabric. Codex Pseudepig. vol. i. p. 344.

Fox hunting

The Genesis record does not distinctly mention a false religious system at Babel, but the statement "nothing will be restrained from them" Gen11:6 would certainly include one

The whole tenor of Scripture supports this

the first systematic apostasy from pure religion was consummated at Babel, and that from that centre it spread itself over the whole world. The prophet of the Apocalypse styles Babylon or Babel *the mother of harlots and abominations of the earth:*[1] by which, it need scarcely be observed, is meant, in the figurative language of Scripture, that all the abominations of apostate idolatry originated from that city as from a common parent. St. John is indeed speaking of a mystic Babel; but, unless the type accurately correspond with the antitype, the whole propriety of the allusion is destroyed. What the figurative Babel therefore has been in the Christian world, we may be sure that the literal Babel was in the patriarchal world. But, in the Christian world, the figurative Babel has been the mother of an idolatrous apostasy, which, reviving under a new name the ancient pagan demonolatry or worship of deified men, long disfigured in almost every part of the Church universal the pure simplicity of the Gospel. Therefore the literal Babel must have been the mother, in the patriarchal world, of that mixed system of demonolatry, which seduced men from the truth, and which was thence diffused throughout every part of the habitable globe. This conclusion seems to me to be inevitable from the language used by the apostle: and, *in the abstract*, it must be equally drawn both by Papist and by Protestant; for, whatever community may be meant by the mystic Babel, since its characteristic is that of being the parent and author of an idolatrous system which spreads itself over the earth, its prototype, the literal Babel, must necessarily have been distinguished by a similar characteristic. In other words, the *one* idolatrous system, which with certain modifications prevailed alike in every pagan nation, must have originated at Babel, and must from that first postdiluvian city have been carried into all quarters of the globe by them of the dispersion. This character of Babel agrees very exactly with what we read of it in various parts of the Hebrew Scriptures. It is uniformly represented as being given up to the vain imaginations of a gross idolatry: and there are two passages in particular, which, if I mistake not, decidedly and literally confirm the opinion, that *must* apparently be drawn from the language employed by St. John respecting the antitypical

[1] Rev. xvii. 5.

The one became many by dispersion

and mystic Babel.   The literal city of Nimrod is said by Jeremiah to have been *a golden cup, that made* ALL *the earth drunken : the* NATIONS *have drunken of her wine ; therefore are the* NATIONS *mad.*[1] If we inquire what is intended by this *intoxicating potion*, which Babel figuratively administered to all the nations of the earth, and which produced the effect of completely disordering their spiritual understanding, we are afterwards plainly told that it was *idolatry.*[2]   In a similar strain we find the same city addressed by the prophet Isaiah.   *Persist now in thine inchantments and in the multitude of thy sorceries, in which thou hast laboured* FROM THY YOUTH ; *if peradventure thou mayest be profited, if thou mayest be strengthened by them.   Behold, they shall be as stubble, the fire shall burn them up.   Such shall these be unto thee, with whom thou hast laboured ; thy negociators, with whom thou hast dealt* FROM THY YOUTH.[3] Sorcery and inchantment formed a constituent and essential part of the false theology of the Gentiles ; that theology, with the fumes of which Babel *made* ALL *the earth drunken.*   But in such practices Babel is here said to have *laboured* FROM HER YOUTH.   Now the allegorical youth of an empire is the earliest period of its existence.   Therefore Babel must have been idolatrous from the very first.

Babel idolatrous from the very first

   Thus, so far as I can judge, it indisputably appears, that the idolatry, by which *all* the nations of the earth were infatuated, was a system, originally invented at Babel under the auspices of Nimrod and his Cuthites, and afterwards, in the progress of replenishing the world with inhabitants by the various scattered members of his broken empire, carried off alike to the nearest and to the most remote countries of the globe.   Such being the case, though the hypothesis of Mr. Bryant is certainly not affected by *this* circumstance, all those theories, which would deduce the origin of pagan mythology either from Egypt or from Hindostan or from any other country peopled after the dispersion from Babel, *must*, according to the scriptural account of the matter, fall to the ground.

BRYANT wrong in ascribing origin of pagan mythology to Egypt.

It is also confirmed by profane history.

   4. Though Scripture teaches us that Babel was founded by Nimrod and consequently that the first empire was that of the Cushim, and though it

[1] Jerem. li. 7.   [2] Jerem. li. 17, 18, 19.   [3] Isaiah xlvii. 12, 14, 15.

further informs us that the idolatry of the whole world originated from this centrical point, it is silent respecting the subsequent fortunes of the house of Cush. In the account which it gives of the settlement of the earth by the posterity of Noah, it simply enumerates the future nations by the names of their several ancestors, specifying however in some instances the regions where they were planted : thus the isles of the Gentiles, or the maritime countries of Europe, are said to have been originally divided by the children of Japhet ; while the borders of the Hammonian Canaanites are distinctly pointed out by the specification of certain well-known cities. Nothing therefore can be gathered from Scripture either to confirm or to confute the supposition, that, from the natural operation of political causes, when the Cuthic empire of Babel was dissolved, each tribe would for the most part emigrate under the guidance of a Cuthic priesthood and military nobility. For I cannot deem the mere silence of Scripture any *confutation* of such a theory: because, since these Cushim would bear but a very small arithmetical proportion to the several families over which they presided, each Japhetic, each Shemite, and each Hammonian, tribe would obviously be enumerated, not with reference to their supposed governors, but with an eye to the descent of their chief population from some common ancestor ; just as, in a genealogical catalogue of the modern European nations, the English would be described as Saxons without any regard to the small admixture of Danish or Norman military rulers. If then any such circumstance occurred at the epoch of the dispersion from Babel, as I have been led, merely from the consideration of political cause and effect, to esteem probable; we must seek for evidence in its favour, if indeed any evidence exist, in the records of pagan history.

In pursuing this inquiry, the first matter, that will naturally strike us, is the evidence of names. Each ancient nation seems naturally to have called itself after the appellation of its peculiar ancestor. Of this we have repeated instances afforded us in Scripture : and the practice continues to this day among the Arabs, a people remarkably tenacious of old usages. Thus the Egyptians were called *Mizraim* from their father Mizr ; the Assyrians, *Ashurim* from their common parent Ashur ; and the greater part of the first occupiers of Palestine, *Canaanites* from their ancestor Canaan : but we find no Mizraim out of Egypt, no Ashurim out of Assyria, no Canaanites out of the district which they occupied. In each case, the name is confined to *one* particular region, and occurs not without its limits. The same remark may be applied to the various other national appellations borne by the different Noëtic tribes: with some few exceptions, produced by the original settlement of a tribe in one district and its subsequent emigration and final settlement in another district, the name of each patriarchal ancestor, as Bochart has shewn at large in his elaborate work on the subject, is to be found only within the precincts of a single country. But very different is the case with the name of *Cush*. Independent of those nations, which were composed of his unmixed offspring, which by the Greeks were styled *Ethiopic*, but which among themselves never ceased to bear the appellation of their great forefather; there is scarcely any region on the face of the earth, where that widely-spreading name, either in a simple or compounded form, will not be found to occur.

Another matter, which deserves to be noticed, is the singular and frequent intercourse that appears to have subsisted between the governing powers of ancient communities, notwithstanding the obstacles presented both by local difficulties of access and by vast remoteness of situation. When we consider the various tribes, through which such an intercourse must have been carried on, it is difficult to conceive, how it could have been accomplished except by the friendly agreement of the different ruling powers: and it is still more difficult to conceive, how this friendly agreement should have subsisted, unless we suppose, that, in the early ages of the world, before the minds of nations were alienated from each other by the wars which an increase of numbers would infallibly produce, a distinct recollection of the common origin of the priesthood and military nobility of every people was carefully preserved. I greatly doubt, whether any other supposition except this will solve the problem: but, according to the present theory, an inquisitive traveller of the sacerdotal or military caste would still find his brethren, into whatever intervening region he penetrated, possessed of sovereign authority, adhering to the same religion, and probably speaking some peculiar common dialect different from those of their respective subjects and esteemed a sort of sacred tongue. Something not

the ubiquitous name of Cush

unlike what I have here described once subsisted between the nobility of France and England: and the dissolution of a singular sort of harmony, produced by sameness of origin and language, which formerly united them, can scarcely be said to have been effected, until the unfortunate claim, preferred by our third Edward to the crown of the almost sister nation, introduced a long series of bloody wars and mutual injuries.

But there is yet a third matter, much more definite than either of those, which I have last adduced: this, if it do not absolutely *prove* the point in question, at least serves to render it in a high degree historically *probable*. It is a remarkable circumstance, that in very many nations, some of them most widely separated from each other, there is precisely the same division into castes: that identical division in short, which I suppose to have naturally originated at Babel from the very organization of the Cuthic empire of Nimrod as briefly described to us in Scripture. In the *inferior* castes indeed of different countries we find a variation, both in numbers and arrangement; which is no more than might be expected, as they constituted the bulk of the population, and as the increasing wants of growing communities would call forth new employments and thus create new castes: but in the two *superior* castes, among whatever people we meet with them, we find an accordance so exact and uniform, that it can scarcely have been produced by a repetition of lucky accidents. These two, wherever they occur, are invariably linked together in a politico-theological compact. The influence of the priest is repaid by the protection of the soldier, and the sword of the soldier acquires additional force from the moral dominion exercised by the priest. Nor is this all: the superiority of the priest is always acknowledged by the warrior; and, with a strange uniformity, the unarmed sacerdotal caste constantly takes precedence of the armed military caste. Such a combination, thus invariable both in its arrangement and in its ends, might alone be sufficient to induce the suspicion, that it was either effected by the conquest and subjugation of a less warlike by a more warlike people, or that it was originally brought from some common centre where its first establishment had taken place. Each of these modes of accounting for this phenomenon would lead to the belief, that, in all instances where the regular division into castes is found to occur and where the two ruling castes are always the priests and the soldiers ranking in the precise order of their present enumeration, the governors were of a different race from the governed. On the supposition of conquest in each separate instance, such for example as that of the Anglo-Saxons by the Normans, or on a larger scale that of the western empire by the Goths, a difference of origin must *necessarily* be admitted. And, on the other supposition, which seems more probable, because a mere repetition of independent and distant conquests could scarcely have produced that undeviating regularity both in precedental arrangement and in necessary descent from father to son which forms so striking a characteristic of the caste system; we shall still, by the train of reasoning already exhibited, be brought to the same conclusion. For it is hard to conceive, how such a system could have been established in the first instance, while the various Noetic tribes were assembled together in one community during the infancy of society, except by the ambition of some enterprizing individual operating, in the manner which has been described, upon his own peculiar tribe: and, accordingly, Scripture plainly enough intimates, that Nimrod was the first sovereign of Babel; and that he acquired that sovereignty by being a mighty hunter, or, in other words, by gradually training certain hardy associates to the use of arms and by thus laying the foundation of a caste of military nobility. Hence it appears, that, in whatever way this singular system be speculatively viewed, we are almost inevitably led to the conclusion, that, where it is established, there the governors must be of a different origin from the governed. Now it is a curious and highly-interesting circumstance, that, in more than one instance where the caste system has prevailed, a tradition has been distinctly and immemorially preserved, that such was actually the case: it has been allowed, that the rulers did *not* spring from the same ancestry as their debased subjects. To boast a special descent from the gods whom they served, to style themselves *children of the Sun and Moon,* and to guard carefully the purity of their lineage from all inferior admixture, has been the ordinary pride of such rulers: but the Hindoos, to the more usual notions, have superadded an account of the origin of their war-tribe, remarkable at once for its precision and for its direct corroboration of the theory which I have advocated. Their military nobility is acknowledged to be of the same family as the Sacas or Chasas, who maintain that their great common ancestor was Cusha or Cush: and, agreeably to this recognition, the war-tribe bears the name of *the Cuttree tribe*, that is to say, *the Cuthite or Cushite tribe*. It may be added, that the genealogy of the Brahmens is similarly traced up to the Sacas or Chasas, while the origin of the main population of Hindostan is left in a state of uncertainty.

5. Yet, while Scripture is silent in regard to the supposed occurrences which I have last mentioned, it repeatedly speaks of nations descended with more or less purity from the line of Cush. Numerous were the minor settlements of this great and warlike family; but we read in a special manner of two lands of Cush, the Asiatic and the African. These were by the Greeks called *the two Ethiopias*, a mode of expression which our translators of the Bible have generally adopted: but by the Hindoos, as by the sacred writers, they are denominated *the land of Cush within* and *the land of Cush without*.[']

The Scythians of Touran were the unmixed descendants of the Babylonic Cuthim of Nimrod.

The Asiatic land of Cush was a most extensive territory, reaching from the banks of the Indus to the shores of the Mediterranean sea: and it was rather governed, than exclusively peopled by the descendants of that patriarch. The African land of Cush stretched southward from the Thebais to the source of the Nile and the mountains of the Moon, including likewise (according to the Hindoos) within its ample limits the whole land of Egypt: and it was planted or subjugated at a later period by a tribe of pastoral Cushim from upper India.

These military Shepherds were a branch of the unmixed Cushim, whose primeval settlements, after they had withdrawn from their Iranian brethren who still adhered to the fortunes of Nimrod and his successors, appear to have been made in that high range of country, which, skirting the north of Persia, extends, under the general name of *Touran*, from upper India to Armenia. The descendants of those, who established themselves throughout this wide region, are still among the Hindoos denominated *Chasas* or *Chusas*: and they themselves, acknowledging the appellation, claim to have received it from their ancestor Chusa or Cusha, the grandson of the ark-

---

[']*Cusha dwip within* and *Cusha-dwip without*, as the Hindoos speak.

preserved Menu. His name was equally bestowed upon the country : for the Sanscrit compound *Chasa-Ghiri*, and the Persic compound *Coh-Cas*, alike denote *the mountain of Cush*. From the Persic *Coh-Cas* the Greeks have manifestly formed their word *Caucasus :* and, as the warlike Chusas spread all the way from upper India to Armenia, we indifferently find a mount Caucasus at the head of the Ganges, on the south of the Caspian sea, and on the north-east of the Euxine sea. In fact, the whole range was properly the Caucasian mountains ; which jointly constitute, as the oriental writers speak, the stony girdle of the earth. Such being the settlements of the Touranian Chusas, their very locality proves them to be the Scuths or Scythians of the Greek writers ; a great nation of whom were ordinarily termed *Indo-Scuths* from their vicinity to Hindostan. These, like the modern Chasas, dwelt in the recesses of the Indian Caucasus : as their brethren, the more westerly Scuths, called *Celto-Scuths* from their vicinity to the originally extensive possessions of the Celtic tribes, occupied the defiles of the Iberian Caucasus.

In all ages, so far as circumstances would allow, the character of this powerful race seems to have preserved its uniformity. Just as we might have supposed would be the case with the peculiar descendants of Nimrod's military nobility, the Scuths or Chasas have ever been more addicted to war and the chase than to the peaceful occupations of husbandry and commerce. Hence was generated a roving unsettled life : which displayed itself in frequent hostile expeditions into other countries ; and which, partly from a hatred of manual labour and partly from the facility which it affords to loco-motion, peculiarly affected the pastoral occupation. Hence also was produced that love of liberty, and that impatience of restraint, which has always characterised the warlike shepherds of Scythia. Where all, from a long preserved remembrance of their origin, were equally noble, though the herds of one might exceed in number the herds of another, the distinction of all castes, save that of the two superior ones, was unknown.[1] The whole nation consisted of priests and soldiers. To the ministers of their

---

[1] To this remark there are some exceptions, as we shall hereafter see : but, wherever such exceptions occur, we may pronounce, that there was an admixture of other blood. See below book vi. c. 2. § VI. c. 4. § I, II. 5.

religion these fearless warriors paid a ready submission: but they disdained the shackles of any human authority; and, while their limited kings were advanced to the throne by virtue of their noble birth from the regal family, the only influence, which their military leaders possessed over them, was that procured by long tried superior valour and experience. Yet, wherever they made a settlement by conquest, an image of the ancient constitution established by their first sovereign immediately and indeed naturally appeared. The victorious nation portioned out their new territory among themselves according to the rank and power which each had held in the invading host: the vanquished were reduced to the condition of slaves, and were tied down to the soil which they were doomed to cultivate for the benefit of their imperious masters: the professions of theology and arms were alone accounted noble: each chieftain held his land by the free and honourable tenure of military service: and the whole country resembled a huge camp, properly provided with the ministers of religion, and duly served by a race of captive slaves. In short, while the Scythians were unmixed in their native mountains and forests, or while they continued unmixed by a new establishment in a *vacant* region, their only castes were the sacerdotal and military: but, whenever they subdued an *already* inhabited country, an inferior race, which naturally resolved itself into the two grand occupations of artizans and husbandmen, was forthwith produced; the warlike nobility meanwhile at once disdaining the degradation of all plebeian alliances, and yet, after the manner of their ancestors, readily granting precedence to the priesthood.

This enterprizing people, who, by a singular fate, have ever been, at different periods, the corrupters and the reformers, the disturbers and the civilizers, of the world, were known by various names, either general to the whole, or particular to certain divisions. They were called *Scuths, Chusas, Chasas, Cissèans, Cossèans, Coths, Ghauts,* and *Goths,* from their great ancestor Cush; whose name they pronounced *Cusha, Chusa, Ghoda, Chasa, Chasya,* or *Cassius.* They were styled *Palli, Bali, Bhils, Philistim, Palistim, Bolgs,* or *Belgæ,* from their occupation; for the term denotes *Shepherds.* And they were partially denominated *Phanakim* or *Phenicians,* and *Huc-Sos* or *Shepherd-kings,* from their claiming to be a royal race; *Sacas, Sagas, Sucasenas, Sachim, Suchim, Saxe,* or *Saxons,* from their god Saca or Sacya; *Budins* or *Wudins,* from their god Buddha or Woden; *Teuts* or *Teutons,* from their god Teut or Taut; and *Germans* or *Sarmans,* from their god Saman or Sarman and his ministers the Samanèans or Sarmanèans or Germanèans, as they are indifferently called according to a varied pronunciation of the same word.

Though pagan Idolatry was fundamentally the same in every part of the world; yet it was divided into two great heresies, which may be termed Scythism, and Ionism or Buddhism and Brahmenism. Each of these is as old as the dispersion, though Buddhism seems the more ancient of the two.

6. But, though pagan mythology be fundamentally and substantially the same in every quarter of the globe, we may, I think, independently of those minor differences which mere separation and lapse of time would naturally produce, observe a grand division of the Gentiles into two leading sects. In many countries these have been long completely and amicably blended together: in others they severally subsist in a state of well marked distinction: and in one at least they are separated by the bitterest hostility; though, with an apparent inconsistency, the objects of their worship confessedly melt into each other, and the same deity is in effect venerated by both. It is difficult to fix upon the proper appellations, by which the two kindred theological systems of these two predominating sects may be best designated. From their supposed founders (adopting the phraseology, with which Epiphanius has been furnished by certain ancient *records*) we may call the one *Scythism,* and the other *Ionism :* or, from the deities who were especially venerated, we may call the one *Buddhism* or *Hermetism* or *Tautism,* and the other *Sivism* or *Osirism* or *Dionusism:* or lastly, from the officiating ministers of religion, we may call the one *Samanianism* or *Sarmanianism,* and the other *Brahmenism* or *Druidism.* I shall in future use the terms *Buddhism* and *Brahmenism,* not as being any way peculiarly apposite, but as being somewhat more familiar than any of the others.

The question has often been agitated, which of these two systems is the most ancient: but the grounds of the controversy do not appear to me to have ever been laid down with so much precision as might have been desired. *Local antiquity* seems to have been a good deal confounded with *general and proper antiquity:* it has been disputed, which of the two was prior *in Hindostan;* and that, to which the palm has been adjudged by its own advocates, has thence been pronounced to be the more ancient system. But this is not an accurate way either of stating or of deciding upon the merits of the case. Brahmenism may be prior to Buddhism, or Buddhism may be prior to Brahmenism, in the *particular* country of Hindostan: but this will not establish the superior antiquity of either, so far as its *primeval* origin is concerned. Without attempting to determine the question of *local* priority, the settling of which is no way necessary to my present plan, I certainly think it manifest, that each system is *as old* as the dispersion from Babel: and I think it equally manifest, both for reasons which will hereafter appear, and because Buddhism is on the whole more simple than Brahmenism, that Buddhism is the more ancient system of the two, having been struck out even *prior* to the building of the tower.

I am fully aware, that Sir William Jones places the origin of Buddhism no higher than about a thousand years before the Christian era; that he supposes the system to have been introduced by a younger Buddha, whom he distinguishes from that earlier Buddha who is placed by the Hindoo records in the age of the deluge; and that he conceives the younger Buddha or Sacya to be the Sesac of Scripture, whom he makes to conquer the whole country between Egypt and Hindostan and to promulge wherever he was successful the then novel doctrine of the Buddhists. To this opinion I am unable to assent. The name indeed of *Sesac* is doubtless a name of Buddha, for *Se-Sac* denotes *the illustrious Saca;* and this *fatal resemblance,* as it has been not ill termed, seems to have been the chief thing, or at least *one* chief thing that gave rise to the opinion. Such a coincidence of names however will by no means prove the point: Sesac, if I mistake not, received his appellation merely in honour of the god Saca or Se-Saca, agreeably to a custom very generally prevalent in the gentile world;[1] and, though I pretend not positively to say how far he *might* have pushed his conquests, there is certainly no *scriptural* evidence that he passed beyond the limits of Judèa. He is simply represented, as taking the fenced cities of Rehoboam and as pillaging the temple of Jerusalem, and then to all appearance as returning with his booty into Egypt.[2] Hence there seems to me, so far as we have any *authentic* account of his actions, to be just as little reason for identifying him with a

---

[1] Thus Nebuchadnezzar, Esar-Haddon, and Belshazzar, were all called after the gods venerated by their fathers.

[2] See 2 Chron. xii. 1—9.

younger Sacya who was the first promulgator of Buddhism, as with the fabulously victorious Sesostris.   The evidence for the remote antiquity of Buddhism rests upon exactly the same foundation as that for the remote antiquity of Brahmenism.   There is scarcely a country, in which we do not find both systems more or less blended together : and Buddha, as much as Siva or Osiris, under his various names of *Buddha, Saca, Taut, Teut, Thoth, Bod, Wod, Hermaya, Hermes,* or *Mercolis,* has been worshipped from Japan in the east to Ireland in the west.   The theory of Sir William Jones is inadequate to account for this circumstance: no conquests, which a king of Egypt *could* make, and which after all it remains to be proved that he *did* make, could have spread his name and novel theology over the face of the whole globe; I say *name,* because, if I do not misunderstand Sir William, Buddha first received his title of *Sacya* from the circumstance of Sesac's being venerated as a new incarnation of Buddha.   This opinion however, if it *be* the opinion of that able writer, is most certainly an error.   The appellation *Saca* or compoundedly *Se-Saca* existed *before* the time of the Egyptian prince, and was communicated from the god to a great tribe of his Cuthic worshippers, who were thence called *Sacas* or *Sachim* or *Saxons.*   Some of these Sachim formed a part of the Indian Shepherd-kings; who once conquered Egypt, and who afterwards founded the kingdom of African Ethiopia or Cusha-dwip without: for we find a detachment of them expressly mentioned with their brethren the Cushim, as serving in the army of Sesac.[1]   If then there was a whole tribe of Sachim or Sacas in the days of Sesac, both the name and the worship of Saca must inevitably have been *prior* to that prince.   Thus, in whatever light the question be viewed, we cannot, I think, ascribe a more recent origin to Buddhism than the dispersion from Babel.

There is some reason for believing, that, immediately before that period, a great disagreement arose respecting the particular modification of the apostate system of theology: one party advocating a form more simple, though directly tending to atheism when pushed to extremities; another, advocating a form more complex and naturally productive of polytheism by repeated

---

[1] 2 Chron. xii. 3.   The word is expressed by our translators *Sukkiim* after the Masoretic punctuation; but it is just as properly pronounced *Sachiim,* which is the plural form of *Sach* or *Sachi.*   In *our* language the plural of *Sach* would be *Sachs.*

distinct personifications of the various names and attributes of the great father and mother; and a third, willing to accommodate matters by adopting both forms, and blending them together, as far as might be, into one. However this may be, the two theories of Brahmenism and Buddhism appear to me to have existed from the very days of Nimrod; because there is no country upon the face of the earth, in which I do not find distinct traces of one or both of them. When examined, they melt into each other: and, notwithstanding the hatred that subsists between their respective votaries in Hindostan, they are plainly, at the bottom, mere variations of one and the same system. Nor will this appear strange to any one, who has observed the operations of the human mind: by a singular fatality, the smaller the difference of opinion between varying sects and the less important the points of discrepancy, the greater has usually been the bitterness of contention. So far as I have been able to observe, Buddhism seems in all ages to have been the favourite theory of the unmixed and warlike Cuthim; while Brahmenism, generally more or less blended with Buddhism, has chiefly prevailed among the mixed nations of the earth. Their original identity, and the circumstance of their being so frequently blended together, render it not always easy to distinguish the one from the other. If in some particulars it shall appear that I have been mistaken, I have only to subscribe to the trite apophthegm that *to err is human.*

7. As I find myself compelled by the force of historical evidence to give the sceptre of the world to the warlike posterity of Cush, I feel it necessary to offer in this place some observations on the celebrated prophecy of Noah.

An opinion has, I know not how, very generally prevailed, that a curse was pronounced upon Ham, which devoted his posterity to servitude: hence the epithet *accursed* has been liberally bestowed upon that patriarch, as his stated and appropriate designation. Nor has this notion been taken up merely by ordinary and superficial theologists: even such writers as Bochart and Mede are to be found among its advocates. Bochart, in one place, styles Ham *accursed;* and, in another, he represents Noah as *execrating* him and as foretelling that *his children should be slaves:* while Mede, not content with calling upon us to *tremble at the horrible curse of impious Ham* and with intimating that he was destined to be *a servant of servants to all his brethren,* roundly asserts, that *there hath never yet been a son of Ham that hath shaken a sceptre over the head of Japhet, that Shem hath subdued Japhet and Japhet hath subdued Shem, but Ham never subdued either*.[1] Yet, notwithstanding this general persuasion, Scripture contains not a single syllable respecting either any curse pronounced upon Ham or any prediction of the general servitude of his posterity. Canaan indeed, the youngest of the four sons of Ham, is the subject of an imprecatory denunciation: but Ham himself was never cursed; consequently neither the curse nor the prophecy can affect any of his descendants except the Canaanites.

Those writers, who have been the most zealous in applying the curse and the prediction to Ham, were sensible, that Scripture, as it stands at present, directly opposed their opinion: but so fully were their minds preoccupied with the common idea, that, rather than relinquish it, they have, with mischievous ingenuity, attempted to make the Bible speak the language, which they had concluded it *ought* to speak. Hence, because the Arabic version reads *cursed be the father of Canaan*, and because some copies of the lxx substitute *Ham* in the place of *Canaan;* they would, throughout the prophecy, wherever the word *Canaan* occurs, correct it to *Ham the father of Canaan.*

With respect to this supposed improvement of the text, it not only runs directly counter both to the Hebrew and the Samaritan copies of the Pentateuch which perfectly agree in their reading of the prediction, to say nothing of the common reading of the lxx; but it seems to me to bear also the strongest internal marks of spuriousness. Why should Ham throughout the whole prophecy be called *the father of Canaan*, rather than *the father of Cush* or of *Mizr* or of *Phut?* Why should this long unmeaning title be thrice repeated? Why should Ham be particularized as the father of Canaan, rather than Japhet as the father of Gomer, or Shem as the father of Elam? When I compare the projected emendation with the commonly received reading, and when I consider the joint high authority of the Hebrew and the Samaritan Pentateuchs, I cannot hesitate long in determining where to fix my choice. But I have yet an additional reason for protesting most strongly

---

[1] Boch. Phaleg. lib. iv. c. 1. p. 203. lib. i. c. 1. p. 3, 4. Mede's Works. book i. disc. 49. p. 271. disc. 50. p. 283. Dr. Hales has fallen into the same error. See Chronol. vol. i. p. 351—353.

against any correction or rather alteration of the text. I have termed such critical ingenuity *mischievous*; nor was the epithet applied lightly and without cause. If the prophecy had *really* been penned in the form which has been recommended instead of its present form, its falshood would have been clearly evinced by the testimony of history; and thus a vantage-ground would have been afforded to the enemy of revelation, from which it would be no easy matter to expel him. So far from Ham never having shaken a sceptre over the head either of Japhet or Shem, as Mr. Mede most incautiously asserts, it may be clearly proved, that his posterity in the line of Cush have been at the head, not only of the Babylonian empire of Nimrod, but of the Persian, the Grecian, and the Roman, empires. Nor did their sway cease with the downfall of the last mighty power: the Goths or Scuths, penetrating into the west from their original settlements in Touran and Cashgar, have established and retained their sway over the fairest provinces of Europe; and thus, to the intrepid and free-born children of the Hammonian Cush or Cusha, are committed the destinies of the world.[1]

Here I might be allowed to stop, since it is sufficient for my present purpose to have shewn that no curse was pronounced upon Ham, and that no part of his posterity was devoted to servitude except the descendants of Canaan. Yet, since the Goths, who established themselves in Europe at the downfall of the Western empire, were certainly Scuths or Scythians; since

---

[1] The account, which Josephus gives of Noah's prophecy, is very curious and important. He says, that Noah blessed two of his sons, but that he refrained from cursing Ham on account of his near relationship to him. The curse however, from which Ham was thus exempted, was laid upon his posterity. Yet, of that posterity, the others escaped the evil consequences of the malediction; and the children of Canaan were *alone* subjected to its direful influence. Ant. Jud. lib. i. c. 6. § 3. edit. Huds. Hence it appears, that Josephus knew nothing of the mischievous correction which would exhibit Ham as being *himself* accursed, and consequently had never heard of any reading of the original Hebrew which would authorise such a correction. Hence also it appears, that, although he laboured under the vulgar mistake that the *whole* posterity of Ham were devoted to servitude, he was too good an historian to assert the accomplishment of the prophecy when *thus* understood: he fairly confesses, that it was fulfilled in the children of Canaan *alone*, and that none of the *other* descendants of Ham were in the least affected by it. Had he only attended to the express words of Noah, he might have spared the latter part of his comment.

the Scythians were doubtless the same race as the Indo-Scythæ; since the Indo-Scythæ of the Greeks were the ancestors of the modern Chasas or Chusas; since those Chusas declare themselves to be descended from the patriarch Cusha, who communicated to them his own appellation, and who is described as being the grandson of the ark-preserved Menu; since this Cusha, as Sir William Jones well remarks, is clearly the scriptural Cush, who was similarly the grandson of the ark-preserved Noah;[1] and since there-fore the Gothic conquerors of Europe must have sprung from Cush, and consequently from Ham: since such is the genealogy of those, who now pos-sess the sovereignty of the most civilized part of the world, and whose do-minion or influence extends either more or less over all the other quarters of it; it may not be altogether uninteresting to make some inquiries into the character of that patriarch, which, after a long and attentive survey of the prophecy, seems to me to have been much misunderstood and much misre-presented.

That Ham beheld his father in an unseemly posture, is indisputable: but the question is, whether he thus beheld him *designedly* and therefore *crimi-nally*, or *undesignedly* and therefore *innocently*. Dr. Jennings justly remarks, that the *merely seeing* the exposure of Noah *might be accidental, unavoid-able, and no way criminal*: but he completely mars this sensible observation by immediately adding, as one whose mind was prepossessed by the common opinion, *we must therefore suppose, that there was something more in the case than is plainly expressed.*[2] Now I would ask, *why* must we suppose something more than Moses has told us? *what* is there in the history, which gives us any warrant for branding the memory of this calumniated patriarch with a most foul and disgraceful aspersion? If indeed a curse had been pronounced

---

[1] When we see Cush or Cus (for the Sanscrit name is variously pronounced) among the sons of Brahma, that is, among the progenitors of the Hindoos, and at the head of an ancient pedigree preserved in the Ramayan; when we meet with his name again in the family of Rama; when we add, that one of the seven dwipas, or great peninsulas of this earth, has the same appel-lation : *we can hardly doubt,* says Sir William Jones, that the Cush of Moses and the Cush of Valmic was the same personage and an ancestor of the Indian race. Asiat. Res. vol. iii. p. 432. See also p. 427.

[2] Jennings's Jewish Ant. b. i. c. 1. p.12.

upon Ham, and if his whole posterity had been devoted to servitude and in-feriority, we should then have been most amply authorized in supposing this *something* which is allowed not to be plainly expressed : we might then have been sure, that he had been guilty of a brutal want of filial piety in offering a *designed* insult to his erring parent ; we might then have been sure, that his base criminality had met with an adequate punishment.   But nothing of the sort is found to be recorded : as no intimation is given of any *purposed* sin on the part of Ham, so neither is any curse denounced against him.   If then the denunciation of a curse would have been an infallible proof of his guilt; are we not bound by every principle of fair reasoning to conclude, that the non-denunciation of a curse is a manifest proof of his innocence? The curse would surely be pronounced upon the offender, whoever that offender might be : and, since it is pronounced, not upon Ham, but upon his youngest son Canaan; I see not how we can fairly avoid the inference, that Canaan, not Ham, was the guilty person.   The remarkable terms, in which the prophecy is delivered, have not been left unnoticed, for indeed it was scarcely possible that they *should* be left unnoticed, by those who have paid attention to the subject. It has been inquired by those, who still laboured under the pre-conceived impression of Ham's criminality, why the curse, due to *him*, was pronounced upon his son *Canaan?* The answer, which the Jewish doctors give, is this : that Canaan first beheld the exposure of Noah, that he imme-diately communicated the discovery to his father, and that the two united in cruelly mocking and insulting the old man.[1]   Such a solution however does but half remove the difficulty.   If Ham and Canaan were *equally* guilty, why was the one punished, and the other suffered to escape? Why was Ca-naan cursed, and Ham not cursed? Why were the children of Canaan de-voted to servitude rather than the other descendants of Ham, since all were alike the offspring of him who had treated his father with the most brutal and unfeeling disrespect? Which ever way we turn, the usual opinion respecting

---

[1] Operosè quæritur, cur Chami maledictionem in caput filii Channaan Noa contorserit. Re-spondet. Theodoretus in Genes. quæst. 57. ab Hebræo quodam se didicisse, primum Channan avi sui verenda animadvertisse, et patri ostentasse tanquam de sene ridentem. Et vero tale quid legitur in Beresith Rabba sect. 37, qui liber scriptus fuit ante Theodoretum.   Boch. Phaleg. lib. iv. c. 37. p. 308.

the criminality of Ham presents, so far as I can judge, insuperable obstacles to any thing like a consistent interpretation of the prophecy. But every difficulty will be removed, if we can only be content to lay to his charge nothing more than Scripture has done.

The ancient tradition of the Jewish doctors is by no means to be hastily set aside, though it has unfortunately been injured by that pertinacious ascription of deliberate wickedness to Ham, which marks the writings of Hebrew no less than of Christian commentators. Since Canaan is *solely* cursed, I believe Canaan to have been *solely* guilty. Connecting together the Jewish tradition with what has been revealed in Scripture, I seem to draw out the following account of the whole transaction. Noah, in consequence of his unhappy intoxication, lay exposed in his tent. In this state he was discovered by his grandson Canaan. Hitherto no crime was committed, for the discovery appears to have been accidental : but the graceless youth, instead of throwing with dutiful haste a mantle over his aged parent, exultingly leaves him as he found him, and sets forth in quest of others whom he may make joint spectators of the shameful sight. The first person, with whom he happens to meet, is his own father. To him, I apprehend, he does not precisely *communicate* the discovery which he had made ; but rather, with much laughter and mockery, invites him to behold a ludicrous spectacle, which could not fail to amuse him. The very same invitation would probably have been given to either of his uncles, if one of them had crossed his path instead of his father ; and it might have been accepted with the same unconscious and unsuspecting innocence, as I am inclined to believe that Ham accepted it. Entering the tent, and little anticipating the sight which was about to be revealed to him, Ham *unwarily* and *undesignedly* beholds Noah in a state of exposed nudity. Instantly however he retires, and tells his two brethren who were without; no way desirous to have his eyes shocked by the repetition of such a spectacle. They, being thus made acquainted with the condition of their father, piously contrive to throw a garment over him without beholding his exposure. Noah, at length coming to himself when the fumes of the wine were dissipated, learns, not what *his younger son* (meaning *Ham*) had done unto him, but what *his little son*, or, as the idiom of our language requires, *his grandson* (meaning *Canaan*), had done unto him: for such, when the immediately subsequent context is attended to, seems to be the meaning of the expression, as the Jewish Rabbins have well remarked. The whole, that follows, is exactly such as might have been anticipated from *this* statement of the matter, but by no means such as might naturally have been expected from the *common* account of it. Noah pronounces a curse, not upon Ham who had done nothing to deserve one, but upon the guilty and depraved Canaan; while the dutiful caution of Shem and Japhet is rewarded by a blessing invoked upon the head of each of them. Respecting Ham he is totally silent: as that patriarch did not merit a curse, so neither had he done any thing to call for a special blessing; hence, in a manner perfectly according with his conduct, he is passed over without either blessing or curse.[1]

That something of this sort is to be received as the proper account of the transaction, seems to me almost necessarily to follow, not only from the Jewish tradition, but from the general context of the whole narrative itself. If Ham were the *sole* guilty person, why was his youngest son Canaan cursed rather than Cush or Mizr or Phut? If *both* Ham and Canaan were guilty, why was Canaan *exclusively* cursed and Ham suffered to escape? The circumstance of the curse being pronounced upon Canaan *alone* surely does all but absolutely prove Canaan *alone* to be the offender: for, if Ham were *really* guilty, it is impossible to assign any satisfactory reason, why he should have borne no mark whatsoever of his father's displeasure. At least, it has never been *my* lot to find any satisfactory reason adduced: and indeed it is sufficiently evident, how little satisfied those expositors themselves are who assume the criminality of *Ham*, from the very circumstance of their labouring to alter the text. As it stands at present, it is utterly irreconcileable with that criminality: but, the criminality having been once taken for granted without a shadow of proof, the advocates of such an hypothesis find it absolutely necessary for their theory to alter the text; and, by this depravation of Holy Scripture, they transform a prophecy which has been accomplished with admirable minuteness into a prophecy which is directly contradicted by the voice of history.

[1] Thus Balak says to Balaam, *Neither curse them at all, nor bless them at all.* Numb. xxiii. 25.

The opinion, that Canaan *alone* was the culprit, exactly corresponds with the peculiar manner in which that patriarch is mentioned.

When Moses specifies the three sons of Noah that went forth of the Ark, he subjoins emphatically, that *Ham was the father of Canaan:*[1] and afterwards, when he begins to relate the humiliating story of the just man's departure from the path of righteousness, the title of *the father of Canaan* is remarkably bestowed upon Ham.[2] Now the turn of this expression is evidently designed, by every rule of composition, to point out to the reader's especial attention not *Ham* but *Canaan*. When we say that *Philip of Macedon was the father of the victorious Alexander*, Alexander, not Philip, is doubtless the prominent figure in the sentence : or again, when we say that *Richard Cromwell was the son of the great protector*, who does not perceive, that the mind is immediately directed not to Richard but to Oliver ? In a similar manner, when Ham is styled *the father of Canaan*, particularly when he is so styled in a sentence which merely speaks of the egress from the Ark, the expression has all the force of the demonstrative pronoun ; it is as if Ham were called *the father of* THAT *Canaan*. Here *Canaan* is the person pointed out to notice, certainly not *Ham:* for, if *Ham* had been the prominent figure on the historical canvass, the turn of the phrase would have been exactly inverted ; if *Ham* had been the person who was a standing and proverbial disgrace to his posterity, Cush or Mizr or Phut or Canaan might have been equally and severally branded as *the son of* THAT *Ham*, but in such case 1 see not with what propriety Ham could have been pointed out to us as *the father of* THAT *Canaan*. The expression certainly imports, that Ham was memorable for being the father of Canaan, not that Canaan was memorable for being the son of Ham, a circumstance no more characteristic of him than of either of his three brethren. Why then is Ham styled *the father of Canaan*, rather than *of Cush* or *Mizr* or *Phut ?* There evidently must have been something remarkable in the conduct of Canaan, to procure such a badge of distinction, either honourable or dishonourable, for a youngest son. What then was this remarkable *something ?* The answer to such a question appears to me sufficiently ob-

[1] Gen. ix. 18.   [2] Ver. 22.

vious.   Ham is denominated *the father of* THAT *Canaan* at the commencement of a narrative, which terminates in declaring that Canaan had a curse
of servitude denounced against him.   Hence it is plain, that Canaan possessed the bad celebrity of being an accursed person : and it is also plain,
that he must have been guilty of some enormous crime, both to call down
upon him such a curse, and to purchase for him such an evil preëminence
in disgrace.   This obvious deduction at once serves to corroborate the view
which I have taken of the matter, and directly tends to establish the genuineness of the common Hebrew reading which some would so rashly undertake to correct.   Had the curse been pronounced upon *Ham*, and had
Canaan been altogether out of the question, as the proposed alteration
would represent the affair to have been ; we might then have easily understood, why Cush or Mizr or Phut or Canaan should be emphatically styled
the son of THAT *Ham :* but it would puzzle the greatest critical ingenuity
to discover a reason, why Ham should be called *the father of* THAT *Canaan.*

This difficulty has been felt by commentators : and therefore, where a
reason *must* be given, a reason *must* of course be invented.   It is commonly said, that Moses thus peculiarly specifies Canaan as the son of the
accursed and servile Ham, in order to encourage the Israelites with the
hope of a sure and speedy victory over the Canaanites already prepared to bow
their necks to the yoke in consequence of an ancient imprecatory prediction.
I am at a loss, whether most to admire the perfect inutility of such a specification, or the total disregard to context evinced by such a mode of solving
the difficulty.   *The specification* would have been thoroughly useless ; both
because Moses plainly informs the children of Israel in his general table of
genealogies[1] that Canaan *was* the son of Ham, because at that time of day
the descent of the Canaanites must have been so well known as to supersede the necessity of any incidental mention of it, and because conquest
was promised to the Israelites much more definitely and explicitly by God
himself than by any interpretation which could be given of Noah's prophecy : *the context* of the narrative imperiously requires us to conclude,

[1] Gen. x. 6.

that Ham was called *the father of Canaan*, not with a view of encouraging the Israelites who wanted no such encouragement, but because Canaan was, in a theological light, a much more remarkable person than any one of his brethren on account of the curse under which he laboured.

I have only to notice a single matter more, and the subject shall be dismissed. They, who by an alteration of the text, would prove Ham to be the person accursed and therefore his posterity in general to be destined to servitude, sometimes adduce, as a proof of the accomplishment of the prophecy according to *their* view of it, the subjugated condition of Egypt or the land of the Mizraim.

Now, in the first place, this does not prove enough ; and therefore, so far as the exact completion of the prophecy is concerned, it proves just nothing. If *all* the descendants of Ham were doomed to servitude, we shall have gained but little in shewing the depression of Canaan and Mizr, unless we also point out the subjugation of Cush and Phut. Perhaps, in regard to Phut, the slave-trade may be adduced ; indeed, I believe, it *has* been adduced by some writers. Whether the negroes are or are not descended from that patriarch, I shall not now stop to determine ; neither is it any way important to my present object, that the question *should* be determined : I shall content myself with asking, when were the warlike Cushim subdued, at least permanently and generally, either by Japhet or Shem ?[1] But, unless *all* the children of Ham were brought under the yoke, it is a clear case, that the prophecy, according to the common exposition of it, has never been accomplished.

So again, in the second place, it may well be inquired, whether the constant subjugation of Egypt from the time of Nebuchadnezzar down to the present day, can in any respect be deemed a completion of Noah's prophecy. I certainly think, that it cannot. The remarkable servitude of

[1] In the great revolutions of empires, Cush may have occasionally suffered as well as his brethren. The Philistim were subdued by the Israelites after a long struggle for superiority ; and the Carthaginians, ill deemed by many the descendants of Canaan, were conquered by the Romans, who seem in a large sense to have been a Japhetic people under Cuthic governors. But the Cuthim, in every age and in every country, have generally managed to preserve a decided ascendancy over all the other children of Noah.

Egypt is the consequence, in the hands of Divine Providence, not of Noah's prediction, but of an eminent prophecy delivered by Ezekiel.[1] Mizr is become a servant, not because he was a son of Ham, but because he was doomed *long afterwards* to a state of degradation on account of his pride and faithless tyranny.[2] This very sentence indeed proves, that heretofore he laboured not under *any* judicial imprecation : for, if he were *already* destined to servitude, and if the prophecy of Ezekiel were solely intended to specify the time of its commencement, it seems natural to conclude that some reference would have been made to his descent from Ham; whereas the alleged grounds of his predicted subjugation are of a totally different nature, and not the least allusion is made to the fancied curse pronounced upon his great ancestor.

In short, after all that has been said on the subject, Bochart himself allows, that Ham, *cursed as he was*,[3] had his full share of earthly blessings.[4] His ample sway extended over at least a third part of the globe : and many are the regions, in which neither Shem nor Japhet, to adopt the phraseology of Mr. Mede, ever shook a sceptre over the head of Ham. I pretend not to say, that this exposition obviates *all* difficulties, though I think it encumbered with fewer than any other that I have met with : but I would again observe in conclusion, that the matter, by which the present work is *alone* affected, is *the supposed curse of servitude upon Ham ;* and, whatever may have been the character of that patriarch, this at least is certain, that no curse of any description was pronounced upon *him.*[5]

V. The human mind rarely tolerates any great changes if they be violent

---

[1] Esek. xxix. 14, 15.   [2] See Esek. xxix. 2—16.

[3] *Licet maledictus* is the expression used by this learned author, as if it were too palpable a case to be controverted.   [4] Boch. Phaleg. lib. iv. c. 1. p. 203.

[5] One difficulty would be in a great measure obviated, if we suppose the verb ירא in the 22d verse to be the defective third person future of the conjugation Hophal, instead of the same person and tense of Kal. The verb occurs in this defective form in Hiphil, in 2 Kings xi. 4, as it is justly remarked by Buxtorf: and it is well known, that the third person future of Hophal is the same as the third person future of Hiphil in such verbs as ראה. According to such a supposition, the translation would run, *And Ham the father of Canaan was caused to see,* that is to say *was shewn, the nakedness of his father.*

and sudden, particularly in matters of religion. This circumstance calls for an inquiry into the steps, which Nimrod and his Cuthites may be supposed to have taken with a view to introduce that theological apostasy, which, perfected at Babel, thence extended itself over the whole world.

1. It seems natural to suppose, that that apostasy was not in the first instance a violent and abrupt setting aside of true religion, that it was not a sudden plunge from the worship of Jehovah into the grossness of rank idolatry. I should rather apprehend, that it must have commenced with a specious perversion of sound doctrine and with an affectedly devout adoption of authorized rites and ceremonies and phraseology: in other words, I am inclined to believe, that Gentilism was a fantastic structure erected upon the basis of ancient Patriarchism.

It emanated from Patriarchism under a shew of superior wisdom.

The mode, in which the edifice was raised, appears to have been by an affectation of superior wisdom and by a pretence of deep philosophical research. Many hints to this purpose are thrown out in Scripture. St. Paul remarks in general terms, that *the world by wisdom knew not God:*[1] and he elsewhere more largely explains the force of his observation, by tracing the origin of idolatry to the vain refinements of this spurious wisdom. He tells us, that, *when men as yet knew God, they glorified him not as God; but became vain in their imaginations, and their foolish heart was darkened. Professing themselves to be wise, they became fools: and* the consequence of this misnamed wisdom was, that they *changed the glory of the uncorruptible God into an image made like to corruptible man, and to birds, and four-footed beasts, and creeping things.* Corrupt worship was speedily followed by corrupt manners: indeed, as we have seen, the latter naturally sprang from the former; and were even esteemed a constituent part of it. *Wherefore,* the Apostle solemnly proceeds, *God also* judicially *gave them up to uncleanness through the lusts of their own hearts, to dishonour their own bodies between themselves; who changed the truth of God into a lye, and worshipped and served the creature rather than the Creator, who is blessed for ever.* He then particularizes the unnatural abominations, which arose out of the theologico-philosophical theories of paganism; ob-

[1] 1 Corinth. i. 21.

serving, in a very remarkable manner, that the circumstance of their being divinely abandoned to such vile affections was *the meet recompence of their error.*[1]   The same account of the origin of idolatry is given both by Isaiah and Jeremiah : and it is particularly worthy of observation, that they are alike speaking of Babylon, which was the universal mother of the spiritual adulteries of the postdiluvian world.   *Thy wisdom and thy knowledge,* says the former of these prophets to the apostate city of Nimrod, *it hath perverted thee.*[2]   *Babylon,* says the latter of them, *hath been a golden cup in the Lord's hand, that made all the earth drunken : the nations have drunken of her wine ; therefore the nations are mad.   Every man is brutish by his knowledge: every founder is confounded by the graven image ; for his molten image is falshood, and there is no breath in them.   They are vanity, the work of error : in the time of their visitation they shall perish.   How is Sesac[3] taken ! and how is the praise of the whole earth surprised ! how is Babylon become an astonishment among the nations !*[4]

2. What then were the fancied refinements of wisdom and knowledge, *The different steps by which it arrived at maturity* which elicited a mixed philosophical idolatry out of the pure doctrine and simple worship of Patriarchism ; which began with insidiously seducing the world from genuine religion under the pretence of conveying a superior degree of information, and which ended in plunging it into the thickest spiritual darkness and into the grossest moral depravity ?

The early inhabitants of the earth after the flood well knew, that the world had been originally created out of a turbid chaotic water, that it had been destroyed by a deluge, and that it had recently been created anew (as it were) out of the overflowing ocean.   This was the simple history of the globe, which they tenanted : but *Wisdom* discovered an endless succession of worlds, each formed by a particular modification of preëxisting matter ; and consequently established the independent eternity of crude matter or

---

[1] Rom. i. 21—27.   [2] Isaiah xlvii. 10.

[3] *Sesac is the illustrious Saca or Buddha.*   He was the favourite god of the Cuthim ; and communicated his name to the great Scythic family of the Sacas, or Sachim, or Saxons. From him also, as we have seen, the Egyptian Sesac borrowed his appellation.

[4] Jerem. li. 7, 17, 18, 41.

substance. The first postdiluvians knew, that each of the two worlds commenced from a man who had three sons, and that there were many other striking points of mutual resemblance which have been already pointed out: but *Wisdom* was not satisfied with a plain story; the doctrine of an endless succession of worlds was improved into that of an endless succession of exactly similar worlds, each invariably commencing with the same great parent and his three sons, whose souls passed by transmigration from one set of bodies into another and thus incessantly reappeared and reacted their parts upon the earth. The first postdiluvians knew, that one omnipotent and omnipresent Being was the sole creator and moderator of the Universe; a Being, who alone could claim to himself the attribute of proper independent eternity: but *Wisdom* had conferred this very attribute of eternity upon matter, and afterwards upon the souls of the great father and his three sons (to say nothing of the souls of all their offspring) who had everlastingly been disappearing and reappearing at the commencement of every successive world; hence both matter and the triplicated great father had usurped an attribute, which was necessarily peculiar to the Godhead. What then was to be done under such circumstances? Some were taught by *Wisdom* to adopt the theory of two independent principles: others naturally enough exclaimed against the palpable absurdity of such a system; and for *them*, *Wisdom*, ever kindly ready to solve all difficulties, had provided another expedient. This was, since the great triplicated father was confessedly eternal, to identify him with the Deity; and, since matter was also eternal, to make the soul of the great father the Soul of the World, and to give him the whole Universe for his body. But here it would readily be objected, how can the mere man Adam or Noah, whose office it is to appear at the beginning of every new world, be admitted as God, when his form has always been that of a simple mortal? To this question *Wisdom* is at no loss for a reply: the body indeed was the body of a man; but the immortal soul was the deity himself; from time to time he descends and becomes incarnate in the person of the great father, and on special occasions appears in the form of other eminent characters: the spirit of this eternal great father, with whom when multiplied into three forms each world commences, is to be revered as the true plastic arranger and governor of the Universe; beside him there is no god, for his three forms or his eight forms are equally a delusion emanating from him and resolveable into his sacred essence.

Thus, as the Apostle speaks, did *Wisdom* teach mankind at Babel to *change the truth of God into a lye, and to worship the creature more than* or *in preference to the Creator.*[1]

3. With the rites and ceremonies of Patriarchism we are but little acquainted, at least when we view it under the name of *Patriarchism.*

We know however, that sacrifice was a standing ordinance; that the first postdiluvian sacrifice was offered up on the summit of a lofty hill; that the early patriarchs were wont to plant consecrated groves for the purposes of devotion; and that they occasionally set up a large massy stone to mark the place where they had worshipped God, anointing the top of it with oil. Each of these practices, though in a distorted state, was adopted into the new ritual of Paganism. Sacrifices, the object of which was to avert the wrath of the venerated deity, still continued to be offered up: mountains, or artificial high places constructed in imitation of mountains, were still selected as the most appropriate for sacrificial devotion: consecrated groves were still duly planted, either simply, or round the temple of the god: and the massy stone column was still erected, and still anointed with oil, though it now became the adored symbolical representation of the great father and the great mother.

For Patriarchism more in detail we must look to the worship of the ancient Israelites. Unless I am greatly mistaken, that worship was no other than Patriarchism, adapted, by various additions and special institutions, to the peculiar situation of a people, which had been selected by Jehovah from the mass of mankind to accomplish certain high and beneficent purposes. In the Levitical dispensation we behold pure and uncorrupted Patriarchism, serving as a basis to some additional ordinances, by which God thought fit to distinguish his people from the rest of the world: in the degraded philosophical idolatry of the Gentiles we behold the very same Patriarchism, diverted from its original intent, and serving as a basis to the

What were the peculiarities of Patriarchism.

---

[1] Gr. παρα τον κτισαντα.

apostate worship of a mixed human, astronomical, and material, demiurgic hermaphrodite. Each was drawn from one primeval source, though with a different application: hence we may naturally expect to find a striking similitude between them.

This similitude has often been remarked; and more than one writer has attempted to account for it.

Some have imagined, that the Gentiles were servile copyists of the Israelites, and that each point of similitude was immediately borrowed from the Mosaical Institutes. But this theory will by no means solve the problem: both because we find the very same resemblance in the ceremonies of nations far distant from Palestine, as we do in the rites of those which are in its more immediate vicinity; because it seems incredible, that all should have borrowed from one which was universally disliked and despised; and because the pagan system, originating (as the sacred writers expressly inform us) from Babel, was *anterior* to the promulgation of the Law of Moses, and had both been witnessed by the Israelites in Egypt and was found by them in its worst state of depravity when they entered the land of Canaan.

Others have fancied, that the devil was the copyist, and that various nations in different parts of the globe pervertedly though unwarily adopted certain parts of the Levitical ceremonies in consequence of his infernal suggestion or inspiration. Such, at one period, was deemed no contemptible theory, particularly as some of the early fathers seem inclined to favour it or at least to favour the notion of the imitative propensity of the evil spirit:[1] but, since it appears to have died a natural death, I shall only say, may it rest in peace!

Others again have precisely inverted the first hypothesis: instead of supposing that the pagans borrowed from the Israelites, they have supposed that

---

[1] Sed quæritur, a quo intellectus interpretetur, eorum quæ ad hæreses faciant? A diabolo scilicet, cujus sunt partes intervertendi veritatem, ipsas quoque res sacramentorum divinorum, in idolorum mysteriis æmulatur. Tinguit et ipse quosdam, utique credentes et fideles suos: expiationem delictorum de lavacro repromittit, et sic adhuc initiat Mithræ. Signat illic in frontibus milites suos, celebrat et panis oblationem, et imaginem resurrectionis inducit. Tertull. de præscript. adv. Hæret. lib. c. 40. Nam et sacris quibusdam per lavacrum initiantur, Isidis alicujus aut Mithræ, ipsos etiam deos suos lavationibus efferunt—Idque se in regenerationem et impunitatem perjuriorum suorum agere præsumunt. Tertull. de baptism. c. 5.

the Israelites borrowed from the pagans. Nor has this opinion been advanced merely by infidels, as at the first glance might be shrewdly suspected: no less names than those of Spencer and Warburton stand pledged to advocate it. The thing in itself appears so utterly incredible, that nothing short of strict mathematical demonstration can be allowed to establish such a theory. That the purity of God should submit to transcribe the base worship of Gentilism; that Egyptian rites should form the basis of the Law delivered amidst the thunders of Sinai; that by a pliant system of accommodation, more worthy of the school of Loyola than of Moses, the idolatrous propensities of the Israelites should be humoured at the very time, when it was the divine purpose wholly to proscribe idolatry and to separate the chosen people from the contagious influence of a pagan neighbourhood: all and each of these propositions may well be deemed alike unworthy of the holiness and wisdom of Jehovah; of his holiness, as ascribing to him an unmeet concord with Belial; of his wisdom, as supposing him to adopt a measure for the preservation of the Israelites from idolatry which of all things would have been the most likely to seduce them into it.

The resemblance in question is too palpable indeed to be denied; but not one of the three preceding theories appears to me to account for it at all satisfactorily. Its true origin I believe to have been such as I have already stated: Judaism and Paganism sprang from a common source; hence their close resemblance in many particulars is nothing more than might have been reasonably anticipated. Such being the case, their rites and ceremonies will throw a mutual light upon each other: and thus, to omit at present smaller matters, the sacred ark and cherubic symbols of the Gentiles, though neither borrowed from nor communicated to the Institutes of Moses, may possibly, when rightly understood themselves, lead to a right understanding of the sacred ark and cherubim of the Israelites. Certain it is, that the cherubim were no way peculiar to the Levitical dispensation. They were exhibited at the gate of Paradise, when man was banished from Eden; and they are recognized under the Gospel by the prophet of the Apocalypse. Their form therefore must have been well known to Noah and his immediate posterity, even if we suppose, which there is no reason to suppose, that their station at the entrance of the garden was merely of a temporary nature: for Adam,

Cherubim

who certainly beheld them, was contemporary in his old age with Lamech the father of Noah. Accordingly, it is worthy of notice, that, when God commands Moses to make the cherubim which were to be placed over the ark of the covenant, he says nothing whatsoever respecting their particular form; yet we find not, that either Moses or the workman had the least occasion to make any inquiries after what model they were to be fashioned.[1] So completely silent indeed is the Hebrew lawgiver on this point, which in *his* days appears to have required no elucidation, that we should have been altogether ignorant of the form of the cherubim, had not Ezekiel furnished us with a most ample and elaborate description of them. Now, since the cherubim were first displayed in the very infancy of the world, and since they were afterwards again displayed at the promulgation of the Law; analogy seems to require, that, whatever was their use and import under the Levitical dispensation, such also was their use and import under the Patriarchal dispensation: and, since among the pagans we find a remarkable set of symbols, which sometimes single and sometimes compoundedly still correspond with the blended forms of the cherubim; it appears naturally to follow, that, as the Hebrew cherubim were exact transcripts of the patriarchal both in form and import, so the Gentile cherubim (if I may be allowed so to speak) were corrupted transcripts of the patriarchal both in form and import.

The phraseology and ideas of Paganism, though still after a perverted manner, correspond, no less than its rites and ceremonies, with those or Judaism and even Christianity, which is the completion of the Law and the consummation of Patriarchism: whence we may infer, that such also were the phraseology and ideas of the first race of men; for I see not how the palpable coincidence can be rationally accounted for, except by the hypothesis of a common origin. In some instances indeed, we may do more than *infer:* and thus the existence of an actual though partial demonstration of a kindred ideal phraseology may reasonably warrant the conclusion, that, where Judaism, Christianity, and Paganism, all employ the same peculiar language, that language was primarily derived from the one source of Patriarchism.

---

[1] See Exod. xxv. 18—22. and Exod. xxxvii. 7, 8, 9.

4. It may here be inquired by those, who espouse the opinion that the triads of Paganism were all equally corruptions of the Trinity, why, upon *my* system of origination, I do not feel myself *ultimately* compelled to adopt the same theory? It may be asked, since I esteem Gentilism a perverted transcript of Patriarchism; since I myself adduce the notion, that the Deity successively became incarnate in the person of each reappearing great father; and since I thence draw the conclusion, that the worship of the Godhead in unity was blasphemously transferred to the great father as viewed in unity: it may be asked, why, on the same principle, I should hesitate to suppose, that, as the worship of *Jehovah in unity* was transferred to *the great father in unity*, so the worship of *Jehovah in trinity* was transferred to *the great father considered as triplicating himself?* It may be added, that, if the one opinion be adopted, analogy seems imperiously to require the adoption of the other: for, if the pagans confounded Jehovah with the great father, they would scarcely overlook so inviting a resemblance, as that of the twice-told three sons or (as they mystically termed them) emanations of the great father to the three persons of the Holy Trinity. Thus, although by a more circuitous route, we should at length find ourselves brought to the hypothesis, that the various triads of the Gentiles, which exhibit their chief god as being three and yet but one, were all ultimately corruptions of the mysterious doctrine of a triad of persons in the divine unity.

I should be most happy to adopt this theory, if I could see it cleared from certain difficulties, with which at present it appears to me to be incumbered. I do indeed derive Paganism from Patriarchism: but, in the course of such a derivation, though Paganism may superadd many *inventions* of its own, it certainly can *borrow* nothing from Patriarchism except what Patriarchism itself *already* possessed. Hence it is manifest, that, before we can admit the hypothesis in question, we must have it shewn to us, that the doctrine of a plurality of persons in the divine essence was known to the early patriarchs: for, if it were *not* known to them, they plainly could not *communicate* what they never had. That they were ignorant of the doctrine, I shall not take upon me to *affirm*: but I can discover no evidence, at least no *scriptural* evidence, for believing that it had been revealed. [1] The first intimation of

Margin note: No sufficient evidence to affirm that the pagan triads were ultimately borrowed from a patriarchal belief in the Trinity.

---

[1] I cannot thoroughly understand the writings of the Hutchinsonian school on this subject: they seem to me to *assume* the very thing, which they ought to have *proved*.

any plurality, that I have been able to find, occurs in the intercourse of God with the family of Abraham. •We then begin to perceive a person spoken of under the name of *the Angel* or *Messenger of Jehovah*; or, if we choose so to render the original expression, under the name of *Jehovah the Messenger*. This person, as his very title indeed implies, is represented as being *sent* by Jehovah: yet divine worship is invariably paid to him without any censure of the worshipper; and, in one place, he is expressly declared, under his official appellation of *the Messenger* or *Angel*, to be the God of Abraham, Isaac, and Jacob.[1] But the God of those patriarchs is perpetually denominated *Jehovah*: therefore the Messenger, whom they adored, must also have been Jehovah. If then Jehovah be a messenger, he must be sent by some one: otherwise how could he be a messenger? Accordingly, he is described both as acting from Jehovah, and as being sent by Jehovah.[2] This Messenger-God is the person, who wrestled with Jacob;[3] who appeared so frequently under a human form, during the period of the Levitical dispensation; who was the Deity and allegorical husband of the Mosaical Church;[4] who is announced as the divine Messenger of the covenant, that, sent by the Lord, should suddenly appear in his temple;[5] and who, in fulness of time, became incarnate in the person of the man Jesus.[6] Here then we have two distinct beings, each of whom is called *Jehovah*, and each of whom is exhibited to us as a proper object of adoration; while yet there is declared to be but one God. The patriarchs therefore of the Hebrew nation must have been acquainted with the existence of at least a duad in the essence of the Deity: and, since it is thus clear that a plurality of persons had been revealed to them, and since afterwards frequent mention is made of a third divine being under the name of *the Spirit of Jehovah*;[7] the presumption is, that they were not ignorant of the precise number comprehended within that plurality.

[1] See Gen. xlviii. 15, 16.   [2] See Gen. xix. 24. and Zechar. ii. 8—11.
[3] Compare Gen. xxxii. 24—30. with Hos. xii. 2—5.   [4] Isaiah lxiii. 9.
[5] Malach. iii. 1.   [6] John i. 1—14.
[7] In one remarkable passage we have the three divine persons mentioned conjointly : Jehovah the messenger professes himself to be sent both by God and by his Spirit. *Come ye near unto me, hear ye this; I have not spoken in secret from the beginning; from the time that it was, there am I : and now the Lord God and his Spirit hath sent me.* Isaiah xlviii. 16. Here a person, who had existed from all eternity, and who by the style in which he speaks is manifestly Jehovah, yet declares that he is sent by the Lord God and by his Spirit.

But I find not any hint given, that the same knowledge had been communicated to the patriarchs *before* the time of Abraham: consequently, if neither Adam nor Noah possessed it, the apostates of Babel could not have borrowed their doctrine of a triad in the great father from the doctrine of the Holy Trinity.

Perhaps it may be said, that, long anterior to the days of Abraham, God had plurally expressed himself *Let* us *make man in* our *image after* our *likeness,* and yet more remarkably *Behold the man is become as* one of us: whence it seems necessary to infer, that a plurality of persons in the Deity was not unknown even to the earliest patriarchs.

I certainly think, that this peculiar phraseology implies a plurality in the divine essence; and I am the more confirmed in my opinion by observing the painfully fruitless attempts of the apostate Jewish Rabbins to elicit tolerable sense from such expressions on the *exclusively* unitarian scheme: ' but that is not precisely the question. God *did* indeed employ this language, and I believe that it was not employed without meaning: but, unless it can be shewn that the early patriarchs actually *knew* that it had been used by the Supreme Being, we shall find ourselves no further advanced in our inquiries. That they were acquainted with many particulars relative to the creation, which seem to have been revealed to Adam, and which were afterwards revealed afresh and perhaps more fully to Moses, is sufficiently clear from the correspondence of the gentile cosmogonies with that of the Hebrew legislator: but, whether the plural phraseology used by the Deity formed a part of the *earliest* revelation, we cannot positively say; nor, so far as I can judge, have we any means of determining the point. It *might* have been revealed *both* to Adam and Moses, or it might have been revealed to Moses *alone:* we *know,* that it was revealed to one; we have no *authority* for asserting, that it was revealed to the *other.* Hence, I think, we have not

---

' I say *exclusively ;* because the title *Unitarian,* as assumed by the modern Socinian, is improper. It implies, that *he alone* believes in the unity of God, and that *all others* disbelieve it. Now, since this most assuredly is not the case, the fitness of a title, which involves such an idea, cannot be recognized. He is *exclusively* unitarian indeed, that is to say, antitrinitarian; but he is not *solely* unitarian, and therefore ought not to have assumed the name as a *distinctive* appellation.

sufficient ground for building an hypothesis on a mere opinion, which *may* be erroneous, and which can never be *proved* to be well founded.

The writers of the Hutchinsonian school, in the absence of more conclusive arguments, have maintained, that the cherubim were symbols of the Trinity in Unity, and that from their station at the gate of Paradise as well as from their subsequent position in the holy of holies they silently declared that important doctrine to fallen man.

Now, even supposing that this conjecture had been more satisfactorily established than it *has* been, we should still in addition have to require a proof, that the discovery of certain ingenious men in the eighteenth century of the Christian era was a matter well known to the early patriarchs: for, unless this point can *also* be demonstrated, it will be of little avail towards determining the question to have shewn even with the clearest evidence that such was the import and intent of those compounded hieroglyphics. It is here that the Hutchinsonians especially fail. They are right in saying, that the Gentiles venerated a triad; they are right also in saying, that that triad was a material one, though they err in treating of it as if it were *solely* a material one: but they, far too confidently, perhaps likewise somewhat too dogmatically, assume without any sufficient proof; that this material triad was a perverted copy of the Trinity, that the doctrine of such a plurality in the Godhead was fully known from the earliest ages, and that it was expressly and allowedly taught together with the future incarnation of the second person by the mysterious configuration of the cherubic symbols.

I have only to add, that, whenever it can be proved that Adam and Noah worshipped a Trinity in Unity, I will chearfully subscribe to the opinion, which *ultimately* derives the triads of the Gentiles from the patriarchal adoration of a triune God: until then, I do not feel myself warranted in the adoption of it.

CHAPTER II.

Concerning the pagan doctrine of a succession of similar worlds·

THE doctrine of a succession of similar worlds, more or less systematically and explicitly maintained, may almost be considered as the key to ancient mythology. As such therefore it merits a particular examination. With it the theory of the Metempsychosis is immediately connected, forming indeed a constituent part of it : but this will be discussed at present no further, than is absolutely necessary to the leading subject of our inquiry.

I. As knowledge of every kind flowed from the central regions of the east, and as it seems to have been retained in a more regular form throughout those parts of the globe than elsewhere, I shall commence with the mundane philosophy of Hindostan, which exhibits the doctrine now under consideration in a manner peculiarly explicit.

1. The Hindoo sages view their principal hero-god as triplicating himself, and as thus sustaining under his three grand forms the characters of the creator, the preserver, and the destroyer. They do not however use the term *creator* in the scriptural sense of the word, as denoting *one who causes something to exist out of nonentity,* but rather as meaning *one who gives regular form and activity to crude preëxisting materials.* The creative power disposes such materials into definite shape, and thus fashions a

The same events take place, and the same persons reappear in every world.

world: the preserving power upholds the world, when it *is* fashioned: and the destroying power reduces it at length to its constituent elements, sometimes by a deluge of water, and at other times by a deluge of fire. Every thing is then absorbed into the unity of the great father: and this mysterious being, during the period that elapses between each two mundane systems, reposes on the surface of the mighty deep, floating securely either in a wonderful *egg*, or in the calix of the lotos, or on a naviform leaf, or on a huge serpent coiled up in the form of a boat, or in a sacred ship denominated *Argha* of which the other vehicles are consequently symbols. To destroy however is but to create afresh: for destruction affects *form* alone; it reaches not to *substance.* Hence, when the great father has slept a whole year of the creator, the space which ever intervenes between world and world, he awakes from his slumber and produces a new order of things. Out of the chaotic materials of the prior world, another world is fashioned: the preserver again supports it: the destroyer again dissolves it: and, as it was preceded by a world, so in due time it is likewise succeeded by one. This alternate destruction and reproduction is thought to be repeated again and again: so that, in the lapse of countless ages, an enormous number of successive worlds is believed to have existed.[1]

But the worlds are not merely successive; they are also perfectly similar. As they resemble each other in their mode of production and dissolution, so do they correspond likewise in their histories and their inhabitants. It is acknowledged, we are told, by the Hindoo mythologists, that, at every renovation of the world, the same events take place; the same heroes reappear upon the stage; and the same Sama, Cama, and Pra-Japati, are born again to every Menu.[2] There cannot, I think, be a reasonable doubt, that, by these three distinguished personages, we are *properly* to understand the Shem, Cham, and Japhet, of Moses; because they are described

---

[1] Moor's Hind. Pantheon, p. 5, 12, 15, 35, 48, 49, 89, 102, 103. Asiat. Res. vol. vi. p. 523.

[2] Asiat. Res. vol. viii. p. 255. *Pra-Japati* denotes *The Lord Japati.* It may not be improper to take this early opportunity of observing, that the final *A* in such words as *Sama* or *Cama* is quiescent in pronunciation, like the final *E* of the French. Moor's Hind. Panth. p. 173.

as the children of one, who was preserved in an ark with seven companions at the time of an universal deluge : yet they are said to reappear by transmigration at the commencement of every successive mundane reproduction.

The Menus are feigned to be seven in number : but these are reduplicated to fourteen. The first is sirnamed *Swayambhuva* or *the son of the self-existent ;* and the seventh, *Vaivaswata* or *the child of the Sun.* These, as we may collect from the several legends attached to them, are plainly Adam and Noah ; the only two Menus or patriarchs of successive worlds, that ever really lived. Accordingly, the first and the last of the primary seven are those, who are chiefly mentioned : and these, from the many points of resemblance between their characters, are not unfrequently confounded together. The number *seven,* to which the two only proper Menus have been extended, seems to have been selected in reference to the number both of the Adamitical and Noëtic families, each of which consisted of seven persons exclusive of its head : and the reduplication of seven, by which the fourteen Menus are produced, is most probably the mere adding together of the members who composed the two patriarchal families.[1] *The Hindoo chronology,* says Mr. Wilford, *presents us with a series of fourteen dynasties, equally repugnant to nature and reason. Six of these are elapsed: we are in the seventh, which began with the flood : and seven more we are taught to expect. The rulers of these dynasties are called* Menus: *and from them their respective dynasty or period is called* a Manwantara. *Every dynasty ends with a total destruction of the human race, except the Menu or ruler of the next period, who makes his escape in a boat with the seven Rishis. The same events take place : the same persons, though sometimes under different names, reappear. Thus the history of one dynasty serves for all the rest.*[2]

Our minds are almost bewildered in following the Hindoos through those vast periods, which they have duly specified in consequence of their adopting the theory of a succession of similar worlds. A year of mortals, they tell

[1] Instit. of Menu. chap. i. p. 9. Moor's Hind. Panth. p. 83, 86, 88.
[2] Asiat. Res. vol. v. p. 244, 245.

us, is but a day and a night of the gods. Twelve thousand years of the
gods constitute each revolving period of the four famous ages: the golden
age containing 4000 such years, while the twilight preceding it, and the twilight succeeding it, are each equivalent to 400; the silver age containing
3000 of the same years, and each of its twilights 300; the brazen age
2000, and each of its twilights 200; and the iron or earthen age 1000,
and each of its twilights 100. Every quaternion of the golden, the silver,
the brazen, and the iron, ages, thus comprehending 12,000 divine years, is
called *an age of the gods*. But 71 ages of the gods, or 71 quaternions of
the golden, the silver, the brazen, and the iron, ages, form only one Manwantara. And 14 Manwantaras, or 1000 ages of the gods, are equal to
no more than a single day of Brahma, his night being also of the same duration.[1] Through each Manwantara, every Menu, with whom a new world
commences, transmits his sceptre to his sons and grandsons: and, at the
close of it, he is succeeded by the new Menu of a new world, who similarly
transmits his sceptre to his posterity during a period of a similar length.
He himself however is not personally visible throughout the whole of his
reign: the Hindoos, thinking it incongruous to place a holy character in
times of impurity, suppose, that the sovereign Menu appears only in every
golden age and disappears in the three human ages that follow it, continuing
to dive and emerge like a water-fowl (such is their whimsical illustration)
until the close of his peculiar Manwantara.[2]

Hence it appears, since fourteen Manwantaras constitute but *a single
day* of Brahma, that, in *every* day of that god, fourteen Menus are successively invested by him with the sovereignty of the reproduced earth.
Hence also it appears, that, as the only two real *individual* Menus, Adam
and Noah, are multiplied first to seven and then to fourteen in the course
of *each day* of Brahma; so the whole *class* of fourteen Menus is itself
again multiplied into 365 similar classes during the course of *each year* of

[1] This statement of the Hindoos is not perfectly correct, being given in round numbers: for
1000 divine ages, at the specified rate of 71 such ages to a single Manwantara, are equal, not
to 14, but to $14\frac{6}{71}$ Manwantaras. I know not why they have contrived their periods, so as
to produce this frcational sum.

[2] Asiat. Res. vol. ii. p. 126, 127, 112, 116. Instit. of Menu. chap. i. p. 9, 10, 11.

the divinity.   Through 1000 repetitions of the four ages, golden, silver, brazen, and iron, Menu succeeds to Menu, until the number of 14 Manwantaras be completed.   But no more than a single *day* of Brahma has then elapsed; though a whole *class* of Menus has appeared and discharged its functions.   Another day of Brahma introduces another class of Menus, and another chiliadal repetition of the four ages: and Menu continues to follow Menu, and class to follow class, through a period of which it is difficult to form an adequate conception.   *There are numberless Manwantaras, says* the ancient author of the Institutes of Menu, *creations also and destructions of worlds innumerable.   The being supremely exalted performs all this with as much ease as if in sport, again and again, for the sake of conferring happiness.*[1]

Such language and such philosophy seem almost necessarily to imply and to require an *eternal* succession of worlds and Menus and Manwantaras: yet the Hindoo sages, unlike those of the west, as if startled by the magnitude of their own conceptions, instead of pushing their theory to its utmost limits, suddenly stop short, when we might suppose them on the point of asserting the absolute eternity of crude matter and an everlasting succession of similar worlds framed out of its substance.   The complete life of Brahma, however vast, is finite.   It is limited to five successive centuries of his own divine years, every day of which beholds the reign of fourteen Menus.   At the end of each of these enormous periods, Brahma dies: at the commencement of each, he revives: and, at the close of them all, the whole creation is absorbed into the supreme being.[2]   The final consummation of the Universe is described under the image of a monstrous demon swallowing up the world.   Him they call *Maha-Pralaya* or *the great deluge*, in contradistinction to the smaller Pralayas or floods, which regularly occur at the end of every Manwantara.[3]   *Through Brahma generations pass on succes-*

---

[1] Instit. of Menu. chap. i. p. 11.   In point of arrangement, the vast cycles of the Hindoos have certainly been constructed, like the Julian period, on mere retrospective astronomical calculations.   See Hales's Chronol. vol. i. p. 292.   [2] Asiat. Res. vol. v. p. 247, 248.

[3] Moor's Hind. Panth. p. 30, 150, 151.   Mr. Moor gives a print of Maha-Pralaya in the act of swallowing a city; while Brahma, Vishnou, and Siva, are irresistibly drawn towards him to be similarly ingulphed.

sively; ages and periods are by him put in motion, terminated, and re-
newed; and, while he dies and springs to birth alternately, his existence or
energy continues a hundred of his years, during which he produces and
devours all things of less longevity.[1]

But, though the Hindoos thus appear to reject the doctrine of an *eternal*
succession of worlds, we find them occasionally employing a phraseology
which might almost lead us to believe that they hesitatingly adopted it.
Thus Brahm, or Vishnou in the character of Brahm, is introduced in different parts of the Gita as saying of himself: *I am of things transient the*
beginning, the middle, and the end: the whole world was spread abroad by
me in my invisible form. At the end of the period Kalp, all things return
into my primordial source: and, at the beginning of another Kalp, I create
them all again. I am the understanding of the wise, the glory of the
proud, the strength of the strong. I am the eternal seed of all nature. I
am the father and mother of this world, the grandsire, and the preserver.
I am death and immortality. I am entity and nonentity. I am never-
failing time. I am all-grasping death. I am the resurrection. The great
Brahm is my womb: in it I place my fœtus: and from it is the production
of all nature. The great Brahm is the womb of all those various forms,
which are conceived in every natural womb: and I am the father that
soweth the seed.[2] All things in short are in a perpetual state of solution
and reproduction. *The earth is perishable,* say the Hindoo bards in one
of their funereal hymns: *the ocean, the gods themselves, pass away. How*
should not that bubble, mortal man, meet destruction? All, that is low,
must finally perish: all, that is elevated, must ultimately fall: all com-
pounded bodies must end in dissolution: life must be concluded with death.[3]
Brahm or the great father is *that, whence all beings are produced; that,*
by which they live when born; that, toward which they tend; and that,
unto which they pass.[4]

2. The three powers, who sustain the offices of creator, preserver, and
destroyer, are termed by the Hindoos *Brahma, Vishnou,* and *Siva:* and

[handwritten margin note: The Hindoo monad and triad are composed of mere]

---

[1] Asiat. Res. vol. iii. p. 127.   [2] Moor's Panth. p. 211.

[3] Moor's Hind. Panth. p. 310, 311.   [4] Yajurveda apud Moor's Hind. Panth. p. 274.

these are believed to emanate from or to be a triplication of a yet older *mortals, being Adam and his triple offspring transmigrating into Noah and his triple offspring* deity, whom they call *Brahm*, and to whom they ascribe so decidedly the peculiar attributes of the godhead that many have supposed them to worship the true God under that appellation. This however I am inclined very greatly to doubt: and, the more I have studied the subject, the more my doubt has approximated to full conviction.

In the preceding citations from the Gita, we may observe, that Vishnou or Crishna is identified with Brahm although one of his three emanations: and we may also observe, that in the single character of Brahm all the three offices of Brahma, Vishnou, and Siva, are united. He is at once the creator, the preserver, and the destroyer. He is the primeval hermaphrodite, or the great father and great mother blended together in one person. Consequently, he is the same as the hermaphroditic Siva in the form which the Hindoos call *Ardha-Nari;* the same also as Brahma and Vishnou, for each of these is similarly an hermaphrodite by an union with his proper Sacti or heavenly consort; the same moreover as the Orphic Jupiter and the Egyptian Osiris; the same as Adonis, Dionusus, and Attis; the same in short as the compound great father in every part of the pagan world.

Yet this compound great father, as the whole of his history shews, is not the true God; but a being, who has been made to usurp his attributes. He is primarily Adam and the Earth, and secondarily Noah and the Ark. In the former case, his three emanations or children, who partake of his nature and who discharge his pretended functions, are Cain, Abel, and Seth: in the latter, they are Shem, Ham, and Japhet. Accordingly, Brahm himself is declared to be the same as Menu: and Brahma, Vishnou, and Siva, are identified with those three sons of Menu, who appear at the commencement of every Manwantara, whose proper human names are said by the Hindoos to be *Sama* and *Cama* and *Pra-Japati*, and who *Sama = Shem* *Cama = Ham* *Japati = Japheth* transmit to their descendants the sceptre of sovereignty throughout the whole duration of their allotted period.

On this point the Hindoo writers are sufficiently explicit; though, by their wild system of personal multiplication and repeated Avatarism, they have superinduced a certain degree of confusion. The evidence may be summed up in the following manner.

We are taught, on the one hand, that Brahma, Vishnou, and Siva, are essentially but a single person; that this single person is Brahm, who unites in himself the divided attributes of the three; and that the triplicated Brahm is materially the World, astronomically the Sun, and mystically the great Hermaphrodite who is equally the father and the mother of the Universe.[1] But we are told, on the other hand, that Menu-Swayambhuva is conjointly and individually Brahma, Vishnou, and Siva; that he had three sons, who sprang in a mortal shape from his body and who married his three daughters; and that these three sons were severally Brahma, Vishnou, and Siva.[2]

Such are the declarations of the Hindoo theologists: and the inference to be drawn from them is abundantly obvious. Since Brahma, Vishnou, and Siva, are conjointly Menu-Swayambhuva; and since they are also conjointly the imagined supreme god Brahm: it is evident, that Brahm and Menu-Swayambhuva must really be the same person. And again, since Brahma, Vishnou, and Siva, are severally the three sons of Menu-Swayambhuva; and since they are also three supposed emanations from Brahm: it must plainly follow, that the famous triad of Hindoo theology, which some have incautiously deemed a corrupt imitation of the Trinity, is really composed of the three sons of a mere mortal, who under the name of *Menu* is described as the general ancestor of mankind.

Brahm then at the head of the Indian triad is Menu at the head of his three sons. But that by the first Menu we are to understand Adam, is evident, both from the remarkable circumstance of himself and his consort bearing the titles of *Adima* and *Iva*, and from the no less remarkable tradition that one of his three sons was murdered by his brother at a sacrifice.[3] Hence it will follow, that Brahm at the head of the Indian triad is Adam at the head of his three sons, Cain, Abel, and Seth.

Each Menu however with his triple offspring is only the reappearance of

---

[1] Moor's Hind. Panth. p. 44, 6, 9, 13, 33, 277, 294, 7, 13, 278, 295. Asiat. Res. vol. i, p. 267.   [2] Asiat. Res. vol. v. p. 247, 248, 249.   [3] Ibid.

a former Menu with his triple offspring: for, in every such manifestation at the commencement of each Manwantara, the Hindoo Trimurti or triad becomes incarnate by transmigrating from the human bodies occupied during a prior incarnation; Brahm or the unity appearing as the paternal Menu of a new age, while the triad of Brahma Vishnou and Siva is exhibited in the persons of his three sons.[1] The first Menu therefore with his three sons must be viewed as reappearing in the characters of Menu-Satyavrata and his triple offspring Sama Cama and Pra-Japati. But the ark-preserved Menu-Satyavrata and his three sons are certainly Noah and his three sons Shem Ham and Japhet. Hence again it will follow, since Menu-Satyavrata is only a reappearance of Menu-Adima, and since the triplicated Menu-Adima is the same as the triplicated Brahm, that Brahm at the head of the Indian triad is likewise Noah at the head of his three sons.

Agreeably to such a conclusion, even those, who contend that the Hindoos worship the one true God, have been compelled to acknowledge, that they do not sufficiently discriminate the creature from the creator:[2] and the Puranas themselves unequivocally teach, that the world, at its reproduction in what is called the *lotos-creation*, was formed indeed by a god; but by a god, who appeared in the shape of a man, and who primarily is the same as Adam, though the attributes of the Deity are blasphemously ascribed to him. *The great God; the great, omnipotent, omniscient, one; the greatest in the world; the great lord; who goes through all the worlds, incapable of decay, and without body: is born a moulded body of flesh and bones, made, whilst himself was not made. His wisdom and power pervades all hearts: from his heart sprang this lotos-like world in times of old. It was then in this, that appeared, when born, the god of gods with four faces, the lord of the lords of mankind, who rules over all, the lord of the world. When this flower was produced by Vishnou, then from his navel sprang the worldly lotos abounding with trees and plants; then the dimensions of this worldly lotos became obvious to the sight.*[3] Now, when we compare this passage with what has already been said respecting the allowed incarnation

---

[1] See Asiat. Res. vol. viii. p. 254, 255. vol. v. p. 293. vol. vi. p. 463.

[2] Asiat. Res. vol. viii. p. 397. [3] Asiat. Res. vol. viii. p. 352.

of the Trimurti in the persons of Menu-Swayambhuva and his three sons, I see not what conclusion we can draw from it except this: that the only great god of the Hindoos is the Menu; who appears at the commencement of every Manwantara, who successively destroys and reproduces the world, and who is invested by them with the usurped honours of the Deity. Accordingly, not only is Menu-Swayambhuva declared to be the first Brahma in a human shape; but Brahma himself is considered as man individually, and as mankind collectively. Hence he is said to be born and to die every day, as there are men springing to life and dying every day; to die collectively every hundred years, this being the utmost limit of human life; and to die at the end of every century of divine years, because at the end of the world the whole race of mankind die.[1]   The Hindoos, in short, however their system may be disguised, acknowledge no god except the universal parent of man, whom they suppose to reappear at the commencement of every new world; because there was a certain degree of resemblance between the beginning of the postdiluvian and that of the antediluvian world: the god of the Hindoos, however disguised in the borrowed plumes of Deity, is Adam, fancifully believed to have appeared again as Noah, and venerated in conjunction at once with the Sun and with the Universe. It is worthy of observation, that such a conclusion has in substance been drawn by one sect of the Hindoo philosophers. Perceiving that the human character, so plainly supported by all their gods, was irreconcileable with the lavish ascription of the divine character to them, they insist, that no incarnations ever took place, but that the pretended deities were mere mortals, whom the Supreme Being was pleased to endow with qualities approaching to his own attributes.[2]

II. The same doctrine of a succession of worlds, each springing from the chaotic wreck of an antecedent world, prevailed also among the ancient Egyptians.

In the theological books imputed to Hermes Trismegistus, which contain an account of the old Mizraimic philosophy, it is laid down as an established maxim, that *nothing in the world perishes, and that death is not the destruc-*

---

[1] Asiat. Res. vol. v. p. 247.   [2] Asiat. Res. vol. iii. p. 146,

THE ORIGIN OF PAGAN IDOLATRY.

tion but only the change and translation of things.[1] Agreeably to this maxim, it is further taught, that, *when the world becomes degenerate, then that lord and father, the supreme god and the only governor, beholding the manners and deeds of men, by his will, which is his benignity, always resisting vice and restoring things from their degeneracy, will either wash away the malignity of the world by water or else consume it by fire, and then restore it to its ancient form again.*[2]

The prevalence of such an opinion among the Egyptians, respecting the successive destructions of the world by inundation and conflagration, is mentioned also by Julius Firmicus :[3] and it is eminently set forth in the curious dialogue between Solon and the Egyptian priest as recorded by Plato. Solon, we are told, wishing rather to learn the sentiments of the Egyptians, than to declare his own, put many questions to one of their priests on various points of antiquity. Thus, from a desire to reduce chronology to some degree of certainty, he asked the opinion of his sacerdotal friend respecting the age of Phoroneus esteemed the first of men, and Niobè, and Pyrrha and Deucalion after the flood, and other matters which enter so largely into the mythological genealogies of the Greeks. To this the priest replied, *O Solon, Solon, you Greeks are always children, nor is there an old man among you. Having no ancient traditions nor any acquaintance with chronology, you are as yet in a state of intellectual infancy. The true origin of such mutilated fables as you possess is this. There have been and shall again be, in the course of many revolving ages, numerous destructions of the human race ; the greatest of them by fire and water, but others in an almost endless succession at shorter intervals.*[4] This is perfectly the Hindoo theory of smaller destructions of the world at the end of each Manwantara, and of more complete ones at the end of each Kalpa.

[1] Cudworth's Intell. Syst. p. 326. Cudworth seems to me rightly to conclude, on the authority of Jamblichus, that the Trismegistic books really contain the Hermaic opinions. His argument is now much strengthened by the circumstance of the same theory respecting the world being found to prevail throughout the east.

[2] Cudw. Intell. Syst. p. 328.   [3] Ibid.

[4] Plat. Tim. fol. 22, 23.

The same doctrine is mentioned also by Origen. *They hold*, says he, *a succession from age to age of many conflagrations and many inundations, and esteem the flood of Deucalion as an event but of yesterday. Indeed to such as are disposed to listen to their speculations, they teach, that the world was never produced, but has existed from all eternity.* [1] And he adds, that the wisest among the Egyptians had communicated their theory of successive conflagrations and inundations to his opponent Celsus. [2]

The Hermetic books, whoever may have been the compiler of them, are full of allusions to the doctrines upon which these notions are founded. The great god of the Egyptians, though clothed with the attributes of the Deity, was no more the Supreme Being than the great God of the Hindoos. He is described, as being the Soul of the World, and as partaking of the nature of both sexes; precisely in the same manner, as that Siva Ardha-Nari, who floated in the ship Argha on the surface of the deluge. From him, their common parent, all human souls are derived. He is ever pregnant, and ever productive. Death is nothing more than a change of body and a passing from visibility into invisibility. Every day, some part of the world passes into this invisibility. It does not utterly perish, but only disappears to our sight, being either translated into some other place or changed into some other form. In a similar manner, animals are dissolved by death, not that they might be utterly destroyed, but that in due season they might be made again. As for the world, which is the body of the great father, it makes all things out of itself, and unmakes all things into itself: it perpetually dissolves all things, and it perpetually renews all things. In the whole Universe nothing utterly perishes. *Itself* is unchangeable: its *parts* only admit of alteration. Yet of these, subject as they are to mutation, none utterly perishes or is absolutely destroyed: for what is incorruptible cannot be corrupted, and what is a part of the great god cannot be annihilated. [3]

III. The fourteen Menus of the Hindoos are manifestly the same as the fourteen Mahabads or great Buddhas of the ancient Iranians: for the first of them, like the first Menu, is said to have been the author of a sacred book in a heavenly language; and the whole fourteen either had appeared, or

---

[1] Orig. adv. Cels. lib. 1.   [2] Ibid.   [3] Cudworth's Intell. Syst. p. 332, 333.

would appear, in a human shape for the government of the world. The diluvian Menu indeed is clearly one with the diluvian Buddha or Maha-Bad: consequently the series of Menus must be the same as the series of Mahabads.[1]

From this palpable identity it seems natural to conclude, that the Iranians held the same doctrine respecting a succession of worlds that the Hindoos have adopted : and the conclusion is rendered more probable, both from the common Gothic or Cuthic descent of the Indo-Scythæ and the military and sacerdotal castes of the Persians, and from the circumstance of the primeval Babylonian empire comprehending within its limits that part of Iran which still bears the name of *Chusistan.* I am not able positively to shew, that such was the case : but there is a tenet of the ancient Magi, preserved by Theopompus, which is so nearly allied to the doctrine in question, that I have little doubt of its having been maintained by them. It was their belief, that men would live again in another state of existence and become immortal: nor are we to suppose, that this means simply their belief of a resurrection in the Christian sense of the word ; for it was additionally their opinion, that the things which now are would for ever continue to be designated by the names of their possessors.[2] There is some degree of obscurity in this statement: but, since the doctrine held by the Hindoos is precisely that which renders it perfectly intelligible, I am inclined to believe that it has been regularly deduced *from* that doctrine. If men are to live again and become immortal, it may reasonably be inquired what we are to understand by the things of this world for ever bearing their names. The answer is afforded by the theology of the Hindoos: whenever the immortal great father reappears at the commencement of a new world, he still bears the appellation of *Menu* or *Mahabad*; and his reign over the perpetually existing materials of each renovated system is still from him called a *Manwantara*.[3]

IV. I suspect, that the same doctrine formed a part of the theology of the Chinese.

---

[1] See Asiat. Res. vol. ii. p. 59.　　　[2] Diog. Laert. in Proœm.

[3] That the *ancient* Persians held this doctrine is rendered more probable by the circumstance of its being undoubtedly maintained by the *present* philosophers of that nation. *To destroy, according to the Vedantis of India, the Sofis of Persia, and many philosophers of our European schools, is only to generate and reproduce in another form.* Asiat. Res. vol. i. p. 250.

We are informed, that the mystic philosophy of the book *Yeking* bears a close resemblance to that of the Pythagoreans; and that it largely treats of natural principles, of judicial astrology, and of generation and corruption. Eight Koua or symbols, each composed of three lines, hieroglyphically express certain general things, on which the nativity and corruption of all particular things are allowed to depend. Of these the first represents the heaven; the second, the earth; the third, lightning; the fourth, mountains; the fifth, fire; the sixth, clouds; the seventh, water; and the eighth, wind. From them variously combined the perpetual variety of nature originates. [1]

Now the Pythagoreans expressly held the doctrine of a succession of worlds and a transmigration of souls; and taught much, respecting the potency of numbers and a perpetual destruction and reproduction of the Universe. If then the theology of the Chinese, which similarly treats of generation and destruction, resemble that of the Pythagoreans, it must have inculcated the tenet of a succession of worlds. Their eight Koua, each composed of a triplet, are nearly allied to the eight material forms of the triple Siva: and their ascribing to them the power of generation and corruption has originated, most probably, from the Adamitical and Noëtic triads and ogdoads. The substance of what they teach, though like all the other heathen systems strongly tinctured with Materialism, seems plainly to be this: that destruction and reproduction, in perpetual vicissitude, spring from the numbers three and eight, with which every new world invariably commences.

V. In supposing such to be the doctrine contained in the book *Yeking* I am the more confirmed by the circumstance of Buddhism prevailing so generally in China: nor do I speak of the comparatively recent introduction of a mere modification of that theology; there is considerable reason to believe that the worship of Buddha or Fo was the religion of the Chinese from the very commencement of their empire. Now the doctrine of a succession of worlds is held no less decidedly by the Buddhists than by the Brahmenists: nor is it set forth with greater precision in any country than in that of the Burmas, who are both determined Buddhists and near neighbours to the Chinese.

[1] Mart. Hist. Sin. lib. i. p. 14, 15, 16. Du Halde's Hist. of China, vol. i. p. 270.

The Universe, we are informed, *is called by the Burmas* Logha, *which signifies* successive destruction and reproduction : *because it is conceived, that the Universe, after it has been destroyed either by fire, water, or wind, is again of itself restored to its ancient form—They say, that the age of man has not always been the same with what it is at present, and that it will not continue to be the same; but that it is lengthened or shortened according to the general merit or demerit of men's actions. After the first inhabitants, their children and grandchildren had gradually and successively shorter lives in proportion as they became less virtuous: and this gradual decrease continued, until men came to live ten years only, the duration of the life of men in their greatest state of wickedness.* The children of these, considering the cause of their parents' short life, and dedicating themselves more to the practice of virtue, had their lives gradually lengthened. *Now this successive decrement in the duration of the life of man, followed by an increase, must take place sixty four times after the reproduction of a world before that world will be again destroyed. In the present world eleven of these changes have taken place; nor will it be destroyed, until it has passed through fifty three more changes—The Burma writings allege three remote causes for the destruction of a world; luxury, anger, and ignorance. From these, by the power of fate, arise the physical or proximate causes; namely fire, water, and wind. When luxury prevails, the world is consumed by fire; when anger prevails, it is dissolved in water ; and, when ignorance prevails, it is dispersed by wind. The Burmas do not suppose, that a world is destroyed, and a new one instantaneously regenerated: but that the destruction takes up the space of an Assenchiekat, that the reproduction takes up another, and that a third intervenes between the end of the old world and the beginning of the new.* At the end of each of the sixty four changes in the life of man, which take place during the existence of every world, an almost total destruction befalls the human race. *After the greater part have perished, a heavy rain falls, and sweeps away into the rivers the unburied bodies and filth. Then follows a shower of flowers and sandal wood to purify the earth; and all kinds of garments fall from above. The scanty remains of men, who had escaped from destruction, now creep out from caverns and hiding places ; and, repenting of their sins, henceforth enjoy longer lives—The Burma writings relate, that a thousand years before the destruction of a world, a certain Nat[1] descends from the superior abodes. His hair is dishevelled, his countenance mournful, and his garments black. He passes every where through the public ways and streets with piteous voice, announcing to mankind the approaching dissolution—When it is to happen by fire, as soon as the Nat has ceased to admonish men, a heavy rain falls from heaven, fills all the lakes, causes torrents, and produces an abundant crop. Mankind, now filled with hope, sow seed more plentifully: but this is the last rain; not a drop falls for a hundred thousand years, and plants with every vegetating thing perish. Then die all animals; and, passing on to the state of Nat, are from thence transferred to the abodes Zian or Arupa. The Nat of the Sun and Moon having now become Zian, these luminaries are darkened and vanish. In their stead two Suns arise, which are not Nat. The one always succeeds to the other, rising when it sets; so that there is no night: and the heat consequently becomes so intense, that all the lakes and torrents are dried up, and not the smallest vestige of a tree remains upon the surface of the earth. After a long interval, a third Sun arises: then are dried up the greatest rivers. A fourth Sun succeeds: and, two being now constantly above the horizon, even the seven great lakes disappear. A fifth Sun arises, and dries up the sea. A sixth Sun rends asunder this and the other 1,010,000 earths; while from the rents are emitted smoke and fire. Finally, after a very long interval, a seventh Sun appears; by which Mienmo[2] and all the inhabitants of the Nat are consumed: and, as in a lamp, when the wick and oil are exhausted, the flame goes out; so, when every thing in this and the other 1,010,000 worlds is consumed, the fire of its own accord will die away. Such is the manner, in which the world is destroyed by fire. When the destruction is produced by water or wind, the circumstances are very similar. For, when water is to destroy a world, at first there fall very gentle showers; which, by degrees increasing, at length become so prodigious, that each drop is a thousand juzana in magnitude. By such rain the abodes of men and Nat,*

---

[1] *Nat* or *Nath* signifies *Lord*, and is used in composition with the names of the gods much in the same manner as the Canaanites used *Baal*, which is a word of the same import. Thus we have *Jagan-Nath*, *Suman-Nath* or *Sumnaut*, and the like.

[2] The Burman centrical mount Meru.

some of the Zian, and all the other 1,010,000 worlds, are entirely dissolved. When a world is destroyed by wind, the Nat having finished his warnings, a fine rain falls: but it is the last rain during that world. After a hundred thousand years the wind begins to blow, and gradually increases. At first it only raises sand and small stones: but at length it whirls about immense rocks and the summits of mountains. Then shaking the whole earth, it dissipates this and the others, with all the habitations of the Nat and Rupa and Arupa; and scatters them through the immense space of the skies.

The conceptions of the Burmas, relative to the reproduction of a world, now come to be explained. They allege three causes of destruction, fire, rain, and wind: but, according to them, the only cause of reproduction is rain. One Assenchickat after the destruction of a world rain begins to fall like mustard seed, and increases by degrees till each drop becomes a thousand juzana in size. This rain fills all the space, which had been formerly occupied by the destroyed habitations, and even a greater: for by the wind it is gradually inspissated to the precise bulk of the former world. The rains, thus inspissated by the wind, form on their surface a crust; out of which arise first the habitations of the Zian, and then Mienmo with all the abodes of the Nat who dwell near that mountain. The rain, continuing to be inspissated, forms our earth, and finally all the other 1,010,000: all these are exactly in the same disposition, order, situation, and form, which they had in their former existence. These changes, both in the destruction and reproduction of worlds, take place, not by the influence of any creative power, but are occasioned by the power Damata which is best translated by our word fate—On the surface of the newly regenerated world a crust arises, having the taste and smell of butter. This smell, reaching the nostrils of the Rupa and Zian, excites in these beings a desire to eat the crust. The end of their lives as superior beings having now arrived, they assume human bodies, but such as are shining and agile, and descend to occupy our earth and the other 1,010,000 worlds which are adjacent. These human beings for some time live on this preternatural food in tranquillity and happiness. But, being afterwards seized with a desire and love for property, the nectareous crust disappears as a punishment for their crime; and their bodies, being deprived of transparency and splendor, become dark and opaque. In the place of the crust comes up a plant, which has also the taste of butter: and, when men degenerate still further, the plant itself disappears, and is succeeded by rice. In consequence of the use of this last food, *the different organs of sex appear; for before that time mankind were neither male nor female. Those, who in a former life had been males, now obtain the male organs of sex; and those, who had been women, obtain female organs.* Marriage is the consequence; and, as men begin to multiply, contentions and quarrels arise among them: *for, avarice prevailing, every one consults his own immediate interest without attending to the injury which he might do to his neighbour. At length these disputes come to be determined by strength: and, to put a stop to this violence, it is determined in common council to elect a prince, who should be able to reward according to merit, and to punish according to the atrocity of crimes. And a certain man being found amongst them, who excelled the rest in stature and beauty, and who had always been more observant of the laws than the others, this person is created king and lord of the earth. Because he had been chosen by common consent, he is called* Mahasamata; *and, because he was made lord of the earth, he is called* Kattia.'

Such is the doctrine of the Burmas respecting a succession of similar worlds. Much as it is blended with wild fiction, and tinctured as it is with atheism, we may still very easily discern whence it has originated: and *its* origin is the origin of that doctrine wherever it prevails. The notion of the Hindoos, that at the end of *each* world a Menu with seven holy companions is preserved in a boat while the rest of mankind are overwhelmed by the waters of a deluge, evidently proves, that their *succession* of worlds is a fable grafted upon the real occurrence of a *single* world succeeding, by the intervention of a general flood, that which was first created. And, in a similar manner, the belief of the Burmas, that an unavailing preacher of righteousness appears towards the close of every world, that men regularly degenerate after the commencement of each new period, and that at a time of increasing anarchy an universal empire is invariably founded by a prince named *Kattia* or *Cassia*, equally proves, that their successive worlds are but an arbitrary multiplication of the postdiluvian and antediluvian worlds. The story, how-

' Asiat. Res. vol. vi. p. 174—249.

ever frequently repeated, is still the same: and it is alike impossible not to recognize the character of Noah in that of the warning *Nat,* or the character of Nimrod the Cassian or Cushite in that of the first universal sovereign *Kattia.* I may add to these obvious remarks, that the cycle of *sixty four,* which, according to the Burmas, completes the duration of every world, immediately connects their system with that of the Chinese philosophers, and thus affords an additional argument that the same doctrine is taught by the latter. The eight primary *Kouas* of the Chinese, each of which is composed of the number three, are multiplied by them into sixty four, which is the square of eight: and this very number *sixty four* thus produced, which is accounted of so much importance by the Burmas, is reckoned a symbol of the Universe.[1]

VI. The same notions, varied according to their humour, are held by the Buddhists of Ceylon.

According to the opinions of the Singhalais and from what appears in their writings, the Universe perished ten different times, and by a wonderful operation of nature was as often produced a-new. For the government of the world at those different periods, there were twenty two Buddhas, a proportionate number of whom belonged to each period. Besides this, the Singhalais assert, from record, the total destruction and regeneration of the Universe many other times; the written authorities for which are no longer to be found—The Buddhists speak of twenty six heavens, which they divide in the following manner: the Deveh-Loke, consisting of six; the Brachmah-Loke, consisting of sixteen, five of which are considered as triumphant

---

[1] Martin. Hist. Sin. lib. i. p. 14, 15. Traces of this universally prevalent doctrine of the pagans may be observed also among the Kayn or rude mountaineers of Arracan, who have been subjected to the Burman empire. Col. Symes gives the following account of a conversation, which passed between a Kayn and himself. *We asked the man, where he expected to go when he died? He replied, that he should again become a child. Who will make you a child? The Mounzing. Who are the Mounzing? The father and mother of the world, who grow on the earth as two trees in a field, one ever green, the other dry. What he meant by this metaphor we could not tell, unless it was a type of successive and eternal renovation and decay. He added, that the Mounzing resided on the great mountain Gnowa, where the images of the dead are deposited.* Embass. to Ava. vol. iii. p. 246. To Col. Symes's very just conjecture I may add, that the sacred mountain Gnowa is certainly the local Ararat or Meru of this people.

heavens; and the Arroopeh-Loke, consisting of four.   They say of the vir-
tuous, that they do not enjoy the reward of their good deeds, until after
having repeatedly died and appeared as often in the six first heavens called
Deveh-Loke, in order to be born again in the world to great wealth and con-
sequence: and that, having at length enjoyed a foretaste of bliss in the
eleven inferior Brachmah-Lokes, they ascend to the five superior Brachmah-
Lokes or triumphant heavens, where their transmigration ends, and where
they enjoy the fulness of glory and the purest happiness.   Buddha, before his
appearance as man, was a god, and the supreme of all the gods.   At the
solicitations of many of the gods, he descended on earth, and was frequently
born as a man; in which character he exercised every possible virtue, by
extraordinary instances of self-denial and piety—The learned Singhalais
do not acknowledge in their writings a Supreme Being, presiding over and
the author of the Universe—In support of their denial of a Supreme Power,
who created heaven and earth, they urge, that, if there existed such a creator,
the world would not perish and be annihilated; on the contrary, he would be
careful to guard it in safety, and would preserve it from corruptibility.   In
the first instance, Buddha interferes in the government of the world; next
to him, Sahampattee-Maha-Brachma; and afterwards the respective gods, as
they are by their relative qualifications empowered.   The world, say they,
perished frequently in former times, and was produced anew by the operation
of the above power; gods and men from the same source.   The latter, on
dying, ascend the six inferior heavens; are judged, according to their me-
rits, by one of the most inferior gods; and regenerate of themselves, on the
earth, either as men or brutes: which regeneration continues, until they
arrive at the heavens of the superior gods, and so on by degrees at the tri-
umphant heavens, until they at length reach the supreme heaven.[1]   With
more consistency than the Hindoos, the Singhalais push their doctrine of a succession of worlds to absolute eternity.   In their opinion, *there has been no*
proper creation: Maha-Brahma, all the Sakreia, and the Brahmes, have
existed from all time; and so have the worlds, the gods, the human race, and
all the animated beings—Their calculations only relate to the immense number

of transmigrations of Buddha, from the time he first thought of becoming Buddha, until the time that he became Nivani: and this period they compute at an unit followed by sixty three Zeros, that is, by the number *sixty four,* which is introduced so conspicuously into the systems of the Chinese and the Burmas. The Singhalais have twenty six heavens, which they divide in the same manner as their brethren of the Burma empire: and their opinions respecting them sufficiently shew, that they are in reality twenty six worlds, termed *heavens* most probably from the union of astronomy and demonolatry. *When the Maha-Kalpa ends,* in the use of which term they agree with the Brahmenists, *that is, when the system of the worlds is overturned and when all is in disorder, some of the heavens are in a state of conflagration, others are laid waste by violent winds, and others are inundated.*[1]

This atheistical system, which is nothing more than paganism boldly pushed to its utmost limits, throws a strong light on the real nature of heathen theology. The being worshipped by the Gentiles, though sometimes decorated with the borrowed attributes of proper divinity, is here fairly confessed not to be truly God: while yet, in consequence of the doctrine of an eternal succession of worlds and the everlasting duration of the human race, the Supreme Being, after having been first robbed of his attributes to trick out a mere mortal, is next denied to have any existence whatsoever. The twenty two Buddhas, like the fourteen Menus, may all be reduced to two, Adam and Noah: for Buddha is the very same person as Menu. A later Buddha is described as living at the time of the flood, as being the sovereign prince in the belly of the symbolical fish, and as marrying Ila the daughter of Menu-Satyavrata who was preserved with seven companions in an ark when the whole earth was inundated. But Menu is also said to have espoused his own daughter: therefore Buddha must be the same as Menu. Accordingly, as Menu and his three sons are allowed to be an incarnation of the Hindoo Unity and Trimurti: so Buddha is at once confessed to be an Avatar of Vishnou, and pronounced to be no other than the mystic Om by which name the Trimurti is wont to be designated. Buddha however is here acknowledged not to be any real and proper god: and his diluvian character proves him to be the patriarch Noah. If we cast away therefore the idle figment of nu-

[1] Asiat. Res. vol. vii. p. 399, 411.

merous Buddhas appearing in numerous worlds, we shall have a single hero-god, with whom commenced a prior world separated from the present by the intervention of a deluge, preceding a second hero-god, who lived at the time of the flood, and with whom the present world commenced. Of these, as the one is certainly Noah, so the other must be Adam.

VII. When the Goths, who were a branch of the Chasas or Chusas or Indo-Scuths, emigrated from the east and invaded the Roman empire, they brought with them the Buddhic theology of their ancestors; and, as a part of it, they have preserved with a considerable degree of accuracy the doctrine of a succession of worlds and of a destruction both of gods and men at the close of the present mundane system.

According to the Scaldic philosophers, a world, luminous, glowing, not to be dwelt in by strangers, existed before all things. This world is named *Muspelsheim.* There the black deity Surtur, the Maha-Cali of the Hindoos, holds his empire. A flaming sword shines in his hand. He shall come at the end of all things : he shall vanquish every god : he shall give up the Universe a prey to the flames. Next in order to Muspelsheim the abode of Surtur, was created what is evidently the antediluvian world; because at the close of it all the families of the giants are destroyed by a flood, except a single giant who saves himself in a ship with all his household. The antediluvian world commences with the first man and his three sons, born from a mysterious cow: and these are unreservedly acknowledged to be the great gods of the Goths. The same triad appears again at the commencement of the postdiluvian world; and, in a wild manner which bears a singular resemblance to the fictions of the Babylonians and the Hindoos, it is represented as being the destined author of a new mundane creation. At the close of the present system, that is, in the Maha-Pralaya of the Hindoos, gods and men will be involved in one common destruction. The great ship Naglefara is then set afloat: the mighty serpent vomits forth floods of poison: the black deity and his genii invade the perishing Universe: all the gods are slain: and the power of dissolution wraps the whole earth in fire and flame. But to destroy in one form is only to reproduce in another. *There will arise out of the sea a new earth most lovely and delightful: covered it will be with verdure and pleasant fields : there the grain shall spring forth and grow of*

*itself without cultivation. Vidar and Vale shall also survive; because nei-
ther the flood, nor the black conflagration, shall do them any harm. They
shall dwell in the plains of Ida;*[1] *where was formerly the residence of the
gods. The sons of Thor, Mode*[2] *and Magne,*[3] *repair thither: thither come
Balder and Hoder from the mansions of the dead. They sit down and converse together; they recall to mind the sufferings which they have formerly
undergone.* Nor do the gods alone tenant the renovated Universe: *while
the fire devours all things, two persons of the human race, the one male and
the other female, lie concealed under a hill. These feed on the dew; and
propagate so abundantly, that the earth is soon peopled with a new race of
mortals. The Sun also,* at once a female and the brilliant monarch of fire,
*before it is devoured by the wolf Fenris, shall have brought forth a daughter
as lovely and as resplendent as herself; who shall go in the track formerly
trodden by her mother.*[4] Every thing in short shall be renovated: and the
destruction of one world shall only be the harbinger to the creation of another.

The opinions of the Goths respecting alternate destruction and reproduction are so well summed up by Mr. Mallet, that I cannot refrain from giving
his statement at some length.

---

[1] The *Ida-vratta* of the Hindoos.　　　　[2] The *Mo-Deo* or *Mah-Deo* of the Hindoos.

[3] Or *Manne*; the *Menu* of the Hindoos, and *Menes* or *Manes* of various other nations.

[4] Edda. Fab. ii, iii, iv, xxxii, xxxiii. Bp. Percy supposes there to be some defect or ambiguity in the original, because the Sun in the same sentence is spoken of as both masculine
and feminine; a mode of phraseology carefully preserved both in the French translation of
Mallet and the Latin one of Goranson. There may be an ambiguity, but there is no defect.
This very ambiguity indeed, which perfectly accords with the opinion entertained by the
pagans respecting the hermaphroditic nature of the great father whom they venerated in the
Sun, is the best proof of the genuineness of the ancient verses referred to as an authority by the
compiler of the Edda: and I greatly doubt, whether the Bishop's attempt to remedy this supposed erroneous reading, by using the word *parent* rather than *mother*, has not completely
marred the intentional mysticism of the writer. The version of Mallet is; *Le Roi brillant du
feu engendrera une fille unique, avant que d'etre englouti par le loup; cette fille suivra les traces
de sa mere, apres la mort des dieux.* That of Goranson: *Unicam filiam genuit rubicun-
dissimus ille rex, antequam eum Fenris devoraverit; quæ cursura est, mortuis diis, viam ma-
ternam.* Such language exactly describes the solar Siva in his double character of *Ardha-
nari;* and ought, in my judgment, to be scrupulously retained, as exhibiting a faithful picture of the theological notions which the Goths brought with them from the east.

*The philosophers of the north[1] considered nature as in a state of perpe-
tual labour and warfare. Her strength was thus continually wasting away by
little and little; and her approaching dissolution could not but become every day
more and more perceptible. At last, a confusion of the seasons, with a long
and preternatural winter, was to be the final mark of her decay. The moral
world is to be no less disturbed and troubled than the natural. The voice
of dying nature will be no longer heard by man. Her sensations, being
weakened and as it were totally extinct, shall leave the heart a prey to cruel
and inhuman passions. Then will all the malevolent and hostile powers, whom
the gods have hitherto with much difficulty confined, burst their chains, and
fill the Universe with disorder and confusion. The host of heroes from Val-
hall shall in vain attempt to support the gods: for, though the latter will
destroy their enemies, they will nevertheless fall along with them. That is,
in other words, in that great day, all the inferior divinities, whether good
or bad, shall fall in one great conflict back again into the bosom of the grand
divinity;[2] from whom all things have proceeded as emanations of his essence,
and who will survive all things. After this the world becomes a prey to
flames: which are however destined rather to purify than destroy it; since it
afterwards makes its appearance again more lovely, more pleasant, and more
fruitful, than before—In this new earth, which is to succeed that which we
inhabit, there are to be again subaltern divinities to govern it, and men to
people it. This, in general, is what the Edda means to tell us. Although
the circumstances of the relation are darkly and allegorically delivered; yet
they are not detailed so obscurely, but that one easily sees it was the idea of
the northern philosophers, that the world was to be renovated and spring forth
again more perfect and beautiful.*

[1] We ought to add, *whose ancestors came from the east.* The idle dream of an inexhaustible
northern hive of men in the barren and uncultivated regions of Scandinavia is now sufficiently
exploded.

[2] Not *the Supreme Being,* I am persuaded, but *the great hermaphroditic triplicated father;*
who was esteemed the demiurge, who was thought to appear at the commencement of each
mundane renovation, who was believed to sleep floating on the surface of the ocean during
the intermediate period of destruction, and whom the Buddhists fairly confess to be no proper
god.

Mr. Mallet adds, that *by the fable of the two human beings, who are to survive the destruction of the world, they meant to say, that there still existed in the earth a vivifying principle and seed, proper to repair the loss of the former inhabitants.* He is right, in asserting their belief in the existence of such a principle; but mistaken, as it appears to me, in deducing it from *this* part of the fable. The man and the woman, who escape in the general destruction, seem plainly to be the great father and great mother of the new world: or, as the Hindoos would speak, the Menu and his consort; who appear at the end of each Manwantara, who are preserved in a boat with six companions during the prevalence of the intermediate deluge, and with whom commences every successive Manwantara.[1] Mr. Mallet also speaks somewhat too exclusively of its being the opinion of the Goths, that the present world would be destroyed by fire. In reality, they have blended together into one fable the *two* notions of *a destruction by fire* and *a destruction by water;* each of which is indifferently called by the Hindoos a *pralaya* or *flood.*

This will be evident to any one, who examines either the preceding extracts from the Edda or the more ancient poem Voluspa where it treats of the same subject. In both, mention is made, not only of devastating fire, but likewise of a wonderful ship being set afloat on the swelling ocean: and we are further taught, that the new earth is to arise out of the sea. *The giant Rymer*, they are the words of the Voluspa, *arrives from the east, carried in a chariot: the ocean swells: the great serpent*[2] *rolls himself furiously in the waters, and lifteth up the sea. The eagle screams, and tears the dead bodies with his horrid beak. The vessel of the gods is set afloat. The vessel comes from the east: the host of evil genii arrives by sea: Loke is their pilot and director. Their furious squadron advances, escorted by the wolf Fenris: Loke appears with them. The black prince of the genii*

---

[1] Their hiding themselves under a hill means their being concealed in the cavern of a mountain: but, by the cavern of a mountain, was meant the Ark resting on mount Ararat. Vide infra book v. c. 7. § I. 2. (1.)

[2] The dracontine Typhon of Egypt, who is expressly said by Plutarch to be a personification of the sea, that is, the deluge.

issues forth from the south, surrounded with flames: the swords of the gods beam forth rays like the Sun. The rocks are shaken, and fall to pieces. The female giants wander about weeping. Men tread in crowds the paths of death. The heaven is split asunder: the Sun is darkened: the sea overwhelms the earth: the shining stars vanish out of heaven: the fire furiously rages: the ages draw to an end: the ascending flame licks the vault of heaven.[1]

Here the agents of destruction are both fire and water: and, while the whole world is convulsed, we are presented with an image of the ship of the gods floating on the surface of the agitated ocean. This agrees with the periodical voyage of the Indian Menu, which is doubtless borrowed from the voyage of Noah: but the Goths, in the course of their progress westward from their original settlements in Cashgar and Bokhara, have deviated somewhat from the genuine tradition, though they have not altogether lost it. It may be observed, that in many pagan accounts of the deluge fire and water are blended together as joint agents in the work of devastation: and each world closes with a deluge, which is the very counterpart of a former deluge at the end of a former world.

The Voluspa proceeds, like the Edda, to describe the production of a new world out of the ruins of its predecessor, in a manner which exactly corresponds with the rising of the present world out of the waters of the flood. *Then,* namely after the death of the gods and the dissolution of the prior system, *Then we see emerge from the bosom of the waves an earth clothed with a most lovely verdure. The floods retire: the eagle soars wheresoever he lists, and seizes his fishy prey on the tops of the mountains. Balder and his brother, those warrior gods, return to inhabit the ruined palaces of Odin. The gods assemble in the fields of Ida; they discourse together concerning the heavenly palaces, whose ruins are before them: they recollect their former conversations and the ancient discourses of Odin.*[2]

Every occurrence, which is here specified as *about* to take place when

---

[1] Mallet's Notes to Edda. Fab. xxxiii.

[2] Volusp. in Mallet's Notes to Edda. Fab. xxxiii.

the world which we now inhabit shall be destroyed, really *took* place, if we make due allowances for the pagan mode of detailing the facts, when the earth arose out of the ocean subsequent to the flood of Noah. The Gothic Ida is the Idavratta or Meru of the Hindoos, and the Ida of the Phrygians and Cretans. It is the Paradise of the hero-gods, and the mountain where they first appeared at the commencement of the new world. It is, in short, the arkite mount Ararat, which there is reason to believe coincides even literally with the Paradise of Adam. Here the deified patriarchs were manifested, when the waters of the deluge abated, after their allegorical death or sleep on the surface of the ocean: here, in the belief of the speculative Gentiles, they had been previously manifested at the commencement of a former world: and here, they will be again manifested, when the present mundane system shall be succeeded by another.

VIII. It is observed by Mr. Mallet, that the doctrine of the Gothic philosophers is precisely the same as that espoused by the Stoics: and, as a proof, he adduces several passages from the writings of Seneca. The observation is perfectly just; yet I think it proper to remark, that the doctrine in question was by no means *peculiar* to the Stoics: it was held also by the philosophers of the other schools. As their sectarial differences however are of no importance in the present inquiry, which respects an hypothesis common in a great measure to them all; I shall notice their sentiments on a succession of worlds *conjointly*, as exhibiting a specimen of what was the wisdom of Greece and Rome.

The principle, which they universally laid down as indisputable, and which formed the basis of all their subsequent reasoning, was *the absolute eternity of matter.* This was declared to be at once uncreated, and incapable of annihilation. *There was among the heathen physiologists*, as it is well observed by Mr. Bayle, *a great variety of opinions about the origin of the world and the nature of the element or elements of which they pretended particular bodies to have been formed. Some maintained, that water was the principle of all things; others gave that preëminence to the air; others, to fire; others, to homogeneal parts: but they all agreed in this, that the matter of the world was unproduced. They never dis-*

puted among themselves upon the question, whether any thing was made out of nothing: *they all agreed, that that was impossible.*[1]

But, though the eternity of crude matter was thus maintained, a frequent change of figure in that matter was fully acknowledged. *Matter itself, they taught, is indeed eternal: but, in addition to the changes of form which we daily witness, it successively undergoes, at the end of certain vast periods, mutations, which are equivalent to the destruction of one mundane system and to the production of another from its ruins.* This point is argued, with some degree of ingenuity, by the philosopher Sallust. Justly drawing a distinction between substance and form, he allows the corruptibility of the latter, but denies that of the former.[2] In a similar manner, Timèus, though he admits the creation or rather the generation of the world by a deity (for he represents it as being the *offspring* of his god), yet acknowledges nothing more than a production out of already existing materials.[3] Precisely the same language is held by Ocellus Lucanus:[4] and, accordingly, it is on this identical principle, that he undertakes to answer those writers, who made the history of Greece commence with Inachus. *That epoch,* says he, *was no real beginning, but only a change: for, as Greece had been in a state of barbarism before the days of Inachus, so will it again relapse into a similar state at some future period.* At the same time he intimates the existence of certain physical, as well as moral, revolutions. *The different parts of the earth are liable to corruption and change, sometimes in consequence of a deluge produced by the sea, and sometimes by the more silent operation of dissipating winds or undermining waters: meanwhile the substance of the earth itself is incapable of corruption.*[5] Such also is the doctrine mentioned by Macrobius. *Nothing can be properly said to perish throughout the whole world. Those things, which seem to be destroyed, only change their appearance. The world itself remains, though the human race has often been almost totally swept*

---

[1] Bayle's Diction. vox *Epicurus*.　　[2] Sallust. de Diis et mund. c. vii, xvii.

[3] Tim. Loc. de anim. mund. p. 545, 546. See also Cudw. Intell. Syst. p. 214, 738. 30—35.　　[4] Ocell. Lucan. de Univ. c. i, ii.

[5] Ocell. Luc. de Univ. c. iii.

away either by inundation or conflagration.[1] In this tenet, with some smaller varieties, the Stoics, the Epicurèans, and the Platonists, were all agreed.[2]

To the doctrine of the eternity of substance and the successive destruction and reproduction of worlds either by fire or water, was added the opinion, that the hero-gods invariably perished at each revolution, and appeared again at the commencement of each new system; the great universal father existing alone during every intervening period. Hence, as it has been justly remarked, the pagan cosmogonies were also theogonies.[3] The devouring Jupiter of the Stoics swallows up, at the close of each world, the whole host of hero-gods: and, as it was the universal doctrine of those philosophers, that, during the intervals of the successive conflagrations by which the mundane system is destroyed, that god retires into himself and converses with his own thoughts; so, at the end of each interval, he produces a new frame of nature, together with a new family of inferior divinities, out of his own substance.[4] Such speculations are plainly the same as those of the Indian school. The devouring Jupiter occupies the place of Siva, or Maha-Cali, or the destroying power: and his solitary abstraction during every intervening period is palpably no other, than the profound solitary meditation of the creative Brahma while he floats inactive on the surface of the chaotic abyss. *The world*, says Seneca, *being melted and having reëntered into the bosom of Jupiter, this god continues for some time totally concentered in himself, and remains concealed as it were, wholly immersed in the contemplation of his own ideas. Afterwards we see a new world spring from him, perfect in all its parts. Animals are produced anew. An innocent race of men is formed under more favourable auspices, in order to people this earth, the worthy abode of virtue. In short, the whole face of nature becomes more pleasing and lovely.*[5] And again, speak-

---

[1] Macrob. in somn. Scip. lib. ii. c. 10. p. 108. c. 12. p. 113. See also Clem. Alex. Strom. lib. v. p. 599.

[2] Minuc. Fel. Octav. p. 322.

[3] Cudw. Intell. Syst. p. 211, 212, 213, 234, 239.

[4] Cudw. Intell. Syst. p. 425, 426. cited by Mallet.

[5] Senec. Epist. 9. et Quæst. Nat. lib. iii. c. ult.

ing of a mundane dissolution as involving the destruction or death of all the hero-gods, he teaches us, that, *when the laws of nature shall be buried in ruin and the last day of the world shall come; the southern pole shall crush, as it falls, all the regions of Africa, and the north pole shall overwhelm all the countries beneath its axis. The affrighted Sun shall be deprived of its light: the palace of heaven falling to decay shall produce at once both life and death: and some kind of dissolution shall equally seize upon all the deities, who thus shall return into their original chaos.*[1]

Immortality of the Soul

The system was completed by the doctrine of *the preëxistence of souls,* as well as *their postexistence:* which indeed was a necessary part of the theory, that there was a perpetual succession of hero-gods appearing at the commencement of each world and absorbed into the unity of the great father at the close of each. For the hero-gods, as we have seen, were no other than the chief patriarch and his offspring, with whom every world invariably began: and, in consequence of the children being deemed mere delusive emanations of the first parent, springing from him at the commencement of a world and returning into his essence at the end of one, the gods of paganism were ever considered in the light of *one and many.*[2] Now this doctrine is in fact the doctrine of the Metempsychosis; which is so closely united with that of a succession of worlds, that, wherever we find the one, we may be morally sure of finding the other. As similar worlds succeed similar worlds, and as similar hero-gods succeed similar hero-gods: so the souls, which have existed in one world, exist again in another, for ever dying in this body and for ever reappearing in that. Such was the notion of Plato. *Our soul,* says he, *was somewhere, before it came to exist in this present human form: whence it appears to be immortal, and as such it will subsist after death.*[3] And again: *In the perpetual circle of nature, the living are made out of the dead, as well as the dead out of the living.*[4] The same philosopher informs us, that some of the ancients, who held these opinions, were not without suspicion, that what is now called *death* is rather a nativity into life, and that what is now called *a generation*

PLATO'S statement of the immortality doctrine

[1] Herc. Œt. ver. 1102. apud Mallet.   [2] Cudw. Intell. Syst. p. 377.

[3] Cudw. Intell. Syst. p. 38.   [4] Ibid. p. 42.

into life is rather to be accounted a sinking into death. *Who knows,* says he, *whether that, which is denominated* living, *be not indeed rather dying; and whether that, which is styled* dying, *be not rather living.*[1] The ancients, to whom he refers, were doubtless the first inventors of this system, from whom all nations have equally derived their tenets : and the absolute immortality of the soul, passing however through a long series of different forms, is at once the doctrine taught in the Bhagavat-Gita, in the traditions of the Celtic Druids, and in the books of the old Babylonians and Egyptians. Similar to the notion of Plato was that of Empedocles. *There is no production,* says he, *of any thing which was not before ; no new substance made, which did not really preëxist. Therefore, in the generations and corruptions of inanimate bodies, there is no form or quality really distinct from the substance produced and destroyed, but only a various composition and modification of matter. But, in the generation and corruption of men and animals where the souls are substances really distinct from the matter, there is nothing but the conjunction and separation of souls and particular bodies existing both before and after ; not the production of any new soul into being which was not before, nor the absolute death and destruction of any into nothing. In short, nothing dies or utterly perishes : but things, being variously concreted and secreted, transposed and modified, change only their form and shape, and are merely put into a new dress.*[2]

It were more easy to multiply citations, than to avoid tedeousness ; yet I cannot refrain from noticing the curious account of the Pythagorèan system, which has been delivered to us at considerable length by Ovid. To the generally professed doctrines of the eternity and imperishableness both of spirit and matter, the Samian philosopher superadds the precise tenets which Buddha at his last incarnation is said to have promulgated ; namely, that it is unlawful to eat animal food, or to take away animal life. Such an opinion naturally flowed from the doctrine of the Metempsychosis ; which was certainly the source, whence it originated. If souls were in a constant state of migration, not merely from one human body to another or from one

Vegetarianism of Buddha stems from Metempsychosis

---

[1] Ibid. p. 42.   [2] Ibid. p. 40, 41.

world to another, but likewise through the bodies of every description of animals, it was not unreasonable to hold in abhorrence a banquet procured by the shedding of blood. Such banquets accordingly were alike proscribed by Buddha and Pythagoras: and the latter assigns as a reason this very doctrine of the Metempsychosis.

Why should fearful man, says he, *tremble at the prospect of death? Our souls are immortal: and, as soon as they quit any former corporeal vehicle, they immediately pass, instinct with undiminished vitality, into new habitations. I myself, in the time of the Trojan war, occupied the body of Euphorbus; and lately recognized in the temple of Juno the identical shield, which I bore when the dart of the younger Atrides pierced my breast. All things are changed: nothing really perishes. The soul sometimes animates one set of limbs, and sometimes another. It flits here, and it flits there. Now it passes from bestial forms into human; and now from human, into bestial: yet in no lapse of time is it annihilated. As wax may be moulded into an infinite variety of shapes, and is still the same wax: so the soul always preserves its identity through whatever outward forms it may pass. Cease then from shedding kindred blood: disturb not the souls of your relations to gratify the propensities of unrestrained and impious appetite. I, who have floated a fish in the mighty ocean stream, and have sailed a bird through the wide fields of ether, know, that nothing is permanent throughout the whole world. All things are in a state of incessant mutation. As day succeeds to night, and night to day; as the seasons follow each other in endless revolution; as youth is ever followed by puberty, and puberty by old age; as the four elements melt into each other in an eternal cycle: such also is the case with the vast Universe itself. Innovating nature for ever repairs form out of form. Nothing perishes: for substance merely assumes new shapes in a perpetual succession. Birth is but an alteration in the mode of existence: death is only the cessation of a single period of being. We have passed from an age of gold to an age of iron; and we shall again and again pass through a similar series. Many are the revolutions even of the great globe itself, which I have witnessed I have beheld the earth inundated by the ocean: I have seen land emerge from the sea and occupy its place. I have gathered marine shells in the centre of solid continents: I have contemplated an anchor on the summit of the loftiest mountain. Plains I have seen rise into hills, and hills sink into plains. In fine, heaven, and earth, and whatsoever they contain, are subject to perpetually successive revolutions. To destroy is only to reproduce in another form: matter itself, as it knew no beginning, knows no end.*[1]

In presenting us with this account of the Pythagorèan system or rather the general system of the whole pagan world, Ovid furnishes us with a key to understand the whole of his curious mythological poem. The various transformations, which he celebrates, are built upon the doctrine of a succession of worlds, a perpetual Metempsychosis both through beasts and vegetables, and a consequent belief in the sacredness both of plants and animals.

IX. The opinions of the ancient Druids on these points have not come down to us with so much regularity and precision as might have been desired: yet we have, I think, sufficient proof, that they fully symbolized in such speculations with their pagan brethren in most other parts of the world.

Cæsar assures us, that they held the doctrine of the imperishable nature of the soul, and that they believed it after death to pass from one body into another. He adds, though unfortunately without descending to particulars, that they largely disputed concerning the nature of things, the motion of the heavenly bodies, the size of the world, and the power of the gods.[2] Lucan however explains *how* they held the doctrine of transmigration. They did not merely suppose, that souls passed from one body to another in the *present* world; but they taught, that the same spirit would animate a new body in a *different* world.[3] Hence they must evidently, like the Hindoos, have maintained the tenet of a succession of similar worlds; and have believed, that every soul, which acted a part here, would act the same part again in a new world to be framed out of the wreck of the present. Diodorus says, that they held the opinion of Pythagoras, supposing that the souls of men after certain determinate periods would pass into other

[1] Ovid. Metam. lib. xv. ver. 60—478. See also Porph. de vit. Pythag. passim.

[2] Cæsar. de bell. Gall. lib. v. c. 14. [3] Lucan. Pharsal. lib. i. ver. 450—460.

bodies : and, according to Valerius Maximus, so fully were the Gauls impressed with the idea that they should animate new vehicles hereafter in a renovated world, that they were wont to lend money on condition of its being repaid them when they should again become incarnate.[1] Agreeably to these notions, they burned on the funeral pile of the deceased whatever he had best loved, whether servants, or clients, or animals, with an intention, I apprehend, of sending them to accompany their master to that world where he should assuredly live again : and I have little doubt, that the same opinion dictates the diabolical immolation of the widows of Hindostan, which has been known to disgrace that country even from the time of Alexander the great.[2] But we are not left merely to *infer*, that they believed in a succession of worlds : Strabo has put the matter out of all doubt by expressly asserting, that they taught the immortality of the soul and a destruction of the world by fire and water.[3]

X. It is a curious circumstance, that we find the doctrine of a succession of worlds and of a death and revival of the hero-gods held also by the Mexicans. They doubtless brought it out of eastern Asia, together with a mythology which is substantially the same as that of the larger continent, agreeably to their own standing tradition respecting the progress of their ancestors.

They supposed the world to have been made by the gods : but, professing themselves ignorant of the precise mode in which it was formed, they imagined, that, since the creation, four Suns had successively appeared and disappeared ; and they maintained, that that, which we now behold, is the

---

[1] Diod. Bibl. lib. v. p. 306. Val. Max. lib. ii. c. 6.

[2] Cæsar. de bell. Gall. lib. v. c. 19. Bernier mentions, that a woman, whose self-immolation he witnessed, audibly pronounced in the midst of the flames the words *five* and *two ;* by which she intimated, that, in the progress of transmigration, she had already burned herself five times with the same husband, and that only two similar sacrifices more remained towards the attainment of blissful perfection. Yet the Institutes of Menu, in prescribing the duties of a widow, are wholly silent respecting this horrible abomination : whence it is evident, both that that Code must have been written prior to the time of Alexander, and that such a practice not being enjoined might surely be abolished by a judicious application of sovereign power. Bernier cited by Southey. Kehama vol. i. p. 152.

[3] Strab. Geog. lib. iv. p. 197.

fifth. The first Sun perished by a deluge of water, and with it all living creatures. The second fell from heaven, at a period when there were many giants in the country; and, by the fall, every thing that had life was again destroyed. The third was consumed by fire. And the fourth was dissipated by a tempest of wind. At that time, mankind did not perish as before, but were changed into apes: yet, when the fourth Sun was blotted out, there was a darkness which continued twenty five years. At the end of the fifteenth year, their chief god formed a man and a woman, who brought forth children; and, at the end of the other ten years appeared the fifth Sun, then newly born. Three days after this last Sun became visible, all the former gods died: then, in process of time, were produced those whom they have since worshipped.[1]

We cannot but observe the striking resemblance between this system and that of the Burmas in particular; though the sum of the doctrine, which it teaches, is precisely the same as that which prevailed in perhaps every part of the gentile world. The Egyptians had a legend, which in some respects is so nearly allied to that of the Mexicans, that, however it may have been altered in lapse of time, I am almost inclined to suspect that it originated from the same source. They told Herodotus, that, according to their records, the Sun had four times deviated from his regular course, having twice risen in the west, and twice set in the east: this change however had produced no alteration in the climate of Egypt, neither had a greater prevalence of disease been the consequence.[2]

XI. Ovid represents Pythagoras, as adducing the story of the phenix by way of exemplifying the perpetual destruction and reproduction of the world: and, in point of application, there is much reason to believe that the fable originated from this very doctrine.

The poet's account of it is nearly the same as that which is given by Herodotus. That historian informs us, that the Egyptians have a sacred bird called *the phenix*, which he never saw except in a picture. Its form, according to the delineation of it, was that of an eagle; and its wings were of the blended colour of gold and ruby. It was wont to make its appear-

[1] Purchas's Pilgr. b. viii. c. 13. p. 806. [2] Herod. lib. ii. c. 142.

ance only once at the end of five hundred years, and *that* upon the death
of the parent bird.   The Heliopolitans asserted, that, whenever that event
took place, it came from Arabia to the temple of the Sun, bearing the
dead body of its parent inclosed in a ball of myrrh, which it prepared in
the following manner.   First it made a ball shaped like an egg of such a
size as it found itself by trial able to carry.   Next it hollowed out the ball,
and introduced the body of the dead bird into the excavation.   Lastly, it
closed the aperture with myrrh: and, the ball being thus again made of the
same weight as it originally was, it carried it to the temple of the Sun at
Heliopolis.[1]   In several of these particulars, Ovid agrees with Herodotus:
but he adds to them some others not specified by the Greek historian.   He
tells us, that the phenix possessed the power of self-reproduction, which
peculiarly fitted it to be a type of the world.   When its long life of five
centuries was drawing to a close, it prepared for itself an aromatic nest in
the branches of an oak or on the summit of a palm-tree.   Its work being
finished, it placed itself upon it; and ended its life in the midst of sweet
odours.   From the body of the deceased bird soon sprang a young phenix,
destined to live through the same long period as its parent had done before it.   With pious care it still hovered near the nest which had given it
birth: and, as soon as its strength was equal to the task, it bore away that
which had equally been its own cradle and the tomb of its parent, and deposited it before the gates of the temple of the Sun.[2]   Nonnus extends
the life of the phenix to a thousand years: and alludes to the familiar
story, which however is mentioned neither by Herodotus nor Ovid, of the
parent bird burning itself upon the odoriferous pile which it had carefully
prepared, and of a young phenix springing to life from the ashes of its
sire.[3]

   The fable almost explains itself: and so obviously indeed does this hieroglyphical legend shadow out the doctrine of one world rising out of the ruins
of another at the close of certain stated immense periods, that the fathers
were accustomed to employ it as an exemplification of the resurrection,

[1] Herod. lib. ii. c. 73.   [2] Ovid Metam. lib. xv. ver. 392—407.

                    [3] Nonni Dionys. lib. xl. ver. 395—398.

when the microcosm man will issue forth in renovated beauty from the decayed ruins of his former self.' Unless I am greatly mistaken, the pagans themselves likewise used it in a somewhat similar manner. The life of Brahma or of man collectively is the life of the world : and, at each great change, the world and all its inhabitants, whether hero-gods or mortals, are involved in common destruction or absorbed into the essence of the great father, from whom in due time emanates another mundane system. Hence, since some held fire rather than water to be the agent of dissolution, and since others believed in an alternation of igneous and aqueous deluges, it was deemed a pious act of faith to burn the body of the dead in imitation of that destruction terminating in reproduction, to symbolize which the legend of the phenix was invented. Hence also in Hindostan it has long been esteemed peculiarly meritorious for a widow to burn herself with the corpse of her husband, in the firm persuasion, that, as she has already lived in a former world, so she assuredly shall reappear in a future world. It is worthy of observation, that the cycle of five hundred years, the reputed duration of the life of a phenix, is precisely the same as that by which the life of Brahma is measured. His are indeed *his own* years, each of a stupendous length ; but the cycle of five hundred equally occurs in the life of Brahma and in that of the phenix. The other period of a thousand, to which the life of the bird is sometimes extended, may either be reckoned a mere reduplication of five hundred, as the fourteen Menus are an evident reduplication of their proper number seven : or it possibly may allude to another mundane cycle employed no less by the ancients than that of five hundred; a thousand divine ages constitute, we are told, a single day of Brahma, which comprehends within its ample space fourteen Manwantaras. Sometimes also the phenix was said to live six hundred years ; sometimes, three hundred and forty years ; and sometimes, four hundred and sixty.' All these again are but so many different cycles or revolutions, invented by the heathen sages, partly in reference to certain astronomical calculations,

' See Tertull. de resurr. c. xi. p. 410. with note in loc.

' Orient. Collect. vol. ii. numb. iii. p. 203, 204.

and partly in allusion to their favourite doctrine of a perpetual succession of worlds.

Herodotus mentions, that the phenix was one of the sacred birds or hieroglyphics of the Egyptians: and it is a curious circumstance, that we find nations the most remote from each other well acquainted with this celebrated symbol. The ancient Irish ascribed a longevity of six centuries to *their* phenix; and considered the production of the young bird as a restoration to life of the old one. *There is but one of the species in the world,* say they, *and she makes her nest with combustible spices. When the Sun sets them on fire, she fans the flames with her wings, and burns herself. Out of the ashes arises a small maggot, which becomes another phenix.* At the same time they remarkably explain the fable by declaring this hiero-glyphical bird to mean only a celestial cycle:[1] that is to say, as the whole character and imagined fate of the phenix sufficiently prove, a cycle or revolution of those immense years which were thought to be commensurate with the duration of each successive mundane system. By the Japanese the phenix is called *Kirin;* and by the Turks, *Kerkes.* According to the latter, it *lives a thousand years. When the thousand years are past, it gathers pieces of wood in its bill; and, kindling a flame, is consumed in the fire, and becomes ashes. Then, by the command of the Almighty, the air restores these ashes to life, and it again lives a thousand years; and so on to the day of judgment.*[2] The phenix is also very plainly the same as the Simorgh of Persian romance: and the account, which is given us of this last bird, yet more decisively establishes the opinion, that the death and revival of the phenix exhibit the successive destruction and reproduction of the world, which many believed to be effected by the agency of a fiery deluge. When the Simorgh was asked her age, she informed Caherman, *that this world is very ancient, for it has been already seven times replenished with beings different from man, and seven times depopulated: that the age of the human race, in which we now are, is to endure seven thousand years: and that she herself had seen twelve of these revolutions, and knew*

[1] Orient. Collect. vol. ii. numb. III. p. 203, 204.
[2] Orient. Collect. vol. ii. numb. III. p. 205, numb. I. p. 64.

not how many more she had to see.[1]   On this Mr. Wilford justly re-marks, that the numerical part of the fable has been borrowed, with some corruptions, from the Hindoo statement of the doctrine of successive worlds and Manwantaras.   The Simorgh ought properly to have been made to declare, that she had beheld the world a perfect void *six* times; for, according to the Hindoos, we are now in the age of the *se-venth* Menu, who is styled *Satyavrata* and who is certainly the same as Noah.   She ought likewise to have asserted, not that she had seen twelve revolutions of seven thousand years each, but seven of twelve thousand each; the current period being the seventh.[2]   I am inclined to be-lieve, that the Simorgh is in reality the same as the winged Singh of the Hindoos and the Sphinx of the Egyptians.   It is said, that the former will appear at the end of the world; and that such will be the size of this mon-strous lion-bird, that as soon as he is born he will prey upon an elephant, which will shrink into absolute insignificance compared to the bulk of its mighty devourer.[3]   Perhaps also both may be identified with the fantastical compound Viratarupa, which certainly is designed to symbolize the destruc-tion of a world.   This creature, like Maha-Pralaya or the great flood, is represented in the act of swallowing a city.   Its neck and head are those of a peacock: its left forefoot and shoulder are those of an elephant: its back rises into the hump of a camel: its body and right hind foot are those of a tyger: its left hind foot and haunch are those of a horse: a human hand and arm supply the place of its right leg and foot: its four wings are those of the horse Kalki, on which Vishnou will appear when he comes to destroy the Universe: and its tail terminates in the head of a snake. Though its form in part has been borrowed, I suspect, from the form of the Paradisiacal cherubim, to which may also be referred both the eagle-phenix and the winged-lion: yet, from the style of its action and composi-tion, it seems designed to symbolize the Universe receiving all things into itself at the close of a great period and afterwards producing all things from itself at the commencement of another great period.[4]

---

[1] Orienta Collect. vol. ii. numb. ii. p. 119.

[2] Asiat. Res. vol. v. p. 245.   [3] Asiat. Res. vol. ii. p. 335.

[4] See Moor's Hind. Panth. p. 327, and plate 93.

From the representations of Paganism and the legends attached to them, the Rabbins appear to have borrowed their fable of an enormous bird, sometimes standing on the earth and sometimes walking in the ocean; the waters of which reach no higher than its legs, while its head props the sky:[1] and with the symbol they have also strangely adopted the doctrine, to which it relates.   They teach, that there are to be seven successive renewals of the world, that each reproduced system will last seven thousand years, and that the total duration of the Universe will thus be forty nine thousand years.   In this series our world holds the second place; as may clearly, say they, be collected from the circumstance of the first Hebrew letter in Genesis being *Beth*, which arithmetically expresses the number *two*.[2]   It might seem from such a mode of arguing, that they made no distinction between the Adamitical and Noetic worlds, but considered them only as parts of the same renewal; while they feigned the existence of a distinct world of seven thousand years prior to that, of which Adam was the first-created.   This last opinion was at least as old as the time of our Saviour: and the whole hypothesis was most probably borrowed from the oriental sages during the period of the Babylonian captivity.   We find the disciples of our Lord inquiring of him, whether a man, whom he restored to sight, had been born blind in consequence of his own sin or that of his parents.[3]   Now it is obvious, that no sin of *his* could have been deemed the cause of a blindness which was coëval with his *birth*, unless it had been committed *before* his birth : but it could not have been committed *before* his birth, unless he had lived in some prior state: the question therefore of the disciples necessarily implies, that they had adopted the doctrine of the preëxistence of souls.   The same tenet appears to be inculcated in the apocryphal book of Wisdom; the author of which represents Solomon as declaring, that he had come into an undefiled body, because he was good.[4]   But, if his goodness was the *cause* of his being thus born, he must have lived, in the judgment of that writer, *previous* to his birth into the present world.   From these speculations of the Jews, and ultimately from the pagan doctrine of succession, the Mohammedans

---

[1] Bava Bathra. fol. 73. 2. 2653. 2654. 2287.   Buxtorf. Synag. Jud. c. l. p. 737, 738.
[2] Orient. Collect. vol. ii. numb. II. p. 118.   [3] John ix. 1, 2.
[4] Wisd. viii. 19, 20.

have evidently borrowed some of their legends respecting the far celebrated king of Israel. D'Herbelot informs us, that the Arabs, not content with a single pre-Adamite Solomon, have invented a whole race of them; who, according to some, governed the world successively to the number of forty, or, according to others, to the number of seventy two.[1] It is almost superfluous to say, that this fable is a mere varied repetition of the imaginary series of Menus or Mahabads or Buddhas.

The Hebrew Rabbins, having adopted the pagan doctrine, next attempted to prove its truth from Scripture. For this purpose they adduced the passage in Deuteronomy, which represents the covenant of God as being made both with such as were then present and with such as were not then present; in other words, both with the persons of that generation and with their yet unborn posterity.[2] Whence they argued, that, since the covenant was made with the latter as well as with the former, the latter must then have been actually in existence, though they had not as yet been born into this world. They also adduced a passage from the book of Jeremiah, in which God declares to the prophet, that, before he had formed him in the womb, he knew him, or (as they would translate it) had endowed him with wisdom.[3] Whence they argued, that, if Jeremiah possessed wisdom before his birth, he must have existed antecedently to it.[4] I need scarcely remark, that in this childish interpretation of such texts, they have made *the mere prevision of God* to imply *the actual existence of the objects of such prevision.* The first of them is plainly a mode of speech similar to our familiar expression of conveying property to a man and his heirs for ever; from which it might with equal cogency be proved, that the English law, like that of Moses, taught the doctrine of the preëxistence of souls. The second of them relates, even admitting the Rabbinical translation of it, not to the wisdom which Jeremiah possessed before his birth, but to God's mental foreknowledge of the prophet as an instrument well adapted to subserve his future high purposes: just in the same manner as God is said to foreknow the objects of his predestination, not as then actually existing, but only as about to exist at some future determinate period.[5]

[1] D'Herbelot cited by Southey. Thalaba, vol. i. p. 198.   [2] Deut. xxix. 14, 15.
[3] Jerem. i. 5.   [4] See More's Myster of godliness. b. i. c. 8.
[5] Rom. viii. 29, 30.

The commencement of the Mosaical history of the creation was designed to strike at the root of this fantastic doctrine, which formed the very basis of pagan idolatry.

152   THE ORIGIN OF PAGAN IDOLATRY.

XII. I am much inclined to believe, that, so far from Scripture sanctioning any such vain speculations, Moses, who was learned in all the wisdom of Egypt and who was therefore well acquainted with the prevailing doctrine of a succession of worlds, delivered his cosmogony, at the beginning of Genesis, in terms studiously selected to oppose such an opinion and to guard the chosen people against adopting a theory, which directly tended to establish the impious tenet of the independent eternity of matter.[1]

By the Hebrew legislator not merely *the formation* of the world is ascribed to the Supreme Being, but likewise *the proper creation* of the rude materials themselves out of which the world was formed. He declares, without giving the least intimation of any prior system, that, in the beginning, God created *the very substance* of the heavens and *the very substance* of the earth; for such is the force of the particle or rather substantive, which he employs in the original.[2] After specifying this *primary* operation, by which matter was produced out of nothing; for the phrase *very substance* necessarily implies, that *strict creation*, nor *mere formation*, is here spoken of: he proceeds to describe the condition of the newly produced matter, before it was brought into order and regularity by a *subsequent* operation: *the earth was without form and void, and darkness was upon the face of the deep;* that is to say, the earth was as yet a rude chaotic mass, dark, confused, and shapeless.[3]

[1] The opinion of Dr. Hales on this point is the same as my own. See Chronol. vol. i. p. 317.

[2] Majorem verisimilitudinis speciem habet Aben-Ezræ judicium, sensus vocis אֵת est quasi *substantia rei*—Hæc certe vocis genuina explicatio ordinem nobis ostendit creationis Universi. Ut enim nuda tantum, rudis, et indigesta, inferioris mundi denotatur moles per הָאָרֶץ אֵת *essentia terræ* initio creata: הַשָּׁמַיִם אֵת vero id duntaxat, quod perfectionem cæli contineret *essentialem:* ita reliquam διαχοσμησιν sequentibus reservare Creator, ut gradibus opus suum perficeret, voluit diebus. Hottinger. Hist. Creat. quæs. xiii.

[3] The Hebrew word תֹהוּ, rendered in our translation *without form*, seems to convey much the same idea as the Greek *chaos*. Quis harum rerum (scil. תֹהוּ et בֹהוּ) in sacris usus? Raro occurrunt, et eodem quidem sensu (usitatissimum enim est Hebræis idem exprimere diversis verbis), hæ voculæ in sacris literis; et vel *privationem* notant *decori et perfecti inesse*, ex idea Creatoris debiti—vel *negationem*. Priori sensu sumitur hoc loco (Gen. i. 2.). Græci verterunt αορατον και ακατασκευαστον, non quidem (ut recte observat Sever.) ὅτι ουκ εφαινετο, αλλ', ὡς αν ειποι τις, αχοσμητος—Sic Ibn-Sina, qui Græcos Arabicè transtulit, *sine specie et apparatu.* Hotting. Hist. Creat. quæst. xxi. Sapientes dixerunt, quod תֹהוּ est *res informis*, apta ad recipiendum omnem formam, quam Græci vocant ὑλην. בֹהוּ vero est forma, quæ dat esse materiæ. Ibid. quæst. xxii.

Having thus described the condition of the newly created matter, he then, with much regularity, details the steps by which it was moulded into the form of a habitable world.   First substance itself is created: next, that substance is brought into shape and order.   And, since the formation of the present world is described as immediately succeeding the original production of matter, or at least since it is represented as being the very first mundane system that was formed out of substance created for that express purpose; this present world, according to the Mosaical cosmogony, must have been the first, nor could it have been preceded by any one anterior to it.

That the word employed by Moses to designate the production of substance means *proper creation*, is sufficiently evident from the very manner in which he uses it.   All are agreed, that it must denote either *strict creation* or *mere formation out of preëxisting materials*.   Now, if we interpret it in the *latter* sense, we shall make the Jewish lawgiver flatly contradict himself: because we shall exhibit him, as first saying that God *formed* the substance of the heaven and the earth; and then as adding immediately afterwards, that the earth, notwithstanding it had *been* formed, had after all *no form*, but was a rude chaos which still required to be reduced into the regular form of a habitable world.'   The *latter* sense therefore involving a palpable contradiction, nothing remains to be adopted except the *former* one: in other words, Moses, at the beginning of Genesis, speaks of *a strictly proper creation of matter;* and then describes, how the matter, thus created, was brought into form, which last operation (he teaches us) occupied the space of six days.   Such, accordingly, is the sense in which the Jewish commentators understand the word here employed by their lawgiver.   *It is a fundamental principle in our Law,* says Maimonides, *that God created this world from nothing.'*   He likewise observes, speaking of three different opinions which were entertained of the antiquity of the world, that *the first is peculiar to those, who believe*

' This contradiction will appear in glaring colours, merely by reading the exordium of Genesis, with the word ברא translated, as meaning only *to form* and not *to create*.   *In the beginning God* FORMED *the substance of the heaven and the substance of the earth: and the earth was* WITHOUT FORM.   That is to say, notwithstanding it had been *formed*, it was still *without form*; notwithstanding it had been reduced into order, it was still a disorderly chaos.

' More Nevochim. par. ii. c. 30.

in the Law of our master Moses: namely, that the whole world, which comprehends every being except the Creator, after being in a state of non-existence, received its existence from God. So that at the first God existed alone, and beside God nothing; neither the angels, nor the heavens, nor the things which are contained in them: but that afterwards, in consequence of his good pleasure, they began to exist as they are, being called into existence from nothing. [1] In a similar manner, the author of the book of *Cosri* asserts, that *it is our duty to believe the Law, when it declares the newness of the world and its creation by the hand of God:* [2] and Aben-Ezra informs us, that *most interpreters agree, that to create is to produce something out of nothing.* [3]

[1] More Nevochim. par. ii. c. 13.   [2] Lib. Cosri. par. i. § 91.

[3] Hottinger. Hist. Creat. quæst. viii. It is somewhat singular, that Dr. Geddes should so roundly assert the opinion of the Jews to be the same as his own, when the passages, which he cites, so far from proving that the word ברא signifies only *to form out of preëxisting materials,* merely declare (what no one ever thought of denying), that God *formed* the world out of a chaos, which he had previously *created* for that purpose. *Nothing, I think,* says he, *but the false idea, that absolute creation is necessarily implied in the Hebrew word* ברא, *could have led commentators to adopt an opposite opinion;* namely to that, which supposes ברא to describe only *formation.* *That it was not the opinion of the ancient Jews themselves,* he continues, *is evident from the book of Wisdom; the author of which expressly says, that the almighty hand of God created (the word is κτισασα) the world out of unfashioned matter.* Preface to translat. of Bible. p. 3. Justin Martyr uses much the same expression. But what does all this prove? It simply tends to shew, that God *formed* (for *that* is the proper sense of κτιζω, its occasional sense of *absolute creation* being purely Hellenistical) a beautiful and orderly world (such is the strict meaning of κοσμος) out of unformed matter, εξ αμορφου ὑλης. Still the question will occur, Whence came this αμορφος ὑλη, out of which the κοσμος was formed? Now it appears to me, as it did to those Jewish commentators whom I cite in the text, that God is said first to create *the very substance* (את) of the heavens and the earth; that is, the תהו of Moses or the αμορφος ὑλη of the book of Wisdom: and afterwards to reduce the originally chaotic substance into *form* or κοσμος. The two first verses of Genesis speak of the *creation* and *nature* of the materials: the rest of the Mosaic cosmogony describes the *formation* of the world and its various parts and inhabitants out of those materials. In addition to the opinions of the Jewish writers so contrary to that of Dr. Geddes, may be adduced the text in 2 Maccab. vii. 28. *I beseech thee, my son, look upon the heaven, and the earth, and all that is in them; and consider, that God made them (ουκ εξ οντων) not out of materials which had previously existed.* That is to say, he not only reduced them into shape, but created their very substance: they were not formed out of the already existing fragments of a former world; but the materials, out of which they were formed, were then created for that express purpose.

Agreeably to this just interpretation we may observe, that, when Moses wishes to describe *mere formation* as contradistinguished from *proper creation*, he uses a totally different term. This circumstance has not been left unnoticed by Maimonides. He remarks, that *there are four words which occur in describing the relation that the heavens bear towards God. These are the three verbs* Bara, Gnashah, *and* Cheneh; *and the substantive* El. *All these are comprehended under the verb* Gnashah; *as it is said,* He made them. *But the verb* Yatzar *no where occurs in this sense: because it signifies only* a making of form and figure or any other accident. *Thus it is said,* who forms the mountains; *that is,* who describes their outlines. *But, with regard to the Universe as comprehending heaven and earth, Moses makes use of the word* Bara, *which signifies* to call something into existence out of non-existence.[1]

Thus it appears, that, while the Gentiles had for the most part embraced the doctrine of *the eternity of matter* and of *a succession of similar worlds resolved into and produced out of that matter;* the prophet of the Hebrews was directed authoritatively to set aside such fantastical tenets, and to inculcate the belief in an all-wise Creator, who once existed in solitary independent majesty, and who produced matter itself out of nothing. And I am the more confirmed in my opinion, that such was the express purpose of the Mosaical cosmogony, by finding the Supreme Being, in another part of Scripture, setting himself in decided opposition to the Persian doctrine of the two eternal and independent principles: Goodness or Mind, of which light was the symbol; and Evil or Gross Matter, which was represented by darkness. In a prophetic charge addressed by name to the victorious Cyrus, the Almighty solemnly declares: *I am Jehovah, and none else; beside me there is no God: I will gird thee, though thou hast not known me; that they may know from the rising of the sun and from the west, that there is none beside me. I am Jehovah, and none else; forming light, and creating darkness; making peace, and creating evil. I Jehovah am the author of all these things.*[2] The belief or the disbelief of the eternity and independence of matter is in fact a point of no trifling importance: for the belief of it almost necessarily

---

[1] Mor. Nevoch. par. ii. c. 30.   [2] Isaiah xlv. 5, 6, 7.

156   THE ORIGIN OF PAGAN IDOLATRY.

leads to some modification or another of atheistic Materialism, which accordingly pervaded more or less every system of pagan theology.

XIII. The belief in an infinite series of similar worlds will account for a very curious local variety in the character of Cronus or Saturn; and will likewise throw some light on the conduct of Lot's daughters after the destruction of Sodom and Gomorrha.

In most of the traditions relative to Cronus, he is manifestly Noah, the head of the postdiluvian world: and, in several, he is plainly Adam, the head of the antediluvian world; who was supposed to have appeared again, at the commencement of a new system, in the character of Noah. Yet there was also a local Cronus, known only to the Phenicians and Canaanites, whom circumstantial evidence necessarily determines to be Abraham. Sanchoniatho tells us, that this person sacrificed his only son; and that, having adopted the rite of circumcision himself, he enjoined it to all his followers. To these particulars Porphyry adds, that the son whom he sacrificed was called *Jehud* or *the only begotten ;*[1] that he was born to Cronus from the nymph *Anobret ;*[2] that Cronus himself formerly reigned in Palestine; and that he was the person, whom the Phenicians denominated *Il* or *Ilus.*[3] Thus it cannot be reasonably doubted, that the character, here described under the appellation of *Cronus* or *Il,* is the patriarch Abraham. Yet this very name of *Il* is applied by the Phenicians to one, who is certainly Noah: and the name itself was clearly, I think, brought by them into Palestine, when they emigrated from the neighbourhood of Hindostan: for the Phenician *Il* is the masculine *Ila*[4] of the Hindoos and Indo-Scythæ; and *Ila* was a title of Menu or Buddha, who was preserved in an ark at the time of the deluge.[5] Such

---

[1] Heb. יחיד

[2] Heb. חן־עברית, *the gracious Hebrew woman.*

[3] Euseb. Præp. Evan. lib. i. c. 10. lib. iv. c. 16. The name stands at present *Israel* instead of *Il :* but it is generally allowed, that the true reading is the latter. Some transcriber of the work of Eusebius, meeting with Iλ, and struck with the manifest identity of this history and that of Abraham, fancied, that Iλ was a contraction of Iσραηλ, and that Porphyry or the Phenicians had by mistake substituted a name of Jacob for that of his grandfather Abraham. Hence he was led to corrupt the genuine reading Iλ, by writing a misdeemed contraction, as he supposed it ought to be expressed at full length.

[4] Pronounced *Il,* the final *a* being quiescent.

[5] *Il* seems to me to have been too hastily concluded to be the same word as *El* or *God.* It is not Hebrew, but Sanscrit: neither does it signify *God,* but *the World;* a title bestowed upon

being the case, the question is, how we are to account for the application of a title of the great father to Abraham: since the application of a title, already bestowed successively upon Adam and Noah, leads us to conclude; that they, who thus applied it, imagined Abraham to bear some such resemblance to Noah as Noah bore to Adam.

Now the prevailing doctrine of a succession of similar worlds will be found most completely and satisfactorily to explain this curious circumstance. It was well known to the ancient pagans, that, in the tenth generation from Adam, a preacher of righteousness arose; who, after having long fruitlessly warned a corrupt world to repent of their sins, was himself preserved in an ark together with his family, while the rest of mankind was swept away by the waters of a deluge. From this personage the new world commenced, with so many strong features of resemblance to him with whom the former world had begun, that the one was esteemed a reappearance of the other. Hence arose the notion; that, as the postdiluvian world was destined perfectly to resemble the antediluvian world; so there had been and would be a succession of similar worlds, in which the same persons would perpetually be manifested again and again to act and react the same parts. When this persuasion was fully impressed on the minds of men, since there were ten generations *between* the creation and the flood, they would naturally be impressed with strong apprehensions of another dissolution of the world, as they approached to the tenth generation *subsequent* to the deluge. Now precisely at this period, when a great corruption of manners a second time prevailed; in the tenth generation after the flood, reckoning from Shem and esteeming Noah the last person of the first Decad; Abraham was chosen out of an idolatrous nation, was honoured by a frequent intercourse with God, and by his whole conduct strongly testified against the wickedness of the times. Under these circumstances, the first impression on men's minds would obviously be, that the warning Ila or Menu, who was to usher in the destruction of one world and

---

the great father in reference to his supposed material character. Had Philo designed to express the Hebrew אל, he would not have written Ιλ but Ελ; as we may safely conclude from his expressing אלהים, which begins with the syllable אל, by Ελωειμ not by Ιλωειμ. For the Indo-Scythic origin of the Phenicians, so often strangely misdeemed the children of Canaan, vido infra book vi. c. 5. § V. 2.

Abraham

afterwards to become the patriarchal head of another, had now made his appearance. With such sentiments, the Phenicians and Canaanites, among whom he sojourned, would anxiously inquire, whether there were any other points of resemblance between the formidable stranger and each reappearing father of a world. To persons, who held the doctrine of Transmigration, and who viewed their chief hero-god in so many different points of paternal and filial and fraternal relationship, nothing would be more familiar than the identification of a father and a son. Inquiring then into the origin of Abraham, they would learn, that his father Terah, who stood in the tenth place of descent from Noah, was, like that patriarch and Adam, the parent of a triple offspring: and, when this characteristic mark of an Ila or a Menu was sufficiently ascertained, they would find no difficulty in blending Abraham with Terah, and in thus reckoning him both as one of a triad and as the parent of a triad; for such perpetually were the variations of a theory, which fundamentally acknowledged but one great father, which deemed his triplication of himself a mysterious delusion, and which esteemed him the same both generally and severally as all and each of his three emanations. While such speculations occupied their minds, they would be deeply struck by a most ominous change in the name of their visitor. They had been accustomed to designate the patriarchal head of each world by the appellation of *the great father;* justly esteeming him the common parent of the whole race both of hero-gods and of men, who were destined to preside and flourish during his appointed mundane period. In the midst then of their suspicions, that such might be the future character of the righteous sojourner, they would learn, that, by the special command of the God whom he served, he had assumed the lofty title of *Abraham* or *the father of a mighty multitude,* and that this name was emphatically imposed upon him as the future parent of many nations and as the sire of numerous potent kings. How they would interpret this prophecy, particularly when they learned that God had entered into a covenant upon the occasion with their visitor as he had heretofore done upon a well-remembered similar occasion with Noah, it is almost superfluous to intimate: they would doubtless view it as foretelling the destruction of the world and the repeopling of a future mundane system with the posterity of the new great father. At length an awful event occurred, which might well seem a confirmation of all their fears: and even, when the first alarm had subsided, according to the doctrine of smaller and partial floods as well as of larger and general ones, according also to the doctrine both of fiery, of aqueous, and of mixed fiery and aqueous, inundations; the destruction of Sodom and Gomorrha by fire from heaven, which occurred precisely in the tenth generation as the flood of Noah had previously done, and which was succeeded by a partial deluge that inundated the whole plain of Jordan and constituted the asphaltite lake, would be deemed, in addition to other circumstances, an abundantly sufficient reason for considering Abraham, to whom the impending catastrophe had been prophetically announced as the approaching dissolution of the antediluvian world had been announced to Noah, in the light of a new Il or Menu or Cronus.[1] This at least is certain, that, in point of matter of fact, the name of *Il* was bestowed upon Abraham by a people, who were of Scythic or Hindoo origin; and that this same appellation was also borne by Menu or Buddha. Hence, when the prevailing notions respecting transmigration and mundane succession are taken into the account, I know not any more satisfactory method of explaining so remarkable a circumstance.

The propriety of this mode of elucidating it appears to receive additional confirmation from the language and conduct of Lot's daughters. Having witnessed the destruction of Sodom and the other cities of the plain; observing from the higher ground the whole country deluged by a spacious lake; and finding (I apprehend) that the little town of Zoar was abandoned by its terrified inhabitants not very long after they had entered it, an example which they themselves together with their father speedily followed: from a supposition that the Zoarites, of whom they saw nothing more after leaving the town, had perished by the calamity which they sought to escape by flight; they were led, in the deep solitude of the mountain, to imagine, that there was not a man left upon the face of the earth by whom they might become mothers, save their miraculously-preserved parent.[2] Wishing therefore to repeople the now desolated world from their own family, which they believed to have alone

[1] See Asiat. Res. vol. v. p. 248, 289. vol. vi. p. 507—510.
[2] See their language in Gen. xix. 31, 32.

survived the new deluge, they were led to the commission of the crime of incest in despair of obtaining posterity by any other method.[1]

With respect to the ten generations from Shem to Abraham which succeeded the first ten generations from Adam to Noah, they could only have been known in the western part of the Asiatic continent: hence we find the Phenicians and Canaanites alone supposing Abraham to be a Cronus or Ilus. And, that they were well acquainted with and had duly remarked the place which he held in the postdiluvian genealogy, may be abundantly gathered from the language used by Berosus and Eupolemus. Each of these writers mentions a just person, who lived in the tenth age after the flood: and, both from this circumstance and from the actions which they attribute to him, Abraham alone can have been intended.[2]

[1] Calmet and Lyranus suppose, like myself, that Lot's daughters committed incest with a view to repeople the world, thinking it to have been destroyed: but the Bereshit Rabba (par. 23.) accounts for their crime on the ground of their wishing to become the parents, either more or less remote, of the Messiah. Dr. Allix rejects the first of these opinions, and adopts the second. In doing so, he appears to me to act injudiciously. I believe them both to be right, and I believe them moreover to be intimately connected with each other. I understand the whole history in the following manner. The tenth generation after the flood having now arrived, and having ushered in so terrible an event as the blasting and submersion of Sodom and the neighbouring cities, Lot's daughters believed the world to have been destroyed partly by fire and partly by water. They conceived their own family to have been alone preserved, as that of Noah had been preserved from the deluge. And they thence imagined, all the inhabitants of Zoar with whom they took refuge having disappeared, that their father was the only man remaining upon the face of the earth. Under these circumstances, they were induced to commit incest with him, partly to repeople the world, and partly from an apprehension that the promise of the Messiah could not otherwise be fulfilled. Their crime, in short, seems to have originated from a mixed and contradictory feeling of faith and want of faith. They believed in the promise: but they could not trust God with the accomplishment of it in his own way. See Allix's Reflect. on Script. par. 1. c. 15.

[2] Joseph. Ant. Jud. lib. i. c. 7. Euseb. Præp. Evan. lib. ix. c. 17.

As there is a succession of worlds, and thus of souls, material is eternal, as is equally, man. As man is eternal and nothing is eternal that is not divine, man is therefore divine. That Man is divine is not a doctrine derived merely from his own imagination, but from reasoned, experiential existence.

CHAPTER III.

Respecting the Materialism of the great god and goddess of the pagans.

Tнε doctrine of the eternity of matter necessarily produced a belief in its divinity : for, as eternity is a special attribute of deity, it is difficult to con- ceive, how that which is eternal can be less than god.   At the same time, while matter was allowed to be eternal, the pagans held, that an intelligent being successively appeared at the commencement of each world, that he was the demiurgic framer and moderator of that world, that he was himself properly eternal though assuming different human forms in each different world ; and that he was the fountain whence every soul emanated and into which every soul finally returned.[1]   The character of this intelligent being, who is peculiarly described as being the parent of three sons, or (as it is sometimes expressed) who is said to have mysteriously triplicated himself at the beginning of every mundane system ; who is likewise represented as sleeping or dying at the end of one world, and as awaking or reviving at

[1] Cicer. de divin. lib. i. c. 32, 49, 57.   Tuscul. Disp. lib. v. c. 13. Fragm. de consolat. De nat. deor. lib. i. c. 11.   Plut. de placit. philos. lib. iv. c. 7. lib. v. c. 20.   Diog. Laert. de vit. phil. lib. i. § 3. lib. viii. § 28.

the commencement of another; who is celebrated as reposing, during the space between each two worlds, on the surface of the ocean; and who is asserted to appear as the first man of every new world, from whom all the future inhabitants of that world are descended : such a character can leave no room to doubt, that the intelligent being who sustains it, though he may be decorated with the usurped honours and attributes of the Deity, is in reality no other than Adam fancifully deemed to have reappeared after the deluge in the person of Noah.

Since then the doctrine of an endless succession of worlds involved the belief in the eternity of that matter out of which they were formed, and since the doctrine of the endless reappearance of the great father at the beginning of each world similarly involved the belief in *his* proper eternity retrospective as well as prospective; the pagans, who impiously sought to thrust God out of his own creation and to invest a mere mortal with his honours and titles, found, that their system inevitably produced *two* eternal beings, neither of whom as such could be esteemed less than divine, though the one was intellectual and the other material. Here then a question arose, how these two eternals should be disposed of, and in what manner they ought respectively or jointly to be considered. Some were inclined to view them separately; and, by way of accounting for the origin of evil, imagined, that they existed in a state of everlasting warfare and dissention. The Intellectual Principle was light and goodness : the Material Principle was darkness and evil. These opposites were in their nature irreconcileable : and, each being eternal, their struggle knew no end, as it had known no beginning. Such a theory, which exhibited Mind and Matter at variance, though doubtless of high antiquity, was probably not so old, and certainly was not so general, as an opposite hypothesis which intimately united them together. Rude Matter and presiding Intellect each being allowed to be eternal, and it being found very difficult to form an idea of two distinct unconnected independent eternals, the two were combined into one, and a single compound being possessing two characters was thus produced as the grand object of idolatrous veneration.[1]

---

[1] Orig. cont. Cels. lib. v.

In this union, Mind was the Soul and Matter was the Body: and, as it was observed that man consisted of two parts intimately associated, the circumstance was analogically extended to the world at large.   The spirit of man for a season animated a body: and, when that body was worn out and its component particles were resolved into their original substance; the spirit occupied another tenement, and again at a stated interval quitted it for a new one.   In a similar manner, the intellectual great father for a season animated his body the world : and, when that body at each great catastrophe was resolved into the primeval crude matter out of which it had been framed, the soul soon formed to itself another body in a new world, which it again occupied and again quitted at the close of the next period. Hence we are told, that physiologists were accustomed to style the world *a great man*, and man *a small world:* arguing at the same time, that, although the world like man was in one respect mortal, yet in another it was immortal; for that nothing really perished within the whole compass of the living mundane frame, but that what seemed to perish only changed its appearance and was resolved into its original constituent elements.[1]   This Soul they supposed to permeate the whole Universe, uniting all the parts of it together, and pervading matter (such was the singular illustration of the Stoics) as honey does the honey-comb.[2]   Agreeably to this theory, they held, that the Soul of the World was present just as much in the vilest substances, as in those which are the most glorious and estimable; because it was diffused through all things, whether small or great, with equal intenseness.[3]   The two supposed component parts of the Universe being thus united, the whole World, consisting of a material body animated by a soul or spirit, was esteemed the only real god.[4]   The souls of men consequently were reckoned to be emanations from the great Soul, and were considered as fellows and members of the principal deity.[5]   In a similar manner, as the World was deemed the body of god, the Sun and the Stars were all supposed to be parts of

---

[1] Macrob. in somn. Scip. lib. ii. c. 12.
[2] Cudworth's Intell. Syst. b. i. c. 4. p. 503, 504.   Virg. Æneid. lib. vi. ver. 724—732.
[3] Ibid.
[4] Senec. Epist. 94.   Lactan. Instit. lib. vii. c. 3.   Cudw. Intell. Syst. p. 327, 331.
[5] Senec. Epist. 94.

him, and were considered in the light of intelligent and animated beings.[1] Pursuant to such a mode of speculation, the different parts of the Universe were sometimes said to be members of the chief deity, and sometimes, as in the theological phraseology of the Hindoos, they were styled his *varied forms.* The sum and substance therefore of the system was this : that, since god was all things and since all things were god, god ought to be worshipped in all things.[2]

The mystic union of Spirit and Matter was not however always conveyed under the idea of soul and body : it was just as frequently represented under the image of the conjugal alliance. In this case, the Earth or Matter was the wife ; and the Soul, which was often identified with heaven or the subtle ether, was the husband. By their conjunction all things were produced : yet so inseparable was their union deemed, that the two blended together formed but one great hermaphroditic deity ; from whom, both as father and mother, sprang every varied part of the Universe. The Pythagoreans were fond of expressing such notions by numbers, which were borrowed in different combinations from those, of which the two successive primeval families were composed, or from which they proceeded. Thus they tell us, that the animating Mind is a monad, which enlarges itself into the two mystic numbers eight and seven, while itself is at once male and female.[3] Similar to this is the Chinese opinion, that one produces two, that two produce three, and that three produce all things.[4] and nearly allied to it is the speculation of the Hindoos, that Siva and his consort Parvati or Isi are equally manifested in eight forms, while the junction of the two composes one hermaphroditic deity called *Ardha-nari*, from whom originate all things.[5] In the material system therefore, the Intelligent Being, who was thought to appear at the commencement of every world, was sometimes esteemed the

[1] August. de civ. Dei. lib. iv. c. 11.   Macrob. in somn. Scip. lib. i. c. 14.   Cudw. Intell. Syst. p. 514.

[2] Cudw. Intell. Syst. b. i. c. 4. p. 308, 342, 343, 346, 409, 363, 386, 462, 463, 514.

[3] Macrob. in somn. Scip. lib. i. c. 6. Tim. Loc. de anim. mund. p. 545. Virg. Georg. lib. ii. ver. 325.

[4] Du Halde's Hist. of Chin. vol. iii. p. 30.   Le Compte's Journ. through Chin. p. 318.

[5] Moor's Hind. Panth. p. 12, 105, 28.   Asiat. Res. vol. i. p. 253.

animating Soul and sometimes the husband of the Universe, while the Universe on the other hand was sometimes reckoned the body and sometimes the wife of the Intelligent Being: and, as the one theory supposed an union as perfect as that of the soul and body in one man, so the other produced a similar union by blending together the husband and wife into one hermaphrodite.

I. This Intelligent Being, who was indifferently esteemed the Soul and *The Pantheistic Great Father* the husband of the World, was the great father or principal Demon-god of the Gentiles; while his body or consort, the Earth, was their primeval great mother or chief goddess. The two were allowed to be the most ancient of their deities, and the first of the Cabiric gods: and they were ever venerated conjointly in different countries under the names of *Coelus* and *Terra, Osiris* and *Isis, Taautes* and *Astarte, Saturn* and *Ops, Woden* and *Frea,* or *Isam* and *Isi.*[1] But the great father, as manifestly appears from the particulars related of him, was Adam reappearing in Noah: and the great mother was the Earth melting into the character of that smaller world the Ark. These two being blended into one, whatever is said of the former is equally said of the latter: and, as the great god was also a goddess, and as the great goddess was also a god; each of them, by whatever name they may be distinguished, is alike pronounced to be one and all things. Such is the character of Janus, Jupiter, Pan, and every other chief god: they are declared to be each the same person, and in their human capacity they are each plainly Noah succeeding to the demiurgic honours of Adam; yet are they each nevertheless declared to be the whole world, composed of an intelligent soul and a material body. Such also is the character of Isis, Isi, Venus, and the other kindred goddesses: they are each declared to be one person, and properly they are the Earth and the Ark viewed conjointly; yet, from their hermaphroditic union with the great father, they are each like him declared to be the Universe. What I am at present concerned with is their material character.

1. Macrobius informs us, that, although Janus was astronomically the *JANUS PANTHEUS*

---

[1] Varr. de ling. Latin. lib. iv. p. 17. Mallet's North. Ant. vol. i. c. 6. p. 91, 92. Asiat. Res. vol. i. p. 253.

Sun, yet he was likewise venerated as the World or Heaven; and he adds, that he was sometimes represented with four faces in allusion to the four quarters of the Universe.[1] This idea is drawn out at considerable length by Ovid. According to that poet, Janus was the primitive Chaos, in whose substance the four elements were mingled together. All things, which we behold, whether the heaven, the sea, the air, or the earth, are shut and opened at his discretion. To him the custody of the vast world is intrusted, and the seasons revolve under his superintendance.[2]

ZEUS PANTHEUS

2. The character of Janus perfectly identifies itself with that of Zeus or Jupiter. Each was alike the World animated by its supposed Intelligent Soul. Accordingly, while Austin observes that Jupiter was the Mind or Soul of the Universe; he remarks, that it was contradictory to divide him and Janus into two gods, since each was equally the World.[3] The materialism of Jupiter is set forth in a very elaborate manner by the Orphic poet. He speaks of him as being an hermaphrodite, at once the father and the mother of all things. The subtle ether he ascribes to him as a soul: and, while he represents the Universe as being engendered in his womb, he makes the different parts of it serve as members to the mighty pantheus.[4] When viewed separately from his consort or body, he was the Mind of the World identified with Heaven or Ether: when viewed conjointly with it, he was the hermaphroditic Universe consisting of Matter animated by Spirit.[5]

DIONUSUS PANTHEUS

3. Orpheus informs us, that Zeus was the same as Pluto or Dionusus:[6] and accordingly we find, that so decidedly were the physiologists of opinion that Dionusus was the Soul of the World that they even supposed his name to denote *the soul of Jupiter.*[7] With the propriety of this etymology I am

---

[1] Macrob. Saturn. lib. i. c. 9. p. 158.

[2] Ovid. Fast. lib. i. ver. 103—160.

[3] Aug. de civ. Dei. lib. iv. c. 11. lib. vii. c. 10.

[4] Orph. Fragm. p. 365, 366. edit. Gesner.

[5] Macrob. in somn. Scip. lib. i. c. 17. p. 60.

[6] Orph. Fragm. apud Macrob. Saturn. lib. i. c. 18. p. 202.

[7] Physici Διονυσον, Διος Νουν, quasi solem, mundi mentem esse dixerunt. Mundus autem vocatur cœlum, quod appellant Jovem. Macrob. Saturn. lib. i. c. 18. p. 201.

no way concerned : it is enough for my purpose, that it clearly shews the light in which Dionusus was viewed by the materialists.

4. A similar derivation, doubtless under the influence of the same opinion, is given by Apollophanes of the name of *Saturn*. He supposes it to mean *the Mind that created or planted all things*.[1] Saturn therefore was the Soul of the World · and, agreeably to the doctrine of a succession of mundane systems formed by the great father out of his own material body, he is celebrated by the Orphic poet as destroying and reproducing all things, as the general parent of an age or (as the Hindoos would speak) a Manwantara, and as intimately dwelling in every part of the Universe.[2]

5. The same great father was sometimes venerated under the name of *Pan*. Thus Herodotus tells us, that Pan was one of the eight chief gods of Egypt and even the most ancient of those gods ; and we are informed by Porphyry, that the Egyptians were wont to represent their deities sailing together in a ship :[3] hence there can be little doubt respecting the human character of this divinity. Yet, according to the Orphic poet, Pan is the Universe. Heaven, and earth, and sea, and fire, are all equally his members : and by his pipe the harmony of the whole world is moderated.[4]

6. Another title of the pantheistic divinity was *Cupid* or *Eros*. In familiar poetry, the god of love is represented as no better than a mischievous urchin armed with a bow and arrows : yet we find him also described, as the first and oldest of all the deities, and as produced immediately out of the bosom of chaos. Accordingly, as he identifies himself in this capacity with Janus and Saturn; so, like them, he is declared to be the whole world, which unites in itself the opposite qualities of the most florid youth and the most remote antiquity.[5]

7. Much the same character was sustained by Osiris, and Hammon, and Phtha or Vulcan. Each was esteemed the Soul of the World : and the latter peculiarly bore that title in his quality of the great artizan or plastic

SATURN PANTHEUS

PAN PANTHEUS

CUPID PANTHEUS

OSIRIS HAMMON PHTHA VULCAN...

---

[1] Satorem Νουν, quasi divinum sensum creantem omnia. Fulgen. Mythol. lib. i. c. 2.
[2] Orph. Hymn. xii.
[3] Herod. Hist. lib. ii. c. 145.   Porph. de antr. nymph. p. 256.
[4] Orph. Hymn. x. Phorn. de nat. deor. c. 27.
[5] Phornut. de nat. deor. c. 25.

demiurge.[1] He was really the framer of the Microcosm or the Ark : but, according to the speculations of the materialists, he was likewise thought to be the reproducer of the Megacosm at the commencement of every new system. I think it manifest, that he is the grand artificer Twashta of Hindoo mythology, who is declared to have been peculiarly venerated in the west. Hence he is certainly the great father Tuisto of the Goths or Scythians.

8. If we pass to Hindostan, we shall still find a similar propensity to Materialism All the gods of that country resolve themselves into three material deities, and those three finally terminate in one whose essence comprehends both them and the Universe.[2] In the Bhagavat, the divine spirit is exhibited to us as the animating Soul of the whole World : and Crishna, one of the incarnations of Vishnou, is described in the same poem as not a little surprizing his foster-mother, by opening his mouth, and displaying to her within the cavity of it the boundless Universe in all its plenitude of magnificence.[3] Vishnou himself, agreeably to his character of Crishna, is at once the Sun, the Earth, Air, and Water :[4] and Siva is said to have been manifested in eight material forms; Earth, Water, Fire, Air, Ether, the Sun, the Moon, and the Person who performs a sacrifice or (as Calidasa enumerates them) Sacrifice itself.[5] In short, the great father of Hindoo mythology, who multiplies himself into three deities, is evidently the same as the western Jupiter, when considered as the all-pervading Soul of the World diffused through and influencing every particle of his material body. In the well-known speech, which Lucan puts into the mouth of Cato concerning the Ammonian oracle, *Jupiter is, wherever we look, wherever we move:* and, in the estimation of the Vaishnavas, who ascribe that preëminence to the preserving power which the Saivas give to the destroying power, their favourite god Vishnou is the principle of Mind, in union and separation, existing every where always.[6]

[1] Cudw. Intell. Syst. b. i. c. 4. p. 489, 490.   Orph. Hymn. lxv.
[2] Moor's Hind. Panth. p. 7, 13.   [3] Asiat. Res. vol. i. p. 267.
[4] Moor's Hind. Panth. p. 16.
[5] Moor's Hind. Panth. p. 12.   Asiat. Res. vol. i. p. 253.
[6] Asiat. Res. vol. i. p. 247, 245.

II. Exactly the same character is assigned to the great mother under whatever name she may be venerated. According to the material system indeed, the great father is properly the Soul of the World or the masculine principle, while the great mother is the body or the female principle : but, the two being intimately united in the person of one hermaphrodite, whatever is said of the one is also said of the other. Thus the great father and the great mother are each indifferently celebrated as Matter animated by Mind : or, as the Hindoos express the idea, the Sacti or consort of each god represents the active power of her lord and displays in her own person every attribute of her husband ; while the two united, Siva for instance and Parvati, form that compound deity partaking of both sexes whom they call *Ardha-Nari*.

1. Agreeably to this mystic intercommunion, Isi or Parvati is no less Universal Nature than her consort Siva or Isa : and, as the three Sactis of the three principal gods all blend together into one great goddess of whom they are allowed to be no more than three varied forms, the sea-born Lacshmi is venerated as the Earth, as the Mother of the World, and as Maya or the Universal Mother ; while Vach or Saraswati is celebrated as the Supreme Universal Soul, in whom the elements were produced and in whom the Universe was framed.[1]

ISI, PARVATI, PANTHES

2. The triplicated Isi is certainly the Isis of ancient Egypt; and, accordingly, we find the character of the latter precisely the same as that of the former.[2] Plutarch has preserved an inscription relative to Isis, which he copied from her temple at Sais, and which describes her as being the Universal Frame of Nature. The goddess is represented as saying of herself, *I am all, that hath been, and is, and shall be ; and my veil no mortal hath ever removed.*[3]

ISIS, PANTHEA

3. Isis was the same as Neith or Minerva :[4] whence the inscription at Sais was likewise applied to that goddess. Athenagoras informs us, that

NEITH, ATENA MINERVA

---

[1] Asiat. Res. vol. i. p. 223, 253, 254. vol. vii. p. 303. vol. viii. p. 402. Moor's Hind. Panth. p. 21, 22, 33, 119, 134, 136, 111, 132.

[2] Athenag. Legat. § 19.

[3] Asiat. Res. vol. i. p. 253. Cudw. Intell. Syst. b. i. c. 4. p. 409.

[4] Cudw. Intell. Syst. b. i. c. 4. p. 342.

this Neith or the Athena of the Greeks was supposed to be Wisdom passing and diffusing itself through all things.' Hence it is manifest, that she was thought to be the Soul of the World; for such is precisely the character sustained by that mythological personage.

VENUS

4. Ovid gives a similar character of Venus. He represents her as moderating the whole world; as giving laws both to heaven, earth, and ocean; as the common parent both of gods and men; and as the productive cause both of corn and trees.' She is celebrated in the same manner by Lucretius, who ascribes to her that identical attribute of universality which the Hindoos give to their goddess Isi or Devi.'

It is superfluous to say any thing more on this part of the subject; because, what one goddess is, the others are. The identity of all the heathen gods on the one hand, and of all the heathen goddesses on the other, is so repeatedly asserted by the ancient authors, and is indeed so manifest in itself, that, the Materialism of Isis or Venus or Minerva being established, the materialism of the rest must follow as a thing of course.'

III. From the preceding remarks I think it evident, that the imaginary Soul of the World is the same being as that great universal father both of gods and men, whom the Gentiles adored under so many different names: for Janus, Jupiter, Cronus, Dionusus, Osiris, and Brahm, are all undoubtedly the great father; and, at the same time, they are all equally described as being the pervading Soul of the World. Hence it follows, that, whatever the great father is, that also the Soul of the World must be. But the great father, as clearly appears from his legendary history, is Noah considered as a revival of Adam at the commencement of a new world. Therefore the pretended Soul of the World, however the character may be disguised by the refinements of the material system, is fundamentally no other than Adam reappearing in the person of Noah.

1. The opinions entertained of this Soul exactly accord with the conclusion, to which we have been brought.

The notions entertained of it is exactly quadrate with this opinion

---

' Cudw. Intell. Syst. b. i. c. 4. p. 486.   Athenag. Legat. § 19.
' Ovid. Fast. lib. iv. ver. 90—96.   ' Lucret. de rer. nat. lib. i. ver. 1—21.
' See this identity fully established below, book iv. c. 1. and book v. c. 1.

II   THE SOUL OF THE WORLD IS REALLY THE GREAT FATHER   OR
CHIEF HERO - GOD

In every part of the globe there was an idea, that the great father had triplicated himself, or (as the opinion was sometimes literally expressed) that he was the parent of three sons—Precisely in the same manner, the demiurgic Mind or Soul, which Proclus rightly identifies with the creative hermaphrodite Jupiter of Orpheus and Plato, is said by Amelius to have triplicated itself; so that this one Mind became three Minds or three Kings: and these three Minds or demiurgic principles, as Proclus subjoins, are the same as the Platonic three kings, and as the Orphic triad of Phanes and Uranus and Cronus. [1]

So again: there was a common tradition, that one of the three younger gods or emanations had dethroned his father and had usurped his empire; a fable, when the history of the whole triad is considered, which evidently appears to have arisen from the circumstance of the retired life of Noah and of the first universal empire having arisen in the line of Ham—A similar idea prevailed respecting the demiurgic Mind: the elder or paternal Mind, having accomplished the work of creation which was supposed to take place after every mundane dissolution, is said to have resigned his empire to a second Mind whom men were accustomed to venerate as the first. [2] This is nothing more, than the story of Jupiter dethroning Saturn and becoming the chief of the gods, recited in the cabalistic language of Materialism.

Again: we perpetually meet with a legend of the great father being born out of an egg; and we no less frequently may observe fables respecting his being exposed in an ark upon the surface of the ocean, or of his being preserved in a ship during the period of an universal deluge: so that the same person is indifferently said to have been produced out of an ark, and out of an egg which had been tossed about by the fury of the elements—In like manner, the three Orphic principles, which are declared by Proclus and Amelius to be the very same as the three demiurgic Minds of the Platonists, although they are esteemed the creators of the mundane system which they animate as the soul does the body, are yet themselves said to have been first manifested in the famous mythological egg. [3] The creative Soul of the World

[1] Cudw. Intell. Syst. b. i. c. 4. p. 305, 306.
[2] Orac. Magic. p. 22. Opsop.
[3] Orph. Fragment. p. 410. Gesner.

therefore, which triplicates itself at the renovation of the mundane system, is produced out of an egg which floated during the intermediate period between two worlds on the surface of the ocean, notwithstanding it is described as being the productive cause of all things.

How we are to understand the fable of this birth of Mind from an egg, we are sufficiently taught, not only by the indiscriminate birth of the great father from an egg and from a ship, but likewise by every thing which is said respecting it. Thus Eusebius tells us, that Mind is the same as Prometheus;[1] and Syncellus makes an exactly similar assertion:[2] but Prometheus, according to Diodorus, lived at the time of a flood which inundated the land of Egypt, a mere local appropriation of the general deluge;[3] and, according to Eschylus, he was the builder of the first ship that ever swam the ocean.[4] Thus also Proclus positively declares, that Mind is the same as Saturn, while the greatest Mind is Jupiter:[5] but the whole history of Saturn demonstrates him to be primarily Adam, and secondarily Noah; while Jupiter, considered as a son of Saturn, is evidently Ham or (as the Egyptians called him) Hammon, that second Mind who acquired the empire of the elder Mind. The three sons of Cronus were the celebrated royal triad of Minds, to whose sceptre the three divisions of the world were committed: hence we are told, that those three gods all sprang from one Mind who preceded them.[6]

Respecting the Sanscrit name Menu.

2. This opinion respecting the Soul of the World is confirmed in a very curious manner by the etymology of the name of the Indian Menu. Sir William Jones remarks, that, like *Menes*, *Mens*, and *Mind*, it is clearly derived from the Sanscrit root *Men* which signifies *to understand;* whence, as all the Pundits agree, it denotes, particularly in the doctrines of the Veda, *Intelligent:*[7] and he elsewhere observes, that perhaps all the fourteen Menus are reducible to one; who was called *Nuh* by the Arabs and probably by the Hebrews, though we have disguised the word by pronouncing it *Noah.*[8] Such being the case, it seems evident, that *Menu* is no other than the proper name *Nuh* in composition with *Men:* consequently, *Menu* or *Men-Nuh* will

[1] Euseb. Hist. Syn. p. 374.   [2] Syncell. Chronog. p. 149.
[3] Diod. Bibl. lib. i. p. 16.   [4] Prom. Vinct. ver. 471, 472.
[5] Proc. in Plat. Theog. l. v. c. 5. p. 256.   [6] Proc. in Plat. Tim. lib. ii. p. 94.
[7] Pref. to Inst. of Menu. p. x.   [8] Asiat. Res. vol. i. p. 239.

signify *the Intelligent Nuh* or *Nuh the Mind.* It appears then, that Menu, who is manifested with his three sons at the commencement of every world, and who with them is allowed to be an incarnation of the Trimurti or triplicated great father, is the Mind or Soul, which is feigned to renovate the mundane system after each dissolution and to animate it after it has been renewed. But Menu is indisputably Noah considered as a revival of Adam. Therefore the Mind or Soul of the Universe is the great primeval father: who, with his three sons (the three younger Minds of the Platonists, and the three intelligent monads or kings of the Orphic theology), is transmigratively revealed at the commencement of every world; who is said to be the common parent both of gods and men; and who is that principal hero-deity of the Gentiles, into whose essence all things are resolved at the close, and from whose essence all things are reproduced at the beginning, of each successive mundane period.

3. A somewhat similar observation may be made on the name, which the Greeks employed to designate the all-pervading Mind or Intellect, that was thought to animate and govern the world as the human soul does the body. In point of matter of fact, this Mind was certainly the great father, or Noah viewed as a reappearance of Adam. The Adamitical Noah therefore being the fabled Mind of the World, the Greeks borrowed the proper name of that patriarch, and employed it to describe Mind or Intellect. As Noah was the Mind of the World, *Noös,* and contractedly *Nous* or *Nus,* was made to signify *Mind;* not only *the Mind of the World,* but thence also *Mind generally.* Hence we are told, that Cronus, who in his human capacity is clearly the Adamitical Noah, was the primordial Noös or Nous; and that from this primordial Noös emanated the royal triad of the younger Noës: in other words, the elder Noös was the father of three sons, among whom the world was supposed to have been once divided.

4. I fully agree with Mr. Bryant, that the *name* of the Platonic Noös has been borrowed from that of the patriarch; because, since the *persons* are manifestly the same, so singular a coincidence of sound can scarcely be deemed altogether casual: but he seems to me to have been mistaken, in charging the Greeks with a complete misprision of terms, and in asserting

[margin note:] Respecting the equivalent Greek name Nous.

[margin note:] The name Nous was originally borrowed from the proper name of Noah. It was applied to the Soul of the world because the great father was deemed that Soul

that they everlastingly rang changes upon *Mind* and *Intellect* and *Intelligent*, when all the while the Hellenic words which convey these ideas had really no relation whatsoever to them, but were mere corrupted variations of the name of Noah.' The true state of the case I believe to be as I have already drawn it out. It was not, that the Platonists did *not* hold the doctrine of a Soul of the World; nor was it, that the doctrine *originated* from a mere casual resemblance of the word *Noös* to the name *Noah:* such a doctrine prevailed throughout the whole of the east, and was no way peculiar to the philosophers of Greece. But the real state of the circumstance was this: the Greeks embraced the doctrine of a Mind of the World; and they learned that that Mind was a person, who was the productive demiurge of the Universe, who triplicated himself at every mundane renovation, and whose name was variously pronounced *Noös*, *Noah*, *Nous*, *Nus*, or *Nuh*. Such therefore being the appellation of this fabled Mind, the name, though truly a proper name of an altogether different signification, was employed as a common name to designate *Mind* or *Intellect itself*.

But it is of little moment to the main question, whether this etymological speculation be admitted or rejected. In point of matter of fact, whether the, *names* be the same or not the same, the *person*, whom the Platonists called *the Noös* or *divine Mind*, is the *person*, whom Moses calls *Noah;* and the persons whom they celebrated as the three younger royal Noës, are the three sons of Noah considered as a reappearance of Adam.

' See Brysut's Anal. vol. ii. p. 272—282.

CHAPTER IV.

Respecting the mundane and arkite egg.

I. THE ancient pagans in almost every part of the globe were wont to symbolize the World by an egg. Hence this hieroglyphic is introduced into the cosmogonies of nearly all nations: and few are the persons, even those who have not made mythology their peculiar study, to whom the mundane egg is not perfectly familiar. The symbol was employed to represent not only the Earth, but likewise the Universe in its largest extent: though I am inclined to believe, that in its primary application the Earth alone was intended. It is remarkable, that the word, used by Moses to describe the motion of the Spirit of God on the surface of the chaotic waters, properly denotes the tremulous fluttering of a bird over the nest in which she has deposited her eggs. This sacred philosophy seems to have been not unknown to Noah, as we may collect from the very general practice among his descendants of employing an egg to represent the Earth: for such a symbol would naturally spring out of such a theory. If the action of the Creator upon Chaos was compared to the incubation of a bird; the globe of the Earth, which the ancients supposed to float like a vast ship in the chaotic fluid, would obviously be compared to an egg. The circular form of the Earth, and its internal structure, respecting which the theory of the pagans very nearly agreed with what is

The egg was a symbol of the World.

revealed to us in Scripture, would tend the more completely to establish the general use of this symbol. There seems reason to believe, that the globe which we inhabit consists of a shell inclosing what is usually called the great abyss of waters: perhaps also, as some have plausibly conjectured, there may be a solid nucleus in the centre, formed of those fragments of the shell which the waters of the deluge would carry with them when they retired into the mighty receptacle. In either of these cases no hieroglyphic could have been more appositely chosen than an egg. Its shell would represent the shell of the Earth; and its liquid contents, the centrical abyss: or, if we adopt the hypothesis of a nucleus, the liquid white would represent the waters of the abyss, and the moist though more solid yolk, the ball of earthy matter at the centre. That some such idea as this was entertained, may be gathered from the Egyptian fable of Typhon breaking the mundane egg during his contest with Osiris. Typhon, according to Plutarch, was a personification of the ocean; and he is said to have violently inclosed Osiris within an ark, and then to have set him afloat. Such a fable sufficiently explains itself: but, if Typhon be the ocean, which compelled the great father to enter into an ark, then his bursting of the mundane egg and his causing it to discharge its contents must denote, I apprehend, the bursting forth of the diluvian waters from the central abyss.

II. But there was another world, which the hieroglyphical egg was employed to represent, as well as the Earth or the Universe. At the period of the deluge, the rudiments of the new world were all inclosed together within the Ark; which floated on the surface of the ocean, in the same manner as the globe of the Earth was thought to have floated in the waters of chaos. Hence the Ark was esteemed a microcosm or little world: and hence arose a complete intercommunion of symbols between the Ark and the Earth. The egg, accordingly, being made a symbol of the Earth, was also made a symbol of the Ark: and we find it so running into other common symbols and likewise so blended with the literal Ark, that it is almost impossible not to conclude that the hieroglyphic has been transferred from the greater world to the smaller world. By way of establishing the position, some instances of this traduction shall now be noticed.

1. The character of Phanes or Dionusus is such, as evidently marks him,

..from the character of Phanes or Dionusus..

in his human capacity, to be the patriarch Noah. He was the patron of agriculture, and the first planter of the vine. He was exposed in an ark on the surface of the ocean: and he was thought to have died for a season during the flood of Deucalion, and afterwards to have returned to life; whence, we are told, originated the fable of his double birth. Yet this very personage, while he is celebrated by the Orphic poet as the first-born, as remarkable for his two-fold nature, as having once hidden himself, and as the general parent both of gods and men, is declared to have been tossed about at the mercy of the elements and to have been produced from an egg. [1] When these different matters are put together, I see not what the egg, out of which Dionusus or Noah was born, can possibly mean except the Ark.

2. From the description which the Orphic poet gives of the first-born Phanes exulting with his golden pinions, it is manifest, that he is the same person as the primeval Love or Cupid celebrated by Aristophanes. Blend- *From the character of the primeval Cupid...* ing together, agreeably to the doctrine of a succession of similar worlds, the original creation and the reproduction of the earth after the deluge, he teaches us, that *Chaos, and Night, and black Erebus, and wide Tartarus, first existed. At that time there was neither earth, air, nor heaven. But, in the bosom of Erebus, black-winged Night produced an aërial egg; from which in due season was born beautiful Love, decked with golden wings. Out of dark Chaos, in the midst of wide-spreading Tartarus, he begot our race, and called us forth into light.* [2] If then, in this legend, Cupid be the same as Phanes; the egg, out of which he is born, must certainly be the Ark, though it has likewise a reference to the Earth at the epoch of the creation: and, in a similar manner, his begetting our race and his calling us forth into light will relate to his being the general father of mankind and to that emerging from the gloom of the Ark into the light of day, which was so much celebrated in the ancient Mysteries.

Agreeably to such a conclusion, the Maneros or Cupid of the Egyptians may be shewn to be no other than Osiris, who was compelled by the diluvian Typhon to enter into an ark: the Cupid of the Persians still appears seated *Cupid is Osiris*

[1] Orph. Hymn. v.   [2] Aristoph. Aves. ver. 694.

on the rainbow in the front of one of the rock temples of Mithras : the Cupid
of Greece and Rome is represented as a maritime deity, either floating on the
ocean in a shell, or riding on the back of a fish, or gliding over the waters on
a pitcher or cup, the navicular Argha of the Hindoos, while he expands his
sail to the wind: and the Cama or Cupid of Hindostan is literally said, like
the classical Dionusus, to have been inclosed in an ark and to have been cast
into the sea.   These fables have all evidently a similar allusion: and, so far
as I can judge, the egg, out of which Cupid or Dionusus was born, must be
the same as the ark within which that god was confined.

*... Venus or
Derceto ...*

3. As Cupid is indifferently said to have been produced from an egg at a
time when the whole world was in disorder and from the womb of the maritime goddess Venus, the egg and the womb of that goddess must denote the
same thing.

Accordingly we shall find, that, on the one hand, Venus is immediately
connected with the symbolical egg; and, on the other hand, that she is identified with Derceto and Isis, and is declared to be that general receptacle out
of which all the hero-gods were produced.   Now there can be little doubt,
in what sense we are to understand this expression, when we are told, that
the peculiar symbol of Isis was a ship; and when we learn, that the form
assumed at the period of the deluge by the Indian Isi or Bhavani, who is
clearly the same as the Egyptian Isis, was the ship Argha, in which her consort Siva floated securely on the surface of the ocean.   Venus therefore, or
the great mother, the parent of Cupid from whom all mankind descended,
must be the Ark: consequently, the egg, with which she is connected, must
be the Ark also.   Aristophanes, as we have just seen, informs us, that the
egg, out of which Love was born, was produced by Night in the bosom of
Erebus.   But the goddess Night, as we learn from the Orphic poet, was the
very same person as Cupris or Venus; and he celebrates her, as the parent
of the Universe, and as the general mother both of the hero-gods and of men. [1]
The egg therefore produced by Night was produced by Venus: but Venus
and the egg meant the same thing; even that vast floating machine, which
was esteemed an epitomè of the world, and from which was born that deity
who is also literally said to have been set afloat in an ark.

[1] Orph. Hymn. ii.

Sometimes the order of production was inverted; and, instead of the egg being produced by Night or Venus, Venus herself was fabled to have been produced from the egg.   There is a remarkable legend of this sort, which ascribes Venus and her egg to the age of Typhon and Osiris, in other words, to the age in which Noah was compelled by the deluge to enter into the Ark. Hyginus tells us, that an egg of an immense size was reported to have fallen from heaven into the river Euphrates.   While it floated in the sacred stream, doves perched upon its exterior.   Soon however it was rolled out to land by fishes: and at length it produced that Venus, who was afterwards called *the Syrian Goddess.*[1]   Ampelius relates the same story; but with greater numerical accuracy states, that only a *single* dove perched upon the egg as it floated in the Euphrates, that the egg itself was produced by a fish, and that in its turn it produced a goddess kind and merciful to mortals.[2]   The fish, that produced the egg, was Venus: for here again, though the egg and Venus are really the same thing (unless we choose to consider the egg as the Ark, and Venus as the genius of the Ark), with a confusion not uncommon in ancient mythology, the goddess appears at once the producer and the produced.   This is manifest from the legend, which connects the present fable with the age of Typhon or the deluge.   When the rage of Typhon caused Osiris to be inclosed within an ark, and compelled all the hero-deities to betake themselves to a precipitate flight; Venus is said to have assumed the form of a fish and to have plunged into the waters of Babylonia, that is to say, into the river Euphrates, that she might escape the fury of the destructive monster.[3]   Venus therefore was the sacred fish of the Babylonians, and the same as the fish-goddess Derceto of Palestine: hence, from the exact coincidence of locality and person, we may conclude that the fish Venus was the fish which produced the egg that floated in the river Euphrates. But the period, to which this egg is to be ascribed, is that of Typhon or the deluge; and the circumstance of a dove perching on its exterior leaves but little room to doubt, that we are to understand by it the smaller world or the Ark.   The Euphrates, in which it is said to have floated, was the sacred

---

[1] Hyg. Fab. 197.

[2] Ampel. in lib. ad Macrin. Beyer's Addit. in Seld. de diis Syr. p. 303.

[3] Manil. Astron. lib. iv. ver. 572.   Ovid. Fast. lib. ii. ver. 461.

symbolical river of the Babylonians: and, like the Nile which the Egyptians designated by the name of *the ocean* and on the waters of which Osiris was launched in his ark, and like the Ganges which is feigned to support the ship of the infernal Menu or Buddha, it represented the deluge.

... Oan or Dagon...

4. As the great father and the great mother were worshipped in conjunction and represented by kindred hieroglyphics, the fish-goddess Derceto is evidently the mate of the fish-god Dagon: and Dagon himself is clearly the same character as the fish-god Oan of the Babylonians, who was similarly the mate of their goddess Venus or Mylitta. The Babylonians held a succession of four of these Oans, who at different times emerged from the Erythrèan sea, and instructed mankind in the arts of civilized life. But, like the Menus of Hindostan, they may all be reduced to two; the first of whom is Adam, and the second Noah. The last of them was the most famous, and he is plainly the great diluvian patriarch; for we may pronounce him to be that Oan, who, according to Helladius, was represented by many writers as a just man that lived at the renewal of time. Such a character only answers to that of Noah: yet this just Oan, in whose days time was renewed, is said to have been born out of the primeval egg.[1] Consequently, the egg, in *his* case, must mean the Ark: and, since he was the allegorical consort of Venus or Derceto, it must be immediately connected with that, which was said once to float, surmounted with the propitious dove, on the waters of the Euphrates.

... Vishnu, Brahma, Siva...

5. Oan or Dagon is the Vishnou of Hindostan in the fish-Avatar, and the Buddha of Cashgar in his character of the sovereign prince in the belly of the fish: Vishnou and Buddha indeed are fundamentally the same, for the one is allowed to be an incarnation of the other. But the fish-Avatar of Vishnou was manifested at the time of the deluge: and Buddha or Menu is literally said to have been preserved in an ark, of which a large sea-fish was one of the most obvious symbols. Here therefore we are again referred to the period of the flood: and here again we shall find the sacred egg introduced in such a manner as evidently to shew its close connection with the Ark.

It is related in the Scanda-Purana, that, when the whole earth was covered with water, and while Vishnou slept extended on the bosom of Devi or the great mother, a lotos sprang from his navel, and its ascending flower soon

[1] Hellad. apud Phot. Bibl. p. 1594.

reached the surface of the flood. From that flower Brahma was produced; who, looking round the vast expanse of water on which he floated without perceiving any creature, claimed to be the first-born. His claim however was contested both by Vishnou and Siva: and the priority of the last (whence I presume the fable was thus modified by one of the Saivite sect) was finally acknowledged by both the other gods.[1] In the delineation of this story Vishnou is represented, not sleeping upon the bosom of Devi at the bottom of the ocean, but reposing with his consort Lachsmi at his feet on the great serpent Ananta, the folds of which, as it floats on the surface of the deluge, are coiled up into the exact form of a boat, while its numerous heads serve as a canopy to the head of Vishnou.[2]

The import of the legend is in both cases much the same: for Devi and the serpent thus coiled up mean each the Ark. This is manifest from the forms, which Devi or Parvati (for *Devi* or *the goddess* is only an emphatic title of Parvati) is said to have assumed at the time of the flood: she first became the ship Argha, and thus bore her consort Mahadeva in safety over the waves; afterwards, while the waters were retiring she flew away in the shape of a dove. Hence it appears, that the birth of Brahma took place at the epoch of the flood; or, as the Hindoos are wont to express themselves, while the great power slept on the surface of the all-prevailing ocean during the period which intervenes between two succeeding worlds. But the navel or womb of Vishnou, considered as an hermaphrodite, is allowed to be a symbol of the great mother or female principle of nature: it is also acknowledged to denote the very same as the aquatic lotos: and the aquatic lotos is pronounced to be an hieroglyphic of precisely the same import as the ship Argha containing the god Siva.[3] So again: Brahma, Vishnou, and Siva, however they may be apparently discriminated from each other, are confessed by the Hindoos to be really and fundamentally one deity, even the great father both of gods and men. Consequently, what is said of one is said of all. Hence, as the navel of Vishnou, the lo-

[1] Asiat. Res. vol. iii. p. 147.

[2] See Plate II. Fig. 1. and Moor's Hind. Panth. p. 26, 27.

[3] Asiat. Res. vol. iii. p. 132—138.

tos, and the ship Argha, denote one and the same thing; namely the World viewed under the twofold aspect of the greater or literal World, and the smaller or mystical World, that is to say the Ark: the birth of Brahma from the lotos in which he sailed on the surface of the deluge, his ultimate birth from the navel or womb of the hermaphrodite Vishnou, the slumber of Vishnou on the serpent Ananta coiled up into the form of a boat, and the voyage of Siva during the prevalence of the deluge in the ship Argha, must all have a precisely similar import. Therefore, since the tenor of the legend directs us to the era of the flood, the birth of Brahma from the lotos and the divine navel can only mean the allegorical birth of Noah from the Ark. But Brahma is also said to have been born from an egg, which floated upon the mighty waters of chaos. In this egg he sat inactive during a whole year of the creator; the period, during which Noah was inclosed within the Ark, and which was thence thought by the Hindoos (fancifully indeed extended by them to what they call *a year of Brahma*) to be the constant intervening period between two successive worlds. Afterwards he caused it to divide asunder: and framed out of its substance the whole material creation. From the circumstance of his moving on the waters, while he floated on their surface concealed within the egg, he acquired the name of *Narayana;* which, for a similar reason, was also a title of Vishnou.[1] Now, since Brahma was born both from the lotos, from the navel of Vishnou, and from the sacred egg; they must all mean the same thing. But this will finally bring us to the conclusion, that his birth from the egg must denote a birth from the ship Argha, and therefore that the egg and the ship Argha must be identified.

With such a conclusion the whole context of the legend respecting Brahma's egg perfectly accords: and it cannot but be evident, that the Orphic fable of the production of the first-born Dionusus from an egg is the very same as the Hindoo fable of the production of the first-born Brahma from an egg, and that the story of the egg-born Dionusus having been exposed in an ark at sea during his infancy is the same as the story of the egg-born Brahma sailing either in the lotos or (as identified with Siva) in the ship Argha on the surface of the deluge. The Hindoos indeed refer the birth of Brahma from the

---

[1] Instit. of Menu. chap. i. § 8—13.

floating egg to the era of Menu-Swayambhuva or Adam, and thus introduce the circumstance into their history of the creation: but it must be remembered, that with *them* the creation of the world is only its renovation after a preceding deluge; that every world terminates with a flood and with the salvation of a Menu and his seven holy companions in an ark; and that the great father, whether distinguished by the name of *Brahma* or *Vishnou* or *Siva*, floats inactive during the intermediate period of the great year either in his egg or his lotos or his mysterious ship, before he awakes from his slumber and proceeds to the creation or rather the restoration of a world. Hence, as the World and the Ark are represented by common symbols, so the histories of the creation and the deluge are perpetually mingled together.

The sum of the matter, in short, is this. Brahma is indifferently said to have been born from a lotos, which was produced out of the navel of Vishnou during the intermediate period between two worlds, and which floated with the god seated in its calix on the surface of an ocean that was bounded by no shores; and from an egg, which similarly floated on the mighty waters during the intermediate space of a great year. The lotos therefore and the egg must mean the same thing. But the lotos is declared to be an hieroglyphic of the same import as the ship Argha, which sailed on the waters of the deluge, and which consequently must be the Ark; though, like the lotos, it is also esteemed a symbol of the greater World, which was supposed to float on the mighty deep after the manner of an immense ship. Hence the egg, being the same as the lotos, must also be the same as the ship Argha. Therefore the floating egg, out of which Brahma was produced, must be the Ark or smaller World, though without excluding an ulterior reference to the Earth or greater World: and the year of the god's inactivity, during which he was confined within it as it drifted to and fro on the surface of the ocean, must be the year of Noah's confinement within the Ark.

The propriety of such a conclusion will further appear from the circumstance of not only Brahma, but likewise Vishnou and Siva being said to have been each produced from an egg. According to some Hindoo treatises, Bhavani or the great mother, who is the consort of Siva, laid three eggs, from which were born the three principal deities, themselves a triplication of a yet older god named *Brahm*. Now, when we recollect, that Bhavani floated on the waters of the deluge in the form of a ship, and that she afterwards assumed the shape of a dove; that her offspring and husband Siva was the mariner that sailed in this ship; and that the three Hindoo deities are most intimately connected both with each other and with the history of the flood: we can have little difficulty in perceiving what is meant by the triplicated egg.[1]

Puoncu

6. These remarks will serve to shew the manner, in which we are to understand the exactly similar fable of the Chinese. Their mythologists say, that the first man was Puoncu: and they assert, that he was born out of chaos, as it were out of an egg. From this egg the Universe was afterwards produced: the heavens being formed out of its shell; the atmosphere, from its white; and the globe of the earth, from its yolk.[2]

Father Martini justly compares the egg of the Chinese to that which was consecrated in the Orgies of Bacchus. They doubtless meant the same thing: and, according to Porphyry, that thing was the world.[3] Yet his assertion must be understood with a certain mystical extension of import; for the egg certainly symbolized the arkite Microcosm, as well as the literal Megacosm. The World, of which the Mysteries treated, was a World of double signification. It was doubtless, in some measure, the greater World, that common parent both of hero-gods and mortals: but it was chiefly, as the whole tenor of the Orgies sufficiently proves, Noah and his family and the birds and beasts and plants and seeds and reptiles (the rudiments of a new World) inclosed together in the Ark, which was thence deemed a World in miniature and symbolized by the mundane egg. Accordingly, in the Dionusiaca, in the rites of the Eleusinian Ceres, and in other similar Mysteries which are for the most part commemorative of the deluge, one part of the nocturnal ceremony consisted in the consecration of an egg;[4] and another part, which serves literally to explain the meaning of the former, in placing the image of Osiris or Bacchus in a boat shaped like the

[1] Maurice's Hist. of Hind. vol. i. p. 60.
[2] Martin. Hist. Sin. l. i. p. 13.
[3] Porph. apud Euseb. Præp. Evan. l. iii.
[4] Platon. Sympos. l. ii. quæs. 3

lumar crescent, which the Egyptians set afloat on their holy river the Nile.[1]

7. The notion of the Persians, that Oromasdes formed mankind and afterwards inclosed them in an egg; and the tradition of the Syrians, that their ancestors the hero-gods were the Titans and sprang from eggs; both originated from this mode of symbolizing the Ark: for the Titans were certainly the diluvians; and the war of the Titans, in which an incorrigible race was destroyed, while seven Titanic heroes and the head of their family (afterwards venerated as the great gods of the Gentiles) were preserved, relates to the awful catastrophè of the flood.[2]

... Fables of the Persians + Syrians

8. From a similar source proceeded a curious fable prevalent among a tribe of Tartars seated in the peninsula of Corea. A daughter of the god Hoang-Ho became pregnant by the action of a sun-beam. In due time she brought forth an egg: and from the egg was born a man-child; who, when he attained the age of puberty, was distinguished by a name which signifies *a good pilot*. The king of the country, jealous of his address, sent assassins to murder him. By these he was pursued to the bank of a river; and was on the point of falling into their hands, when he addressed a prayer to his father the Sun. Scarcely had he finished it, when the fishes, rising to the surface of the water, formed a bridge for him, over which he passed in safety, and thus made his escape.[3]

... Hoang-Ho and his egg-born descendant ...

It is easy to perceive, that this legend is the very same as that of the Indian Crishna, one of the principal incarnations of Vishnou; who in his infancy is persecuted by the tyrant Cansa, and who escapes from him by being conveyed across the river Jumna. The fable of Crishna again must be identified with that of Osiris fleeing from the rage of Typhon, and with that of Apollo closely pursued, while yet in the womb of the great mother, by the serpent Python. These different stories all equally relate to the escape of Noah from the fury of the deluge. The egg, from which the fabled *good pilot* of the Coreans was produced, is the Ark, the mythological parent of

[1] Jul. Firm. de error. prof. rel. p. 53. Plut. de Isid. p. 368.
[2] Voss. de idol. vol. i. p. 33. Plut. de Isid. p. 370. Arnob. adv. gent. l. i. p. 20.
[3] Banier's Mythol. vol. i. p. 146.

the far-famed maritime god of the Gentiles: the Sun is ascribed to him as a father, precisely in the same manner as the Menu, who was preserved in a ship at the time of the flood, is styled *Vaivaswata* or *the child of the Sun:* and, though I wish to build upon circumstance rather than etymology, the close resemblance of the two names *Hoang-Ho* and *Oannes* or *Oan* renders it not improbable, that they are but one appellation somewhat differently pronounced.

...The Japanese fable of the bull & egg.

9. The egg, which floated in the river Euphrates surmounted by doves is said to have been rolled to the shore by fishes: the Japanese revere the very same symbol, but in the place of fishes they substitute a bull. One of the principal objects of worship in the temple of Dai-Bod at Meaco is a very remarkable groupe of hieroglyphical statuary. From a low altar, which serves as its basis, rises a rude and rocky sort of cup. The shallow cavity of the cup is filled with water: and in the water stands a bull in the act of butting a floating egg to the dry circumference, which serves as a shore to the miniature ocean.[']

This is a mere variation of the same idea. A bull, in every quarter of the globe, was one of the most common symbols of the great father; and, as such, is obviously connected with the sacred egg. Thus the egg-born Phanes of the Orphic poet is compared to a bull: and thus a bull is ever the hieroglyphic and companion of Siva, who is indifferently said to have been born from an egg and to have sailed over the waters of the deluge in the ship Argha; from which, as a form of Bhavani, the egg itself was produced. The Japanese groupe has, I believe, a double allusion to the history both of the creation and of the flood: but it chiefly, if I mistake not, relates to the events of the deluge. It seems intended to describe the great taurine father, in the act of impelling to land that floating egg, from which he was himself produced.

What we are to understand by the egg of the Japanese is further exemplified by the mode in which they delineate their triple deity. A single human body with three heads rises out of an egg marked with the characters of the country. It is so joined to the egg, that we may either

---

['] Maur. Hist. of Hind. vol. i. p. 69. and plate opposite p. 47.

conceive the god to be proceeding out of it, or we may suppose the egg to constitute his womb. I am inclined to believe, that both ideas were meant to be expressed. The egg is the Ark, from which was born the triplicated Noah: but, when he is viewed as an hermaphrodite, the great father united to the great mother; it is then his womb out of which was produced the Universe. In the one case, the egg-born triple god of Japan must clearly be identified with the three egg-born kings of the Orphic theology, and with the egg-born Trimurti of the Hindoos: in the other case, he is the same as Orphic hermaphrodite Jupiter, from whose womb or from an egg Eros or Phanes is indifferently said to have been produced; and as the Ardha-Nari of Hindostan, in whose single compound person are united Siva and that very Bhavani, who at once floated as a ship on the waters of the deluge and is feigned to have laid those eggs from which were born her husband Siva and the other two principal divinities.[1]

III. I may here properly observe, that the mystical egg is not always represented in a simple state: it is frequently united with other hierogly-phics of a similar import, which serve indeed to explain its true meaning, but which have sometimes given rise to much wild fiction.

1. We have already seen, by a regular comparative induction, that the egg and the lotos denote the same thing, and that both are equally to be identified with the ship Argha: while this diluvian ship is confessedly a form of the goddess Bhavani or Isi; who therefore, as the great mother, is at once the Ark or smaller World and the Earth or larger World. *With the lotos which is expressly declared to typify the ship of the deluge*

Such being the case, we shall perceive the reason, why the egg, out of which proceeds the triple Japanese divinity, is represented as resting in the calix of the expanded lotos. The egg and that aquatic flower are hiero-glyphics of the very same signification: hence the great father and the great mother are sometimes said to have been born from an egg, and at other times are described as sitting on the lotos while it floats on the surface of the ocean. Here the egg and the lotos are associated together, and thus form one double symbol.

2. We find the egg also not unfrequently conjoined with a serpent. Much *With the serpent*

the same reason is to be assigned for such an union as for that which I have last noticed. Though the malignant serpent appears to have been among the ancients a symbol of the evil principle, chiefly considered as producing the deluge; yet they also venerated the agathodemon or beneficent great father under the form of another serpent, to which they ascribed various good and mysterious qualities. But they did not confine this hieroglyphic to the great father alone: agreeably to their system of arranging the sacred symbols in pairs, as the bull was adored in conjunction with the cow, the horse with the mare, or the merman with the mermaid; so the male serpent was employed to represent the principal Demon-god, and the female serpent the principal goddess or great universal mother. The ophite superstition shall be discussed more largely in its proper place:[1] at present I content myself with merely mentioning the circumstance as tending to throw additional light on the worship of the egg.

The serpent: among the Tyrians and Egyptians

(1.) Such then being the character of the beneficent serpent, we shall perceive the reason why the Tyrians were wont to depict the mundane egg encircled by the folds of a large snake.[2] The snake denoted the great father, and the egg the great mother: the two united were that compound hermaphroditic being, from which the Universe was thought to have been produced. In the kindred theology of Egypt, the winged serpent Cnuphis, a form (as it is well known) of the Orphic Phanes or Dionusus, was both worshipped in a temple shaped like an egg; and was perpetually, like the Tyrian snake, represented as half coiling round a globe, which is in fact an egg flattened into a spherical shape. The famous hieroglyphic of a globe, serpent, and wings, as it has often been described, or rather of a globe and winged serpent, still decorates the front of numerous Egyptian temples, whose solid structure has hitherto bid defiance to the ravages of time. It differs only from the Tyrian symbol in a single immaterial circumstance: the serpent in one case has wings, in the other case it is without them; but both hieroglyphics were equally intended to shadow out the egg-born great father and his mysterious parent and consort the mundane Ark.[3]

[1] Vide infra book ii. c. 7.   [2] See Plate I. Fig. 1.
[3] See Plate I. Fig. 8. Kircher supposes the Egyptian symbol to represent the Holy Tri-

(2.) As the globe, which is a solid circle, is sometimes substituted for the egg; so the circle or ring, which is a plain sphere, sometimes occupies the place of the globe. Allowing for this variation, we find the form of the Persian Azon or Azonac closely corresponding with the Egyptian hieroglyphic: the god appears in the centre of a ring, which is attached to a winged snake. Sometimes also he is represented floating in the air: and then he holds a ring in his hand; while a cloud, so disposed as to exhibit the semblance of wings, is joined beneath him to a fillet coiled like a serpent.[1] The connection, in which the ring is here placed, demonstrates it to be an emblem of the same import as the globe or egg: for each is equally united, in an exactly similar manner, with a serpent and wings.

The serpent: among the Persians

(3.) Since the globe or egg therefore symbolizes both the World and the Ark, the ring or circle must likewise be understood to symbolize them. And this we shall find to be precisely the case. Ila, the daughter and consort of Menu or Buddha who was preserved at the time of the deluge, is evidently the same as Bhavani or the great mother or the ship Argha: for her name signifies *the World*, and Bhavani or Argha is declared to be a type of the World; though it is plain from the whole legend of Argha, that that ship must be identified with the Ark considered as a Microcosm. Now the peculiar sign of Ila is a circle, named *Ila-Vralta* or *Ida-Vralta*, that is to say *the circle of the World:* and this circle is feigned to be a ring of hills crowning the summit of mount Meru, which is at once the region of Paradise and the region where the Ark is supposed to have grounded

The serpent: ring of Ila

nity, worshipped, as he imagines, after a corrupt manner, by the early idolaters. Cudworth is not dissatisfied with his opinion; and Maurice very warmly adopts it. I suspect however, that they have been much too hasty in advancing or admitting this opinion. To say nothing of its total repugnance to the whole analogy of paganism, what becomes of the fancied third person when the serpent is divested of his wings? See Cudw. Intell. Syst. b. i. c. 4. p. 413. properly 353; and Maur. Ind. Ant. vol. iv. p. 695. Though I have myself felt the fascination of such a theory, a more thorough investigation of the subject has led me heartily to wish that it had never been advanced. The eloquent enthusiasm of the ingenious author of the Indian Antiquities has, I fear, been wasted on the baseless fabric of a vision. For the proof of the doctrine of a Trinity we must look to Scripture, and to Scripture alone.

[1] See Plate I. Fig. 9, 10.

when the waters of the flood retired into the great abyss. From the character of Ila then, no less than from the identification of the mystic circle with the egg, we must conclude, that this fabled ring on the summit of Meru was designed, like the lotos, the egg, and the ship Argha, to represent both the World and the Ark.[1]

The serpent: among the British Celts

(4.) The story of a ring of mountains gave rise to those circular temples, which were constructed with vast upright stones, and which have been called perhaps too exclusively *Druidical structures*.[2] Some of the most remarkable edifices of this description, in which large perpendicular columns supply the place of the fancied hills that form the circle of Ila, are to be found in our own country. Among these the gigantic monument of Stonehenge is conspicuously preëminent; and the varied allusion, with which it was erected, is sufficiently manifest from its several British appellations which have come down to us. It was indifferently called *the circle of the World*, or *the circle of the Ark*, or *the circle of the mundane Ark:* and it represented at once the inclosure of the Noëtic Ship, the egg of the Earth, and the zodiacal circle of the Universe in which the Sun, the astronomical representative of the great father, performs his annual revolution through the signs. As the temple, such was the worship. Hu and Ceridwen, the British Bacchus and Ceres or the great father and the great mother, were venerated conjointly within its mystic inclosure. But, while Hu was astronomically the Sun, his whole history proves him to have been in his human capacity the patriarch Noah: and, while Ceridwen was astronomically the Moon, her character similarly demonstrates her to have been truly the Ark.

Into the Mysteries of these deities the serpent and the egg, which is the same symbol as the ring, the one expressing solidly what the other expresses superficially, were introduced in a very conspicuous manner. The most usual name of the British Proserpine, the mythological daughter of Ceridwen, was *Creirwy* or *the symbol of the egg*. But this Proserpine, as in the Greek and Hindoo system, is the same person as her fabled mother: each is equally the Ark of Noah, viewed under the double aspect of the

---

[1] See Plate III. Fig. 21.   [2] See Plate III. Fig. 22.

termination of one World and the commencement of another. Hence the daughter, whose mystic name was *the Symbol of the Egg*, bore the additional and (as it were) explanatory title of *Creirddylad* or *the Token of floating ;* was described as the allegorical offspring of the chief, who governed or steered the diluvian vessel; and was said to have been forcibly hurried away by the king of the great abyss : and hence the mother was represented as the deity of a ship formed by the dragon-chief of the world, which passed through the dales of grievous waters having the fore part stored with corn, and which with well-connected serpents mounted aloft through the tempest. The import of such language cannot well be mistaken : all possibility of misapprehension however is removed by the circumstance of our being expressly informed by Taliesin, that this goddess, the great mother of the Britons and the mystic consort of the diluvian Hu, was a ship floating on the water ; which was supposed to carry the aspirant into the sea of that Dylan, who was preserved in an ark at the time of the deluge. As for the dragon-chief of the world, who formed the ship of the British Mysteries, and who was the allegorical parent of the goddess styled *the Symbol of the Egg* and *the Token of floating,* he is certainly Noah worshipped in conjunction with the Sun : for both his whole history proves him to be that patriarch, and he is even sometimes designated by the very appellation of Noë.

From this fable of his being the parent of the egg-goddess, and from this mode of representing him by a dragon or serpent, evidently originated the fiction of the Druids that their sacred eggs were produced by serpents. Pliny recites the story at large : and his account perfectly accords with the language used by the ancient bards. One of these eggs was the distinguishing badge of a Druid : and the person, who bore it, agreeably to the pagan custom of the priests assuming the names and characteristics of the god whom they worshipped, was called *an adder.* Both the snake and the egg immediately related to that regeneration, which was ever taught in the Mysteries, and which was in fact no other than the doctrine of a succession of similar worlds exemplified in the birth of Noah and his family from the arkite egg : for the snake, which annually casts his skin and returns to a second youth, was thought to be an apt representation of the twice-born patriarch ;

and the egg, containing within itself the rudiments of life in a dormant state, was supposed to shadow out a resurrection from the dead, which phrase was constantly used synonymously with regeneration.[1]

A curious circumstance is mentioned by Pliny respecting the British hieroglyphic, which seems decidedly to confirm the opinion that it was designed to typify a boat. He informs us, that, after it was produced, the test of its genuineness was its ability of floating against the stream even when circled with gold. Hence it is evident, that the ceremony of its consecration consisted in trying, whether the egg which was made of glass was sufficiently buoyant, even with its setting of gold, to remain on the surface of the water. The priests, I apprehend, cast it when duly prepared into one of their sacred rivers, which, like the Nile, the Euphrates, and the Ganges, represented the deluge; and drew it against the stream by a string which they had attached to it for that purpose. If it were light enough to swim, it then served as an emblem of a floating vessel: if it sank, it did *not* serve as such, and required to have its circlet of gold made lighter before it could be fit for use.[2] It may be further observed, that an egg, when divided longitudinally, exhibits the form of a boat: and, when whole, presents in some measure that of a decked vessel such as the Ark; for the ancient mystagogues, particularly those of Britain, appear to have been well aware that this was the manner in which the ship of Noah was constructed. The divided egg is one of the forms of the Indian Argha; the vessel, which is used in every sacred rite, and which is venerated as a copy of the navicular Argha in which the great father sailed over the waters of the deluge. Another of its forms is the circle, which is the divided globe. Here it coincides with the circular temple and with the sacred

---

[1] This emblem has been borrowed from the pagans both by Jews and Christians. Dean Addison mentions, that in Barbary the Jewish mourners at funerals are wont to eat eggs, thereby expressing their belief in the resurrection of the dead: and it is said, that, on Easter day, which is the anniversary of our Lord's rising from the tomb, the oriental Christians present each other with eggs richly adorned with painting and gilding. See Harmer's Observ. vol. iii. p. 423. Hence the Russians of Narva, who are members of the Greek church, eat painted eggs at their funeral feasts, which are held among the tombs.

[2] Davies's Mythol. of Brit. Druids, p. 208, 209.

circle of Ila on the summit of Meru, the prototype of which holy mountain is certainly the Ararat of Scripture. The Argha likewise is plainly
the navicular goblet, which Jupiter is said to have given to Semelè the
mother of the arkite Bacchus: it is also that celebrated cup, in which
Hercules and the Sun (they were both the same god) are each feigned to
have performed a wonderful voyage over the ocean. This brings us back
again to the Druids: for they had not only a floating egg of glass, but they
had likewise a sacred glass boat, which must have been either of an oval or
circular form, probably sometimes of one and sometimes of the other, because they variously denominated it *a house of glass* and *a circle of glass*.
It manifestly was designed to represent a ship: for, in allusion to the
Druidical ceremony of initiation, Merdin and his bards are said to have
put to sea in it.

There is another British temple at Abury, which in one respect is even
more remarkable than Stonehenge. It is at present nearly destroyed, but its
original form has been very accurately determined to be that of an immense
serpent attached to a circle. The serpent, like that with which the Tyrians
encompassed the mundane egg, is devoid of wings ; which seem to have
been at pleasure either added to the hieroglyphic or omitted.[1] When the
whole analogy of the Druidical superstition is considered, or I should rather
say the superstition of the universal gentile world, there cannot be any doubt, as
it appears to me, that the serpent was designed to represent the great serpent-
god Hu ; and the circle or superficial egg, that mysterious vessel which the
Druids were accustomed to style *the Ark of the world*. In short, the serpent and the ring or egg, whether they occur in Britain, Persia, Egypt,
Phenicia, or Hindostan, symbolize alike the great father and the great mother of pagan mythology.[2]

(5.) The sacred rings of the Samothracians, famed for their devotion to
the Cabiric or diluvian Mysteries, were emblems of an exactly similar import. The Druids had the same sort of consecrated rings. They are also
familiar to the Hindoos : and, as they are placed in the hands of most of

[1] See Plate 1. Fig. 5.
[2] Cooke's Inq. into the patriar. and druid. rel. p. 30.

The serpent:
among the
Samothracian
Druidical,
Indian,
Egyptian, and
Persian rings

their gods, so the Sakwell or circle of Buddha-Sacya, which is clearly the same as the Ila-Vratta or circle of Ila, for Ila was his consort, is peculiarly celebrated. They were no less used among the ancient Egyptians: and it is a curious circumstance, that that people and the Hindoos had in common a mode of delineating them, which decidedly proves the symbolical identity of the circle and the egg. The old Egyptian hieroglyphic of a triangle within a circle is well known to the modern Hindoos: but these last explain the triangle to mean their Trimurti or triplicated great god :[1] the triangle therefore within the circle will denote the triplicated deity within that egg out of which he was supposed to be born; in other words, it will symbolize Noah and his three sons, the three egg-born kings of the Orphic poet, inclosed within the Ark. It was with the same idea, that the Persians, as I have already observed, placed their god Azonac in the midst of the circle attached to the winged serpent. Hence also the regeneration of the Mysteries, which was procured sometimes by passing through the figure of a cow, sometimes by quitting a boat within which the aspirant had been exposed on the ocean, and sometimes by being born as it were from a rocky cavern within which he had been confined, was supposed to be no less efficaciously brought about by forcing the body either through a ring or through a circular hole in a rock.[2] Whatever mode was adopted, the allegorical birth from the Ark or great mother was equally intended.

(6.) The hieroglyphical serpent was occasionally so managed, that, instead of being joined to a distinct ring or globe, it was made itself to represent the mystic circle. Agreeably to the ever blended astronomical and diluvian speculations of the Gentiles, they were wont to place in the hand of Cronus, whose name has been justly pronounced to be the same as Chronus or Time, a snake which formed a ring by the insertion of its tail within its mouth. Now Cronus or Time is certainly Noah, the Cali of the Hindoos and Persians; whose name similarly denotes *Time*, and in whose days a great deluge is said to have taken place: and he was emphatically styled *Time*, because his life was marked by a great renovation of time and by the commencement of a new mundane period. The serpent therefore at once

The serpent identified with Cronus (Time or Noah)

---

[1] Moor's Hind. Panth. p. 400.   [2] Vide infra book v. c. 6. §. VIII.

represented eternity as taught in the doctrine of a succession of similar worlds, an astronomical cycle, and the hermaphroditic great father as symbolized by a snake united to a globe or circle. I may add, that the caduceus of Thoth or Hermes, who is the Buddha of the eastern world and who is equally with Cronus the patriarch Noah, is composed of a rod, surmounted by a winged globe, and encircled either by one or two serpents.

3. As the egg was frequently joined with a snake, so we likewise find it united with another emblem of great celebrity among the pagans: I mean the lunar crescent. This navicular form, which the Moon assumes in her first and last quarters, rendered her a peculiarly fit astronomical symbol of the Ark: and the circumstance was not overlooked by those, who wished to inscribe their theological tenets on the sphere. Hence we may observe, that the great mother, who in one sense is declared to be the Earth and in another is said to have floated as a ship on the surface of the deluge, is in a third pronounced to be the Moon. This mixture of character, material, diluvian, and astronomical, has given rise to many singular fables which will be noticed in their proper places, but to none more curious than those which connect the mystical egg with the Moon.

[The egg in association] With the lunar crescent

(1.) The god Lunus of Heliopolis and Carrhœ was an egg, on the top of which rested a crescent formed like a boat. But Lunus was the same as Osiris, who was exposed (we are told) in an ark which in shape resembled the new moon; the same also as Siva or Iswara, who floated in the ship Argha on the waters of the deluge. Hence we can have little difficulty in understanding what is meant by the egg and navicular lunette joined together in one common symbol.[1]

(2.) In a similar manner, the forms of Jagan-Nath and his brother Bal-Ram are each a larger egg surmounted by a smaller one, which latter supports a boatlike crescent containing the head of the deity. The whole presents a mishapen human figure: the lower egg supplying the place of a womb to the semi-female god, the upper egg being his chest, and the horns of the crescent furnishing him with arms.[2] But Jagan-Nath and Bal-Ram are one person divided into two characters: and in the worship of this deity, as

[1] See Plate I. Fig. 11, 22.   [2] See Plate I. Fig. 16.

in a common point of union, the worship of Buddha and the worship of Vishnou meet together; for Jagan-Nath is each of those cognate diluvian gods.[1]

(3.) The Egyptians employed exactly the same symbols, though they combined them in a somewhat different manner. Kircher has given a representation of Osiris in a sitting posture with a crescent on his head, which, like that of Jagan-Nath and Bal-Ram, contains another head. Above is the hieroglyphic of the globe or egg placed in a ring and attached to a flying serpent. The connection of these several symbols with the arkite god Osiris sufficiently shews, how we are to interpret them.[2]

(4.) The union of the egg with the lunette will lead us to understand that part of the Babylonian fable, which describes the egg of Venus as having fallen from heaven previous to its floating in the river Euphrates.[3] By its fall from heaven was meant its fall from the Moon: but the Moon here alluded to was not the literal Moon in the firmament; but the arkite crescent, which rested on the summit of mount Ararat whence the Euphrates takes its rise, and which was the prototype of the lunette that received the body of Osiris when he was set afloat on the Nile by Typhon or the deluge.

(5.) That such was the meaning of its fall from heaven, we may collect by comparing the Babylonian legend with another fable of similar import.

The egg, whence Helena and the Dioscori were produced, is said by the poets, according to Plutarch, to have fallen from heaven:[4] but Athenæus mentions, that some mythologists, such as Neocles of Crotona, asserted it to have fallen from the Moon.[5] By the fall therefore of the egg from heaven we are to understand its fall from the Moon: and the notion of its fall from the Moon must be referred to that mode of symbolizing the god Lunus, which prevailed so eminently among the Heliopolitans, though the preceding remarks shew that it was equally familiar to other nations. They worshipped an egg surmounted by a lunette: consequently, when the lunette was interpreted to mean the literal Moon, the egg would appear to be

---

[1] Vide infra book iv. c. 6.

[2] See Plate I. Fig. 12.

[3] Hyg. Fab. 197. Ampel. c. 2.

[4] Plut. Symp. lib. ii. quæs. 3.

[5] Athen. Deipnos. lib. ii. p. 57.

dropping from it.[1] The Moon however and the egg really meant the same thing: and the whole of the curious fable of Leda has been built upon these two symbols of the Ark.

The most common, though the most corrupted, story is, that Leda, the wife of Tyndarus, was debauched by Jupiter in the form of a swan, while at the same time she cohabited with her husband. In consequence of this she produced two eggs: out of the first of which proceeded Pollux and Helena, who were the children of Jupiter; and out of the second Castor and Clytemnestra, who were the offspring of Tyndarus. Hesiod however, according to the scholiast on Pindar, makes both Castor and Pollux to be the sons of Jupiter; and asserts, that Helena was his daughter by one of the nymphs of the ocean: the egg therefore and the oceanic nymph must mean the same thing; and that nymph, I doubt not, is in reality the sea-born Venus or the diluvian great mother.[2] Such a modification of the fable would leave only *one* egg: and, accordingly, the scholiast on Aratus mentions only *one* egg which produced Helena and the Dioscori.[3] This, I apprehend to have been the original number, the addition of the *second* egg being a subsequent corruption. But the primitive fable seems to have been most accurately preserved by Tzetzes. He informs us, that Jupiter, having changed himself into a swan, enjoyed, in that shape, the person of Nemesis daughter of the Ocean; who had previously, according to the author of the Cyprian verses, assumed the form of a sea-fish, in order that she might escape his embraces.[4] She produced an egg, and left it in a marsh or lake; where a shepherd found it, and brought it to Leda. That princess carefully preserved it in an ark: and, in due season, Helena, Castor, and Pollux, issued from it.[5] The same story is related by the scholiast on Callimachus, who adds that the circumstance happened at Rhamnus in Attica.[6]

The whole of this fable appears to me sufficiently to bespeak both its origin and import. Nemesis and Leda, as we are told by Lactantius, are

[1] See Plate I. Fig. 11.
[2] Schol. in Arat. Phæn. p. 38.
[3] Tzetz. in Lycoph. ver. 88.
[4] Schol. in Callim. Hymn. ad Dian. ver. 232.
[5] Schol. in Pind. Nem. x. ver. 150.
[6] Athen. Deipnos. lib. viii. p. 334.

See also Apollod. Bibl. lib. iii. c. 9.

the same person.' But Leda, as the very name imports, though the history has been transferred into Greece, is no other than the Babylonian Venus, who bore the title of *Mylitta* or *Mileda*, in her character of the female principle of generation.' The egg of Leda, sometimes said to have been produced by Nemesis in the form of a fish, is the egg of Venus similarly produced by a fish. Both equally meant the Ark: whence originated the legend of the egg of Leda being deposited in an ark, after it had been found floating in a lake which among the ancients was a symbol of the deluge. Accordingly, the Dioscori are said to have been born from the egg: but these Dioscori presided over navigation, and are allowed to be the same as the Cabiri whose whole history proves them to have been the Noetic family.' Such being the character of the Dioscori, the egg, from which they were born, must inevitably, as it appears to me, represent the Ark.

There is indeed a variation in the fable of Leda from that of the Babylonian Venus: in the one, the egg is either produced or fostered by Leda; in the other, Venus is herself produced from the egg. But this variation is perfectly in character with those speculations of Paganism, which represented Noah both as the father and as the son of the Ark, and which analogically transferred the same sort of involved genealogy to the arkite goddess likewise. Hence Venus or Leda is indifferently said to have produced an egg and to have been produced from an egg: just as the great father, under the name of *Phanes* or *Brahma* or *Eros*, is represented as having been born from an egg; while, under that of *Cneph*, he himself produces an egg from his own mouth, which again produces the god Phtha or Vulcan, who nevertheless, if his character be analysed, will prove to be the very same person as Eros or Brahma or Cneph or Phanes.'

(6.) The Druids were no less inclined, than the mythologists of Greece and the East, to connect the sacred egg with the Moon: and, when the evident drift of their superstition is considered, we can scarcely doubt,

---

' Lactan. Instit. lib. i. c. 21.

' Herod. lib. i. c. 131. Mileda, whence the Greek Leda, is evidently the Chaldee מילדה or מולדתא.

' Sanch. apud Euseb. Præp. Evan. lib. i. c. 10. Pausan. Phoc. p. 686.

' Euseb. Præp. Evan. lib. iii. c. 11.

that the same idea produced the same combination also in Britain. Mr. Davies conjectures, that the egg, which we have already seen connected with the hieroglyphical serpent, contained within it a small lunette of glass, and that this lunette was the boat which the Druids used in their Mysteries as the symbol of the ship Ceridwen.[1] Whatever degree of probability there may be in a conjecture, which represents the Druids as inclosing within the egg that boatlike crescent which the Heliopolitans attached to the exterior surface of it, this at least we learn from Pliny, that the British anguinum or serpent-egg was always procured at a certain time of the Moon. The time in question I apprehend to have been during either the first or the last quarter, when the crescent of that planet exhibits the shape of a boat.

IV. I am inclined to refer the egg of the Phenix to the same mixed superstition, which so perpetually represented by common symbols the greater or literal World and the smaller or arkite World.

The fable of the Phenix, as I have already observed, was invented to shadow out the favourite pagan doctrine of a succession of similar mundane systems. Hence the ball or egg of myrrh, within which it was feigned to inclose the body of its deceased parent, will denote, according to the universal analogy of gentilism, the World. But it will also denote the Ark or Microcosm: for the idea of inclosing the dead Phenix in the egg is precisely the same, as that of inclosing the dead body of Osiris within the arkite lunette in the ceremony which was called his funeral. In this lunette he was afterwards set afloat and bewailed as one dead: but, after a proper interval, he was supposed to return to life, and to be born again (as it were) out of his floating coffin. Unless I am greatly mistaken, the death and revival of Osiris is but another mode of representing the death and revival of the Phenix. In both cases, the renovation of the World, and the new birth of the great father who floats during the intermediate period on the surface of the mighty waters, are alike intended.

The Phenix is palpably the Simorgh of Persian romance, and the Garuda of Hindoo mythology who is ever considered as the celestial vehicle

[1] Davies's Mythol. p. 210, 211, 212.

of the egg-born Vishnou : I think it probable, that the Rokh of the Arabian fabulists is likewise fundamentally the same hieroglyphical bird. Romantic fiction has in most countries derived its origin from misunderstood theological fiction : and I strongly suspect, that the mysterious egg of this fabulous monster of the feathered creation has been borrowed from the sacred mundano-arkite egg of the diluvian Orgies. In the curious Arabic story of the wonderful lamp, a mischievous inchanter persuades Aladdin to demand of the servant-genius the egg of a Rokh, in order that it might be suspended as the most suitable decoration in the ample dome of his magic-built palace. The demand is made : but, in a voice of thunder, the slave of the lamp reproves him for his temerity in daring to ask for the master whom he obeyed, merely that he might hang him up as the ornament of a dome.' Now it was in this precise manner, that the sacred egg was sometimes suspended from the dome of a temple ; which itself, like the egg, was intended, as we shall hereafter see, to represent both the World and the Ark. An instance exactly in point is afforded us by Pausanias. He mentions a temple in Laconia, from the roof of which hung the identical egg that was feigned to have been produced by Leda and to have given birth to the Dioscori.' It was doubtless, I think, that mysterious egg, respecting which I have been treating, and of which sufficient has now been said.

' Arab. Nights' Entertain. story of Aladdin.   ' Paus. Lacon. p. 190.

CHAPTER V.

Heathen Cosmogonies.

Tʜᴇ remarks, which have been made on the mundane egg and on the doctrine of a succession of similar worlds, will have served to prepare the way
for a consideration of the various cosmogonies of the Gentiles.

Perhaps, in absolute strictness of speech, that is to say, in the sense of
proper creation, they had *no* cosmogony ; because they held, that each world
was produced from the wreck of a former system : yet their various theories
respecting this production are of such a nature as to shew very evidently that
they must have sprung from some common primeval origin. In many points
they bear so close a resemblance to the Mosaical cosmogony, that it can
scarcely have been the effect of mere accident : but it seems to me in the
highest degree incredible, that they should have been borrowed from it, as
some have imagined. The Israelites were neither so universally celebrated, nor
was their commonwealth of so ancient an origin compared with that of many
other nations, as to warrant the belief, that mythologists flocked from every
quarter of the globe to derive wisdom from the books of Moses. In fact,
the very same idolatry, which has subsisted even to the present day in Hindostan, was established, substantially at least, both in Egypt and in Palestine, *previous* to the exodus of the children of Israel : and so intimately, in
every region, is the prevailing idolatry combined with some hypothesis respect-

ing the creation, and with some account of the deluge; or rather, I should say, so evidently is pagan idolatry *built* upon traditions of the creation and the deluge; that, where the former is found, there we may rest assured that the latter must also have prevailed. Hence it is manifest, that the Canaanites and the Egyptians cannot have borrowed their theories from Moses: and, if *they* did not, how strangely improbable is it, that the remote and ancient nations of the Hindoos, the Chinese, and the Scythians, should have been indebted to him.

These observations necessarily lead us to adopt the opinion, which Dr. Allix, though from a different train of reasoning, was induced with so much sound judgment to advance: namely, that, in writing the book of Genesis, Moses declared nothing but what was then generally known.[1] Inspiration is of a two-fold nature, agreeably to the circumstances of those matters respecting which it may be concerned. Sometimes it enables a prophet to reveal things, with which neither he nor any other human being was previously acquainted: at other times, it only directs him to give a perfectly accurate statement of points which in the main were already well known. The first kind of inspiration comprehends the whole of prophetical and doctrinal theology: the second kind comprizes every thing of an historical nature. To this latter sort I refer the greatest part of the book of Genesis. It is impossible, that mankind should have known nothing of the deluge until Moses gave an account of it: and it is utterly incredible, that all the early patriarchs from Adam to the Hebrew legislator, should have been profoundly ignorant of the history of the creation. Moses therefore did not now for the first time reveal the origination of the world and its inhabitants, neither did he now for the first time declare that the whole race of mankind except a single family had been swept away by the waters of a flood: he simply rectified the mythological errors, which had been superinduced over the primitive account of those great events as possessed by Adam and Noah; and, while others had disfigured the truth by the wildness of philosophical and idolatrous fiction, *he* was taught by the Holy Spirit of God to give a clear and perfectly unerring recital of early history.

In fact, had Moses been the first who asserted a cosmogony and a deluge,

---

[1] See Allix's Reflex. on Script. part i. c. 18.

and had such events never been heard of, until he, in the full sense of the word, *revealed* them : it is easy to perceive, that he must have been immediately rejected as an impostor even by the Israelites themselves.

He gives a regular history backwards from the period in which he lived to the deluge. Now, as the Israelites must have been well acquainted with their ancestry at least as high as Abraham, Moses could never have persuaded them that they were descended from that patriarch if they really were not: and as little could he have induced them to believe, that an universal flood had taken place in the tenth generation before Abraham, if an event of such stupendous magnitude had been utterly unknown both to them and to their neighbours until it was declared by Moses. With just as much facility might a pretended prophet start up in the present day, and convince the English by an alleged revelation from heaven, that their whole island was inundated in the days of William the conqueror, and that the Norman invader planted a country just emerging from the ocean and completely destitute of inhabitants. A revelation, which now for the first time described and chronologically determined a wonderful circumstance hitherto altogether unknown, would in itself be sufficient to convict a man of impudent imposture. The very account, which Moses gives of the deluge in the tenth generation before Abraham, necessarily involves the persuasion, that he only described with the infallible accuracy of divine truth a circumstance, of which the existence was well known both to the Israelites and to all the rest of the world.

An extension of the same reasoning will lead to a similar result respecting the creation. At the period in which Moses flourished, as he could by no revelation have induced the Israelites to believe in an universal deluge ten generations before Abraham, if hitherto they had never heard of such a thing; so neither could he have led them to admit a cosmogony which he similarly places ten generations before Noah, minutely specifying every one of those ten generations, if they had never had any previous reason to believe, that the world was then actually created and that the human race then actually commenced.

What applies to the Israelites, applies with equal force to all other ancient nations. If primeval events had *not* occurred as Moses represents them to have done, the Gentiles could never have had accounts of the creation and the deluge so nearly resembling those contained in the book of Genesis : for, were they *first* revealed by Moses, he could still less have persuaded the Gentiles to adopt them than the Israelites. If, on the other hand, primeval events *did* occur agreeably to the representation of the Hebrew lawgiver; *then* the Gentiles must in the main have been well acquainted with the history of the creation and the deluge long before the time of Moses, however they might have corrupted them by the speculations of an idolatrous philosophy.

On these principles, since we actually find among all nations certain accounts of the creation and the deluge, which bear a strong general resemblance to the Mosaical history of those events; and since they assuredly could never have been borrowed from Moses had *he* been the original inventor of them, because the very promulgation of such a history of matters hitherto unheard of would alone have been sufficient to brand him with the indelible mark of shameless imposture: on these principles, I say, the existence of such accounts among the Gentiles, in every part of the world, proves, that the facts themselves must have been universally known and universally received as truth *prior* to the time of Moses, and consequently that the acquaintance of the pagans with them could not have been *derived* from the Pentateuch. We are brought, in short, to the following conclusion : that the history of the creation and the deluge had always been admitted as indisputable long before the composition of the book of Genesis ; and that Moses, although inspired, did not reveal any novel historical circumstances, but only detailed with infallible accuracy the *real* mode in which events had occurred that were themselves universally acknowledged to *have* occurred.

And with this conclusion the fact, so far as we are able to judge, will be found exactly to agree. The pagan traditions and the Mosaical history are plainly of common origin : if the events in question *really* happened, the traditions could not have been *borrowed* from the history, but must have existed *anterior* to it; if they did *not* happen, then the traditions could have had *no* existence whatsoever : but the traditions *do* exist, and yet could not have been borrowed from the history : therefore Moses can only have delivered, in the naked simplicity of truth, what was already well known though disguised by the extravagance of mythologic fiction. Accordingly, if any person will compare together the history and the traditions, though it is impossible that the latter could have been borrowed from the former, he will not fail to perceive, that they chiefly differ in this single circumstance: the one details the events in the unadorned manner of a plain authentic record, without adding any thing more of the marvellous, than what inevitably belongs to such events, supposing them to have really happened; the others detail the self-same events, but disguise them with such a profusion of grotesque ornaments, that the corrupting hand of theologic fable is manifest upon the very face of them. The leading circumstances in both are alike: but, if we descend to particulars, the legends of Paganism bear much the same relation to the narrative of Moses, that the reign of Charlemagne, as exhibited in the life of Archbishop Turpin and in the romances of Boyardo and Ariosto, bears to the reign of Charlemagne, as detailed in the page of sober history.

But, in addition to the reveries of mythologic fiction, a variation from genuine history of a different description has been admitted into those traditions of the Gentiles which respect the origin of the world. As they believed in an endless succession of similar mundane systems, each both commencing from and terminating with a flood: it is obvious, that, with such sentiments, their histories of the creation, though in the main they describe the same event as that with which the book of Genesis opens, will contain perpetual references to the deluge and to a reproduction of the earth after its submersion beneath the chaotic waters of the ocean; and, on the other hand, that their histories of the deluge, though in the main they describe that deluge from which Noah and his family were preserved in an ark, will contain very frequent allusions to the creation. Viewing the reproduction of the earth from the flood in the same light as that which Scripture teaches us to esteem its original production from chaos, and believing that the same great father appeared with his triple offspring at each epoch, they continually blended the two together; and in some instances they treated of them in so singularly inseparable a manner, that it is impossible to give the history of the cosmogony without also giving that of the deluge, or of the deluge without that of the cosmogony. The doctrine of a succession of similar worlds will alone explain this curious circumstance, and account for a confusion sufficiently notorious but otherwise wholly inexplicable. With that doctrine however for a key, we shall be able to understand very readily the greatest part of what the pagans have written on the subject.

I. The inhabitants of Chaldèa, long celebrated for their astronomical observations and deducing their origin from the most remote antiquity, are now extinct as a separate people, and their learning has in a great measure perished with them. Some remains however of their sentiments respecting the creation of the world are preserved by Syncellus and Eusebius from Alexander Polyhistor and Berosus: Whatever knowledge they had of this event, they ascribed to the teaching of an amphibious creature denominated *Oannes*. Like the Vishnou of Hindostan and the Dagon of the Philistines, his form consisted of the body of a man terminating in the tail of a fish. By day he ascended from the waters of the Erythrèan sea, and in a human voice conveyed his instructions to the assembled multitudes: but at night he retired from the land, and concealed himself within the recesses of the ocean.

The fish-god Oannes or Dagon

1. Oannes taught his auditors, that there was a time, when all things were darkness and water, in the midst of which resided various monsters of most horrible forms. Of these, some resembled men with two wings, or with four wings, or with two faces. Others were hermaphrodites, having a single body, which bore the distinguishing characteristics of both sexes; and furnished with two heads, the one of a man, and the other of a woman. Some had human figures, but provided with the legs and horns of goats. Some had the feet of a horse: while others united the body of that animal to the body of a man, resembling in shape the fabulous centaur. There were also bulls with the heads of men: dogs with fourfold bodies and the tails of fishes: horses with the heads of dogs: and men and various other animals with the tails of fishes and the heads and bodies of horses. Snakes, reptiles, and fishes, likewise there were; which mutually assumed each other's aspect, form melting (as it were) into form. Over these monsters and the chaotic mass in which they moved presided a female named *Omoroca*, who long reigned in gloomy and solitary independence. But at length the destined hour of creation arrived. The woman was slain and cut asunder by Belus: the earth was formed by the victorious god out of the one half of her, and heaven out of the other half: and the deformed animals, which had composed her empire, were annihilated. Oannes however taught, that this physiologi-

cal description was to be taken purely in an allegorical sense, and that the whole fable alluded to the aqueous origin of the Universe: for Omoroca was a personification of the sea, though the name might likewise be interpreted to signify *the Moon*. Afterwards Belus cut off his own head: and the other gods, mixing the blood with earth, formed out of the compound the human species. Hence man is endowed with reason, and partakes of the divine knowledge. This same Belus moreover, whom men call *Dis* or *Pluto*, divided the darkness from the light, separated the earth from the heavens, disposed the world in order, and called the starry host into existence.[1]

2. The whole of the preceding cosmogony, though in many respects it relates to that creation of the world which Moses describes at the beginning of Genesis, is yet mingled with perpetual allusions to the deluge. What first attracts our notice is the character of Oannes, the supposed revealer of it. According to Eusebius, who writes from Berosus, his whole body was like that of a fish: but under the fish's head he had another head like that of a man, and human feet subjoined to the fish's tail. He not only instructed the Babylonians in the history of the creation; but he likewise taught them the use of letters, and made them acquainted with the principles of architecture, of jurisprudence, and of geometry. He shewed them how to collect fruits, and how to distinguish the seeds of the earth. He gave them an insight into the whole circle of the arts and sciences. In short, he was their instructor in every thing, that could tend to soften and humanize their manners. It is said, either that four of these mermen successively appeared, or that the same merman exhibited himself at four different times: and Berosus promises to give an account of them, when he treats of the history of the Babylonian kings. Under one of his manifestations the merman was called *Odacon*. This last circumstance, as well as his form, sufficiently shews, that he was the Dagon of the Philistines, *Odacon* being nothing more than a Greek corruption of *Dagon*.[2] He is also the same as the Dac-Po of Thibet; under which name is venerated Po or Buddha, who is celebrated as the sovereign prince in the belly of the fish, and who thus coincides with Vishnou in the fish Ava-

The character of Oannes discussed

---

[1] Syncell. Chronog. p. 29. Euseb. Chron. p. 5.

[2] Instead of ὁ Δαγων some Greek transcriber wrote Ωδαχων. Vide Seld. de diis Syr. Synt. ii. c. 3.

tar. The Philistines were Cuthites or Scythians of the same race as the Babylonians and the Thibetians: and they doubtless brought with them from their original settlement in Cashgar the worship of Dac-Po or Dag-On. This deity was sometimes called *Annedotus;*[1] which seems to be a compound of the two Buddhic titles *Jain* or *Oan*, and *Dot* or *Thoth*. The genuine prototype of the Babylonian man of the sea, the teacher of all the useful arts, and the revealer of the process of creation, is clearly the patriarch Noah: but, agreeably to the doctrine of a succession of similar worlds, four of these beings are said to have emerged from the sea at different intervals. Like the various Buddhas and Menus, who are feigned to have been successively manifested, I have no doubt, that the four Annedoti ought to be reduced to two, of whom the first is Adam and the second Noah.

The various monsters of this cosmology were hieroglyphics

3. Those different monsters, which are feigned to have tenanted the mighty deep previous to the creation, were all delineated, we are told, in the temple of Belus at Babylon. I think it sufficiently evident from the description given of them, that they were hieroglyphics or sacred symbols. Several of such combinations occur very frequently in the mythology of the Gentiles: the bull, for instance, with the man's head; the man with the tail of a fish; the hippocentaur; and the hermaphrodite. All these, floating in the waters of chaos during the intermediate space between two worlds, were designed, if I mistake not, to represent the great father and the great mother, who die at the end of one mundane system only to revive at the commencement of another. Such hieroglyphical representations, which adorned or disfigured the walls of the Babylonian temple, seem plainly to be alluded to in a remarkable vision of Ezekiel. The prophet is directed by the Holy Spirit to enter into one of those cells or caverns, which were so very generally used in the celebration of the Mysteries. He obeys; and beholds, pourtrayed upon the wall, every form of creeping things and abominable beasts, even all those idols of the house of Israel which they had borrowed from the astronomical mythology of the neighbouring nations.[2] These, I have little doubt, were figures of much the same nature as those, over which Omoroca was said to have presided, and which were painted on the walls of the temple of Belus.

Omoroca is the great mother

4. Their sovereign Omoroca, from the description which is given of her,

[1] See Seld. de diis Syr. Synt. ii. c. 3.   [2] Ezek. viii. 7—12.

appears to be no other than the great mother, whose character comprizes at *who united in her own mythological character the Earth and the Ark and who was astronomically represented by the lunar boat or crescent* once both the World and the Ark. She was a marine goddess, and lay floating many a rood in the mighty deep until the hour of creation or rather of renovation arrived. The whole World was then formed out of her body. An exactly similar account is given of the mundane egg: consequently Omoroca and the egg mean the same thing. She is the same also as Isis, or Isi, or Bhavani: who similarly comprehends within herself the whole Universe, and who similarly floats on the ocean during the period that it covers the surface of the earth. Agreeably to this character, she is said, in the mystical jargon of Paganism, to be at once the Sea and the Moon. Such discordant attributes are not easily reconcileable, unless we look beyond the letter. What the ancients meant by the Moon was no further the Moon in the firmament, than as that planet, when it assumes the figure of a boat or crescent, was the astronomical representative of the great mother; by whom they doubly intended the smaller ship of the Ark and the larger ship of the World: for they ascribed to the Earth the form of a ship, and supposed it to float on the bosom of chaos. Such was the Moon, which they identified with Omoroca, as may easily be collected from their perfect correspondence of character. Omoroca, though positively declared to be in some sense the Moon, floats nevertheless on the surface of the ocean during the intermediate space between the destruction of one world and the creation of another; and afterwards, by the agency of Belus or the great father, becomes herself the all-productive parent of a new mundane system. In a similar manner the Moon, which the Gentiles venerated, was, as they explicitly assure us, a Moon that was the child of the sea, a Moon that was born out of the deluge, a Moon that was the parent of that egg-born Bacchus who was exposed in an ark, a Moon within which Osiris was inclosed and set afloat on the water, a Moon that was a prison within which the hero-gods were confined, a Moon that was the residence of the ancestors of mankind, a Moon that was the saviour of the great father in his character of Lunus or Chandra, a Moon that was the mother of the whole world, a Moon that was esteemed the same as the Earth. These characteristics sufficiently determine what we are to understand by the Moon, which the pagans venerated: but that Moon was the same person as Omoroca; consequently, what the one is, the other is also.

But Omoroca is further declared to be the Sea: this part of her character is perfectly consonant with the mystic theocrasia of the ancients. Isi, who floated as a ship on the surface of the deluge, is yet pronounced to be the same both as Water and as the Moon; or, in the language of the Hindoos, the Moon and the aqueous Element are no less forms of Isi than the diluvian ship Argha: and, in like manner, a notion prevailed, that, as the Moon was born out of the sea; so, after some incomprehensible and ineffable manner, the Moon and Water were the same thing.

Belus is the great father

5. Belus, who produces the Universe from the body of Omoroca, is doubt-less the great father; that is to say Adam reappearing in the person of Noah: hence Nonnus rightly identifies him with Hercules, Ammon, Jupiter, and the principal god of each nation under whatsoever name he might be adored.[1]

The fable of his losing his head, from the streaming blood of which mingled with earth the human species was produced, seems, as Sir William Jones has justly remarked, to be the same legend, as that of the decapitation of the Indian Brahma by the being who floats on the waters during the intermediate space between the death and revival of that deity. In this last tradition there is so much wild obscurity, that the elucidation of it has been despaired of both by Sir William Jones and Mr. Wilford: I am inclined however to think, that at least a considerable degree of light may be thrown on the subject by following the method of comparative analysis.

The chief point to be ascertained is the opinion, entertained by pagan mythologists, of the human head viewed as a symbol or hieroglyphic. From the fable of Belus, they plainly supposed it to represent something, out of which the human species was born or produced: and the tradition respecting Brahma will lead to the same conclusion; for Brahma is both esteemed the same as man collectively, and is venerated as that hermaphroditic being from whom at the commencement of each world is born the whole race of man-kind. Now it is observable, that the form of the human head is nearly that of an egg. But from the floating mundane egg, precisely in the same manner as from the head of Belus, the great father, and through him all the genera-tions of men, were thought to have been produced. Hence, according to

[1] Nonni Dionys. lib. xl. p. 683.
[2] Asiat. Res. vol. i, p. 246. Moor's Hind. Panth. p. 102.

one fable, mankind are born out of a head severed from the body and consequently made to resemble an egg : while, according to another fable, they are
born out of the egg itself. Thus there is certainly a strong presumption, that
the head and the egg mean the same thing: and we shall find the presumption increase every step that we advance in our inquiry.

The ark, within which Typhon inclosed Osiris, was said to have drifted
on shore in Phenicia : and the Egyptians, as we are informed by Lucian, had
a custom of yearly commemorating this supposed event in a very remarkable
manner. They made a papyrine vessel, which in form represented the head
of the deity; and, committing it to the winds and waves, feigned, that it was
wafted to Byblos in seven days by a supernatural impulse.[1] Now, since this
annual rite was commemorative of the pretended voyage of Osiris in the ark,
the boat or vessel fashioned to represent his head must, I should conceive,
mean the same as the ark within which he was inclosed. The opinion is
strengthened by the mode in which the vessel was shaped. Lucian simply
says, that it resembled a human head : but its exact form has come down to
us in imperishable sculpture ; whence it appears, that the vessel in question
was a human head placed in a lunette or boat.[2] The two united form the
same compound hieroglyphic as the egg and the lunette ; and we have little
reason to doubt that they meant the very same thing. Similar to the Egyptian hieroglyphic is the form of Jagan-Nath, in whose person are united the
characters of the diluvian Vishnou and Buddha. As I have already had
occasion to observe, the head of the deity is placed in a crescent or boat,
which rests upon an egg that again rests upon a larger egg.[3] Here we have
a triplicated hieroglyphic : but the import of the head, the boat, and the egg,
is one and the same. Accordingly, when the form of Jagan-Nath is described
in a sort of cypher annexed to the low pedestal on which rest the images of
himself and Bal-Ram and Sabhudra, we behold the lunar boat or crescent
containing an egg or ball precisely in the same situation as the head of the
god appears in the idol itself : the egg therefore and the head must in point
of import be identified.[4] The head of Belus or Brahma or Osiris in short
symbolized, like the mundane egg, both the World and the Ark : and the

[1] Luc. de dea Syra.
[3] See Plate I. Fig. 16.
[2] See Plate I. Fig. 12.
[4] See Plate I. Fig. 16.

production of mankind from it related both to the original birth of man from the Earth and to his second birth at the commencement of the postdiluvian world from the Ark. It was on this account, I apprehend, that human heads were wont of old to be sacrificed to Hades or Pluto, whom Syncellus or Alexander Polyhistor rightly pronounces to be the same as Belus:[1] and it was on the same account, that Siva and his consort Parvati, who floated together on the deluge as a mariner and a ship, are so frequently decorated with heads or skulls; for Parvati and Cali are one person.

We may hence discover the origin of the superstition respecting magical oracular heads. The ancients had a notion that the Ark was oracular, most probably from the responses brought by the dove: hence the Argo or Argha, and the ship of Osiris or Ammon, were also deemed oracular. But the human head, from its resemblance to an egg, was used as a symbol of the Ark: consequently, when prepared with suitable magic rites, *it* also was thought to possess the power of giving answers to such as consulted it. Sometimes the head of a murdered infant, preserved by proper drugs from corruption, was placed in a golden boat or dish, that is, in such a vessel as the Hindoos call *an Argha:* and, at other times, a brazen head, formed under particular conjunctions of the planets, was more guiltlessly employed. The placing of this head in a golden dish is but a part of the same superstition, which placed the head of Osiris in a boat formed like a crescent or the head of Jagan-Nath in a lunette resting on an egg.[2]

I suspect, that the stories of Minerva and Gunga springing from the heads of Jupiter and Siva have originated from the same source. Minerva is ultimately one goddess with Venus or the great mother; and Gunga, the genius of the river Ganges, which like the Nile symbolized the deluge, is acknowledged to be fundamentally the same as Isi or the ship Argha:[3] the legend therefore of their birth from the head of the great father is but a varied mode of relating the fable of the birth of Venus from the egg which floated in the

[1] Macrob. Saturn. lib. i. c. 7.

[2] See Calmet's Dict. *Teraphim.* and Seld. de diis Syr. Synt. i. c. 2. Mr. Southey has made great use of this superstition in his exquisite poem of Thalaba. Vide infra book v. c. 8. § III. 5.

[3] See Moor's Hind. Panth. p. 417, 429.

river Euphrates. The Roman tradition likewise of the discovery of the bleeding head of Tolus, while the workmen were digging the foundations of the future Capitol, may probably be traced to a similar origin. *Talus*, or *Tulus*, or *Tolus*, was a title of the great father worshipped in the Sun:[1] his head therefore must be a symbol of the same mythological import as that of Osiris, Belus, Brahma, or Jagan-Nath. Now it is well known, that nothing was more common among the ancients, than to consecrate a newly built city by associating it in some manner or another with the mysterious rites of their religion: hence arose the fables of the Theban and Trojan heifers, and hence probably originated the kindred stories of the discovery of the head of Tolus at Rome and the finding of the heads of a horse and a heifer at Carthage. The horse and the mare, the bull and the cow, were symbols of the great father and the great mother: consequently the heads of those animals will be hieroglyphics of the same meaning as the head of a man. Thus the Egyptians venerated not only the head of Osiris, but likewise the head of his representative the bull. This they crowned with what has generally been esteemed the modius or bushel, placing it between the horns which were made to exhibit the precise form of a boat or lunette: but I am much inclined to believe, both from the shape and position of this vessel, that it is no other than the sacred cup or Argha, which, whether round or navicular, is still a symbol of the Earth and the Ark.[2]

II. The Gothic cosmogony, like that of Chaldèa, is largely intermingled with diluvian history. From the close resemblance indeed, which in some particulars subsists between them, it is more than probable, that our Scythian ancestors, who were of the same race as the Chaldèans and northern Indians, brought into Europe, with some variations, the system, which had been held by their brethren of Cashgar, Iran, and Babylonia.

1. *At the beginning of time*, they are the words of the ancient poem Voluspa, *when nothing was yet formed, neither shore, nor sea, nor foundations beneath; when the earth was no where to be found below, nor the heavens above: all was one vast abyss without plant or verdure. Yet before all things*

The first part of the cosmogony

---

[1] Hesych. Lex. Ταλος. Nonni Dionys. lib. xxv. p. 439.
[2] See Plate I. Fig. 15.

*there existed Muspelsheim.   It is a world, luminous, glowing, not to be dwelt
in by strangers, and situate at the extremity of the earth.   Surtur holds
his empire there.   In his hands there shines a flaming sword.   He shall come
at the end of the world; he shall vanquish all the gods; he shall give up the
universe a prey to flames.*

*But what was the state of the world, before there were families of men
upon the earth, and before the nations were formed?*

*The rivers called Elivages flowed so far from their sources, that the venom
which they rolled along became hard, like the scoria of a furnace when it
grows cold.   Hence was formed the ice, which stopped and flowed no more.
Then all the venom, that was beginning to cover it, also became frozen.   And
thus many strata of congealed vapours were formed, one above another, in
the vast abyss.   By these means that part of the abyss, which lies towards
the north, was filled with a mass of gelid vapours and ice; whilst the interior
parts of it were replete with whirlwinds and tempests.   Directly opposite to
it rose the south part of the abyss, formed of the lightnings and sparks which
flow from the world of fire.   By these means a dreadful freezing wind came
from the quarter of Niflheim, whilst whatever lay opposite to the burning
world was heated and enlightened.   And, as to that part of the abyss which
lay between these two extremes, it was light and serene like the air in a
calm.* [1]

2. In this cosmogony, Surtur or the black, who dwells in a world prior to
that of which the formation is here described, and who at the close of the
present system will swallow up both the gods and the Universe, is evidently
the *Maha-Cali* or *Maha-Pralaya* of the Hindoos, to whom a similar office is
ascribed at the end of each mundane revolution.   His character is that of the
great universal father, whom the Hindoos and Egyptians agree in representing
of a black or dark azure colour.   From him all things are supposed to proceed, and into him all things are resolved.   When the energy of creation is
past, he acts as the preserving power: when a world approaches to its final
catastrophè, he appears as the genius of destruction; and, having resolved it
into its original chaos, he floats in deep repose on the surface of the waters,
until the time of creative energy again calls him forth into action.

[1] Edda. Fab. i, ii.

3. *A breath of heat spreading itself over the gelid vapours, they melted into drops; and of these drops was formed a man, by the power of him who governed. This man was named* Ymer; *the giants call him* Aurgelmer. *From him are descended all the families of the giants. He was wicked, as were all his posterity. Whilst he slept, he fell into a sweat; and from the pit of his left arm were born a male and a female. One of his feet begot upon the other a son, from whom is descended the race of the giants. Immediately after this breath from the south had melted the gelid vapours and resolved them into drops, there was formed out of them a cow named* Oedumla. *From her there sprang a man, who was endowed with beauty, agility, and power. He was called* Bure, *and was the father of* Bore, *who married* Beyzla *the daughter of the giant* Baldorn. *Of that marriage were born three sons,* Odin, Vile, *and* Ve: *and it is our belief, that this* Odin *with his brothers ruleth both heaven and earth, that* Odin *is his true name, and that he is the most powerful of all the gods.*

Was there any kind of equality, or any degree of good understanding, between those two different races?

Far from it: the sons of Bore *slew the giant* Ymer; *and there ran so much blood from his wounds, that all the families of the giants of the frost were drowned in it, except one single giant, who saved himself with all his household. He is called* Bergelmer. *He escaped by happening to be aboard his bark; and by him was preserved the race of the giants of the frost. This is confirmed by the following verses. Many winters before the earth was fashioned, was* Bergelmer *born; and well I know, that this sage giant was saved and preserved on board his bark.*

What then became of the sons of Bore?

They dragged the body of Ymer *into the middle of the abyss, and of it formed the earth. The water and the sea were composed of his blood; the mountains, of his bones; the rocks, of his teeth; and of his hollow bones, mingled with the blood that ran from his wounds, they made the vast ocean, in the midst of which they infixed the earth. Then, having formed the heavens of his skull, they made them rest on all sides upon the earth: they divided them into four quarters, and placed a dwarf at each corner to sustain it. These dwarfs are called* East, West, South, *and* North. *After this they went and*

The second part of the cosmogony intermingled with the history of the deluge seized upon fires in Muspelsheim, that flaming world in the south; and placed them in the abyss, in the upper and lower parts of the sky, to enlighten the earth. Every fire had its assigned residence. Hence the days were distinguished, and the years reduced to calculation. For this reason it is said in the poem of Voluspa, Formerly the sun knew not its place, the moon was ignorant of its powers, and the stars knew not the stations which they were to occupy. The earth is round, and about it is placed the deep sea, the shores of which were given for a dwelling to the giants. But higher up, in a place equally distant on all sides from the sea, the gods built upon the earth a fortress against the giants, the circumference of which surrounds the world. The materials, which they employed for this work, were the eye-brows of Ymer; and they called the place Midgard or the middle mansion. They afterwards tossed his brains into the air; and they became clouds.

But whence came the men, who at present inhabit the world?

The sons of Bore, as they were walking one day upon the shore, found two pieces of wood floating on the waves. They took them; and made a man of the one, and a woman of the other. The first gave them life and soul; the second, reason and motion; the third, hearing, sight, speech, garments, and a name. They called the man Aske, and the woman Emla. From these two are descended the human race; to whom the gods have assigned a habitation near Midgard. [1]

4. The decided resemblance between the characters of the Gothic *Ymer* and the Chaldèan *Omoroca*, from each of whose bodies the Universe is created, has been observed by Mr. Mallet. [2] They are indeed evidently the same person, not only in point of character, but, if I mistake not, even in appellation: for *Ymer* or *Umer* is *Omor-Oca* expressed in a more simple form. The difference of sex does by no means invalidate this opinion, which rests upon the perfect identity of their characters: for the great mother, like the great father, was an hermaphrodite; or rather that person, from whom all things were supposed to be produced, was the great father and the great mother united together in one compound being. Ymer and Omoroca are each the same as that hermaphrodite Jupiter of the Orphic theology; who is

[margin note: Ymer is the same mythologic character as Omoroca]

---

[1] Edda. Fab. ii, iii, iv, v.   [2] Note on Edda. Fab. iv.

pronounced to be at once a male and an immortal nymph, and whose different members are described as being the component parts of the Universe. Each in short is the World; viewed, agreeably to the material system, as constituting the mighty body of the great arrhenothelyte parent. Hence originated the notion, that the World was a huge animal, which arose out of the waters of chaos; a notion, that prevailed no less among the Druids of Britain, than among the mythological philosophers of other countries.[1] It is a curious circumstance, that the double character of Ymer, both as the World and as the great father, is most accurately set forth in the Gothic cosmogony. He is plainly the Earth: because the blood, which spouted out from his body when he was slain, is both declared to be the water of the deluge; and, when the World was subsequently reproduced out of his body, is said to have become the ocean. Yet is he also represented as the first man, from whom descended a race of wicked giants that lived in a state of lawless violence, until, with the exception of a single family which was preserved in a ship, they were swept away by the waters of the flood. Now this is the precise character of the great hermaphroditic parent, when modelled according to the theory of the materialists. He is that being, who appears at the commencement of each world, who is the general ancestor of mankind, and whose body is nevertheless imagined to be the Universe.[2]

5. It is observable, that, in exact accordance with the prevailing doctrine of a succession of worlds, though the death of *Ymer*, or in other words the dissolution of the antediluvian world over which the great father Adam presided, is unequivocally and literally described as synchronizing with the deluge, yet the creation even of the whole Universe is said to be *posterior* to that event. *Many winters before the earth was fashioned*, says the author of the Voluspa, *was Bergelmer born; and well I know, that this sage giant was preserved on board his bark.* Bergelmer is evidently Noah, considered as a reappearance of Adam: he is the same therefore as Ymer himself, when viewed simply in his human character of the great father and distinctly from

[handwritten marginal note: The character of Bergelmer]

---

[1] See Cudw. Intell. Syst. b. i. c. 3. p. 124, 131, 141. c. 2. p. 113. c. 4. p. 499. and a most curious mystical poem in Davies's Mythol. of Brit. Druids. p. 47, 48.

[2] It is not improbable, that the Gothic name *Ymer* or *Umer* is the same as the Persic name *Cai-Umersh*; an appellation, which is applied to Adam.

his superadded material character of the Universe.   Hence that fashioning of the Earth, which is said to have taken place *subsequent* to his preservation in a ship, must mean the renovation of the World after the deluge, which was esteemed a new creation: and, agreeably to the prevailing doctrine, not only is the Earth said to have been then created out of the body of Ymer, but even the whole mundane system.

6. The first man Ymer is represented as being the parent of a lawless race of giants; who are contemporary with another race and are even connected with them by marriage, but who yet live in a state of continual hostility with them.   The heads of this second race are a patriarch and his three sons;[1] who are born from a mysterious cow, who flourish during the whole antediluvian period, who produce the deluge by slaying Ymer, who afterwards create the World anew out of his body, and who in subsequent ages are revered as the greatest of the gods.

Here we have again the great father presented under a somewhat different aspect.   The heifer-born patriarch is still Adam reappearing as Noah; and his three sons are the triple offspring of the one reappearing in the triple offspring of the other.   Hence they are said to have lived during the whole period of the antediluvian world, to have contracted marriages with the contemporary lawless race of giants, to have produced the deluge, and again to have lived subsequent to that event.   The cow, from which they were born, symbolizes, like the lotos, the ship Argha, the egg, and various other double hieroglyphics, both the Earth and the Ark or the greater World and the smaller World; that mighty mother, from whose womb were successively produced the hero-gods that presided over each creation.   She is the same as the wonderful cow Surabbhee, which in the mythology of the Hindoos emerges from the deluge, and which is a form of Isi or Devi; that goddess, who is at once declared to be the Earth and who is said to have floated in the form of a ship on the surface of the flood.   She is the same also as the Io, the Isis, and the Astartè, of the Greeks, the Egyptians,

---

[1] I say *a patriarch*, because Bure and Bore, though the one is made the father of the other, are evidently but one person.   The same relationship and the same identity may be observed in the Osiris and Horus of Egypt.   If however we choose to consider them as Adam succeeded by Noah, the import of the legend will still remain much the same.

and the Phenicians. She is the same, in short, as the heifer, which was called *Theba* or *the Ark*, and within which Osiris was inclosed when he was set afloat by Typhon : for that god is indifferently feigned to have been shut up in an ark, or in the Moon, or in an ark resembling the Moon, or in a wooden cow whose curving horns exhibited the shape of the lunar boat or crescent.

In the preceding detail, however distorted and corrupted, it is impossible not to perceive a striking resemblance to the antediluvian and diluvian history of Moses. The sons of Cain are there represented to us as a race, according to some translations, of giants ; but certainly as a lawless and violent race.[1] They are said to have contracted marriages with another race termed *the sons of God* ; an ancient expression of ambiguous import, which in the traditions of the Gentiles might easily have converted that race into a distinct family of superior beings, but which seems with sufficient plainness to allude only to the offspring of the righteous Seth. Wickedness, after such incongruous connections, diffused itself yet more rapidly ; until at length, in the days of Noah and his three sons, the old world was destroyed by the waters of the deluge. In subsequent ages, these, considered as a reappearance of Adam and his three sons, became the great gods of the nations : and the destruction and reproduction of each successive world was attributed to them.

7. It appears, that the Goths had an idea that the race of the giants was specially perpetuated in the descendants of Bergelmer, who preserved himself in a ship at the time of the deluge. They also had a second distinct postdiluvian race produced from two pieces of wood, which the sons of Bore found floating in the waves of the sea.

Thus, although with a clear and decided reference to the diluvian origin of all the present race of mankind, do they account for a new and remarkable classification which took place not very long after the flood. By the warlike descendants of Bergelmer they meant, I have little doubt, the children of Ham chiefly in the line of Cush ; who established the first universal monarchy at Babel, and who subjugated their less enterprizing brethren here

The race of the giants is perpetuated in the family of Bergelmer

---

[1] Gen. vi. 4.

described as a distinct and inferior race sprung from two pieces of floating wood. Of the family of the Cuthic giants were the Scythians or Goths: and, in all ages, they seem to have been fully conscious to the proud pre-ëminence of their military ancestors.

8. The centrical fortress, which the gods constructed from the eye-brows of Ymer, and which towered from the midst of the earth equally distant on all sides from the sea, is certainly the Meru of the Hindoos and Indo-Scythæ, which is described in a manner precisely similar. Accordingly, as the Goths termed the flat summit of this holy abode *the plain of Ida,* so the Hindoo mythologists denominate it *Ida-Vratta* or *the circle of Ida.* It was the peculiar residence of the hero-gods immediately after the deluge: and it is at once described with all the characteristics of a Paradise, and is represented as a fortress which might secure the deities against any further attacks from the giants. This lofty abode seems very evidently to be the mountain, upon which the Ark rested, and which (there is reason to believe) coincides even geographically with the pristine terrestrial Paradise. The giants, against whom it was to secure the gods, are the impious antediluvians, the rebellious Titans of Greek mythology: and, in exact accordance with the notions of the Hindoos, it is represented not only as rising out of the centre of the earth, but as being in some sort even the whole world itself. It cannot, I think, be doubted, that these opinions of the Goths were brought by them into the west from northern India, the ancient settlement of their warlike ancestors the Chasas or Indo-Scythæ.

III. The Phenician cosmogony, as it has frequently been remarked, is altogether founded upon atheistical principles: this may perhaps in some measure be accounted for by the origin of the people, that adopted such a system. The Phenicians were not of the race of Canaan, as many have supposed: but, according to the positive declaration of ancient history, they were Chusas or Indo-Scythæ; who descended, in the first instance, from the mountains of Cashgar to the shores of the Erythrèan sea; and who, from the shores of the Erythrèan sea, again migrated into Palestine.[1] Now the Chusas, or Scythians, or unmixed pastoral Cushim, were peculiarly devoted to the su-

---

[1] Vide infra book vi. c. 5. § V. 2.

The central fortress of the gods is the Paradisical Ararat

perstition of Buddha: and to this day, wherever that religion is professed, a system of philosophical atheism naturally engendered by Materialism will, I believe, almost invariably be found to prevail. Hence we need not wonder at the atheism of the Phenician cosmogony: the whole theory is evidently, indeed professedly, a modification of Buddhism, which the emigrants brought with them from Babylonia and India.

1. Sanchoniatho informs us, that the system, which he details, was taken from the cosmogony of Taautus. But Taautus, or Taut, or Thoth, is the same person as the oriental Buddha; who is likewise called *Tat* or *Datta*, and who is said by the Hindoos to have been peculiarly venerated in Egypt and the west.[1] The Phenician hypothesis therefore is palpably that of the atheistical Buddhists: and every part of it will be found to bear testimony to its parentage.

It was copied by Sanchoniatho from the books of Taut or Buddha, and is founded on atheistical principles

According to this system, the Universe originated from a dark air and a turbulent evening chaos. These were boundless, and long remained destitute of order and regular figure. But, when the air became enamoured of its own principles, a certain mixture was produced, which bore the name of *Poth*. This mixture was the beginning of the creation: and from it and the air, ignorant of its own production, was begotten Mot; which some pronounce to be the same as Ilus, and which others interpret to mean a putrid watery mixture. Ilus or Mot was the seed of the World, and the productive cause of all things. But there were likewise certain animals destitute of intelligence; whence were born other animals, which possessed intelligence. These last were each shaped like an egg, and were called *Zophesamen* or *overseers of the heavens*. Thus did the Sun, the Moon, and the greater and smaller Stars, all equally shine out of Mot.[2] The air now be-

---

[1] Vide infra book iv. chap. 5. § IX, X, XI, XIX.

[2] Such clearly appears to me to be the proper translation of the Greek of Eusebius: Και εξελαμψε Μωτ, ἡλιος τε και σελνηη, αστερες τε και αστερα μεγαλα. He had just before told us, that *Mot* was the productive cause of all things; and now he goes on to state, that the whole host of heaven was born out of Mot. Bp. Cumberland entirely ruins the sense by supposing *Mot* to be the nominative case, and by translating the passage, *Thus shone out Mot, the Sun and the Moon, the less and the greater Stars*: whereas the undeclinable word *Mot* is the genitive, governed of εξ in composition with ελαμψε. It was not *Mot* that shone out *along with* the host of heaven; but the host of heaven, that shone out of, or was produced from, *Mot*.

ginning to emit light, winds and clouds were produced by its fiery influence on the seaa nd on the earth. These, being separated by the heat of the Sun, dashed against each other, and thus caused thunder and lightning. The noise awoke the intelligent animals : males and females were stirred up in the earth and in the sea : and thus appeared the various tribes of the brute creation. Lastly, from the primeval wind Colpia and his consort Baau or Baaut were born the two first mortals named *Eon* and *Protogonus ;* to the former of whom we are indebted for the knowledge of deriving nourishment from the fruit of trees.[1]

Remarks upon the cosmogony

2. All the foreign words, which occur in this theory, Bochart has resolved into Hebrew. In some of his etymologies he is right; but, I suspect, not in all of them. Thus the name *Zophesamen* is clearly composed of two Hebrew words, which jointly signify *the overseers of the heavens :*[2] but it may be doubted, whether *Colpia* ought to be understood as denoting *the voice of the mouth of Jah.*[3] Most of the terms have in fact been borrowed from oriental Buddhism: and this is what we might naturally expect would be the case with a theory, which was professedly inculcated by Taut or Buddha, and which was brought from the confines of India by a colony of Buddhic Chasas.

Poth, which is said to have been the appellation of the primeval chaotic mixture, is but the name of *Bot* or *Pot* or *Buddha,* pronounced and written as it is very frequently pronounced and written in the east. Hence the Greeks borrowed their Pothus or Eros or aboriginal egg-born Cupid, who is the same person as Buddha or the great father. The character given of Poth in this cosmogony exactly accords with the notions, which were entertained respecting the principal Demon-god. He was not only supposed to have floated in a state of deathlike sleep on the surface of the chaotic abyss during the intermediate period between two worlds ; but he was likewise identified with the abyss itself, or, in the language of the Hindoos, the all-pervading ocean was one of his material forms. Thus both Iswara and Osiris are each said to be the element, on the surface of which

---

[1] Sanchon. apud Euseb. Præp. Evan. lib. i. c. 10.
[2] Heb. צופי שמים.   [3] Heb. קל פי יה.

they nevertheless severally floated in a mysterious ship: and thus Janus, whose whole history proves him to be the great father, is yet declared by Ovid to be the same as Chaos or that turbid mixture of water and mud, whence the world was originally created, and whence it a second time arose as by a new creation while the deluge was retiring into the central cavity.[1] Accordingly, Epiphanius informs us, that Chaos was the same as Buthus, by which the Greeks understood *the abyss :*[2] nor were they mistaken in their opinion, though the name *Buth,* like the name *Poth,* is really the name of the chaotic god But or Buddha.

Sanchoniatho represents Poth as being the parent of Mot or Ilus : but this is merely a genealogical reduplication ; for Poth is defined to be a watery chaotic mixture, and Mot is also defined to be a watery chaotic mixture from which all things were subsequently produced. *Mot* I take to be a Chaldee or Hebrew word, which properly signifies *Death.*[3] It was a title of Buddha or the great father, in his quality of an infernal divinity: for the chief Demon-god was venerated under the character of Death or Hades from Hindostan in the east to Britain in the west.

Ilus or *Il,* on the other hand, is a regular Cuthic name of Buddha, which the Phenicians, I have no doubt, brought with them from their settlements on the Erythrèan sea: for Buddha or Menu, in the character of Ila, is said to have married his own daughter Ila, who is described as the offspring of an ancient personage that was preserved in an ark at the time of the general deluge. Sanchoniatho afterwards tells us, that *Il* or *Ilus* was a title of him; whom the Greeks called *Cronus,* who was the parent of three sons, and who was certainly that supposed transmigrating personage whom the Gentiles venerated as the great father both of gods and men. He was well known to the Iliensians, who were another Scythian colony: and it is declared, that from him the city of Ilium received its appellation. It is worthy of remark, that the Greeks have preserved the word in their language precisely according to its oriental import. *Ila,* in the Sanscrit, denotes *the World,* as produced out of the slimy chaotic mixture of mud and water

---

[1] Ovid. Fast. lib. i. ver. 103.

[2] Epiph. adv. Hær. vol. i. p. 164,   [3] Heb. מות.

described by Sanchoniatho: and, in a similar manner, *Ilus*, among the Greeks, signified such *mud* or *slime* as subsides to the bottom of lakes.

The Zophesamen or overseers of the heavens appear to me, as they did to Bp. Cumberland, to mean the celestial bodies: indeed the subsequent context of the Greek of Eusebius seems almost necessarily to require such an interpretation; for, after describing the Zophesamen, he immediately adds, *thus did the Sun, the Moon, and the Stars, shine out of Mot.*[1] The notion of their being all formed like eggs has arisen from the well-known symbol of the mundane egg: and the supposition, that they are animated and intelligent beings, perfectly accords with an opinion which prevailed very generally throughout the pagan world. Sometimes the souls of the hero-gods were thought to be translated to the heavenly bodies: and, at other times (such was the theory of the Stoics), all the Stars were accounted parts of Jupiter or the great father, all were supposed to live and to have rational souls, all therefore without controversy were to be worshipped as gods.[2] In a similar manner, the Platonists delighted to talk of an intelligible World, an intelligible Heaven and Earth, an intelligible Sun and Moon:[3] and it is worthy of observation, that this pagan hypothesis has been adopted by some of the Rabbinical writers among the Jews. Thus Maimonides asserts, that the Stars are all animated, and endued with life and knowledge and understanding: and he maintains, that each of them, according to its degree and excellence, praises and honours God after the manner of the holy angels.[4]

With respect to the wind Colpia, the name of which Bochart resolves into three Hebrew words, I cannot help suspecting that the true origin of the appellation is to be sought in the Sanscrit *Calpa*. The term has indeed been misapplied, for the Calpa is that grand period which comprehends

---

[1] Bochart supposes them to be angels, but, so far as I can judge, without any sufficient reason. Boch. Canaan. lib. ii. c. 2. p. 706.

[2] August. de civ. Dei. lib. iv. c. 11, 9, 27, 31. lib. vii. c. 6.

[3] Cudw. Intell. Syst. b. i. c. 4. p. 554.

[4] Jesude Hattorah c. iii. § 9. apud Cudw. Intell. Syst. b. i. c. 4. p. 471. It seems, that they attempted to prove the truth of this pagan speculation from Scripture, by taking in a literal sense that expression of Nehemiah, *The host of heaven worshippeth thee.* Nehem. ix. 6.

fourteen Manwantaras and is equal to a day of Brahma: but the deducing of the birth of the first man from the commencement of a Calpa, thus making the Calpa his allegorical parent, accords so exactly with the prevailing notion of a succession of worlds, that I cannot but think the derivation of *Colpia* from *Calpa*, especially when the Cuthic descent of the Phenicians is considered, a more probable etymology than that of Bochart.

Eusebius says, that the name of Baau or Baaut, who is assigned as a wife to *Colpia*, signifies *Night*. If the word ever bore any such signification, which probably was the case, I should be inclined to think that it was an acquired one. What I mean is this: the proper name of the goddess Night was *Baaut*, whence *baaut* came to denote *night* in general. *Baaut* itself is no other than the title *Buddha*, or, as it is sometimes written, *Baoth*, considered as a feminine appellation, and applied to the great mother. All the chief gods of the Gentiles were hermaphrodites: but, when they are divided into two distinct persons male and female, the two perpetually bear a name common to both. Thus, as Isa is the husband of Isi, and Ila of Ila; so *Baaut* will be no less a feminine than a masculine name. The goddess Night, whom the Phenicians called *Baaut* and esteemed the mother of the first man, is said by the Orphic poet to be the same as Venus; and is celebrated by him as the common parent both of gods and men, and as the all-productive matrix of the Universe.[1] What they meant by her was both the World and the Ark: for such was the character of Venus, Isis, Bhavani, or the great mother, under whatever name she may be venerated.

Hence, agreeably to the doctrine of a succession of similar worlds, her offspring Protogonus or the first-born will be both Adam and Noah; or, as the matter ought to be expressed according to the speculations of Paganism, the great father successively appearing by transmigration in the persons of those two patriarchs. This Protogonus is evidently, as the very name implies, the first-born Brahma of the Hindoos; who was produced from an egg that floated on the waters of the abyss. He is also the Protogonus, or first-born Phanes, of the Orphic theology; who is similarly said to have been produced from an egg and to have been the parent both of gods and

[1] Orph. Hymn. ii.

men. The egg and the goddess Night or Baaut mean the same thing: and the person, who is born from the egg, is also represented as having been exposed in an ark, as floating on the surface of the ocean in the calix of the lotos, or as sailing in a ship over the waters of the deluge.

Eon, who is described as a male, I take to be really the same character as Protogonus. The Greek title, which he bears, and which we may conclude to be a translation of the corresponding Phenician word, sufficiently points out his real character; and at the same time proves his identity with the Grecian Cronus and the Indian Cali: for *Eon* signifies *an Age* or *Cycle;* and *Cronus* and *Cali* equally denote *Time,* which is nearly equivalent to it. This appellation of *Time* or *Age* was applied to the great father, because with him postdiluvian time or a new age commenced; and indeed, according to the notion of the pagan theologists, the beginning of every new time or new mundane system, which was invariably preceded by a flood, was marked by his appearance when awaking from his deathlike slumber on the surface of the ocean: hence we find Protogonus and Eon placed at the head of the age, respecting which Sanchoniatho undertakes to treat. Some have thought, that the Eon, whom he joins with Protogonus, ought to be esteemed a female; and indeed that part of the legend, which makes this person the first who plucked fruit from trees, seems to contain no obscure allusion to the transgression of Eve: but Philo, his Greek translator, speaks of Eon as a male; and it is not improbable, that, instead of *Protogonus* AND *Eon,* Sanchoniatho wrote, without the conjunction, what in English would be equivalent to *The first-born Age,* in Greek to *Protogonus-Eon.* This Eon of Sanchoniatho is clearly the Eon mentioned by Nonnus in his remarkable episode of the birth of Beroè: for the former of these writers professedly treats of Phenician mythology, and the latter is here giving us a curious portion of the same mythology. The sea-nymph Beroè, whence the city Berytus derived its name, is represented as being the daughter of Oceanus and Tethys: and she is celebrated, as the root of life, as the house of Venus and Jupiter and the Loves, as the hall of Mars, as the habitation of Bacchus, and as the firm abode of Hermes or Taut. She is certainly the same character as the Atergatis of Syria, and as the navicular Isis or Baris of Egypt: for each of these goddesses is similarly described, as being the common receptacle of the hero-gods. Her birth is said to have taken place, when the whole earth was washed by the ocean, when the star of Orchomenus or Noah rode high in the heavens, and when all the brute creation dwelt together in peace and amity: and she herself is exhibited to us as the first apparent female, as equalling the world in antiquity, and as being produced at the commencement of a new age. The whole of this relates to the allegorical nativity of the Ark from the deluge, after it had conveyed in safety over the mighty waters both birds and beasts and hero-gods. Accordingly, as soon as Beroè is born, or in other words as soon as the Ark grounds on the summit of mount Ararat, a venerable personage named *Eon* is introduced to our notice. He is said to have been a prophet; and he is described, as having been washed in the swelling floods of justice. In consequence of this oceanic purification, he is restored from the decrepitude of old age to the vigour of youth, in the same manner as a serpent at stated intervals casts its skin and becomes young again. Approaching to the newly born Beroè, with whom he is represented as being strictly coëtaneous, he looses the veil of justice with which she had been swathed, and removes the mysterious covering that shrouded her. This veil is doubtless the same as the veil of Isis or Juno:[1] and, by the removing of it, we must evidently, I think, understand the opening of the door or hatchway in the side of the Ark. Such events were supposed to occur at the beginning of every world: hence Sanchoniatho rightly places Eon at the head of his mythological genealogy.[2]

3. The fable of the mundane egg, which gave birth to Protogonus, was well known to the Phenicians. Damascius gives an account of their cosmogony from Mochus, in which *Ether and Air are the first principles. From them is produced Ulomus: who, by commerce with himself* (that is, with his female half, after he has divided himself into two persons, like the Brahma, Menu, and Viraj, of the Hindoos), *begets Chusorus the first opener and afterwards an egg. The egg is heaven: but, when it is broken in two, both heaven and earth are formed out of it.*[3]

Phenician Cosmogony as detailed by Mochus

---

[1] See Plate I. Fig. 13.　　　　[2] Nonni Dionys. lib. xli. p. 698.

[3] Damas. de princip. apud annot. in Phorn. de nat. deor. c. xvii. p. 179.

In this legend, Chusorus the first opener is certainly the great father, in his character of the god of the door or the god of opening : though, in the present instance, Cush, agreeably to the doctrine of repeated transmigration, appears to have usurped the honours of Noah; for Chusorus is Cush the Aurite, from whom the royal Phenician Shepherds were descended. What he opens is the mystic floating egg, from the broken parts of which is framed the renovated Universe: and that opening is the same as the removal of the veil of Beroè by the hand of the regenerated Eon.

IV. The Egyptian cosmogony, like the Phenician, is professedly of the Buddhic school: for the fullest account, which we have of it, is contained in a book ascribed to Hermes or Thoth : but Hermes or Thoth is the same person as Taut, who is said to have drawn up the Phenician system; and Taut again is the same as the oriental Tat or Buddha.

As exhibited in the books of Taut

1 According to this treatise, the materials of which (like those of the Persic Zend-Avesta) are probably genuine, whoever may have been the compiler of it; according to this treatise, *there was originally a boundless darkness in the great abyss: but water and an Intelligent Ethereal Spirit acted by divine power in Chaos. Then sprang forth holy light : then the elements were compacted of the moist sandy substance of the chaotic mixture: then all the gods made an orderly distribution of things out of seminative nature.*[1]

The Intelligent Ethereal Spirit here mentioned is the great father, to whom the pagans were wont to ascribe the office of creator : and he is styled *an Intelligent Spirit*, because he is the person, who was considered as the Soul of the World, who by the Hindoos is called *Menu* or *Mind*, and who under the appellation of *Nous* is celebrated by the Orphic Platonists as the parent of the three younger egg-born Noës or divine creative kings.

Demiurgic Triad

2. With this celebrated demiurgic triad the Egyptians, like most other ancient nations, were well acquainted. In the Hermetic theology, as we learn from Jamblichus, *Emeph* was reputed to be the ruler of all the celestial gods, and was described as a self-understanding Nous or Intellect. Yet before Emeph was placed another Intellect, denominated *Eicton ;* who was

[1] Serm. Sac. c. iii. init. apud Jackson's Chron. Ant.

deemed the first of beings, and who was to be worshipped only in the silence of deep abstraction. To these two Noës was added a third; who was specially esteemed the creator of the world, and who bore the names of *Phtha* and *Ammon.*[1]

The Egyptian triad, thus stated, will teach us how to understand a curious form of adjuration, which Cyril and Justin Martyr give to Orpheus, but which John Malela and the author of the Paschal Chronicle ascribe to Thoth or Hermes-Trismegistus. The difference however is immaterial; for the Orphic and Taautic systems were fundamentally the same. In the Paschal Chronicle, the oath is exhibited in the following terms. *I adjure thee, the Heaven, the wise work of the great God: be propitious. I adjure thee, the Voice of the Father, which he first spake when he established the whole world by his counsel; the Voice of the Father which he first uttered, his only-begotten Word.*[2] To the genuineness of this oath, in its *present* very suspicious form, I am inclined to give but little credit: it is evidently an adjuration to the triplicated god of the Gentiles dressed up in a Christian garb. Finding that the pagans universally worshipped a triad of deity, and mistaking (as many modern writers have done) this triad of hero-gods for the Holy Trinity, the fathers have been apparently led, with more zeal than judgment, to heighten the colouring and to fill up the outline of the original form. In this opinion I am the rather confirmed by observing, that the author of the Paschal Chronicle has thought proper to add the *last* clause of the adjuration to a fragment already sufficiently corrupted: the other writers, who have preserved the oath, are silent respecting *the only-begotten Word.*

I apply the same remark to the response, said to have been given by an oracle to Thulis one of the early kings of Egypt, when he inquired who that being was that ruled all things. *First God, then the Word, and the Spirit with them. All these coalesce together, and proceed jointly into that unity, whose strength is the strength of ages.*[3] The preceding response con-

---

[1] Jamb. de Myster. sect. viii. c. 3.

[2] Chron. Pasch. p. 47. Comp. Cyril. cont. Julian. p. 23. Justin. Mart. Cohort. p. 78. Mal. Chronog. p. 30.

[3] Chron. Pasch. p. 46.

tains the precise doctrine of the Hindoos respecting their Trimurti; so far
therefore I believe it to be genuine: but the dress in which it is exhibited by
the author of the Paschal Chronicle, to whom we are indebted for its preservation, has, I think, but too evidently been borrowed from the Christian sanctuary.   Not indeed that the term *Word* was *unknown* to the Platonists;
they seem to have received it, as much of their theology was confessedly of
barbaric origin, from the *Mimra* of the Targumists: yet so remarkable a
combination as *God, the Word, and the Spirit,* appears to myself at
least of so very suspicious an aspect, that I cannot easily believe it to have
been a genuine portion of the ancient oracle.

The cosmogony as exhibited by Diogenes Laertius and Diodorus Siculus

3. The account, which Diogenes Laertius gives of the Egyptian cosmogony, exactly agrees with that contained in the book ascribed to Hermes-
Trismegistus. *In the beginning was rude matter: then the four elements
were separated out of it: and next animals were perfected.*[1] It was in
reality an atheistic system : for Diodorus Siculus represents it as founded,
like that of the Phenicians, on mere physical principles, yet as deducing
the origin of all things from the matter of heaven and earth blended together in a chaotic state.[2]

The goddess Night or Darkness was highly venerated by the Egyptians

4. We may observe, that the Egyptians, no less than the Phenicians, venerated the goddess Night or Darkness: for the *Night* of one cosmogony
seems evidently to be the *Darkness* of the other.   This primeval deity, as
I have already observed, is declared to be the same as Venus or the great
mother.   I am inclined to think, that, as the character of Venus is two-fold,
so the identification of that goddess with Night or Darkness has arisen
from a two-fold source.   We are told by the sacred historian, that at the
time of the first creation *darkness was upon the face of the deep:* and,
from the account which he gives of the construction of the Ark, the interior of that smaller World, immediately before what the pagans deemed
another creation, could have had little or no light except what was artificial:
Both these circumstances were well known to the Gentiles, and are perpetually alluded to in their Mysteries.   But Venus or the great mother is
certainly both the Earth and the Ark: hence, from the darkness which pre-

[1] Diog. Laer. in Proœm.   [2] Diod. Bibl. lib. i. p. 7.

_ach creation, she was esteemed the goddess of Night or Darkness, and all things are feigned to have been produced from the womb of Night. Damascius, in an inquiry respecting the first mundane principle, tells us, that the Egyptians have chosen to celebrate the primal cause as unspeakable; that they style it *Darkness unknown*; that they mention it with a three-fold acclamation; and that they hold this principle to be an inconceivable Darkness, night and Darkness past all imagination.[1] He further informs us, from Heraïscus and Asclepiades, that to this unknown Darkness, the principle of all things, they added water and sand; and that from the combination of these they supposed a triad to have been produced, of which they made Camaphis the head.[2] We also learn from Plutarch, that, agreeably to the Mosaical cosmogony, they conceived darkness to be older than light; an opinion, which is equally true whether considered with reference to the first or to the second creation.[3] Their *threefold* acclamation to Darkness related, I have no doubt, to the triplicated character of the great mother: for, by way of preserving a strict analogical correspondence between her and her mystic consort, she was also feigned either to have multiplied herself into three goddesses or to possess three combined forms. In a similar manner, the triad of gods, produced from darkness water and sand at the beginning of the world, is clearly, I think, the great triple father; who, according to the speculations of the pagans, was manifested as three emanating from one at the epoch of every new creation.[4]

[1] Bryant on the plagues of Egypt, p. 170. Cudw. Intell. Syst. b. i. c. 4. p. 414, properly 354.

[2] Damas. apud annot. in Phornut. de nat. deor. c. xvii. p. 179.

[3] Plut. Sympos. lib. iv. p. 670.

[4] I suspect, that the *Mother Night* of the ancient Goths was the very same as the *Universal Mother Night* of the Orphic theology, and as the *all-productive Night* or *Darkness* of the Phenician and Egyptian systems. They applied indeed this title to the longest night in the year: but their notion, that the world was created on such a night, sufficiently shews how we are to understand the appellation. At every annual recurrence of the longest night, they had a festival named *Iuul* in honour of their solar god Thor, who then astronomically begun to rise from the grave of the southern hemisphere and thus to represent on the sphere the resurrection or new birth of the great father from the Ark which was esteemed his coffin. Mallet's North. Ant. vol. i. p. 130, 358. The Gothic or Scythian *Iuul* is evidently the *Huli* of the

V. The cosmogony of the Persians is contained in the Zend-Avesta, a composition ascribed to their prophet Zeradusht or Zoroaster and translated into French by M. Anquetil de Perron, who in his earliest youth had the merit of undertaking a voyage to India with no other view than to recover the writings of that ancient personage. How far this curious work is to be admitted as containing fragments at least of genuine antiquity, is a point which must be reserved for our future consideration:[1] at present I shall merely give some account of its history of the creation.

According to the system of Zeradusht then, as it is set forth in the Zend-Avesta, the god Ormuzd created the world, not indeed in six days, but, what is very similar to it, at six different intervals. Each of these periods comprehended a considerable number of days, though not an equal one; yet, in the sum total, the six times amounted exactly to a whole year. During the first period were created the heavens; during the second, the waters. The third was allotted to the production of the earth; the fourth, to the formation of trees and vegetables. During the fifth, the various tribes of animals, aërial, sylvan, and aquatic, received their existence; and the sixth space of time, in almost exact conformity with the sixth day of the Mosaical cosmogony, was devoted solely to the creation of man. This was the most honourable of all the productions of Ormuzd: and the person so produced, the general father of the human race, was compounded of a man and a bull. That being was succeeded by a second bull-man, a reappearance of the first, who flourished at the period of an universal deluge.[2]

VI. The preceding cosmogony bears a striking and curious resemblance to that of the ancient Etrurians; a singular race of men, who were nearly

Hindoos, and the *Gule* of the ancient Irish. Hence, on account of the time when it was celebrated, the Saxons named Christmas *Yeol* or *Yule.* Both *Thor* or *Taranath,* and *Iuul* or *Gul* or *Goles,* were titles of Buddha, who is the same as the Gothic Wod or Woden. The Goths or Scythians brought both the worship of this deity and the great outlines of their mythology from their ancient settlements in Casbgar and Bokhara. They were universally and from a very remote period votaries of Buddha or Sacya. General Vallancey has given a Dissertation on the Irish Gule in Collect. de reb. Hibern. vol. iii. p. 468.

[1] Vide infra book iii. chap. 3. §. II.

[2] Zend-Avest. vol. iii. p. 348. Hyde de rel. vet. Pers. p. 161, 162.

allied to the Hindoos and Egyptians, and from whom the Romans seem to have borrowed the most mysterious and recondite part of their theology. We are informed by Suidas, that a sage of that nation wrote a history, in which it is said, that God created the world in six thousand years, and appointed the same period of time to be the extent of its duration. In the first millenary he made the heaven and the earth; in the second, the visible firmament; in the third, the sea and all the waters that are inthe earth; in the fourth, the sun, the moon, and the stars; in the fifth, every living soul of birds, reptiles, and quadrupeds, which have their abode either in the air, on the land, or in the waters; and lastly, in the sixth, man alone. According therefore to the system of the old Etrurians, five millenaries preceded the formation of man, to which the whole of the sixth was devoted: while a remaining period of six thousand years comprehends the duration of the human race. So that the age of the world, from its commencement to its termination, will amount precisely to twelve thousand years. [1]

1. Respecting this cosmogony it may be observed, that, among the ancients, millenaries and days appear to have been used convertibly, perhaps from an idea, sanctioned even by revelation, that a thousand years constituted a great day of the Creator. [2] Such a mode of speaking remarkably prevails among the Hindoos in computing the duration of the life of Brahma: and there can be little doubt, I think, that the twelve chiliads of the Etruscans are the same as the famous Indian period of twelve thousand years. [3] How this number came to be selected, we may gather from the cosmogony now under consideration. Because God reduced the world to order in six days, the old Etrurians extended the divine labour to six millenaries: and, on the other hand, from an imaginary analogy to the six days of the creation, they concluded, that the mundane system would last six thousand years ere it was resolved into its component chaos. The opinion has been adopted both into the Jewish, and into the Christian, church; into the latter, on the professed ground of the analogy of six millenaries to six days, and of a concluding seventh sabbatical millenary to a seventh day of rest; and, in support of the

Respecting the ancient opinion that the world is to continue six millenaries.

---

[1] Suid, Lex. Τυρρηνια.
[2] See Psalm xc. 4. and 2 Pet. iii. 8.
[3] See Asiat. Res. vol. v. p. 242, 245.

theory, the convertibility of a day and a millenary has been seriously urged from the language used (as I have already intimated) both by a prophet and by an apostle.[1] That the earthly reign of the Messiah will be closed by a triumphant period of a thousand years, is expressly foretold in the Apocalypse: but that that chiliad will be the *seventh* chiliad of the world, is no where intimated. Analogy might seem indeed to teach us, that, as the seventh day was the sabbath, so the sabbatism of the Millennium would coincide with the seventh mundane chiliad: but, as we have nothing to depend upon beyond a tradition deduced from this specious analogy, and as there is considerable reason for believing that we are already far advanced into the seventh chiliad from the creation, we are certainly not warranted in speaking so positively on the subject as some have done.[2]

Respecting the general mode of computing time by weeks

2. Whatever may be the fate of such speculations, which at least are harmless, it is difficult to account for the universal division of time into weeks and for the very general notion that the seventh day was peculiarly holy, except from some tradition of the creation similar to those preserved by the Persians and Etrurians. A year is the revolution of the sun: a month is the revolution of the moon: the month of thirty days with the five epagomenæ is an attempt to adjust the course of the moon to that of the sun. None of these, except possibly the last, can be deemed arbitrary; because such admeasurements of time are founded on the physical motions of the heavenly bodies:

---

[1] *Six thousand years the world shall subsist, and during one it shall be in a state of devastation.* R. Ketina in Gemar. Sanhed. cap. Cheleck. apud Huls. Theol. Judaic. lib. i. par. 2. p. 497. *The tradition of Rabbi Elias. Six thousand years are the age of the world: two thousand are chaos; two thousand are the Law; two thousand are the days of Messiah.* Gaulmin de vit. et mort. Mosis. lib. iii. c. 2. To this tradition the later Jews, as it has been proved by Peter Galatin, have added the following words: *But, on account of our many and great sins, out of these there have passed away what have passed away.* See Mede's Works. b. v. c. 3. p. 893. Iren. lib. v. c. 28, 30. Just. Mart. Dial. cum Tryph. Jud. Lactant. Instit. lib. vii. c. 14. Cyprian. lib. de exhort. mart.

[2] There can scarcely, I think, be a doubt, that we ought to adopt the longer scheme of chronology, as it is called, in preference to that curtailed one which appears in the common Hebrew Pentateuch. I am myself inclined to follow the Seventy in their antediluvian chronology, and the Samaritan Pentateuch in early postdiluvian chronology. See however Hales's Chronol. vol. i.

hence their universal adoption cannot occasion any surprize; it is nothing more than might have been expected. But a week is a portion of time wholly arbitrary: the general prevalence therefore of *such* a mode of computation cannot be accounted for in a similar manner; still less can the opinion respecting the superior sanctity of the seventh day. Yet it is indisputable, that both the one and the other *have* obtained very widely throughout the world in all ages. The key to this remarkable circumstance is found in the Mosaical history of the creation, and in the singularly parallel cosmogonies of Etruria and Persia.

3. With respect to the fact itself, Eusebius cites several of the ancient poets, who speak of the seventh day as being holy. Thus Hesiod and Homer unite in ascribing to it a superior degree of sanctity; and thus Callimachus and Linus assert, that, when it arrived, all things were finished.[1] Eusebius further tells us from Porphyry, that the Phenicians consecrated one day in seven to their god Cronus:[2] Aulus Gellius mentions, that some of the heathen philosophers had a custom of teaching only on the seventh day:[3] Lampridius observes of Alexander Severus, that on the seventh day he was wont to ascend to the capitol and to frequent the temples:[4] and Lucian speaks of the seventh day being given to schoolboys as a holy-day.[5] We may trace the same idea in the tradition, that Apollo instituted the Pythian games on the seventh day after he had slain the serpent Python;[6] perhaps also in the curious legend of Theodorus the Samothracian, preserved by Ptolemy Hephestion, that Jupiter after his birth laughed incessantly seven days:[7] but we re-

Respecting the prevelant opinion among the Gentiles that the 7th day was holy

---

[1] Euseb. Præp. Evan. lib. xiii. c. 13.   Fragmen. Lini ex Aristob. Poes. philos. H. Steph. p. 112.

[2] Euseb. Præp. Evan. lib. i. c. 9.

[3] Aul. Gell. Noct. Attic. apud Gale.   Suetonius says the same of Diogenes the grammarian of Rhodes. In Tiber. xxxii.

[4] Lamprid. in Alex. Sev. apud Gale.

[5] Lucian. in Pseudol. apud Gale.

[6] Schol. Pind. in proleg. ad Pyth.   The victory of Apollo over Python, as we shall hereafter see, is the victory of Noah over the deluge. Why it was celebrated on the seventh day, may be learned from Gen. viii. 10, 12: but Noah's observance of weeks must be deduced from the creation.

[7] Ptol. Heph. Nov. Hist. lib. vii.   See also Cœl. Rhodig. Lect. Ant. lib. xxii. c. 12.

cognize it with perfect distinctness in the observance of a sabbath by the ancient inhabitants of Arabia previous to the era of Mohammed, and in the hebdomadal devotional rest of the natives of Pegu and Guinea.[1] The very names indeed of the days, differing in different nations, yet always amounting to the number *seven*, prove the universality of a mode of computation, which prevailed alike among the Indians, the Egyptians, the Celts, the Sclavonians, the Greeks, and the Romans.[2] It was not therefore without reason, that Eusebius observes, that not only the Hebrews, but almost all the philosophers and poets, acknowledged the seventh day as being peculiarly holy; that Josephus affirms, that there was no state, whether Greek or Barbarian, which did not own a seventh day's rest from labour; that Clemens Alexandrinus remarks, that Greeks as well as Jews observed the seventh day as holy; that Dion Cassius deduces the universal practice of computing by weeks from the Egyptians, or, as he should rather have said, from the primitive ancestors of the Egyptians who were equally the ancestors of all mankind; that Theophilus of Antioch speaks of the every where prevailing sanctification of a seventh day, as a palpable matter of fact; and that Philo declares the sabbath to be a festival, not of this city or of that city, but of the universe.[3] A practice so general, a practice which may be carried back at least as high as the deluge,[4] could not have been borrowed from the Jews. As Abp. Usher justly observes, *the heathens had their knowledge of God and the sabbath by tradition from the first fathers, who lived before the dispersion.*[5] Even the Mosaical method of reckoning by nights instead of by days, or rather of making the evening precede the morning, has prevailed in more than one nation. The Athenians computed the space of a day from sunset to sunset:[6] and, from a similar custom of our Gothic ancestors during their abode in the forests

[1] Purch. Pilgrim. b. iii. c. 2. b. v. c. 5. b. vi. c. 15.

[2] Dion. Cass. lib. xxxiii. Isid. lib. v. c. 30, 32. Helmold. lib. i. c. 84. Philost. lib. iii. c. 18. apud Grot.

[3] Euseb. Præp. Evan. lib. xiii. c. 14. Joseph. adv. Apion. lib. ult. Clem. Alex. Strom. lib. v. Dion. Cass. lib. xxxiii. Theoph. ad Autol. lib. xi. Phil. apud Grot. et Gale.

[4] See Gen. viii. 10, 12.

[5] Usher's Disc. on the sabbath. p. 73.

[6] Aul. Gell. Noct. Attic. lib. iii. c. 2. In lib. iii. c. 10, there are various refined remarks on the number *seven*, much in the manner of the Pythagoreans.

of Germany,[1] words expressive of such a mode of calculation have been derived into our own language.[2] The same custom, as we are informed by Cesar, prevailed among the Celtic nations; and it evidently originated from the circumstance of night preceding day both at the literal and at the postdiluvian creation. *All the Gauls,* says he, *conceive themselves to be sprung from father Dis,* that is to say, the great father of gods and men, who in every quarter of the globe was esteemed an infernal deity: *and they assert it to have been handed down to them by the Druids. For this reason they measure time, not by the number of days, but of nights. Accordingly, they observe their birth-days and the beginnings of months and years in such a manner, as to cause the day to follow the night.*[3]

VII. From ancient Persia and Etruria we may next proceed to Hindostan. The Institutes of Menu are supposed by their translator Sir William Jones to have been composed no less than 1280 years before the Christian era: consequently, the author of them must have flourished not very long after the days of Moses.[4] This Hindoo tract commences with the following account of the creation.

Menu sat reclined, with his attention fixed on one object, the supreme God; when the divine sages approached him; and, after mutual salutations in due form, delivered the following address: Deign, sovereign ruler, to apprize us of the sacred laws in their order; for thou, lord, and thou only amongst mortals, knowest the true sense, the first principle, and the prescribed ceremonies, of this universal supernatural Veda, unlimited in extent and unequalled in authority.

He, whose powers were measureless, being thus requested by the great sages, saluted them all with reverence, and gave them a comprehensive answer, saying, Be it heard!

This universe existed only in the first divine idea, yet unexpanded, as if involved in darkness, imperceptible, undefineable, undiscoverable by reason, undiscovered by revelation. Then the sole self-existing power, himself undiscern-

---

[1] Tacit. de mor. Germ. c. 11.

[2] Such as *fortnight, se'nnight.*

[3] Cæsar. de bell. Gall. lib. vi. c. 18.

[4] I suspect, that the documents at least, on which this work is founded, are still older: that they are as ancient in fact, as the building of the tower:

ed by making this world discernible, appeared with undiminished glory, dispelling the gloom.   He, whom the mind alone can perceive, whose essence eludes the external organs, who has no visible parts, who exists from eternity, even he, the soul of all beings, whom no being can comprehend, shone forth in person.

He, having willing to produce various beings from his own divine substance, first with a thought created the waters, and placed in them a productive seed. The seed became an egg, bright as gold, blazing like the luminary with a thousand beams : and in that egg he was born himself, in the form of Brahma, the great forefather of all spirits.   The waters are called nara, because they were the production of Nara or the Spirit of God: and, since they were his first ayana or place of motion, he is thence named Narayana or moving on the waters.

From that which is the first cause, not the object of sense, existing every where in substance, not existing to our perception, without beginning or end, was produced the divine male, famed in all worlds under the appellation of Brahma.   In that egg the great power sat inactive a whole year of the creator ; at the close of which, by his thought alone, he caused the egg to divide itself.   And from its two divisions he framed the heaven above, and the earth beneath : in the midst he placed the subtle ether; the eight regions, and the permanent receptacle of the waters.   From the supreme soul he drew forth Mind, existing substantially, though unperceived by sense, immaterial : and, before Mind or the reasoning power, he produced Consciousness, the internal monitor, the ruler.   And before them both he produced the great Principle of the soul, or first expansion of the divine idea—He framed all creatures—

From his image, or appearance in visible nature, proceed the great elements, endued with peculiar powers, and Mind with operations infinitely subtle, the unperishable cause of all created forms.   This universe therefore is compacted from the minute portions of those seven divine and active principles, the great Soul or first emanation, Consciousness, and five perceptions ; a mutable universe from immutable ideas—

He too first assigned to all creatures distinct names, distinct acts, and distinct occupations—He, the supreme ruler, created an assemblage of in-

ferior deities, with divine attributes and pure souls, and a number of genii exquisitely delicate: and he prescribed the sacrifice ordained from the beginning—He gave being to time, and the divisions of time; to the stars also, and to the planets; to rivers, oceans, and mountains; to level plains, and uneven vallies; to devotion, speech, complacency, desire, and wrath; and to the creation, which shall presently be mentioned: for he willed the existence of all those created things.

For the sake of distinguishing actions, he made a total difference between right and wrong; and enured these sentient creatures to pleasure and pain, cold and heat, and other opposite pairs. With very minute transformable portions of the five elements, all this perceptible world was composed in fit order. And, in whatever occupation the supreme lord first employed any vital soul, to that occupation the same soul attaches itself spontaneously, when it receives a new body again and again. Whatever quality, noxious or innocent, harsh or mild, unjust or just, false or true, he conferred on any thing at its creation; the same quality enters it of course on its future births—

That the human race might be multiplied, he caused the Brahmen, the Cshatrya,[1] the Vaisya, and the Sudra,[2] to proceed from his mouth, his arm, his thigh, and his foot. Having divided his own substance, the mighty power became half male, half female, or nature active and passive; and from that female he produced Viraj. Know me, O most excellent of Brahmens, to be that person, whom the male power Viraj, having performed austere devotion, produced by himself me, the secondary framer of all this visible world.

It was I, who, desirous of giving birth to a race of men, performed very difficult religious duties, and first produced ten lords of created beings, eminent in holiness—They, abundant in glory, produced seven other Menus, together with deities, and the mansions of deities, and great sages unlimited in power, benevolent genii, and fierce giants, blood-thirsty savages, heavenly choristers, nymphs and demons, huge serpents and snakes of smaller size,

---

[1] It is sometimes written in a more pronounceable form *Kettree* or *Cuttree*.

[2] These are the four great Hindoo castes; the priest, the soldier or military nobleman, the tradesman, and the labourer.

birds of mighty wing, and separate companies of *Pitris* or progenitors of mankind, lightnings and thunder-bolts, clouds and coloured bows of *Indra*, falling meteors, earth-rending vapours, comets, and luminaries of various degrees, horse-faced sylvans, apes, fish, and a variety of birds, tame cattle, deer, men, and ravenous beasts with two rows of teeth, small and large reptiles, moths, lice, fleas, and common flies, with every biting gnat, and immoveable substances of distinct sorts.

Thus was this whole assemblage of stationary and moveable bodies framed by those high-minded beings, through the force of their own devotion and at my command, with separate actions allotted to each—

All transmigrations, recorded in sacred books, from the state of *Brahma* to that of plants, happen continually in this tremendous world of beings; a world always tending to decay. He, whose powers are incomprehensible, having thus created both me and this universe, was again absorbed in the supreme spirit, changing the time of energy for the time of repose. When that power awakes, then has this world its full expansion; but, when he slumbers with a tranquil spirit, then the whole system fades away. For, while he reposes as it were in calm sleep, embodied spirits, endued with principles of action, depart from their several acts, and the mind itself becomes inert: and, when they once are absorbed in that supreme essence, then the divine soul of all beings withdraws his energy, and placidly slumbers. Then too this vital soul of created bodies, with all the organs of sense and of action, remains long immersed in the first idea or in darkness, and performs not its natural functions, but migrates from its corporeal frame. When, being again composed of minute elementary principles, it enters at once into vegetable or animal seed, it then assumes a new form. Thus that immutable power, by waking and reposing alternately, revivifies and destroys in eternal succession, this whole assemblage of locomotive and immoveable creatures.

He, having enacted this code of laws, himself taught it fully to me in the beginning: afterwards I taught it to *Marichi* and the nine other holy sages. This my son *Bhrigu* will repeat the divine code to you without omission; for that sage learned from me to recite the whole of it.

Bhrigu, great and wise, having thus been appointed by *Menu* to promulge his laws, addressed all the *Rishis* with an affectionate mind, saying: *Hear!*

From this Menu, named Swayambhuva or sprung from the self-existent, came six descendants, or Menus, each giving birth to a race of his own, all exalted in dignity, eminent in power—The seven Menus (or those first created, who are to be followed by seven more), of whom Swayambhuva is the chief, have produced and supported this world of moving and stationary beings, each in his own antara or the period of his reign[1]—There are numberless Menwantaras; creations also and destructions of worlds, innumerable: the being supremely exalted performs all this, with as much ease, as if in sport; again and again, for the sake of conferring happiness.[2]

1. We might easily be led to imagine by taking a hasty view of the exordium of the preceding cosmogony, that the Hindoos ascribed the creation of the world to the true God, and that the Institutes of Menu treated exclusively of the same primeval transactions as those detailed in the beginning of the book of Genesis: but, if we advance further and carefully attend to the general drift of the whole, we shall find that such is by no means the case.

The Hindoo creator of the world is not the true God, but merely the great father

The imagined supreme being is represented as casting a seed into the all-prevailing waters: the seed becomes an egg, floating upon their surface: and the creator is himself born in the character of Brahma, the universal father of spirits, out of that egg, after he had sat inactive within it during the space of a great year. From the circumstance of his thus floating on the waters, he receives the name of *Narayana:* which is also a title of Vishnou, and for precisely the same reason; that kindred deity being similarly described, as floating in a state of deep repose on the surface of the vast abyss, during the intermediate period between two worlds, either in an egg, or on the navicular leaf of the Banian tree, or on a mighty serpent coiled up in the form of a boat. Now the characters of Brahma and Vishnou are allowed by the Hindoo mythologists to melt into each other, and both again to melt into that of Siva; so that their Trimurti being really but one deity who triplicates himself, whatever is true of the one is equally true of all. But Siva floats in the ship Argha on the surface of the deluge: consequently, the floating of Brahma and Vishnou in the several marine vehicles in which they are placed must mean the very same as the voyage of Siva in the Argha.

Thus we shall be brought to the conclusion, that the Hindoo history of the

[1] Here follows the monstrous chronological system of the Hindoos.
[2] Instit. of Menu. chap. i.

creation is largely intermingled with allusions to the deluge, that the imagined creator is no other than the great father, and that the year during which he is inclosed within the floating egg has been borrowed from the year during which Noah was shut up in the Ark.

The character of Menu

2. This will be yet further evident, if we consider the character of Menu.

The personage, to whom the Institutes are ascribed, is the first Menu or Menu-Swayambhuva. But Menu-Swayambhuva is certainly Adam, as the seventh Menu or Menu-Vaivaswata is no less certainly Noah. Now in the persons of Swayambhuva and his three sons the Hindoo Trimurti is believed to have been incarnate : and, since exactly the same events take place and the same persons reappear at the commencement of every world, we must deem the Trimurti to have been similarly incarnate in Vaivaswata and his three sons. Hence, as the imagined creator proves to be the egg-born Brahma; so Brahma himself, in conjunction with Vishnou and Siva, proves to be the triplicated Swayambhuva.

Accordingly, we are told, that Brahma is man both collectively and individually; and there are certain parts of his history, which clearly demonstrate him to have been the first man. In his hermaphroditic quality, he identifies himself with Siva, with the Orphic Jupiter, and with the great father wheresoever worshipped. He is the same also as Viraj his supposed son, and Viraj again is the same as Menu: for exactly the same actions are given to Viraj, which are also given to Brahma. In a curious passage in the Yajur Veda, which I have already had occasion to notice, Viraj, like Brahma, appears as an hermaphrodite, and then divides himself into man and woman: from this pair is descended the whole human race. The man and the woman next successively assume the forms of different animals : and from the several pairs, into which they are metamorphosed, is produced the brute creation. Much the same idea is entertained of the first Menu; who, as I have just observed, is Brahma incarnate, and consequently is one person both with Viraj and the pretended demiurge. Menu produces from himself a daughter named *Satarupa*, and by an incestuous connection with her becomes the parent of all mankind : in a similar manner, Viraj produces from himself a female ; who at first hesitates to admit his embraces lest she should incur the guilt of incest, but who afterwards by a varied intercourse with him becomes the universal mother both of men and animals. Thus, as the demiurge, Brahma, Menu, and Viraj, all melt into each other, and are evidently, as the Hindoo theologists declare and as their own actions testify, one and the same person ; so we may rest assured, that that person is no other than the great father, who was believed to appear with his three sons at the commencement of every world, and to whom the office of creation or rather of renovation is ascribed to the exclusion of the real first cause.

With this opinion the whole of the preceding cosmogony exactly accords. We are told indeed, and we might be hastily led to imagine, that it was really a history of the creation ; that is to say, in the same manner as the exordium of Genesis is properly a history of the creation : but, as we proceed, we find that it treats but of one creation among thousands ; and, as all those thousands are exactly similar, an account of one is in effect an account of them all. Hence, as the Hindoos believe that the process of the creation over which Adam presided exactly resembled that of the creation over which Noah presides, their cosmogony is more or less a history of the renovation of the earth after the deluge ; and again, on the other hand, their account of the deluge is more or less a cosmogony.

3. That the view which I have taken of this cosmogony is a just one, namely that it has throughout a double reference to the creation and the deluge in consequence of the received doctrine of a succession of similar worlds, is manifest from the following compressed statement which Sonnerat exhibits of Hindoó philosophy.

On the death of Brahma, all the worlds will suffer a deluge: all the Andons will be broken: and Cailasa and Vaicontha (or the highest summit of mount Meru which towers above the surrounding waters, and the floating Paradise of Vishnou in the sea of milk where he reposes on the bosom of Lacshmi ; in other words, mount Ararat and the Ark) *will only remain. At that time, Vishnou, taking a leaf of the tree called* Allemaron, *will place himself on the leaf under the figure of a very little child, and thus float on the sea of milk sucking the toe of his right foot.*[1] *He will remain in this posture, until Brahma anew comes forth from his navel in a tamarind flower. It is thus, that the ages and worlds succeed each other, and are perpetually renewed.*[2]

[The Hindoo Cosmogony doubly relates to the creation and to the deluge]

[1] A rude attempt to mould the body of the deity into the form of a circle.
[2] Sonnerat. vol. i. p. 226. apud Moor's Hind. Panth. p. 103.

The infancy of the floating Vishnou is doubtless the same as the infancy of the solar god of the Egyptians, who was represented as a child floating in the calix of the lotos. Such a mode of exhibiting him alludes very plainly to the regeneration of the great father: who, in the capacity of one born again from the womb of his mother at the beginning of every new world, is thence consistently enough depicted as an infant. From this source originated the fable of the infant Bacchus being exposed in an ark on the surface of the ocean, and a variety of other kindred tales respecting the supposed infancy of the gods. The fable indeed of Bacchus affords an excellent comment both on the Hindoo and the Egyptian legend: What Sonnerat calls *the Allemaron leaf* is the leaf of the Banian tree: and the tamarind flower, which he describes as being the watery cradle of Brahma, is in reality the cup of the lotos. Mr. Moor rightly conjectures, that the leaf and the lotos mean the same thing. But that thing, as we learn from the more literal Greek fable, is an ark, which was set afloat on the sea: and, in exact accordance with the Greek fable, the lotos is declared by the Hindoos to be a symbol of the ship Argha, which safely bore the god Siva over the waters of the deluge.

4. It is observable, that in the present cosmogony there is a certain degree of confusion respecting the genealogy of Menu's descendants. Swayambhuva is described, as first producing ten lords of created beings; who again, in *their* turn, produce seven other Menus: yet the head of the seven Menus is Swayambhuva himself; from whom accordingly, it is afterwards said, that the six younger Menus were successively born.

The best method of solving this difficulty is that proposed by Mr. Wilford. Let the seven Menus, produced from the ten lords, be the same as the seven Rishis, who, when each successive world is destroyed by a deluge, are the companions of Menu in the ark: and the whole confusion will be removed in a manner perfectly according with the scriptural account. In this case, Menu-Swayambhuva or Menu-Adima will be Adam, as both his name and his history indeed evidently shew him to be: the ten lords descended from him will be the ten generations of patriarchs from Adam to Noah: and the seven Menus, or more properly the seven Rishis, who succeed the ten lords, and who are therefore contemporary with Menu-Vaivaswata or Noah, will be, as *their* history equally shews, the family of the arkite great father,

[handwritten margin note: Confusion in the genealogy of Menu]

inasmuch as they are jointly preserved with him in a ship from the fury of the deluge.

5. I take it that Menu, whether considered as Adam or as Noah, is in reality the head of that curious triad of abstract ideas (if I may so speak), which the speculative Hindoos have introduced so conspicuously into their cosmogony. We are told, that from the great Soul, that is from the great father, who was believed to be at once the Soul of the World and the universal parent of human souls, Brahma produced a triad consisting of Mind, Consciousness, and psychic Principle.

Menu is the head of a philosophical triad of abstract ideas

This, I am persuaded, is a mere philosophical refinement almost exactly similar to that of the Platonists, who educed from the elder Nous or Mind three younger Noës. And I am the more confirmed in my opinion by the signification of the word *Menu*, the import of which in the Sanscrit is *Mind*: so that, when we are taught that Mind was generated from the great Soul, we are in effect taught that Menu was thus generated. Such refinements, as I have already observed, arose from the character of Mind or Intellect being attributed to the great father in contradistinction to inert Matter, which was sometimes given to him as a body and sometimes as a consort. Agreeably to these notions, we may observe, that, while Brahma is awake, the world is said to have its full expansion; but, when he slumbers, the whole system fades away. Then every soul, which had emanated from him, is absorbed into his essence: all things are resolved into their first principles: and the world, his visible image, ceases to exist, until the deity awakes from his placid slumber, and a new order of things commences exactly similar to that which had preceded it.

VIII. The cosmogony of China bears a considerable resemblance to that of Hindostan.

The first of men was Puoncu. He was born out of chaos, as it were out of an egg. From the shell of this egg, in the deep gloom of night, were formed the heavens; from the white of it was made the atmosphere; and from the yolk, the earth. In point of order, the heavens were first created; the foundations of the earth were next laid; the atmosphere was then diffused round the habitable globe; and last of all men were called into existence.'

1. Most of the remarks, which have been made on the Hindoo cosmogony, are equally applicable to this: and the character of Puoncu in particular decidedly confirms all that has been said respecting Brahma. The ex-

It relates both to the creation and to the deluge

actly similar birth of each from the sacred egg indisputably proves them to be the same person. Now I have contended, that Brahma, though represented by the Hindoos as the creator, is in reality no other than the great father; who appears with his three sons at the commencement of each world, and from whom the whole human race is descended. Agreeably to this opinion, the Chinese inform us, that the egg-born Puoncu, who clearly must be identified with Brahma, is neither a god nor a creator, but merely the first of men. Arguing from the analogy of other cosmogonies, I apprehend, that Puoncu unites in his own person the characters both of Adam and Noah: in other words, he is that great universal father, who was thought to be successively produced in a human form, at the beginning of every world, from the egg which floated on the waters of the circumfluent ocean during the intermediate period of a divine year.

The world was created by a triad

2. Further light is thrown on the cosmogony of the Chinese by some curious passages in their book Y-king. This volume is said to be as old as Confucius, who flourished five centuries before Christ: and it is the most ancient, the most obscure, and the most esteemed, of all their national records. The word *Y-king* signifies *the book of Y*: and the book received its name from the mystery of which it treats; for the mystery in question was hieroglyphically represented by a figure, resembling the Greek *T* or the Roman Y.

This book teaches, that the heaven and the earth had a beginning, and therefore much more the human race: that, after the heaven and the earth, all material things were formed: then, male and female; and then, husband and wife: that (what they call) the great Term is the great Unity and the great Y: that Y has neither body nor figure: and that all, which have body and figure, were made by that which has neither body nor figure. It further teaches, that the great Term or the great Unity comprehends three: and it describes this comprehension to be of such a nature, that the one is three, and that the three are one. *Tao, it informs us, is Life: the first has produced the second: the two have produced the third: and the three have made all things. He, whom the spirit perceiveth and whom the eye cannot see, is called* Y. This character Y is explained by Hin-chin in the following words: *At the first beginning, Reason subsisted in the Unity: that is it, which made and divided the heaven and the earth, which changed and perfected all things.*[1]

[1] Memoires Chinois apud Bryant in Phil. Jud. p. 285—287.

3. Mr. Bryant is willing to refer the preceding tradition to the knowledge *[That triad is the triplicated great father]* which the Chinese had of the triple nature of God. In this opinion I find it impossible to agree with him.

The triad of the Chinese is described in terms so exactly similar to those, by which the Hindoos set forth the attributes of their Trimurti, that we can scarcely, I think, doubt, that whatever the one means the other must also mean. Now the Hindoo Trimurti, springing from the unity of a yet more ancient god, is believed to become incarnate, at the commencement of every new world, in the persons of Menu and his three sons. But Menu is that great father; who, immortal in his nature and perpetually reappearing, is said at the close of each mundane system to be preserved with seven companions in an ark from the fury of an universal deluge. Hence it is sufficiently evident, that by the Hindoo Trimurti we are to understand the great father triplicating himself, or (in other words) begetting three sons, at the beginning of every similar renovated world. The triplication itself they are wont to style *delusion ;* intimating, that all things really spring from the unity of the great father, and that his three sons or three powers are such mere varied multiplications of himself that they are mutually the same with each other and collectively the same with the paternal unity.

Precisely similar are the ideas entertained of the Chinese triad. The three are virtually identified with the one, and the one is virtually identified with the three. To this triplicated monad, as was universally the case throughout the pagan world with respect to the great father, the office of creator is ascribed: and we may observe exactly the same notions concerning *Reason* or *Intellect* or *Mind* in the philosophy of the Chinese, as those which make so prominent a figure in the systems of the Hindoos and the Greek Platonists. Reason, we are told, subsisted at first in the Unity. This *Reason* is the *Mind* or *Menu* of the Hindoos, and the *Nous* of the Orphic and Platonic philosophers: for the Chinese *Reason* afterwards triplicates itself, precisely in the same manner, as *Menu* (in whom the Trimurti is incarnate) begets three sons, and as *Nous* produces three younger demiurgic Noës. By *Reason subsisting in the Unity,* they meant *the great father considered as the Soul or Intellectual Principle of the Universe :* and, by the same *Rea-*

son multiplied into three, they meant *the great transmigrating father of the human race at the head of his triple offspring.*

I need scarcely observe, that they plainly invented the hieroglyphical figure Y to exhibit this mystic union of their three in one.

Propriety of this opinion established

4. The propriety of this opinion will, if I mistake not, be yet further established by inquiring a little more minutely into the character of the Chinese triad.

In the legend, as translated by the author of the *Memoires Chinois* and as cited above, *three* persons only are mentioned, of whom *Tao* or *Life* is the first: but in the same legend, as it is rendered both by du Halde and le Compte, *four* persons are mentioned, of whom the three younger, just as in the case of the Hindoo and Platonic triads, proceed from a fourth *anterior* to them. According to du Halde, *Tao or Reason hath produced one, one hath produced two, two have produced three, and three have produced all things.*[1] According to le Compte, *Eternal Reason produced one, one produced two, two produced three, and three produced all things.*[2]

Here we have Reason or Mind placed at the head of the triad which emanates from it; that Reason, which, as I have just observed, the pagans constantly identify with the great father, and which they represent as the animating Soul of the World. Now it is obvious, that such a generation as this, while it accurately corresponds in point of number with the great father and his three sons, does by no means agree with what we are taught to believe respecting the Jewish and Christian Trinity. Yet such is the very generation, which is set forth in the book Y-king: for the great Term is said to be at once the great Unity and the great Y; the Unity comprehending within itself the Triad, and the Triad emanating from the Unity.

Nor is this all: we are further taught, in exact accordance with those speculations of the pagans which constituted the very basis of their mythology, that, powerful as the great Term is supposed to be, his existence has nevertheless in one sense had a commencement. *We must know,* says Vang-Chin in his commentary, *that, in the beginning, when as yet the great Term*

[1] Du Halde's Hist. of China. vol. iii. p. 30.
[2] Le Compte's Journ. through Chin. p. 318.

was not in being, there existed an active and inexhaustible Reason, which no image can represent, which no name can designate, which is infinite in every respect, and to which nothing can be added.[1] The non-existence of the Term, spoken of in this passage, relates, I apprehend, to that supposed intermediate period between two worlds, when both the demiurgic triad and the whole Universe are absorbed into the single essence of the great father. At that time, Reason or Intellect or Mind, the cabalistic name of the paternal unity considered as the Soul of the World, alone exists, floating on the surface of the ocean either in the egg or on the lotos or in the sacred ship, and either sunk in a state of deep repose or engaged in profound meditation upon his own nature. When the hour of creation arrives, then he changes the season of rest for the season of energy. First he produces from himself the mysterious triad of the great Term: and afterwards, by the instrumentality of that triad, he calls the Universe into renovated existence.

This, judging both from the general tenor of the Chinese cosmogony and from the analogy of other parallel gentile systems, is meant, I have little doubt, by the solitary existence of Reason or Mind, the Menu of the Hindoos and the Nous of the Platonists, previous to the birth of that great triplicated Term, who is represented as the creator of the world.

IX. From China we may pass to the neighbouring empire of Japan : and here again we shall find the cosmogony to be deeply tinctured with diluvianism.

According to the tradition of the Sintoists, the most ancient sect of idolaters in that country, all things indeed originated from a chaos : but the general tenor of the legend shews with sufficient plainness, that the chaos alluded to is that produced by the flood ; or, to speak perhaps more properly, by that flood which was equally supposed to precede *every* mundane renovation. It is said, in their mysterious book *Odaiki*, that, *in the beginning of the opening of all things, a chaos floated, as fishes swim in the water for pleasure. Out of this chaos arose a thing like a prickle, moveable and transformable. This thing became a soul or spirit : and*

---

[1] Mem. Chin. apud Bryant in Phil. Jud. p. 287.

this spirit is called Kunito-Ko-L'ats-No-Mikotto.[1] He was the first of the seven original spirits, whom they divide into the three elder and the four younger. The three elder are said to have had no wives: but the four younger had each his proper consort. The last of them is held in peculiar veneration by the Japanese as being the parent of the second race of hero-gods, whom they suppose to be five in number, but inferior both in purity and dignity to the first race. Respecting the origin of the third race or that of ordinary men, there appears, so far as I am able to collect from Kœmpfer, to be a difference of opinion among them; some deducing it from the eldest of the five hero-gods of the second race, and some from the youngest of them. The lives of the first race they extend to an enormous term of years: the lives of the second race they diminish in length; yet, diminished as they are, they far exceed the duration, to which human life is now limited. The hereditary ecclesiastical emperors of the Japanese claim their right to dominion by the patriarchal tenure of primogeniture in a direct line from these two successive races of hero-gods.[2]

1. The very first expression in this cosmogony is familiar to those, who are in the least accustomed to mythological studies. *The opening of all things*, with which the Japanese history of the creation commences, relates, I have no doubt, to the bursting or opening of the sacred egg, from which the great triplicated father and the whole world are equally produced. But, as that egg is a symbol of double import representing both the World and the Ark; the notion of its having once been opened and of the whole Universe having proceeded from its interior, after it had floated a divine year on the surface of the ocean, must have chiefly originated from the opening of the door in the Ark and from the egress of all the living creatures and vegetable seeds, which had been preserved of the first creation, and which constituted the rudiments of the second. Hence the great diluvian patriarch, who is said to have been born out of the opening egg, was worshipped under the name of *Baal-Peor* or *the lord of opening*: and, from an idea that the

[1] Kœmpfer's Hist. of Japan. b. iii. c. 1.

[2] Kœmpfer's Hist. of Jap. b. i. c. 7. b. ii. c. 1.

Ark was an universal mother, he was considered as the masculine principle of generation, and was adored by his apostate descendants with all the abominations of the phallic worship.[1] Hence also Mylitta or Venus, the goddess of the Ark, was called *Prothyrèa* or *the tutelary patroness of the door*; and, being ever worshipped in conjunction with the great father, was esteemed the female principle of generation. And hence Janus, whose history proves him to be the same as Noah, was venerated as a divinity, who presided over doors, and who was connected in a peculiar manner with shutting and opening.

2. The long lives ascribed to the seven great spirits, and the shorter lives ascribed to their five successors though still of a duration far exceeding that of the present life of man, are in themselves sufficient to teach us the true eras of these Japanese demigods: we have in fact only to compare the fabulous narrative with the literal history of Moses. The life of the human race was of the same average length *before* the deluge: but, in the very first generation *after* that awful catastrophè, it began to shorten; and its gradual abbreviation continued, until it was ultimately fixed at its *present* average length. Hence it is evident, that the seven elder hero-gods of Japan must represent the antediluvians, and that the five younger must shadow out the yet long-lived postdiluvians ere the age of man finally settled at its present curtailed duration.

Such an arrangement, which seems to point out its own propriety, is confirmed by the parallel theory of the Hindoos. I think it evident, that the seven primeval long-lived spirits are the same as the seven Menus, whose series commences with Swayambhuva or Adam and terminates with Vaivaswata or Noah, and who clearly run parallel with the ten antediluvian patriarchs or lords of created beings though the Hindoos make them the heads of seven successive worlds. For the ten lords descend from Swayambhuva, and the six younger Menus also descend from him: but the ten lords are said to produce seven *other* Menus, whom (I think with Mr. Wilford) we must necessarily identify with the seven Rishis that are preserved in an ark with Vaivaswata or the seventh Menu: hence the seventh Menu must

Respecting the seven great Spirits

[1] See my Dissert. on the Cabiri. vol. ii. p. 109. note k.

chronologically coincide with the tenth lord; and the series of Menus, however each may be feigned to preside over his own renovated world, must in
reality synchronize with the period between Adam and Noah; Swayambhuva (as I have just observed) being certainly the former of those patriarchs,
and Vaivaswata the latter.   But, if the seven Menus be the same as the
seven long-lived spirits of the Japanese, of which there can scarcely be a
shadow of doubt; then those spirits must represent the antediluvians; a conclusion, to which we had already been brought by the circumstance of their
longevity being succeeded by an abbreviation in the life of man before it was
finally reduced to its present narrow limits.

It is observable, that the Japanese divide their seven spirits into three
and four.   I think it most probable, that they have adopted this arrangement in order that they might thus be enabled to place a triad at the head
of their cosmogony; for, like the Hindoos, they worship a triple god springing out of an egg that rests upon the mysterious lotos.'   They also contrived
by such a plan to exhibit a complete ogdoad of four males and four females, corresponding with the two successive ogdoads of the Adamitical
and Noetic families: for to each of the four spirits they assign a consort,
thus making up the precise number eight.

Though it is easy to arrange the chronological epoch of the five younger
hero-gods, who with shortened lives succeeded the seven great spirits, it
must of course be a matter of conjecture why the number five has been
pitched upon rather than any other number: yet a conjecture *may* be adduced, which at least is not devoid of plausibility.   As the seventh of the
great spirits must, according to the analogy of the seventh Menu, be the
same as Noah; and as human life began to shorten not with him, but with
his sons: he must plainly be excluded from the number of the five hero-
gods.   And again, since the dispersion from Babel took place in the days
of Nimrod, I should doubt whether we ought to look for any one of them
posterior to the time of that prince.   Now there is reason to believe, that
the Japanese are of Cuthic or Scythian origin; at least they seem to have
among them a very considerable mixture of Cuths: hence we must look for

' See Plate I. Fig. 14.

the later of their five demigods in the line of Ham, rather than in that of either of his brethren.[1] If then we inquire within these defined limits, we shall find that Scripture furnishes us with exactly five patriarchs, who with shortened lives succeed Noah the supposed seventh great spirit : namely, Shem, Ham, Japhet, Cush, and Nimrod.

I may remark, that the idea of the seven spirits being superior to men, and yet being at once their ancestors and of the same chaotic origin with them, very nearly corresponds with the notion of the Egyptians, that their country was first ruled by the immortals, and with the Greek division of the intelligent beings who sprang from chaos into the immortal gods and mortal men.

X. The Greek accounts of the cosmogony indeed appear evidently to have been borrowed from the systems of more ancient nations, whether they occur in the writings of the philosophers or of the poets. As such therefore the preceding detail will throw considerable light on them : nor are they in themselves destitute of interest.

1. It was well remarked by Cudworth, though he has not built upon the remark the superstructure which I conceive he ought to have done, that the cosmogony of the pagans was in reality one and the same thing with their theogony.[2] This arose from the circumstance, which I have so frequently had occasion to notice, of their confounding the proper creation of the world with its re-formation after the deluge : and the confusion itself originated from the doctrine of a succession of similar worlds, at the close of each of which all the hero-gods are absorbed into the essence of the great father, as at the commencement of each they are all reproduced from his essence. Hence it happened, that the Demon-gods of the Gentiles, whose history when analysed shews them to be chiefly the family of Adam reappearing in that of Noah, are represented, sometimes as effecting the creation, and sometimes as themselves originating out of it. This last is eminently the case with the theogony of Hesiod. His account of the production of the Universe is so immediately connected with the whole train of

[handwritten note: That of Hesiod]

[1] Vide infra book vi. c. 4. § II. 3. (2.)

[2] Intell. Syst. b. i. c. 4. p. 234.

diluvian hero-gods whose birth he deduces from the chaotic mixture ; with
the Eros, Uranus, and Cronus, of the Orphic poet; and with the twice-told
story of a tetrad, composed of an older god and three younger deities his
children : that it must necessarily be viewed as relating in a great measure
to the reformation of the earth after the deluge, though by no means without a decided allusion to a yet prior creation.

First, says he, *existed Chaos. Next was produced the spacious earth,
the firm seat of the Olympian immortals ; Tartarus hid within the recesses of the ample globe ; and Eros, the most beautiful of the immortals,
the dispeller of care, and the author of wise counsels both to gods and men.
From Chaos sprang Erebus and black Night ; and, from the union of
Night and Erebus, were born Ether and the Day.*[1]

These first principles gave birth to various oceanic gods; among whom we
recognize the Uranus and Cronus of the Orphic poet, and Rhea the fabled
mother of all the deities.   Uranus is twice represented as being the parent
of three sons : and the same legend is afterwards repeated in the story of
Cronus, who is similarly made the father of a triple offspring.   I say *repeated*, both because Uranus and Cronus may be proved to be the same
person, and because the two fables carry along with them a sufficiency of
internal evidence to establish the point of their origination from a common
source.   Uranus is said to have been mutilated by Cronus : and Cronus
himself, according to the Orphic poet, experienced afterwards the same
treatment from Jupiter or (as he was called by the Egyptians) Hammon.
It is added, that Cronus was intoxicated at the time when the affair happened.[2]   If the very contexture of this story did not plainly shew whence
it was derived, the name of that son of Cronus, to whom the crime against
his intoxicated father is attributed, would inseparably connect it with a
well-known event in the life of Noah.   The Gentiles indeed, and especially
the Hindoos, have, after their manner, explained the fable in a physical
sense, as alluding to the successive destructions and renovations of the
world; and the general story of the mutilation of the principal hero-god
appears to me in itself to relate also to the supposed hermaphroditic nature

[1] Hesiod. Theog. ver. 116.   [2] Porph. de antro nymph. p. 260.

of the great father: but yet, as the event stands connected in the Greek legend, it is almost impossible not to refer it to the indignity which Noah suffered from Canaan. Since then the gods of Hesiod are manifestly diluvian or arkite gods, the chaos, from which they are produced, must be the chaos, out of which the world was created anew after the deluge; though, for the reasons already assigned, neither a prior creation nor a prior race of hero-gods are to be excluded.

2. Much the same remarks apply to the cosmogony preserved by Aristophanes.

Chaos, and Night, and black Erebus, and wide Tartarus, first existed. At that time, there was neither earth, air, nor heaven. But, in the bosom of Erebus, black-winged Night produced an aërial egg; from which, in due season, beautiful Love, decked with golden wings, was born. Out of Chaos, in the midst of wide-spreading Tartarus, he begot our race, and called us forth into the light.[1]

The Love or Eros of Aristophanes is the same mythological character as the Phanes-Protogonus of the Orphic poet, as the first-born Brahma of the Hindoos, and as the primeval Puoncu of the Chinese. They are all equally produced from the egg, that floated upon the waters of the chaotic mixture: and they are all equally represented as being the parents of the human race. The Orphic Phanes is styled *hidden*, from his being inclosed within the ark: the Love of Aristophanes, in allusion to the egress from the arkite egg, is said to have called forth mankind into light. From the Orphic Phanes the immortal gods derive their origin: the Eros of Hesiod is the wise counseller both of gods and men. But these immortal gods are not beings, that have existed from eternity. Their mythological birth synchronizes with the birth of the world. They are produced, at the commencement of each system; which, according to the Hindoos, is invariably preceded by a deluge: they are produced, with their general parent Eros himself, from ancient Chaos and that allegorical egg which once within narrow bounds inclosed the Universe. The earth, as Hesiod truly tells us, when it emerged out of the same Chaos, was their first habitation. Then it was, that

That of Aristophanes

---

[1] Aristoph. Aves. 694.

Eros performed the task of dispelling the anxious cares of the hero-gods. In short, as Homer asserts that all the pagan deities sprang from the ocean;[1] so Pindar delivers it as an undoubted truth, that the origin of gods and of men is the same, that they were all born from one common mother.[2] This great universal parent, the Panthea of antiquity, who is the same as the black goddess or Night or Venus that produces the mundane egg in Chaos, was certainly the arkite ship and ultimately the larger mundane ship floating (as it was supposed) in the waters of Chaos.

Those of Thales and Anaxagoras

3. The opinions of some of the ancient philosophers, respecting the aqueous origin of the Universe, are, I think, to be referred to the same double source: for the world, both at its first creation and at its subsequent postdiluvian renovation, equally arose out of water. Of such a conjecture the propriety is confirmed by the character of the agent, to whom the work is ascribed. Thales and Anaxagoras agree in teaching, that water was the matrix of all things, and that the Universe remained in a state of chaotic confusion until Nous or Intellect came and arranged it in order.

This demiurgic Nous is evidently the same person as the Nous of the Platonists; who was the head and parent of three younger demiurgic Noës, and whom Proclus rightly identifies with the Orphic hermaphroditic Jupiter.[3] He is also pronounced to be one with the ark-preserved Dionus or Bacchus, and with the navicular Cronus who is similarly described as the father of a triple offspring.[4] The creative Nous therefore is plainly the same person as the transmigrating great parent, who appears with his three sons at the commencement of every mundane system: and the Greek word *Nous*, like the Sanscrit word *Menu*, was made to signify *Mind* or *Intellect*, because Nuh or Noah was deemed the Soul of the World.

XI. I shall take this opportunity of making some remarks on the Orphic and Platonic triads, which have not unfrequently been esteemed primeval corruptions of the doctrine of the Trinity. That such was their

[1] Plut. de placit. philos. lib. i. p. 875.
[2] Pind. Nem. Od. vi.
[3] Cicer. de nat. deor. lib. i. c. 10. Diog. Laer. in vit. Thal. et Anax.
[4] Fulgen. Mythol. lib. i. c. 2. Macrob. Saturn. lib. i. c. 18. p. 201.

origin, I thoroughly disbelieve: for, though one of the most prominent features of ancient mythology is the notion that the world was created or rather formed anew by the instrumentality of a triplicated divinity or a triad of great gods, circumstantial evidence demonstrates, that this demiurgic triad, emanating from a paternal monad, is really composed of no other persons than the three sons of Noah viewed as a reappearance of the three sons of Adam.

1. *In the beginning, according to the doctrine of Orpheus,* says Cedrenus from the Christian chronographer Timotheus, *was created the Ether. Chaos, and gloomy Night the first of all things, enveloped it on every side, and occasioned an universal obscurity. Nevertheless, there was a being, incomprehensible, supreme, and preëxistent ; the creator of all things, as well of the Ether itself, as of whatsoever is under the Ether. The earth was hitherto invisible on account of the darkness, until the light, bursting through the Ether, illuminated the whole creation. That light was the being before mentioned, even he that is above all things. His name is Wisdom, Light, and Life: but these three powers are one power ; the strength of which is the invisible, the incomprehensible, God. From this power all things were produced, incorporeal particles, the sun, the moon, their influences, the stars, the land, and the sea ; together with all things in them, whether they be visible or invisible. The human race was formed by an immediate act of the deity, and received from him a reasonable soul. Thus were all things created by the three names of the one only God ; and he is all things.*[ ]

Replete as this legend is with much curious and (I believe) genuine matter, it is impossible to avoid recognizing the hand of a modern Christian corrector; who, by a few strokes of his pen properly applied, has transformed the real Orphic triad into an accurate resemblance of the scriptural Trinity. The too palpable similitude would in itself be sufficient to excite suspicion, even if we had no other accounts of the Orphic triad: but, when those accounts are examined, the suspicion (as it appears to me) will nearly be

[ ] Cedren. Histor. Compend. p. 57. The same fragment is preserved also by Suidas, and nearly in the same terms. Lexic. vox *Orpheus.*

[right margin, handwritten: Respecting the Orphic triad]

converted into certainty.   I believe indeed, that Orpheus, or whoever was the author of his remains, taught, that the Universe originated from a triad: I believe also, that he asserted the divinity of that triad; because the triplicated great father of paganism was universally esteemed the principal deity: and I further believe, that he might have described his triad as essentially but one person who multiplied himself into three; because I find exactly the same tenet maintained in the theology of Hindostan, to which the Orphic remains bear so close a resemblance that they must inevitably be considered as inculcating one system.   But I am slow to credit, that he described his triad in the precise words and in the precise manner attributed to him by Cedrenus and Timotheus.

I am the more confirmed in my opinion, both by finding that the very curious cosmogony introduced into the Orphic Argonautics exhibits no such marks of corrective alteration, and by observing that the genuine Orphic triad does not bear the Christianized names which Cedrenus ascribes to it.

I have sung, says the poet, *the immense necessity of ancient Chaos; and Cronus who produced the vast tracts of Ether; and Eros the parent of eternal Night, famed on account of his double nature, whom more recent mortals call* Phanes; *and the birth of mighty Brimo; and the deeds of the earth-born; and the wanderings of Ceres; and the illustrious gifts of the Cabiri; and the ineffable nocturnal mysteries of Bacchus; and Venus beloved by Adonis; and the orgies of Praxidice; and the mourning of the Egyptians; and the infernal rites of Osiris.*[1]   So again, in another part of the poem: *I sang the mystic hymn of ancient Chaos; the alternation of the physical elements; the formation of heaven; the origin of the broad-breasted earth; the profundity of the vast ocean; wise Eros, the most ancient, the perfecter of the Universe, who produced all things and separated each from the other; and Cronus the dire destroyer, until the sceptre of the immortals passed to thunder-loving Jupiter.*[2]

Now I will venture to assert, that the whole cosmogony, as exhibited in the Argonautics, is in a great measure diluvian, though, as usual, with a decided reference to a prior creation.   The demiurgic power is here declared

---

[1] Orph. Argon. ver. 12—32.   [2] Orph. Argon. ver. 419—425.

to be Phanes or Eros, and with him is associated Cronus or the destructive power. But Phanes is certainly the same as the Hindoo Brahma; both because the attribute of creation is ascribed to each contradistinctively to that of destruction, and because each is declared to be that first-born who was produced from the egg that floated in Chaos: and, in a similar manner, Cronus is clearly that person of the Hindoo triad; whose office it is to destroy each world when the appointed hour arrives, who in conjunction with the creative power presides over what the Orphic poet calls *the alternation of the physical elements*, and who bears the name of *Siva* or *Mahadeva*. Such being the case, since, in the account given by Cedrenus of the Orphic cosmogony, the office of creator is ascribed to a god, who multiplies himself into three powers, and who is said to bear the three names of *Wisdom* and *Light* and *Life*; and since, in the Argonautics, the same office of creator is chiefly assigned to Eros or Phanes, though not without admitting even the destroyer Cronus to a share of the labour: it will necessarily follow, however the colouring of the Orphic triad in Cedrenus may have been heightened by some Christian hand, that Eros and the triplicated demiurge are one and the same person. Accordingly, this conclusion exactly agrees, both with the Hindoo theology which makes Brahma a member of a divine triad, and with the Orphic theology itself which similarly makes Eros (who must plainly be identified with Brahma) a member of another divine triad. Hence the Orphic triad, though mentioned in such remarkable terms by Cedrenus, proves eventually to be no other than that Hindoo triad; which is supposed to emanate from a yet older deity, and of which the different members all melt both into each other and into the primeval unity of their common parent. So again, Phanes and Cronus, though separately viewed as the powers of creation and destruction, will be found eventually to be one person: which person is the great father, chiefly indeed Noah, yet not that patriarch exclusively, but rather Noah considered as a reappearance of Adam. Thus the double nature of Phanes relates to Noah's twofold existence, the second period of it commencing with his allegorical birth from the Ark: for the first-born Eros or Phanes, that hidden tauriform god who was the common parent both of gods and men, is declared by the Orphic poet to be the same as Bacchus; to whom he equally assigns a double nature, whom he similarly styles *the tauriform hidden deity*, and who was feigned to have been in his allegorical infancy set afloat in an ark on the surface of the ocean.[1]   Phanes or Bacchus, we may observe, is said in the Argonautics to be the parent of the goddess Night.   This goddess, as the Orphic poet elsewhere informs us, is no other than Venus :[2] and Venus herself is the universal mother, who comprehends under one character both the greater World and the smaller World, both the Earth and the Ark.   Here she is described as being the daughter of the primeval Eros or Cupid, who perfected the Universe and who produced all things : at other times, and according to the more popular mythology, she is represented as being his parent.   But this seeming contradiction, of which instances perpetually occur in the fables of paganism, is easily accounted for (as I have already had occasion to intimate in general terms) by the different degrees of relationship which the great father was thought to bear to the great mother.   He was her parent, considered as the creator of the World and as the builder of the Ark : he was her son, considered as produced out of the Earth and as born from the Ark : he was her husband, considered as jointly with her bringing all things into existence.   This goddess Night or the infernal Venus is the same as Brimo, likewise mentioned in the cosmogony of the Argonautics ; and Brimo again is the same as Hecatè and Ceres :[3] while the Cabiric, the Eleusinian, the Bacchic, and the Egyptian, Mysteries alike describe the wonderful deliverance of the patriarchal family from the waters of the deluge.

Thus we are already brought to the conclusion, that the Orphic demiurgic triad is in reality no other than the Hindoo triad : that is to say, it is a triad, which, so far from having any relation to the holy Trinity, consists of the great father multiplying himself at the commencement of every world into three sons ; it is a triad, in short, springing from unity, of which the unity is Adam reappearing in Noah, and the triad the three sons of Adam reappearing in the three sons of Noah.   But the conclusion is further strengthened by our finding, that the Christianized names, which Cedrenus gives to

---

[1] Compare Orph. Hymn. v. with Hymn. xxix.

[2] Orph. Hymn. ii. ver. 2.

[3] See my Dissert. on the Cabiri. vol. i. p. 139, 279. vol. ii. p. 323.

the three persons of the Orphic triad, are not the names which the poet himself applies to them. He does indeed maintain the ancient tenet of a triad of deity, and considers the great father as multiplying himself into three powers or emanations : but, instead of denominating those three powers *Wisdom, Light,* and *Life,* he styles them, in exact accordance with the language of the Argonautics, *Phanes* or *Eros, Uranus,* and *Cronus ;* and, after the manner of the Hindoos, he chiefly ascribes the work of creation to the first of them who is the same as Brahma, and the work of destruction to the last who is the same as Siva. [1] What we are to understand by the birth of Eros or Brahma from the egg, has already been sufficiently pointed out : the exposure of Bacchus in an ark, and the voyage of Siva in the ship Argha over the surface of the deluge, afford the best comment both upon the production and character of the Orphic demiurge. Further light however is thrown upon the subject by the mythological birth, not only of the creative Eros, but of all the persons of the triad. As the Hindoos suppose, that Brahma, Vishnou, and Siva, were each produced from an egg : so Olympiodorus tells us, that in the Orphic theology an egg gives birth to the three primeval monads or individuals. [2] Now, since Phanes or Eros is himself said to be born from an egg within which he had been hidden, since the triad of which he is the head is also said to be born from an egg within which it had similarly been hidden, since Phanes is declared in the Argonautics to be the creator of the world, and since in the fragment preserved by Cedrenus from Timotheus the three powers of one god whose names are *Wisdom Light* and *Life* are also pronounced to have created the world : we cannot reasonably doubt, that the Orphic triad mentioned by Cedrenus, whatever marks it may bear of the corrective hand of some Christian editor, is the very same as the triplicated Phanes or as that triad which is fabled to have been born out of an egg. But the character of the hidden Phanes or Bacchus, who was exposed in an ark and who is described as the common parent both of gods and of men, proves him to be Noah who was esteemed a reappearance of Adam: consequently the triad, produced by his triplication of himself, can have no reference to the Trinity, but must clearly be composed of the triple offspring of the great transmi-

[1] Proc. in Plat. Tim. p. 93. apud Cudw. Intell. Syst. b. i. c. 4. p. 306.
[2] Olymp. Comment. in Philib. apud Orph. Oper. Gesner. p. 410.

grating father. This matter is literally set forth in the history of Cronus. He is described as one of the persons of the Orphic triad; all which persons, agreeably to the Hindoo doctrine of Maya or delusion, melt at length into the unity of a single monad. But Cronus, whose whole history proves him to be Noah, is said to have had three sons, one of them called *Hammon*, among whom he divided the empire of the world. Here then, as in the Hindoo theology, we have three principles emanating from a fourth: the only difference is, that the fable of Cronus expresses literally what the Hindoo dogma sets forth mystically. Exactly the same opinion will be found to occur in the Orphic system. Not only does the poet celebrate a triad of demiurgic principles jointly produced from an egg, which once floated on the surface of the ocean: but he likewise speaks of there having been *four* primeval kings or kingdoms, which he subdivides into a monad generating a triad. First he places Uranus alone; next Cronus, Zeus, and Dionusus: who here manifestly occupy the place of Eros, Uranus, and Cronus, when arranged as a triad.[1] All these, agreeably to the Hindoo theory, are comprized in the single person of Phanes or Eros; who is, at the same time, one and three, or one producing three. Hence we are told, that Phanes was a tetrad: and hence, since a single eye was the hieroglyphic of the great father worshipped in the unity of Osiris, and since three eyes were the hieroglyphic of the same great father worshipped as the triple Siva or Jupiter; so we find the tetrad Phanes described as having four eyes, because he united in his own person both the aboriginal monad and the triad which emanated from it.[2] The whole of this cabalistical jargon meant no more, than that the great father, whom they venerated as the supreme god and whose origin at the commencement of each successive world they deduced either from a floating egg or from a lotos or from a ship, was the parent of three sons.

As the ancient pagans by triplicating the unity of the great father, because Adam and Noah had each three sons, produced three great fathers; so, by analagously triplicating the unity of the great mother, they produced three great mothers. Such is the triple Devi of the Hindoos; whose three forms, though she is still but one person, constitute to the three wives of their three

[1] Olymp. Comment. in Phæd. apud Orph. Oper. Gesner. p. 408.
[2] Herm. Comment. in Phæd. apud Orph. Oper. p. 405.

chief divinities : such also is the triple Diana or Hecatè of the Greeks : and such is the triplicated goddess Night of the Orphic poet.   He tells us, that Night was the daughter of the primeval Eros, and that she was the same person as the infernal oceanic Venus or the great mother : yet he likewise very remarkably teaches us, that there were three Nights, and that from the last of them sprang Justice.[1]   Now, when the character of the goddess Night is considered, whom the poet identifies with Venus or Isis or Isi, that was born from the ocean and that floated on the waters of the deluge in the form of the ship Argha; it will, I think, be sufficiently evident, that the birth of Justice from her womb means the birth of the just man Noah, the *Sadik*[1] alike of Moses and Sanchoniatho, from the gloomy interior of the Ark.

Enough has now perhaps been said to shew, that the Orphic demiurgic triad can have no connection with the doctrine of the Trinity : indeed Cudworth himself ingenuously confesses, that the appellation of *Logos* or *the Word*, which as well as the title of *Light* has been conferred upon the second person of that triad, is liable to the *suspicion* at least of forgery.[1]

2. What has been said respecting the Orphic triad will lead us, if I mistake not, to a right understanding of the famous Platonic triad, which is similarly represented as being the creator of the world. The idea, which I am disposed to entertain of it, is this : that it was primarily and properly a mere mortal triad, the very same as the triad of the Orphic philosophy, to which, agreeably to a system that prevailed in almost every part of the globe, the creation or rather the renovation of the Universe was ascribed at every great mundane change which matter was destined periodically to undergo; but that afterwards, by an intercourse more or less direct with the Hebrews, some knowledge of a divine Trinity in the essence of God was superadded to the old tradition of a demiurgic triad, springing from a monad, and born out of a wonderful egg which had floated during an entire year on the surface of the chaotic ocean.

With respect to the first part of this opinion, we are plainly told by Proclus, that the three demiurgic Noës or Intelligences of the Platonist Amelius were,

[right margin, handwritten] Respecting the Platonic triad

---

[1] Herm. Comment. in Phæd. apud Orph. p. 406.

[1] Heb. פְדִיק. See Gen. vi. 9. and Sanch. apud Euseb. Præp. Evan. lib. i. c. 10.

[1] Intell. Syst. b. i. c. 4. p. 303.

in the judgment of that philosopher, the very same as Plato's three Kings and as the Orphic triad of Phanes Uranus and Cronus.[1] Here then the identity of the Platonic and the Orphic triads is unequivocally confessed by one, who had thoroughly studied the subject. Hence, whatever subsequent additions might be made from another quarter to the Platonic doctrine, originally and properly it was a mere transcript of the ancient Orphic philosophy. But we have seen, that the Orphic triad was the very same as the Trimurti of the Hindoos and as the demiurgic triads of most primitive nations: and we have further seen, that those various triads were no other than the triplicated great father, who was supposed to appear at the commencement of every new world after floating on the surface of the ocean during the intermediate period either in an egg or on the lotos or literally in the ship Argha. Consequently, if the Platonic triad were properly the same as the Orphic triad, agreeably to the express declaration of Amelius, it must, in a similar manner be the same as the triplicated unity of the mere mortal great father; and must therefore, in the first instance at least, be wholly unconnected with a chief article of Christian belief.

With respect to the second part of the opinion which I have expressed, since it is well known that Plato travelled into Egypt, if not into the east; since his disciple Apuleius affirms, that he went there for the express purpose of learning the rites of the prophets; since Aristobulus the Jew declares, that he had diligently studied the law of Moses; since Josephus another Jew asserts, that he plainly imitated that lawgiver; since Clemens Alexandrinus the Christian speaks of him, as being acquainted with prophecy, and as having revived the light of Hebrew philosophy; since Justin Martyr another Christian declares, that he must have borrowed from the writings of Moses; since, in exact accordance with opinions both of Jews and Christians, Numenius the Pythagorèan even styles him *the Atticizing Moses;* since he himself speaks of certain Phenician (by which he must obviously mean Jewish) fables, that represented man as made out of the dust of the earth; and since, at the time when he travelled into Egypt, the Jews were wont to resort there in considerable numbers: when all these matters are duly weighed, we can scarcely avoid inferring, that the remarkable title of

---

[1] Proc. in Plat. Tim. p. 93. apud Cudw. Intell. Syst. b. i. c. 4. p. 306.

Logos or *the Word*, which he applies to one of the persons of the old Orphic triads, and which is altogether unknown in the Orphic theology whence he confessedly received his doctrine of a demiurgic triad, was borrowed from the school of the Hebrew Targumists.[1] But such an inference seems to be converted into almost absolute certainty by the declarations of the Platonists themselves. Thus Proclus tells us, that their belief in a demiurgic triad was adopted from a divinely revealed theology.[2] Here he speaks of those opinions, which Plato had learned from the Jewish writers, and which he had superadded to the mere mortal triad of the Orphic poet. He does not mean to say, that his notion of a triad was *itself* derived from that source: of *that* Plato was already in possession; because, according to Amelius, his triad was the very same as that of the more ancient Orphic philosophy, and consequently the one must have been borrowed from the other. But when he became acquainted with the writings and traditions of the Hebrews, struck with the apparent analogy between *his* demiurgic triad worshipped by the Gentiles as the supreme god and the *real* demiurgic Trinity of divine hypostases coexisting in mysterious Unity, he not unnaturally mistook the one for the other: whence he denominated his first person *The good one* or *The being that always and truly exists*, simply translating the name *Jehovah*; his second person, *Logos* or *the Word*, fancying that Nous or Intellect, the title which the great father bore as the Intelligent Soul of the World, might properly be identified with the Chaldee *Mimra* and the Hebrew *Dabar*; and his third person, *the Spirit*, which from the exordium of Genesis he had learned to esteem *the oldest of all things* and *the author of motion*.[3] These three persons he mentions conjointly in his epistle to Dionysius.[4] That such an adaptation as I here suppose really took place, may be collected from Photius.

[1] Apul. de dogm. Plat. Euseb. Præp. Evan. lib. xiii. c. 12. Joseph. cont. Apion. lib. ii. Clem. Alex. Strom. lib. i. Pædag. lib. ii. c. 1. Justin. Mart. Apol. ii. Theodor. Curat. Græc. Affect. lib. ii. Plat. de repub. lib. iii. fol. 44. Plat. Phæd. p. 97. Epinom. p. 986. apud Kidder and Gale.

[2] Proc. apud Cudw. Intell. Syst. b. i. c. 4. p. 294. His expression is ἡ θεοπαραδοτος θεολογια.

[3] Plat. de repub. lib. vi. p. 508. Tim. p. 27, 69. Phædr. p. 247. Phædon. p. 97. Epinom. p. 986. De leg. lib. x. apud Kidder.

[4] Ad Dionys. Epist. ii. apud Kidder.

He mentions, that Hierocles divided his book *of fate and providence* into seven parts, and that the object of the fourth part was to reconcile the doctrines of Plato with those writings which were accounted to be oracles; that is to say, with *the divinely revealed theology* spoken of by Proclus, which (I think) must have been the theology of the Hebrews.[1]

Since then, according to the express declaration of Amelius, the *genuine* Platonic triad is the same as the Orphic triad; it will follow, that Plato must have been well acquainted with the triad in question *previous* to his intercourse with the Hebrews: and it will likewise follow, that his mode of arranging it must have been similar to that which prevailed in the Orphic philosophy. Now the Orphic Mysteries ascribed the creation of the world to a triad; which was thought to have emanated from a yet more ancient monad, and which together with the monad was said to have been produced from a floating egg. Hence, from the testimony of Amelius to the identity of the Orphic and Platonic triads, we seem obliged to conclude, that such also was the *original* triad of Plato before his acquaintance with those whom he terms *Phenicians.* However it might be afterwards adapted to the knowledge which he had acquired of a higher Trinity; it was at first, like the Orphic tetrad of one king producing three younger kings, a subordinate triad springing from a more ancient monad. Accordingly we find, that the primitive idea of *one generating three*, which equally occurs in the mythology of Hindostan, China, Phenicia, and Greece, was never wholly lost among the Platonists. Thus Amelius speaks of a Demiurge and three Noës or three kings, whom he designates by the titles of *Him who exists, Him who possesses*, and *Him who sees:*[2] and thus Proclus very distinctly asserts the existence of a monad, which presides over a separate and subordinate triad. This assertion he makes in such a manner, as at once to prevent the possibility of being misunderstood, and to teach us what person was intended by the unity of the primeval Nous. He speaks of three gods, whom he declares to be the same as those celebrated by the Pythagoreans: and then he remarks, that one

---

[1] Phot. apud Cudw. Intell. Syst. b. i. c. 4. p. 292.

[2] Αμελιος δε τριτον ποιει τον Δημιουργον, και Νους τρεις, Βασιλεις τρεις, τον Οντα, τον Εχοντα, τον Ορωντα. Proc. in Plat. Tim. p. 93. apud Cudw. Intell. Syst. b. i. c. 4. p. 303. The passage is obscure; but I think it will not bear Dr. Cudworth's translation of it. If I have erred in my own gloss, let it be rejected.

Nous was alike the father of them all. In the same passage he mentions the three kings, whom Plato supposed to be the creators and governors of the Universe: and, having pronounced that Amelius rightly identified them with the three kings of the Orphic poet, he adds, that it was however a necessary constitution of this triad that the divine number, meaning evidently the monad, should precede it.[1] If we would further wish to know, who is that single Nous or Intellect that is thus placed at the head of three younger Noës, Proclus will give us all the information that could be desired. He teaches us, still in the course of the same passage, that the demiurgic Nous of Plato was the same person as the demiurgic Jupiter of the Orphic poet; and that this Jupiter, the creator of all things, preceded the three sons of Cronus: whence it is manifest, that the primeval Jupiter is the same person as Cronus, the names being used indifferently and convertibly, and each being alike described as the parent of three sons.[2] Agreeably to such a deduction, he elsewhere tells us, that Nous was equally Cronus and Jupiter, though one was ordinarily esteemed the father of the other: and, as he makes Jupiter to be the head of the three sons of Cronus, so he likewise affirms, that Cronus was the first king of the intelligent gods, that is, of the three Noës or demiurgic Intellects.[3] In a similar manner, we learn from Eusebius, that the person, whom Anaxagoras called *Nous* or *Intellect*, and whom he represented as producing an orderly world out of universal disorder, was the same both as Jupiter and as Prometheus.[4]

Thus it appears, that the triad of Plato, however he might afterwards decorate it with names and attributes borrowed from the Jewish Targumists, was in reality the triad of the Orphic poet; and that the Nous, whom he placed at the head of it, was the same as the Orphic Jupiter, as Cronus or Saturn, and as Prometheus. But both Prometheus, Cronus, and the Orphic Jupiter, are all most certainly the great father; that is to say, Adam reappearing in the character of Noah. For Prometheus is said to have flourished at the period of a great deluge: Cronus, as every part of his his-

---

[1] Proc. in Plat. Tim. p. 93, 94. apud Cudw.

[2] Proc. in Plat. Tim. p. 95. apud Cudw.

[3] Proc. in Plat. Theogon. p. 256. apud Cudw.

[4] Euseb. Hist. Synag. p. 374. Diog. Laert. in vit. Anaxag.

tory shews, is a character made up of the two patriarchs who appeared at the commencement of the two successive worlds : and the Orphic Jupiter is described with the precise well-known attributes of the great father inseparably united to the great mother ; for, like the diluvian Siva in the compound form of Ardha-Nari, he is said to be an hermaphrodite from whose womb universal nature is produced. If then the head of the Platonic triad be the great father considered in unity, the triad itself must be composed of his three sons, whom the pagans viewed in the light of the great father triplicated.

The sum and substance, in short, both of the Hindoo, the Chinese, the Pythagorèan, the Orphic, and the Platonic, theology, so far as it respects that being who was considered as the animating Soul and demiurgic Principle of the Universe, is comprized in the words of the oracle, which Patritius cites from Damascius : *Through the whole world shines a triad, over which presides a monad.*[1] This monad, being confessedly the same as Cronus or the more ancient Jupiter, can only be the great father Noah viewed as a reappearance of Adam : and this triad, which shines through the whole world, and among the persons of which there was an old tradition that the world was once divided, must in consequence be the triple offspring of the one patriarch similarly viewed as a reappearance of the triple offspring of the other.

In exact agreement with such a conclusion, as the demiurgic Nous is declared to be one person with Prometheus who flourished at the time of a deluge and with Cronus who was the father of three sons ; so we sometimes find him celebrated, as *the Nous who came forth from a door*, while yet he is cabalistically pronounced in the same sentence to be *the Nous or Intellectual Soul of the Universe.*[2] I need scarcely observe, that the expression manifestly relates to the mystic birth of Noah from the door in the side of the Ark.

XII. As the inhabitants of the great eastern continent systematically blended together the primeval creation of the earth and its reformation after the deluge : so, whatever notions the tribes which peopled the western con-

[1] Damas. apud Cudw. Intell. Syst.

[2] Περι δε την κλησιν διηνεχθησαν, Νουν του παντος, και τον θυραθεν Νουν, και τα τοιαυτα προσαγορευσαντες. Gregor. Nazian. de Spirit. Sanct.

tinent had of a cosmogony, they largely mingled them with allusions to the flood.

1. Thus the Peruvians termed the supposed creator of the Universe *Viracocha*: but the word *Viracocha*, in a manner precisely resembling the title of the Greek *Aphrodite*, denotes *the froth of the sea*. What idea they had of this primitive being whom they esteemed the demiurge, is sufficiently plain from the curious circumstance of their applying the name to the Spaniards on account of their sailing in ships over the surface of the ocean. Accordingly, his sacred rites had immediate respect to the sea; whence this pretended creator, like Brahma, Puoncu, and Phanes, was thought to have derived his origin. Subordinate to Viracocha they revered two triads; connecting, like the nations of the eastern continent, the triple offspring of the great father with the Sun and (as in the case of Jupiter) with the thunder. The first consisted of Chuquilla, Catuilla, and Intyllapa; or the father-thunder, the son-thunder, and the brother-thunder: the second, of Apomti, Churunti, and Intiquaoqui: or the father-Sun, the son-Sun, and the brother-Sun. Nor were they satisfied with these two principal triads. So strongly were they impressed with the notion of three deities inferior to that primeval god, who sprang from the sea and to whom they assimilated the Spanish mariners, that they had likewise three images of Chuquilla, himself a person of their first triad; as the Persian Mithras was not only one with Oromasdes and Ahriman, but was also said to have triplicated himself. They had moreover an idol called *Tangatanga*, which they said was one in three and three in one: that is to say, the paternal monad branching out into a cognate triad of sons; each (agreeably to the theory of the Hindoos) identifying himself with each, and all finally resolving themselves into the unity of that monad whence they had emanated. Added to these they venerated, like the pagans of the eastern hemisphere, a great universal mother: and, what shews yet further the genuine character of their ancient demiurgic man of the sea the superior of their multiplied triad, the badge of the Inca was a rainbow and two snakes; the one allusive to the deluge, the others the symbols of the two general parents both of gods and men.[1]

---

[1] Purch. Pilgrim. b. ix. c. 10, 12. Purchas quaintly calls their triads *an apish imitation of*

That of the Mexicans

2. Remarks not dissimilar may be made on the deity, whom the Mexicans supposed to be the creator of the world. They called him *Mexitli* or *Vitzliputzli;* and believed him to be in a peculiar manner the founder and ancestor of their own nation. His image was seated on an azure-coloured stool placed in a litter. His complexion was also azure: and in his hand he held an azure staff, fashioned into the shape of a waving serpent. Closely attached to him there was a second deity named *Tlaloc.* And besides these two they revered a third, whom they called *Tezcallipuca.* Him they esteemed the god of repentance. His complexion was nearly the same as that of Mexitli, for his statue was formed out of a black shining stone.[1] As for the superior divinity of this triad, he was placed upon the high altar in a small box decked with feathers and ornaments of gold: and the tradition of the Mexicans was, that, when they journeyed by different stations from a remote country to the north-west, they bore his oracular image along with them seated in a coffer made of reeds.[2] Whenever they rested, they placed the ark of their deity on an altar:[3] and at length, by his special direction, they built their principal city in the midst of a lake.[4]

Every particular of this superstition shews its diluvian origin, and proves the supposed demiurge to be no other than the great father. The ark of Mexitli is the same machine as the ark, in which the Hammon or Osiris of Egypt was wont to be similarly borne in solemn procession; the same also as the sacred ark of Bacchus; and the same as the ship of Isis and the Argha of Iswara. His dark azure complexion is the very complexion of the

---

the Trinity brought in by the devil. Their worship was indeed sufficiently diabolical, being debased with all the abominable impurities of the arkite superstition; but I do not believe, that it had any relation whatsoever to the Trinity.

[1] *Attired,* says Purchas, *after their manner, with some ethnick devises.* One of these devises was an azure feather.

[2] *They went forth, carrying their idol with them in a coffer of reeds supported by four of their principal priests, with whom he talked, and communicated his oracles and directions. He likewise gave them laws, and taught them the ceremonies and sacrifices they should observe. And, even as the pillar of cloud and fire conducted the Israelites in their passage through the wilderness, so this apish devil gave them notice when to advance forward, and when to stay.*

[3] Purchas applies the name of *ark* to the coffer, in which the god was seated.

[4] Purch. Pilgrim. b. viii. c. 10, 11. Robertson's Hist. of Amer. b. iv. sect. 8. p. 41, 42, 43.

Vishnou and Cneph of the Hindoo and Egyptian triads.[1] He was oracular, like the ship Argo of the Greek mythologists, like the Baris of Hammon, and like the superior arkite gods of all the gentile nations. And his supposed injunction, that the city should be founded in the midst of a lake, is perfectly agreeable to similar legends which occur in various parts of the eastern continent, and to the Cabiric veneration of lakes and the small islands which they contained. These latter were sometimes feigned to float; and it is not improbable, that there may have been occasionally real floating islands artificially constructed of timber covered with turf. That in the lake Chemmis near the Egyptian city Buto contained a temple of Horus furnished with three altars: and the god was reputed to have been there preserved from the rage of Typhon or the ocean. Such islands were considered as double symbols both of the Earth and of the Ark, each of which was esteemed a World floating on the waters of Chaos : and, from the general connection of the early history of Mexico, I am inclined to believe, that with a similar allusion the capital was built in an island in the midst of the lake.[2] The traditional route of the founders of the nation proves them to have been, as Dr. Robertson justly observes, *emigrants from Asia ;* who, after wandering through the eastern regions of Siberia, crossed over the streights that divide the two continents. And with this hypothesis their religion, so far as we have any accounts of it, exactly corresponds : for in fundamentals it is manifestly the same as that of Egypt, Hindostan, Phenicia, and Greece. The twisted serpent, which Mexitli bore in his hand, was a very general symbol of the great father worshipped in the Sun : and accordingly, next to him (or, as I rather suspect, in conjunction with him), they adored that luminary. Their second god Tlaloc was the deity of the waters, to whom children were sacrificed by setting them afloat on the lake in a leaky canoe. And their third deity Tezcallipuca resembled in complexion their first. His character, as the god of repentance, has been borrowed from that just patriarch, who vainly became a preacher of righteousness to an incorrigible generation.[3]

[1] Asiat. Res. vol. i. p. 261. Cudw. Intell. Syst. b. i. c. 4. p. 412.

[2] This subject will be resumed more at large hereafter, book iii. chap. 6.

[3] 2 Peter ii. 5.

That of the Virginians

3. The cosmogony of the Virginians seems also to be mingled with diluvianism. They believe, that he, whom they esteem the supreme being, created the world by the agency of other inferior gods whom they designate by the general name of *Mantoac*. First were made the waters, out of which these deities formed all things, whether visible or invisible : but mankind originated from the conjunction of a woman with one of the gods. The images of their divinities they call *Kewasowok*. One alone, apparently of superior dignity to the rest, is styled *Kewas*. Of this personage some of their temples contain only a single statue ; others, two ; and others again, three.[']

The triplicated Kewas I conceive to have the same allusion as the various other triads of the gentiles. The duplicated Kewas is probably the same as the double hermaphroditic Jupiter of the Orphic poet, who unites in his own person the two great principles of nature ; the same also as the Hindoo Ardha-nari, or Siva combined with his consort Bhavani, who at the time of the deluge is said to have floated on the ocean in the form of the ship Argha. The single Kewas I take to be *the Monad* or *elder Mind* of the Orphic and Platonic-schools, who was esteemed the Soul of the World, and who in his demiurgical capacity was supposed to have mysteriously triplicated himself. The inferior gods, by whose agency the world was created, seem to be much the same as the chaogenous hero-deities of Hesiod and other ancient mythologists.

That of the Iroquois

4. We still find the same double allusion to the creation and the deluge in the cosmogony of the Iroquois. According to father Laffiteau, they believe, that in the beginning, when as yet there was no earth, there were six men, who were carried about in the air at the mercy of the winds. Having no women, they foresaw that their race must soon come to an end : but they learned that there was one in heaven ; and resolved, if possible, to gain her. The enterprize was difficult and dangerous : but the person, who undertook it, was wafted thither by birds upon their wings. The voyage being happily achieved, he waited until the woman should come out, as her manner was, to draw water. When she appeared, he offered her a present, and

['] Purchas. Pilgrim. b. viii. c. 6.

thus seduced her: but the lord of heaven, knowing what had happened, banished her; and a tortoise received her upon its back. The otter and the fishes then drew up mud from the bottom of the water, and formed of the body of the tortoise a small island, which was gradually enlarged until it became the earth which we inhabit. The woman at first had two sons. One of these, who had provided himself with an offensive weapon, slew his brother who was unarmed. She was afterwards delivered of several children, from whom the rest of mankind are descended.[1]

There is one singular and arbitrary part of this legend, which at once serves to shew the Asiatic origination of the Americans and to point out the union of the present cosmogony with the history of the deluge. The tortoise, which receives the woman, seems very evidently borrowed from the Courma-Avatar of Hindostan; in which Vishnou, assuming the form of a tortoise, supports on his back the mighty hill Mandar, while the assembled genii violently churn the agitated ocean.[2] This fable has been reasonably pronounced by Sir William Jones to relate to the deluge: yet, like that of the Iroquois, it is largely intermingled with references to the creation. The Hindoos have also an account of one of the sons of the first Menu, who is certainly Adam, being slain by his brother at a sacrifice. This tradition, conjointly with the story of the tortoise, has been brought, I apprehend, by the ancestors of the Americans out of Asia. It is almost superfluous to point out the source whence it originated in the first instance, or to remark that evident traces of the fall may be detected in the history of the first woman of the Iroquois. I have only to add, that their considering the earth in the light of a floating island is perfectly analogous to the generally received theory of ancient paganism.

5. Under the present division of my subject, I may not improperly arrange the cosmogonies of two out of the many recently discovered islands, which thickly stud the vast ocean that flows between Asia and America.

That of New Zeland

The New-Zealanders, such is the substance of what Mr. Marsden learned from the native Duaterra, believe, that three gods made the first man, and that the first woman was made of one of the man's ribs. The general term

[1] Moeurs des sauvages. tom. i. p. 43.   [2] Vide infra b. iii. c. 4. § III. 3.

for *bone* is *Eve :* and, if we may credit Duaterra, all his countrymen maintain, that the first woman was formed out of *a bone* or *eve* taken from the
side of the first man. They have also a counterpart to the legendary story of
the man in the Moon ; and they assert, that at some former period the serpent
spoke with man's voice. They further suppose, that the world was originally under water ; and they assign to each of their three gods his own peculiar part in giving to it its present form. Besides these they have another
triad : the god of anger and death, of whom they are much afraid ; the god
of the sea, rain, wind, and thunder ; and the god of reptiles, who is also the
deity of sorrow. They have no written records among them : consequently,
all that they know of past events is traditional.[1]

We have here again the demiurgic triad and another added to it, which I
believe to be a mere repetition of the first. The deity of sorrow is evidently
the same person as the Mexican deity of repentance : the deity of anger
and death identifies himself with Siva or the destroying power of the Hindoos : and the god of the sea similarly coincides with the Mexican Tlaloc,
the Indian Vishnou, and indeed the great diluvian father venerated in every
part of the world. Unless we suppose that the Zealanders have received
the name of *Eve* from the missionaries, and have afterwards represented
themselves as already possessed of her history ; it seems probable, that the
appellation has reached them from Hindostan, where the first Menu and
his consort produced from his side are still known by the titles of *Adima* and
Iva. Their fable, as well as our own, of a man being in the Moon, has
originated, I have little doubt, from an astronomico-diluvian source. The
Egyptians had a legend that Osiris entered into the Moon : they had also a
legend, that he was inclosed by Typhon or the ocean in an ark shaped like
the Moon, that is to say, like the lunar crescent, and was thus set afloat on
the surface of the water.[2] These two legends serve to explain each other ;
and the two conjointly teach us what we are to understand by the apparently
wild fable of a man being transported to the Moon. That planet was the
astronomical symbol of the Ark : and, when the great father was said to

[1] Christian Observer. Novemb. 1810. p. 724.

[2] See Plate III. Fig. 1.

enter into the Moon, it is evident from the parallel story of his entering into a floating ark shaped like the Moon, that his entrance into the Moon and his entrance into the Ark was the very same event. With a similar allusion, the Moon is thought by the Hindoos to have been the hiding-place of Crishna or Vishnou, to have been the saviour of Chandra or the lunar Iswara who is literally represented as floating in the ship Argha on the surface of the deluge, to have been the residence of the ancestors of mankind, and to have been herself the child of the ocean. In short, the man in the Moon, who was a character well-known to the ancient mythologists, whatever whimsical additions may have been made to his story, is really no other than Noah concealed in the preserving Ark.

6. The general analogy of the preceding cosmogonies will shew, that the traditions of Otaheite, separated as it is from the main land, have originated from the same source and involve the very same mythological notions. The inhabitants of that island give a fanciful account of their own immediate creation : but they believe also in a previous universal one, and they speak of lands respecting which they have now no other knowledge than what has been preserved by tradition. Their most remote account reaches to Tatooma and Tapuppa ; the former of whom was a male rock, and the latter a female one. These support that congeries of land and water, which composes the terraqueous globe. The two rock deities produced Totorro, who was killed, and divided into land. After him, Otaia and Oroo were begotten : who, being married, became the parents first of land and then of a race of gods. Otaia was killed : but Oroo married her son, the god Teorraha, whom she ordered to create more land, the whole race of animals, all sorts of food found upon the earth, and the sky which is supported by men called *Teeferei*. The spots observed in the Moon are supposed to be groves of a sort of trees, which once grew in Otaheite. These being destroyed by some accident, their seeds were carried up thither by doves, where now they flourish.' To the Otaheitean account of the creation may properly be subjoined the opinion, which they entertain respecting their principal god. Their general name for deity in all its ramifications is *Eatooa :* but, agree-

That of
Otaheite

_____
' Cook's third voyage. b. iii. c. 9. p. 153. 12mo edit.

ably to those notions of the triplicated great father which pervaded every part of the gentile world, they believe in a triad of supreme demiurgic gods, who stand in a height of celestial dignity to which no others can approach.[1]

Almost every part of this cosmogony bespeaks its origin : while the re-collection of distant lands at present known only by tradition seems to prove, that Otaheite and the neighbouring islets were peopled by some roving Asiatic tribe, driven there probably by stress of weather. Tatooma, I have little doubt, is the Buddha or Tat-Om of the Hindoos and Indo-Scythæ; who is sometimes represented by a large stone, and sometimes by a colossal statue of stupendous dimensions : and Tapuppa is his consort, the great mother, who in various parts of the world was similarly venerated under the form of a stone. This worship of rock deities was both very ancient and most extensively prevalent : and the superstition of the Otaheiteans is, I think, clearly a branch of it. The death of Otaia seems to be the same event as that of Osiris or Adonis; and this deity, with his consort and son, forms precisely the Egyptian triad of Osiris, Isis, and Horus. Totorro, from whose body the earth is produced, coincides so exactly with the Gothic Ymer and the Chaldèan Omoroca, that the resemblance can scarcely be deemed altogether casual. And the persuasion, that it is not accidental, is considerably strengthened by the remarkable legend respecting doves carrying the seeds of certain trees to the Moon. Here, unless I greatly mistake, we may detect precisely the same notions of that planet, as those which entered so largely into the mythological speculations of ancient idolatry. The fable was, I believe, altogether founded on the circumstance of the dove bearing the branch of an olive-tree to Noah in the Ark. When to these arbitrary coincidences we add the Otaheitean belief in a demiurgic triad of supreme gods, we may rest assured, that the popular theology of the island was not of native growth, but was brought thither from some foreign clime by the original colonists. The propriety of such a conclusion is finally, so far as I can judge, placed out of all doubt, by the circumstance of the natives having also their ark-god, their pyramidal temples, and their sacred lake : but the consideration of these matters must for the present be postponed.

[1] Mission. Voyage to south. pacif. ocean. p. 343.

Enough has now been said to shew, that, in accordance with the established doctrine of a succession of similar worlds, each commencing with a demiurge who triplicates himself, and each terminating with a deluge from the rage of which the future great father of a new mundane system is preserved in an ark, the pagan accounts of the creation, though approaching in many particulars to the scriptural verity, are yet very intimately and almost universally blended with allusions to the flood. Hereafter we shall find, that, for the same reason, the gentile traditions of the deluge contain perpetual references to the history of the creation.

THE ORIGIN

OF

PAGAN IDOLATRY.

BOOK II.

PLATE I.

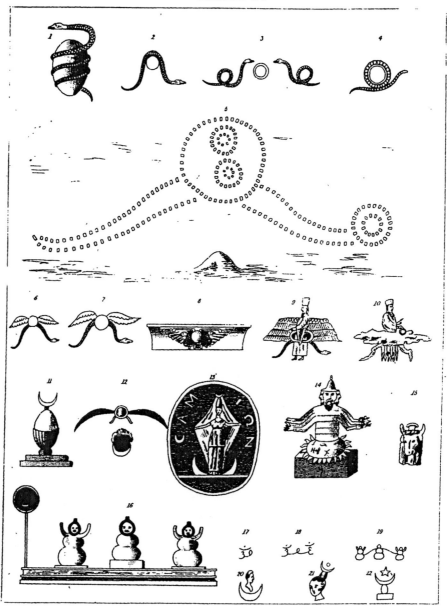

To the Right Hon.ble and Revnd GEORGE, LORD VISCOUNT BARRINGTON,
this Plate is respectfully inscribed by his obliged humble Servant.
THE AUTHOR.

CHAPTER I.

Concerning the garden of Paradise and mount Ararat.

THERE is reason to believe, that the situation of the garden of Paradise coincides geographically with that of mount Ararat. This circumstance was one of the various causes, which served to produce the theory of a succession of similar worlds. Adam, the parent of three sons, appeared, at the epoch of the first creation, in Paradise: Noah, likewise the parent of three sons, appeared, at the epoch of what was deemed another creation, on the summit of mount Ararat. But Paradise locally coincided with Ararat. Consequently, each world commenced, as it were, from the same spot: and, each world also commencing with a father and his three sons, Noah and his triple offspring were considered as a new manifestation of Adam and his triple offspring; a manifestation, which again and again took place in the self-same lofty and sacred region at the beginning of every successive mundane system.

I. Before any attempt be made to ascertain the true situation of Paradise and to determine its geographical coincidence with mount Ararat, it will be necessary to inquire what changes the deluge may be supposed to have effected in the surface or general constitution of the earth.

1. Now, if either the theory adopted by the writers of the Hutchinsonian

[margin annotations:]
AN ENQUIRY into what changes the deluge may have wrought on the surface of the earth

Theories of the Hutchinsonian school, and of M. de Luc

school, or that preferred by the celebrated geologist M. de Luc, be well founded it is obvious, that any search after the situation of Paradise is perfectly nugatory.

The writers of the Hutchinsonian school maintain, that the operation of the deluge was such, as to resolve or melt down the globe of the earth into its primeval chaotic state; and that, when the waters of the flood abated, the process was in every respect the same as *the gathering together of the waters into one place* and *the appearing of the dry land,* which is said to have occurred at the time of the original creation.[1] According to this theory, in short, the old world was not so much overflowed by the deluge, as it was reduced to a sort of confused muddy pulp; and, when the waters retired, instead of the primeval continents and islands reappearing in their ancient places, an entirely new world emerged, bearing not the least superficial resemblance to its predecessor, but exhibiting a wholly different arrangement both of sea and land.[2]

Mr. de Luc, on the contrary, does not admit of any such solution as the Hutchinsonians contend for; but supposes, that the surface of the globe experienced a complete inversion of its component parts in consequence of the operation of the diluvian waters. What were once tracts of land sank below their proper level, and were inundated by the ocean: what was once the bed of the sea retained its original level, and, being now higher than the land of the old world, became, when the flood retired, the land of the new world. In other words, the present race of men inhabit what was formerly the bed of the sea; while the ocean, navigated by modern keels, for ever hides from the curiosity of mortal eyes the more ample tracts of land possessed by their antediluvian forefathers.[3]

Should either of these theories be well founded, Paradise in local situation exists no longer: according to the first of them, it was melted down and lost in the chaotic mixture, out of which a new world was formed by a

---

[1] Gen. i. 9, 10.

[2] See Catcott on the deluge, and other writers of the same school.

[3] See de Luc's Lettres Morales et Physiques sur l'histoire de la Terre, vol. i. p. 227. vol. v. p. 449.

process similar to the formation of the old world ; according to the second of them, it lies buried and concealed beneath the overwhelming waters of the ocean.

2. Our knowledge respecting the precise mode, in which the deluge operated on the surface or general constitution of the earth, is inevitably so limited and imperfect, that whatever is advanced on the subject beyond the express revelation of God can at the best be deemed nothing more than a plausible or ingenious conjecture. But, if a theory, instead of merely going *beyond* Scripture, be found plainly to *contradict* it, then it must necessarily be rejected by every believer. Should such then be the case with the hypotheses in question, neither the piety nor the talents of their framers must prevent them from being discarded as erroneous and untenable.

No theory can be admitted, which contradicts Scripture

3. The language employed by Moses in the account which he gives us of the deluge, so far from favouring either of these theories, appears to me most positively and decidedly to contradict them both. Instead of intimating, either that the substance of the earth was dissolved, or that the ancient continents sank below their proper level, he describes, according to the most plain and obvious acceptation of his words, first a gradual inundation by which every portion of habitable land was covered, and afterwards a gradual subsiding in consequence of which the identical land that had been covered again appeared.

The above two methods are contradicted by the Scriptural account of the deluge

It may be said, that, although such be the popular language employed by Moses, it does not absolutely contradict the theory of de Luc, whatever be the fate of the Hutchinsonian hypothesis : because the gradual sinking of the old continents would *apparently* produce the very same phenomenon as the rising of the waters ; in each case, the sea would equally *seem* to elevate itself above the land, and, after inundating the plains and valleys, to creep up the sides of the mountains and at length cover their summits.

This no doubt is true, but it does not meet the whole of the objection. Moses informs us, that, at the height of the flood, all the mountains were covered ; and he afterwards tells us, that, as the waters abated, the tops of the mountains were seen. Now, according to the ordinary rules of composition, when we are taught in a continued narrative, that the mountains were *first* entirely covered by the waters, and *then*, as the waters gradually retired, that the tops of the mountains appeared : we *must* conclude, that the *self-same* mountains are spoken of in both parts of the history ; that the mountains, which appeared while the deluge was subsiding, were the *identical* mountains which had been previously inundated. Such is the obvious purport of the Mosaical narrative, and such (I will venture to say) is the manner in which it would be understood by any plain reader who had no particular hypothesis to form on the subject. But, in the Hutchinsonian theory, the primeval mountains are all melted down : and, in that of de Luc, they never appear again above the water, being succeeded by an entirely different set of mountains which heretofore were vast inequalities in the bed of the ocean. That is to say, in each theory, Moses is arbitrarily made to speak of two totally *distinct* classes of mountains which have nothing between them in common, though he himself gives no intimation of any such distinction, but *apparently* at least is speaking all the while of the *same* mountains.

Still it *may* be asserted, that it is as much a gratuitous assumption to consider Moses as speaking of the *same* mountains, as it is to pronounce that he speaks of *different* mountains. He himself does not, *in so many words,* settle the question either way : consequently, the system of de Luc is rather *supposed,* than absolutely *proved,* to contradict the sacred history.

Let us then examine, whether the language of the Jewish lawgiver does not throw some still further light on the subject.

In describing the manner in which the antediluvian mountains were covered by the encroaching deluge, he informs us, that the waters prevailed above the summits of the highest hills fifteen cubits upwards : hence he plainly intimates, that, whatever might be the depth of the waters above the *plains* or above the tops of *lower* mountains, they reached no further than fifteen cubits above the *loftiest* peak in the old world. This assertion however, so far as I can judge, is utterly irreconcileable with either system. The waters cannot properly be said to have prevailed *above* the tops of the highest hills, if, as we are taught by the Hutchinsonian school, the hills were melted down into the common mucilaginous mass, and therefore *ceased* to be eminences : neither is it possible, that they could have prevailed *no more* than fifteen cubits, if the theory of de Luc faithfully exhibit the phy-

tical operations of the deluge.   Whatever the present continents may have
been before the flood, the loftiest hills which we now behold were assuredly
covered by its waters : because we are both told, that they successively appeared as the waters abated, and that the Ark of Noah did not rest on the
summit of Ararat until they had sufficiently retired.   Now, if the high
hills, covered during the rise of the waters, were the hills of the antediluvian continent, which was gradually sinking below its primeval level ; if the
hills, which appeared when the waters subsided, were once eminences at the
bottom of the antediluvian ocean ; and if, as Moses positively asserts, the
waters prevailed *no more* than fifteen cubits above those hills which were
confessedly antediluvian : it is clearly impossible, that in *that* case they could
have covered *any* part of the present continents, still less therefore the tops
of the loftiest hills of the new world ; for it is plain, that, in order to hide
the summits of such hills as the Alps or the Andes, the water must have risen
immensely more than only fifteen cubits above the tops of the *antediluvian*
mountains, which even now, when the deluge has completely retired, are
still, according to the theory, plunged many fathoms deep beneath the waves
of our present oceans.[1]

    There is yet another circumstance, noticed in the Mosaical history, which
can as little be reconciled with the system of de Luc ; because it necessarily
leads to the belief, that the continents which we now inhabit are the very
same as the antediluvian continents, which, after having been overflowed by
the deluge, reappeared in their present form when the waters retired.   The
sacred writer informs us, that, when the dove returned to Noah the second
time, there was in her mouth an olive leaf plucked off from the parent tree :

---

    [1] I speak of course on the presumption, that the deluge, while it continued, was a sea
without a shore, and that no land, either antediluvian or postdiluvian, was visible.   If indeed
M. de Luc should contend, that the bed of the old ocean rose above the waves, as the antediluvian continents sank beneath them, so that *some* land was always visible and consequently
that the flood was never properly *universal ;* he will remove the present objection : but then
he will contradict the plain tenor of the scriptural account, which represents the waters as
not retiring from the lands which we now inhabit *until* the close of the allotted period of the
deluge ; whence it is evident, that those lands must have been under water during the whole
of its continuance, and consequently that the inundation must have been universal.

and he adds, that the patriarch naturally gathered from this incident that
the waters were abated from off the earth.   Now, according to the theory
either of de Luc or of the Hutchinsonians, such a circumstance could neither have happened, nor, if it *had* happened (most unaccountably on *their*
systems), would it have been any indication to Noah that the waters were
abating.   The physical strength of the dove requires us to suppose, that the
small twig which she plucked off was green and tender, not dead and un-
yielding.   But, agreeably to either of the theories in question, she could
have plucked it from no tree except one, which had accidentally been torn
up by the roots, and which had afterwards been tossed about on the surface
of the waters for the space of at least seven months.'   A tree however
under such circumstances must, I should apprehend, have been entirely
dead and stripped of all its leaves and soft young twigs; consequently, supposing the dove to have found it, she would scarcely have been able to tear
from it the twig mentioned by Moses.   Or, even if she *had* met with a
dead leaf which still adhered to one of the boughs, her returning with *this*
in her mouth could have been no proof to Noah that the waters were abated;
which the sacred historian clearly intimates was the case: because it might
equally have been produced by the dove at *any* period of the deluge, provided only she had been sent out of the Ark.   In order to be an indication

---

' The flood commenced on the seventeenth day of the second month; and the period of its
increase until it attained its greatest height was forty days: consequently, it had attained its
extreme elevation on the twenty sixth day of the third month.   The olive-tree therefore,
which, if we adopt the hypothesis either of de Luc or of the Hutchinsonians, we must suppose to have been tossed about on the surface of the waters, could scarcely have been torn
up later than the end of the forty days.   But, on the first day of the tenth month, the tops
of the mountains were seen; and, at the end of forty seven days afterwards, Noah sent forth
the dove the second time, which in the evening of the same day brought back the twig.   This
consequently must have happened on the seventeenth or eighteenth day of the twelfth month.
Now, between this day and the twenty sixth of the third month when the waters attained
their greatest elevation, there is a period of almost nine months.   I am moderate therefore
in supposing seven to be the least time, that the tree could have been floating on the waters:
and, according either to the hypothesis of de Luc or that of the Hutchinsonians, there is no
way of accounting for its appearance, except by supposing that it *was* torn up and that it
did float.

to Noah that the waters were abated, we must necessarily conclude that it was plucked from a *living* tree, which had firmly fixed its roots in one of the clefts of mount Ararat, and which, after having been overwhelmed by the waters during the time that the flood prevailed at its greatest height, had shot forth new suckers by that 'tenacious principle of vitality which so eminently distinguishes the roots of trees.' Except this, I see no satisfactory method of accounting for the existence of the olive-tree, so as to accord in *all* points with the circumstances specified by Moses : for we must not forget, that the dove is not only said to have plucked off a leaf or twig, but that the producing of the twig was *a proof to Noah that the waters were retiring*. If then the root of the tree had survived the deluge, and was putting forth new leaves after it had emerged from the waves, the mountain of Ararat, where it was growing, could not possibly have been a *submarine* antediluvian mountain, but must have been one of the peaks of an antediluvian *continent*. In this case therefore, the antediluvian continents can neither form the beds of our present ocean, nor can the beds of the antediluvian oceans have become our present continents. The olive tree alone, which must have been growing *before* the flood in the *very* place where it was found *after* the flood (if we would render the account of Moses at all consistent with itself), is amply sufficient, on scriptural grounds (and I seek for no other), to overturn both the systems now under consideration.

We are brought exactly to the same conclusion by attending to the general phraseology of Moses. I have already observed, that, when he speaks of the mountains being covered by the waters, and when he afterwards says that the mountains appeared as the flood retired, we are inevitably led by every rule of composition to infer, that the mountains, which appeared as the deluge abated, were the same mountains as those which were hidden during its prevalence. A similar conclusion must be drawn from the language which he holds respecting the earth. He informs us, that God declared to Noah that he would bring a flood of waters upon the earth

---

' We need not suppose the root to have been under water much more than 150 days, for that was the extreme period of the greatest height of the flood : and the submersion of a root, which all the while was drawing nutriment from the earth, would not during that space be sufficient to destroy the principle of vitality.

to destroy all flesh: he then proceeds to tell us, that rain was upon the earth forty days, that the Ark was lifted up above the earth, and that the waters prevailed exceedingly upon the earth: and at length he remarks, that the waters returned from off the earth continually, that the waters were abated from off the earth, and that the earth was dried. Now the necessary purport of such language is, that the self-same earth, which had been inundated, was in due time forsaken by the waters: for, when we are told that God would bring a flood upon the earth, and when we are afterwards taught that the waters returned from off the earth, I see not what we can possibly understand but this: that the same waters, which had deluged the antediluvian continents, at length retired and left them dry. But, if such be the plain import of the Mosaical history, then each theory must be abandoned as equally untenable; since we learn from Scripture itself, that, so far from either the whole earth being dissolved into a mucilage or the primeval continents forming the bed of our present oceans, we now inhabit the identical tracts of land that were tenanted by our earliest forefathers, tracts which the deluge once indeed overwhelmed but afterwards relinquished.

The same conclusion results from the scriptural account of the Antediluvian Paradise and its rivers

4. We shall be brought to precisely the same result, if, quitting the inspired history of the flood, we direct our attention to the remarkable geographical account which Moses has given us of the garden of Paradise. He tells us, that this garden was watered by a river, which afterwards divided itself into four distinct heads or streams; and of these streams he both gives us the names, and marks out with much preciseness the situation. One of them is the well-known river Euphrates: the others therefore must be streams in the neighbourhood of the Euphrates. Hence it is manifest, that, according to the Mosaical account, this river existed in its present situation before the deluge. But, if it then existed, the continent, through which it now flows, must also have existed. Whence it will plainly follow, both that the earth was not dissolved by the operation of the flood, and that the antediluvian continents do not form the bed of the present oceans: for, if the former had been the case, both Paradise and its rivers must have been utterly destroyed, whereas Moses assures us that one of those rivers was the Euphrates which is still in existence; and, if the latter, then the ancient channels of the Paradisiacal streams must now be lost at the bottom of the

sea, whereas Moses by intimating that one of them was the Euphrates does in effect declare, that their course before the deluge as well as after it was through the continent which is now called *Asia*.

Should it be said in reply, that the Paradisiacal Euphrates corresponds with the modern Euphrates in *name* alone; or, in other words, that the postdiluvian Euphrates is *not* the same river as the antediluvian Euphrates, but that the appellation of the one has been transferred to the other, as the planters of newly settled countries are wont to bestow upon rivers and mountains the familiar names of those which they have left behind in their native land: should such an answer as this be attempted, the minute geography of Moses will at once shew its complete futility.

He not only gives us the *names* of the Paradisiacal rivers, but he likewise distinctly points out their *course*. Thus he tells us, that Pison compasseth the whole land of Havilah, that Gihon is the identical river which circuits the land of Cush, and that Hiddekel is the stream which forms the boundary of Ashur. Respecting the situation of the Euphrates he says nothing; for the course of that mighty river was so well known to the Asiatic nations which lay to the westward of it, that any geographical specification might well be deemed wholly unnecessary. Now it is almost superfluous to observe, that such a local description as that which is given by Moses necessarily implies, that the very rivers which watered Paradise had reappeared after the flood and were actually in existence at the time when he wrote. Havilah was a son of Cush; Cush was a son of Ham; and Ashur was a son of Shem. They were all postdiluvians: and the regions, which were called after their respective names, were well known in the time of Moses, not to say even in the present day. Consequently, when he tells us that three of the Paradisiacal rivers were the boundaries of Havilah, of Cush, and of Ashur; he tells us, by a necessary implication, that the rivers still existed when he was himself composing his history: for how could those rivers be said to water lands which bore the names of three *postdiluvian* patriarchs, if either the earth had been dissolved by the operation of the flood, or if the antediluvian continents and therefore the channels of all the Paradisiacal rivers are sunk at the bottom of the present ocean? Should any great convulsion of nature swallow up the continent of Asia, and should the same convulsion produce a new tract of land by elevating the bed of the Pacific ocean, no future historian could, with the least semblance of accuracy, describe the course of the Ganges or the Indus, *previous* to such convulsion, as compassing certain regions of a continent which had been *recently* produced from the bottom of the sea and which had not the slightest geographical coincidence with the absorbed continent of Asia. Let us only apply this mode of reasoning to the narrative of Moses, and the conclusion must certainly be the very same. Since he informs us, that three of the rivers of Paradise watered countries, which *subsequent* to the deluge had received their names from Havilah and Cush and Ashur; it is impossible, if Scripture be true, that the channels of those rivers, together with the antediluvian continent through which they flowed, should now lie concealed at the bottom of the ocean. The language of Moses necessarily implies, that the rivers both existed in his time and that their course was through the continent of Asia. Hence it will plainly follow, that the present continents, with their present mountains and rivers, existed before the deluge: and that, instead of our either inhabiting an entire new world formed out of the chaotic wreck of the old, or of our tenanting lands which formed the bed of the antediluvian ocean; we now possess, by the reflux of the waters which once inundated the whole globe, the very same tracts of country, bearing the very same great characteristic marks, as those possessed by our earliest ancestors.

II. If there be any force in this train of reasoning (and I see not how it can be combated upon *scriptural* principles), there will assuredly be nothing visionary in an attempt to ascertain the situation of the terrestrial Paradise: for, if the rivers of Paradise yet exist, the tract of land which once was Paradise, whether its outward lineaments be defaced or not defaced by the flood, must also exist. The question then is, where we are to seek for it.

1. Now it will readily be granted, that neither the well-known Euphrates, nor any of the neighbouring rivers, can be made, in their *present* course, to produce a situation, which will geographically answer to the Mosaical description of Paradise: but this does by no means weaken the credit of the sacred historian, nor does it at all disprove the actual present existence of the

Certain partial changes must have taken place in the course of the Euphrates and the other Paradisical rivers

four rivers; for it is in fact nothing more than what might be naturally expected from so great a convulsion as the deluge. We may indeed very unequivocally collect from Scripture, that the waters of the flood first deluged the ancient continents and afterwards retired from them, so that the present tracts of land are *in their great outlines* geographically the same as those which were inhabited by the antediluvians: but this does not prove, that no *minor* and *partial* alterations have taken place on the surface of the globe. The rivers of Paradise, for instance, certainly appeared again after the deluge: and the course of the postdiluvian streams so far coincided with that of the antediluvian ones, as to be amply sufficient to establish their proper identity. But we are not hence bound to conclude, that the coincidence was *absolutely* perfect: we are not bound to suppose, in order to preserve the historical verity of Moses, that the postdiluvian Euphrates flowed through *every furlong* of the channel which contained the antediluvian Euphrates. Much weaker causes than the flood produce very considerable changes. The course of the Ganges experiences a yearly alteration, and the mouths of the Nile are not now what they were in the days of Herodotus: yet the Ganges and the Nile still flow on the Ganges and the Nile. Some mutation therefore must obviously be expected to have taken place in the four rivers of Paradise by the operation of so mighty a cause as the deluge. We are prepared to *expect* such a change; and a comparison of modern geography with the antediluvian geography of Moses only proves, that the change *has* occurred, not that the historian has been in any respect inaccurate. When the Hebrew legislator wrote, the rivers flowed as he described them in the vicinity of countries known by postdiluvian names; but never, since the flood, have they so met together, as to water what once was Paradise in accurate correspondence with antediluvian geography. This has been felt by every writer, who attempted to settle the local position of Eden: each hypothesis has been built on the postulate, the necessary postulate, that the course of the four rivers has experienced *some* change.

2. The general opinion, however it may be marked by smaller shades of difference, has been, that Paradise was situated somewhere in the flat rich country below Babylon. To this region therefore has been directed every

[handwritten margin note: The most common opinion has been that Paradise lay in the flat country below Babylon]

attempt to point out, how the four rivers could be supposed to have once met together in a single garden.

(1.) Morinus conceives, that the Euphrates and the Hiddekel, which is certainly the Tigris, united together into one channel; and, after flowing in conjunction for a short distance, branched out again into two other streams, called the *Pison* and the *Gihon*, which discharged themselves into the Persian gulph. Such a confluence and diffluence make, he supposes, the four heads mentioned by Moses; and the region, which comprehended them, he determines to have been the scite of Paradise. Hence, as appears by his explanatory map, the garden was divided into four quarters: one, above the confluence of the Euphrates and the Hiddekel; another, on the eastern side of the large single stream formed by their conjunction; a third, on the western side of the same stream; and a fourth, below its supposed diffluence into the Pison and the Gihon.[1] This opinion was held by Calvin, and it has received the approbation of Bochart.[2]

It has also, with a slight variation, been adopted by Dr. Wells. Agreeing with Morinus in other respects, that writer, instead of making the Euphrates and the Tigris fall into one stream, draws a channel between them at right angles for the river of Eden; and then assigns the name of *Pison* to that part of the Euphrates which is below this intermediate river at its western extremity, and the name of *Gihon* to that part of the Tigris which is similarly below it at its eastern extremity. Such an arrangement will, equally with the other, divide the garden into four quarters, though after a somewhat different form.[3]

(2.) Dr. Shuckford similarly looks for Paradise below Babylon; but the principle, which he adopts, is altogether unlike that of the last-mentioned authors. He supposes, that all the four rivers united into one stream called *the river of Eden*, and that on the bank of this single stream was situated the garden.[4]

3. Both of these opinions seem to me to labour under insuperable objec-

Objections to this arrangement

[1] Morin. Dissert. de Parad. terres. in init. Bochart. Geog. sacr.
[2] Bochart. Epist. ad Ludov. Cappel. ibid.
[3] Wells's Geog. of the O. Test. part i. c. 1.
[4] Shuckford on the Creation and Fall. chap. viii. p. 144—147.

tions, and the last of them has difficulties peculiarly its own. The account which Moses gives, is, that *a river flowed out of Eden to water the garden, and that from thence it was divided into four heads.* But with this account neither of the theories now under consideration can be reconciled.

(1.) The hypothesis of Morinus makes two rivers flow into the garden, there become one stream, and afterwards branch off into two other rivers: and the slightly varied theory of Wells does in effect produce no more than two rivers in the whole, united together by a transverse canal. Such a scheme may in some sort be said to exhibit four heads, but it certainly does not exhibit them in the manner set forth by Moses. *He* describes *one* river as running *into* the garden, and *four* rivers, into which the first single river divides itself, as issuing *out of* the garden : *Morinus*, on the contrary, makes *two* rivers run *into* the garden, and *two* run *out of* it. Nor is this the only point of discrepance: *the head of a river*, according to a very natural metaphor, denotes perhaps in every language, certainly in the Hebrew, *its commencement, fountain, or origin.* This being the case, since the single river of Eden branched off from the garden into the four heads of four other rivers; the garden itself must plainly have been situated at the *commencement* of all the four rivers, or at the point where they branched off from the single one. But the region, in which the garden is placed by Morinus and Wells, does not at all answer to such a description of country. Instead of the four heads of all the four rivers being within the circuit of the garden, we find but two of them: for the Euphrates and the Hiddekel, instead of *commencing* in Paradise, are made to *terminate* there; and the heads, or originating points, of the Pison and the Gihon are alone apparent within its boundaries.

(2.) That such is the necessary import of the word *heads*, Dr. Shuckford was fully aware, and explicitly allows: hence he frames his hypothesis in such a manner, as at least to avoid the palpable contradiction of making *the head of a river* indifferently denote both *its commencement* and *its termination ;* a contradiction, which so glaringly marks the theory both of Wells and Morinus. But, while he escapes one difficulty, he falls into another, from which he vainly attempts to extricate himself.

According to Moses, the single river of Eden divided itself, when it was quitting the garden; and branched out into four heads, which afterwards became four mighty rivers: according to Shuckford, the very reverse was the case, for he makes the four rivers, at a vast distance from their respective heads, coalesce into the single river of Eden; and, on the bank of that single river, he places the garden. It may seem strange at first, how such an opinion, which directly contradicts the inspired narrative, could ever have been hazarded. In fact, it could not have been hazarded, without an attempt to alter the commonly received translation, to which it stands diametrically opposite. Our English version is, *A river went out of Eden to water the garden; and from thence it was parted, and became into four heads:* the proposed version of Dr. Shuckford, on which he plainly founds the whole of his theory, is, *A river went out of Eden to water the garden, and from thence it was parted: and it was from four heads.*

The ground, on which he produces so complete an inversion of the sense, is the double import of the Hebrew preposition here used by Moses: it generally signifies *to* or *into*, but it sometimes denotes *of* or *from* or *out of*. On this I would remark, that, although it does sometimes occur in the latter meaning; yet it so occurs only in the sense of *from*, as *a man from a tribe* or as *a vessel made from gold* and the like: I doubt, whether it is ever thus used in the sense of *locality*, as *a man coming from such a place.* Dr. Shuckford does indeed give for his authority a passage, where the Seventy render it *from* in the sense of *locality:* but we may well question, whether that passage, as it occurs in our present Hebrew Bibles, be perfectly genuine.[1]

Granting however that the word is capable of such a translation, we must still, as he himself very justly and fairly observes, be guided by the necessary sense of the place in determining whether its import be *to* or *from.* Now the context of the present passage seems to me most clearly to decide in favour of our common version, and against that proposed by Dr. Shuck-

[1] 2 Chron. i. 13. The passage, rendered by the lxx Εκ βαμα της εν Γαβαων and by our own translators *to the high place that was at Gibeon*, seems to be an interpolation which has crept in from ver. 3: for it does not occur in the parallel passage in 1 Kings iii. 15. We there simply read, that Solomon *came to Jerusalem* without any mention of the Gibeonitish high-place. If however it be not an interpolation, I should rather conclude, that the copy used by the lxx read מבמה, than that the present reading לבמה would bear to be rendered *from the high place.* This passage is the sole groundwork of Dr. Shuckford's criticism.

ford. We are told by Moses, that *a river went out from Eden to water the garden, and* that *from thence it was parted* or *divided.* After we have received this information, we are naturally led to expect, that the historian, if he says any thing further on the subject, will proceed to teach us, *how it was* parted. Accordingly we find, that, if we only translate a Hebrew preposition in the very sense in which it almost invariably occurs, we shall have precisely the information which we looked for: *from thence it was parted, and became into four heads;* its division was of such a nature, that the single stream became four streams.

In such an interpretation we are confirmed by finding, both that it is the sense given to the passage by the Greek translators, and that it is the sense which has been universally received as the plain and obvious meaning of the passage. We are further confirmed in it by the very aspect of the Hebrew text, if I may use the expression. Of this the mere English reader cannot be a judge: but any moderate Hebraist, upon a bare inspection of the original passage, will be convinced, that it cannot, without the utmost violence, be rendered otherwise. On the contrary, Dr. Shuckford, by translating the preposition in a sense peculiarly rare and unusual, departs entirely from what might seem to be the natural context; and exhibits Moses, as clumsily introducing a needless obscurity, which with the very slightest possible transposition of the words might have been easily avoided. Had he meant to intimate what this writer ascribes to him, he would surely have said, *A river from four heads went out of Eden to water the garden, and from thence it was parted:* he never would have so strangely expressed himself, as to lead all commentators in all ages to understand him, *inevitably* to understand him, in a sense diametrically opposite to that which he intended. The translation in short of Dr. Shuckford is so forced, and so evidently contrived merely to serve a turn; it is so contrary to the universal sense of expositors, and so incongruous to the spirit of Hebrew syntax; that it cannot, I think, be tolerated for a single moment. But, if *it* be untenable, the whole hypothesis must be untenable likewise: for the hypothesis is altogether built upon the translation.

(3.) What has been urged against both these theories may alone be deemed sufficient to overturn them: but there yet remain two distinct objections, one to each of them, which must not be passed over in silence.

When we are told that God put Adam into the garden to dress it and to keep it, and when we are further informed that he had permission to eat of every tree in it except one; we are *necessarily* led to conclude, that he had easy and free access to *all* parts of the sacred inclosure: for how could he cultivate that, which was inaccessible; or how could he enjoy the privilege of eating of every tree with a single exception, if many of those trees were from local circumstances completely out of his reach? Now, according to the system of Morinus, Paradise was divided into four quarters by four immense rivers; for immense they needs must be, since he places the garden below the scite of Babylon and not very far distant from the present influx of the Tigris and the Euphrates, themselves two of the rivers, into the Persian gulph. Let us conceive then what would be the situation of Adam in a garden so circumstanced. Whatever quarter of Paradise he might originally occupy, such rapid and gigantic streams as the Euphrates and the Tigris, the last proverbially violent, whether they flowed separately at their entrance into the garden, or conjointly through its centrical region, or separately again when they quitted it under the new names of the *Gihon* and the *Pison:* such streams as those would have as effectually confined Adam to a *single* quarter of the garden, as if an ocean had flowed between him and all the *remaining* quarters. He plainly could not pass rivers of that magnitude without either a bridge or a ship; and, since no hint is given that he possessed either, it would be worse than idle to conjecture, that he moved from one quarter of the garden to another by the aid of such accommodations. Yet the language of Moses unequivocally intimates, that *every* part of Paradise was open to him: how this was accomplished, they, who adopt the system of Morinus, do not inform us.

The present difficulty is avoided in the theory of Dr. Shuckford; because he represents the river of Eden, which he supposes to have been formed by the confluence of the other four rivers, as *bordering upon* the garden, and not as *flowing through* it: but the question is, whether by such an arrangement he faithfully adheres to the description of Moses. When the historian teaches us, that a river went out of Eden to water the garden, and that from thence, namely from the garden, it was divided; the obvious import of his language seems to be, that the stream did not merely *flow along one side of the garden*, but that it *ran through the midst of it*: for how can a river be properly said to water a garden simply by being one of its lateral boundaries? The watering of a garden surely implies, that the irrigating stream glides in a meandring course through the inclosure itself, blessing the land on either bank with glad fertility. Such, accordingly, is the sense, in which the words of Moses have been ordinarily and (I think) rightly understood; for in fact, without great violence, they are scarcely capable of any other meaning. Hence it follows, that, if Dr. Shuckford places Paradise only on the margin of the river of Eden, he ascribes to it a situation irreconcileable with the language of Moses: if he makes the river flow through the midst of it, thus dividing it into two parts, he then completely separates the one part from the other by the intervention of a gigantic stream formed by the confluence of no less than four mighty rivers.

III. The preceding remarks will serve to prepare the way for ascertaining, in what quarter of the globe the terrestrial Paradise was once situated. We have learned from them *negatively*, that it is vain labour to look for the garden *below* Babylon; both because it is impossible to find the four heads of any four rivers in that region, and because, if the vast streams of the Tigris and the Euphrates had flowed through it in the manner which it has been conjectured they did, every part of it except one must have been utterly inaccessible to the first man: let us now endeavour to learn *positively* where we *are* to seek it.

1. Moses informs us, that a river went out of Eden to water the garden, and that from thence it branched out so as to constitute the four heads of four other rivers, which he denominates *Pison*, *Gihon*, *Hiddekel*, and *Euphrates*. From this account, according to its most natural and obvious interpretation, we may collect, that, in the antediluvian world, previous to the effecting of any partial alterations by the action of the flood, a stream flowed out of a region called *Eden* into the garden, which God had planted for the reception of the first pair. Here it fell into a lake or reservoir: and from this reservoir it again issued through four distinct glens or channels. The four new streams, produced by such a division of the waters, soon quitted the limits of

According to the Scriptural account it must have been situated at the source of the Euphrates ie Armenia

the garden; for we are told, that the original river, which rushed a *single* stream into Paradise, was divided from it, or left it, in *four* brooks, which were the heads or beginnings of *four* great rivers. Having quitted the garden, the four streams pursued their course: and, by the gradual reception of other streams, at length became rivers, which flowed contiguous to certain countries very accurately described by Moses, and of which two at least may be positively ascertained without the slightest difficulty.

This seems to me to be evidently the substance of the inspired account, which has been handed down to us, of Paradise and its rivers. If then the heads of all the four rivers met together in the garden, the garden must clearly have been situated in a high region at the sources of all those four rivers, not surely in a low country far distant from the head or origin of *any* river and removed but a little distance from the sea. To such a conclusion we are necessarily brought, both by the plain import of the language used by Moses, and by the very reason of the thing itself. If *the heads of rivers* mean *their beginnings*, as the signification of the Hebrew word here employed absolutely requires;' and if the *single* river of Eden, in quitting the garden, was divided into *four* heads of rivers: then the garden must have been situated at the *beginnings* or *fountains* of the rivers, not near the *mouths* through which they emptied themselves into the sea; in other words, it must have been situated in a high inland region where the courses of the four rivers all *commenced*. And, if the words of Moses clearly imply that every part of the garden was equally accessible to Adam; and if nevertheless that garden, as his words also intimate, was divided into several different parts by the course of the streams which watered it: then the very reason of the thing proves, that it cannot have been planted near the sea where rivers are broad and deep, but that it must have been planted near the sources of its irrigating streams where they flow only in the condition of shallow brooks which might easily be passed over. With this conclusion every idea, which we are taught to form of Paradise, exactly accords. No tract of country could possibly produce more exquisitely beautiful and romantic scenery, than one, which contained a stream, running through a finely wooded vale into a glassy lake,

---

' The word רֹאשׁ always involves the idea of *priority*. See Parkhurst's Heb. Lex.

and afterwards discharging itself by four rivulets murmuring through the same number of deep rocky glens: while, on the other hand, the charms of the dead flat country below Babylon, where commentators have generally agreed to place the garden, might indeed rival the beauties of Holland and Batavia; but they would be physically incapable of ravishing any eyes except those of a Dutch burgomaster.

If then Paradise, according to the description of Moses, must have been seated in a high country and at the source of the four rivers which issued from it; since one of those rivers is declared to be the well-known Euphrates, Paradise must have been seated in the region whence the Euphrates takes its rise. But the Euphrates rises in Armenia. Therefore Paradise must have been seated in Armenia.

This seems to be the inference, which must necessarily be drawn from the language of Moses interpreted according to its most plain and obvious acceptation: and with such an inference I might rest satisfied; for I only proposed to shew, that there is considerable reason for believing that the terrestrial Paradise was seated in the same lofty region where the Ark rested after the deluge; and in establishing this position I have now made some progress, since Ararat is generally supposed to have been one of the Armenian mountains. But it may be curious to push the inquiry somewhat further, and to examine how far it is possible to ascertain the three other rivers mentioned by Moses. Before I commence this inquiry however, I wish distinctly to specify, that, whether I be right or wrong in my determination, the main question respecting the scite of Paradise will not be at all affected: for, since the garden was seated at the head of the Euphrates, I see not where it can be found except in the land of Armenia.[1]

---

[1] *This whole country*, says a modern author speaking of Armenia, *is so extremely beautiful, that fanciful travellers have imagined that they had found here the situation of the original garden of Eden. The hills are covered with forests of oak, ash, beech, chesnuts, walnuts, and elms, encircled with vines growing perfectly wild but producing vast quantities of grapes. From these is annually made as much wine as is necessary for the yearly consumption: the remainder are left to rot on the vines. Cotton grows spontaneously, as well as the finest European fruit trees. Rice, wheat, millet, hemp, and flax, are raised on the plains, almost without culture. The valleys afford the finest pasturage in the world; the rivers are full of fish; the mountains abound in minerals; and the climate is delicious: so that nature appears to have*

An attempt to identify the three other rivers of Paradise

2. In forming any hypothesis respecting the remaining rivers of Paradise, it is necessary that three things should concur: that they should be in the same part of the world as the Euphrates; that they should take their rise in the same high tract of country as that river, for, though the heads of all the four no longer now meet together in one point, we cannot suppose that their channels were so far altered by the deluge as to be diverted into a totally different region; and that in their course they should correspond with the geographical description, with which we have been furnished by the sacred historian. If, in addition to these indispensable marks, there should, in the rivers which we may pitch upon, be a close correspondence of name with the rivers particularized by Moses; the probability, that we have not been mistaken, would be much increased: for, though neither mere etymological coincidence would be sufficient to establish a theory nor the want of it be enough to overthrow one; yet a *triple* resemblance of appellation, when all the necessary marks had been found to meet together, would at least furnish a corollary to the argument not wholly contemptible.

The Hidekel is the Tigris

(1.) The Euphrates being indisputably one of the Paradisiacal rivers, if we simply cast our eye upon a map, we shall immediately be led to conclude, as all commentators invariably *have* concluded, that the Tigris is another. Nor shall we be mistaken; for it exhibits every mark which has been laid down as necessary.

With respect to its locality, it is to be found in the same part of the world, and it rises in the same high country, as the Euphrates. It also bears the precise geographical relation to Assyria, which Moses ascribes to the

lavished on this favoured country every production that can contribute to the happiness of its inhabitants. Memoir of a map of the countries between the Black sea and the Caspian. p. 46. Armenia then is so beautiful a region, that from the mere aspect of it travellers have been led to deem it the land of Eden. Nor were they mistaken in their opinion; though, in forming such an opinion by guess alone and without adducing any arguments in favour of it, they themselves may certainly be considered as fanciful. Let us however contrast the outward appearance of this lovely country with the monotonous Batavian aspect of Babylonia, and we can scarcely hesitate in determining which bids fairest to have comprehended the primeval garden of Paradise. It is not unworthy of observation, that Milton, as a poet of the picturesque, found himself absolutely compelled by his subject to place the holy garden in a romantic mountainous country.

river Hiddekel: whence it must clearly, I think, be identified with that river. In our common English translation indeed, the Hiddekel is said to go *toward the east of Assyria*, whereas the Tigris flows *to the west of that country*: but this apparent contrariety arises solely from an erroneous rendering of the original. The phrase, which is translated *toward the east of Assyria*, ought to have been translated *before Assyria*, as it is rightly understood by the Greek interpreters.[1] The expression *may* indeed denote *eastward*: but it likewise means *before*, in the sense either of *time* or *place*. Here it relates to *place*: and, since Moses composed his history in a region far to the *west* of Assyria; a river, which, with reference to *him the speaker*, flowed *before* Assyria, would of course be the *western* boundary of that country, as is precisely the case with the Tigris. Hence the Greek interpreters, agreeably to their very just translation, explain the Hiddekel of Moses to mean the Tigris of the classical writers: and in this opinion Josephus agrees with them.[2]

As for the *Greek* appellation of the river, it departs indeed very widely from the sound of the Hebrew: but the *oriental* name of the Tigris, as well as its geographical situation, seems ever to have pointed out its identity with the scriptural Hiddekel. By Josephus, the Chaldee Paraphrasts, the Arabians, and the Persians, this river is called *Diglath;* by the Syrians, *Diklat;* by Pliny, or rather by those who communicated to him its eastern name, *Diglito;* and by the Levanters and other modern orientals it is still denominated, with a slightly varied pronunciation, *Diglath* or *Degil* or *Degola*.[3] That each of these is a mere abbreviation of the word *Hiddekel*, the first syllable being omitted, is abundantly evident: and some have even supposed, that *Tigris* itself is but an Hellenic corruption of *Diglis* or *Tiglis*.[4]

Be that however as it may, there is yet another argument, by which the identity of the Tigris and the Hiddekel may be sufficiently established. Daniel mentions, that he himself was once on the banks of the Hiddekel during his sojourn in Babylonia.[5] Now, as the Hiddekel *cannot* be the Euphrates,

---

[1] Κατεναντι Ασσυριων.
[2] Joseph. Ant. Jud. lib. i. c. 1. § 3.
[3] Wells's Geog. of O. Test. part i. c. 1. § 23.
[4] Ibid.
[5] Dan. x. 4.

it *must*, when *thus* mentioned, if we would preserve geography consistent with itself, be the Tigris, which is not distant from Babylon more than fifty or sixty miles. That it cannot be a mere canal or petty tributary stream to the Euphrates, is evident from the descriptive language of the prophet. He says, that he *was by the side of the* GREAT *river which is Hiddekel:* but there is no river, which can merit the appellation of *great*, in the Babylonian neighbourhood of the Euphrates, except the Tigris: the Tigris therefore must be the same as the Hiddekel.

The Pison is the Absarus or Batoum which seems to have been the real Phasis

(2.) Hitherto commentators are very generally agreed; and indeed there can scarcely be more than one opinion respecting the Hiddekel and the Euphrates: but it is not quite so easy to determine the situation of the Pison and the Gihon. That it is vain to seek for these two rivers where they have commonly been placed, I have already pointed out: and not more satisfactory is the conjecture of Josephus (though it is a conjecture which may easily be accounted for, as will appear in the sequel), that they are the Ganges and the Nile. Yet, if we do not attain to absolute certainty, we may at least be able to reach a moderate degree of probability.

The river Pison is described as compassing a land, named after the patriarch Havilah and abounding in gold. Hence, in order to ascertain the river, it has been usual to inquire into the scite of the country.

The region, generally selected for this purpose, is that mentioned by the author of the first book of Samuel, when he says, that *Saul smote the Amalekites from Havilah until thou comest to Shur that is over against Egypt:*[1] and, in order to make it answer to the proposed arrangement of the Pison, it is arbitrarily extended all the way from Egypt westward to the Persian gulph eastward.[2] But such a disposition ill accords with the obvious purport of the language employed by the sacred historian. The pursuit of the Amalekites is positively declared by that writer to have commenced from one of *their* own cities, and Saul is afterwards said to have smitten them *from Havilah to Shur.*[3] This Havilah therefore must have been a district, which bordered upon the Amalekitish city where the pursuit commenced, or which not impro-

[1] 1 Sam. xv. 7.
[2] Wells's Geog. par. i. c. 1. § 9.
[3] 1 Sam. xv. 5. compared with ver. 6, 7.

bably comprehended it. But the land of Amalek, thus immediately contiguous to the land of Havilah, was distant scarcely less than a thousand miles from the lower Euphrates which Wells and Morinus would identify with the Pison, and it was also completely separated from Babylonia by the vast intervening desert of Arabia. Hence it is not very easy to conceive, how the land of Havilah, from which Saul chased the Amalekites, can have been compassed by the Pison, if we suppose that river to mean the lower Euphrates. Nor would the matter be much mended, even if it could be shewn that there was a country bearing the name of *Havilah* on the western bank of the lower Euphrates: for still that country could not be the Havilah intended by Moses in his description of Paradise. The Havilah, of which we are in search, is declared to be compassed by a river, the head or beginning of which was close to that of the Euphrates; for the heads of both are said to have been alike comprehended within the garden. But no large river empties itself into the sea in that part of the world, which at all answers to such a description.

Perhaps it is impossible to determine positively the scite of that land of Havilah, which is mentioned by Moses, in his account of Paradise, as watered by the river Pison: but, since Havilah was a son of Cush, and since there were several countries denominated from that patriarch owing to the very great extension of his posterity, it is reasonable to conclude, both that there might in a similar manner be more lands of Havilah than one, and that the regions so called would frequently be in the vicinity of countries which bore the name of Cush. Of this we may at any rate be sure, that the Havilah, of which we are in quest, was a district bounded by some river that rises like the Tigris and the Euphrates in the lofty region of Armenia, and that it was a country celebrated in old times for the production of gold. Taking theseparticulars for my guide, I am inclined to believe, that the Pison of Moses was the Absarus of the classical writers or the Batoum of modern geographers. This river and the Phasis appear to have been a good deal confounded together by the ancients. For the latter stream was sometimes called *the true Phasis*, by way of distinguishing it from other rivers which bore the same name; and it was imagined, as we learn from Dionysius, to take its rise from a mountain of Armenia, though its real source lies far to the north of that country :[1] while the former stream was also a Phasis; and does in fact originate from the very district, whence the Greek geographer erroneously deduces the other.   Hence I suspect, that the Absarus or the false Phasis ought to be deemed the true one, and that the name itself is a corruption of the scriptural *Pison*.   But, however this may be, it answers with sufficient accuracy to the account given by Moses.   The Colchians, whose territory was encompassed by the winding stream of the Absarus, were certainly a race of Cuthites, probably through the line of Havilah : and their country was famed in ancient times for the abundance and excellence of its gold, as Strabo, Appian, Eustathius, and Pliny, all concur in testifying.[2]

The Gihon is the Gyndes

(3.) It only now remains, that we should ascertain the river intended by the Gihon.

This is said by Moses to have compassed the whole land of Cush ; a description in itself somewhat ambiguous, since, as I have just observed, there were more countries than one which bore the name of that patriarch.   But the ambiguity is sufficiently corrected by the manner, in which he particularizes the rise of the river.   Its head before the deluge was close to that of the Euphrates and the Tigris: its head therefore after the deluge must at least be sought for in the same tract of country as that, whence those streams now originate.

Of the various lands of Cush, the two most celebrated were the Asiatic and the African.   Each of these was styled by the Greeks *Ethiopia*, as being occupied by two great branches of the same family : and the two are still denominated by the Hindoos, in language perfectly corresponding with that of Scripture, *the Cusha continent within* meaning the Asiatic, and *the Cusha continent without* meaning the African.[3]   It was partly from a mistaken notion that the African Ethiopia was intended by Moses, and partly (I apprehend) from a correspondence of names, that Josephus was induced to pronounce the Gihon the same as the Nile.   The ancient pagans were strongly

---

[1] Diog. Perieg. ver. 691—694.

[2] See Bochart. Phaleg. lib. iv. c. 31. p. 290.

[3] They so call them in reference to the situation of their own country, as the Romans were wont to speak of the nether and the further Gaul.

addicted to local appropriation: hence, in whatever countries they settled, there they alike placed both Paradise and mount Ararat; and, in more than one instance, applied to their sacred river, which flowed from the supposed scite of the garden and the arkite mountain, the name of one of the rivers of Eden. Thus the Nile was called both compoundedly *Ogen* or *Ogeon*, and simply *Geon*: thus the Oxus is still denominated *Jihon* or *Gihon*: and thus the present Indus was formerly known by the appellation of *Phison*.[1] The Ganges or Ganga also, which, as we shall presently see, flows from the Paradise and Ararat of the Hindoos, is most probably a mere variation of *Gihon*, pronounced contractedly *Gawn*. But neither can the Ganges, the Nile, nor the Oxus, be the *scriptural* Gihon; nor yet can the Indus be the *scriptural* Pison: because both those rivers are said by Moses to rise from the same country as the Euphrates; consequently the origin of both must be sought for in the high tract of land, which bears the name of *Armenia*. This being the case, since the Gihon is described as compassing the whole land of Cush, and since it is also represented as rising in the same range as the Euphrates; the Ethiopia, which it compasses, must doubtless be the Asiatic, not the African, Ethiopia.

The Asiatic Ethiopia however in its largest sense, or the interior Cusha-dwip of the Hindoo geographers, is a most extensive tract of country, comprehending the whole of the ancient empire of Iran from the river Indus to mount Caucasus or even to the shores of the Euxine, and therefore receiving its general appellation rather from its Cuthic governors than from the great mass of its inhabitants.[2] This region consequently is so ample, that it contains both Babylonia and Assyria: whence we must plainly look for some specific part of it, which will answer to the description given by the sacred historian. Now there was a portion of it bordering upon the Persian gulph, which of old was called *Cissia*, and which is even yet denominated *Chusistan* or *the land of Cush*, as being peculiarly occupied by the descendants of that patriarch. This then I conceive to have been the Ethiopia intended by Moses.

And now, if we consult a map, we shall perceive, that the western bound-

[1] Chron. Pasch. p. 30, 34.   [2] Asiat. Res. vol. ii. p. 43, 44.

ary of Chusistan is the ancient Gyndes, which empties itself into the Tigris a little before that river falls into the Euphrates. The Gyndes therefore,
judging both from its name and its situation, I suppose to be the scriptural
Gihon. Its name is nothing more than *Gihon*, with a Greek termination
suffixed: in its course it compasses the whole of Chusistan, or the proper
Asiatic land of Cush: and it rises, though not in Armenia, yet in the same
mountainous region which may be deemed a continuation of that country.

Respecting the changes experienced by these rivers in their courses, and respecting the lake at their heads

3. These then I suppose to be the four rivers of Paradise; and, whatever
alteration has taken place in the higher part of their courses, I attribute to
the violence of the deluge. The Euphrates and the Tigris appear to have
suffered the least change, for their heads are still very near to each other:
and it may be remarked, that even the present face of the country seems to
indicate, that the form which it exhibited before the flood was not very
different from what I have supposed. Those two rivers both rise in the
neighbourhood of a considerable lake, formerly denominated the *Palus Ar-
sesa* and now *Lake Van*. This inland sea, though more than one stream
falls into it, has no visible outlet: consequently its waters must be discharged
through certain subterraneous passages. Where they reappear, it is impossible, and would be useless, to attempt to determine: but there is no absurdity in conjecturing, that, before the great convulsion of the flood, they may
have quitted the lake through visible channels. I think it, in short, not improbable, that this very lake may be an enlargement of the pool, into which
the river of Eden once flowed, and from which the four rivers of Paradise took
their rise. Should this speculation be well-founded, the garden may be considered as submerged beneath the surface of the present more ample sheet of
water.[1]

IV. The country, where the Ark rested after the deluge, is not pointed
out by Moses with the same geographical precision as he marks the scite of
Paradise. He simply intimates, that the place of its appulse was one of
the mountains of Ararat: but, in what part of the world Ararat was to be

---

[1] The annexed map may serve to explain more fully the theory, which I have here advanced.
The black lines mark the present courses of the four rivers: the dotted lines exhibit the channels, through which they are supposed to have flowed from Paradise: and the small lake,
formed by the river of Eden before the deluge, appears in the middle of the garden.

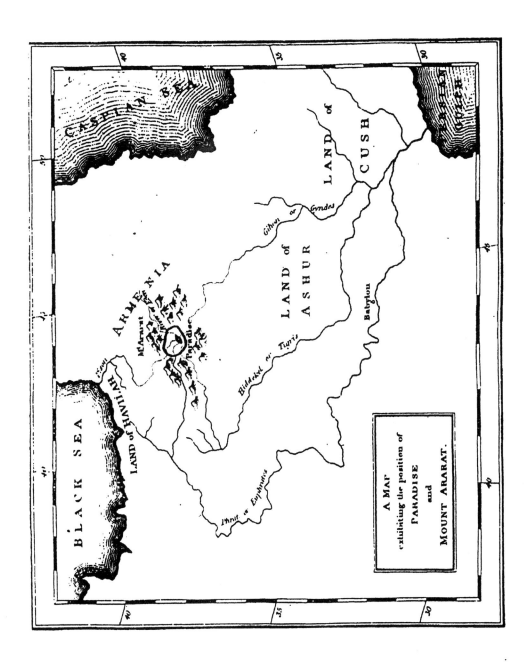

A Map
exhibiting the position of
PARADISE
and
MOUNT ARARAT.

sought, he does not determine. Hence a field is opened for inquiry, and room is left for difference of opinion. Accordingly, there has been a considerable difference of opinion respecting the precise situation of Ararat. Most persons have placed it in the high land of Armenia near the fountains of the Euphrates: but some have supposed, that it lay in the mountainous country of Cashgar to the north of India, and that it was a part of that lofty chain of hills which the Greeks called *the Indian Caucasus*. The latter of these opinions was held by Heylin and Shuckford :[1] and it has lately been revived, with much ingenuity and with the advantage of great local knowledge, by Mr. Wilford.[2]

1. In each of these regions a lively tradition yet prevails of the appulse of the Ark, which the advocates for either system have not failed to adduce. But this argument proves nothing at all ; because it will just as much prove, that the Ark grounded in a hundred different places.

A very large part of heathen mythology originated from the history of the deluge : and numerous were the rites of Paganism, which were instituted in commemoration of that awful event. Wherever mankind settled after the dispersion from Babel, they carried with them rites of this description : and the natural consequence of celebrating such rites was a perpetual recurrence of local appropriation. Each tribe, in the country which it planted, had a sacred mountain, of which Ararat was the prototype : and in that mountain was laid the scene of the appulse of the Ark and the egress of the Noëtic family. Thus the ship, in which the second father of mankind was preserved, was not only said to have landed in Armenia and in Cashgar: but it was likewise reported to have first touched ground on the summits of Athos, of Etna, and of Parnassus ; near the Syrian city of Hierapolis ; and in the countries of Phrygia, Wales, and even America. Mere *tradition* therefore will not decide the point ; for, so far as tradition *alone* is concerned, it is impossible to determine whether Ararat is to be sought for in Cashgar or in Armenia.

Somewhat on the same principle, the argument deduced from the nu-

---

[1] Heylin's Cosmog. p. 7. Shuckford's Connect. b. ii. p. 98.

[2] Asiat. Res. vol. vi. p. 524, 525.

merous olive-trees which still flourish in the former of those regions can
scarcely be deemed altogether conclusive; because Strabo mentions, that
Armenia likewise produced the olive:[1] and, even if we had had no proof
positive whatsoever, it still could never have been shewn negatively, that
there was not a single olive-tree in all that country from which the dove
could pluck a twig.

There is however another argument, which is much more promising, which
in fact is the only effective argument in favour of the appulse of the Ark in
Cashgar, and which therefore has always been brought forward by those
who advocate the remote oriental situation of Ararat. The first important
event mentioned as taking place after the deluge is the building of the tower
of Babel. Now the persons, who built this edifice, are said to have *journeyed from the east* previous to their arrival in the plain of Shinar.[2] Hence
it is argued with much plausibility, that the Ark must have grounded far to
the east of Babylon; because mankind travelled from the east to reach the
country where they built the tower: and hence it is further argued, that it
could *not* have grounded in Armenia; because, if mankind had journeyed
from *that* country to Shinar, their course would have been not from the
east but from the north.

It does not appear to me, that even *this* argument would *decisively* prove
the appulse of the Ark to have been in Cashgar, supposing our common
English version *accurately* to express the sense of the original: because we
are not obliged to allow, that the early postdiluvians travelled in a *direct*
course from Ararat to Shinar. They, who contend that Ararat is to be
sought for in Armenia, might easily reply, that the builders of Babel first
journeyed eastward, then inclined to the south, and lastly turned their faces
towards the west; which course would obviously make them arrive at Shinar
from the east: and they might very fairly adduce in favour of this conjecture
the testimony of Berosus, who expressly asserts, that the ancestors of the
Babylonians, in order to reach the place of their settlement, *travelled by a
circuit,* or *in a circuitous route,* from the country where the ark of Xisuthrus landed after the deluge.[3] But I do not conceive that this is the pro-

---

[1] Strab. Geog. lib. xi. p. 528.   [2] Gen. xi. 2.

[3] His expression is περιξ πορευθηναι.

per answer, neither do I imagine that *the circuit* mentioned by Berosus would correspond with such a line of march.[1] The truth of the matter is, that Moses does not speak of *the route by which* mankind arrived at Babel, but of *the time when* they journeyed there. The Hebrew word, ill rendered in our English translation *from the east,* denotes *before,* in the sense either of *time* or *place.* When used to describe the course of the Hiddekel, it intimated, as we have already seen, that that river flowed *before* Assyria, not *to the eastward* of it : and here it teaches us, in a manner exactly agreeable to the general context of the history, not that the builders of the tower discovered the plain as they journeyed *from the east,* but as they *first* journeyed ; that is to say, in the course of their first general migration from Ararat, near which they would doubtless remain after the flood until their numbers had sufficiently increased for the forming of new settlements. In this sense accordingly the passage is rightly understood by Josephus, who says not a single syllable respecting any supposed journey *from the east ;* but simply intimates, that, when men *first* ventured to descend from the high ground where the Ark had rested, they travelled to the plain of Shinar, which was the *first* country that they planted.[2]

Thus, I think it evident, the two arguments from tradition and from the existence of olive-trees will prove neither Armenia nor Cashgar to be country of Ararat : and the third argument from the supposed oriental route of the builders of Babel will neither establish the pretensions of Cashgar, nor overthrow those of Armenia. In reality, if we would settle the question, we must pursue a totally different method from that which has been hitherto noticed.

[1] More will be said on this subject hereafter. book vi. c. 1. § IV.

[2] Joseph. Ant. Jud. lib. i. c. 4. § 1. He uses the same repetition which I have done. His expressions are πρωτοι κατελθοντες, and πεδιον εις δ πρωτον αυτους κατψκισαν. These are plainly his translation of the Hebrew word, which is rendered both by the Seventy and in the English *from the east.* Bochart, though he prefers this last version, yet fairly mentions, that both the Chaldee and the Jerusalem Targums understood the word as denoting *at first :* and, to shew with how much strict propriety it may be so translated, he adduces Habak. i. 12, where it evidently is incapable of any other meaning. *Art thou not, O Lord, from everlasting* or *from the first ?* not, it is almost superfluous to observe, *from the east ?* Boch. Phaleg. lib. i. c. 7. p. 30.

Proof that
Ararat was
in Armenia

2. When Moses speaks of the Ark resting on the mountains of Ararat, he evidently speaks of a country well known to his contemporaries, because he deems a geographical description of its scite wholly unnecessary. The first matter then to be inquired into is the opinion, which the Israelites themselves, and which writers who may be supposed to borrow from them, have entertained respecting it; also what sentiments have prevailed among the nations closely connected with them, if any such can now be discovered: and the next is, how far this opinion, whatever it may be, will be found to correspond with other passages of Scripture, in which, no less than in the Mosaical history of the deluge, mention is made of Ararat. Now, if I mistake not, both these topics of investigation will at once decidedly prove, that Ararat is to be sought for in Armenia, and that it cannot possibly have been situated in Cashgar.

From the
opinions both
of the Jews,
of early Christians
and of the
Pagans

(1.) As for the Jews, Josephus informs us, that the mountain, on which the Ark rested, was a high peak in the land of Armenia: and, in thus delivering his opinion, there can be little doubt that he expressed the sentiment which had long prevailed among his countrymen.[1] This is evident from the language adopted by the Greek translators: for, in two parallel passages of Holy Writ where *Ararat* occurs in the original Hebrew, they write the word in the one place *Ararat* and in the other *Armenia*.[2] Hence we may collect, that, in *their* day no less than in that of Josephus, it was commonly believed that Ararat was an Armenian district.

From the Jews the opinion passed universally to the early writers among the Christians, who seem to make no doubt that Ararat was situated in the land of Armenia. Such for instance was the sentiment of Eustathius and Chrysostom; such also that of Epiphanius and Jerome. This indeed is rather a proof how widely the notion had extended itself, than any demonstration of its propriety: yet it may serve to shew, since the Christians copied from the Jews, that it had ever been the prevailing belief of the latter, a belief most probably handed down to them by tradition from their fathers, that by the land of Ararat their great prophet meant the land of Armenia.

In such an opinion they were by no means singular: for exactly the same

---

[1] Joseph. Ant. Jud. lib. i. c. 3. § 5.   [2] 2 Kings xix. 37. and Isaiah xxxvii. 38.

idea prevailed among the writers of the neighbouring nations, as appears from those fragments of their works which are still preserved in the pages of Syncellus, Josephus, and Eusebius. Thus Berosus the Chaldèan, Nicolas of Damascus, Melo, and Alexander Polyhistor, all concur in asserting, that the Ark, which preserved the second father of mankind by whatever name he might be called, rested on one of the mountains of Armenia : and some of them assert, with what truth I shall not pretend to determine, that fragments of that vessel were still even in their days shewn in the country of its appulse.[1] Thus generally, from the most remote antiquity, prevailed the belief that Armenia was the land where the Ark first grounded.

(2.) We must next inquire, whether this opinion will accord with those other passages of Scripture in which Ararat is mentioned : for, since Holy Writ is the most satisfactory interpreter of its own geography, nothing can be allowed to stand which contradicts what may be clearly deduced from it. *from the tenor of other passages of Scripture*

When the prophet Jeremiah foretold the destruction of Babylon by the Medes and Persians, he was led to enumerate some of those countries from which the invading army should be collected. Among these he specially mentions *Ararat* and *Minni:* and he further intimates, that the troops, which were destined to subvert the Chaldèan empire, should come *out of the north.*[2] Thus it appears, that we must look for Ararat and Minni *to the north* of Babylon. But this geographical description at once directs us to look to Armenia for the mountains of Ararat, and effectually prevents our seeking them in Cashgar which lies far *to the east* of Chaldèa. And with such an arrangement history exactly accords. The conquests of Cyrus, previous to his attack upon Babylon, lay to the north and the west: Lydia and Armenia had been subjugated by him : and we are expressly informed, that from these countries he drew a considerable part of the troops with which he subverted the empire of the Chaldèans.[3] On the contrary, his dominions, even in their greatest extent, never reached beyond the In-

---

[1] Syncell. Chronog. p. 30. Joseph. Ant. Jud. lib. i. c. 3. § 6.   Euseb. Præp. Evan. lib. ix. c. 12. Chron. lib. i. p. 8.

[2] Jerem. l. 3. li. 27.

[3] Herod. Hist. lib. i. c. 84, 85, 177, 191.   Xenoph. Cyrop. lib. ii. iii. v. vii.

dus : and his army most assuredly, when he marched against Babylon, had received no recruits from the far distant land of Cashgar. We are told however by Jeremiah, that Ararat should furnish the Medo-Persian conqueror of Babylon with a part of his invading forces, and that the progress of those forces should be from the north. Hence, by comparing Scripture and profane history together, we are brought to as decisive a proof as can well be desired, both that Ararat lies in Armenia, and that it does not lie in Cashgar. Accordingly, *Minni*, which the prophet joins with Ararat, has been generally and rightly supposed to be the prototype of the word *Armenia* : for *Armenia* is no other than *Meni* or *Minni* or *Mena*, united in composition with *Ar* which signifies *a mountain* ; so that *Ar-Meni* is equivalent to *the mountainous country of Minni*.

We are led exactly to the same conclusion by two more passages of Scripture, which are parallel to each other, and in both of which mention is made of Ararat. Isaiah and the author of the second book of Kings concur in asserting, that, after the murder of Sennacherib, his two parricidal sons escaped into the land of *Ararat*.[1] This word, as I have already intimated, is, in one of the passages, expressed by the Greek translators *Armenia;* while, in the other, they retain the original Hebrew name. The question then is, whether they give a right geographical interpretation of *Ararat* when they write it *Armenia :* that is to say, whether we are to understand that the two princes fled into *Armenia* when they are said to have fled into *the land of Ararat.* Here we might fairly argue from a mere inspection of the map, how much more probable it is, that two Assyrian princes should escape into the comparatively near country of Armenia than into the distant region of Cashgar : but we can adduce evidence of a far more decisive nature. Josephus has preserved a curious fragment of the Babylonian history of Berosus ; in which that ancient writer, after giving exactly the same account of the unsuccessful expedition and subsequent murder of Sennacherib as that which is recorded in Scripture, adds, that his two sons fled into *Armenia*.[2] Now he had already specified in a former part of his history,

---

[1] Isaiah xxxvii. 38. 2 Kings xix. 37.

[2] Joseph. Ant. Jud. lib. x. c. 1. § 4, 5. Edit. Hudt.

that the ark of Xisuthrus rested in the mountains of Armenia. The two sons of Sennacherib therefore, according to Berosus, fled into the very country where the Ark was believed to have grounded. But Scripture declares that they fled to Ararat, where also it places the appulse of the Ark. Consequently, since Berosus asserts that they fled into Armenia, he undesignedly proves from the historical records of his own country, that Armenia and Ararat were the same region, or at least that the mountains of Ararat were a certain district comprehended within the limits of Armenia.

3. Thus, as we were before brought to Armenia in our search after Paradise, so are we again conducted to the very same country in pursuing our inquiries after the situation of mount Ararat. It is probable, that the two might not be exactly coincident; though it certainly is not impossible, that the very hill, which Moses calls *Ararat*, might have been inclosed within the circuit of the garden, or at least might have belonged to the more ample region of Eden: but, at any rate, if there be some degree of conclusiveness in the preceding arguments, the geographical correspondence of Paradise and Ararat will be such as to warrant the assertion, that mankind twice derived their origin from the same country, and that the second great father appeared after the deluge in the identical lofty tract of ground which had been the primeval habitation of the first great father in his state of innocence and happiness.

[Margin, handwritten:] Whence it will follow that Ararat and Paradise were certainly in the same range of country

CHAPTER II.

Respecting pagan transcripts of Paradise and mount Ararat.

WITH the conclusion, to which we have now been brought, the legends of Paganism respecting Paradise and mount Ararat will be found very remarkably to correspond.

Fables of the Hindoos respecting mount Meru

I. The tradition of the Hindoos seems to be more embodied and better connected than that of any other nation. Perhaps also it may serve as a kind of key to the right understanding of parallel legends. Hence it will properly demand our first attention. Now it is rather a curious circumstance, that this very tradition, when thoroughly examined, will serve to establish the belief that Paradise and Ararat are to be sought for in Armenia; though ostensibly it teaches, what Mr. Wilford has adopted for historical truth, that they are situated in the high land of Cashgar and Cashmir to the north-west of modern India.

Fabled Meru a transcript of Paradise

1. In the fabled Meru of Hindoo theology may be recognized, with singular exactness of correspondence, the Mosaical garden of Eden.

The summit of this sacred mountain is represented as a circular plain of vast extent, surrounded by a ring or belt of hills. The whole is called *Ila-Vratta* or *the circle of Ila ;* and it is considered as a celestial earth, the abode of the immortals or hero-gods : it is likewise designated by the cognate name of *Ida-Vratta* or *the circle of Ida, Ida* and *Ila* being the same word somewhat differently pronounced. It is said to be of four different colours towards the four cardinal points ; and is believed to be propped by four enormous buttresses of gold, silver, copper, and iron. Some imagine its form to be that of a square pyramid ; by others it is thought to be of a conical shape ; and others again compare it to an inverted cone—Moses tells us, that a river went out of Eden to water the garden, and that from thence it was divided into four heads or beginnings of four other rivers. The Hindoos imagine, that one vast river rises either from the head of Siva or from under the feet of Vishnou ; whence, after passing through the circle of the Moon, it falls upon the summit of Meru, where it is divided into four streams flowing towards the four cardinal points : and the Pauranics use the very same expression as the author of the Pentateuch to denote the quadruple division of the one original river ; but, taking the word *heads* in a literal sense, and confounding also these four river heads with the four heads of the cherubim, they suppose, that its four branches actually pass through four rocks carved into the shape of the heads of four different animals, a cow, a horse, an elephant, and a lion—Moses informs us, that in the midst of the garden of Eden was the tree of knowledge. The Hindoos believe, that the four rivers of Meru spring from the roots of Jambu, a tree of a most extravagant size, which is thought to convey knowledge and to effect the accomplishment of every human wish. *ffp. 325*

2. It may appear at the first sight to be no easy matter to give geographical locality to such a mountain as Meru ; which, though pretty evidently a copy of the scriptural Paradise, is a copy embellished in the very wildest style of oriental fabulizing : yet, as Mr. Wilford has admirably shewn, the region, where this sacred hill was placed by the old Hindoo mythologists, may be ascertained with a sufficient degree of precision. *Its general locality ascertained*

That it lies to the north of India has been so generally allowed, that it has even been assumed by the geographers of that country to be the north-pole : but the description which is given of it, united with a variety of traditions still prevalent in the high range of land to which we are brought by attending to that description, clearly proves that the north-pole can never have been originally intended by it.   In fact, such a notion stands directly opposed both to numerous passages in the Puranas, and even to the maps constructed by the Brahmens themselves.   The immense country of Curu is repeatedly declared in those writings, and is allowed by the Brahmens in conversation, to be situated to the north of mount Meru : and, in the Hindoo maps of the seven dwipas, that holy hill is placed far to the south of Siddha-puri, which is universally acknowledged to be exactly under the north-pole.

How it came in time to be esteemed the north-pole, is not very difficult to discover.   The old Hindoo geographers considered the earth as a flat table with the immense conical mountain of Meru rising in the middle of it ; and they represented it by the flower of the lotos, with its central petal, floating, like a vast ship, on the bosom of the great abyss.   Hence, from a notion that the north-pole was the highest part of the globe, mount Meru, which was deemed the highest land in the world, was pronounced to be the north-pole.   Yet the truth was not altogether lost even after the adoption of this opinion.   Some Hindoo astronomers, aware that, agreeably to the language of the Puranas, mount Meru must be situated in the centrical part of Asia, allow that such is its true position ; but, unwilling to give up the idea that it is *also* the north-pole, actually place that pole on the elevated plains of the lesser Bokhara, and thus force the sun out of the ecliptic.   So firmly was the old tradition established, that mount Meru lay immediately to the north of Hindostan.

Its particular locality ascertained to be the high land of Cashgar and Bokhara

3. Hitherto we have only *generally* ascertained the situation of mount Meru, having learned both from the Puranas and from the maps constructed by the Brahmens themselves, that it is to be sought for in the centrical part of Asia, north of Hindostan and south of Curu ; which last is acknowledged to be the vast tract of land, that includes Russia and Siberia.   We may now endeavour to fix it more *particularly*.

Meru is described as a country, from which four rivers flow in four opposite directions to the four cardinal points of the compass.   All these are supposed to issue from four rocks, carved into the shape of the heads of four different animals.   One of the heads is said to be that of a cow ; and this is placed on the southern side of Meru.   Now it is the universal persuasion of the Hindoos, that such is the origin of the Ganges: and there is actually a rock not far from its source, through which the river is precipitated, that bears the name of *the cow's head.* The Vaishnavas indeed honour their favourite god, by supposing the sacred stream to spring in the first instance from beneath the feet of Vishnou; and the Saivas pay a similar compliment to *their* peculiar deity, by making it issue from the head of Siva: but both concur in maintaining, that, when it quits mount Meru, it again bursts from the rocky head of a cow. Hence, in every pictured representation of the holy mount with its celestial inhabitants, though the Ganges first springs from the head of Siva, *it* never fails afterwards to reappear as flowing from the mouth of the cow and as thence descending down the side of the hill to carry sanctity and abundance to the favoured realms of Hindostan. The Ganges therefore is clearly one of the four rivers of Meru, as the Hindoos themselves indeed positively declare: and, agreeably to this notion, they esteem it a sacred stream, introducing it conspicuously into the due celebration of their religious mysteries precisely as the Egyptians were wont to do the Nile.

If the Ganges then flow from Meru, Meru must certainly be sought for at the source of the Ganges. But, by pursuing its course upwards, we are brought to the high land of Cashmir and Cashgar; that is to say, to the lofty tract of country, which the Greeks called *the Indian Caucasus*, and which may be considered as including little Bokhara deemed (as we have already seen) by some Hindoo astronomers at once mount Meru and the north-pole.

Now in this very country, which literally appears to be no other than Meru, the Hindoos place the garden of Paradise, traces of which are introduced so conspicuously into the legend of their sacred hill. Here, in exact accordance with my own theory of the antediluvian geography of Eden, they suppose, that a river first flows round the city of Brahma; that next it discharges itself into the lake Mansarovara; and that thence it issues through the rocky heads of four animals, constituting four streams which run to the four quarters of the globe.

Though it is easy to perceive whence such an opinion originated, I need scarcely observe, that, so far as the lake and the primary river are concerned, it will not be found to correspond with the accuracy of modern geography. Yet, to a certain extent, it *does* agree with it; since four rivers, such as the legend describes, really flow in different directions from the same high centrical region which to me appears to be indisputably the literal Meru of Hindoo theology. These are enumerated by Mr. Wilford from the legend itself, and are identified with their four proper corresponding streams as laid down in our common maps of Asia. Towards the south is the cow's head; and from it issues the Ganga or Ganges: towards the west is the horse's head; and from it issues the Chocshu or Chocshus, which is evidently the Oxus: towards the east is the elephant's head; and from it proceeds the Sita-Ganga or Hoang-ho: lastly, towards the north is the tyger's or lion's head; and from it flows the Bhadra-Ganga or the Siberian river Jenisea.

With this arrangement, which is corroborated to a sufficient extent by true geography, the fanciful maps of the Brahmens, which depict the earth as a lotos floating on the ocean and mount Meru as the centrical petal of the flower, will be found exactly to correspond. The four principal leaves of the flower represent the four supposed great continents : Curu or Siberia, to the north of Meru; Bhadrasua or China. to the east of it; Bharata or India, to the south of it; and Cetumala or the land of the Cetim (evidently the scriptural Chittim of Greece and Italy, for in this continent is placed the city of Romaca), to the west of it. The eight smaller leaves of the flower shadow out eight supposed principal islands, which are placed in a manner not very far removed from the truth : between Cetumala and Curu to the north-west, Suvarneya and Avartana or Juvernia and Bartana, that is Hibernia and Britannia; between Curu and Bhadrasua to the north-east, Mandara and Ramanaca, which are probably Jesso and Japan; between Bhadrasua and Bharata to the south-east, Mahalanca and Sinhala or Malacca and Ceylon; and between Bharata and Cetumala to the south-west, Sancha and Harina or Zanguebar and Madagascar. From the centrical Meru issues a river: and thence it is divided into the four streams, which are supposed to flow from the heads of four animals. A map thus constructed, in addition to the arguments already adduced, proves irrefragably, so far as I can judge, that the literal situation of the fabled Meru or the

Hindoo Paradise coincides with the high land of Cashmir and little Bokhara.[1]

4. With this conclusion the traditions both of the Puranas and of the country itself perfectly accord.

Traditions of the Puranas and of the Cashgarians respecting Cashgar being the region of Paradise

The Puranas declare, that Menu-Swayambhuva or the first Menu, who is known also by the name of *Adima* as his consort is by that of *Iva*,[2] lived in the north-west parts of India about Cashmir: and the natives of that region believe, that Bamiyan and the adjacent countries, by which they understand all the lofty tract that reaches from Sistan to Samarcand and extends eastward as far as the Ganges, were the first abode of the antediluvian progenitors of mankind. This notion is of great antiquity, having most probably originated from the very first settlers of the country: and it is countenanced equally by Persian authors, and (as I have just observed) by the sacred books of the Hindoos. There lived the primeval heroes of Persian history; there flourished their holy instructors in religion; and there were erected the first temples.

With respect to the most ancient Menu, whose place of abode is said to have been in the very same country, even if his name *Adima* did not sufficiently point him out to be the scriptural Adam, both the chronology and the general tenor of his real character would amply identify him with the protoplast. He is described as being eminently the first Menu, as being the son of the Self-Existent, as being the universal parent of mankind, as being the husband of Iva, and as living before the time of the deluge which took place in the days of a younger Menu surnamed *Satyavrata*. He is supposed to have been an incarnation of Brahma: and, as the Hindoo triad is also believed to become incarnate in the persons of the three sons of the great father at the commencement of every mundane system, he is thence, in the character of Dacsha, evidently confounded with the scriptural Abel. When Brahma, according to the Matsya-Purana, assumed a mortal shape, he was pleased to manifest himself in Cashmir; that is to say, in the very country where we have been led to place the Paradisiacal Meru of Hindoo theology. Here,

[1] See a map of this description in Asiat. Res. vol. viii. p. 376.

[2] Pronounced *Eva*.

one half of his body sprang from the other, which yet experienced no diminution; and out of the severed moiety he framed a woman, denominated *Iva*
and *Satarupa*.   Her beauty was such as to excite the love of the god; but,
deeming her his daughter, he was ashamed to own his passion.   During this
conflict between shame and love, he remained motionless with his eyes fixed
upon her.   Satarupa perceived his situation, and stepped aside to avoid his
ardent looks.   Brahma being unable to move but still desirous to see her, a
new face sprang out upon him toward the object of his desires.   Again she
shifted her situation, and another face emanated from the enamoured god.
Still she avoided his gaze; until the incarnate deity, become conspicuous with
four faces directed to the four quarters of the world, beheld her incessantly
to whatever side she withdrew herself.   At length he recovered his self-
possession, when the other half of his body sprang from him and became
Swayambhuva or Adima.   Thus were produced the first man and woman;
and from their embrace were born three sons, in whom the Trimurti became
incarnate.   On this occasion, Iswara or Siva became Cardameswara or the
destructive power united to a form of a clay.   In that shape he attempted to
kill his brother Brahma, who, being immortal, was only maimed: but, afterwards finding him in a mortal form as he sustained the character of
Dacsha, he killed him as he was performing a sacrifice.   Previous to the
murder, some animosity had long subsisted between the two brothers in their
human shapes: and Siva, on account of his bad conduct which is fully described in the Puranas, had given much uneasiness to his parents Adima and
Iva.   He is said to have been of a libidinous disposition, and to have gone
about in a state of nudity brandishing a large club in his hand: on which account he was deprived of his right of primogeniture, and his brother Brahma
or Dacsha set up in his room.   One day when Dacsha entered into the assembly of the gods, they all rose to honour him; but Siva, indignant at his degradation, gloomily kept his seat.   The affront was resented by Dacsha,
who, cursing him in his human shape, wished that he might always remain a
vagabond on the face of the earth, and ordered that he should be carefully
avoided and deprived of his share of the sacrifices.   Siva, now irritated to
the last pitch, cursed Dacsha in his turn, and wished that he might die.   A
dreadful conflict took place between them; the three worlds trembled; and

the gods themselves were alarmed. Brahma and Vishnou in their divine forms, which the Hindoos ever distinguish from their human forms, interfered and separated the combatants; who returned to their respective homes. They even effected a reconciliation between them, but it proved of no long continuance. Dacsha, it appears, though married, was not blessed with a son. This was a subject of much concern both to his wife and to himself, and they agreed to offer up a solemn sacrifice in order to obtain one. On such an occasion, Dacsha convened both gods and men; but could not be persuaded to invite Siva. The wife however of the latter deity thought proper to attend: but, being treated with contempt by Dacsha, she in a rage threw herself into the holy fire, and thus spoiled the sacrifice. After this, Siva, approaching Brahma in his character of Dacsha, began to vilify and beat him. The confusion soon became general, and the whole assembly took the part of Dacsha: but Siva, striking the ground, brought two heroes at the head of a whole army of demons to his assistance. In the midst of the conflict, he slew Dacsha and cut off his head. Then the gods humbled themselves before him; and peace was reëstablished. He even promised, at their request, to restore Dacsha to life: but the severed head could not be found; for during the fray it had fallen into the fire, and was burnt. It was supplied therefore by that of a he-goat: and the lifeless corpse of Dacsha instantly revived. But he remained weak and without power, a mere non-entity in the antediluvian world, until he was born again after the flood in the person of a son of Menu-Satyavrata who was preserved in an ark from the general destruction. The country, where this famous sacrifice was offered up which occasioned the death of Dacsha, was that which lies at the head of the Ganges; for the offering was performed in the hills on the banks of the tributary river Chinab.

Thus we are again brought to the same region, where we are clearly to seek for the Hindoo Paradise of Meru, and where both local and written tradition places the early antediluvian residence of Adima or the first Menu. As Adima then is manifestly Adam, for the preceding legend requires no explanation; as Meru, with its tree of knowledge and its four rivers springing from a common source, is clearly Paradise; as Adima is said to have first lived in Cashmir; and as Meru, by an independent train of reasoning, has already been shewn to coincide literally with the high land of Cashmir and Bokhara: we have here an additional proof, that the locality of Meru has been rightly settled; for, Adima being Adam and Meru being Paradise, where Adima flourished, there must be mount Meru; but Adima flourished in Cashmir, therefore Meru on this account also must be placed in Cashmir.

The other traditions of the country all tend to the same conclusion; and prove at once, that the locality of Meru has been ascertained according to the geographical notions of the old Hindoo mythologists, and that the prototype of Meru was the scriptural Paradise.

Thus the Musulmans, who live in the countries adjacent to Bamiyan, and who have thence adopted the popular belief that Paradise was situated in this region, contend, that Adam and Eve, the former of whom they call *Keyumursh*, when they had been driven out of the sacred garden, wandered separately for some time, until at length they met in a place, which received the name of *Bahlaca* or *Balk* (as it is usually expressed in our common maps) from the circumstance of their greeting each other with a mutual embrace: Thus also they pretend, that, when Satan was cast out of Eden, he leaped over the mountains and fell on the spot where Cabul now stands. And thus, still under the influence of the same notion, they assert, that two gigantic statues, which are yet to be seen between Bahlac and Bamiyan, represent Adam and Eve; while a third of smaller dimensions is intended for their son *Seish* or Seth, whose tomb, or at least the place where it formerly stood, is shewn near Bahlac.

Such legends perfectly agree with the received opinions both of the Musulmans and Buddhists respecting the burial place of the protoplast or the most ancient Buddha. They say, that his body was at his own request entombed in a cave or vault called *Alconuz*, which was formed in the heart of a mountain situated in the centre of the world. Round that holy mountain his descendants long continued to dwell: but the wicked offspring of his fratricidal son were only allowed to fix their habitations at the foot of it, while those of his other son Seish were seated higher up as far as the top. Here they lived in great sanctity and purity of manners, every day worshipping God on the summit of the mountain, and visiting the body of Adam in the vault as the means of procuring the divine benediction.

This mountain, thus described as being in the centre of the earth, is evidently the Meru of the Hindoos; which is ever thus placed in their systems of geography, and which is represented in such a manner as to leave no doubt of its being a copy of the scriptural Paradise. Nor is such a coincidence the only one which may be pointed out. As the body of Adam is supposed to be buried in the sacred mount of God: so Meru is deemed the worldly temple of the Trimurti; and is considered by the followers of Buddha, who unites the Trimurti in his own person, as the tomb of that son of the great Spirit who successively reappears at the commencement of each world in the character of the first lawgiver and universal great father. Hence the pyramidal temples, which are constructed in avowed imitation of the primeval Meru, are commonly said to contain a portion of the bones of Buddha which are venerated as sacred relics: because the worldly temple of the alleged supreme being, of which they are mere transcripts, is believed to be really the tomb of his first embodied form; that is to say, in the language of the Hindoo theologists, of Adima or Menu-Swayambhuva in whose person Brahma was first incarnate. The legend of Adam being buried in the cave Alconuz is mentioned by Eutychius; and the cave itself is described, as being hollowed out in the mount of Paradise. When the time of the deluge drew near, and when Noah was about to enter into the Ark, he first, attended by his three sons, visited the cave, and reverently kissed the bodies of the early patriarchs which were there deposited: but that of Adam he removed, and carried it with him into the Ark. After the deluge, it was again placed in the same central region of the earth; which was believed to be the scite of Paradise, and to which Noah and his family had bid a solemn farewell when they removed the body from the cave: and, when the second father of mankind himself died, his body was laid by that of Adam; each corpse thus finally resting within the sacred precincts of Eden.[1]

As the traditions of Cashmir represent that country as being the abode of

---

[1] Eutych. Annal. vol. i. p. 36, 44. apud Fabric. Cod. Pseudepig. vol. i. p. 241, 267.

the first parents of the human race, and as we have necessarily been led to place Meru or the Hindoo Paradise in the same lofty region; so, with perfect harmony, other legends of the natives complete the picture by ascribing to it another characteristic of the scriptural Eden.

When Adam and Eve were expelled from the garden, God is said to have placed on the eastern side of it a guard of Cherubim with a flaming sword which spontaneously turned itself in every direction. The particular form of these Cherubim is not specified by Moses: but we learn from other parts of Scripture, that it was compounded of a man, an eagle, a bull, and a lion; and that it was likewise furnished with wings, that wafted the mysterious living creature from the one part of heaven to the other. Now it is remarkable, that, at the entrance of the mountainous eastern passes which lead to the supposed scite of the Cashmirian Paradise, the Hindoos place a destroying angel, whose shape is thought to be precisely that of what may be called an imperfect Cherub. He is represented as a young man with the countenance, wings, and talons, of an eagle: and his peculiar office, in their mythology, is to act as the vehicle or flying car of the god Vishnou; exactly as, in the inspired language of Holy Writ, Jehovah is said to ride upon the wings of the Cherubim. His name is *Garuda*, which possibly may itself be a mere corruption of the word *Cherub:* and, as he is feigned peculiarly to haunt the eastern passes of Cashmir; so, in exact conformity with the hypothesis which supposes the literal Meru to coincide with Cashmir and Bokhara, he is also conspicuously introduced into the synod of the hero-gods assembled on the summit of the Paradisiacal Meru. This being is evidently the fabled griffin-guard of the Arismaspians and old Scythians; who journeyed westward from their original settlements in the Indian Caucasus, and who thence brought into Europe many of the legends of their forefathers. He is likewise the Simorgh or Phenix of Persian romance; who peculiarly appears at the commencement of each new world, and who carries the oriental heroes from one extremity of the globe to the other. We may recognize him also as the manifest prototype of the thunder-bearing eagle of the classical Jupiter; whose seat is the top either of Ida or Olympus, each equally a transcript of Ida-Vratta or Ilapu or Meru. And we may not obscurely perceive, that he is really no other than the avenging bird; which, as Grecian fables tell, was at once the guard and the tormentor of Prometheus, as he lay chained to one of the precipices of Caucasus or Chaisaghar. The Sacas or Saxons, who were ever associated with the Scythians or Goths, introduced the knowledge of him into their western settlements; for, wherever the Sacas went, there also we find some legend respecting griffins, the native country of which is rightly said by classical mythologists to have been the central Asiatic region of Bactria: and thus at length, in the character of the flying griffin-horse, he appears again in the not unlovely visions of Italian poetry, and transports through the air the mailed warriors of the west as he had long similarly conveyed the chivalrous heroes of Persian story. Nor are the other two cherubic forms wanting in the Paradise of the Hindoos, though they have been severed from those of the eagle and the man which are united in the compound figure of Garuda. Two of the sacred rivers are supposed to pour their streams through the mouths of a rocky lion and heifer: and the four animal heads are placed towards the four quarters of the world, in a manner that bears considerable resemblance to the arrangement which has been made by some, both in ancient and modern times, of the four cherubic heads.

The Buddhists of Thibet entertain much the same sentiments respecting Meru, as the Brahmenists of Hindostan. They place the sacred garden at the foot of mount Meru, toward the south-west and at the source of the Ganges. The four holy rivers, for they equally believe them to be four in number, are the Ganges, the Indus, the Sampa, and the Sita-Ganga; by which last they understand the Sirr or Jaxartes, denominated *Sita-Ganga* in the Puranas. They have also the same number of heads of animals, which are disposed in the same manner: and both their divines and those of India consider the four animals as the original guardians of the four quarters of the world. The tree likewise of knowledge, or rather (according to their theology) the tree of life, which however is equally mentioned by Moses as growing in the garden, is conspicuously introduced into their terrestrial Paradise. They call it *Zambu*, which is nothing more than a variation of the Hindoo *Jambu:* and they believe it to be a celestial tree, bearing the Amrita or fruit of immortality (by the Greeks named *Ambrosia*), and adjoining to four vast rocks from which flow the same number of sacred rivers.

It is not unworthy of observation, that the very name of *Eden* seems to be preserved in the Hindoo appellation *Ida;* by which term, or in its compound form *Ida-Vratta,* the circular summit of Meru, girt by a belt of mountains, is wont to be designated. *Ida* signifies *the World;* and *Ida-Vratta* denotes *the circle of the World:* for Meru, as we have seen, is thought to represent the Universe and to be the great original mundane temple of the chief hero-god. This notion, connected with what has already been said respecting the literal scite of Meru, will explain the otherwise almost inexplicable account which Josephus gives of the locality of the terrestrial Paradise. He evidently appears to me to have been not unacquainted with the old oriental notion, that the garden of Eden was situated in the mountainous country of Cashgar: hence he vainly attempts to blend together into one system the narrative of Moses and the tradition of the Indo-Scythians. The latter fixed Paradise at the source of the Ganges; which it made to be one of the sacred rivers, while it described the Chocshu or Oxus as being another of them. From this circumstance the first of these streams received the name of *Phison,* which it continued to bear in the days of St. Jerome; and the second of them, that of *Gihon,* which it still retains. Josephus therefore, being absolutely fixed to the well-known Euphrates and Tigris or Phrat and Diglath as two of the Paradisiacal rivers, and not knowing where to look with equal certainty for the other two, adopted, in utter defiance of geographical accuracy, the Ganges, because it was called *Phison* and was immediately connected with the legend of mount Meru, and the Nile, because it was called *Geon* and likewise undoubtedly compassed an Ethiopia or a land of Cush. That he was not ignorant of the Hindoo fable, is further evident from a very curious coincidence. He tells us, that the river of Eden, previous to its division into four heads, flowed round the whole earth. For this singular assertion he has not a shadow of warrant from Scripture: but it is the natural result of an acquaintance with the Hindoo tradition. Eden in the hands of the Brahmens became Ida, and was made to signify *the World:* the river of Eden therefore was the river of the whole earth.

5. Hitherto I have considered mount Meru as a transcript of Paradise; *Meru was also a transcript of Ararat* and I have shewn, that, according to the notions of the old Hindoo mytho- logists, it was supposed to be literally that high tract of land at the source of the Ganges, which comprehends the countries of Cashgar, Cashmir, and little Bokhara. In exact accordance with this opinion, we found, that the natives of those regions still believe, that they were the peculiar residence of the first antediluvian pair Adima and Iva or Menu-Swayambhuva and Satarupa, and that they were the scite of a holy garden from which flowed four rivers to the four opposite quarters of the world and which was guarded on the eastern side by a being compounded of a man and an eagle. I now proceed to view this same mount Meru under a different character, even that of the lofty peak, by Moses called *Ararat*, on which the Ark rested when left by the retiring waters of the deluge.

recap

We are told in the Puranas, that, during the prevalence of the flood, Brahma or the creative power, who was incarnate at the beginning of the antediluvian world in the severed persons of Adima and Iva, lay asleep at the bottom of the great abyss. Then the generative principles of nature, both male and female, were reduced to their simplest elements, the Linga and the Yoni: of which the latter assumed the shape of the hull of a ship, since typified by the Argha; whilst the former became the mast of the sacred vessel. This mast was no other than the god Mahadeva himself, who is frequently represented as standing erect in the middle of the Argha and as thus supplying the place of a mast: and the ship, in a similar manner, is allowed to be one of the forms of Parvati or Bhavani, the mystic consort of the deity who presides over destruction and renovation. Thus meta-morphosed, they were wafted over the deep under the special care and pro-tection of Vishnou the preserving power. When the waters at length re-tired, the female power of nature appeared immediately in the character of Capoteswari or the dove, and she was soon joined by her consort in the shape of Capoteswara.[1]

Now, as the Trimurti both jointly and individually are believed to have been incarnate in the persons of the first Menu and his three sons; so are

[1] Asiat. Res. vol. vi. p. 523.

they likewise thought to have again manifested themselves in those of Menu-Satyavrata and his triple offspring, who were preserved from destruction at the time of the deluge. Mahadeva therefore or Siva is evidently, in this legend, to be considered as the power of destruction and renovation incarnate in the person of Noah, who presided (as it were) both over the destruction and the renovation of the mundane system: and his mystic consort Parvati, who first bore him over the deluge in the form of a ship, and who afterwards as the waters retired assumed the shape of a dove, is clearly and palpably the Ark out of which a dove was sent as the flood gradually abated. But, in every description and in every delineation of mount Meru, Siva and Parvati, whether viewed as two distinct characters or united together in the single hermaphroditic form of Ardha-Nari, are always represented, as conspicuously seated on the central summit of the sacred hill, and as receiving the homage of the inferior attendant deities: and mount Cailasa, which is one of the three peaks of Meru, is believed to be the peculiar and favourite abode of Siva, who there, in evident allusion to the Noetic ogdoad, is said to manifest himself in eight sacred forms; while the three peaks, severally and conjointly, are supposed to be the mundane temple of the Trimurti, who become incarnate, at the commencement of every new world, in the persons of the great father and his three sons. If then Siva and Parvati be Noah and the Ark, the sacred mountain, whose summit they are specially thought to inhabit, must certainly be that, on which the Ark rested after the deluge and which Moses calls *Ararat.* Hence one of the titles of Parvati is *the mountain-born goddess :* and hence she is sometimes delineated sitting on the top of Meru, and receiving, in her character of the great universal mother, the adoration of the surrounding deities.

The propriety of such a conclusion will further appear from the curious Hindoo legend respecting mount Mandar. At the period of the deluge the Soors and Asoors are feigned to have violently churned the troubled ocean with this mountain; on the summit of which Vishnou is represented sitting on the lotos, the acknowledged symbol of the ship Argha. But Vishnou, whose character melts into that of Siva, and who during the prevalence of the flood appears in the well-known symbolical shape of the mer-man, is like him the patriarch Noah. Vishnou therefore in the lotos or Argha is Noah in the Ark: and mount Mandar, on which he thus appears seated in the midst of the ocean, must necessarily be intended for Ararat. But Mandar is no other than Meru: for the literal scite of this mountain is at the source of the Ganges, which, as we have seen, is the precise literal situation of Meru.

We shall be brought exactly to the same conclusion by following another train of argument. I have already observed, that the Ark was esteemed a microcosm or little world from its containing within its womb the rudiments of the new world: hence it was typified by the mundane egg, which was thought to have floated on the waters of the abyss, and from which the three divine sons of the hermaphroditic Zeus or Siva were believed to have been born. Agreeably to this system of double typification, the Hindoos, as we have just seen, represented the World by the lotos floating on the surface of the ocean; the leaves of that aquatic flower shadowing out the four continents and eight principal islands, and its petal denoting the supposed centrical mount Meru: but they likewise equally employed the same lotos to symbolize the ship Argha and its mariner or mystic consort Mahadeva; in which case the calix of the flower typified the hull of the ship, and its petal the god who navigated the sacred vessel over the waves of the deluge. The diluvian god therefore and mount Meru, and the mystic Ship and the Earth, are severally represented by common symbols: and accordingly, while the ship Argha which floated on the surface of the flood is declared like the lotos to typify the Earth, the Earth itself in return was thought both by the old Chaldèans and the Hindoos to be shaped like a boat and to be suspended upon the waters of the abyss in the manner of a huge ship. Thus immediately was the arkite Siva connected with the diluvian Meru: and hence originated the practice, common to the Atlantians and the Cappadocians, of esteeming the sacred mount in their respective countries at once the temple of the deity and the deity himself.[1]

There is yet another train of reasoning, by which we shall again be brought to the same inevitable result. The summit of the fabled Meru is called *Ida-Vratta* or *Ila-Vratta*. But this compound appellation signifies

[1] Maxim. Tyr. Dissert. xxxviii. p. 374, 375.

the circle of Ida, which is equivalent to *the circle of the World.* Ida however is said to have been both the daughter and the wife of Buddha or Menu-Satyavrata, who was preserved in an ark at the time of the deluge. Now Menu-Satyavrata is certainly the same as Siva, considered as incarnate in the person of Noah, and as thus sailing over the waters of the flood in the ship Argha. But Argha or Parvati is the mystic consort of Siva; and Ila is said to be the wife and daughter of Menu: therefore, since Siva and Menu are the same, Argha and Ila must be the same also. Ila consequently is the Ark: and with this result both her name and her character perfectly agree. Her name denotes *the World;* and the ship Argha, as we have just seen, was considered as being the World, and as such was conjointly typified by the mundane symbols of the egg and the lotos: her character is that of the wife and daughter of him, who was saved in the Ark; and the ship Argha, which conveyed Mahadeva in safety over the waves of the deluge, is declared to be only a form of the consort of that deity. Ila therefore being the same as Argha, or Parvati, or the great mother, or the Ark; Meru must of necessity be the same as Ararat: because the summit of Meru is described as being surmounted by the circle or sacred inclosure of Ila, as Ararat was after the deluge surmounted by the Ark. This circle of mountains represented at once the Ark and the World, or Ila understood in both those senses: and it was the prototype of those round stone temples, which the ancient Druids were wont indifferently to denominate *the circle of the World, the inclosure of the ship-goddess Ceridwen,* and *the Ark of the World.* Sometimes, instead of this belt of mountains, Meru was thought to terminate in three lofty peaks: but the idea was still the same; for the three peaks represented, upon a vast scale, the stem and the stern of the ship Argha with Siva standing in the centre of it like a mast.[1]

Thus, whatever train of argument we follow, we are still uniformly brought to the same conclusion, that Meru is no less to be deemed a transcript of the mountain on which the Ark rested after the deluge, than a copy of the sacred garden of Paradise.

The circumstance of its sustaining this double character will lead us to understand, how it came, like Mahadeva, to be esteemed the masculine

[1] Vide infra book v. c. 7. § 1. 1. II. 1.

power of the Universe : and, on the other hand, its singular identification with the masculine power may serve as an additional proof, that the result, to which we have been led in the progress of our inquiries, is strictly consonant with truth. We have seen, that the lotos, floating on the surface of the ocean, is at once a symbol of the Earth with mount Meru rising in the centre of it, and a type of the ship Argha with the regenerative god Mahadeva supplying to it the place of a mast. We have also seen, that the calix and petal of the lotos, and the hull and mast of the Argha, are equally supposed to represent the masculine and feminine principles of nature ; which are fabled to have been reduced to their simplest form during the prevalence of the deluge. Consequently, mount Meru, which, like Mahadeva, is shadowed out by the petal of the flower and the mast of the ship, is esteemed the great masculine power whence the whole World was produced : just as Mahadeva, agreeably to the nature of his constant symbol, is peculiarly held to be the president of generation ; which, in the theory of the old mythologists, ever followed destruction, to destroy being only to reproduce in a new form. Now the reason, why such an attribute was ascribed both to the mountain and the god, is sufficiently evident from the opinion which we have been led to form of their real characters. Paradise was the cradle of the *primitive* human race : the mountain, where the Ark grounded, was, in a similar manner, the cradle of the *postdiluvian* human race. And again ; Adam was the parent of the inhabitants of the *first* world : Noah was the parent of the inhabitants of the *renovated* world. But Paradise and the arkite mountain, as the Hindoo mythology teaches us in exact correspondence with what may be deduced from Scripture, were geographically coincident ; that is to say, the Ark rested in the self-same high tract of land after the deluge, where the garden had been situated before it : and Adam, the father of three sons at the commencement of one world, was believed by the Gentiles to have appeared again in the person of Noah, himself similarly the father of three sons, at the commencement of another world ; each with his triple offspring being deemed equally, severally, conjointly, and successively, an incarnation of the Trimurti ; who are thus manifested in the character of the great father and his children, at each similar mundane renovation. Hence Meru, which is the transcript both of Paradise and Ararat; and Siva, who, intimately blended with Brahma and Vishnou, is alike the representative of Adam and Noah; came both to be esteemed the masculine principle of nature, both to be deemed the origin or patron of generation, and both to be venerated by a symbol as familiar throughout the whole pagan world as it was disgraceful to the inventors of so degrading a mode of worship. Such, in short, was clearly, if I mistake not, the foundation and leading idea of a superstition; which, in a discussion like the present, cannot be wholly passed over in silence, though decorum requires that it should be consigned as soon as possible to modest oblivion: such was the cause, why the great father and the great mother of gentile antiquity, or Adam reappearing in Noah and the Earth identified with the Ark, were so perpetually esteemed the deities of love and the patrons of fecundity; and were thence venerated, by their fanatical devotees, with abominations but too perfectly analogous to the symbols, by which they were mysteriously represented.

Traditions of the Puranas and of the Cashgarians respecting Cashgar being the region where the Ark landed

6. As both the legends of the Puranas and local tradition concur, in making the high mountainous region of Cashgar and Bokhara to have been the abode of the first antediluvians and to have geographically coincided with the scite of the garden of Eden; which identifies that country with the Paradisiacal Meru: so they equally concur, in representing that same region, as the place where the Ark rested after the deluge, and as the district peculiarly inhabited by the first postdiluvians; which again identifies it with Meru viewed in its diluvian character.

The natives, we are told, look upon Bamiyan and the adjacent countries as the abode of the progenitors of mankind, no less *after* the flood than *before* it: and, in this very ancient opinion, which places in the same region both Menu-Swayambhuva and Menu-Satyavrata or (to speak of them by their scriptural names) both Adam and Noah, they are countenanced, to its full extent, alike by Persian authors and by the sacred books of the Hindoos.

According to the Puranas, Swayambhuva or Adima before the deluge, and Satyavrata or Noah after it, equally lived in the north-west parts of India about Cashmir. There, as we have already seen, flowed the four rivers of Paradise; there flourished the sacred tree of life and knowledge; there Iva was produced from the body of Adima; and there, at the offering up of a memorable sacrifice, Dacsha fell by the hand of his jealous brother, who was doomed by an awful curse to become a vagabond on the face of the earth: there also, as we now further learn, dwelt the second father of mankind; and there rested the wonderful vessel in which he was preserved from the fury of the deluge.

Respecting the precise mountain indeed, on which the ark is supposed to have grounded, there is some diversity of opinion: but it is universally agreed, that the mountain in question was one of those, which constituted the high range by the Greeks denominated *the Indian Caucasus.*

Many believe it to be the famous peak of Chaisa-ghar or Cashgar, which the Musulmans call *Tuct-Suleiman* or *the throne of Solomon.* This mountain is seen at the distance of one hundred coss, and begins to be visible near the extensive ruins of the city of Sangala. Its summit is always covered with snow; in the midst of which appear several streaks of a reddish colour, supposed by pilgrims to be the impression made by the feet of the dove that Satyavrata let out of his ark. Agreeably to this supposition, it is the general and uniform tradition of the country, that the ship of the great father was built on the summit of Chaisa-ghar; that, when the deluge abated, that was the first land which emerged from beneath the waters; and that thus it became the resting-place of the dove, which left the impression of her feet in the mud, by time hardened into a solid rock.[1] The ark itself is thought to have grounded about half way up the mountain on a projecting plain of very small extent. With respect to the footsteps of the dove, they are known only by tradition; for the inhabitants of the country assert, that they have never heard of any body going up so high on account both of the snow and of the ruggedness of the mountain. The Buddhists, who were the first inhabitants of this lofty region, are, it is said, of the same

---

[1] From traditions of such a nature, the mountains of Coh-Suleiman are sometimes called by the natives *the mountains of the dove;* a title, which exactly accords with that bestowed by Ptolemy on the whole range as far as Gazni: for he denominates this range *the Paruëti mountains,* most probably from the Sanscrit *Parvata* or *Paravat* which signifies *a dove.* It may be observed, that the consort of Siva, who sailed over the deluge in the form of the ship Argha and who afterwards flew away in the shape of a dove, seems to have derived her name *Parvati* from the latter of these metamorphoses.

opinion as to the place where the ark rested : hence they assert, that Shama
or Shem descended from the mountain of Chaisa-ghar, previous to his building the sacred town of Bamiyan.

On the other hand, the Pauranics insist, that, as it is declared in their
sacred books that Satyavrata made fast the ark with a cable of prodigious
length to the celebrated peak called from that circumstance *Nau-bandha*,
he must have built it in the adjacent country.[1] This mountain is situated in
Cashmir, three days journey to the north-north-east of the purganah of Lar:
and, in consequence of the tradition by which it is distinguished, pilgrims
resort to it from all parts of India, who scramble up among the rocks to a
cavern beyond which they never go. A few doves, alarmed by the noise,
fly from crag to crag : and these the pilgrims esteem their guides to the
holy place, believing them to be the genuine offspring of the dove which
was let out of the ark.

In reply to the Pauranics, who advocate the cause of mount Nau-bandha,
the followers of Buddha urge, that, although the Ark might have been
fastened to that peak in the vicinity of Cashmir, yet it does not therefore
follow that it floated perpendicularly above it during the whole prevalence
of the deluge. On the contrary, they ingeniously contend, that so vast
was the length of the cable by which it was secured, that while it
was moored to the summit of Nau-bandha, it was riding above that
of Chaisa-ghar. The rival claims of these two celebrated mountains are,
I believe, equally well founded; for I am fully persuaded, that it was
the mere vanity of local appropriation which ascribed the appulse of
the Ark to either of them. It is however remarkable, that, in the midst of
the controversy, some evident vestiges of the truth are still apparent : for
both the Pauranics and the Buddhists agree in this particular, that the name
of the mountain on which the Ark rested was *Aryavarta* or *Aryawart*,
plainly the *Ararat* of Moses.

As the high land to the north-west of India is thus supposed to have been
the residence of Noah after the flood, so is it likewise believed to have
been the place of his sepulture ; a notion, which exactly accords with the

---

[1] *Nau* signifies *a ship*, and *bandha* denotes *to bind* or *to make fast.*

legend preserved by Eutychius, that the body of Noah was deposited in the same cavern of the holy Paradisiacal mountain that contained the corpse of Adam. In the Varaha-Purana, the father of Satyavrata, who corresponds with the scriptural Lamech, is declared to have been king of Cashmir and the adjacent countries; and to this day a tomb is shewn at Naulakhi, where that patriarch is thought to have been interred. The character however of the person, to whom the sepulchre is said to belong, plainly shews, that he was not Lamech, but Noah: and Mr. Wilford has pointed out, with much plausibility, the origin of the mistake. The Musulmans call him *Peer Maitlam;* a name, which they received from the natives when they conquered the country. Now *Maitla* or *Maitlam* is the same as Vaivaswata or Menu-Satyavrata, both in his divine and human character: for that title is a derivative form from the Sanscrit *Mait,* which implies the consort of Lacshami and the owner of her wealth. But the Musulmans probably pronounced the word *Maiter Lam,* which combination would denote *the lord Lam:* and, finding also a tradition that the father of him who had been preserved in an Ark once reigned in that country, they thence inferred, that the *Maiter Lam,* whose tomb continued to be shewn, was Lamech the father of Noah. Such a mistake is easily rectified by the strong characteristic marks, which infallibly point out the person to whom the tomb ought properly to be ascribed. The Buddhists say, that he is *Buddha-Narayana,* or *Buddha dwelling in the waters:* and the Hindoos, who live in the country, call him *Machodar-Nath,* or *the sovereign prince in the belly of the fish.* These titles are by no means applicable to Lamech, but evidently belong to Noah: for, by the belly of the fish, they understand the cavity or interior of the Ark. Thus there is a place underground at Banares, which they call *Machodara.* The centrical and most elevated part of that sacred city bears also the same appellation; because, when the lower parts of the town are laid under water by some unusual overflowing of the Ganges, this remains free from the partial deluge like the belly of a fish. The whole city itself likewise is sometimes thus called; because, during the ordinary periodical floods, the waters rise like a circular wall around it. In short, any place in the middle of waters, either natural or artificial, which can afford shelter to living beings, is called *Machodara.* The evident allusion contained in such notions cannot well be mistaken : and it is sufficiently manifest, that the fish-prince, whose pretended tomb is shewn in Cashmir, is the same person, as Vishnou in the fish-incarnation, which is supposed to have taken place at the period of the deluge; the same also, as the *Oannes* or *Annedot* of the old Babylonians, and as the *Dagon* of the Philistines. The sepulchre, which contains, as it is pretended, the body of this ancient personage, is about forty cubits in length; corresponding, if we may believe tradition, with the stature of the hero-god : and under it is a vault of the same dimensions, with a small door that is never opened out of respect to the venerable deposit. They say, that the body is yet in high preservation, and that it is sitting in a corner of the vault on its heels with its arms crossed over its knees and its head reclining upon its hands; a favourite posture among the inhabitants of India.[1]

How the Indian legend in effect identifies the Paradisiacal Meru with mount Ararat

7. From what has been said respecting the celebrated mount Meru, we may clearly gather the following particulars.

In exact accordance with the result, to which we had already been brought by a previous investigation, the old tradition of the Hindoos and the Chasas places the garden of Paradise and the peak where the Ark rested after the deluge in one and the same lofty region; which, under the name of *Meru*, has been made the celestial abode of the deified ancestors of mankind, both antediluvian and postdiluvian. In exact accordance also with the Mosaical account, whatever discrepance there may be respecting the precise mountain where the Ark grounded, Brahmenists and Buddhists unite in confessing, that one of the names of that mountain was *Aryavarta* or *Ararat*. But, contrary to the conclusion which I had been led to draw from my preliminary discussion, the *literal* scite of the Paradisiaco-diluvian Meru is placed in the high land of Cashgar and Bokhara, to the north-west of Hindostan. The point then of *the geographical identity* of Paradise and Ararat being thus established, both by deductions from Scripture and by a very remarkable combination of gentile traditions; the only question, which remains to be finally determined, is this : whether the real prototype of

---

[1] Asiat. Res. vol. vi. p. 455—539. vol. viii. p. 284—374. vol. i. p. 248, 419. vol. v. p. 261. vol. vii. p. 406. vol. ii. p. 334, 335. Moor's Hind. Panth. passim.

Meru is to be sought for in the mountains of Armenia, as I contend; or in those of Cashgar and Bokhara, as Mr. Wilford, following the Hindoo legend, strenuously maintains.

Now the well established point of *the geographical identity of Paradise and Ararat* is in itself sufficient; even independent of the arguments, by which I proved, that the scriptural Ararat cannot have been situated in Cashgar, but must have been situated in Armenia: this well established point is in itself sufficient positively to decide the matter now under litigation. The mode, in which I argue from it, is as follows.

Moses represents two well known rivers, the Euphrates and the Tigris, as being rivers of Paradise; and he asserts, that the primeval river of Eden branched off from the garden into the heads of those two rivers. Paradise therefore must have been situated in a country, which lies at the sources of the Euphrates and the Tigris. But the country, which lies at their sources, is Armenia. Therefore Paradise must have been situated in Armenia. Paradise however and mount Ararat geographically coincide with each other, as we collect both from Scripture and pagan tradition. Consequently, since Paradise was situated in Armenia, Ararat must also have been situated in Armenia. Thus the Hindoo legend, by tending to establish the geographical coincidence of Paradise and Ararat, undesignedly serves also to establish their real situation.

I am perfectly aware, that Mr. Wilford (as indeed was absolutely necessary to his hypothesis) attempts to identify the four rivers mentioned by Moses with four eastern streams, the course of which does not forbid him to fix the terrestrial Paradise in the mountains of Cashgar: but, so long as the Euphrates stands upon record as one of those rivers, no ingenuity can transport the garden from Armenia to the source of the Ganges. This learned writer does indeed say, that of the *Phrat* (as Moses writes what we call *the Euphrates*) no particulars are recorded: whence he feels himself at liberty, as one unhampered by any geographical fetters, to pronounce it the river of Cunduz. What he says no doubt is perfectly true: but the silence of Moses in one particular passage will by no means warrant the arrangement, which places the scriptural Phrat very far to the east of every country with which the Israelites were acquainted. The brevity of Moses in simply saying that *the fourth river is the Phrat*, while he largely and geographically particularizes the three other rivers, is not the brevity of ignorance or of indecision. He is silent respecting the course of the last Paradisiacal stream, solely because it was altogether unnecessary to specify what was so well known : just as any foreign topographer, who wrote for the instruction of our continental neighbours, would judge it wholly superfluous to say that the *Thames* is a river in the south of England ; though he would feel himself called upon to mark out with geographical precision, to his otherwise ignorant readers, the obscure northern *Ouse* or *Ribble* or *Swale.*[1] But the silence of the Hebrew historian in this particular passage does by no means leave undetermined what we are to understand by the Phrat, nor does it authorize a commentator to place that river in what part of the world he pleases. So often, and with such unambiguous local characteristics, is the Phrat elsewhere mentioned in Scripture, both by Moses himself and by the other inspired writers, that there cannot be a shadow of doubt, that what he calls *Phrat* is the same as what we after the Greeks are wont to call *Euphrates.* Suffice it to remark, that this very Phrat, which Mr. Wilford would place in the neighbourhood of the Indian Caucasus, is ever emphatically described in Holy Writ, as the great river that should be the eastern boundary of the Israelitish empire, when it should attain its widest extent in the prosperous reign of Solomon : and, if this be not sufficient to fix its geography, we find it also mentioned as the stream to whose banks Jeremiah resorted during the Babylonish captivity, as the river which was the eastern limit of one of the enemies of king David, and lastly and literally as the peculiar flood of Babylon itself.[2] The

[1] This is strongly expressed in the original Hebrew ; the literal translation of which is, *The fourth river is THAT Euphrates :* as much as to say, *that well-known Euphrates.* In Latin it would run, *Quartum vero flumen est ISTE Phrat.* It is not improbable, that the word *Euphrates* has been made up of the very phrase here used by Moses, which may have been the common mode of speaking of that great river. His expression is *Eu Phrat* or *That Phrat.*

[2] See Gen. xv. 18. Deut. i. 7. xi. 24. 2 Sam. viii. 3. 2 Kings xxiv. 7. 1 Chron. v. 9. Jer. xiii. 4, 5, 7. Jer. xlvi. 10. li. 63, 64. All these passages clearly prove the Phrat to be the Euphrates. Hence the Greek translators and Josephus, and after them all the fathers, were

Phrat therefore is indisputably the Euphrates. But, if the Phrat be the Euphrates, it is impossible, according to the scriptural account at least, that Paradise should have been situated in Cashgar. And, if Paradise be not situated in Cashgar, then neither can we look for Ararat in that country.

II. The legends of Hindostan perhaps connect together, more distinctly than those of any other nation, the garden of Paradise and mount Ararat; yet there are few traditions respecting either, in which the two are not more or less united.

Some traces both of the fable and of the very name of Ida-Vratta occur in countries far remote from India: and we may still collect from them the ruling idea, that the mountain of the Ark coincided geographically with the holy Paradisiacal mountain of the deified patriarchs. Thus Ida-Vratta is evidently ths same as the Ida both of the Cretans, the Iliensians, and the Goths. Each was esteemed the blissful abode of the hero-gods: and yet each was connected with the history of the deluge and the navicular great father and mother.

1. The Cretan Ida was supposed to be the birth-place of that Jupiter, *Ida of Crete* who was nourished in his infancy by doves, and whose whole legend points him out to be the diluvian Siva of the Hindoos. A cave on the summit of Ida witnessed his nativity: and the Idèi Dactyli or Cabiri were the guardians of his mystic childhood. But the sacred caves of the ancients, like their various other two-fold symbols, typified equally the Earth and the Ark:[1] and every fable respecting the Cabiric deities, whether Phenician, or Samothracian, or Egyptian, or Indian, decisively refers them to the era of the deluge.

2. In a similar manner, the Trojan Ida was famous for the worship of *Ida of Troas* Cybelè. But Cybelè, or the great Idèan mother, like the Indian Ida, is at once the Earth and the Ark. Hence *she* also was called *the mountain-born goddess :* and hence the figure of a boat, doubtless the Argha of Hindostan, was conspicuously introduced into her Mysteries. To the rites of this ancient su-

---

perfectly warranted in supposing the Euphrates and the Phrat to be one and the same river.

[1] Respecting these sacred caves more will be said hereafter, book v.c. 7. § I. 2. II. 2.

perstition the whole of the early fabulous history of the Iliensians is to be referred. Their city is said to have received its name from Ilus; who, I doubt not, was the very same character as the masculine Ila or Ida of the Hindoos, and as the Ilus of the Phenicians who is identified with Cronus and Dagon. This fabled prince is supposed to have been directed by a heifer to the place where Ilium was destined to be founded, precisely as Cadmus was led by the same animal to the scite of the Grecian Thebes.[1] Now a heifer is equally the symbol of Parvati and of Isis; and the name of *Theba*, which was alike bestowed upon the sacred beast and upon the city which was called after it, properly signifies *an ark*.[2] Theba in short is the same as the ship Argha; and the name was communicated to the heifer, only because a heifer was symbolical of the Noetic ship. Agreeably to the preceding legend of Ilus and the cow, the Iliensians had also a literal tradition that one of their first princes was set afloat in an ark on the surface of the sea.[3] Of a similar nature is the whole fable respecting Dardanus, who is said to have flourished during the period of a deluge which inundated the island of Samothrace. This island was famous for the worship of the Cabiric gods, which Dardanus is feigned to have imported with him into Troas. They were equally venerated, as we have just seen, in the region of the Cretan Ida; and the whole of their fabulous history is diluvian. In fine, however varied and corrupted, the same notions and the same superstitions are attached to both the classical Idas as to the Meru or Ida-Vratta of Hindostan and Cashgar.

Ida of the Goths   3. But this holy mountain is even yet more palpably the Ida of the ancient Goths; whose ancestors certainly travelled westward from the neighbourhood of the Indian Caucasus, and whose religion (as the Edda both explicitly testifies, and as its own internal evidence sufficiently demonstrates) was imported from the east by the Asæ or Asiatics.

The Ida-Vratta of Hindoo theology is supposed, as we have already seen, to be a vast circular plain on the summit of Meru surrounded by a ring of

---

[1] Apollod. Bibl. lib. iii. c. 11. Tzetz. in Lycoph. ver. 29.

[2] Etym. Magn. Vox Θηβα. Tzetz. in Lycoph. ver. 1206.

[3] Conon. Narrat. 29.

mountains.   Agreeably to this representation of it, the Gothic celestials of
the golden age are fabled to assemble in the lofty plain called *Ida*, in the
midst of the divine abode, the sacred city of the gods; or, as the Hindoos
denominate it, the *Ilapur or holy city of Ila*.   Here they administer justice under the shade of the ash Ydrasil.   *This is the greatest and the best
of all trees.   Its branches extend themselves over the whole world, and
reach above the heavens.   It has three roots widely remote from each other:
the first is among the gods; the second, among the giants, in the place
where the abyss formerly was; the third covers Niflheim or hell.   Under
this root is the fountain Vergelmer, whence flow the infernal rivers: it is
gnawed upon below by the monstrous serpent Nidhoger.   Under that, which
extends towards the land of the giants, is a fountain, in which are concealed
wisdom and knowledge.   He, who possesses it, is full of wisdom, because he
drinks thereof every morning.*[1]*

It need scarcely be observed, that the great ash Ydrasil is palpably the
Jambu of the Indian mount Meru, and that they are equally transcripts of
the Paradisiacal tree of knowledge.   The Goths have added to it an infernal
serpent, which perpetually gnaws its roots from below; a curious part of
the tradition, which sufficiently bespeaks its own origin.   They have likewise made the sacred rivers to be infernal rivers: an idea, in which they
are by no means singular; for the Ganges, one of the Hindoo rivers of Paradise, is also a river of Patala or Hades; and the infernal regions themselves, as we shall presently see, stand immediately connected with Elysium
or Eden.

But, though they thus blend together Hades and Paradise, a combination
which will shortly be explained, they by no means lose sight of the four holy
rivers.   These, on the contrary, are elsewhere duly particularized; and *that*
too in such connection, as to leave but little doubt whence the fable was
borrowed.

The Hindoos imagine, that of the four rivers of Meru the Ganges *only*
flows through the head of a cow, while the three others spring from the
heads of three different animals: but the Gothic mythologists feign, that

---

[1] Edda. Fab. vii, viii.

four rivers of milk issue from the teats of the primeval cow Oedumla.[1] This animal is certainly the same as the sacred cow of the Hindoos; the station of which is sometimes said to be on the summit of mount Meru, and which is also acknowledged to be one of the forms of that very goddess Parvati who floated on the surface of the deluge in the character of the ship Argha. She represents in short, like the calix of the lotos, both the Earth and the Ark: and the four rivers are described as proceeding from her, because the four rivers of Paradise flowed from the same high tract of land as that where the Ark rested at the close of the flood.

I am much mistaken, if these rivers of milk are not nearly allied to the Hindoo sea of milk, in which is placed the fabulous Vaicontha or Paradise of the god Vishnou. Here, floating on the folds of the huge serpent Shesha-naga, and reposing on the lap of his consort Lacshmi, he enjoys the happiness of profound abstraction, during the period of universal inundation which ever intervenes between each two successive worlds. In this legend, which compares the foamy deluge to a sea of milk, we may again trace the generally prevalent opinion, that mount Ararat and the Ark were immediately connected with the garden of Paradise. The Elysium of Vishnou is the lap of the great mother, who floats together with him on a large sea-serpent coiled up into the form of a boat: in other words, the Ark is his Paradise. But all possibility of mistake is removed by its being further intimated in the fable, that, during the prevalence of each intermediate deluge, every thing is completely destroyed or laid under water, except mount Cailasa and the floating Elysium of Vaicontha; that is to say, mount Ararat (for Cailasa is one of the three peaks of Meru), and Paradise singularly identified with the Ark.[2]

The gods, who inhabit the Gothic Ida, are precisely of that character, which, according to the present theory, they might be expected to support. Wod or Odin, as I shall elsewhere shew at large, is the Buddha of the oriental Chasas, whose worship the Goths brought with them into the west, and whose character comprehends both that of Adam and that of Noah. The elder Buddha is the former of those patriarchs; and the younger, who is

---

[1] Edda Fab. iii.   [2] See Moore's Hind. Panth. p. 23, 103, 415, 418.

venerated within the recesses of the Cashgarian mount Meru as the sovereign prince in the belly of the fish, is the latter. Woden accordingly is represented as being one of three brothers, the children of Bore; for Noah, in every mythological system of the pagans, was confounded or rather identified with one of his three sons: and his whole family is described as having been produced from the womb of the sacred cow Oedumla, which doubly symbolizes the Earth and the Ark. This family is placed before the deluge, in the capacity of the Adamitical family: but, in that of the Noetic family, it is said to have flourished at a time when the whole world was inundated, and to have created it anew when the waters abated.[1] The inhabitants, consequently, of the Gothic Paradise are the first race of men both before and after the flood.

To what has been said may be added, that the western Chasas or Goths describe the Earth and the sacred mountain of the gods in a manner which so perfectly corresponds with the notions of their eastern brethren, that there can be little doubt of the source whence the doctrines of the Edda originated. According to the received opinions of the Pauranics, the Earth is a flat surface, surrounded on all sides by the ocean, and swelling out into an immense convexity in the centre. This convexity is mount Meru or Ida-Vratta; and, from its being deemed the birth-place of man both antediluvian and postdiluvian, it is considered as the great masculine principle of nature. Such being the case, when the plain of the Earth was described as circular or oval, and when the whole was exhibited as a vast island floating on the sea, a resemblance was produced of a boat with its mast; and this mundane boat was symbolized alike by the lotos and the diluvian ship Argha supporting the god Mahadeva.[2] In a similar manner, it is the geographical hypothesis of the Edda, that the Earth is round, and that about it is placed the deep ocean: that its coasts or flat lower districts were given for a dwelling to the giants; by whom, since this description is applied to the postdiluvian world, we must understand the daring architects of Babel, for these, when they left the mountainous region of Ararat, first settled in the plain country of Shinar and in the comparative neighbourhood of the sea:

---

[1] Edda Fab. iii, iv.   [2] Asiat. Res. vol. viii. p. 312.

but that, higher up, in a place equally distant on all sides from the circum-ambient waters (the very scite of the fabled Meru), the hero-gods, or the deified mariners of the Ark, built upon the solid earth a fortress against the giants; the circumference of which fortress, agreeably to the idea conveyed by the Sanscrit compound *Ida-vratta*, surrounds the world.[1]

III. The sacred mountains, which I have hitherto mentioned, at once bear the name and exhibit the characteristics of the Hindoo Ida or the Mosaical Eden: some others may now be noticed, which are, I believe, equally transcripts of the Paradisiacal Ararat, though they bear not, at least not so palpably, the appellation of *Ida* or *Ila*.

So closely are the Hindoo deities allied to those of Greece and Rome, that it is impossible to read a description of mount Meru without im-mediately recognizing the classical Olympus. Whether the very word *Olympus* be a variation of *Ilapus* or *Ilapur*, which denotes *the city of Ila*, I shall not pretend to determine. This conjecture of Mr. Wilford is, I think, very probable: but, whatever may be thought of it, the identity of the Greek Olympus and the Hindoo Ilapus requires not for its establishment the aid of perhaps an uncertain etymology. Each is mythologically the abode of the immortals: and each is peculiarly the residence of that deity, whom the Hindoos call *Siva*, and the classical writers *Zeus* or *Jupiter*.

I am speaking at present of the *fabulous* character of these two celebrated hills: Olympus however, like Meru, is not solely a poetical mountain; it has a real geographical situation, or rather many geographical situations; and this circumstance seems to me to give additional probability to the con-jecture that the word itself is but a corruption of the Hindoo *Ilapus*. According to the scholiast on Apollonius, there were no less than six moun-tains, all of which equally bore the name of *Olympus*. These, he tells us, were situated in Macedon, Thessaly, Mysia, Cilicia, Elis, and Arcadia.[2] There was likewise, as we learn from Strabo, a mount Olympus in Lycia; and another in Cyprus.[3] Several towns also in different regions were called either *Olympus*, or *Olympia*, or *Olympè*. At one of these in the territory of

[1] Edda Fab. iv.   [2] Schoe. in Apoll. Argon. lib. i. ver. 598.
[3] Strab. Geog. lib. xiv. p. 666, 682.

Elis, not far distant from the Olympus of that country, were celebrated the famous Olympic games: but there were games of a similar name and description also celebrated in the vicinity of the Thessalian Olympus.[1]

From such a remarkable multiplication of the title, I am inclined to draw the following inference: that *Olympus* was not the specific proper name of any one of those hills; but that each hill, being a copy of the original Paradisiaco-diluvian mountain to which the appellation of *Ida* or *Ila* was wont to be applied, came thence to be equally styled an *Ilapus* or *Olympus*. The word, in short, was rather descriptive of the light in which each hill was considered, than, strictly speaking, its own peculiar appellation. Every sacred mountain of the pagans, whether natural or artificial, was but a transcript of that hill, which the Hindoos call *Meru*, but which was really no other than the Paradisiacal Ararat: every such hill therefore, being alike devoted to the worship of the Paradisiacal and arkite hero-gods, might equally be called *a Meru*, or *an Ida*, or *an Ilapus*, or *an Olympus*. Agreeably to this supposition, we are told by the Hindoo theologists, that each pagoda, each pyramid, and each montiform high-place (of which we read so frequently in Scripture), is invariably to be esteemed a copy of the holy hill Meru.[2] And I am the more confirmed in the propriety of it by finding, that, as every Olympus was deemed the special residence of Jupiter or Siva, so the Arcadian Olympus bears the very same fabulous characteristics as those which mark the Cretan Ida: whence it will evidently follow, that the two hills sustain but one mythological character, and that Ida was as much the Olympus of the Cretans as Olympus was the Ida of the Arcadians. Pausanias tells us, that the Arcadians maintained Jupiter to have been born and educated in *their* sacred mountain, and that they denied the claim of the Cretan Ida to that honour. This, in fact, proves, that the very same tradition was attached to *both* hills, and, I have no doubt, for the very same reason. In neither of them was the real Jupiter born: but each was equally a transcript of that sacred mountain, where the first great father was originally produced at the beginning of the world; and where the second great father, at the commencement of the renewed world, was born from the womb of the universal arkite mother, and was nursed by doves during the period of his mystic infancy: It is remarkable, that Pausanias further informs us, that the specific name of the holy mount of the Arcadians was *Lyceum;* though some called it *Olympus,* and others merely *the sacred hill.* This exactly accords with the preceding supposition respecting the use of the word *Olympus;* and serves to prove, that that appellation was general to every high place, not peculiarly appropriated to any one in particular.[1]

The different accounts, which are given of the origin of the Olympic games, all serve to shew, that I am not far mistaken in identifying the mythological character of Olympus with that of Meru and Ida, and in thus ultimately resolving it into the Paradisiacal Ararat. The town of Olympia, where the most famous of those games were celebrated, was situated (as I have already observed) in the territory of Elis, not far distant from the Olympus of that country. Such of the Eleënsians, as were best versed in mythological antiquity, asserted, that a temple was first dedicated in Olympia to Cronus or Saturn by that primeval race of men, who flourished during the golden age: hence the sacred mount of Olympia was sometimes called *the hill of Saturn.* Afterwards, when the infant Jupiter was committed by Rhea to the care of the Idèi Dactyli, who are the same as the Curetes or Cabiri; these personages came from mount Ida in Crete to Olympia, and there instituted the games in question. Two of the Idèi Dactyli were called *Hercules* and *Ida:* but these are evidently one person; for the origin of the games was generally ascribed to Hercules-Idèus or Hercules-Ida. The victor was crowned with a wreath of olive: and the original tree, which produced the first chaplet, was supposed to have been brought into Greece by Hercules from the northern country of the Hyperboreans. Some mythologists further asserted, that the contest of Jupiter and Saturn took place in Olympia: others contended, that the games were instituted on account of the victory over the Titans: and others again

---

[1] Paus. Arcad. p. 517.

ascribed their origin to the Cretan Clymenus, who was a descendant of Hercules-Ida, and who flourished fifty years after the flood of Deucalion.[1]

It is easy to decypher these various traditions, all of which tend to prove, that the Paradisiacal Ararat was the real prototype of Olympus. The golden age was the age of man's innocence in Eden; though, agreeably to the doctrine of a perpetual succession of similar worlds, every new mundane system was feigned to commence with it. The most ancient Cronus, who flourished during that period and who was the primitive god of Olympia, is certainly Adam: but the younger Cronus, or rather Cronus reappearing at the beginning of a new world, is no less certainly, as every part of his history abundantly testifies, the patriarch Noah. Hence it necessarily follows, that the sacred hill, which sometimes was called *Olympus* and sometimes *the hill of Cronus*, must at once have been the representative of Paradise and Ararat. The war of the Titans, which terminated in their being plunged beneath the waves of the ocean, and which was immediately connected with the far-famed oath of Jupiter by the waters of hatred, relates altogether to the destruction of the impious antediluvians. But the Olympic games were thought by some to have been instituted in commemoration of this war; and accordingly an antiquity is by others assigned to them, which falls short of the deluge only by fifty years. So again: Hercules-Ida, whom the legend brings from the sacred mountain of Crete, is evidently no other than the masculine Ida or Ila of Hindostan, and the Ilus or Saturn or Dagon of Phenicia. His character accordingly comprehends those both of Adam and Noah: for we at once find him sailing over the sea in a wonderful cup, the navicular Argha or sacrificial cup of the Hindoos; and placed in a sacred garden, which in almost every particular identifies itself with Paradise.

IV. This celebrated garden is styled by the Greek mythologists *the garden of the Hesperides:* and additional light will be thrown on the present subject by considering the legends attached to it.

We are told by the poets, that it produced golden fruit, which was guarded by a serpent; that this reptile encircled with its folds the trunk of a mysterious tree; and that Hercules gained the fruit by overcoming the

[1] Paus. 1 Eliac. p. 299, 300. Lycoph. Cassand. ver. 42. Tzetz. Schol. in loc.

serpent.[1] The principal actors in the fable have been elevated to the sphere: and Eratosthenes relates the story, and describes the constellation, in so remarkable a manner, that we are almost constrained, with Sir Walter Raleigh and many others, to apply the whole to the primitive history of mankind.[2] *This serpent*, says he, *is the same as that, which guarded the golden apples, and which was slain by Hercules. For, according to Pherecydes, when all the gods offered presents to Juno on her nuptials with Jupiter, the Earth also brought golden apples. Juno, admiring their beauty, commanded them to be planted in the garden of the gods: but, finding that they were continually plucked by the daughters of Atlas, she appointed a vast serpent to guard them. Hercules overcame, and slew, the monster. Hence, in this constellation, the serpent is depicted rearing its head aloft; while Hercules, placed above it with one knee bent, tramples with his foot upon its head, and brandishes a club in his right hand.*[3] The same fable is very curiously represented on the reverse of a coin of Antoninus Pius: Hercules appears plucking apples from a tree, round the trunk of which a serpent is enfolded.[4]

Some tradition of the original promise made to the woman seems pretty evidently to have been introduced into the present legend: and the serpenticide Hercules, the Ila of Hindoo theology, is here very nearly allied to Vishnou in his character of trampling on the head of a snake which at the same time bites his heel.[5] Be that as it may, since Hercules bears the double attributes of Noah and Adam, the garden of the Hesperides, which is described as terminating his successful voyage over the ocean, must be viewed as equally representing Paradise and Ararat, and as thus affording another proof of their geographical coincidence.

The Greeks in general placed this fabled garden close to mount Atlas, and removed it far into the regions of the western Africa:[6] but its

---

[1] Lucret. de nat. rer. lib. v. ver. 33.   [2] Raleigh's Hist. of the world. p. 73.

[3] Erat. Catast. c. iii, iv.   See also Hyg. Poet. Astron. lib. ii. constell. 3. p. 361. and Arat. Phænom. p. 13.

[4] Gurtler's Orig. Mundi. p. 9.   [5] See Maurice's Hist. of Hind. vol. ii. p. 290.

[6] Hyg. Poet. Astron. lib. ii. cons. 3. p. 361.

true situation was in the north, on the summit or in the neighbourhood of the Armenian Ararat. All knowledge of its real scite was by no means erased from the memory of the classical mythologists: for Apollodorus tells us, that certain writers placed it, not on the Libyan Atlas, but on the Atlas of the Hyperboreans; and he adds, that the serpent, like that of the Mosaical Paradise, possessed the faculty of uttering various articulate sounds.[1] With this accords the Olympian tradition, that Hercules-Ida brought the original olive-tree, which furnished the chaplet for the first victor at the games, from the northern country of the Hyperboreans. I need scarcely remark, that the olive branch of Ararat was the stock whence the Olympic olive-tree of Hercules was produced.

V. To this sacred northern hill, northern with respect to so large a portion of the ancient civilized world, there is more than one allusion in Scripture: and the language of inspiration is such, as to leave but little doubt, that Eden was the prototype of the Olympic synod or holy garden of the pagan hero-gods.

In the sublime epiniceon of Isaiah, the king of Babylon is described as boastingly saying in his heart, *I will ascend into heaven, I will exalt my throne above the stars of God; I will sit also upon the mount of the congregation in the sides of the north.*[2] The sentiments, here placed in the mouth of the arrogant tyrant, seem evidently to refer to that apotheosis of sovereign princes which prevailed so extensively among the Gentiles: and the specific idea, which is meant to be conveyed, I take to be this; that the Babylonian monarch, not content even with the impiety of an ordinary deification, claimed, in the pride of his high speculations, the loftiest seat of the holy northern mount, that hill of the congregation or synod of the demon-gods, whether known by the name of *Meru* or *Ida* or *Olympus* or *Atlas*. Such a supposition is rendered the more probable by the curious circumstance, that the summit of Meru is actually called by the Hindoos *the hill of the assembly*. In short, Isaiah appears to have adopted in his song of triumph the very phraseology of the Pauranics: for we are told, that he describes the fall of the king of Babylon almost in the same words, in which

The location of Eden according to Scripture

[1] Apoll. Bibl. lib. ii. c. 5. p. 117.   [2] Isaiah xiv. 13.

they celebrate the fall of the principal Daitya from the Hindoo Olympus.' What then are we ultimately to understand by this *lofty northern mountain*, to which the prophet so pointedly alludes? We may safely, I believe, answer, *the garden of Paradise :* which was situated (as we have seen) in the northern mountains of Ararat, often specifically called in Holy Writ *the north country ;* and which was the true original whence every pagan Olympus was copied.

Such an answer, in fact, is even literally furnished by another of the prophets. Ezekiel describes the pride of the king of Tyre much in the same manner as Isaiah does that of the Babylonian sovereign. Each of them proudly seats himself on the summit of the holy mountain; each elevates his throne above those of the stars of God; and each is contemptuously ejected from the synod of the assembled hero-deities. The two paintings, in short, prove, by their striking mutual resemblance, that they have been copied from the same original. Now Isaiah represents the mount of the congregation as being situated in the north, which, as I have shewn, was the precise geographical situation of Paradise: and Ezekiel explains how we are to understand such imagery, by unreservedly calling this holy mountain by the name of *Eden the garden of God*, and by alluding to the cherub or humano-taurine apparition whose character seems to have been assumed by the king of Tyre. Eden then, according to Ezekiel, was situated in a high mountainous country; for with him *the garden of God* and *the holy mountain of God* are plainly synonymous terms: and this holy mountain, according to Isaiah, is to be sought for in the north.'

Thus do we at once learn, what we are to understand by the Hyperborean mountainous garden of the fabled Hesperides; and find ourselves furnished with another argument to prove, that Paradise cannot have been situated in the *flat* and *southern* country below Babylon, because we are taught to look for it in a *mountainous* and *northern* region. It may not be improper to remark, so thoroughly exact and consistent with itself is Holy Scripture, that St. John, when describing the mystical new Jerusalem under imagery plainly borrowed from the garden of Eden, most accurately places it, agree-

---

' Asiat. Res. vol. vi. p. 489.   ' Ezek. xxviii. 12—17.

ably to the real situation of Paradise, not in a dead flat, but on the summit of a great and high mountain.[1] Such covert allusions as these all tend to establish the position, that the first abode of man coincided geographically with some part of the lofty northern region of Armenia.[2]

VI. Mr. Wilford observes, that the high range of the Paropomisean hills, by which name the mountains of the Indian Caucasus were sometimes designated, is called by Dionysius-Periegetes, Priscian, and Avienus, *Parnasus* and *Parnessus*. This latter appellation has often been deemed only a corruption of *Paropomisèus*, though there is little resemblance between the two words except in their common initial: but the researches into Hindoo literature, which have recently been prosecuted with so much success, prove that the two words are perfectly distinct, and that the name of *Parnasus* was very accurately applied to the range in question.

The mountains, of which it consists, and which (as we have seen) geographically coincide with Meru, are, in the sacred books of the Hindoos, generally called *Devanica;* because they are full of Devas or gods and of holy Rishis and Brahmens, who are emphatically denominated *the gods of the earth*. These hero-deities, as the whole fabulous history of Meru sufficiently testifies, were the members of the two primeval families antediluvian and postdiluvian: and they lived, according to the Puranas and agreeably to what might be expected at those two early periods, in bowers or huts; which received the name of *Parnasalas* or *Parnasas*, because they were constructed with the leafy branches of trees.

---

[1] Rev. xxi. xxii.

[2] As mount Ararat thus locally coincides with the garden of Eden, we shall perceive the strict accuracy of the Rabbinical tradition, that the olive-branch, which the returning dove brought to Noah, was plucked from the groves of Paradise. The Hebrew doctors account for its existence precisely according to the notions of the Hindoo mythologists. As the latter conteud, that the sacred white island of the Moon, which is the Paradisiacal abode of the ark-preserved Pitris, is incapable of decay; and that, with the summit of Cailasa or Meru, it always appears above the surface of each intervening deluge: so the former maintain, that the holy garden was borne above the tops of the highest hills, and that the waters of the flood were thus unable to reach it. The notion clearly originated from the geographical coincidence of Eden with Ararat, and from the circumstance of the buoyant Ark having rested upon the top of the holy mountain. See Bochart. Hieroz. par. ii. lib. i. c. 5. p. 28, 29.

The most celebrated of them was that of the famous Atri; who is certainly the same as Edris or Idris or Atlas, and whose worship was carried far into the west by the early colonists from Asia.   This ancient personage may clearly be identified with Buddha or Menu, considered both as Adam and as Noah: and accordingly the Puranas say, that one of his favourite places of abode was a lofty mountain near the sea-side in a sacred island of the west.   By that island and mountain we are to understand the peak of Ararat or Eden; which was surrounded by the ocean when it first emerged from the deluge, and which lies directly to the west of Hindostan: and of it both the Mauritanian mount Atlas, and the British mount Cader-Idris,[1] are evidently mere local transcripts.   Ararat then was the real Parnasa of Atri: but, agreeably to the prevailing humour of national appropriation, he had also an Indian Parnasa; which was situated on an insulated mountain, in the Puranas denominated *Meru*, and by the Greeks expressed *Merus*. The Hindoos suppose it to be a splinter from the larger Meru; and believe, that the gods occasionally reside upon it.   To this day it is called *Mer-Coh;* which denotes *the mountain of Mer* or *Meru:* and not far from it is the spot, where Alexander encamped near the celebrated city of Nusa, which extended all round the hill.   Here, according to the Puranas, was the Parnasa of Atri or Idris; and here was formerly shewn a cave, to which he used occasionally to retire.[2]   Here also, as the Greeks acknowledged, was born that far-famed Dionusus, the Deo-Naush of the Hindoos; who was exposed, during his mythological infancy, in an ark on the surface of the ocean.   What was meant by the birth of this diluvian god in the city of Nusa and in the region of Meru, need not be formally pointed out: all that I have occasion at present to intimate is, that he is the same character as Atri; and th atthe Greek Parnassus, like the Mauritanian Atlas and the British Cader-Idris, was a local Meru or a transcript of the Paradisiacal Ararat.

Every particular respecting the classical mountain demonstrates, that it

---

[1] *Cader-Idris* signifies *the chair of Idris:* and tradition still reports it to have been the observatory of the gigantic astronomer who bore that name, just as mount Atlas was deemed the observatory of the gigantic astronomer Atlas.

[2] Asiat. Res. vol. vi. p. 496, 497.

was what the Hindoos call *a Parnasa*. Here, as well as at the cognate oriental mount, the original temple was a humble bower of green branches. Here was specially worshipped the Sun and Dionusus, venerated indeed as two distinct persons, though allowed by the old mythologists to be really but one. Here also was a cave sacred to the Earth, or the arkite great mother; whom the Hindoos emphatically call *Devi* or *the goddess*, and who is said to have floated in the form of a ship on the waters of the deluge. And here, if not a city, there was at least a peak of the sacred mountain which bore the appellation of *Nusa*.

Such an opinion exactly tallies with the fabulous history of the Greek Parnassus. We have already been brought to the result, that, like Olympus and Ida, it was certainly a Meru; in other words, that it was a copy of Paradise combined with mount Ararat. Accordingly, a notion prevailed, that it was once tenanted by a mighty serpent; which possessed the power of speech, and which was wont to deliver oracular responses previous to the establishment of the Delphic oracle of Apollo.[1] The chief deity who presided there was likewise esteemed the god of knowledge; and he was said to have encountered and slain the serpent, which during his infancy sought the destruction both of him and of his mother. Yet was this legend completely intermingled with arkite allusions: for the serpent Python is feigned to have been produced after the deluge; and, considered as the origin of evil, he seems to have been a personification of the avenging flood itself. That such was his super-added character we may gather from his manifest identity with Typhon; who was esteemed by the Egyptians the same as the ocean, and who equally compelled Osiris to enter into an ark and Horus to take refuge in a floating island. But this tale is evidently the counterpart of the Greek fable, respecting the flight of Latona from the rage of Python while she was pregnant of Apollo, and her finding an asylum in the floating island of Delos.[2] Both traditions alike relate to the escape of Noah into the Ark which was symbolized by a floating island, when pursued, as it were, by the

[1] Hyg. Fab. 140.
[2] Hyg. Fab. 53. Ovid. Metam. lib. i. ver. 438. Herod. Hist. lib. ii. c. 156.

waters of the over-whelming deluge.   The same double character may be
observed in Dionusus, the other god worshipped in mount Parnassus; nor
need we wonder at it, for he was really the very same person as Apollo.   In
the Mysteries sometimes the form of a bull was ascribed to him, and sometimes that of an immense snake with the head and hair of a man:[1] and,
during the celebration of the Bacchanalia, baskets filled with fruit and containing serpents were borne in procession by virgins of noble families, while
the whole multitude joined in reiterated exclamations of the word *Evoë*, by
many supposed to be only a variation of the name of our first mother.[2]
Yet was this deity, as we have already seen, thought to have been exposed
in an ark on the surface of the ocean; and was universally allowed to be the
same as the Egyptian Osiris, who was similarly exposed in an ark, and who
again may be clearly identified with the Hindoo Iswara floating in the ship
Argha.

As the mythological genii of Parnassus are thus immediately connected
with the deluge, precisely in the same manner as the demon-gods of the
oriental Parnasa or Meru: so we have a literal tradition of the resting of
the Ark on the summit of that mountain, which similarly corresponds with
the literal tradition of its appulse on the top of Chaisaghar.   It was on Parnassus, that Deucalion and Pyrrha are feigned to have landed, when the retiring waters of the flood left the ship aground in which they had been preserved.   Here, in the celebrated Corycian cavern, the double symbol of the
World and the Ark, they venerated the Corycian nymphs, or (as some
mythologists say) the nymph Corycia.[3]   By this pretended nymph Corycia
(for the Greeks transformed every thing into nymphs and heroes),[4] we are to
understand, I have little doubt, the mystic Cor or sacred circle, which was
believed to crown the summit of mount Meru.   The nymph Corycia was
the same as the Ida-Vratta, or circle of Ida: for *Cor* and *Vratta* equally

---

[1] Jul. Firm. de error. prof. rel. p. 52.   Eurip. Bacch. ver. 1015.   Orph. Hymn. xxix.
Plut. Quæst. Græc. p. 299.   Orph. Fragm. apud Athenag. Apol. p. 72.

[2] Potter's Grec. Ant. vol. i. p. 383.

[3] Ovid. Metam. lib. i. ver. 320.   Pausan. Phoc. p. 619, 671.

[4] Thus they pretended, that Parnassus was so called after a hero Parnassus.

denote *a circle;* and the Hindoos, as much addicted to personification as the Greeks, similarly esteemed Ida or Ila a nymph or goddess. Corycia and Ila, in short, were alike that mystic circle; which at once represented the inclosure of the Ark and the circumference of the World.

With respect to Cader-Idris, I am not aware that any local tradition supposes the Ark to have grounded on the summit of that mountain: but the gigantic astronomer Idris, whose observatorial chair it is feigned to have been, is so palpably the same as the gigantic astronomer Atlas or Edris or Atri, that we may reasonably pronounce it a Celtic Parnasa or Meru or Ararat; and consequently we may attach to it the same mythological ideas, as those which belonged to its prototype in Armenia. It may be observed, that, as two peaks in the Indian Caucasus contest the honour of being the landing place of the Ark, so it is probable, that in former times a similar controversy may have been maintained respecting Cader-Idris and Snowdon. If this were ever the case, Snowdon has obtained a decided victory over its antagonist; for, at present, it appears to enjoy the exclusive privilege of being the Parnassus of Druidical theology. On its summit they, who were preserved from a deluge which is said to have occurred in the days of Seithinin the drunkard, took refuge: and, in exact accordance with the notions entertained by the Hindoos of their Meru, it was supposed to be peculiarly sacred to the higher powers or the Paradisiaco-diluvian patriarchs; whose ambrosial city Emrys plainly identifies itself with the sacred Brahmapur or Ilapur, which contained the Amrita tree of life and knowledge. The deluge of Seithenin is indeed, in the legends of the Druids, a local one, appropriated only to a part of Wales: but such likewise, in classical lore, was the flood of Deucalion. Each however was equally a transcript of that great event, which alike affected the whole world; and which was so frequently represented as being particular to this or that region, only because the most conspicuous hill of each newly settled country became the commemorative Meru or Ararat of the infant colony. In the present case, the drunkard Seithenin is certainly Noah the planter of the first vineyard, who was venerated by the Gentiles as the god of wine under the names of *Bacchus* and *Osiris:* for not only does this part of the character of Seithenin answer to the corresponding part of that of Noah.; but he has likewise been proved to be the same person as the mystic husband of the ship-goddess Ceridwen, the Argha or Parvati or Ceres or Isis of other pagan nations.[1]

[1] Davies's Mythol. of Brit. Druids. p. 242, 243. The name of *Seithenin* I take to be the same as *Seth*, which was an appellation of Typhon. The character of Typhon melts into that of Osiris, notwithstanding he appears as his decided enemy, agreeably to the material doctrine of the Hindoos, that water or the ocean is one of the forms of the great father. *Seth* was sometimes written *Siton* or *Seth-On*, which means *Seth the sun*. In this form, it was a title of Dagou or Cronus, as we learn from Sanchoniatho.

CHAPTER III.

As the Earth was esteemed an immense island with the holy mount rising aloft in the centre of it, so each smaller island was not unnaturally reckoned to be a mountain rising out of the sea. This being the case, all such islands were deemed symbols or representations of the larger mundane island: and the peak, which almost invariably rises in the middle of every small island, was considered in the light of a Meru or an Ararat. The Ark however, being esteemed a little World and having once floated on the surface of the deluge surrounded on all sides by water, was typified by exactly the same symbols as the larger World. Hence, as the Earth with its centrical mount was thought to be shadowed out by the ship Argha and its mast, so the Ark in return was symbolized by an island with its centrical mountain, which island was often supposed to have once floated erratically over the ocean.

There is reason to believe, that in the sacred lakes, which were used in the Mysteries as types of the deluge, artificial floating islands were frequently constructed. These appear to have been frames of timber, covered with earth and green turf, and supporting small shrines or temples either of the great father and mother or of the sacred triad which emanated from them and which blended itself with them. To an islet of such a description, which was shewn in the Egyptian lake Chemmis, Horus was believed to have fled from the rage of Typhon or the diluvian ocean : and to the fabled floating Delos Latona was thought, in a similar manner, to have escaped from the fury of Python, when she was pregnant with Apollo and Diana.

These remarks will lead us to a right understanding of other pagan legends ; in which, as is ever found to be the case, Paradise is inseparably united with mount Ararat.

How mount Ararat can be esteemed an island

I. The isles of the blessed, or the fortunate isles, were esteemed by the ancient mythologists the peculiar abode of illustrious heroes and legislators, who, during their life-time, had civilized or benefited mankind. What persons we are to understand by such heroes, is intimated to us very unequivocally by those who have written on the subject. We are told, that they were eminently that primeval race, which flourished during the period of the golden age. But the golden age, as we shall hereafter see, was equally the first age both of the antediluvian and of the postdiluvian world.[1] This being the case, those happy isles, where the hero-gods enjoy unutterable felicity, in the midst of shady groves watered by beautiful streams, and in a climate undisturbed by the perpetual vicissitudes of less favoured regions, must inevitably be the particular country which was occupied by our earliest progenitors. But that country was Paradise, viewed as coinciding with mount Ararat. Therefore the isles of the blessed must necessarily be the same.

1. Here however it may be asked, with what propriety mount Ararat can be esteemed an island? The answer to this question is not very difficult. As the waters of the deluge retired, the summit of the Paradisiacal mount emerged as an island from the great deep: and, after it had thus emerged, it received within the recesses of what had once been the sacred garden another island, even the floating island of the Ark. The seagirt top then of Ararat, and the Ark of the chief hero-god, are the isles of the blessed, when those isles are mentioned plurally.

---

[1] Vide infra book iii. c. 1.

2. Tzetzes, in elucidating a difficult passage of Lycophron, has furnished us with some very curious information respecting the present subject.

He begins with telling us, that, when his author speaks of *the isles of the blessed,* he must be understood as bestowing that appellation upon Thebes ; notwithstanding, as he observes, by the general consent of Hesiod, Homer, Euripides, Plutarch, Dion, Procopius, and others, those same isles are placed in the midst of the ocean. And then, after remarking that Britain and Thulè correspond with such a description, he proceeds to inform us, that, in his days, there was a wild superstition prevalent respecting the first of those islands, which described it as being tenanted by the souls of the dead : so completely had the old Celtic mythological tradition survived that literal knowledge of Britain, which the western Romans had acquired by their conquest of it.

A certain tribe, it seems, that lived on the sea-coast of Gaul, had been reduced to subjection by the invading Franks : yet the members of it were exempted from all taxation, by virtue of their somewhat unusual employment, which consisted in ferrying over the souls of the deceased to the neighbouring shores of Britain. The brethren of this Charonic society were accustomed to sleep, at proper intervals, in houses looking towards the west. Ere long, in the dead of night, they were roused by the sound of jarring doors, and were summoned by an audible voice to their appointed occupation. Obedient to the awful call, and unconsciously impelled by a fatal necessity, they rose from their beds, and proceeded without delay to the sea-shore. Here they found light skiffs, not their own ordinary boats, ready prepared for them. Into these they entered, apparently empty of men : but, though they could see nothing, they could readily perceive, that the vessels sustained other burdens besides themselves. Having thus embarked with their invisible companions, in a single moment of time they were wafted over to the British coast, though in their own ordinary ships such a voyage would occupy a whole day and night. When they reached the place of their destination, still they were unable to see any thing : but they could distinctly hear the voices of persons welcoming the arrival of their ghostly fellow-mariners, and hailing them both by their names, their families, and their recent professions or occupations. On reëmbarking, their vessels were sensibly lighter in consequence of their having landed the spiritual part of their crew: and, in another short moment of time, they found themselves conveyed back to the coast of Gaul. From this circumstance, adds Tzetzes, many were of opinion, that here we ought to place the islands of the blessed and the fabled voyage of the dead.[1]

We may evidently, I think, perceive, that the whole of this legend, like that of the Egyptian Charon and the Acherusian pool, has arisen from the celebration of the old Druidical Mysteries; which in substance were the very same as those of Greece, Egypt, Phenicia, and Hindostan. The voyage of the dead or of the departed patriarchs is in reality no other than the voyage of Noah in the Ark: for, in the theology of every ancient pagan nation, we invariably find, that the great father, who was believed to have been preserved during the period of an universal deluge, was either esteemed the god of obsequies, or was supposed to have descended into the infernal regions and afterwards to have returned from them, or was imagined to have died and to have been restored to life. Charon himself, the infernal ferryman, was the same person as Osiris: for the ship or ark of each is equally called *Baris* or *Theba*; each navigates it either upon the sacred Nile or upon a pool formed by the Nile; and each is equally a god of that Hades, of which the Nileotic Acherusia was deemed the venerable lake. He was the same also as the Hindoo Buddha or Menu-Satyavrata, who was preserved in an ark at the time of the deluge: for their attributes so perfectly correspond, that there can be no mistake respecting their identity of character. Buddha or Menu is said to have been constituted, after the flood, the god of obsequies: and, accordingly, his office is to waft the souls of the deceased in a mysterious ship over the holy river Ganges, considered like the Egyptian Nile as a stream of Patala or Hades. Thus closely are the Paradisiacal isles of the blessed connected with the history of the deluge: and thus may we again observe the prevalence of that ancient and (I believe) true opinion, that the garden of Eden coincided geographically with the mountainous region of Ararat.

But there is another remarkable part of the preceding commentary of Tzetzes, which must not be passed over without due notice. Lycophron, as

---

[1] Tzetz. in Lycoph. ver. 1200.

he rightly observes (for the whole context of the passage shews it), certainly speaks of Thebes and the islands of the blessed as being, in some manner or another, the same. Tzetzes makes the remark, plainly without understanding the drift of such singular phraseology: for he adds immediately after, that the real situation of those islands was in the great western ocean. The question then is, how Lycophron came to identify them with Thebes. The true state of the case, I have little doubt, was this. Both the Grecian and the Egyptian city, which bore the name of *Thebes*, was so called from *Theba;* which properly signifies *an ark*, and secondarily was made to denote *a cow* because a cow was a symbol of the Ark: hence Osiris is indifferently said to have been inclosed in an ark and in a wooden heifer. Theba was the same as Argha or Argo: for we are told, that the Argo was the ship of Osiris, as the Argha was that of Siva or Iswara. But Argha was a form of the goddess Parvati; and another of her forms, like the Egyptian Isis, was the mysterious Theba or cow. Now we have seen, that each sacred island was a symbol at once of the World and of the ship Argha, and that its centrical mountain alike represented Meru and the mast of the Argha. Hence we may readily understand, why Lycophron speaks of Thebes and the islands of the blessed as being the same. Each island, representing the World with the Paradisiacal Meru in the centre, was esteemed a Theba or Argha; because the Argha, though properly the ship of the deluge, was also a symbol of the Earth with the centrical Meru. Each island, in short, though the Paradisiacal abode of the patriarchs, was also a type of the Theba or Ark, which rested in the very country where the garden of Eden was originally planted. Lycophron, who appears to have used language which he understood as little as his commentator Tzetzes, says, that Thebes was the islands of the blessed: he ought, I apprehend, to have said, that all those islands were symbolical Thebæ or arks. They were mythologically of the very same description as the Vuicontha or floating Paradise of Vishnou, on which, as I have already mentioned, the god reclines during the intermediate period between two worlds, when every thing is laid under water except this navicular Elysium (doubtless the same as the ship Argha) and the towering peak of Cailasa or Meru or Ararat.

II. Such insular Edens were adopted into the system of the ancient

Druids no less than into that of other old mythologists, as may indeed be obviously collected from the preceding legend detailed by Tzetzes. They have now passed, such is the usual progress of theological fiction, into what the Welsh call *Mabinogion* or *fairy-tales*. One of these tales is given by Mr. Davies; and every part of it seems to me to bespeak its origin.

In the mountains near Brecknock there is a small lake; near which, on a certain day in the year, a door in the rock was in ancient times regularly found open. Those, who had the resolution and curiosity to enter, were conducted by a secret passage, which terminated in a small island in the centre of the lake. Here the visitors were surprized with the prospect of a most enchanting garden, stored with the choicest fruits and flowers, and inhabited by *the fair family;* which was composed of a kind of fairies, whose beauty could be equalled only by the courtesy and affability which they exhibited to such as pleased them. They gathered fruit and flowers for each of their guests, entertained them with the most exquisite music, disclosed to them many events of futurity, and invited them to stay as long as they should find their situation agreeable. But the island was sacred, and nothing of its produce must be carried away. The whole of this scene was invisible to those, who stood without the margin of the lake. Only an indistinct mass was seen in the middle: and it was observed, that no bird would fly over the water, and that a soft strain of music breathed at times with rapturous sweetness in the breeze of the mountain. It happened on one of these annual visits, that a sacrilegious wretch, when he was about to leave the garden, concealed a flower with which he had been presented: but the theft boded him no good. As soon as he had touched unhallowed ground, the flower vanished, and he lost his senses. Of this injury the fair family took no notice at the time: they dismissed their guests with their accustomed courtesy; and the door was closed as usual. But their resentment ran high: for, though (as it is devoutly believed) they and their garden undoubtedly occupy the same spot to the present day, though the birds still keep at a respectful distance from the lake, and though some broken strains of music are still occasionally heard; yet the door which led to the island has never reappeared, and from the date of this sacrilegious act the Cymry have been unfortunate. It is added, that some time afterwards an adventurous person attempted to draw off the water in order to discover its contents, when suddenly a terrific form arose from the midst of the lake, and commanded him to desist unless he wished to see the whole country inundated.[1]

From this legend Mr. Davies rightly infers, that, in times of Druidical Paganism, the lake was furnished with a floating raft, which, like the Egyptian Chemmis, represented the Ark; while the sacred pool, which contained it, shadowed out the deluge. Hence, agreeably to the various traditions which occur in different parts of the world respecting the flood having proceeded from a lake, we find attached to the present fable a threat made by the genius of the place that he would drown the adjacent country: That by an artificial floating island was meant the Ark, he proves from an ancient mythological poem of Taliesin, which throughout treats of the deluge and of the wonderful escape of the far-famed eight in a mysterious vessel. This vessel is denominated *a Caer* or *a fenced inclosure;* which was likewise a name of Stonehenge, because it represented the holy circle of Sidi or Ila, that surmounted Meru and symbolized at once the Ark and the World : yet the Caer, though it is spoken of as the ship in which the eight sailed over the waters of the flood, is nevertheless described as an island. The obvious conclusion therefore is, that a floating island typified the Ark.

Now such a conclusion perfectly accords with the mythological notions, which prevailed in every part of the world, but which are specified with peculiar accuracy by the divines of Hindostan. The Earth and the ship Argha, as I have repeatedly had occasion to observe, are constantly represented by symbols common to both. That ship is deemed a type of the Earth ; the Earth again is supposed to resemble a ship ; and each is considered in the light of an island, surrounded by, and floating on the bosom of, the ocean. The fairy island therefore of the tale now before us, when we recollect the nature of the old Druidical superstition, may reasonably be conjectured to have been a representation of the Ark. This supposition is confirmed by the manner in which the island is furnished. Precisely as the

[1] Davies's Mythol. of Brit. Druids. p. 155, 156, 157.

sacrificial vessels of the Hindoos, which are called *Arghas* from their being avowed representations of the ship Argha, are always filled with fruits and flowers; so the fairy island is described as abounding in the choicest specimens of those productions of nature.

On the whole, I think it evident, that the island in question was a sacred Argha or Theba. The music, which proceeded from it, related to those songs of the arkite priestesses; which, according to Taliesin, were chaunted from the Caers or sanctuaries that floated on the bosoms of the consecrated lakes. The door in the rock, and the dark winding passage, are both well-known appendages to the due celebration of the Mysteries. Through apertures of this description the aspirant was wont to be conducted: and at length, when his initiation was completed, he emerged, like the visitors of the fairy island, from gloom and darkness into an amazing light and into all the fabled beauties of Elysium. Lastly, the sacrilegious conduct of one of the guests, the anger of the fairies, the disappearance of the island, and the subsequent misfortunes of Wales all of which are attributed to this rash profanation, seem pretty evidently to relate to the suppression of the old arkite idolatry; to which the enraged priests both of Britain and throughout the Roman empire never failed to ascribe every calamity, with which their respective countries were visited after the establishment of Christianity upon the ruins of Paganism.

Thus far I understand our fairy-tale exactly in the same manner as Mr. Davies: and my comment upon it, though with some additions, is in substance the same as his. With him I believe the lake to have been one of the sacred commemorative lakes of the Druids, and the island to have been a floating raft constructed as a representation of the Ark: but I think his hypothesis defective, because it only explains the fable partially. From the description which is given of the island, we may, I think, very clearly collect, that it was not intended to exhibit the Ark *solely*. It is said to have displayed the appearance of a beautiful garden, well stocked with trees and fruits and flowers; and to have been inhabited by a celestial race, who there enjoyed a state of happiness superior to what falls to the lot of mere mortality. Hence I am persuaded, that the island, which has given foundation to this curious fairy-tale, was a raft covered over with earth and green turf, and of sufficient bulk to be able, like the Egyptiam Chemmis, to sustain trees or at least shrubs of a moderate size.' It was, in short, a copy of one of those islands of the blessed, which appear, from the language employed by Lycophron, to have been called *Theba* or *Arghas*: and I believe it, equally with Chemmis and various other artificial floating islands of a similar description, to have been what the Hindoos would style a *Vaicontha* or *floating Paradise of Vishnou*; to have been, in other words, a mingled representation of Paradise and the Ark; mingled, because the Ark rested in the same lofty region which once contained the garden of Eden.

III. The Paradisiacal islands of the blessed, in which dwell the spirits of departed heroes and patriarchs, are evidently the same as the fabled Elysium of classical antiquity, which is equally described as the abode of those illustrious dead who were the parents and benefactors of mankind. Accordingly, while some writers place it in the centre of the earth, others represent it as geographically coinciding with those western fortunate islands which we have last considered.' To this second opinion Virgil, though he makes his hero descend to Elysium through a sacred cave near the lake Avernus in Italy, as Homer similarly conducts Ulysses through a cavern in the land of the Cimmerii,' seems to me very plainly to allude in a part of the phraseology

---

' Herod. lib. ii. c. 156.

* Bocat. de geneal. deor. lib. i. c. 14. p. 19. Pindar. Olymp. Od. ii.

³ Bochart supposes Homer to have placed the Elysian fields in Spain near the pillars of Hercules, but Lycophron considers him as fixing them to Italy in the same manner as Virgil does. Bochart. Canaan. lib. i. c. 34. p. 600, 605. Lycoph. Cassan. ver. 681—711. Whatever may have been the idea of Homer, each sacred cavern, where the Mysteries were celebrated, was esteemed a descent into Hades: and, since the old Cimmerii or Cymry or Celts appear to have occupied all the west of Europe previous to the arrival of the victorious Goths or Chasas or Scythians; the poet's land of the Cimmerii may be placed either in Spain, or Italy, or Gaul, or Britain, or Ireland. I am much inclined myself to think, that the country, which he really had in his eye, was one of those sacred islands of the west, which were the ancient abode of the Cymry. The lake in Brecknockshire, where is laid the scene of the Mabinogion which I recently considered, was plainly a Celtic Avernus; for exactly the same notion was prevalent both in Wales and in Italy, that no bird could fly over the waters of the consecrated pool: and St. Patric's purgatory in a small island in one of the Irish lakes, which the Romanists have adopted into the mythology of their semi-pagan superstition, has evidently been no other than a Celtic grotto, like that of Trophonius, through which there

which he employs: for he speaks of the seats of the blessed under the name of *the fortunate groves,* in evident reference to what were sometimes called *the fortunate islands.*[1]

Such a discrepancy in the local arrangement of Elysium is more apparent, than real: for the two opinions, though seemingly different, are (if I may so speak) mythologically or mystically the very same. The islands of the blessed, as I have already shewn, were esteemed Thebœ or Arghas: and, from that interchange of ideas which I have so frequently had occasion to notice, they represented at once the greater World with the Paradisiacal Meru rising in its centre, and the smaller World or Ark with Siva supplying the place of the mast. So again, the Earth and the Ark being each esteemed a world, and each therefore constantly being typified by symbols common to both, the central cavity of the one was mystically blended with the gloomy interior of the other: and the same geographical coincidence of Paradise and mount Ararat, which led the ancient mythologists to place the sacred garden in a floating island or Theba, led them also to place it in their subterraneous Hades. One idea was designed to be conveyed by both arrangements: for, as the floating or insular Paradise meant also the Ark, so the central cavity of Hades denoted likewise the dark and hollow interior of the diluvian ship.

This conclusion would inevitably follow from that curious intercommunion of symbols, by which the Earth and the Ark, each considered as a World, were indifferently represented: because, since they were both equally typified by the egg, the lotos, the floating island, the gloomy cavern, and the sacred ship Argha or Theba; the interior of the Ark must have been viewed

---

was a fabled descent into hell. Much stress has been laid upon the circumstance of Ulysses having reached the land of the Cimmerii from the territories of Circè in a single day, as if this incident could fix the geography of his infernal regions. I can build very little upon it, since the gale is said to have been *preternaturally supplied by magic;* which implies, that it was not the voyage of an ordinary day, even supposing we could determine the situation of Circè's country. The voyage is clearly represented as being *miraculously rapid:* and there seems to me to be a strong resemblance between it, and the voyages of those Celtic ferrymen of the dead from Gaul to Britain which are described as being accomplished in a single moment.

[1] Virg. Æneid. lib. vi. ver. 639.

as the central cavity of the Earth, and the central cavity of the Earth must conversely have been viewed as the interior of the Ark. But we are not merely brought to such a conclusion in the way of inference: we have it explicitly set forth to us in a manner which can hardly be mistaken. Throughout the whole of pagan mythology, the great father, who is preserved in an ark at the period of the deluge, is invariably either represented as a god of the infernal regions, or is said to have descended into them and afterwards to have emerged again to the light of open day. This mystic descent and return, or death and revival, or disappearance and reappearance, as the same circumstance was variously and indifferently denominated, constituted the most prominent feature in the celebration of the ancient Mysteries: but, if we inquire into the import of it, we shall find that it really means nothing else than the in-closure of the great father within the gloomy interior of a floating ark and his subsequent liberation from the darkness of his temporary prison. Accordingly we may observe, that the Egyptian Osiris is said to have been *slain* by Typhon or the Ocean, at the time when he was shut up in an ark by that fabled monster and set afloat on the waters of the Nile; and afterwards to have been restored to life, when he was taken out of the ark. We may also observe, that the ark, in which his supposed dead body sailed on the surface of that sacred river which the Egyptians denominated *the Ocean* from its being deemed a symbol of the deluge, was, in exact conformity with the mystic death of the god, styled his *coffin*. And we may further observe, that, as this deity is said to have been slain, to have been inclosed in a floating ark or coffin, and to have been restored to life: so he is likewise said to have descended into the infernal regions or the realms of death and darkness, and to have again returned from them to the light of heaven; to have disappeared for a season from the eyes of men, and afterwards to have reappeared. Putting these different things together, I think it sufficiently evident, that they all represent one and the same event in the history of Osiris: consequently, if the inclosure of his dead body within a floating ark or coffin mean the same as his descent into Hades or the invisible world, and his restoration to life when he quitted that floating ark mean the same as his return from Hades or his reappearance after his mystic aphanism; the interior of the ark must inevitably have been identified in the ancient Orgies with the infernal regions, which the old mythologists placed in the interior of the Earth.

Hence we may readily perceive the cause, why Elysium or Paradise was sometimes placed in those western isles of the blessed which were considered as Thebæ or arks, and sometimes plunged down to the central cavity of the Earth which was deemed the peculiar region of Hades. Different as the two situations are *ostensibly*, they prove, as I intimated above, to be *really* the same : for in both we find Paradise and the Ark inseparably united together, agreeably to that true matter of fact, the geographical coincidence of mount Ararat and the primeval garden of Eden.

IV. So many writers have pointed out the close resemblance between the pagan Elysium and the scriptural Paradise, thence rightly inferring that the one was but a transcript of the other, that it is superfluous to enter into a laborious comparison of them. The notions, which the Gentiles entertained of their Elysium, are familiar to every classical reader : and, when we consider both the nature and the most probable origin of that idolatry with which the posterity of Noah were so generally infected, we can scarcely, as it appears to me, entertain a doubt, that the garden of Eden was the prototype of those happy shades and blissful retreats which were thought to be occupied by the illustrious spirits of the progenitors and benefactors of mankind. I know not however, that any author has viewed the pagan Elysium or Paradise in the close relation, which it bears to the history of the deluge. In this light then I shall now proceed to consider it ; such a connection affording an additional proof of the widely prevalent belief, that the sacred garden was planted, and that the Ark rested, in one and the same tract of country.

1. I have already shewn, that, whether Elysium was placed in the western isles of the blessed, or concealed within the central cavity of the Earth, the reigning idea was still the same. In each case, there was a reference to the Ark : and Paradise was thus in a manner blended with the ship of Noah, because the place of the Ark's appulse coincided geographically with the scite of man's primitive abode in his state of innocence. This circumstance will explain much of the machinery of the classical Inferum : and, in discussing such a topic, let Virgil, who certainly appears to have written

The rivers of Hades are the rivers of Paradise

the sixth book of his Eneid in direct reference to the ancient Orgies, act as our principal mystagogue.

We have seen, in the way of a necessary conclusion from the legend of Osiris, that the central cavity of the Earth, where the pagan Hades was wont to be placed, mythologically identifies itself with the gloomy interior of the Ark ; and *that* on a singular principle of intermixture, which pervades the whole system of Gentilism. Hence, since Paradise was the abode of man during the short period of his pristine happiness, since the Ark was immediately connected with a most signal punishment of his iniquities, and since that vessel grounded in the region which once contained the garden ; the seat of bliss, and the seat of woe, were fixed by the old mythologists to the same place, severed from each other only by a narrow interval, and subjected to the controul of one infernal sovereign. This circumstance caused the rivers of Paradise to become also the rivers of Tartarus : for the chief stream of Eden, whether it were locally deemed the Nile, or the Ganges, or the Styx, was also esteemed a symbol of the ocean which punitively overwhelmed the impious inhabitants of the antediluvian world, and was thence considered as a river of hell or death. Accordingly, as the rivers of Paradise were four in number, and as the four seem to have equally proceeded from a common lake or reservoir : so the rivers of Hades were also four in number, and they are usually associated with a lake or pool which is sometimes produced by and sometimes identified with the principal infernal stream. This opinion is not a mere licentious conjecture: it is confirmed by the express declarations of the ancient mythologists themselves. Thus the Puranas teach us, that the Ganges is the chief river of Meru or Paradise, where also the Ark is supposed to have grounded : but we are likewise told, that it is a river of Patala or Inferum ; and that the Menu, who was preserved in a ship at the period of the deluge, was constituted the god of obsequies or the deity of the infernal regions. Thus also an ancient notion prevailed, that the Nile was a Paradisiacal stream : yet, in the theology of Egypt, it was also made a river of hell, and was associated in that capacity with the Acherusian pool.

2. On this account it is, that, in the Hades of the pagans, we find a ship set afloat on the river or lake of hatred ; and that the office, assigned to its

[margin note:] The ship of Hades is the ship of Osiris or the Ark of Noah

mariner, is that of ferrying over the souls of the deceased. The general coherence of the whole system will obviously lead us to conclude, that this mariner and this ship are Noah and the Ark: but we shall find ourselves brought to the opinion in a much more express manner than that of inference and deduction. The Charon of Greek mythology was borrowed from Egypt: and the local Styx of Arcadia was the no less local Acherusian pool formed by the superfluous waters of the Nile. What then are we to understand by the character of the Egyptian Charon? Diodorus informs us, that the vessel, in which he plied on the Nileotic lake, was no other than the celebrated Baris.[1] But the Baris was the ship of Osiris, the same as the ship Argo or Theba; for the Argo is declared to be the ship of Osiris, as the Argha is similarly said to be the ship of the diluvian Iswara: and Osiris, the mariner of the Argo or Baris, is represented as an infernal god, and is feigned to have descended into the nether world.[2] Osiris therefore is the same as Charon, whether floating on the Styx, or sailing over the Acherusian pool: for each is the navigator of the same vessel, each is equally a deity of Hades, and each is described as floating on the surface of the Nile, by the Egyptians at once styled and deemed a type of the Ocean. With this the speculations of the Hindoo theologists will be found exactly to accord. Having made the Ganges a river of Patala, and the chief divinity of the Ark an infernal god, they set him afloat on the waters of that mystic stream as it winds its darkling way through their Hades, and ascribe to him the office of ferryman of the dead. Now there is so perfect a resemblance between the mythological characters of the Greek Charon, the Egyptian Charon, and the Hindoo Menu under the name of *Buddha* or *Salivahana;* and again between those of the classical Styx, the Egyptian Nile forming the Acherusian lake, and the Indian Ganges: that it is impossible not to conclude that they must have had a common origin. But, the Grecian Charon being thus evidently the same as the Egyptian Charon, the Egyptian Charon being the same as Osiris, Osiris being the same as the Argonaut Iswara, and Iswara being the same (for his history proves it) as the infernal Menu who is literally said to have been preserved in an ark

---

[1] Diod. Bibl. lib. i. p. 82, 83.

[2] Plut. de Isid. p. 359.

at the time of the deluge : it will inevitably follow, that the pagan ferry-man of the dead, by whatever name he may be designated and in whatever mythology he may appear, is really no other than the patriarch Noah. It will likewise follow, that the vessel which he navigates, sometimes styled *Baris*, sometimes *Argo*, sometimes *Theba*, and sometimes *Argha*, must certainly be the Ark ; and that the water, on which he sails, whether deno-minated *Styx* or *Nile* or *Ganges*, must equally represent the deluge, that water of indignant hatred by which the race of wicked antediluvians was swept away from the surface of the earth.

Agreeably to this last conclusion, and in perfect harmony with the my-thological attributes of the Egyptian Nile, we find the fabled bark, which conveyed the souls of the dead, sometimes set afloat on the ocean itself. Thus, in the old Druidical Mysteries, as we may collect from the curious legend which I have already recited from Tzetzes, the hierophants, who were ever deemed the immediate representatives of the gods that they worshipped, pretended that they ferried the ghosts of the deceased from the shore of Gaul to that of Britain.[1] Here that arm of the sea, which separates two mighty modern rivals, occupies the precise place of the Styx, the Nile, and the Ganges ; and thus serves to explain, in what light we are to understand the mystical character of each of those celebrated streams.   The Styx in short, though in one point of view one of the four rivers of Paradise, is in another point that vengeful deluge, which sustained indeed the Ark, but which plunged an impious race into the central abyss of Tartarus.   On this account, the Styx was mythologically said to be the daughter of the Ocean, because the flood proceeded out of the great deep.   On this ac-count also, the pagans had a fable, that the Styx with all her numerous streams assisted Jupiter in his war with the rebellious Titans ; who, when subdued, were cast down to Tartarus and overwhelmed in the central abyss of the earth: though eight of those Titans are specially distinguished from their brethren ; are identified with the diluvian Cabiri ; and are considered as those eight great gods, who were represented sailing together in a ship on

---

[1] It is not unworthy of observation, that the ferryman of the dead was by the ancient Bri-tons styled *Garan hir* which is evidently the same word as *Charon*.   Davies's Mythol. p. 392.

the surface of the ocean. On this same account likewise, they connected the waters of Styx with Iris or the rainbow; assigning to this last goddess a sister, whom they called *Arca*, and whom I believe to have been no other than the ship Argo or Argha. And on this account, in allusion to the post-diluvian oath of God, they had a remarkable legend, that Jupiter swore by the waters of Styx, either going to the war of the Titans, or (as some writers more properly say) returning from it; and that ever after, in memory of the signal service rendered him by Styx, he decreed such an adjuration to be peculiarly sacred and inviolable.[1]

Charon, the three judges, Cerberus, the lake Avernus, all connected with the Mysteries

3. In strict conformity with the character of Charon as the mariner of the ship Argo or Baris, Servius tells us, that he was the same as Cronus or Saturn, who was venerated under the appellation of *Time* both by Hindoos, Persians, and Greeks, and whose whole history proves him to have been the scriptural Noah viewed as a reappearance of the scriptural Adam.[2]

Being thus identified with Cronus, he must also be identified with the Egyptian Anubis, whose character again, like that of Charon, melts into that of Osiris: for Plutarch informs us, that some mythologists deemed Cronus the same as Anubis, considering him in the light of an hermaphroditic being, who both begot and produced all things.[1]

The canine deity Anubis is nearly allied to the infernal three-headed dog Cerberus: who was himself a symbol of the Trimurti or great triple divinity of the Gentiles. Hence, as the Hindoos believe their triad, when viewed astronomically, to represent the Sun in the west, in the east, and in the zenith; so we learn from Porphyry, that Cerberus was described with three heads, in reference to the rising, the meridian altitude, and the setting, of the Sun.[4] Cerberus therefore was an hieroglyphic of the Trimurti; which astronomically was venerated as the Sun, but which humanly represented the great father multiplying himself into his triple offspring. Accordingly

---

[1] Apollod. Bibl. lib. i. c. 2. Schol. in Hesiod. Theog. ver. 776. Lycoph. Cassand. ver. 706. Ptol. Heph. Nov. Hist. lib. vi. p. 331. Schol. in Arat. Phænom. p. 52. Hyg. Poet. Astron. lib. ii. c. 39. Hesiod. Theog. ver. 729. Orph. Hymn. xxxvi.

[2] Serv. in Æneid. lib. vi. Bocat. de geneal. deor. lib. i. c. 33.

[3] Plut. de Isid. p. 368.

[4] Asiat. Res. vol. iii. p. 144. vol. v. p. 254. Porph. apud Euseb. Præp. Evan. lib. iii.

we find, that Cerberus was in reality the same as Pluto, for each is indifferently denominated *Orcus*.[1] But Pluto was allowed to be no other than Osiris or Serapis.[1] He was the same, consequently, as the mariner Charon, or the great diluvian father: whence the dog Cerberus was no less an attendant upon the Egyptian Serapis, than upon the classical Pluto.[3] Some representation of this dog appears to have been introduced into the Mysteries: for Pletho speaks of certain canine phantoms, rising from the bowels of the earth, and exhibiting themselves to the initiated.[4]

As Pluto then was the diluvian patriarch; so both his consort Proserpine and her fabled mother Ceres were the same as the ship Argha, which was equally a form of Isis, Parvati, and Ceridwen: for all the goddesses of Paganism melt at last into the single character of the great mother; and this great mother was the Earth and the Ark throughout represented by common symbols.

If we proceed yet further in our inquiries, we shall find the Trimurti again appearing as the three judges of hell. Of these the most celebrated was Minos: but Minos was, I think, indisputably the very same person as the Indian Menu, the Egyptian Menes or Menuis, and the Gothic Mannus; each of whom was the patriarch Noah, not indeed simply, but Noah considered as a reappearance of Adam.

With the whole of the mixed scenery of Hades, the entrance, which Virgil ascribes to it, exactly corresponds. He represents the place of descent as being in the neighbourhood of the Italian lake Avernus, respecting which it was fabled, that no bird could fly over its surface. To this sacred pool he brings his hero: and, from a tree, which grew near its banks in the midst of a thick grove, Enèas is described as plucking a wonderful branch, the token of amity and propitiation, having been conducted to it by two doves, the peculiar birds of his oceanic mother Venus.

The lake Avernus was clearly one of those consecrated lakes, which in the celebration of the Mysteries shadowed out the deluge, not without a final reference to the Paradisiacal lake whence issued the four holy rivers.

---

[1] Sil. Ital. lib. xiii. ver. 845.

[1] Plut. de Isid. p. 361, 362.

[1] Macrob. Saturn. lib. i. c. 20.

[4] Pleth. Schol. in Orac. Magic. Zoroast. p. 131.

We may observe, that precisely the same notion of the impossibility of a bird's flying over its surface prevailed respecting the Welsh lake in Brecknockshire, where the scene of the insular fairy Paradise is laid; and, I believe, for precisely the same reason. There was an ancient idea, that the waters of the deluge acquired a highly poisonous quality from their having been employed to wash away the manifold corruptions of a guilty world. With this idea was associated the long-preserved story of Noah sending birds out of the Ark; which were unable to fly over the widely extended ocean, and which therefore could find no rest for the soles of their feet. The two conjointly produced the fable of the lake Avernus: and, agreeably to the perpetually mixed allusion both to Paradise and mount Ararat, we find on its banks a grove with a central tree, from which a mysterious branch is plucked by doves, and which (if I mistake not) was designed at once to represent the tree of knowledge in the garden of Eden and the olive which furnished the branch that was conveyed to Noah. Mysteries of precisely the same nature and import, as we may abundantly collect from what has been handed down to us of pagan mythology, were celebrated on the margin both of the Italian and the British lake. In those Mysteries the aspirant was conducted through the gloom and darkness of an infernal cavern to the light and joy of an Elysium or Paradise. The remembrance of Eden was still retained in the midst of Orgies, which chiefly related to the entrance into the Ark and the subsequent liberation from its dark inclosure: for, as the entrance into it was considered as a descent into Tartarus, so the liberation from it was deemed a passage into Elysium.[1]

V. With the view, which I here exhibit of the notions that formed the groundwork of the classical Hades, the sentiments entertained by the Hindoos respecting their goddess Parvati will be found exactly to correspond.

Parvati, or the great mother, is considered as the Earth and even as Universal Nature: yet she is said to be the same as the female Cali or the goddess Time, in the days of whose consort the general deluge took place; to have been born on the summit of that mountain, where the ark of Satyavrata is thought to have rested; and to have herself assumed the form

[1] Vide infra book v. c. 6. § viii. 1, 2.

of a ship at the period of the flood, and afterwards that of a dove when the waters abated. So far therefore she appears in the double character of the Earth and the Ark, each of which was accounted a World, and each represented by the same symbols. But there is yet another light in which she is exhibited: she is also described as an infernal goddess, the consort of Yama or the Indian Pluto; and, as such she bears the name of *Patala*, which is likewise the name of Hell: while conversely, Hell is sometimes denominated *Bhuvana* or *Bhavani*, which is a title of Parvati.

Thus it appears, that Parvati is at once the Earth, the Ark, and the Infernal Regions or the Female Genius of the Infernal Regions: and this mixed character both confirms the hypothesis which I have here advanced, and is itself explained by it. The same goddess, who floats as a ship on the surface of the deluge, is nevertheless a personification of Hades, which was believed to be situated in the centre of the Earth: and she is likewise the Earth itself, the hollow interior of which was supposed to contain the fabulous Hades. Hence it will follow, that, the characters of the Ark and the Earth being inseparably blended together in the person of one goddess, what the interior of the one was deemed, the interior of the other was also deemed. But Hades was placed in the central cavity of the Earth. Therefore Hades was likewise placed in the hollow interior of the Ark. Hence the entrance into the Ark was considered as a descent into hell, and the Ark itself was viewed in the light of a coffin. Hence also the great father was indifferently said to have been shut up in a floating ark, to have died, to have vanished, and to have descended into Hades. This varied phraseology, which necessarily arose from the singular speculations of the pagan hierophants, was employed to denote one and the same circumstance: and, if that circumstance were not already expressed with sufficient clearness, the infernal consort, whom the Hindoos assign to Parvati in her character of Patala, might be adduced as indisputably determining it. Yama is allowed to be no more than a form or modification both of Brahma, Vishnou, and Siva: and he is likewise the same as Menu, in his character of Dhermarajah or king of justice, and of Sradda-deva or god of obsequies. The consort therefore of Parvati or Patala is that primeval character, who was preserved in an Ark at the time of the deluge, and who was considered as a reappearance of a yet more ancient personage.[1]

Parvati, as Patala, is evidently the same as the infernal Venus, or Isis, or Diana, or Ceres, or Proserpine; for all these goddesses were but one mythological being. Accordingly, if we examine their fabulous histories, we shall find each of them connected either with a ship, or with a dove, or with both; precisely as the ship and the dove were two forms of Parvati.

VI. Since Parvati is the same as Ila, whose mystic circle at once represented the World and the Ark, and whose consort bore the name of *Isa* or *Esa* no less than that of *Menu* or *Siva*, we may probably ascertain from the varied legend of this goddess the real etymology of the word *Elysium*.

When I consider the close affinity, in many instances even the verbal affinity, of the superstitions of Greece, Egypt, and Hindostan, I am much inclined to believe, that Elysium, or the arkite Paradise, was so called, as being the Ila of the god Esa, contractedly expressed *Il-Esa* or *El-Isa*.

To the same origin, and for the same reason, I trace the Gothic appellation of Inferum. That the Goths or Scythians migrated from the vicinity of the Indian Caucasus and brought with them into Europe the religion of their fathers, may be established both by the evidence of history, and by their curious theological system as it is exhibited in the Edda. Now the Inferum of the Goths bears so close a resemblance to that of the Greeks and Romans, which I have been last considering, that their common origination cannot, as it appears to me, be reasonably doubted of. But the Goths called their Inferum *Hela*, whence is plainly derived the English word *Hell:* and their brethren of Cashgar have ever had a ship-goddess of Hades or Patala, whom they denominate *Ila*, pronouncing the title *Ela* or with the aspirate *Hela*. Such being the case, we need hardly scruple to identify the Gothic *Hela*, and the Hindoo or Hindoo-Scythic *Ila*. It may be observed, that, although in our modern usage of the word *Hell*, we have restricted the

---

[1] Moor's Hind. Panth. p. 112, 148, 151, 392, 305, 405. Asiat. Res. vol. i. p. 252. vol. ix. p. 281.

term altogether to Tartarus or the place of punishment, it was formerly of by no means so limited a signification. The sense, which it conveyed, and which it still conveys in the Creed, is that of the invisible world of departed spirits, whether good or bad. As such, it nearly corresponds with the Hades of Paganism, which was divided into Elysium or Paradise, and Tartarus or Gehenna.

CHAPTER IV.

Respecting the connection of Paradise and the Ark with the symbolical Moon.

It may be remembered, that the great river of Meru, which afterwards branches out into four streams towards the four quarters of the heavens, is said to pass through the circle of the Moon.[1] What idea was meant to be conveyed by this fiction, is not at first sight perfectly clear: yet we must not too hastily ascribe it to the mere unrestrained licentiousness of a wildly extravagant imagination. Would we learn the real purport of the fable, we must inquire into the notions which the old mythologists entertained respecting the Moon; notions, which originated from the astronomical reveries that so largely tinctured their curiously systematic superstition.

I. The Hindoos, as we have seen, place the spirits of the departed Pitris or patriarchs in the sacred isles of the west: and some of the classical mythologists, in a similar manner, describe their Elysium as being situated in the fortunate islands or the islands of the blessed, surrounded by the waters of the great Atlantic ocean. These islands, as we have likewise seen, were esteemed Thebæ or Arghas or Arks: and, in strict consonance with the

---

[1] See above book ii. c. 2. § I. 1.

mixed principles of gentile theology, they jointly represented Paradise and the Ark, because the Ark rested on mount Ararat which geographically coincided with the primeval scite of Paradise. The same notions, as we have further pointed out, prevailed in the ancient superstition of the Celts : and their perfect correspondence with those of Hindoo and classical mythology clearly proves, that they are to be traced to a common source. Now the Hindoos not only place the souls of the patriarchs in the sacred western islands, but they also teach that the Moon is their residence.[1] And again, they not only describe Siva as dwelling in their Paradise on the summit of Meru, but they likewise feign that the Moon is his peculiar abode.[2] Thus it is evident, that, in their theology, Paradise is placed, with mystical indifference, on the top of Meru, in the sacred isles of the west, and in the circle of the Moon. Just the same speculations prevailed in other pagan countries. Lucian tells us, that some placed Elysium in the Moon.[3] Psellus, commenting on the old Chaldèan oracles, teaches us, that the abode of souls after death was a region above the Moon resplendent with marvellous light, while all beneath that planet is gloom and darkness.[4] And Macrobius describes it as being an essential part of the mysticizing philosophy of the Platonists, to consider the Moon, as the confines of life and death, and as the abode of human souls : and he adds, that, according to the doctrine of the Metempsychosis (which we have already seen to be most closely connected with the pagan theory of a succession of similar worlds[5]), those souls passed from the Moon to the Earth when they were born in fleshly bodies, and returned from the Earth to the Moon when they were delivered from their carnal prisons.[6] Much the same fantastic system is exhibited by Porphyry : for he tells us, that the Moon was to be esteemed the president of generation, because the souls of men were born from it; and that there was a constant migration of those souls, ascending and descending, through the two astronomical gates.[7]

[1] Asiat. Res. vol. vii. p. 267. Moor's Hind. Panth. p. 93.

[2] Moor's Hind. Panth. p. 39.   [3] Lucian. Oper. vol. ii. p. 483.

[4] Psell. Schol. in Orac. Chald. p. 52—55.

[5] Vide supra, book i. c. 1. § I. 6. c. 2. § I.

[6] Macrob. in somn. Scip. lib. i. c. 11.   [7] Porph. de ant. nymph. p. 261—265.

From the pagans, through the medium of some of the early gentilizing heresies, a similar opinion was strangely adopted into the Christian church: and Paradise, wholly removed from the grosser atmosphere of the Earth, was transferred to the purer orb of the Moon.[1] This notion prevailed among various writers of the Romish school; and has aptly served as a foundation for sundry marvellous legends. Thus we have been told (a fable palpably drawn from the oriental belief, that mount Cailasa and the floating Paradise of Vaicontha were alone unaffected by the deluge): we have been told, that the sacred garden was separated from our habitable world, and elevated to the circle of the Moon; by which expedient it was placed out of the reach of Noah's flood. Thus also we have been edified with a wonderful tale respecting a stupendous voyage of St. Brandon, and another of a no less surprizing expedition performed by Ninias. The saint, it appears, once sailed in a ship from Ireland to the Moon, by which feat he ascertained the real situation of Paradise. On his way thither he met with Judas, who experienced a regular hebdomadal remission of his pains from every saturday to every sunday evening: and he also landed upon a large fish, which his crew mistook for an island, until a fire, which was unluckily kindled on the back of the animal, convinced them of their mistake. A voyage of a similar description was undertaken by another adventurer of the name of *Ninias*. This great navigator, sailing beyond Thulè, advanced so far north, that at length he came to the Moon, which seemed a resplendent Earth: and here he beheld many strange sights, which may claim at least an equal degree of credibility with the discoveries accomplished by St. Brandon.[2]

It is not difficult to perceive, that these wild fictions have been borrowed from the old mythology of Paganism; which always blended together Paradise and the Ark, which never lost sight of the diluvian voyage of Noah, and which so pertinaciously preserved the memory of the northern mountains of Ararat (strictly *northern* to the early colonists of Shinar) that they were sometimes even confounded with the north-pole itself.

---

[1] See various authorities in Clasen. Theol. Gentil. par. ii. c. 11. p. 300. See also Calmet's Dict. vox *Paradise*.

[2] Purchas. Pilgrim. b. i. c. 3. p. 18.

As the notion of Paradise being situated in the Moon was thus borrowed by the monkish framers of ecclesiastical romance, so we may likewise observe, that heroic romance has been equally enriched by the adoption of it. When Ariosto sends Astolpho in quest of the lost intellect of Orlando, that hero, mounted on his Hippogriff, the Garuda of Indo-Scythic mythology, flies to the Moon from a lofty mountain at the source of the Nile: and in that planet, where all things are infallibly to be found that have been lost on Earth, he discovers the blissful regions of Paradise.[1]

II. Thus extensively has the fable been received, that Paradise, or Elysium, or the residence of the deceased patriarchs, though sometimes placed on the summit of a lofty mountain, sometimes fixed to a sacred island clipped by the far distant western ocean, sometimes set afloat on the surface of the deluge, and sometimes concealed within the central cavity of the Earth, was yet situated in the circle of the Moon. We have now to account for the origin and import of such an apparently extravagant fiction: and the mode, in which alone this can be done, will furnish an additional proof of the connection, which was ever believed to subsist, and which in fact really *did* subsist, between the garden of Paradise and mount Ararat.

The self-same opinion, which placed Elysium in an island, or which described it under the name of *Vaicontha* as floating on the surface of the deluge, was likewise the cause of its being translated to the Moon. That planet, from the boat-like form of a crescent which it periodically assumes, was made the astronomical symbol of the Ark: while the mystic consort or god of the Ark was sometimes venerated in the orb of the Sun, and sometimes worshipped as Lunus or Chandra; a character, which relates to his being the masculine genius or husband of the Moon, considered as the sidereal hieroglyphic of the diluvian Ship or the ship Argha. This curious speculation will be found to pervade the whole of ancient mythology: and, as its actual existence admits of a very easy proof, so it serves to explain various matters, which otherwise are utterly unintelligible.

That such a speculation really existed, may be shewn in a manner which cannot easily be controverted.

[1] Orland. Fur. Cant. xxxiv.

In the theology of the Hindoos, the goddess Parvati, whose character melts into those of Lacshmi and Saraswati, as that of her consort Siva does into the characters of Vishnou and Brahma, is said to be at once the Earth and the ship Argha which floated on the surface of the deluge. Yet the triplicated great mother of the Hindoo superstition, whether adored as Parvati or Lacshmi or Saraswati, is positively declared to be also the Moon. Hence the Moon, in some sense or another (astronomically, as I myself am persuaded), was identified first with the ship Argha, and afterwards by mystic intercommunion with the Earth. The ship Argha being thus identified with the Moon, we find Siva the navigator of that ship, notwithstanding he is worshipped in conjunction with the Sun, yet esteemed the same as Lunus or Chandra, that is, the god or male genius of the Moon : and he doubtless sustained this character as being the deity of the ship, which the Moon astronomically represented. Hence he is ever depicted, bearing the crescent or lunar boat on his forehead, and holding in his hand a trident which is composed of a lunette with a spike rising perpendicularly from the centre of it. This last hieroglyphic, as I shall hereafter prove at large, shadows out the ship Argha under its sidereal form of a crescent with Siva standing in the midst of it and supplying the place of a mast.[1]

The same notions prevailed in the theology of the Egyptians, which indeed is palpably no other than that of the Hindoos. The identity of Parvati and Isis is established both by name and character : for one of the titles of Parvati is *Isi;* while the two kindred goddesses are alike symbolized by a cow, and are alike declared to be at once the Moon, the Earth, and a Ship floating on the surface of the ocean. That ship was the ship of Osiris or Iswara : and, as it was deemed a navicular Moon, the sacred heifer Theba, which represented it, bore a lunette impressed upon her side, and had her horns studiously polished that they might exhibit the exact figure of a boat-like crescent. Such being the case, Osiris is sometimes said literally to have entered into an ark, sometimes into the ship called *Baris* and *Argo*, sometimes into the Moon, and sometimes (as we learn from Diodorus) into a wooden heifer or ark mystically constructed in the shape of

---

[1] Moor's Hind. Panth. p. 22, 111, 405.　Asiat. Res. vol. vi. p. 523.

a cow. The ark, the ship, the Moon, and the heifer, therefore mean one and the same thing; because the god is indifferently feigned to have been inclosed in each of them. If however there might yet be any doubt on the subject, Plutarch has effectually removed it by the explanation which he gives us of this mystical jargon. The Moon, he observes, into which Osiris entered, was in reality an ark shaped like a lunette; shaped, that is to say, like the horns of a cow. Hence it appears, from the united testimony of Plutarch and Diodorus, that the ark of the deity was sometimes made in the form of a cow whose horns represented the lunar crescent and whose side exhibited the same crescent artificially impressed upon it, and some-times simply in the form of a lunette or a life-boat or a pair of bovine horns.[1] It is manifest therefore, since Isis was symbolized by the heifer Theba, since she was astronomically venerated as the Moon, since the hei-fer and the Moon both represented the ark in which Osiris was set afloat, and since the word *Theba* literally and properly signifies *an ark:* it is mani-fest, that the ship Argo was sidereally represented by the Moon. As the character of Isis thus minutely coincides with that of Parvati or Isi, so the character of Osiris no less minutely corresponds with that of Siva or Iswara. Each is the navigator of the ship called *Argo* or *Argha:* each is astronomi-cally venerated as the Sun: yet each is likewise worshipped as the god Lu-nus, or the masculine deity that presides over the Moon.

A similar idea may be clearly traced in the mythology of Greece and Rome. The triple character of Diana, who is the Moon in heaven, Diana on earth, and Hecatè or Proserpine in Hades, is well known to every school-boy: but it is not so generally known, that the very same triple cha-racter is equally sustained by the Devi or Isi of Hindostan.[2] Isi therefore must undoubtedly be identified with Diana, no less than with the Isis of Egypt. How this triple character originated, is sufficiently plain from the preceding disquisition. On the surface of the earth, the great mother is the Ark: hence we find Diana represented as a maritime goddess who presided over navigation; hence also we meet with a legend of her being born in a

---

[1] Plut. de Isid. p. 366, 368. Diod. Bibl. lib. i. p. 76. See Plate III. Fig. 1.
[2] Moor's Hind. Panth. p. 136. Asiat. Res. vol. xi. p. 110, 111, 112.

floating island, to which her mythological parent had been compelled to flee in order to escape the rage of Python or Typhon or the deluge. In heaven she is the Moon: because the Moon or crescent was the astronomical symbol of the Ark. In Hades she is Hecatè: because the central cavity of the Earth, and the dark interior of the Noetic ship, were by mystic inter-communion alike esteemed the Inferum of pagan mythology.

The same idea prevails, with equal uniformity; in the old Druidical superstition. Ceridwen or Sidi, the Ceres of the classical writers and the Sita of Hindostan, was venerated as the Moon, was esteemed the same as the circle of the World, and was symbolized by a cow. Yet her hieroglyphic was a sacred boat, represented by the lunar crescent: and she is described as being the ship, which was formed by Menwyd the sovereign of the world at the period of the deluge, and which bore him in safety through the dale of the grievous waters.[1] Menwyd is plainly the Menu-Satyavrata of the Hindoos, and Ceridwen is certainly the same character as Parvati in the form of the ship Argha: but the arkite goddess of the Britons, like the great mother of Hindostan, Egypt, and Greece, is also astronomically the Moon and mystically the Earth.

III. The circumstance of the Moon being thus made the sidereal representative of the great mother, under which character the ancient mythologists venerated conjointly the Earth and the Ark, will serve to explain some matters not otherwise intelligible: and these matters themselves, when thus explained, will all tend to confirm the supposition, that the Gentiles did not worship the Moon simply, but the Moon considered as the astronomical hieroglyphic of the Magna Mater.

A notion very generally prevailed, that the chief goddess, from whose fruitful womb all the hero-gods were produced, was herself born from the ocean. Such was the origin ascribed to Venus, whom the Syrians thence depicted as a mermaid: such also was the origin ascribed to the Indian Lacshmi, who is allowed to be essentially the same character as Parvati or Argha.[2] Both these goddesses are astronomically the Moon. Hence the

---

[1] Davies's Mythol. of Brit. Druids. p. 270, 256, 285, 176.

[2] Asiat. Res. vol. i. p. 240.   Moor's Hind. Panth. p. 10, 29, 132, 136, 137, 183.

Moon is also said, sometimes to have been born from the sea, and some-times to have emerged from the deluge.[1] Hence likewise the Egyptians re-presented both the Sun and the Moon, by which they meant the arkite patriarch and his ship, sailing in boats on the surface of the ocean.[2] And hence the lunar goddess was depicted by the Hindoos, bearing a crescent on her forehead, and seated on the aquatic lotos which is the symbol of the ship Argha.[3]

The cow being a form or type of the great mother, we find also the very same legends respecting this mystic animal. We are taught by the Hindoo theologists, that the cow, which represented each of their three principal cognate goddesses or rather the one Devi conspicuous in three forms, was produced from the ocean: yet they sometimes likewise make her the child of the Sun, because the Sun was the astronomical representative of the great father; just as they inform us, that the sea-born Moon, which being both Lunus and Luna is an hermaphrodite, ought to be deemed at once the husband, the wife, and the child, of the solar divinity.[4] So likewise the Egyptians indifferently set Osiris afloat in a wooden cow and in an ark shaped like a lunette: and the old Druids had a legend, that their sacred cow was tossed about, or (as they mystically expressed it) was boiled, by the waters of the deluge ; and that, where her troubles were accomplished, there their chief god, who had been preserved in an ark, at length found rest.[5]

The great mother however is the Earth, as well as the Ark. Hence there was an idea, that the Moon is another Earth, the abode of departed spirits : and hence both the Moon and the Earth bore the common appellation of *Olympia* or *Olympias*, by which was meant that each was an Ilapu or Meru.[6]

So again, the Hindoo Magna Mater, under the names of *Lacshmi* and *Saraswati*, while she is on the one hand described as Narayani or the goddess that floats on the surface of the waters, is said on the other hand to

[1] Moor's Hind. Panth. p. 183.   Maurice's Hist. of Hind. vol. i. p. 585.
[2] Asiat. Res. vol. iii. p. 535.   [3] Porph. de ant. nymph. p. 256.
[4] Moor's Hind. Panth. p. 139, 138, 141, 292.
[5] Davies's Mythol. of Brit. Druids. p. 177.
[6] Macrob. in Somn. Scip. lib. i. c. 11.   Euseb. Chron. p. 45.   Plut. in vit. Thes.

be the mother of the World and to have produced all the elements within her womb: and, in a similar manner, the Syrian fish-goddess Atargatis is represented as being the common receptacle of all the hero-gods; and the Egyptian Isis is feigned to comprehend within herself the first rudiments of all things.[1] Precisely the same character is ascribed to the Moon: for, in the theology both of the Hindoos and the Egyptians, that planet is esteemed the hermaphroditic mother of the World.[2] Now it is obvious, that such sentiments can only have been entertained respecting the Moon, in consequence of her being the symbol or representative of something which *really* corresponds with them: and, what that *something* is, may be learned from the circumstance of the Moon being astronomically identified with that great goddess of Paganism, who is said to have been produced from the ocean and to have floated on its surface in the form of a ship during the prevalence of the general deluge.

IV. From the preceding observations we may learn, why so many lofty mountains in different parts of the world were reputed to be mountains of the Moon, and were even specifically designated by the name of that planet. Each of these, with the sole exception of the real Ararat, was a local transcript of the Paradisiaco-diluvian mountain: each was what the Hindoos would call *a Meru*, or *an Ida-vratta*, or *an Ilapu*; and the Greeks, *an Ida* or *an Olympus*: each was devoted to the celebration of the commemorative Mysteries of the Cabiric gods: and each, partly in consequence of the celebration of those Mysteries and partly through the common vanity of national appropriation, came in time to be actually considered as the proper scite of Paradise and as the true place of the Ark's appulse after the flood. We may commence with Ararat itself; and from it, as from a centre, extend our inquiries into other regions.[3]

1. In the dialect of the ancient Scythians who colonized both Armenia and Cashgar, the word *Ararat* or *Ar-Art* denotes, we are told, *the mountain of the Ship*: and the name was clearly bestowed upon the peak thus

Ararat,
Luban,
Lubar,
Baris

---

[1] Moor's Hind. Panth. p. 74, 134, 132, 136, 137, 127. Simp. in Aristot. de Ausc. Phys. lib. iv. p. 150. Plut. de Isid. p. 374.

[2] Plut. de Isid. p. 367. Moor's Hind. Panth. p. 22, 132, 136, 137.

[3] See Plate III. Fig. 2.

designated from the circumstance of the Ark having grounded upon its summit.[1] But this *mountain of the Ship* was known to the Armenians by other appellations also: they called it sometimes *Baris*, sometimes *Luban*, and sometimes *Lubar*.[2] The first of these terms was the very name, by which the Egyptians, whose country was once occupied by the Scythian Shepherds, designated the Argoan ship of Osiris or Charon. Now the Baris, as we learn from Plutarch, was represented by a boat formed in the shape of a lunette; whence, he tells us, the inclosure of Osiris within the ark was sometimes called his entering into the Moon. Just the same idea may be traced among the inhabitants of that region, where the Ark really grounded. *Luban* or *Laban*, which is another of the names of Ararat, signifies *the Moon*.[3] Mount Luban therefore is the mountain of the Moon: but by this Moon the Scuths meant the planet no further than symbolically; for the mountain of the Moon was likewise the mountain of the Ship; and, the Moon being thus made the astronomical hieroglyphic of the Ship, the word *Leaban* or *Leabarn*, which properly denotes *the Moon*, came also, in the dialect of the Armenian Scuths, to denote *a ship*.[4] Sometimes, instead of *Luban*, they called the hill *Lubar*. This appellation is said to have acquired among them the sense of *the place of egress*. Such a sense perfectly accords with the history of the mountain: yet there is reason to believe, that it has only been superadded from circumstances, and that it is not the proper and genuine import of the word. As the hill bore also the two names of *Luban* and *Baris*, it seems to me the most probable, that *Lubar* is a title made up of those two names contractedly united together in composition. From Ararat the idea was extended to the whole of the lofty region, where that hill is situated. The word *Armenia* seems to be the compound appellation *Ar-Men-Aia*. But *Mena* or *Minni*, as it is expressed by the scriptural writers, signifies *the Moon*: and *Ar* denotes *a mountain*. Hence *Armenia* or *Ar-Men-Aia* will be equivalent to *the land of the mountain of the Moon*.

[1] Vallancey's Vind. of anc. hist. of Irel. pref. p. xxxvii.
[2] Epiph. adv. Hær. lib. i. p. 5, 6. Euseb. Præp. Evang. lib. ix. c. 11, 12. Cedren. Hist. Compend. p. 11, 12. Joseph. Ant. Jud. lib. i. c. 3. § 6.
[3] *Luban* or *Laban* is the Chaldee or Hebrew *Labuna*.
[4] Vallancey's Essay on British isles. p. 33.

Meru, Cailasa, 2. As Ararat was thus esteemed a lunar peak, so we find a similar notion
Chandrasichara entertained respecting numerous local copies of Ararat in various parts of the
world.

..One of the most eminent of these is the Meru of Indian theology: and
accordingly, like Ararat, it is venerated as a lunar mountain. In mythologic
poetry, the sacred river of Paradise, which descends in a copious stream on
the top of that holy hill, is said to fall from the circle of the Moon: while
the favourite terrestrial haunt of the ark-preserved Siva, which is declared to
be the Cailasa peak of Meru, bears the name of *Chandrasichara* or *the
mountain of the Moon*.[1] But, in literal matter of fact, Meru coincides with
the high land of Cashgar at the head of the Ganges: and, in exact accordance with such an arrangement, that country, the fabled region of Paradise
and the Ark, presents us with two *mountains of the Moon*, which are still
venerated by the natives under that mystic appellation.[2]

Mountain of the 3. There is another mountain of the Moon at the source of the Nile;
Moon at the which is much celebrated in the ancient geography both of the west and of
head of the Nile the east, and which by the Hindoos is esteemed a second Meru as the Nile
is deemed a second Ganges.[3] Both these sacred streams however were but
mythological copies of the Euphrates, that first holy river of the Cuthic
founders of Babel: and the Indian and the African lunar Meru was each
but a transcript of that original Armenian mountain of the Moon, where the
Ark truly rested, and from which the rivers of Paradise truly descended.
It was to the African lunar mountain, that Ariosto, on the faith of ancient
pagan legends, sent his hero in search of that Paradise, which at length he
happily found in the Moon: but the Moon, which gave its name to the Egyptian Meru, was in reality that Moon or luniform Ark, within which Osiris
was annually set afloat on the water of the Nile.

Lebanon 4. The Osiris and Isis of Egypt are undoubtedly the very same deities as
the Adonis and Venus of Phenicia, and the Phenicians themselves were descended from a common stock with the Indo-Scythic Shepherd kings of Egypt:
hence we find a mountain of the Moon near Tyre no less than at the sources

---

[1] Asiat. Res. vol. i. p. 248. vol. viii. p. 320. [2] Asiat. Res. vol. vi. p. 482.
[3] Asiat. Res. vol. iii. p. 56, 60, 66, 88, 104.

of the Euphrates, the Nile, and the Ganges. Lebanon, which is precisely the same word as the Armenian Luban, was sacred to Adonis and Venus or the great father and the great mother: and the latter, who, agreeably to the prevalent mysticism of pagan theology, unites in her own character the Moon, the Ark, and the Earth, was there worshipped under the title of *Architis;* a word compounded of *Argha* and *Is*, and denoting *the ship Argha.*[1] Somewhat higher up on the same coast was the city of Berytus or Beroë; which, like the Armenian Baris, took its name from the ship of the covenant. This is sufficiently manifest from its fabulous history. Sanchoniatho tells us, that the eight Cabiri, who were the builders of the first ship and whose whole history proves them to be the family of Noah, received a grant from Cronus of the city Berytus, where they solemnly consecrated the relics of the ocean:[2] and Nonnus celebrates the imaginary nymph or goddess, from whom it derived its appellation, in language which at once refers us to Paradise and the deluge.[3] The sacred writers mention a deity, who was worshipped in Palestine under the name of *Baal-Berith.* This lord of the Baris was clearly, I think, the same as Adonis, or Osiris, or Iswara, or Menu: he was the navigator of the lunar ship Baris or Argha.

5. We find another mountain of the Moon in Latium, for mount Albanus is the same as mount Alban or Luban or Lebanon: and on the top of this Latin mount Alban a mysterious ship was venerated, which was supposed to be the ship of Juno.[4] The form of the vessel I have little doubt was that of a lunette, like the Baris of Osiris; because the Samian Juno was represented standing in a boat, which exactly resembles a lunar crescent floating in the water.[5] Juno herself indeed was the same character as Isis or Parvati, in her varied capacity of the ship Argha, the Youi, and the sacred dove.

[margin: Mount Alban in Latium]

6. As the ancient Britons venerated their goddess Ceridwen under the symbol of a luniform boat, we may be sure that their Celtic brethren of the neighbouring continent were addicted to a similar superstition. Such being

[margin: Alpin, Jura]

---

[1] Macrob. Saturn. lib. i. c. 21.

[2] Sanchon. apud Euseb. Præp. Evan. lib. i. c. 10.

[3] See Nonni Dionys. lib. xli. and a translation of the passage in my Dissert. on the Cabiri. vol. ii. p. 313.

[4] Dion. Cass. lib. xxxix. p. 62.   [5] See Plate I. Fig. 13.

the case, we shall be prepared to expect a mountain of the Moon at the head of a large river or rivers in these western regions, no less than in Armenia, Cashgar, Phenicia, and African Ethiopia: nor shall we, I apprehend, be disappointed. The four holy rivers of the Celtic Paradise were the Rhine, the Rhone, the Danube, and the Eridanus: and all these take their rise from a lofty chain of hills, which received their appellation from the mysterious worship of the symbolical lunar planet. The word *Alps* or *Alpin* is but a variation of *Alban*, which signifies *the Moon:* and one of the highest peaks of the Alpine mountains is called *Jura* or *Ira;* which is a name, both in the Celtic and the Babylonic, of precisely similar import.

Agreeably to these conjectures which are perfectly in character with the Druidical mythology, while the Danube is styled *Danaw* or *Noas* or *the river of Noah* from the god *Deo-Naush* or *Dio-Nusus;*[1] Virgil describes the Po or the Eridanus, as descending, like the Ganges or the Styx or the Nile, from the upper to the nether world, and as watering with a copious stream the Elysian fields of the blessed.[2] That river therefore was a river of Paradise: and, since the chief Paradisiacal stream was ever viewed as closely allied to the deluge, we find the ship Argo or Argha, the ship of Osiris and Iswara, floating on the waters, not only of the Nile and the Ganges, but likewise of the Phasis, the Danube, the Rhone, and the Eridanus; not only on the waters of those rivers, but likewise on the mightier floods of the Mediterranean, the Euxine, the Adriatic, the Baltic, and the Ocean which surrounds the sacred British islands.[3] By such legends it was simply meant, that the veneration of the Argha or lunar Ark prevailed in every country that was washed by those various holy streams. Agreeably also to the preceding conjectures, we learn by an arbitrary coincidence of a very singular nature, that the Eridanus was the Ganges of the Italian Celts. When that river, like the Argo, was elevated to the sphere, it was represented as flowing from the foot of Orion:[4] just as the Vaish-

[1] Herod. Hist. lib. iv. c. 49.   Valer. Flacc. Argon. lib. vi. ver. 100.   Asiat. Res. vol. iii. p. 57, 244, 245, 247.

[2] Æneid. lib. vi. ver. 658, 659.

[3] Apoll. Argon. passim. Schol. in Apoll. Argon. lib. iv. ver. 259.   Orph. Argon. passim,

[4] Hyg. Poet. Astron. lib. iii. c. 31.   Arat. Phæn. p. 47.

navas teach us, that the Ganges flows from the foot of Vishnou. The Saivas however maintain, that the holy stream proceeds in the first instance from the head of Siva: and we may gather from Homer, that the Nile was believed in a similar manner to fall from Deva or Jupiter.[1] Such coincidences serve to prove, how striking an uniformity of sentiment prevailed throughout the whole pagan world.

[1] Hom. Iliad. lib. xvii. ver. 263. The description, which the poet gives of this river, proves it to be the Nile. It is not unworthy of observation, that the Eridanus of the sphere was by some mythologists asserted to be the Nile. In this case, we shall have just the same double account of the poetical origin of that river, that we have of the Ganges. In reality, the Nile, the Ganges, and the Eridanus, were all sacred rivers, and were all viewed in the same light by the votaries of one common superstition. The real Eridanus of the sphere however was neither the Po nor the Nile, but the Euphrates; to the banks of which we may ultimately trace all the cognate systems of pagan theology. See Eratosth. Catast. *Eridanus*. and Schol. in Arat. Phæn. p. 48. This last writer says, that the natives called the Eridanus *Bodincus*. The name was probably borrowed from Bod or Buddha, who is substantially the same as Vishnou, and whose foot was equally venerated.

CHAPTER V.

— ◆ —

Respecting the Holy White Island of the West.

— ◆ —

As I have supposed the isles of the blessed to relate jointly to Paradise, mount Ararat, and the Ark, it will be proper for me to discuss more at large the geographical situation of the Brahmenical Swetadwipa; respecting which, so far as I can judge, a very erroneous opinion has been pretty extensively adopted.

The sacred isles of the west, says an eminent orientalist, *of which Sweta-dwipa or the White Island is the principal and the most famous, are the holy land of the Hindoos. There the fundamental and mysterious transactions of the history of their religion, in its rise and progress, took place. The White Island, this holy land in the west, is so intimately connected with their religion and mythology, that they cannot be separated: and of course divines in India are as necessarily acquainted with it, as distant Musulmans are with Arabia. This I conceive to be a most favourable circumstance; as in the present case the learned have little more to do, than to ascertain, whether the White Island be England, and the sacred isles of the Hindoos the British isles. After having maturely considered the subject, I think they are.*[1]

[1] Asiat. Res. vol. viii. p. 246.

This opinion has been finally adopted by Mr. Wilford in preference to his former conjecture, which exhibited Crete as the sacred White Island of the west: and the theory, which he has inevitably been led to deduce from it, is not a little extraordinary. Since the Brahmens declare that the holy western isle was the very cradle of their theology and the grand stage where the creation and renovation of the world were alike accomplished, and since that isle is pronounced by Mr. Wilford to be Britain: he is thence compelled to suppose, in direct opposition to the general testimony of history, which brings knowledge of every kind, not from Europe into Asia, but from Asia into Europe; he is thence compelled to suppose, that, at some remote period, Britain was the religious instructor of Hindostan.

I confess myself, except in a very secondary manner, unable to adopt any part of this hypothesis, and utterly unable to adopt the whole of it.

I. As the White Island of the west is positively declared to have been the region whence the diluvian mythology of the Brahmens was imported, this single circumstance plainly seems to me to exclude both Britain and Ireland and their dependencies, on the one hand; and Crete, Cyprus, Rhodes, Naxos, Samothrace, Delos, Leucè, and every sacred European or African island, on the other hand. For, since history both sacred and profane exhibits the march of knowledge and colonization as being from Asia into Europe and Africa, we cannot, without paradoxically contradicting the most unexceptionable evidence, deduce the theology of Hindostan from any one of the above-mentioned western islands. And, if this be impossible, then is it equally impossible, that any one of them should be the *real* sacred White Island of the Brahmens; because that island is unequivocally pronounced to be the cradle of their mythological system.

II. Yet, as the very name imports, the *western* holy island of the Brahmens must of course be sought for *to the west* of Hindostan; otherwise it could never have been designated by such an appellation: where then, it may be asked, shall we find a country which answers to the description given of the White Island, if we at once exclude all the consecrated isles of the west?

I readily answer, that the same important particulars, which shut out Britain and every other island of Europe or Africa from being the Brahmenical White Island, will conduct us with perfect facility to the region of which we are in quest.   To these particulars let us carefully attend.

There is a tribe of Brahmens in India to this day, actually descended from a sacerdotal race which resided originally in the White Island.   Learned men in India readily acknowledge, that the Brahmenical tribes are by no means aboriginal in that country: they came from the north, entering India through the pass of Hari-dwar ; and their first settlement was at Canoge. They also acknowledge, that the light of revelation came from the west, and that the Vedas reside in the White Island in human shapes.   This notion is openly avowed in their sacred books: as well as, that the fundamental Mysteries of their religion are intimately connected with the White Island ; and that the momentous events, which took place in consequence of them, either to create the World, or to bring on the regeneration of mankind and to shew them the path to heaven and eternal bliss, actually came to pass in the White Island or its adjacent sea.   The White Island in short is the holy land of the Hindoos, and to it they refer every thing.[1]

And now let us ask, *What* sacred country was the undoubted cradle of the Paradisiacal and diluvian theology of Hindostan?   *Which* was the holy land, that witnessed all its fundamental and mysterious transactions, being so intimately connected with the entire system that they cannot be separated? *Where* lived the sacerdotal ancestors of the Brahmens, ere, shaping their course to the east, they at length entered the southern peninsula of Hindostan from the north?   In *what* region are we to seek the origin of those sacred books, which are said to have been preserved during the time of the deluge, and which are uniformly ascribed to the great transmigrating father?[2] *Where* did that great father, who evidently unites in his own person the two characters of Adam and Noah, flourish equally at the commencement of each successive world?   With *what* special land is a religion inseparably connected ; which, so far as its demonolatrical part is concerned, is wholly built upon traditions relative to Paradise and the mountain of the Ark? *Where* was it, that the light of revelation or the revealed will of heaven,

---

[1] Asiat. Res. vol. xi. p. 69, 70.
[2] For an account of the sacred books, see below book iii. c. 5.

however early it might be corrupted by the apostates of Babel, was first communicated to the postdiluvians, as it had heretofore been to the antediluvians? In fine, *what* was the island and *what* was the adjacent sea, which are to be viewed as the particular stage at once of the primeval creation of the world and of a wonderful regeneration of mankind by which they were again stationed on the lost mount of Paradise?

The answer to these questions will of course give us the sacred White Island and its circumambient sea. But that answer necessarily specifies the Paradisiacal mount of Ararat and the diluvian ocean; which, as its waters retired, left the holy hill in the condition of an island. Therefore mount Ararat must clearly be the White Island of Brahmenical theology, which accordingly is described as the peculiar abode of the hero-gods and of the deified Pitris or patriarchal ancestors of mankind: while the sea, which surrounds it, must inevitably be the deluge.

But this is not the only proof of the opinion, which is here advanced. Ararat is indeed the sacred White Island of the west, but it is not the *sole* island. The Brahmens ever speak of the holy western isles in the *plural* number: and their traditions point out with sufficient plainness, what we are to understand by a *second* consecrated island; and thus demonstrate, that I have rightly identified the *first* with the sea-girt top of the Paradisiacal Ararat. A White Island, or an Island of the Moon (for the appellations are synonymous), is described by them as floating in an erratic state, like Delos and Chemmis, on the surface of the ocean; and it is said to have at length become fixed or rooted immoveably to the earth. From this floating island, as well as from that which is stationary, they deduce all the Mysteries of their theology. They inform us, that it is a navicular Moon; that it was born out of the ocean; that it once served as a receptacle for all living creatures; that it sheltered its worshippers from danger in a mysterious Paradise; that it is incapable of decay, being exempt from the periodical destruction of each successive world by the waters of an universal deluge; that it is immediately connected with the regeneration or renovation of every mundane system; that it is the abode of the mighty Isa who navigated the flood in the ship Argha, of the fish-god Vishnou or Crishna who reposes on the boat-like folds of the serpent Sesha, of the god of wisdom, and of those seven blessed Rishis who once performed within it a wonderful penance and who were literally preserved in an ark with Menu-Satyavrata; that it was created or made a short time before the war of the hero-gods with the giants; and that its female tutelary genius is the White goddess, who sailed in the form of a ship over the waters of the deluge, and who contained within her womb the Trimurti or the triplicated great father.[1]

Such legends require not much penetration to decypher. So long as the flood remained upon the face of the earth, the Ark, which in every particular agrees with the second holy island of the Hindoos, and which in the Orgies was astronomically represented by a lunette or crescent, was the *only* white or lunar island, the sole floating Moon: but, when the summit of Ararat emerged from the waves while the lower adjacent regions were still over-flowed, the top of the mountain was obviously for a season another island; and thus the holy white islands, being ultimately *two* in number, are always by the Brahmens mentioned *plurally*. As the waters retired, the stationary island of the Moon received the floating island of the Moon, which then became immoveably fixed to the earth: and thus henceforth the two sacred islands were necessarily viewed as immediately contiguous to each other.[2]

Nor does the geographical arrangement of the Brahmens less decidedly conduct us to the Ark and mount Ararat, than the circumstantial evidence which has just been considered. The White Islands are ever styled *the sacred isles of the west:* hence, as such phraseology is Indian or Indo-Scythic, we must necessarily look for the isles in question *to the west* of India and the Indian Caucasus. This, accordingly, is the precise relative situation of the Armenian mount Ararat.

To circumstantial evidence and accurate geographical arrangement may be added such proof as can be drawn from correspondence of appellation. As the sacred western isle of the Brahmens is said to be at once the White Island and the Island of the Moon: so the once insular peak of Ararat,

[1] Asiat. Res. vol. viii. p. 246. vol. xi. p. 21, 35, 43, 44, 47, 69, 88, 90, 91, 92, 97, 110, 111, 112, 114, 120.

[2] Agreeably to this opinion, and in exact accordance with the Armenian appellation *Lubar*, the Hindoos call the stationary White island *the mountain of the Moon*, and the sea which once surrounded it *the sea of the mountain of the Moon.* Asiat. Res. vol. viii. p. 301.

from its having supported the floating lunar island of the Ark, was called *Luban* or *Laban* or *Alban;* a title, which, in the language of those who founded Babel, jointly expresses the idea of the Moon and of Whiteness.

Here then, associated with a wonderful floating island, we have the true sacred White Island of the west, which the Brahmens rightly describe as the cradle of their theology: for here, in Paradisiacal innocence, dwelt Menu-Adima; and here was mystically born again the god Chandra or Lunus or the ark-preserved Siva from the womb of the ship Argha, which is declared to have been a form of Parvati who herself is identified with the lunar White goddess.

III. As the ancestors of the classical mythologists emigrated from the region of the Indian Caucasus,[1] they still, after their arrival in Europe and Africa, spoke of the holy *western* isles, when, from the relative situation of their new settlements, the phrase was no longer appropriate: and, under the same impression, their descendants, forgetting the true scite of the happy isles, were led at length to place them in the midst of the great western Atlantic ocean. Such an error was rendered the more easy from the localizing humour of their religion. Of the primitive White Island, whence originated the whole theological system both of the Hindoos and of all the other Gentiles, each literal sacred island was an avowed imitative transcript. Such was the case with the various Greek islands, which I have already enumerated: such was the case likewise with Teneriffe and the Canaries, well known by the name of *the Fortunate Islands* and lying not far from the coast of the ancient Cuthic Atlantians: and such was eminently the case with Britain and Ireland, which, as we learn from Tzetzes, were esteemed by many the Elysian islands of the blessed.[2] In this *secondary* sense therefore, but no further, they may all, if we please, be reckoned the sacred islands of the west. Hence we have the legend of a deluge attached to Samothrace: hence Delos, where the Moon was born, was thought to have once floated: hence Leucè was deemed the abode of departed heroes, and bore a name which signifies *White:* hence Crete, famed for its local Ida or

[1] Vide infra book vi. c. 4. § II. 2. c. 5. § V, VI. 1, 2.
[2] Schol. in Lycoph. ver. 1200.

Ararat, always had the notion of whiteness associated with it: and hence a well-known appellation of Britain was specially borrowed from that of the real White Island, on which the navicular Moon rested at the close of its long voyage.[*]

[*] The island Leucè, which I have mentioned in this catalogue, is situated in the Euxine sea. In aspect it resembles a serpent or a large fish floating on the water: and it is still the popular opinion, that it abounds with serpents. Arrian says, that it was sometimes denominated *the course of Achilles*, that Thetis was fabled to have given it to that hero, that his ghost still inhabited it, and that his temple and statue both of ancient workmanship were to be seen there. With the hero-god Achilles was worshipped his friend Patroclus. No human being inhabited the island: but certain aquatic birds alone had the care of the temple. Every morning they repaired to the sea, wetted their wings, and sprinkled the sacred edifice: afterwards, they carefully swept its pavement with their plumage. But this marvellous region was not solely tenanted by the shades of the two Grecian warriors: it was likewise thought to be the general abode of the souls of ancient heroes. Arrian. Perip, Pont. Eux. p. 21. Strab. Geog. lib. vii. p. 306. Paus. Lacon. p. 200. Pind. Nem. iv. Pompon, Mel. lib. ii. c. 7. Fest. Avien. Orb. Descript. See Clarke's Travels. vol. i. c. 25.

It is not difficult to learn, whence these several wild notions have originated respecting the island Leucè. The peculiarity of its form rendered it an apt symbol of the huge navicular sea-serpent, on which the great father Vishnou floated during the period of the intermediate deluge: and, agreeably to this supposition, we find the Brahmens declaring, that Crishna dwells with the snake Sesha in the holy White island of the west. During the celebration of the Mysteries, real serpents were not unfrequently introduced; the great father himself was believed to have taken the figure of a serpent; and his idolatrous descendants sometimes asserted, that they were the children of the serpent: hence arose the persuasion, that Leucè abounded with those reptiles. Lastly, the aquatic birds, which were feigned to minister in the temple, were doubtless priests; who assumed the names of such birds, and who in accordance with the doctrine of the Metamorphosis disguised themselves with suitable vizors that they might resemble them. Of this description were the sacred birds of Memnon, the black oracular doves that were said to have come from Egypt, and the holy ravens of the Mithratic Orgies: they were all equally either priests or priestesses of the great father and mother. From a similar source originated the classical fable, that the swan, though it had perseveringly screamed all its lifetime, yet sings melodiously at the point of death. Each such musical swan was not a bird, but a priest or priestess, who affected the name and form of one of the metamorphoses of the great father Zeus or Theuth: and the dying strains, which it uttered, were the funereal songs of the Mysteries, chaunted sometimes in honour of Linus and sometimes in praise of the untimely slaughtered Maneros. These ancient melodies are universally represented, as being most sweetly melancholy.

In the name of *Albin*, *Albion*, or *Albanich*, the two ideas of *Whiteness* and *the Moon* are equally expressed: for the Babylonians and other early post-diluvians denominated the Moon *Labanah* or *Albanah* from the circumstance of its whiteness.   Armenia, being peculiarly the land of the floating Moon, was thence called *Albania*; and the peak, where that Moon was thought to have rested, *Luban* or *Laban* or *Alban*.   *Albany* therefore denotes either *the white land* or *the land of the Moon*: and, as, in the former signification, it identifies itself with the White Island of Indian theology; so, in the latter, it identifies itself with the same region when denominated *the lunar island*.   Into our own country the name, with the theological system attached to it, was brought, I believe, by the Celts or Gomerians under their Cuthic leaders from the Armenian mount Laban or Alban: for it is most idle to conjecture, that it was imposed upon the island in after ages by the Phenicians on account of its chalky cliffs.   The appellation in fact is perfectly familiar in Celtic North-Britain, where the Phenicians never came: we still meet with lakes and rivers styled *Leven* from the worship of the Moon: and the whole country was viewed by the Druids, as eminently sacred to that mystic navicular planet.   Nor was another name of the Armenian peak omitted by the first planters of Albion.   The arkite mount Alban was likewise called *Baris* or *Barit* or *Brit* from the sacred ship so denominated: and, in a similar manner, the holy white island of Albin was styled *Britain* or *the land of the ship Barit*, evidently from the same mysterious vessel.[1]   Nor was the country in general only called *Britain* and *Albin*: the Celtic Druids, no less than their oriental forefathers, had also their mount Baris and their river of the Moon, names preserved in more than one instance even to the present day.   Ros-Bari, or inversely *Bari-Ros*, denotes, we are told, in the Celtic *the mountain or promontory of the ship*: and *Leven* or *Leben* is equivalent to *the Moon*.[2]   Hence in Cleveland, widely overlooking the sea, we have a remarkable conical hill; the precise shape in which the ancient pagans peculiarly delighted, from its literal resemblance to the Armenian hill Masis or Baris which is still shewn

---

[1] Britain is Brit-Tan, like Hindos-Tan, Chusis-Tan, and other similar compounds.

[2] Vallancey's Vindic. p. 100.

as the mountain that received the Ark:[1] we have a remarkable conical hill, which to this day bears the name of *Ros-Bari* or corruptedly *Roseberry*; while, through the district beneath it, flows the once holy river *Leven*. Hence also in Scotland we have another *Roseberry* or *Ros-bari*, and another *Leven* as the name both of a sacred lake and of a sacred river.[2] All these were severally the mountains or lakes or rivers of the holy lunar ship: and, accordingly, the same localizing spirit, which has given us a mount Baris in the far western Albion, produced another mount Baris near the eastern Ecbatana, where, as we learn from Strabo, the navicular goddess of that name was duly worshipped.[3] Doubtless the Armenian Baris and Laban were the prototypes of all other consecrated places thus denominated.

IV. Every particular, adduced even by Mr. Wilford himself, tends to establish the opinion here adopted.

As he states, that, in Asia and the eastern part of Europe, Britain was esteemed the land of spirits: so he thinks it probable, that, in Britain, the holy island was placed still further to the west; and observes, that the savages of America, who it seems have the same article of belief, actually fix it yet again more westerly as if it were in Asia. He mentions also a notion, hat the White Island had been brought into various parts of Hindostan. And he cites a commentator on the Bhagavata, as pronouncing that the two White Islands are really but one.[4]

The whole of this perfectly accords with what I have said on the subject. In Egypt and Greece, Britain was deemed the holy western isle; because the Indo-Scythic invaders of those countries used the term *western*, when from their change of situation it was no longer proper: but, in America, which was peopled from eastern Asia, the natives retained the idea that the White Island lay far to the west without at all departing from the accuracy of truth. The fable of its being brought into India relates to the practice

---

[1] Tournefort's Voyage to the Levant. vol. iii. p. 94, 101, 104. cited by Hales.

[2] It has often been justly remarked, that the old Celtic names of rivers and mountains very generally remain throughout England, though its present inhabitants are Saxons.

[3] Strab. Geog. lib. xi. p. 531.

[4] Asiat. Res. vol. xi. p. 88, 100—104.

of local transcription, which prevailed so extensively throughout the pagan world; for every holy island in every consecrated lake was deemed an express image of the true White Island, which in this secondary sense was to be found in all regions of the earth. And the circumstance of the two White Islands really constituting but one was a literal matter of fact, when the Ark became inseparably united to mount Ararat; a peculiarity, which never could have been characteristic of Britain and Ireland.

CHAPTER VI.

On the origin and import of the veneration paid to the bull, the lion, and the eagle.

ARBITRARY points of resemblance afford the most decisive proofs of the common origin of those speculations, in which they occur.

Had the idolatry of every pagan nation sprung up independently and unconnectedly, it could only have resembled the idolatry of other nations in matters which are not arbitrary, while it would have exhibited no similitude in matters which are purely arbitrary. Thus, if we had found the Gentiles in every part of the world *simply* worshipping the Sun, the Moon, and the Stars, without entertaining any other ideas of them than what would obviously result from the knowledge of their physical properties : such a circumstance would by no means have been sufficient to demonstrate, that they had all derived this mode of worship from a common source ; because, if the posterity of Noah had retired to their respective settlements *previous* to the rise of idolatry, and if they had all *afterwards* lapsed into it without any mutual communication, the first objects of veneration, when they forsook the worship of the one true God, would naturally, in every instance, be the host of heaven. But if, on the other hand, we find both notions and symbols of a perfectly arbitrary description attached to a mode of superstition in itself *not* arbitrary: we may rest assured, that such coincidences and combinations cannot have been accidental, but that all the theological systems which exhibit them must have been derived from some primeval common original. Widely separated nations, which had had no intercourse during the formation of their several mythologies, might all have been led, without the least degree of mutual correspondence, to worship the Sun and the Moon: but they could not all have stumbled upon the notion, in itself wholly arbitrary and unnatural, that the god, whom they venerated as the Sun, once sailed over the ocean in an ark; and that the goddess, whom they adored as the Moon, was most properly represented by a ship, because she once in such a form floated on the surface of the mighty deep. In a similar manner, they might all, without any communication, have been induced to worship the Sun and Moon as a god and goddess: but they could not all have happened, in a solitary insulated state, to pitch upon precisely the same sacred symbols. If the various systems of Paganism had originated *independently* of each other, one nation would have venerated the Sun under one hieroglyphic; another nation, under another; and a third, under none at all: but it is impossible to conceive the existence of such a lucky chance, as should lead them all, not merely to worship the Sun and Moon, but to worship them with exactly the same notions and under exactly the same hieroglyphics. This universal agreement in matters arbitrary proves a common origin. But the theological systems of the whole pagan world could not have had a common origin, unless the first exemplar of idolatry was struck out when all mankind were assembled together in one place and in one community. The general prototype therefore of every pagan system must have been invented *previous* to the dispersion of Noah's posterity, and copies of it must have been carried by each tribe into the land of its own peculiar settlement.

This train of reasoning will at once compel us to fix the origin of idolatry to the age of the tower of Babel; and will account for the singular resemblance, even in the most arbitrary particulars, which one gentile system invariably bears to another. I have at present to exemplify such accordance in the universally prevailing veneration paid to the bull, the lion, and the eagle; and afterwards to trace the origin of that veneration, and to ascertain its subsequently acquired import.

I. There is perhaps no part of the gentile world, in which the bull and the cow were not highly reverenced and considered in the light of holy and mysterious symbols. Sometimes they appear as attendants or vehicles of the principal god and goddess : and sometimes they are deemed forms or representations of the deities themselves. Wherever we direct our attention, be it north, south, east, or west, still these hieroglyphics present themselves to our view, and that too invariably in the same bearing and connection.

The great father was universally represented by a bull.

1. Among the Chinese, the great father Fohi, whose whole history proves him to be the scriptural Noah, is said to have had a son named *Shin-Nungh*. But, agreeably to that mystic system of genealogizing which prevailed so universally among the Gentiles, we may safely pronounce Fohi and Shin-Nungh to be one and the same character. Now Shin-Nungh is feigned to have had the head of a bull.[1]

In the neighbouring empire of Japan, this ancient personage is venerated under the title of *the ox-headed prince of heaven* : and his figure is here again that of a man, having the horns of a bull, and exhibiting the lunar crescent impressed on various parts of his body.[2] At Meaco, in the same country, he appears in the uncompounded form of a bull; which is represented in the act of impelling the mysterious egg towards the shore of that ocean, in which it had previously floated.[3]

The crescent impressed on the side of this ox-headed deity is the very device, which was equally impressed on the side of the Egyptian bull Apis. That sacred animal, the living object of national devotion, was studiously selected of a black colour, the holy colour alike of Emphtha and Vishnou : and on his side was artificially imprinted a white figure of the lunar crescent.[4] The priests told Plutarch, that it was produced by a touch of the

---

[1] Couplet. Præf. ad Tab. Chronog. p. 3.

[2] Kæmpfer's Hist. of Japan. b. v. c. 3. p. 413. with the plate there referred to.

[3] See the plate in D'Hancarville's Recherches sur l'orig. des arts. vol. i. p. 65. and in Maurice's Hist. of Hind. vol. i. p. 47.

[4] Plin. Nat. Hist. lib. viii. c. 46.

Moon, which descended from heaven for that special purpose.' By this
pretended Moon we must evidently understand a metal plate cut in the
shape of a lunette, which was either applied hot to the side of the beast, or
was the vehicle of a caustic. Such a descent of the Moon was of the same
nature as that, which both the ancient Brahmens of India, and their brethren the Druids of Britain, claimed to effect. The former, according to
Nonnus, compared that planet to an unyoked heifer, doubtless in reference
to the horns of the animal; and were wont by their incantations to bring it
down from heaven: the latter, as we may collect from Diodorus, pretended,
that at times it was so near their island, that the hills on its surface might be
clearly discerned.' In both these instances, a crescent, or the figure of a
bull whose horns resembled a crescent, was most probably exhibited in the
sacred rites and designated by the name of the Moon. Now, under the
form of the bull Apis or Mneuis, the Egyptians worshipped their great god
Osiris; esteeming him the living representative of the deity, believing that
the soul of the god tenanted the body of the animal, and thence deeming the
bull the very same as Osiris himself.'

The Osiris of Egypt was avowedly the Bacchus or Dionusus of Greece:
hence in this latter country, we find also a notion prevalent, that the god of
wine bore some resemblance to a bull. Nonnus styles him *the tauric deity*:
Euripides introduces a chorus of Bacchantes, inviting him to appear in the
shape of a bull: the Orphic poet celebrates him as the god with two horns,
having the head of a bull: and Plutarch tells us, that the women of Elis
were accustomed to invite him to his temple on the sea-shore, under the
name of *the heifer-footed divinity, the illustrious bull, the bull worthy of
the highest veneration.*

Bacchus or Osiris again was the same as Adonis: hence Adonis is likewise described by the Orphic poet, as having two horns, and as thus wearing
the semblance of a bull.'

' Plut. Sympos. lib. viii. p. 718.
' Nonni Dionys. lib. xxxvi.   Diod. Bibl. lib. ii. p. 130.
' Plut. de Isid. p. 362, 366, 368.   Diod. Bibl. lib. i. p. 76.
' Nonni Dionys. lib. v.   Eurip. Bacch. ver. 1015. Orph. Hymn. xxix. Plut. Quæst.
Græc. p. 299.   ' Orph. Hymn. lv.

The character of Bacchus also, as we shall hereafter see at large, equally melts into those of Jupiter and Neptune. Accordingly it is said, that, on different occasions, the form of a bull was assumed by both those divinities.[1]

The tauric Jupiter was the parent of the Cretan Minos; who is nearly allied to the Minotaur or the bull Minos, and who is the same character as the Menes or bull Menuis of Egypt and as the great father Menu of Hindostan. Hence the bull of Menu is no less celebrated by the Brahmens, than the bull Menuis was by the Egyptians and the bull Minos by the Greeks. He is deemed the personification of justice: because Menu, of whom he is the representative, is the same person as Noah, whom Moses eminently styles *the just man.*[2]

The bull of Menu must certainly be identified with the bull of Siva: because Menu, whether viewed as Adam or Noah, equally and ultimately resolves himself into the character of that deity.[3] Siva however or Iswara is clearly the Osiris or Isiris of Egypt: the bull therefore, which invariably attends upon Siva, is the same mystic animal as the bull Apis. Agreeably to this opinion, we find even to the present day, that sacred bulls are duly maintained within the precincts of the temple of Jagan-Nath, who unites in his own character the mystic Trimurti of the Hindoos: and we may safely venture to pronounce, that the great black bull worshipped in Tanjore was but a figure of the emblematical animal which the Egyptians called *Apis.*[4] Siva himself, under the name of *Ishuren* or *Maid-Ishuren*, that is, *the great Ishuren*, is said by the Tamuli of Tranquebar to have the horns of a bull. Here his mythological history immediately connects itself with that of the tauric Dionusus, with whom, no less than with Osiris, he is most undoubtedly to be identified. The Greeks had a legend that Bacchus was born from the thigh of Jupiter: but the more intelligent among them were

---

[1] Ovid. Metam. lib. ii. ver. 850. lib. vi. ver. 115. Hesiod. Scut. Herc. ver. 104. Tzetz. in loc. Jupiter, as the bull of Europa, is said to be the bull of the sphere: though some say, that the animal there depicted is the heifer Io. There is no real mythological difference in these two opinions; for Io is the cow Isis of Egypt, and the bull Jupiter is the same deity as the tauric Osiris. Nonni Dionys. lib. i. Eratos. Catast. *Taurus.*

[2] Preface to Instit. of Menu. p. viii. Moor's Hind. Panth. p. 296, 297.

[3] Asiat. Res. vol. i. p. 250.   [4] Buchanan's Christ. Res. in Asia. p. 129

fully aware, that this fable originated from a mere misprision of terms. Hence we are told, that what Bacchus was really born from was mount Meru in India; and that the special place of his nativity was the city Nysa or Nusa, which was situated in the immediate vicinity of that mountain.[1] Now this Maid-Ishuren is, in a similar manner, represented as having been born at Nisa-Dabura near mount Meru; and is described, as drinking wine, as having the horns of a bull, and as being attended by eight gigantic demons named *Pudam*.[2] The tauric Ishuren then is clearly the same person as the tauric Bacchus. But Ishuren is the same god as Siva; who like Bacchus floated in an ark on the surface of the ocean, whose favourite haunt is mount Meru, and who is there conspicuous in the eight forms of the eight regents of the world. Ishuren or Siva however is equally the Osiris of Egypt, who again is acknowledged to be no other than the Dionusus of the Greeks. Consequently, Ishuren, Osiris, and Dionusus, who are all described as partaking of the form of a bull, must have had such a form assigned to them from the prevalence of some common mythological idea. The bull of Siva is called by the Hindoos *Nandi*, as those of Osiris were denominated by the Egyptians *Apis* and *Menuis*. But Nandi, though the symbol and attendant of an Indian divinity, is yet said by the Brahmens to reside in the sacred White Island of the west.[3] The assertion is perfectly accurate: for that island, as we have already seen, is the insular peak of the once sea-girt Ararat; where the patriarch, of whom the bull was a symbol, dwelt after the recess of the deluge.

Equally sacred was that animal deemed among the Celtic Druids of the west. By the ancient Britons the bull was not only reverenced in a very high degree: but he was likewise reverenced by them precisely in the same manner, and was exhibited by them exactly in the same connection; as he was by the Egyptians, the Hindoos, and the Greeks. He was the symbol of their great god Hu; the whole of whose character and attributes proves,

---

[1] Diod. Bibl. lib. ii. p. 123.

[2] Bayer. Hist. Bactrian. p. 2, 3. apud Bryant's Anal. vol. iii. p. 559.

[3] Asiat. Res. vol. ix. p. 78.

him to be one with Osiris, Siva, and Bacchus: and it is worthy of observation, that this deity appears to have been moreover represented by living bulls, just as those deities also were.[1] The same mode of worship prevailed among their brethren, the Cimbri or Cymry of the continent. They adored their principal god under the form of a brazen bull, and called him *Tarvos Trigaranos* from the figures of three cranes which appeared perching upon him.[2]

This title, which is pure Celtic, seems to prove very clearly that the Cimbri ought to be ascribed to the Celtic stock.[3] Yet, in their attack on the Romans, they were associated with an apparently Gothic or Scythian tribe: for the Teutones, as we may collect from their name, were of Teutonic or Teutsch or German origin. The religion of the two great families of the Celts and the Goths was fundamentally the same, though subsisting under different modifications. Hence we are told, that the Teutones, no less than their allies the Cimbri, venerated the brazen bull, which symbolized the great god Hu or Esay or Noe, as he was variously denominated. Such veneration is perfectly in character with the accounts, which have come down to us of the Gothic superstition. The three principal deities of that mythology were supposed to have been born from a wonderful cow, which doubtless represented the great mother: for we find, that the chariot of that goddess was wont to be drawn by sacred heifers, previous to the ceremony of solemnly committing her to the waters of a holy lake.[4]

In a similar manner, the shrine of Agruerus, whom the Phenicians venerated as the greatest of the gods, who was supposed by them to be the patron of husbandry, and whose legendary history proves him to be the same as Noah, was drawn about from place to place by a yoke of oxen.[5] This deity, whom

---

[1] See Davies's Mythol. of Brit. Druids. p. 128—143.

[2] Borlase's Hist. of Cornwall. b. ii. c. 16.

[3] The Romans wrote his name *Tarvos Trigaranus,* observing that its import is *the bull with three cranes :* the signification of *Tarw Trigaranus* even in modern Welsh is the very same. Hence the Cimbri must have spoken nearly the same language as the Welsh or Cymry, See Davies's Mythol. p. 132.

[4] Edda Fab. iii. Tacit. de mor. Germ. c. 40.

[5] Sanchon. apud Euseb. Præp. Evan. lib. i. c. 10. See my Dissert. on the Cabiri, vol. i, p. 35, 45—47.

the Greek translator of Sanchoniatho calls *Agruerus* from the circumstance of his being an agricultural god, was worshipped by the Tyrians and their neighbours the Canaanites under the titles of *Baal* and *Moloch:* and, as his shrine was drawn by oxen, so he himself was represented by the figure of a man having the head of a bull and sometimes probably by the simple figure of a bull alone.[1] His rites were of a very bloody and cruel nature: and, from the manifest connection of the fable of Europa and the bull Jupiter with the Phenician mythology, we may safely pronounce, that he was the very same character as the semi-human and semi-bestial Minotaur of Crete, whose sacrificial Orgies were of an equally sanguinary description. He is also, if I mistake not, nearly allied to the brazen-footed bulls of Colchis; which are so conspicuously introduced into the legend of the Argonautic expedition, and which are said to have breathed fire from their nostrils. This last circumstance is by no means to be deemed altogether fabulous: it alludes to the mode of worship that prevailed among the Colchians, who were of the same Indo-Scythic origin as the Goths and the Phenicians. The brazen image of Moloch is said to have been heated red-hot, whenever a devoted infant was consigned to the arms of the mishapen monster: and, from a similar practice, seems to have originated the legend of the fire-breathing bulls of Colchis.

We find the self-same symbol held in equal veneration among the ancient Persians. One of the sacred carved grottos, which still exists near the Campus Magorum, exhibits the tauric Mithras under the too well known symbol of the Linga or Phallus surmounted by the head of a bull.[2] Such a mode of representation is in perfect congruity with the notions entertained by the old mythologists respecting the character of the great father. They universally symbolized him by a bull, and considered him as the patron at once of destruction and of generation: for in their philosophy, which was built on the doctrine of a perpetual succession of similar worlds, to destroy was only to reproduce in a new shape. The tauriform Mithras is the same personage as the bull-man of the Zend-Avesta; who is described, as first

[1] Seld. de Dis Syr. Synt. i. c. 6. Compare Jer. xix. 5 with xxxii. 35.
[2] Bryant's Anal. vol. ii. p. 425, 426.

appearing at the epoch of the creation, and as afterwards reappearing at the time of the deluge. His legend undeniably proves him to be Adam, viewed as again manifesting himself in the character of Noah: and this mixed being, the principal hero-god or *great father* of the Gentiles, is the divinity, who was so universally worshipped under the semblance of a bull or of a man with the head of a bull.

Even in the American world, at the period of its first discovery by the Spaniards, the present symbol was not wholly unknown: for we are told by Cieza, that in some provinces of Peru the image of a sacred bull was highly venerated by the aboriginal inhabitants. This deity was doubtless brought with them by the primitive settlers of the country, when they emigrated from the north-eastern regions of Asia.[1]

2. As the chief male divinity of the Gentiles was represented by a bull, so their principal female divinity was typified by a cow.

Thus the Egyptians depicted Isis, as the Greeks painted Io who indeed was the same as Isis, with the horns of a cow on her head; and on this account, as we learn from Herodotus, they venerated cows beyond all other animals, as being the recognized hieroglyphic of their Magna Mater.[2] Thus the Phenicians represented Astartè or Baaltis with the head and horns of a cow.[3] And thus the Greeks both supposed Diana to ride upon a bull, and sometimes ascribed to her the head of that animal.[4] Thus also the Indian Isi, who unites in her own person the three cognate great goddesses, is symbolized even to this day by a cow; which is occasionally represented with three tails and the head of a woman, and which in that form is used as a domestic idol.[5] Thus again, as we have already seen, the Magna Mater of the Goths was a cow. And thus Ceridwen, the chief goddess of

[Margin handwritten note: The great mother was universally represented by a cow]

---

[1] Cieza c. 50. apud Purch. Pilg. b. ix. c. 10. p. 879.　　[2] Herod. Hist. lib. ii. c. 41.

[3] Sanchon. apud Euseb. Præp. Evan. lib. i. c. 10. Tobit accordingly complains, that the idolatrous tribes of Israel sacrificed to the cow-goddess Baal. Tob. i. 5. Baal, like all the chief deities of the Gentiles, was androgynous. Hence, throughout the Greek translation of the lxx, the word occurs as frequently with the feminine as with the masculine article. See Selden. de Dis Syr. Synt. ii. c. 2. p. 167.

[4] Suid. Lex. *Taurione.* Porph. apud Ger. see Parkhurst's Heb. Lex. p. 388.

[5] Moor's Hind. Panth. p. 138, 136, 141.

Druidical superstition, was attended by three cows, which jointly represented her in her triple capacity: for this deity was evidently the same as the triple Isi of the Hindoos, the triple Diana of the Greeks, and the Triglaf or triple Hecatè of the Goths.[1]

From Ceridwen venerated under the form of a heifer, the island, where her worship eminently prevailed, was called *Mona* or *Ynys Mon*, which signifies *the island of the cow*.[2] *Mon* or *Mena* however equally denotes *the Moon*: and the sacred cow was called by the name of that planet, because she was the symbol of the Moon: but the word itself is ultimately no other than the feminine form of *Menu*; and the patriarch, who bore that name, was esteemed the male genius of the Moon, because the lunette, which the horns of a cow so aptly represent, was the astronomical type of the diluvian ship Argha.

II. Though the hieroglyphic of the lion has not perhaps acquired an equal degree of celebrity with that of the bull, we shall find it just as universally employed, and in point of application employed in the very same manner: for those identical mythologic characters, which are attended or represented by animals of the bovine species, are also attended or represented by lions.

1. Among the Hindoos, Siva is clad in the skin of a lion; and Vishnou assumes the form of that beast in order to destroy a blaspheming tyrant.[3] Among the Greeks, Hercules was similarly clad in a lion's skin: while Bacchus was believed to manifest himself in the semblance of a lion, and was feigned in that shape to have torn asunder a giant in the wars of the gods.[4] It was the same superstition, which prompted Crœsus to dedicate a golden lion to the Delphic Apollo;[5] and which led the ancient Orphic mystagogue to ascribe the head of a lion to that primeval character, whom he called *Hercules* or *Cronus*, and to whom he attributed the production of the World from chaos.[6] It was the same superstition also, which induced the

The great father was represented by a lion

---

[1] Davies's Mythol. of Brit. Druid. p. 177.   [2] Ibid.
[3] Moor's Hind. Panth. plate 17. and p. 146. Maurice's Hist. of Hind. vol. ii. p. 25.
[4] Eurip. Bacch. ver. 1017. Hor. Od. lib. ii. od. 19. ver. 21—24.
[5] Herod. Hist. lib. i. c. 50.
[6] Athenag. Legat. p. 65.

Egyptians to consecrate a lion to Vulcan or Phtha, to worship that animal in a peculiar manner at the city of Leopolis, and to esteem him the symbol of Horus or the younger Osiris.[1] And it was the same superstition, equally operating in countries widely separated from each other, which taught the Persians to represent Mithras with the head of a lion as well as with that of a bull; the Assyrians and Hindoos, to depict the solar Adad and Surya as a man riding on the back of a lion; the ancient Arabs, to venerate Yaghuth under the form of a lion; the Celtic Druids, to consider a lion as a fit type of their god Hu; and the Mexicans of Tabasco, to worship the image of a lion as a present and potent divinity.[2]

2. In strict analogy to the mode of representing the great mother by a cow, while the great father is symbolized by a bull, we find the principal goddess, no less than the principal god, of Paganism, connected with the lion.

A female deity of the Syrians of Hierapolis, whom Lucian calls *Juno*, was represented sitting upon lions: Cybelè, or the universal mother of the hero-gods, who was equally worshipped in Phrygia, Greece, and Italy, rode in a chariot drawn by lions: one of the three heads of Diana or Hecatè was a lion; and in her temple at Olympia there was a winged figure, the right side of which resembled a panther, and the left a lion: the Atargatis of the Assyrians, who was venerated in conjunction with Adad, was seated on a throne supported by lions, in the very manner (as Macrobius justly remarks) that the Phrygians depicted Cybelè: and the Hindoo Parvati, in her character of Durga (the Derceto and Atargatis of Palestine and Assyria), appears riding on a lion, the gift of her mountain-sire Himalaya.[3]

Since then we may safely conclude that the great mother was symbolized

[1] Ælian. de animal. lib. xii. c. 7. Plutarch. Sympos. lib. iv. quæst. 5. Horapoll. Hierog. lib. i. § 71.

[2] Montfauc. Ant. Expl. vol. ii. p. 368, 369. Parkhurst's Heb. Lex. p. 393. Maurice's Hist. of Hind. vol. i. p. 274. plate of Zodiac. Hyde de rel. vet. Pers. c. v. p. 132. Sale's Prelim. Disc. to Koran. sect. i. p. 19. Davies's Mythol. of Brit. Druid. p. 116, 364. Cerem. and relig. cust. vol. iii. p. 167.

[3] Lucian. de dea Syr. vol. ii. p. 901. Macrob. Saturn. lib. i. c. 23. Orph. Argon. ver. 973—977. Pier. Hierog. p. 11. Orph. Hymn. xxvi. ver. 3. Moor's Hind. Panth. p. 153.

by a lioness, as well as by a cow; we may, I think, venture analogically to suppose, that those kindred hieroglyphics, the Chimera and the Sphinx (evidently borrowed by the Greeks from the theology of Egypt), were in reality representations of the chief goddess of the Gentiles. Chimera was a female Cerberus, for she is said to have had three heads; one of a lion, one of a she-goat, and one of a serpent.[1] Cerberus however is declared by Porphyry to be a type of the triple solar god: and he uses language in speaking of him, which exactly corresponds with that employed by the Brahmens in describing the nature of their triple solar deity, Brahma-Vishnou-Siva.[2] If the three-headed Cerberus then be a symbol of the great father; we may reasonably infer, that the three-headed Chimera was a symbol of the great mother. Sphinx is described by Hesiod as being the daughter of Chimera, a circumstance which sufficiently proves their near connection with each other. She was likewise triformed, blending together in one figure a lion, a virgin, and a bird.[3] This in fact was but a variation of the other hieroglyphic: the Sphinx and the Chimera equally represented the Magna Mater.

III. The third sacred animal, which I proposed to notice, was the eagle: and we shall again have reason to observe the characteristic of universality in the worship of this bird.

The great father was represented by a male eagle

1. The Vishnou of the Hindoos rides upon the shoulders of Garuda, a being compounded of a man and an eagle.[4] The Jupiter of the Chinese is the perfect counterpart of the Garuda of the Hindoos, uniting the head of an eagle to the body of a man.[5] The Nesr of the ancient Arabs is said to have been worshipped under the form of an eagle.[6] The Nesroch of the Assyrians has been thought by some to have been also represented by the same bird.[7] The Mithras of the Persians had the wings of an eagle; and

[1] Hesiod. Theog. ver. 319—324.
[2] Porph. apud Euseb. Præp. Evan. lib. iii.   See also Macrob. Saturn. lib. i. c. 20.
[3] Hesiod. Theog. ver. 326.
[4] Moor's Hind. Panth. p. 343.
[5] Lord Macartney's Embass. to China. vol. iii. p. 120. 8vo edit.
[6] Sale's Prelim. Disc. sect. i. p. 19.
[7] Beyer. Addit. in Seld. de dis Syr. Synt. ii. c. 10. p. 325.

the eagle itself was consecrated by his votaries from the most remote antiquity.[1]   The classical Jupiter was not only attended by an eagle, but was likewise himself feigned to have assumed the shape of one.[2]   The British Hu again was symbolized by an eagle.[3]   And that same bird entered also into the composition both of the Gothic Rodigast, of the Celtic Dolichenius, and of the Chinese Lui-Shin.[4]

Such an application of the hieroglyphic will sufficiently account for the high veneration in which it was held, and for the frequency of its occurrence in the temples of the pagans.   The Thebans of upper Egypt worshipped an eagle, as a royal bird, worthy of Jupiter.[5]   In the temple of the Delphic Apollo there were two golden eagles.[6]   Over the door of the temple of the Sun, both at Palmyra and at Balbec, the figure of a large eagle may still be observed.[7]   The eagle was likewise accounted sacred by the Mexicans, and is said to have been their national banner.[8]   And, among the Tensas of the Missisippi, two eagles with extended wings appear in the temple of their solar deity.[9]

The great mother was represented by a female eagle

2. I am not able to produce many instances of the female eagle being venerated as a symbol of the great mother: such however does appear to have been sometimes the case.   Juno or Isis was worshipped in a city of the Thebais under the form of a vulture, which is a bird of the same family as the eagle:[10] an eagle entered into the shape of the Sphinx: and the Gryphin, which was deemed sacred to the Sun, and which is nearly allied both to the Sphinx and the Chimera, united the head and wings of an eagle to the body of a lion.

IV. The preceding account of the universal veneration, in which the bull, the lion, and the eagle, have ever been held by the Gentiles, is in itself suf-

[1] Montfauc. Ant. vol. ii. p. 368.   Xenoph. Cyrop. lib. vii. p. 300.
[2] Nonni Dionys. lib. vii, xxv.   Ovid. Metam. lib. x. ver. 156—158.
[3] Davies's Mythol. p. 119.
[4] Banier's Mythol. vol. iii. p. 331. vol. ii. p. 219.   Embass. to Chin. vol. iii. p. 119, 120.
[5] Diod. Bibl. lib. i. p. 78.   [6] Pier. Hierog. lib. xix.
[7] Univ. Hist. vol. ii. p. 275, 266, 268.
[8] Purch. Pilg. b. viii. c. 10. p. 790, 791. c. 11. p. 797.
[9] Cerem. and relig. cust. vol. iii. p. 86.   [10] Univ. Hist. vol. i. p. 483.

IV. WHATEVER WAS CHARACTERISTIC OF THE DEITIES WAS MADE CHARACTERISTIC ALSO OF THEIR ANIMAL REPRESENTATIVES

ficient to point out the import of those hieroglyphics: the male of each animal is evidently the symbol of their principal masculine divinity, whom they adored under the character of the great father; while the female represents their principal female deity, whom they worshipped as the great mother of all things. Agreeably to this obvious conclusion we shall find, that, whatever was deemed characteristic of the gods, was likewise arbitrarily made characteristic of their animal representatives.

1. Thus the great father was astronomically the Sun. Hence the Egyptians of Heliopolis worshipped the bull Netos, and those of Hermunthis the bull Pacis; each esteeming their tauric god a lively and express image of the solar deity.[1] Hence also they, in common with the Hindoos, the Chaldèans, the Persians, and the Celts, considered the lion as equally a symbol of the Sun.[2] And hence, as we have already seen, the eagle was universally thought sacred to the regent of the day.

[margin note: Exemplification from the animal symbols of the great father]

The great father however in his human capacity was certainly the patriarch Adam, viewed as reappearing in the person of the patriarch Noah. Hence the bull Apis or Mneuis, which was the same mystic animal as that otherwise called *Netos* or *Pacis*, was esteemed the living image of Osiris: and so intimate was the connection between them, that the soul of the God was believed to migrate into each of his successive bestial representatives. Hence, in perfect accordance with this notion, as Osiris is said to have been inclosed in an ark and set afloat on the Nile; so his tauric symbol, when solemnly invested with the honours of deity, was similarly placed in a boat, and conveyed by water to the city of Memphis, after having been previously fed by the priests during the space of forty days, which was the precise period of the increase of the deluge.[3] Hence, agreeably to this rite, the bull Apis, notwithstanding his being a type of the Sun, appears in the Bembine table sailing in a ship. And hence, in perfect accordance with such speculations, the Egyptians were wont to depict the Sun himself, of which the

[1] Macrob. Saturn. lib. i. c. 21. p. 212.
[2] Plut. Sympos. lib. iv. quæst. 5.   Horapoll. Hierog. lib. i. § 71.   Ælian. de animal. lib. xii. c. 7. Pier. Hierog. p. 1.
[3] Plut. de Isid. p. 362, 366, 368. Diod. Bibl. lib. i. p. 76. Gen. vii. 12, 17.

bull was the allowed emblem, floating in a mysterious vessel on the surface of the ocean.

The personage, whom they meant thus to describe, was evidently Noah: and the navigator bull was no otherwise a symbol of the Sun, than as the Sun itself was the astronomical type of the diluvian hero-god. Hence, as in the case of Vishnou, that very deity, who assumes the form of a lion, appears also floating on the waters of the mighty deep; and, as in the case of Bacchus, is inclosed in an ark, and committed to the mercy of the winds and waves. And hence the Assyrian Nesroch, who was worshipped under the form of an eagle, is said likewise to have been exhibited to his votaries in an ark or ship.[1]

2. Much the same remarks apply to the female symbolical animals.

The great mother was at once the Earth, the Moon, and the Ship of the deluge: and these various characters most curiously mix with each other, as they unite together in the composition of one triple imaginary female. Thus, as we have already seen, the ship Argha or Argo, though palpably the Ark because it is said to have floated on the waters of the deluge, is yet considered as an image of the Earth with mount Meru rising in the centre. Thus conversely the Earth was feigned both by the Chaldèans and the Hindoos to resemble a boat; and was thought in that shape to repose on the surface of the great deep, while the centrical holy mountain served it as a mast.[2] And thus, because the navicular lunette was made the astronomical symbol of the Ark mystically blended in point of character with the Earth, the ship Argo or Baris, within which Osiris was inclosed, was sometimes constructed in the shape of a crescent; and the god himself was indifferently said to have entered into an ark and to have entered into the Moon.

In strict analogy with this supposed mixed nature of the principal goddess, her representative the cow was at once a symbol of the Earth, the Moon, and the Ark. Apuleius expressly assures us, that that animal was

[Marginalia: Exemplification from the animal symbols of the great father]

---

[1] Beyer. Addit. in Seld. de dis Syr. Synt. ii. c. 10.
[2] Diod. Bibl. lib. ii. p. 117. Asiat. Res. vol. iii. p. 133, 134.

the fruitful image of the all-productive Isis.[1] Hence, whatever was attributed to Isis or the great mother, was also attributed to the cow. Thus, in the theology both of Egypt and Hindostan, the cow is declared to be a type of the Earth.[2] Thus likewise she is equally pronounced to be a symbol of the Moon, for which she was peculiarly qualified by the crescent-like conformation of her horns : whence the Moon is said to have the countenance of a heifer and to ride in a chariot drawn by bulls ; whence also the sacred cakes dedicated to the Moon were made in the form of an ox.[3] And thus she was called by the Syrians and Egyptians *Theba*, which properly signifies *an ark*.[4]

Nor was this name applied to the cow accidentally: there is sufficient proof that she received it from the circumstance of her being made an hieroglyphic of the Ship of the deluge. As I have already had occasion to observe, Osiris is indifferently said to have been inclosed in an ark, in the Moon, in the ship Baris or Argo which was shaped like a crescent, and in a wooden cow: it is evident therefore that the cow, the Moon, and the ark, all meant the same machine, within which he was compelled to enter by the rage of Typhon or the ocean, and in which his image was commemoratively set afloat on the waters of the Nile. Sometimes the cow Theba was feigned to be a nymph or goddess : and here her mythological history exactly accords with her navicular character. She is described as flourishing at the period of the deluge, and is sometimes feigned to have been the wife of Corybas and the mother of the Corybantes or Cabiri ; who were esteemed the builders of the first ship, who were eight in number, and who are said to have once consecrated the relics of the ocean. She is also reported to have given her name to the Egyptian city of Thebes, which is yet declared to have likewise received its appellation from the sacred cow Theba : and we are further told, that Ogyges, in whose time there was a great inundation of

[1] Apul. Metam. lib. ix. p. 373.
[2] Macrob. Saturn. lib. i. c. 19. p. 204. Asiat. Res. vol. v. p. 254.
[3] Porph. de ant. nymph. p. 262. Pausan. Bœot. p. 559. Ammian. Marcell. lib. xxii. p. 257. Plin. Nat. Hist. lib. viii. c. 46. Nonni Dionys. lib. i. xliv.
[4] Tzetz. in Lycoph. ver. 1206.

the sea, was the first sovereign of that city.[1] Such legends require no explanation: the nymph Theba is clearly the same mythological character as Isis; who, although both the Earth and the Moon, was yet moreover both the mystic cow and the ship Baris or Argo.

The theological speculations of the Hindoos are perfectly analogous to those of the Egyptians. They inform us, that their triple Devi is symbolized by a cow; and that she is at once the Earth, the Moon, and a Ship which floated on the surface of the deluge. Hence they teach us, that their great goddess, the Moon, and the sacred cow, were all equally produced from the waters of the ocean. Sometimes also they assert, that this cow was the daughter of the Sun : but the two fables are fully reconcileable with each other, according to the universally received principles of old mythology. The Ark, though the allegorical child of the sea, was equally the mystic daughter of its architect Noah, who was astronomically venerated as the Sun : hence the very person, whom the Hindoos literally describe as having been preserved in an ark, is represented by them as being in his divine capacity an emanation of the great solar deity.[2]

The symbols of the lioness and the female eagle cannot, like the cow, be throughout discussed separately from the goddess which they represented; nor do they ever appear to have been brought into such general use as the last animal. Yet we may observe some traces of the mode in which they were applied. The ancient gallies, which were constructed with the head of a bull, a lion, or an eagle, seem to point out to us in what light those hieroglyphics were wont to be considered; for the naval, like the sacred, architecture of the pagans partook largely of their religious speculations : and, if the body of an ox bears an almost exact resemblance to the hull of a ship, the wings of an eagle, when the head of that bird adorned the prow of a vessel, might aptly be thought to shadow out the sails. This at least is certain, that another bird, the hen, united with a monstrous horse, and thus producing the fabulous hippogriff, was a form of the British Ceridwen;

[1] Diod. Bibl. lib. i. p. 76. lib. v. p. 323. Tzetz. in Lycoph. ver. 1206. Varr. de re rust. lib. iii. c. 1. Sanchon. apud Euseb. Præp. Evan. lib. i. c. 10.

[2] Moor's Hind. Panth. p. 10, 21, 22, 29, 33, 158, 183, 139. Asiat. Res. vol. i. p. 240.

V. THE ORIGINATION OF THE SYMBOLS OF THE BULL, THE LION AND THE EAGLE, MUST BE TRACED, IN THE FIRST INSTANCE, FROM THE FORMS OF THE PARADISIACAL CHERUBIM

THE ORIGIN OF PAGAN IDOLATRY. 419

who, like the Indian Parvati, is said to have once floated on the sea in the shape of a ship.[1]

It is however in my power to produce a more direct mythological proof of the lion being actually employed to represent the mysterious diluvian vessel Argha. On the upper part of a Sanscrit roll brought from Bengal by Lady Chambers, there is a delineation of the god Siva floating in his sacred ship on the waters of the deluge, which exactly accords with the legend preserved in the Puranas. That Siva is the person intended, is evident from his well-known concomitant the trident, no less than from his being exhibited as sailing in a ship over the ocean. Now this ship, which is clearly the Argha, is composed of two lions united together by the hinder quarters; so that the vessel, which they thus jointly form, is ornamented with the head of a lion both at its stem and its stern.[2] The present curious picture then serves to prove, that the ship Argha was occasionally symbolized by a lion: and, in addition to this, it may likewise explain a mode of representation, which occurs very frequently in the Indian paintings of Siva. That god, attended by his consort Parvati, is often delineated sitting on the skin of a lion, just as Brahma and Vishnou are placed on the aquatic lotos.[3] From the Sanscrit picture we may infer, that by the skin of the lion, no less than by the lotos, we are to understand the ship Argha.

V. Such, so far as I can judge, is the application and import of the three symbols of the bull, the lion, and the eagle, as they were used by the Gentiles in perhaps every quarter of the globe: it may be curious to inquire, whence, in the first instance, they may be supposed to have originated.

That they are of a wholly *arbitrary* nature, it is almost superfluous to remark: hence their universal adoption can only have proceeded from some common source; for it is incredible, that the very same hieroglyphics could *accidentally* have been employed to denote the very same objects in *all* parts of the world. Now the only common source, from which they can be deduced with any reasonable degree of probability, is that primeval society; which, during a certain period after the deluge and previous to the dis-

[1] Davies's Mythol. of Brit. Druids. p. 589—617.
[2] Orient. Collect. vol. ii. numb. ii. p. 183.
[3] See Moor's Hind. Panth. plate 17, 18.

persion, comprehended within its bosom the whole of mankind. This being the case, the peculiar veneration of the bull, the lion, and the eagle, which has just been considered, cannot be ascribed to a more recent epoch than the building of the tower of Babel: because never since that time have the children of Noah been united together in a single community. Here therefore the question will arise, from what source the leaders of that primitive universal society may rationally be supposed to have borrowed symbols, which in themselves are altogether arbitrary.

It is obvious, that, for the first idolatrous application of these hieroglyphics, we have been brought to a very early period even of what are usually called *the patriarchal ages.* For, if we adopt the chronological computation of the Hebrew Pentateuch which makes Noah survive the dispersion from Babel, we have been brought to the very life-time of the second great father of mankind: or, if we prefer that of the Samaritan Pentateuch which with a greater shew of probability would ascribe the building of the tower to a more recent epoch, we have still been brought to those days, which immediately succeeded the death of Noah, and during which many must have been alive who had actually conversed with him.[1] If then we find the self-same hieroglyphics employed in the early unadulterated worship of the true God; it seems only natural to conjecture, that the first idolaters borrowed them from the pure religion of Adam and Noah, and employed them when borrowed in the corrupt system which originated with the ambitious founders of Babel. This supposition is in itself probable *a priori:* let us examine, whether it can be established by any arguments *a posteriori.*

1. We are told by the sacred historian, that, when the first pair were expelled from Paradise, God placed, on the eastern side of the garden, certain beings called *Cherubim,* to preserve the way to the tree of life.

The particular form of these beings is not specified by Moses himself: but it is evident, that the Israelites at the time of the Exodus were well acquainted with it; for we find, that, when the workmen were ordered to make Cherubim for the tabernacle, no directions were given them as to the

Respecting the appearance of the Cherubim

---

[1] The different chronological computations of the early postdiluvian ages will be discussed at large hereafter. book vi. c. 2. § V.

shape of the sacred hieroglyphics, and yet they had not any occasion to make the least inquiry respecting it. But, though Moses is silent on this point, Ezekiel has provided us with a very minute and ample description of the Cherubic emblems. From him we learn, that the Cherubim were not winged boys, as the licence of painters often idly represents them; but that they were creatures, furnished indeed with wings, yet each compounded of a man, a bull, a lion, and an eagle.

So far he is explicit: with respect to other particulars, they must be gathered by induction.

Were an artist employed to depict a Cherub from the description of Ezekiel, he would first wish to learn which of the four forms *predominated* in the compound symbol. He would know indeed, that each hieroglyphic had four heads, four wings, feet like the feet of an ox, and hands resembling the hands of a man; but he would still find it necessary to inquire, with what body these different parts were to be combined. Now, if I mistake not, the prophet himself will tacitly furnish him with the very information which he requires, by presenting us with two distinct paintings of a Cherub as viewed under different aspects. In one place, Ezekiel tells us, that a Cherub had in general the likeness of a man, though three animal heads were joined to his human head:[1] in another place, he not obscurely intimates, that the predominating form of the symbol was that of a bull. This last particular I gather in the following manner. In his first description of the Cherubim, he says, that each of them had four faces; that of a man, that of a lion, that of an ox, and that of an eagle.[2] In his second description he similarly informs us, that each had four faces: but he *then* adds, that they were those of a Cherub, of a man, of an eagle, and of a lion.[3] By comparing the two passages together it appears, that, in the phraseology of Ezekiel, *the head of a Cherub*, and *the head of an ox*, are synonymous terms. This has frequently been remarked: and hence it has been inferred by some, that the word *Cherub* does itself properly denote *an ox*. The inference is not devoid of plausibility: without however pledging ourselves to adopt it, we may at least venture to say, that the prophet would

---

[1] Ezek. i. 5. [2] Ezek. i. 10. [3] Ezek. x. 14.

scarcely have called the head of the ox by way of eminence *the head of a Cherub*, unless the form of the ox so greatly predominated in the compound form of the Cherub as to warrant the entire Cherub being familiarly styled *an ox*. Had the lion, or the man, or the eagle, predominated; the head of the ox could not have been emphatically denominated *the head of a Cherub*. The whole Cherub must have *especially* resembled an ox; otherwise such a mode of speaking would have been plainly improper. Yet, as we have seen, the prophet likewise intimates, that the general aspect of the Cherubim was that of a man. Here then we have an apparent contradiction; but it is a contradiction, which is *only* apparent. The form of a Cherub was, I apprehend, thus compounded. To the body of an ox was joined the body of a man; and the human body was surmounted by the four heads of a man, a bull (emphatically called *a Cherub*), a lion, and an eagle. Each of the bodies was furnished with a pair of wings: and under that pair, which was attached to a human body, appeared of course, when the wings were not extended for flight, the hands of a man. The whole figure in short bore a considerable resemblance to that of the fabulous Centaur; differing from it chiefly, in its being provided with four heads, four wings, and eyes without number. Now, supposing such to have been the shape of a Cherub, we shall find no contradiction in the two apparently different inferences which may be drawn from the language of Ezekiel. When an hieroglyphic of this description was viewed in the front, the body of the ox would be hidden, and the human body branching out into four heads and supported by the legs and feet of a bull would alone be visible: but, when it was viewed laterally, the larger body of the ox would be by far the most conspicuous object, though the smaller human body would still be seen. Hence, just according to the aspect under which the Cherub was beheld, the form of the man or the form of the bull would predominate: and hence Ezekiel, without any contradiction, both tells us that it had a general resemblance to a man, and uses the word *Cherub* as if synonymous with *an ox*.[1]

So remarkable an appearance, as that of the Cherubim when they were

See Plate II. Fig. 6, 7.

first exhibited before the garden of Paradise, could not be easily forgotten, even supposing that their manifestation was only of a temporary nature: but, so far as I can judge, we have every reason to believe that it was *not* merely temporary. The common notion, that they were little better than a sort of terrific scare-crows employed to prevent mankind from approaching to the tree of life, seems to me to be no less childish than irreconcileable with other parts of Scripture. Under the Levitical economy, which was a republication of ancient Patriarchism adapted to the peculiar circumstances of the children of Israel, the Cherubic symbols were placed in the adytum of the tabernacle and afterwards in the corresponding sanctuary of the temple. Whatever they may have been designed to represent, they were clearly religious hieroglyphics of some description or another: arguing therefore from analogy, we may reasonably infer, that, such as their use and import was under the Law, such also it was under the dispensation of primitive Patriarchism. And this inference will be little less than demonstrated to be just, if we attend to the remarkable language employed by Moses in describing the Paradisiacal Cherubim. Our translation simply and imperfectly says, that God *placed* the Cherubim eastward of the garden: but the force of the original Hebrew is, that he placed them *in a tabernacle*. The Cherubim then of Paradise, and the Cherubim of the Levitical economy, were alike placed in a sacred tabernacle: and, since in each case both the emblems and the position were the very same, the obvious presumption is, that the design and purport was in each case the same also. Such a conclusion is confirmed by another particular, which Moses carefully specifies, and which must by no means be passed over in silence. He tells us, that, with these Paradisiacal Cherubim which were placed in a tabernacle, there appeared likewise, what our translators render, *a flaming sword which turned every way;* but what, I apprehend, may more properly be understood to mean *a bright blaze of bickering fire.* Now an exactly similar manifestation of ardent glory was visible between the Cherubim of the Mosaical dispensation. By this was indicated the presence of Jehovah: and the name, which it usually bears, is that of *the Shechinah ;* a word of the same origin as that, which the Hebrew legislator employs to describe the *tabernacling* (if I may so speak) of the Paradisiacal Cherubim. When the preceding coincidences therefore are duly weighed, we can scarcely, I think, doubt, that the bright blaze, which appeared with the Cherubim of Eden, was no other than that fiery symbol of the divine presence, which the Rabbins have denominated *the Shechinah*. Thus we find, that, as the Hebrew church in the wilderness had the Cherubic symbols, placed in a tabernacle, and surmounted by a preternatural blaze of glory: so the patriarchal church, at its earliest commencement, had the very same symbols, placed in the very same manner, and illuminated by the very same fiery apparition. Such being the case, it is almost impossible to avoid concluding, that their use and intent under one dispensation exactly corresponded with their use and intent under the other dispensation.[1]

What that precise use may be, it is foreign to my present purpose to inquire: but I think, that the Levitical ordinance respecting the adytum of the tabernacle will explain what is meant by the assertion, that the tent-dwelling Cherubim and the blaze of burning glory were placed before the garden to keep the way of the tree of life. We are told, that the Cherubim under the Law, similarly illuminated by the fiery token of the divine presence, were stationed in the Holy of holies; and that no one was permitted to enter into that peculiarly sacred place, except the high-priest, and he only once in the course of every year. We are further told by the great apostle of the Gentiles, that the high-priest was a type of the Messiah, and that his annual entrance into the otherwise inaccessible Holy of holies represented the entrance of Christ into heaven. We may also collect from the ordinary phraseology of Scripture, that Paradise itself was a symbol of heaven; and consequently, since the sacred adytum was likewise a symbol of heaven, we may be sure, that the Holy of holies was in the first instance an express and studied representation of Paradise. Now from these premises we seem compelled to infer, that the exclusion of the people at large from the most holy place shadowed out the exclusion of our first parents and all their posterity from the garden of Eden; that the Cherubic blaze of glory, equally and with the very same allusion, precluded any entrance in

---

[1] The Targums both of Jerusalem and of Jonathan suppose, that the glory of God dwelt between the two Cherubim at the gate of Eden, just as it rested upon the two Cherubim in the tabernacle.

both cases; and that the import of what Moses says respecting the Paradisiacal Cherubim, as elucidated by the ordinances of the Levitical economy and as authoritatively explained by St. Paul, is this: that lost mankind can have no access to the forfeited tree of life, but must for ever remain excluded from the spiritual Paradise by the fiery indignation of Jehovah, unless a divine redeemer shall be pleased to recover their privileges, and to open for them a way to happiness and immortality. Accordingly, as the first book of Scripture represents the children of Adam as shut out from the tree of life; so the last exhibits them, at its triumphant conclusion, as having free access to the same mystic plant, through the prevailing merits and potent intercession of their great high-priest.

2. If then the Cherubim of Paradise stood in a similar relation to the antediluvian patriarchal church, as the Cherubim of the Levitical economy did to the Hebrew church, we may naturally, perhaps necessarily, conclude, that their abode in the tabernacle before Paradise was not of a mere temporary nature, but that they there remained surmounted by the divine glory to the very time of the deluge. Corruption in the antediluvian world would produce much the same effects, as it did in the postdiluvian. We read, that a very early separation took place between the children of Cain and those of Seth, the representative of the righteous Abel: and we further read, that, in the course of the rapid progress of irreligion, the church of pure worshippers was more and more diminished, until at length it comprehended only the members of a single family. Under such circumstances, the sincere church of the antediluvian world in the line of Seth would bear a striking resemblance to the separated Hebrew church of the postdiluvian world in the line first of Shem and afterwards of Abraham. That primitive patriarchal church, which ended in Noah and his family, or which (to speak more properly) was continued by them, would doubtless, if I be right in my view of the Paradisiacal Cherubim, remain in the land of Eden and in the immediate vicinity of those holy symbols, until the deluge came and destroyed the old world; just as the rallying point of the church of Israel was the tabernacle in the wilderness, and the temple, that stationary copy of the tabernacle, in mount Zion. Accordingly, the ancient oriental tradition is, that the flood found Noah ready to embark in the neighbourhood of the sacred mountain,

The forms of the Cherubim must have been well known to the antediluvian patriarchs

where his direct forefathers had never ceased to dwell from the very time of the expulsion out of Paradise.[1] And, in exact consonance with this tradition, we are informed by Moses, that Cain indeed *went out* from the presence of the Lord, his presence (I apprehend) as manifested between the Cherubim; and, *quitting* the territory of Eden, dwelt in the land of Nod: while we are thence necessarily left to conclude, both that the presence of the Lord was specially manifested in Eden; and that Adam, and after him Seth, never removed out of that country.

3. Thus, on the one hand, Noah and his family must have been well acquainted both with the form of the Cherubim and with their use in the religious service of the antediluvian church: and, on the other hand, either in the life-time of that patriarch, or in the age immediately subsequent to his death, that system of idolatry, which has diffused itself with so much uniformity over the face of the whole earth, must have commenced in the postdiluvian world about the era of the building of Babel. The knowledge therefore of the Cherubic symbols has been brought down chronologically to the rise of pagan mythology after the flood. Now the Cherubim were used in the worship of the true God; and they united in one compound hieroglyphic the forms of a man, a bull, a lion, and an eagle. Hence, when idolatry sprang up among those who must have been acquainted with the figure of the Cherubim; the presumption is, that they would employ in the worship of their demon-gods the very same emblems, which had been rendered venerable by long consecration to the service of the true God.

With this presumption the fact perfectly accords. In every quarter of the world the bull, the lion, the eagle, and the man, have been accounted sacred symbols. This uniform veneration of them must have proceeded from a common origin. That common origin can only be found in a period, when all mankind formed a single society. The existence of that single society cannot be placed later than the building of the tower. Consequently, the first veneration of those symbols cannot be ascribed to a more recent age than that of Nimrod. But in that age, which was marked by the

---

[1] Fabric. Cod. Pseudepig. vol. i. p. 241. Thus also the Hindoos represent Menu-Satyavrata or Noah as living in the very same country as that, where they place the garden of Paradise and Menu-Swayambhuva or Adam.

They must also have been well known to the early postdiluvian patriarchs and therefore to the builders of Babel

commencement of a mythological system that was afterwards carried into
every region of the earth by them of the dispersion, the form of the Cherubic
hieroglyphics must have been well known.   Since then genuine Patriarchism and the rise of idolatry thus chronologically meet together; since
the latter seems evidently to have been a perverse depravation of the
former; since the three animal figures, which entered into the compound
shape of the Cherubim, are the very three animal figures, which have been
universally venerated by the Gentiles from the most remote antiquity: I see
not how we can reasonably avoid the obvious conclusion, that, in whatever
manner the pagans applied the symbols of the bull, the lion, and the eagle,
they were borrowed in the first instance from those animals as combined
together in the form of the Cherubim.

VI. To this general argument may be added some others, all of which
tend to establish the same opinion.

In the Cherubim the figures of the lion, the bull, the man, and the eagle,
were all conjoined, so as to make up one compound hieroglyphic.   Thus
likewise the Gentiles, though they frequently venerated those symbols
separately from each other, almost as frequently revered monstrous combinations, which exhibited various animals joined together in a single por-
tentous form.   Into these the bull, the lion, the eagle, and the man, are
conspicuously introduced : and, notwithstanding the licentious fancy of the
pagan mythologists has perpetually added other animals, the peculiar mode
in which such combinations are made bears too striking a resemblance to
the composition of the Cherubim to be purely the effect of accident.   The
production of some of these gentile Cherubim, if I may be allowed so to
express myself, will best enable the curious inquirer to estimate the weight
of the present argument; more especially when the very peculiar connection, in which they are occasionally placed, is likewise taken into consideration.[1]

---

[1] This same argument is adduced by Mr. Parkhurst with a view of establishing the same
opinion; and I am indebted to him for several of the illustrations of it. See his Heb. Lex.
vox ברב. I think him perfectly right in the origin which he ascribes to the compound
hieroglyphics of the pagans: but it is not equally easy to adopt his speculations respecting the
symbolical import of the Cherubim themselves. To omit other objections to his theory, it is

The dog of Hades

1. The dog Cerberus had three heads; that of a lion, that of a dog, and that of a wolf: and his body terminated in the folds of an immense serpent. In the Greek mythology, he was given as an assistant to Pluto; in the Egyptian, he was similarly placed near Serapis or the infernal Osiris: in both, he was described as inhabiting Hades or Tartarus.[1] We find an animal likewise of much the same nature in the Gothic Hell, which encounters Odin during his fabled descent into the world of the departed.[2]

Here we have one of the Cherubic symbols combined with three other bestial forms: and the monster thus produced is immediately connected with the great father, who unites in his own person the characters of Adam and Noah; and is placed in the infernal regions, which, as we have already seen, have a mixed reference to Paradise, the Ark, and the deluge.

Hecate

2. Hecatè or the infernal Diana is sometimes said to have had the heads of a horse, a dog, and a lion; sometimes those of a dog, a horse, and a woman; at other times, those of three women; and at others again, those of a dog, a bull, and a lion.[3]

Here also we may observe two or more of the Cherubic symbols variously combined: and here too we may observe the peculiar connection in which they stand. Hecatè was the same as Proserpine or Isis: she was the female president of the infernal regions: and she at once represented the Earth with the mount of Paradise in its centre, the ship Argha floating on the waters of the deluge, and the tauric lunar crescent by which that ship was astronomically symbolized.

Osiris, Molech, Minotaur, Mithras

3. Osiris was sometimes typified simply by a bull; and sometimes depicted under the compound form of a man with a bull's head, or of a

very difficult to believe, that the Cherubim should have been descriptive images of the Trinity combined with the human nature of Christ, when God has so expressly prohibited all attempts to represent him by any material substance. But this subject will be resumed more at large hereafter. Book vi. c. 6. § II.

[1] Macrob. Saturn. lib. i. c. 20. Apollod. Bibl. lib. ii. c. 5. Montfauc. Ant. vol. ii. par. ii. p. 189.

[2] Mallet's North. Ant. vol. ii. p. 220.

[3] Orph. Argon. ver. 973. Pier. Hierog. p. 48. Æneid. lib. iv. ver. 511. Porph. apud Ger.

serpent furnished either with the head of a bull or with that of a lion.[1] Of a similar nature was the form both of Moloch and Mithras: while in that of the Minotaur, by an inversion of the symbols, we behold a human head attached to the body of a bull.

Here likewise the Cherubic symbols present themselves: and here again they occur in the same connection; for the infernal Osiris, or Mithras, or Moloch, or Minotaur, were all equally the Paradisiacal great father Adam reappearing in the diluvian great father Noah.

4. Precisely in the same connection those symbols also present themselves in the old mythology of Persia, as exhibited to us in the Zend-Avesta. Two personages are described as successively appearing, the one at the commencement of the antediluvian, and the other of the postdiluvian, world: each of whom is styled *the bull-man*; and each of whom is said to have been compounded of a man, a bull, and a horse. These two are clearly Adam and Noah: and the mode of their combination seems to have been this; a human body was joined to a bestial body, which had cloven feet, and which partly resembled an ox and partly a horse. It is not improbable likewise, that the figure had three heads; those of a bull, a horse, and a man. On the whole, such an hieroglyphic would bear a strong resemblance to what I conceive the form of the Cherubim to have been: and, since Adam was represented by it as well as Noah, it is reasonable to conclude, that the shape thus ascribed to the first great father was borrowed from the compound symbols which were displayed before the garden of Paradise.

5. The bull-man of the Zend-Avesta is evidently the Centaur of the classical writers; which was similarly composed of a man, a horse, and a bull: that is to say, its figure was the body of a man united to that of a horse with the cloven feet and tail of an ox. Chiron is usually said to have been the son of Cronus or Saturn, who begot him in the shape of a horse: but Cronus himself is emphatically called by Lycophron *the Centaur*, as being that ancient personage who was thus hieroglyphically represented.[2] Nor is

The transmigrating man-bull of the Zend-Avesta

The Centaur Chiron, Saturn. The figure of the Orphic Cronus or Hercules

[1] Kirch. Chin. Illust. p. 143. Mont. Ant. vol. ii. par. ii. p. 204. Bryant's Anal. vol. ii. p. 432.

[2] Lycoph. Cassand. ver. 1203.

this name bestowed upon him erroneously or casually : as the symbol was the very same as that of the Persian bull-man ; so Cronus united in his own person the characters of the two beings, who are said in the Zend-Avesta to have appeared successively under such a form at the commencement of each world. Cronus, as his legend plainly demonstrates, is both Adam and Noah ; or rather, to express myself agreeably to the notions of the old mythologists, Adam reappearing by transmigration in the person of Noah.

This ancient hero-god was sometimes represented by another compound figure, which still however bears a very close affinity to that of the Cherubim. According to the Orphic theology, from the primeval water and mud was produced a being, which to the body of a dragon added the head of a lion and the face of the god Cronus or Hercules. This being generated an egg of an immense size ; which, being afterwards broken into two parts by its parent, was moulded into the heaven above and the earth beneath.[1] Such is the account given by Athenagoras ; but Damascius says, that this Orphic divinity was a dragon, which had the bestial heads of a bull and a lion and the human face of a god, and whose shoulders were furnished with the golden wings of a bird.[2]

Here, with the addition of a dragon, we have nearly the exact form of the Cherubim : and, since we are explicitly told, that the symbol represented Cronus ; we shall readily perceive, why that deity is said to have been born from mud and water, and why he is fabled to have produced an immense egg. Adam was literally formed out of the moist clay of the earth, and the diluvian Noah is mystically feigned to have been the child of the ocean or of the chaotic mixture : the egg symbolized at once the World and the Ark : and, agreeably to the different relations which he was supposed to bear to it, the great father was sometimes said to have been born out of a floating egg, and sometimes himself to have produced one which comprehended the rudiments of the Universe.

6. Other parallel compounds ought all, I think, to be ascribed to the same origin ; for the close analogy, which exists between them, proves, that

Chimera,
Sphinx,

---

[1] Athenag. Legat. p. 65.
[2] Damas. de Princip. apud Cudworth's Intell. Syst. b. i. c. 4. p. 298.

they have sprung from one source, and have been constructed under the prevalence of one idea.

Chimera had the three heads of a lion, a goat, and a dragon. Sphinx, probably the Singh or winged lion of the Hindoos, had the head of a woman, the wings of a bird, and the claws and body of a lion. The sacred dragon of the Chinese is compounded of a bird, a wild-beast, and a serpent. The German Rodigast bore the head of an ox upon his breast, and an eagle upon his head. The Celtic Dolichenius[1] was depicted standing on a bull, beneath which an eagle was displayed. And the West-Indian Chemens or Zemes had the body of a man, with a serpent wreathed round his legs; the head of a bird at his middle; the five heads of a lion, an eagle, a stag, a dog, and a serpent, on his shoulders; and in his right hand the trident, or navicular lunette with its central mast elevated on a pole, which is equally borne by the classical Neptune and the Indian Siva.[2]

VII. The derivation of the bull, the lion, and the eagle, from the Cherubic symbols of Paradise, will appear yet more explicitly, if we direct our attention to the mythology of Hindostan.

Mount Meru, as we have already seen, is an evident transcript of the garden of Eden associated with the diluvian mount Ararat. Now in this very region, which geographically coincides with the high land of Cashgar and Bokhara, the Brahmenical divines place all those three hieroglyphics. Through the mouths of the lion and the cow they bring two of the sacred rivers of Paradise: and, at the eastern passes, which lead to the Eden of their mythology, they station, in a manner which singularly corresponds with the Mosaical narrative, a being compounded of a man and an eagle whom they denominate *Garuda*. The office, which they assign to him, is that of a guard: and a special part of his employment is to resist the approach of serpents. With these he is said to have engaged in a long and exterminating war, which originated in the jealousy of the serpent race. Garuda had espoused a beautiful woman: and the whole family of snakes took the alarm, fearing lest his progeny should bear as great an antipathy to

---

[1] The *Tailgean* of the old Irish, and the *Telchin* of the classical writers.
[2] See Parkhurst's Heb. Lex. vox כרב.

Margin notes: Chinese dragon, German Rodigast, Celtic Dolichenius, West-Indian Zemes or Chemens

VII HINDU CHERUBIM IN THE PARADISE OF MERU, PHENIX, SIMORGH

them as he himself did.   The man-eagle however destroyed them all, except one which he wore in triumph round his neck.   It is almost superfluous to point out whence this legend has palpably been borrowed.   Garuda is likewise described as being the vehicle of the god Vishnou, who is feigned to be borne on his shoulders through the air, as the Hebrew poets represent Jehovah flying on the wings of the Cherubim.   In other respects, the accounts, which are given of this fabled being, contain a double reference to Paradise and the deluge; just as Meru, where he is stationed, is at once the holy hill of Eden and mount Ararat.   He is said to have been born from an egg: and he is depicted, sometimes supporting on his back a cup out of which springs the sacred aquatic lotos, and sometimes bearing Vishnou in the ship Argha.   The egg, out of which he was produced, was laid by the all-prolific Diti or the great universal mother: and it was not until the end of five centuries that he sprang from it; when he instantly bore off the Amrita or water of immortality, which enabled him to liberate his then captive parent.[1]

This legend, which requires as little elucidation as the preceding one, connects Garuda with the hieroglyphical Phenix and the Simorgh of Persian romance.   The Phenix is said by Herodotus to have exactly resembled an eagle; and the stupendous Simorgh or Rokh is ever placed in the mountains of Caf or the Indian Caucasus.   Enough however has already been said respecting these symbols; which, like the griffin Garuda, have been borrowed from the aquiline part of the Paradisiacal Cherubim.[2]   I shall at present only observe, that, as they have been employed to shadow out the favourite pagan doctrine of a perpetual succession of similar worlds, so their special appearance at the commencement of each great revolving period has been taken from the first manifestation of the Cherubim at the beginning of the antediluvian world.

VIII. The light, in which the Gentiles themselves evidently considered the Cherubim of the Levitical tabernacle, will afford another argument in favour of the present hypothesis.

---

[1] Asiat. Res. vol. vi. p. 490, 491, 493, 513, 515.   Moor's Hind. Panth. p. 334, 336, 337, 340, 341.

[2] Vide supra book i. c. 2. § XI.

VIII. RESPECTING LIGHT, IN WHICH THE LEVITICAL CHERUBIM WERE VIEWED BY THE NEIGHBOURING HEATHENS

When the Israelites, during the administration of Eli, were engaged in war with the Philistines, they vainly and superstitiously sent for the ark of the covenant to the lid of which were attached the Cherubim, imagining that the mere presence of the sacred symbols would be sufficient to ensure the victory over their enemies. The Philistines soon heard of their arrival; and not unnaturally, upon their own principles of hieroglyphical idolatry, forthwith concluded, that the compound forms of the Cherubim were those mighty gods who had inflicted so many plagues upon the Egyptians. Animated however with all the characteristic intrepidity of their Scythic ancestors, they ventured to join battle: and the result was the total rout of the Israelites with the capture of the ark and its attached symbols. The Cherubim having thus fallen into the hands of the Philistines, they placed them, together with the ark, in the temple of Dagon: but the maladies, with which they were supernaturally troubled, produced a speedy restoration of the imagined gods of their enemies.

Now, if I mistake not, the peculiar mode of their restoration will serve to point out the opinion, which indeed the Philistines could scarcely avoid entertaining of the Cherubim when once they had beheld them. A sacred ark or ship was introduced conspicuously into the mysterious rites of the Gentiles, wheresoever idolatry had established itself: and the god of that ark was ordinarily typified by a bull, either in a simple form or compounded with other animals. To this mode of worship the Philistines, who were of the same Cuthic race as the Phenicians and the Shepherd-kings of Egypt, were familiarly accustomed. Hence, deeming the Israelites to be idolaters like themselves and like all other nations with which they were acquainted, they would obviously conclude, that the two Cherubim were the mixed tauric figures of the great father and the great mother, and that the ark on which they were placed was the sacred ship Argha or Argo. With such views, in what manner could they, according to *their* notions, more reverently or consistently return them to their own ministers, than by adopting the precise ceremonial with which the bull-god of Phenicia was wont to be moved from place to place? We learn from Sanchoniatho, that the agricultural deity of that country, who was esteemed the greatest of gods, whose history proves him to be the same as Noah, and who was represented under the figure of a bull or a bull-man, was drawn about to his different temples in a shrine or ark, which was placed in a waggon attached to a yoke of oxen.[1] This was the exact mode which the Philistines selected, when they sent back the ark and the Cherubim to the Israelites. They placed them in a new cart drawn by two cows, on which no yoke had ever yet come; and thus, agreeably to the established method of removing the arkite bull-god, they reverently restored what they believed to be the representations of the tauric great father and great mother of their vanquished enemies.[2]

IX. An argument of a parallel nature may be deduced from the conduct and policy of Jeroboam. When the ten tribes renounced their allegiance to the house of David, and made the son of Nebat their king, the new sovereign was scarcely seated on the throne of Israel, when the Levitical ordinance, by which all the people were required at stated times to sacrifice in the temple of Jehovah at Jerusalem, excited his jealous apprehensions. He concluded, that, if this ordinance were still suffered to remain in force, his subjects, when their revolutionary fever had somewhat abated, would be led by their frequent visits to the ancient capital to repent of the step which they had taken, and thence to put to death the late object of their choice and turn again to his rival Rehoboam. With a view of preventing this apprehended danger, he made, we are told, by the advice of his counsellors, two calves of gold: and then, as if kindly desirous of relieving his people from unnecessary labour, *It is too much for you*, said he, *to go up to Jerusalem; behold thy gods, O Israel, which brought thee up out of the land of Egypt.* To the mode of worship thus established by Jeroboam, his successors in the kingdom adhered to the very last: and the policy, as a second cause, certainly appears to have had the desired effect of preventing the reunion of the two Hebrew kingdoms.

1. The question then is, of what nature was the veneration paid to the two golden calves of Bethel and Dan? It clearly differed, in some respect or other, from the worship of Baal, though the form of Baal himself was that of a bull or a bull-man: because we are more than once told, that,

His calves were primarily copies of the Cherubim

[1] Sanchon. apud Euseb. Præp. Evan. lib. i. c. 10.

[2] See 1 Sam. iv. v. vi.

although some of the kings of Israel abolished the rites of Baal, they never could be induced to relinquish the veneration of the calves, which is repeatedly and emphatically styled *the sin of Jeroboam who made Israel to sin*. Now in what are we to suppose that the difference consisted? The general context of the narrative, when compared with other parts of Scripture, will satisfactorily answer the question.

We find, that the two calves were set up expressly to supersede the periodical religious journeys of the Israelites to the temple at Jerusalem; and we also find, that the new worship, however depraved and perverted, was yet a studied imitation of the regular Mosaical service of Jehovah. The king consecrated priests, but they were of the lowest of the people; because he either feared to trust the Levites, or because they refused to sanction his scheme. He likewise appointed a feast, similar to the feast that was in Judah: and, in his sacrifices, he copied the sacrifices of the temple. Unless indeed a considerable degree of resemblance had been preserved, the end would not have been attained: for the evident policy of Jeroboam was to set up a rival ecclesiastical system, and to divert the people from resorting to Jerusalem by providing for them a similar institution at home which (he assured them) would equally answer every religious purpose. Such being the manifest state of the case, the two calves must have been decidedly analogous to something in the temple; otherwise the plan would have been marred even in its very commencement, and the purpose of the monarch would have been self-defeated. Now in the sanctuary of the temple were placed the two Cherubim; whose figures, though compounded, partook most largely of the form of a bull. Hence, when the matter is considered in all its bearings, we must, I think, almost inevitably conclude, that the two golden calves were copies of the two Cherubim.

Had Jeroboam stopped at this point, he would indeed have been guilty of a most presumptuous schism, but he could not have been justly charged with idolatry. Some writers accordingly have strenuously maintained, that, what is emphatically called *his sin*, was not idolatry, but only a schismatical innovation profanely introduced on Machiavellian principles of state policy. This opinion however, so far as I can judge, is directly contradicted by the express language of Scripture. Jeroboam positively declared, that

his two golden calves were the gods who had brought the Israelites out of
Egypt; and agreeably to such a declaration, he offered sacrifices to them as
real divinities.[1]   The phraseology likewise of Hosea, when he speaks of
them, necessarily implies, that they were considered in the light of deities,
that they were worshipped as the heathen worshipped their false gods, and
consequently that in their use they were to all intents and purposes mere
idols.[2]   Jeroboam therefore was not only guilty of a profane schism; but
he also taught his subjects to adore the tauriform Cherubic symbols, as the
very gods that delivered them out of the hand of Pharaoh.

2. Yet this perversion of the hieroglyphics of the sanctuary was not a
mere simple perversion.   Jeroboam had been much in Egypt, and he had
there observed the two sacred bulls venerated by the people of that country.
He had doubtless also seen some of those compound figures; which, in the
arrangement of their parts, bear so close a resemblance to the Cherubim.
Thus instructed in the mystic lore of Paganism, he committed anew the
very sin which seems to have been committed by the first authors of idolatry
at Babel.   He employed the Cherubic symbols as representations of the
hero-gods; and, with a peculiar reference to the well-known superstition of
Egypt, he pronounced the Cherubim to be the bulls Apis and Mneuis, declared them to be the deliverers of Israel from the tyranny of Pharaoh, and
worshipped them with the same rites that Jehovah was worshipped with in
the temple of Jerusalem.   This then was the sin of Jeroboam: and its
enormity was increased by the baseness of the motive which suggested it.
He deliberately corrupted the very fountain of pure devotion: and led his
people into an idolatry the more dangerous from its speciousness, merely
that he might secure his own regal authority and prevent them from renewing their oaths of allegiance to the house of David.

That these calves, though in the first instance copies of the Cherubim,
were, in their use and application, designed to be images of the two sacred
bulls which were the living representatives of Osiris and Isis, is both very naturally asserted by St. Jerome,[3] and may be collected even from Scripture it-

[Margin note: Yet they were also imitations of the bull and cow of Egypt]

[1] 1 Kings xii. 28, 32.   [2] See Hosea viii. 3—6. xiii. 2.
[3] Hieron. Comment: in Hos. iv.

self. Hosea styles the idols of Jeroboam *the calves of Beth-Aven ;* and immediately afterwards speaks of the high-places of the god Aven, whom he denominates *the sin of Israel.*[1] Now we are told, that, when Jeroboam instituted the worship of the calves, he likewise made high-places in which their priests might officiate.[2] The high-places therefore of the calves are the high-places of Aven; the temple of Aven is the temple of the calves; and Aven, the sin of Israel, is the same as at least one of the calves, which are also peculiarly described as being the sin of Israel. But the god, whose name by the Masoretic punctuation is pronounced *Aven,* is no other than the Egyptian deity Aun or On: for the very god, whose worship Hosea identifies with that of the calves, is he, of whom Potipherah is said to have been the priest; the two appellations, which our translators variously express *Aven* and *On,* consisting in the Hebrew of the self-same letters.[3] *On* however or *Aun* was the Egyptian title of the Sun, whence *the city of On* was expressed by the Greeks *Heliopolis ;* and the Sun was astronomically the same as the tauric god Osiris : consequently On and Osiris are one deity. Hence it is evident, that the worship of Jeroboam's calves being substantially the worship of On or Osiris, the calves themselves must have been venerated, agreeably to the just supposition of Jerome, as the representatives of Apis and Mneuis. The opinion, that the calves, though imitatious of the Cherubim, were employed as instruments of an idolatry brought out of Egypt, is further confirmed by the account which is given of the matter in another part of Scripture. We are told by the author of the Chronicles, that Jeroboam not only set up two calves as objects of worship, but likewise what our translators, following the conjectures of the Rabbins, have thought proper to call *devils.*[4] The corresponding Hebrew word however simply signifies *goats :* and so, I think, it ought manifestly to have been here rendered. The goats then, which were venerated along with the calves, serve to shew, with what superadded theological notions the calves themselves were worshipped. Among the Egyptians, and thence

[1] Hos. x. 5—8. [2] 1 Kings xii. 30, 31, 32.
[3] Comp. Hos. x. 5, 8. with Gen. xli. 45, 50. xlvi. 20. and Ezek. xx. 17.
[4] 2 Chron. xi. 15.

among the Greeks, a goat or a goat-man was the figure of the god Pan or Mendes. When Jeroboam therefore perverted the Cherubim to the veneration of Apis and Mneuis, he associated with his calves another Egyptian deity, who was worshipped under the form of a goat. It may be observed, that this last animal enters into the composition of the fabulous Chimera; which, like the Sphinx, I have already considered as an hieroglyphic of the great universal mother.[1]

[1] There is reason to believe, that the Israelites in the wilderness adored the dog-star or the canine Anubis, who was the same person as Saturn or Chiun or Remphan. The Israelitish sculptures, we are told, at Kibroth Hataavah in the neighbourhood of Sinai remarkably abound in hieroglyphics of the dog-star, represented as a human figure with a dog's head. See Hales's Chronol. vol. ii. p. 451.

CHAPTER VII.

———•——•——

On the origin and import of the worship of the serpent.

———•——•——

The origin of serpent - worship is twofold : and with this supposed origin the gentile use of the symbol corresponds

No part of ancient mythology is more curious, though, in some respects, more intricate and perplexed, than the worship of the serpent. Nearly allied to that of the Cherubic symbols, it rivals it in point of universality, and closely resembles it in point of application. There is however a certain degree of confusion in the subject, as it presents itself to us in the theology of the Gentiles, owing to the various and even opposite lights under which the serpent was considered. Yet this confusion is not so great as to bid defiance to all elucidation : on the contrary, it will be found to be the natural result, partly of the origin of the worship, and partly of that mystic *theocrasia* which forms so prominent a feature in the religious system of Paganism.

The origin of the worship seems to me to have been two-fold, agreeably to the double character of evil and good which the serpent has ever sustained. Under the form of that reptile, the tempter seduced our first parents to sin and consequent misery : yet the Seraphim, who are evidently the same as the Cherubim, are designated in the Hebrew, which was apparently the primeval language of the world, by a common name with the fiery flying serpent of the wilderness.

With this supposed double origin the gentile use and application of the symbol perfectly corresponds. The serpent was esteemed a type of evil and corruption : and, since the deluge was eminently the fruit and consequence of evil, we find it represented by a serpent, as if it had specially proceeded from the evil principle. Yet was the same animal also deemed a fit type of goodness and wisdom ; and, as such, it was made an hieroglyphic of deity ; the male serpent shadowing out the great father or Adam reappearing in the person of Noah, and the female serpent shadowing out the great mother or the Ark venerated in conjunction with the World. Certain properties however, which may be observed in that reptile, contributed, with a race of men strongly attached to the symbolical mode of worship, to produce a still further extension of its typical import, though in close connection with that which has been already noticed. Among the old pagans it was a favourite doctrine, that the World was itself immortal ; yet that in its component parts it was subject to great periodical changes, which amounted to dissolution and subsequent renovation. With the fate of the World was linked that of the great father : for, at each mundane dissolution, he was supposed to slumber in a deathlike sleep on the face of the abyss ; and, at each mundane renovation, he was believed to awake in all the vigour of youth to a new existence. Both these ideas are most aptly expressed by the form and natural history of the serpent. When he sleeps, he convolves himself into a circle with his head in the centre ; and, when he is depicted with his tail inserted in his mouth, he exhibits the appearance of a perfect circle. But this mathematical figure, which terminates in itself, and which thus in some sort has neither beginning nor end, may be employed not improperly as a symbol of eternity or immortality. On the other hand, the serpent is said from time to time to cast his skin ; and thus to appear in renovated youth, another and yet the same. Hence he fully shadowed out the peculiar sentiments, which the pagans entertained respecting a perpetual succession of similar worlds and a periodical regeneration or resurrection of the transmigrating great father. For this reason, we find the serpent considered as a symbol of immortality or eternity : not, I apprehend, *simply* and *abstractedly*, but by an obvious deduction from his being *previously* made a type of the World and the great father ; which deduction was itself drawn with reference to his figure and natural history.

I. Such were the various sentiments entertained of the serpent: I proceed to verify my statement by proofs taken from the documents of ancient mythology.

1. That the worship of the serpent was in part derived from the form assumed by the tempter, may be collected from various legends of a very remarkable nature.

Plutarch supposed, that the serpent Python typified destruction: Adamantius conceived, that it represented a race of demons, to whom dragons and serpents perform the part of ministering attendants: Pierius teaches us, that by the serpent the ancients symbolized destruction, misfortune, and terror: and Diodorus Siculus asserts, that a serpent twisted in spiral volumes was the hieroglyphic of evil.[1] What beings we are to understand by the anguiform demons which Adamantius associates with the serpent Python, may easily be collected from other kindred sources. The Greeks had by no means lost all knowledge of certain evil spirits, inimical to man and hostile to God. Thus Porphyry speaks of wicked demons; which had fallen from their once happy condition, and which were perpetually attempting, either by fraud or by violence, to pervert us from communion with the Supreme Deity and to turn us to themselves. *Intemperance, covetousness, ambition, and above all deceit, are produced by their instrumentality. Falshood is their proper element. Their wish is to be gods; and the power that presides over them aspires to be the greatest of gods: but the Most High, with a mighty arm, restrains their machinations.*[2] Thus also Plutarch mentions a very ancient tradition respecting certain malignant spirits, which envy and oppose good men, excite in their minds fears and doubts, and impede their progress in virtue; lest, by a perseverance in that which is good, they should attain to a greater degree of happiness than they them-

[1] See these authorities collected together by Olaus Wormius de monument. Dan. lib. v.

[2] Porph. apud Euseb. Præp. Evan. lib. iv. c. 22, 23. See also Jamb. de Myster. sect. iii. c. 31. sect. iv. c. 13.

[Margin note: Worship of the serpent was in part derived from the form assumed by the primeval tempter]

selves enjoy.' And he tells us, that it was the doctrine of Empedocles, that there were some impure spirits, which had been banished from heaven, and which wandered about unable to find any rest; the divine wrath pursuing them to every part of the creation.' Thus likewise Themistius speaks, on the authority of what he calls an ancient philosophy, not only of evil demons, but of good spirits, who formerly were accustomed to converse with men in a human form.' And thus both the old Chaldèans and Hindoos had a notion, that their sacrificial rites might be interrupted by the intrusion of impure demons.'·

In the Gothic mythology of Scandinavia, Loke, or the evil principle, is described as being the parent of the great serpent of Midgard.' Now we may easily trace the prototype of this monster in some of the fables which are told of him. The god Thor, though he is really no other than *the great father* of gentile mythology, yet appears, through the channel of perverted tradition, to have had certain of the predicted attributes of the Messiah ascribed to him. He was esteemed *a middle divinity, a mediator between God and man :* and, with regard to his actions, he is said to have bruised the head of the great serpent with his mace.' It was further believed of him, that, in his final engagement with the same serpent, he would beat him to the earth and slay him ; but that the victory would be obtained at the expence of his own life, for that he himself would be suffocated by the floods of poison vomited out of the mouth of the noxious reptile.' There is so close a resemblance, in every main particular, between these legends and the first prophecy, that *the seed of the woman should bruise the head of the serpent while the serpent*

' Plut. apud Stillingfleet's Orig. Sacr. b. iii. c. 3. § 17.

' Plut. de vit. ær. alien. p. 830.

' Themist. Orat. vii. p. 90. See also Lactan. Instit. lib. ii. § 14, 15.

' Annot. in Jamb. de Myst. sect. iii. c. 31. *O king, while we are beginning our evening sacrifice, the figures of blood-thirsty demons, embrowned by clouds collected at the departure of day, glide over the sacred hearth, and spread consternation around.* Sacontala. Act iii.

' Edda Fab. xvi. Remarks on Fab. xvi, xvii.

' Edda Fab. xi. in the notes.   ' Edda Fab. xxvii.

' Edda Fab. xxxii.

should bite his heel, that we can scarcely deem it merely accidental. And we shall be less inclined to ascribe it to a lucky chance, when we recollect the oriental origin of the Goths. They were a branch of the Chasas or Chusas; and they emigrated into Europe from their ancient settlements in the Indian Caucasus. Hence, as might naturally be expected, they brought with them into the west the theology of their brethren of Hindostan. Accordingly, we find the same notion prevalent from a very early period in this last country. Two sculptured figures are yet extant in one of the oldest pagodas, the former of which represents Chrishna, an incarnation of Vishnou, trampling on the crushed head of the serpent; while the latter exhibits the poisonous reptile incircling the deity in its folds and biting his heel.[1] A similar idea may be obviously traced in the history of the classical Hercules. On the sphere he is represented in the act of contending with the serpent, the head of which is placed under his foot: and this serpent, we are told, is that which guarded the tree with golden fruit in the midst of the garden of the Hesperides.[2] But the garden of the Hesperides, as we have already seen, was no other than the garden of Paradise: consequently, the serpent of that garden, the head of which is crushed beneath the heel of Hercules, and which itself is described as incircling with its folds the trunk of the mysterious tree, must necessarily be a transcript of that serpent whose form was assumed by the tempter of our first parents.[3] We may observe the same ancient tradition in the Phenician fable respecting Ophion or Ophioneus. According to Pherecydes, from whom the Greeks received the story, this snake-god was the prince of certain evil spirits, that contended with Cronus, and were by him ejected from heaven. Between the character of Ophion thus exhibited and that of the scriptural Satan there is so strong a resemblance, that Celsus could not avoid being struck with it: but his hatred of Christianity induced him to argue from the circumstance, that the Mosaical history of the fall was borrowed from pagan traditions. He is however well answered by Origen;

---

[1] Maurice's Hist. of Hind. vol. ii. p. 290,

[2] Erat. Catast. ὁ εν γονασιν. Hyg. Poet. Astron. lib. ii. c. 3.

[3] Lucret. de nat. rer. lib. v. ver. 33. Raleigh's Hist. of the world. p. 73.

who clearly shews the great priority of the era of Moses to that of either Heraclitus or Pherecydes.[1]

As the deluge was thought to proceed from the evil principle, the great serpent became also a symbol of the deluge.

2. The serpent being used as the symbol of the evil principle, in consequence of Satan's having once assumed the form of that reptile, it was thence employed to represent the deluge: because the deluge, although really a punishment inflicted by the hand of God, was yet considered as proceeding from the author of ill. For this purpose however, with much hieroglyphical propriety, the sea-snake or water-snake was commonly, though not perhaps invariably, brought forward.

In the Egyptian mythology, the monster Typhon is described as terminating in the volumes of two immense serpents, is celebrated as the greatest of all the children of the Earth, and is said to have overtopped the loftiest mountains while his two hands extended to the utmost limits of the east and the west.[2] The accuracy of this hieroglyphical painting, which represents Typhon as rising above the highest hills and as spreading himself over the whole globe, will readily be allowed, when we find the Egyptians assuring Plutarch, that Typhon was literally nothing more than the ocean.[3] If Typhon then be the ocean, he must be the ocean at some time, when it rose above the summits of the mountains, when it spread itself without shore from the west to the east, and when it made war upon the hero-gods; otherwise the thing symbolized will not correspond with the symbol. But all these circumstances occurred at the time of the deluge, and at no other time except that of the deluge. Typhon therefore must be the ocean at the period, when its waters overwhelmed the whole habitable globe, and put to flight those ancient personages who were the hero-gods of the Gentiles. In exact accordance with this inevitable conclusion, we are told, that Typhon inclosed Osiris within an ark and set him afloat on the waters of the Nile, which the Egyptians called *the Ocean*, because in the celebration of their Mysteries it represented the ocean: and we are further taught, that, at the same period, Horus, or the younger Osiris, was compelled to take refuge in

[1] Stilling. Orig. Sacr. book iii. c. 3.

[2] Apollod. Bibl. lib. i. c. 6. § 3.   Anton. Liber. Metam. c. 28.   Æschyl. Prom. vinct. ver. 351.

[3] Plut. de Isid. p. 363.

an island which floated on the bosom of a sacred lake. Hence it is manifest, that Typhon was a personification of the sea at the period of the deluge: because we are positively told, that he was the ocean; and no other period, but that of the deluge, will agree with his mythological character and history. Accordingly, his very name itself has become the name of the deluge; for the Arabs, who are the immediate neighbours of the Egyptians, still express the general deluge by the term *al Tufan.*[1] But the form of Typhon, as we have seen, was that of a man-serpent: and the Egyptians, though they allowed him to be the ocean at the time when the chief hero-god was driven into the Ark, evidently considered him also as a type of the evil principle; for, in addition to the sentiments which they entertained of him as the parent of all ill, he is also said to have been the father, by the snake Echidna, of the serpent which guarded the golden apples of the Hesperides and which is displayed on the sphere with its head crushed beneath the heel of Hercules.[2] The serpent however of the sacred garden of the Hesperides was a transcript of the serpent in Paradise: and we now find it to be immediately connected with Typhon; who was certainly a personification of the deluge, and who was represented under the mixed form of a man and a dragon. Consequently, the deluge was symbolized by an enormous serpent; and it was so symbolized, in allusion to the form assumed by the evil principle in Paradise.

The Greek fable of Latona being compelled by the serpent Python to take refuge in the floating island of Delos, where she brought forth Apollo and Diana, is palpably the counterpart of the Egyptian fable; which describes Latona or Isis, as fleeing with Horus to the floating island Chemmis, in order to escape from the fury of the dragon Typhon. Horus, accordingly, is allowed to be the same as Apollo; and Typhon must therefore be the same hieroglyphical character as the serpent Python. Hence Python must also be the deluge: and, agreeably to this conclusion, we find his history ascribed to the period of the deluge: for he is said to have been slain by Apollo in the arkite mount Parnassus immediately after that catastrophè; a legend, which simply means, that the hero-god, who was driven by him into

---

[1] Anc. Univ. Hist. vol. i. p. 200.   [2] Apollod. Bibl. lib. ii. c. 5. § 11.

that floating island the Ark, afterwards prevailed over him as the waters gradually retired.

The same mode of symbolizing the flood may be traced in the Gothic mythology. The great serpent of Midgard is said to have been precipitated, by the universal father Woden, to the bottom of the ocean; where he increased to so prodigious a size, that he wound himself round the whole globe of the earth.[1] We have here nothing more than a repetition of the Egyptian fable of Typhon; in which the general prevalence of the deluge, and the final victory obtained over it by the principal hero-god, are symbolically described. That such is the import of the Scandinavian legend, may be gathered, both from the manifest identity of Typhon and the serpent of Midgard, and likewise from a curious story respecting the god Thor. That deity, whose character melts into that of Woden, and who like him is the great father, is fabled to have embarked in a boat to fish for the vast sea-serpent, and by main force to have nearly dragged him from his watery bed.[2] The story is, I believe, purely diluvian; for the fictions respecting Woden, Thor, and the other demon-gods of Scandinavian mythology, carry us back to the times of the sacred cow, the Ark, and the flood. Thor therefore in a boat is the same as the chief deity of Egypt and Hindostan in the ship Argo or Argha; and the great water-serpent bears the same relation to this god, as Typhon does to Osiris. Such a coincidence can scarcely be deemed altogether casual: because we find, that both the Goths and the Egyptians equally represented their hero-gods floating in a ship on the surface of the ocean; notwithstanding the latter described the sea as a demon inimical to man, used a fish as a type of hatred, and debarred their priesthood from eating of it.[3]

In a manner precisely resembling the foregoing examples, the Ophion or Ophioneus of Phenician mythology, whose legend the Greeks received from Pherecydes the Syrian, is at once connected with the primeval tempter and with the history of the deluge. He is described as the prince of the evil demons: yet he is likewise said to have been the sovereign of the Titans,

---

[1] Edda. Fab. xvi.   [2] Edda. Fab. xxvii.

[3] Edda. Fab. xxii.   Porph. de ant. nymph. p. 256.   Plut. de Isid. p. 363.   Herod. lib. ii. c. 37.

the whole of whose fabled war against the hero-gods is built upon traditions of the flood; and he has a consort assigned to him, who is the daughter of the Ocean. Agreeably to this part of his character, he is indifferently feigned to have been cast into Tartarus or the central abyss, and to have been plunged, like Typhon and the serpent of Midgard, beneath the waves of the sea.[r]

The same hieroglyphic of the serpent is used also by the Chinese to express the deluge viewed as proceeding from the evil principle: for so I am led by analogy to understand the curious fable preserved by Martinius. *In the time of Thienhoang the son of Puoncu, a celestial spirit, passing about in all directions, gradually introduced civilization, and softened the native ferocity of man. This was the more easily effected, since the great dragon, which disturbed the whole world by confounding together heaven and earth, had been slain. For, after his destruction, matters were arranged, each according to its proper rank and dignity.*[2] The rout of this dragon, which had thrown the Universe into confusion, seems to allude to the same event as the plunging of Typhon into the sea to escape the wrath of Jupiter, the submersion of Ophion and the Titans, the casting of the serpent of Midgard to the bottom of the ocean, and the slaying of Python by Apollo immediately after the deluge. Such an opinion is confirmed by the general connection of the story. The civilization of mankind subsequent to the allegorical death of the dragon, which is said to have been effected by a celestial spirit travelling to every quarter of the globe, is palpably the same as the similar civilization which is feigned to have been produced by the imagined travels of the great father; who, whether designated by the appellation of *Osiris* or *Dionusus* or *Cronus* or *Buddha*, was esteemed, in the material system, the Soul or intellectual Principle of the World. But this civilizing Intelligence, as his history proves, is the patriarch Noah considered as a reappearance of Adam. And accordingly his efforts, which succeed the destruction of the dragon that had reduced all things to chaos, are ascribed by the Chinese to the era of Puoncu: who, as we have already seen, was

[r] Tzetz. in Lycoph. ver. 1191. Apollon. Argon. lib. i. ver. 503.

[2] Martin. Hist. Sin. lib. i. p. 16.

born out of an egg that floated on the waters of the great abyss; and who consequently is the same personage as Brahma, Siva, Dionusus, and Phtha.[1] Puoncu therefore is Adam reappearing in Noah: and the contemporary dragon is the serpent of Paradise viewed as the author and parent of the deluge.

II. But, though the serpent is thus exhibited in pagan mythology as the representative of the evil principle and thence as a symbol of the flood, he was considered also in the opposite light of a great and beneficent deity.

1. This part of his character, like that which has been recently discussed, may be traced to the first age of the world. The Cherubim sometimes bore the name of *Seraphim*, for the identity of the Cherubim and the Seraphim manifestly appears from comparing together the visions of Isaiah and Ezekiel.[2] But the word *Seraph* signifies also *a flying serpent*: which is an animal of great beauty, shining like burnished gold, and exhibiting the semblance of fire as the rays of the sun strike upon it while it rapidly wings its way through the liquid air. Now, since the fiery and flitting appearance of the Seraphim stationed before the garden of Eden would bear a considerable resemblance to that of the fiery flying serpent, and since the very same appellation was employed to designate each of them, it was not unnatural to conclude, that the form of the flying serpent entered into the composition of the Seraphic or Cherubic emblems. We have no warrant indeed from Scripture to suppose, that this was *really* the case: yet the notion itself, however erroneous, seems to have been of very great antiquity; and the existence of such a notion would obviously cause the serpent, particularly the winged serpent, to be viewed as a fit symbol of the agathodemon. Rabbi Bechai observes, *this is the mystery of our holy language, that a serpent is called Seraph, as an angel is called Seraph:* and, in accordance with this supposed mystery, it has been imagined, that Satan tempted Eve under the form of one of those resplendent winged serpents which are denominated *Seraphim*, and that he succeeded the more easily because the

As such, his figure was borrowed from the winged seraph.

---

[1] Vide supra book i. c. 4. § II. 6.

[2] Compare Isaiah vi. with Ezek. i. and x. and see Parkhurst's Heb. Lex. vox שרף.

angelic Seraphim were wont to appear to our first parents under the precise form assumed by the seducer.[1]

The prevalence of some such notion, I mean the notion which ascribed to the Cherubic Seraphim the figure of a fiery flying serpent, may be traced not obscurely in the hieroglyphical mythology of Paganism. I have already referred the gentile symbols of the bull, the lion, the eagle, and the man, whether exhibited singly or compoundedly, to the mixed form of the Paradisiacal Cherubim. Now with these figures is perpetually associated that of a serpent, and very commonly of a winged serpent: whence it is natural to infer, if the derivation of the bull, the lion, the eagle, and the man, from the Cherubic symbols, has been satisfactorily established; that they, who so generally added to them a serpent, believed that reptile, in the Hebrew termed *Seraph*, to have entered into the composition of the Seraphim or Cherubim.

I shall notice some of these blended hieroglyphics, though I may incur the charge of repetition, as they bear so immediately on the point now under consideration; and I shall add to them other particulars, which have not as yet been noticed.

2. The Orphic first principle is sometimes said to have been compounded of a bull, a lion, a winged man, and a serpent; and is sometimes described as a dragon, having the head of a lion and the face of the god Cronus.[2] This being is the same as that, which the Orphic Phanes is reported to have produced; a monster, exhibiting the semblance of a snake with the head of a man.[3] Of a similar description is the old Egyptian hieroglyphic of a serpent having the head of a bull:[4] and since, agreeably to the pagan notions of the mystic generation of the great father by which one and the same person supported the two characters of father and son, the serpent was indifferently feigned to have produced the bull, or the bull the serpent; we may hence perceive both the origin and import of the ancient Bacchic chaunt, *The bull is the father of the dragon, and the dragon of the bull.*[5] Some-

[handwritten marginal note: Hence it was blended with the Cherubic symbols]

---

[1] See Patrick on Gen. iii. 24; Abp. Tennison's Disc. of Idol. c. xiv. p. 354; and Hales's Chronol. vol. ii. p. 13.

[2] Damasc. apud Cudw. Intell. syst. b. i. c. 4. p. 298. Athenag. Legat. p. 65.

[3] Orph. Fragm. apud Athen. Legat. p. 72. [4] Montfauc. Ant. vol. ii. p. 204.

[5] Jul. Firm. de err. prof. rel. p. 52. Clem. Alex. Cohort.

times the sacred serpent of the Egyptians was delineated with the head of a hawk, which is a bird of the same species as the eagle:[1] and his relationship to the Seraph is shewn by his being furnished with wings, a circumstance implied indeed in his very name *Cneph*.

It is easy to point out various other instances, in which the serpent is equally blended with one or more of the Cherubic figures. The Cerberus both of the Greeks and the Egyptians was compounded of a dog, a wolf, a lion, and a serpent.[2] The sacred dragon of China consists of a bird, a serpent, and a wild-beast.[3] The monster Chimera blended together, in one hieroglyphical animal, a lion, a goat, and a dragon.[4] The Zemes of the West-Indians was composed of a man, a lion, an eagle, a stag, a dog, and a serpent.[5] The Persian Mithras was depicted with a human body, a lion's head, and four wings; and was associated with a snake.[6] And the Hieropolitan Belus or Apollo had for his companions a dragon, an eagle, and two female figures.[7]

III. Such I consider to have been the origin of the worship of the serpent as viewed in the light of a benignant genius: and agreeably to this origin was the application of the symbol. As the proper Cherubic figures were employed to represent the greatest of the pagan deities: so the serpent, misdeemed a Cherubic or Seraphic figure, was used precisely in the same manner and was invested with precisely the same character.

The ancient sages, who were much addicted to physiological speculations, gave various reasons deduced from the natural history of the serpent for bestowing upon it a high degree of veneration. With these reasons, which Eusebius has detailed at large, I shall not concern myself: it will be sufficient to state the undoubted fact which he mentions, that serpents were accounted the greatest of gods and the leading principles of the Universe, and that as such they were invariably introduced both into the temples and into the due celebration of the Mysteries.[8] The real ground of their being accounted the greatest of the gods was this: they were employed, according

[1] Euseb. Præp. Evan. lib. i. c. 10.   [4] Macrob. Saturn. lib. i. c. 20.
[3] Parkhurst's Heb. Lex. p. 391.   [4] Hesiod. Theog. ver. 319.
[5] Picart's Cerem. vol. iii. p. 142.   [6] Mont. Ant. vol. ii. p. 368.
[7] Macrob. Saturn. lib. i. c. 17.   [8] Euseb. Præp. Evan. lib. i. c. 10.

to their sexes, to symbolize the great father and the great mother. And, in this manner, like the proper Cherubic figures, we find them venerated in every quarter of the globe; another proof, that the different mythological systems of Paganism must all have originated from a common source, and have been all constructed under the impression of similar ideas.

1. That the serpent was used to represent the great father, by whom the ancients meant Adam reappearing in the person of Noah, and whom they supposed to be manifested at the beginning of each successive new world in the character of its demiurgic regenerator, may be gathered from the whole tenor and arrangement of gentile mythology. Every where we find the great father, exhibiting himself under the form of a serpent; and every where we find the serpent, vested with the attributes of the great father, and partaking of the honours which were paid to him.

Among the Egyptians, the winged serpent Cneph was highly venerated, and was esteemed the creator of the World.[1] This part of his character proves him to have been a symbol of the great father; because Phtha or Vulcan or Osiris was equally supposed to be the demiurge. Accordingly, the serpent Cneph was so immediately connected with Phtha, that the latter was feigned to be the offspring of the former; by which, agreeably to the regular system of pagan genealogies, nothing more was meant, than that each was the same person viewed under a somewhat different aspect:[2] and, in a similar manner, Osiris, who was no other than Phtha, was represented in the midst of the volumes of a serpent.[3] The Phenicians considered the winged snake as the symbol of the Agathodemon or good demon-god: and it was supposed, that their Taut, who was the same as the Thoth of the Egyptians, was the first inventor of serpent worship.[4] Taut however, as we shall hereafter see, was in reality the great father himself; the same, as the Tat or Datta or Twashta of the Hindoos, and as the Codom or Cadmus of the oriental Buddhists the Greeks and the Phenicians. But Twashta, the great artificer of the Universe, whose character perfectly corresponds with

The male serpent typified the great father.

---

[1] Euseb. Præp. Evan. lib. iii. c. 11.

[2] Ibid. Thus Horus is said to be the son of Osiris: but Horus and Osiris were equally Noah. The reason of this confusion has already been stated. Vide supra b. i. c. 1. § I. 10.

[3] Mont. Ant. Suppl. p. 211.

[4] Euseb. Præp. Evan. lib. i. c. 10.

that of the Egyptian Cneph and Phtha, is supposed to bear the form of a serpent:[1] and Cadmus is feigned to have been, at the close of his life, metamorphosed into that reptile.[2] Twashta or Tat melts into the great triad of Hindoo deity, and the members of that triad again meet together in the person of Jagan-Nath ; though this last god is more peculiarly identified with Vishnou. Here we still meet with the universally prevailing form of the sacred serpent. Vishnou is represented, like Osiris, encompassed in the volumes of a snake: Siva is crowned with the great serpent Sesha-Naga, and is ordinarily depicted with snakes twisted round every limb : and Jagan-Nath is said to be sometimes worshipped under the form of a seven-headed dragon, in allusion to the seven Rishis or Titans or Corybantes, who with the great father himself make up the sacred family of eight with which each successive world was supposed to commence.[3]

Agreeably to this use of the serpent as a symbol of their chief deity, the Hindoos highly venerate that animal itself, considering it in the light of a sacred and mysterious being.[4] Equally reverenced was it by the Persians, who accounted it the greatest of gods, as we learn from the Octateuch of Ostanes referred to by Eusebius:[5] and, pursuant to this sentiment, they associated it with their god Mithras or the great universal father.[6] Nor was the worship of the serpent less prevalent among the Babylonians. The apocryphal story of Bel and the dragon, though it cannot be admitted into the canon of Scripture, must yet have been founded upon a well-known superstition of the Chaldèans : and its exact accordance with the temple-adoration of the serpent in other countries sufficiently proves, that in the chief outlines it may be received as agreeable to the truth. The same

---

[1] Asiat. Res. vol. x. p. 39, 40. The ancient heresy of the Ophites engrafted itself upon the pagan legend of a demiurgic serpent. Joseph the carpenter was reported to be the great artificer Twashta; and Christ was impiously said to be an incarnation of the great serpent, which gently glided over the cradle of his mother Mary while she was yet an infant. Mr. Wilford justly remarks, that the serpent-god of the Ophites was obviously the demiurgic Cneph or Agathodemon of the Egyptians, Phenicians, and other oriental nations.

[2] Ovid. Metam. lib. iv. ver. 575.

[3] Maurice's Hist. of Hind. vol. ii. plate 8. Moor's Hind. Panth. p. 39 and plate 17. Bruton. Churchill's Collect. in Southey's Kehama. vol. ii. p. 171.

[4] Maurice's Ind. Ant. vol. v. p. 1015 plate.   [5] Euseb. Præp. Evan. lib. i. c. 10. sub fin.

[6] Ban. Mythol. vol. ii. p. 104. Mont. Ant. vol. ii. p. 368.

superstition still presents itself, if we direct our attention to China: and presents itself likewise in the very same application. Couplet mentions, that Fohi was reported to have the body of a serpent, and his son Shin-Nungh the head of an ox.[1] But Fohi, as the whole of his history demonstrates, was the patriarch Noah; and his mythological ox-headed son was the same person as his parent. The great father therefore in China, as well as in other countries, was symbolized by a serpent: and, since this serpent is made the father of a bull, we may clearly perceive, that the framers of such hieroglyphics must have been well acquainted with the idea expressed in the Bacchic chaunt, which I have already had occasion to notice; *The bull the father of the dragon, and the dragon of the bull.* From China we may turn to the Orphic and classical mythology, and again we shall find the great father similarly represented. All the pagan gods, as we are repeatedly informed by the ancient mythological writers, are ultimately one and the same person: and that person is the great father; who, under whatever name, is described as the head of the diluvian Cabiri, and is perpetually represented as having been exposed at sea in an ark. But Jupiter, Esculapius, and Dionusus, are all equally said, on various fabled occasions, to have assumed the form of a serpent; and all these deities may be shewn from circumstantial evidence to be the patriarch Noah.[2] In a similar manner, the Hindoo Deonaush, who is manifestly the same as the Greek Dionusus, is supposed to have been metamorphosed into a snake:[3] the Orphic Cures or principal Cabirus, the description of whom equally proves his identity with Dionusus, is celebrated as taking the form of a terrific dragon:[4] and the Orphic Cronus and Hercules, each of whom may be shewn by circumstantial evidence to be the great father, are represented, either as compounded of a man a lion and a serpent, or simply as being a winding serpent.[5]

The ancient character, thus symbolized by a snake, was accounted the

---

[1] Couplet Præf. ad Tab. Chron. p. 3.

[2] Athenag. Legat. p. 71. Nonni Dionys. lib. vi, viii. v. Schol. in Arat. Phænom. p. 11. Ovid. Met. lib. xv. ver. 622—744. Eurip. Bacch. 1016.

[3] Moor's Hind. Panth. p. 272.   [4] Orph. Hymn. xxxviii.

[5] Athenag. Legat. p. 65, 69.

common parent of the Ophites or Serpentigenæ; and nearly all the Hellenic tribes claimed to be of this descent. Nor was their claim so irrational as at first sight it may appear; for the serpent-god was in reality the great father, from whom all the nations of the earth may equally deduce their genealogy. Thus the Athenians were reported to be of the serpent brood; and they had a tradition, that the chief guardian of their citadel was a dragon.[1] This dragon-god was the same as their first king Cecrops; who, like the Chinese Fohi (with whom he doubtless must be identified, for the first sovereign of every ancient pagan nation will uniformly prove to be Noah), was feigned to be of a twofold nature, a man blended with a serpent.[2] Cecrops reigned at the supposed period of the contest between Neptune and Minerva, when the former brought an inundation over the land of Attica; a legend founded on the history of the general deluge. Closely connected with Cecrops is another serpent-prince, who is really the same as Cecrops himself: for the form of each is perfectly similar; and, as Cecrops is placed at the time of a flood, so Erichthonius is reported to have been inclosed by Minerva within an ark and thus committed to the care of one of the daughters of Cecrops.[3] Both of them are described as being primeval sovereigns of Attica: but the histories of them both serve only to shew, that the great father was universally symbolized by a serpent.

We have now traced the hieroglyphic of the snake in application to the great father through the mythologies of the most celebrated nations of the earth: we shall equally meet with it, and in precisely the same application, in the mystic theology of the Druids. The god Hu or Noë, who is the allegorical husband of the ship-goddess Ceridwen, who (as we have already observed) is represented by the Cherubic symbol the bull, and who is described as having been preserved in an ark during the prevalence of an universal deluge, is styled, in the writings of the bards, *the glancing Hu, the gliding king*, and *the dragon sovereign of Britain*. From one of those poems we may collect, that a living serpent was venerated as the symbol of the deity: and, as serpents agreeably to their supposed sacred nature were kept by the Egyptians in their temples; so the dragon, which typified the

[1] Herod. lib. viii. c. 41.   [2] Apollod. Bibl. lib. iii. c. 13. § 1.

[3] Apollod. Bibl. lib. iii. c. 13. § 6.

arkite god Hu, is described, as moving round the huge stones of Caer-Sidi or Stone-henge, and as pursuing a retreating goddess who is styled *the fair one*. The whole seems to allude to some then well-known fable; which most probably was nearly allied to the legend of Jupiter violating Proserpine under the form of a serpent and by her becoming the father of the infernal Bacchus.[1]   Hu at least was certainly the same deity as the classical Huas or Bacchus, and was worshipped together with Ceres and Proserpine in a manner which exactly resembled the Orgies of the Samothracian Cabiri.[2] But the ophite Jupiter and the ophite Bacchus, though placed in the relation to each other of father and son, are confessed by the old mythologists to have been fundamentally one deity.

The serpent was equally venerated as the greatest of gods, that is to say as the representative of the great father, by the ancient Russians, Samogitians, and Lithuanians:[3] and, if from the nations of the eastern hemisphere we finally direct our attention to America, we shall still find the same animal appearing in such immediate connection with the principal of the Mexican gods, that we can scarcely doubt its being thus placed in consequence of the prevalence of notions similar to those which were so familiar to the mythologists of the old world.   Vitzliputzli, who was carried from place to place in an ark like Osiris or Ammon or Dionusus, who in short was evidently the great father of Mexican theology, held in his right hand a staff cut in the form of a serpent; while the four corners of the ark, in which he was seated, terminated each with a carved representation of the head of that reptile.[4]

2. As the male serpent was thus employed to symbolize the great father, so the female serpent was equally used to typify the great mother; under which character the pagans jointly venerated the Earth or larger World, and the Ark or smaller World.   Such a mode of representation may both be

The female serpent typified the great mother.

---

[1] Davies's Mythol. of Brit. Druids. p. 116, 121, 561, 562.

[2] Dionys. Perieg. ver. 565.   Artemid. apud Strab. Geog. lib. iv. p. 198. Mnas. apud schol. in Apoll. Argon. lib. i. ver. 917.

[3] See Erasmus Stella, Sigismund Baro, Scaliger, Alexander Guagin, and Boxhorn, cited by Ousel annot. in Minuc. Fel. Octav. p. 267, 268.

[4] Purch. Pilg. b. viii. c. 11. p. 796.

proved by express testimony, and is perfectly agreeable to the analogy of the whole system of gentile mythology. In the same manner as the two great parents were worshipped under the hieroglyphics of a bull and a cow, a lion and a lioness, a merman and a mermaid, or a horse and a mare: so were they adored under the cognate figures of a male and female serpent.

Among the Syrians and the Celts, the great mother was typified by a woman terminating in the volumes of a serpent; who is described as the guardian of Jupiter in the sacred Corycian cave when he fled from the rage of Typhon or the deluge, and as the paramour either of Hercules or Jupiter to whom she bore three sons.[1] The same mode of symbolizing prevails also among the Hindoos. Devi or Isi, who sailed over the deluge in the form of the ship Argha, is fabled to have assumed the figure of a serpent during that intermediate period between two worlds which is ever marked by the mystic slumber of Vishnou.[2] In this shape she bore the god in safety over the waters of the interminable ocean; until at length, at the commencement of a new mundane system, he awoke to the exertion of fresh demiurgic energy.[3] Now, as the serpent is thus declared to be a form of Isi; as the ship Argha is declared to be another of her forms; and as, under each form, she is indifferently the vehicle of the great father on the surface of the deluge: it is manifest, that the serpent, when thus exhibited to us, must inevitably be the Ark of Noah.

This application of the hieroglyphic will lead us to the right understanding of a most curious Hindoo painting, which represents one of the miracles ascribed to Chrishna or Vishnou: and the painting will, in return, serve to confirm and establish the propriety of the foregoing conclusion. An enormous snake is depicted in the act of opening its jaws to their utmost extent: and the god Vishnou, that same god who was borne over the waves of the deluge on the navicular sea-serpent, is seen, driving into its mouth a mixed herd of cattle, and followed by three companions of inferior dignity. The legend, of which this painting is the representation, informs us, that

[1] Apollod. Bibl. lib. i. c. 6. § 3. Herod. lib. iv. c. 9, 10. Diod. Bibl. lib. ii. p. 127.
[2] Moor's Hind. Panth. p. 22.
[3] Moor's Hind. Panth. p. 26, 27. Maur. Hist. of Hind. vol. i. p. 401. See Plate II, Fig. 1.

Crishna, being once in imminent danger from the rage of his numerous enemies, produced a vast snake; which received and sheltered in its capacious stomach his flocks, his herds, himself, and his fellow-shepherds.[1] With the key, of which we are now possessed, it cannot be difficult to unlock the hidden meaning of this very remarkable hieroglyphic. The huge snake produced by Vishnou is the water-serpent, which bore him floating on the surface of the intermediate deluge; in other words, it is the Ark, which, as we have seen, was symbolized by a serpent. He is said to have produced it, because the prototype of his character was the builder of the Ark. He produced it when in great danger from his enemies, because Noah built the Ark while the flood was yet impending: and the enemies, from whom he took refuge within the stomach of the snake, are the same as those, whom the Greeks and Egyptians called *Typhon* and *the Titans*, that is to say, the deluge and the impious antediluvians. Vishnou, in short, entering into the snake with his herds, his flocks, and his three companions, is Noah entering into the Ark with the beasts and his three sons. Thus accurate is the hieroglyphic in all its parts; and thus exactly does it at once tally with and confirm the conclusion, that the Ark or great mother was symbolized by a serpent.

The same hieroglyphic occurs in the mythology of China, and evidently in the very same application. Fohi, the reputed first emperor of that country, whose form is fabled to have been that of a man terminating in the tail of a snake, and whose whole history decidedly proves him to be Noah or the great father, is said to have delivered to the Chinese eight hieroglyphics denominated *Koua*. These *Koua*, we are told, expressed certain general things, on which the corruption or generation of particular things depended; such as heaven, earth, thunder, mountains, fire, clouds, water, and wind: and, when Fohi taught his subjects how to use them, he is reported, by way of exciting a mysterious veneration for his new institutes, to have declared, that he had seen them traced on the back of a dragon-horse which rose from the bottom of a lake.[2] Now, when the character of Fohi

[1] Moor's Hind. Panth. p. 202. See Plate II. Fig. 5.
[2] Du Halde's China. vol. i. p. 270.

is considered, and when we recollect the principles on which the whole of pagan mythology is founded, we shall easily decypher the import of the preceding legend.   Fohi himself is certainly Noah: the philosophy respecting the alternate generation and corruption of things, which he is said to have inculcated, is the identical philosophy, which taught that to destroy is but to produce in another form: the sacred lake was in every part of the gentile world a symbol of the deluge: it only remains therefore, that the dragon-horse, which proceeds from it, must, according to the preceding general analogy of the hieroglyphic of the serpent, represent the Ark.   This supposition is confirmed, both by the compound figure of the Chinese symbol, and by the fable of its having the philosophical system of Fohi inscribed on its back.   The mare, no less than the serpent, was a well-known hieroglyphic of the great mother; being a form equally assumed by the classical Ceres, the British ship-goddess Ceridwen, and the mystic nurse of the diluvian Bacchus: and the pretence, that the institutes of the first Chinese emperor were received from the fabled dragon-horse, exactly corresponds with the widely prevailing oriental tale, that certain sacred books or records were either preserved in the Ark, or were recovered after the deluge from the bottom of the ocean.[1]

We may now direct our attention to classical mythology: and once more we shall find the same symbol applied in the same manner.   Harmonia the wife of Cadmus, and Rhea the wife of Cronus, were each one character with Isis or Parvati; that is to say, were each, as I shall hereafter shew, the Ship of the deluge or the great mother.   But Harmonia and Rhea are both said to have been changed into serpents: the former, when her husband Cadmus underwent the same metamorphosis; the latter, when she attempted to escape the embraces of her son Jupiter himself in the form of a dragon.[2]   This second fable, like other similar pagan tales of incestuous mixtures, originated from the different degrees of relationship, which the great father was supposed to bear to the Ark: he was at once its parent, its husband, and its son.   Accordingly, though Jupiter is said to have been

---

[1] This subject will be resumed at large hereafter, book iii. c. 5.
[2] Ovid. Metam. lib. iv. ver. 590—602.   Athenag. Legat. p. 71.

the offspring of Cronus, we are yet assured by the old mythological writers, that they were really one and the same deity. When Cronus was viewed as the husband, and Jupiter as the son, of Rhea; Jupiter was necessarily considered also as the son of Cronus, though he was the same as Cronus. Hence he stood to Rhea in the double relationship of son and husband: and hence the mystic union of the great father and the great mother was hieroglyphically described by the incestuous conjunction of two serpents. The two, we are informed, when united, presented the figure of the two snakes, which appear twisted round the caduceus of Hermes.[1]

I may here remark, that, as the serpent was deemed oracular and was likewise an hieroglyphic of the ship Argo; so the ship Argo, partly from its being thus represented, and partly from the responses of the dove, was equally thought to be oracular. Rhea and Harmonia were the same as Isis; and, accordingly, among the Egyptians, we find the serpent immediately connected with that goddess. Elian tells us, that the asp-snake called *Thermuthis* was held by them in the highest veneration, and that they were wont to attach it like a royal diadem to the head-dress of Isis.[2] Now this animal, united with the mysterious Yoni and Linga or the ship Argha containing the phallic Siva, constitutes the precise head-dress with which the Indian Devi is sometimes decorated.[3] The combination is remarkable, since it abundantly shews the close relation of the serpent to the diluvian Argha: and it may serve to explain the idea, with which the asp was placed on the head of Isis; for the navicular Isis of Egypt is certainly the same as the navicular Parvati or Devi of Hindostan.

3. From what has been said it appears, that the serpent was universally employed to symbolize the great mother no less than the great father: and, since it was thus used, it necessarily represented whatever the great mother herself represented. But the great mother represented both the Megacosm and the Microcosm, or the Earth and the Ark: whence, as the ship Argha and the aquatic lotos support both these characters, so the serpent likewise will be found to do the very same.

[handwritten margin note: Hence the serpent represented the perpetually renovated world; and, as such, was used in the Mysteries.]

---

[1] Athenag. Legat. p. 71.
[3] Moor's Hind. Panth. plate 6. numb. 4.
[2] Ælian. de anim. lib. x. c. 31.

We have already seen how it symbolized the Ship of the deluge: we may now further observe, that, as a type of the great mother, it was also an hieroglyphic of the World.   This necessarily follows from the very circumstance of its *being* a type of the great mother, even if there were no positive declaration to the purpose: but we likewise have it explicitly declared that such was the case.   Horapollo tells us, that, when the Egyptians wished to express the World, they painted a serpent:[1] and Macrobius says, that the Phenicians similarly represented the World by a dragon devouring its tail ; that is to say, by a snake with its tail placed in its mouth, so as to exhibit the figure of a circle.[2]   The reasons given by these two authors for such a mode of symbolization differ in words, but agree in substance.   Horapollo says, that the World was represented by a serpent, because that animal every year sheds its skin and appears in renovated youth: Macrobius intimates, that the snake formed into a circle shadowed out the World, considered as proceeding from itself and revolving into itself.   The idea was however in both cases the same, though somewhat differently expressed.   Independent of any other origin, both the circular disposition and the natural history of the serpent served admirably to describe the favourite dogma of ancient Paganism, that the substance of the World was eternal; but that there was an endless succession of similar mundane systems, each springing in the vigour of renewed adolescence from its worn out predecessor, and each at the termination of an appointed great period being resolved into its component matter.   It was by pursuing this idea, that the Hindoos made the great navicular serpent, on which Vishnou reposes floating on the surface of the intermediate deluge, a symbol of eternity or immortality.[3]   That serpent, as we have seen, is a type of the ship Argha: and the Argha, as a form of the great mother, is at once the Ark and the boat of the Earth, each considered as borne on the waters of the mighty deep.

The Earth then being deemed eternal in substance, though experiencing successive great revolutions ; and being symbolized by a serpent, because the serpent as an hieroglyphic so aptly expressed both these ideas : the ser-

---

[1] Horap. lib. i. c. 2. p. 4.   [2] Macrob. Saturn. lib. i. c. 9. p. 158.
[3] Moor's Hind. Panth. p. 29.

pent, thus employed to represent the Magna Mater, naturally became itself a type of the abstract idea of *Eternity*, which it was used to express in reference to the supposed nature of the World. It was in mixed allusion to the successive regenerations of the Universe and to the new birth of the great father at the commencement of each mundane system, speculations built wholly upon the renewal of the World after the deluge and the mystic second birth of Noah from the Ark, that a golden serpent was wont to be placed in the bosoms of those who were initiated into the Orgies of Jupiter Sabazius.[1] Each mysta was thought to undergo scenically in his own person whatever had been undergone by the great father : and the regeneration of the aspirants, to which the golden serpent related, was but a transcript of the new birth of the chief hero-god, under whatever name he might be venerated.

4. These remarks on the worship of the serpent bring me again to the conclusion respecting a celebrated hieroglyphic of the gentile world, to which I have already been brought by discussing the worship of the egg.

On these various principles, it was often united with the egg or globe.

The symbol of a serpent, frequently a winged serpent, connected in some mode or other with a globe, or an egg, or a ring, has been used, not merely by the Egyptians, to whom it is commonly given, but by most of the nations of antiquity. It was familiar alike to the Chinese, the Hindoos, the Persians, the Phenicians, the Egyptians, and the Celtic Britons: nor was it unknown to the Greeks, as appears from the serpent twisted in the form of a circle which was placed in the hand of Cronus, and from the caduceus of Hermes which exhibited two serpents, a globe, and wings. The Chinese have a symbol of two serpents with a ring between them:[2] the Hindoos, of a serpent forming a curve and a globe or egg placed within the curve:[3] the Persians, of a winged serpent attached to a globe, and sometimes to a ring in the midst of which is a human figure holding in his hand a smaller snake which forms a circle by the insertion of its tail in its mouth:[4] the Phenicians, of a serpent coiled round an egg:[5] the Egyptians,

---

[1] Jul. Firm. de error. prof. rel. p. 23. Clem. Alex. Cohort. p. 11.
[2] See Plate I. Fig. 3.   [3] See Plate I. Fig. 4.
[4] See Plate I. Fig. 7, 9, 10.   [5] See Plate I. Fig. 1.

of a serpent either winged or not winged attached to or half encompassing a globe, and sometimes of two serpents similarly attached to a winged globe :[1] and the ancient Britons, as appears from the vast dragontian temple of Abury, of a serpent joined to a circle.[2]

Now between these several hieroglyphics there is such a decided and palpable resemblance, both in general composition and in particular arrangement, that no person can behold them exhibited together in a single plate without being immediately convinced of their identity. This being the case, since the mythology of the whole gentile world was in substance the same, originating from one common source; we may rest assured, that, whatever the hieroglyphic in question was designed to express among one people, it was designed likewise to express among all the rest.

Import of the famous hieroglyphic of the globe and winged serpent.

5. Kircher, and after him Maurice, have supposed it to represent the Trinity. In this conjecture they seem to me to have been peculiarly unfortunate in every respect. The Egyptians, like most other ancient nations, did indeed venerate a triad of deities: but neither has their triad, I will be bold to say, the slightest connection with the Holy Trinity; nor does the present hieroglyphic symbolize even the *human* triad of the Gentiles.

The egg or globe or circle, for they were but variations of the same type, represented, as I have already proved, the great mother; that is to say, the ship Argha or Argo or Theba, viewed under the two-fold aspect of the World and the Ship of the deluge: and the serpent, sometimes winged and sometimes not winged, shadowed out the person and character of the great father; that is to say, Adam reappearing in Noah. Hence the globe or egg and the winged serpent (described under the triple formula of *the globe, serpent, and wings,* by those who are bent upon discovering the Father, the Son, and the Spirit, in an ancient pagan hieroglyphic): hence the globe and the serpent, or the egg and the serpent, clearly symbolize the great mother united to the great father, under whatever local appellations they might be worshipped. Thus, among the Persians, they represent Lilith and Mithras; among the Hindoos, Parvati and Siva; among the Phenicians, Astartè and Taut, or Venus and Adonis; among the Egyptians, Isis and Osiris; among

---

[1] See Plate I. Fig. 2, 6, 8.　　　　　　　　[2] See Plate I. Fig. 5.

the Greeks, Ceres and Bacchus; and among the Britons, Ceridwen and Hu. These they represent separately: but, when considered as blended together in one hieroglyphic, they then shadow out the same great father and great mother united in the single mysterious person of the hermaphroditic Ardha-nari, Adonis, or Zeus, of the Hindoo, Phenician, or Orphic, theology. Sometimes the egg is associated with two serpents, in which case the great mother is twice represented by the egg and the female serpent. This we may collect from the fable mentioned by Athenagoras, respecting the incestuous commerce of Jupiter and Rhea under the precise appearance of the two serpents which are twisted round the globe-sur-mounted caduceus of Hermes or Taut. But, whatever may be the sub-ordinate variations of the symbol, it was always designed to shadow out the great father and the great mother, or, when the two were united together in one compound character, the great hermaphroditic parent of the Universe.

This is manifest, I think, both from the import of the two hieroglyphics of the serpent and the egg, considered distinctly from each other; and like-wise from the peculiar manner in which they are sometimes connected, and from the peculiar language used respecting them.

We find it sometimes said, that the serpent was produced from the egg, and sometimes the egg from the serpent. They stand therefore connected mutually with each other in the relation of parent and child. Now this, as I have frequently had occasion to observe, is precisely that contradictory relationship which is feigned to subsist between the great father and the great mother. The one is said to be the husband of the other, and from their mystic embrace all things are generated: yet the great father is described as the parent of his consort, because Noah was the builder of the Ark: and the great mother again is represented as the parent of her hus-band, because the Ark produced him from her womb. Thus the sacred egg of the Universe is feigned to have proceeded from the serpent god Hercules or Cronus;[1] and thus the same egg is described as issuing from the mouth of the snake-deity Cneph or Cnuphis.[2] Yet again, on the other hand, the dragon-god Dionusus or Protogonus is said by the Orphic poet to have been

---

[1] Athenag. Legat. p. 65.   [2] Euseb. Præp. Evan. lib. iii. c. 11.

born from the egg:[1] and a precisely similar origin is ascribed both by the Phenicians and the Hindoos to their respective serpent deities.[2]

With this will be found to correspond the different arrangements of the hieroglyphic. Sometimes the serpent winds himself round the exterior of the egg: at other times he is depicted proceeding out of it. There is yet a third mode of representation, which must not be passed over unnoticed. The Egyptians, as we are told by Eusebius, when they wished to symbolize the World, drew a circle, and placed in the centre of it a hawk-headed snake, denoting the World by the circle, and by the snake in the middle of it the Agathodemon: and he adds, that the hieroglyphic, when briefly expressed, nearly resembled the form of the capital Greek letter Θ *Theta*.[3] Sometimes also they just inverted the hieroglyphic, representing a large house or palace in the midst of a circle formed by a snake; by way of intimating, as we learn from Horapollo, that the World was the royal palace or temple of the deity, which he surrounded and protected on all sides by his powerful influence.[4]

It is easy to perceive, that these two last modes of delineating the symbol are the same in substance as those which were previously mentioned. The snake-god in the centre of the circle is the great father in the midst of the ship Argha, which at once shadowed out the World and the Ark: and the same deity surrounding the palace exhibits him, anxious for the preservation of the vessel which he really constructed and of the Universe which he was thence feigned to have constructed. It is not improbable, that the form of the Greek capital Θ *Theta* was borrowed from the hieroglyphic which I have recently noticed; and that the name of the letter itself, as well as the name of the corresponding Phenician or Hebrew letter *Teth*, is but a variation of *Taut* or *Thoth* or (as the Hindoos write the word) *Tatta*. Eusebius says, that Taut was the reputed inventor of serpent-worship, and that he introduced snakes into the Mysteries.[5] Hence the hieroglyphic of the serpent and the egg was probably ascribed to him, and its transcript *Theta* called after his name.

---

[1] Orph. Hymn. v.
[2] Fragm. Sanchon. apud Kirch. Œdip. Ægypt. Instit. of Menu. chap. i.
[3] Euseb. Præp. Evan. lib. i. c. 10.   [4] Horap. Hierog. lib. i. c. 2.
[5] Euseb, Præp. Evan. lib. i. c. 10.

CHAPTER VIII.

———

On the origin and purport of sacrificial rites.

The Universality of Sacrificial Rites is a Proof of Their Common Origin

In every quarter of the globe, Paganism, both ancient and modern, has never failed to inculcate the necessity of sacrificial rites. This universal accordance, which it is almost superfluous to attempt formally to prove, can only be satisfactorily accounted for on the principle of the common origination of all the mythological systems of the Gentiles: for the same argument, which has already been so frequently employed, may here again be used with equal advantage and propriety.

Throughout the whole world we find a notion prevalent, that the gods could only be appeased by bloody sacrifices. Now this idea is so thoroughly arbitrary, there being no obvious and necessary connection in the way of cause and effect between slaughtering a man or a beast and the recovering of the divine favour by the slaughterer, that its very universality involves the necessity of concluding that all nations have borrowed it from some common source. It is in vain to say, that there is nothing so strange, but that an unrestrained superstition might have excogitated it. This solution does by no means meet the difficulty. If sacrifice had been in use only among the inhabitants of a *single* country, or among those of *some few neighbouring* countries who might reasonably be supposed to have much mutual inter-course; no fair objection could be made to the answer. But what we have to account for is *the universality* of the practice: and such a solution plainly does *not* account for such a circumstance; I mean, not merely *the existence* of sacrifice, but *its universality*. An apparently irrational notion, struck out by a wild fanatic in *one* country and forthwith adopted by his fellow-citizens (for such is the hypothesis requisite to the present solution), is yet found to be equally prevalent in *all* countries. Therefore, if we acquiesce in this solution, we are bound to believe, either that all nations, however remote from each other, borrowed from that of the original inventor; or that, by a most marvellous subversion of the whole system of calculating chances, a great number of fanatics, severally appearing in every country upon the face of the earth, without any mutual communication strangely hit upon the self-same arbitrary and inexplicable mode of propitiating the deity. It is difficult to say, which of the two suppositions is the most improbable. The solution therefore does not satisfactorily account for the fact of *the universality*. Nor can the fact, I will be bold to say, *be* satisfactorily accounted for, except by the supposition, that no one nation borrowed the rite from another nation, but that all alike received it from a common origin of most remote antiquity.

I. The propriety of such a supposition will be rendered yet more evident, when we recollect, that sacrificial rites have not only been universal in their reception; but likewise that they have been adopted in every nation, except one, long prior to the commencement of authentic history. There is no heathen people, that can specify the time when it was without sacrifice: *all* have equally had it from a period, which cannot be reached by their genuine records; and tradition alone can be brought forward by the Gentiles to account for its origin. Let us then attend to the testimony of tradition; which in this instance is so remarkably uniform, that, even if it stood wholly unsupported by better evidence, it would still be eminently worthy of our notice.

Pagan testimonies to this position.

1. We find then, by the general traditionary consent of pagan antiquity, that sacrificial rites, and the worship of the gods which ever involved sacrificial rites, are said to have commenced with that primeval character whom

the nations venerated as their great universal father; that character, who, under whatever name he was adored, is demonstrated by the circumstantial evidence of his legendary history to have been Adam considered as reappearing in the person of Noah.

Thus one of the eight mystic forms of the Indian Siva, a number which evidently alludes to the ogdoad conspicuous in *both* the two first families, is said to be the performer of a sacrifice.[1] Thus the Egyptian Thoth or Taut, who is the same as Buddha or Cadam, is described as the original inventor of sacrificial rites.[2] Thus the Egyptian Osiris, who is clearly no other than the Greek Dionusus and the Indian Siva or Iswara, is celebrated as the person, who first instructed mankind in the worship of the gods; with which, as I have just observed, sacrifice was ever inseparably united.[3] Thus the Etruscan Janus was thought by the Italians to have first taught them to build temples to the gods, and to have instituted the sacred rites with which they were adored.[4] Thus the Argive Phoroneus, who was accounted the first of men and who is made coëval with the flood, is said to have first built a temple and an altar for sacrificial purposes to Juno.[5] Thus the Chinese Fohi is represented as carefully breeding seven sorts of animals, the number according to which Noah was directed to take the clean animals into the Ark, for the purpose of sacrificing them to the supreme spirit of heaven and earth.[6] Thus the Babylonian Xisuthrus, when he quitted the ark within which he had been preserved, is said to have built an altar and offered sacrifices to the gods.[7] Thus both the Greek and the Scythic Deucalion is equally described, as building an altar, and as offering up sacrifices immediately after the deluge.[8] Thus the British Hu, who with

---

[1] Moor's Hind. Panth. p. 12.   [2] Diod. Bibl. lib. i. p. 14.

[3] Diod. Bibl. lib. i. p. 14.   Plut. de Isid. p. 356.

[4] Xenon apud Macrob. Saturn. lib. i. c. 9. p. 157.

[5] Clem. Alex. Strom. lib. i. p. 321.   Hyg. Fab. 225, 274.   The common reading in the last cited place is *arma*: but a comparison of the two fables clearly establishes the propriety of Scheffer's correction, which substitutes *aram*.   In Fab. 143 Hyginus similarly observes, that Phoroneus first instituted sacred rites to Juno.

[6] Le Compte's China. p. 310.

[7] Syncell. Chronog. p. 30.   Euseb. Præp. Evan. lib. ix. c. 12.

[8] Luc. de dea Syra.   Apollod. Bibl. lib. i. c. 7. §2.

seven companions sailed in an ark over the interminable ocean, is eminently styled *the sacrificer.*[1]   And thus the Peruvian Manco-Copac is supposed to have first reclaimed mankind from a savage life and to have taught them the worship of his father the Sun.[2]

The altar, on which the primeval sacrifice was offered up, has been elevated to the sphere: and the legends, which are there attached to it, all tend to refer us to the same period for the origin of the rite.   On the sphere itself we behold the fabulous centaur, the reputed son of Cronus but by Lycophron rightly identified with Cronus himself,[3] issuing from the ship Argo, and bearing on his lance a victim towards the altar for the purpose of sacrificing it:[4] and we are told, that on this same altar Jupiter offered an oblation, when going to the war of the Titans, or rather (as the scholiast on Aratus more accurately gives the tradition) when returning victorious from that war.[5]   The Titanic war however relates altogether to the deluge, and is the very same as the war of Typhon or the ocean against the hero-gods:[6] consequently, the sacrifice of Jupiter on the altar is no other than the first post-diluvian sacrifice of Noah.   Hence, in allusion to the flood, we are informed, that Night, whom the Orphic poet identifies with the infernal Venus or the great arkite mother, was the person that placed the altar among the constellations, in pity of the calamities inflicted upon men by the tempestuous ocean.[7]

Thus universally do the pagans ascribe the origin of a rite, which far precedes the records of authentic profane history, to the age of the great father.   But the great father is he, who was supposed to be manifested anew at the commencement of every similar mundane system.   Now we know, that only *two* such systems have existed; which, from many points of resemblance between their respective commencements, have occasioned the philosophical fable of an endless succession of perfectly similar worlds.

---

[1] Davies's Mythol. of Brit. Druid. p. 121.
[2] Robertson's Hist. of Amer. vol. iii. p. 200, 201.
[3] Lycoph. Cassan. ver. 1203. Schol. in loc.   [4] Eratos. Catast. 40.
[5] Hyg. Poet. Astron. lib. ii. c. 39. Schol. in Arat. Phæn. p. 52.
[6] See my Dissert. on the Cabiri. chap. ix.
[7] Orph. Hymn. ii. 2. Schol. in. Arat. Phæn. p. 53.

Therefore the pagans, by ascribing the origin of sacrifice to the age of the great transmigrating father, do in effect deduce it from the two primeval sacrifices, which were offered up, the one at the beginning of the ante-diluvian world, and the other at that of the postdiluvian.

Such being their traditional account of the origin of sacrifice, if it be well founded, all nations must obviously have borrowed the rite from a common source: and, since the very circumstance of *the universality of sacrifice* can only be accounted for in some such manner as the traditional account has specified; the presumption, even if we had no better evidence, would be, that the account itself, however perverted to serve the purposes of idolatry, is in the main founded on truth.

2. But we *have* better evidence, even the evidence of inspiration itself: for it will be found, that the genuine records of the only nation, whose historical documents reach as high as the commencement of sacrifice, give substantially the same account of its origin as the coincident traditions of the pagans.

Scriptural testimonies to the same.

We are informed by Moses, that, immediately after the deluge, Noah, the first man of the new world, the transmigrating great father of gentile theology, built an altar, and offered up a propitiatory sacrifice upon it: and we are further taught, that the wrath of God was appeased by it, and that he solemnly promised never more to bring upon the earth a flood of waters.[1] From the action of Noah then the practice must have been derived to all his posterity through each of his three sons: and, when the dispersion from Babel took place, it would be carried as from a common centre to every quarter of the globe by the various leaders of those colonies which in time became nations.

But even this is insufficient to account quite satisfactorily for its *continued prevalence*, though it decidedly establishes the truth of gentile tradition respecting the postdiluvian part of its *origin*. A strong belief of the *obligation* and *necessity* of sacrifice must have been *already* predominant in the minds of the Noetic family: otherwise it does not appear, why their descendants should have argued its *general* necessity from its *particular* pro-

[1] Gen. viii. 20, 21, 22.

priety in the case of the second great father of mankind. We must ascend
therefore still higher, as indeed we are compelled to do by the remarkable
distinction which we find subsisting in the time of Noah between cere-
monially clean and unclean animals; a distinction, which relates immediately
to their use or non-use in sacrifice, and which consequently proves that
sacrifice was an antediluvian no less than a postdiluvian institution.

With this necessary conclusion the sacred history perfectly agrees. The
first *observance* of the rite, which has been *positively recorded*, occurs in the
history of Cain and Abel: but it is not difficult to collect, that the *institution* of it must have been *prior* to the sacrifices of the two brethren. We
may observe, that the account of those sacrifices is detailed in a familiar
manner, which by no means resembles the narrative of an entirely novel
transaction: and, in the course of it, Moses employs an expression, which
intimates, that, so far from being the *first* that were offered up, they were
no more than the *ordinary* oblations which took place at regularly stated
periods.   In our translation it is said, that Cain and Abel brought their
offerings *in process of time:* but the phrase, thus rendered generally, ought
to have been translated (as Kennicott, supported by Fagius, has shewn) *at
the end of the days* or *at the close of the appointed season.*[1]   The sacrifices
therefore of the brethren, instead of being the *first* in the antediluvian world,
were but part of a regular series which had commenced from a yet *prior*
era.   If then we are to ascend still higher than the days of Cain and Abel,
we are inevitably brought to some part of the antecedent life of Adam and
Eve.   Now there is not the slightest hint given, that the ordinance commenced during the period that our first parents dwelt in Paradise: but there
is a circumstance mentioned immediately after the account given of the fall,
which warrants our determining that epoch to have witnessed the original
institution of sacrifice.   We read, that God made coats of skins for Adam
and his wife; with which he cloathed them, after they had been convicted of
disobedience, and after the promise of a redeemer had notwithstanding been
made to them.[2]   The question then is, whence were these skins procured?

[1] See Magee on atonement, No. lvii. vol. ii. p. 80, 81. 3d edit. and Kennic. Dissert. p.
177—188.

[2] Gen. iii. 21.

They could not have been the skins of animals, which had died without violence: because as yet death was not in the world. Neither could they have been skins of animals slain for the purpose of food: because our primeval ancestors were not carnivorous; the original grant of diet, which we have no reason to suppose *them* to have transgressed, extended only to the productions of the earth; the use of animal food was permitted for the first time after the deluge.[1] I see not therefore how we can account for their appearance precisely at this time, except by supposing them to be the skins of animals slain for the purpose of sucrifice, which was then originally instituted. But, if this were the case, then, agreeably to the unvarying traditions of the Gentiles, the first sacrifice both of the old and of the new world was equally offered up by the compound personage, whom they believed successively to appear by transmigration at the commencement of every mundane system and to perform anew each action which he had already performed. It is not unworthy of observation, that the Indian Siva, one of whose forms is that of the offerer up of a sacrifice, is frequently represented, perhaps in allusion to the mode in which Adam was cloathed by the Deity, as clad in the skin of a beast; and that the votaries of Bacchus, during the celebration of his frantic Orgies, were arrayed in the skins of fawns.[2] Siva at least, and Bacchus, were equally the great transmigrating father, with whom the rite of sacrifice commenced at the opening of every new world.

Such then, equally according to Scripture and pagan tradition, was the double origin of sacrifice: and the circumstance of an animal oblation having been offered up nearly at the beginning both of the antediluvian and the postdiluvian world, and in each instance by him who was venerated as the great universal father, was one of the many parallel circumstances at the opening of each world, which induced the doctrine of an endless succession of similar mundane systems, constantly divided from one another by the intermediate period of a general deluge. We may now proceed to consider the purport of the rite.

---

[1] Compare Gen. ii. 16. and ix. 3.

[2] See Moor's Hind. Panth. pl. xv. and Potter's Grec. Ant. vol. i. p. 383.

II. Since the rite itself is found to be equally prevalent in the religion of the ancient patriarchs, in that of the Israelites as ordained by the hand of Moses, and in the corrupt system of idolatry which nearly overspread the whole face of the globe; it appears more reasonable to inquire what notions were entertained of its purport by those who received it, than to start a theory of our own devised only to buttress a fabric of preconceived opinions.

The Pagans deemed it piacular or expiatory.

1. In pursuing this inquiry I shall begin with the Gentiles : but I must not omit previously to observe, that so thoroughly has the subject been exhausted, and so very ably has it been treated, by an excellent modern writer, that, with the exception of a small portion of additional matter, I have little more to do than to avail myself of his learning and industry.[1]

Some have contended, that sacrifices ought to be considered only in the light of gifts, with which a suppliant inferior approaches his acknowledged superior. Allowing for a moment that to a certain extent they *may* be thus estimated, still we must obviously inquire with what *sentiments* the heathens offered these supposed gifts to their deities.

Now their whole sacrificial phraseology is built upon the predominant idea, that it was necessary to propitiate the gods, and that such propitiation was best effected by shedding the blood of a devoted victim. Thus we read of appeasing the wrath of the deities with bulls and with lambs, with sprinklings and with oblations, with blood and with slaughter. Thus also we are told, that human sacrifices were offered up for the express purpose of obtaining pardon from the gods, and that the worshippers hoped to ensure their peace with heaven by shedding the blood of such victims. And thus we meet with the phrase of *expiating a crime ;* and sometimes find the analogous idea, that there might be wickedness of so black a die as to be utterly incapable of any expiation.[2]

---

[1] The parts of Dr. Magee's Work on atonement and sacrifice, to which I here acknowledge my obligation, are No. v, xxxiii, liv, lv, lviii, lxi, lxii, lxiii, lxiv.

[2] Hom. Iliad. lib. i. ver. 386. lib. ii. ver. 550. Hesiod. Oper. et dier. ver. 338. Hor. lib. ii. sat. 3, ver. 206. lib. i. od. 2. ver. 29. od. 28. ver. 34. Cicer. de nat. deor. lib. iii. c. 6. Sil. Ital. lib. iv. ver. 768. Justin. lib. xviii. c. 6. Lucan. Phars. lib. i. ver. 443, Virg.

Agreeable to the received phraseology was the uniformly adopted practice. As the prevailing notion was, that without the effusion of blood the gods could not, or would not, forgive the offences of men; so there perhaps has been no people upon the face of the earth, which has not at one period or another been addicted to sacrifices both human and bestial, sacrifices expressly offered up for the purpose of propitiating the angry deities. Animal oblations have never been discontinued by any pagan nation, so long as it retained the profession of Paganism: and, though human victims more or less ceased to be slaughtered in polished and civilized communities; yet perhaps in no idolatrous region were the bloody rites, which required such sacrifices, wholly unknown. The Ethiopians, the Phenicians, the Scythians, the Celts, the Egyptians, the Chinese, the Persians, the Hindoos, the Greeks, the Latins, the Carthaginians, the Canaanites, the Arabians, the Cretans, the Cyprians, the Rhodians, the Africans, the Mexicans, the Peruvians, and the recently discovered islanders of the great Pacific ocean: all these either are, or have been, polluted with the abomination of human sacrifice; polluted with it, from an express persuasion, that the anger of the gods might thus be averted from their worshippers, and that their favour might thus be most effectually procured.[1]

If then we at all allow, that the sacrifices of the pagans ought to be considered in the light of gifts: we must likewise allow, that they were gifts made under the impression of fear, that they were gifts which presupposed the wrath of the gods, that they were gifts which propitiated the indignation of the offended deities only by the destruction of the offered victim. And this will further compel us to allow, that, for some reason or other, man was

---

Æneid. lib. ii. ver. 116. Liv. Hist. lib. vii. c. 2. Macrob. Saturn. lib. iii. c. 5. See Magee on the atonement. No. v.

[1] Heliod. Æthiop. lib. x. p. 465. Euseb. Præp. Evan. lib. i. c. 10. Herod. lib. iv. c. 62. Cæsar. Comment. lib. vi. c. 16. Plut. de Isid. p. 380. Diod. Bibl. lib. i. p. 79. Martin. Hist. Sin. lib. iii. p. 75. Herod. lib. i. c. 132. lib. vii. c. 113, 114. Asiat. Res. vol. i. p. 265. Macrob. Saturn. lib. i. c. 7. p. 153. Porph. de Abstin. lib. ii. § 54, 55, 56, 57. Levit. xx. 23. Acost. Hist. of Ind. p. 379. Anton. de Sol. and Clavig. Hist. of Mex. lib. vi. c. 18, 19, 20. Cook's Voyag. See Magee No. v. See also Cooke's Inq. into the patriarch. and druid. rel. p. 66.

supposed by the Gentiles to be at enmity with the gods ; and that the gods themselves were thought to be so much delighted with the shedding of blood either human or bestial, as freely to remit their indignation against man when thus propitiated. How they came to entertain such opinions, and what led them to connect together in the way of cause and effect the slaughter of an unoffending victim and the propitiation of their gods, things which in themselves have no obvious or natural connection : how such notions as these originated, is another question; I am at present simply concerned with the matter of fact.

The pagans then offered up their sacrifices, whether we choose to call them *gifts* or not, under the manifest impression, that their gods required propitiation, and they might be propitiated by the shedding of blood : we have next to learn, in what precise manner they believed the propitiation to be effected and the wrath of the deities averted. Now this manner, if we may argue from the *avowed* intention of *some* sacrifices to the *implied* intention of *others* which bear a perfect outward resemblance to them, was as follows : the wrath of the gods and the consequent necessity of propitiation being assumed as indisputable circumstances, the animal or person sacrificed was devoted in the stead of the sacrificer ; and the indignation, which would otherwise have descended upon the sacrificer, now descending upon the substituted victim, was thought to be appeased and entirely turned away from the former by the death and sufferings of the latter. In short, the victim was considered not so much in the light of a gift, as of a proxy: it was supposed to stand in the place of the offerer, and to endure in his room those penalties which *he* must otherwise have endured : its pangs, by which the deity was propitiated, were deemed purely and properly *vicarious*.

That such was the leading idea of the pagans with respect to sacrifice, might almost be inferred from their ordinary phraseology, which has already been noticed : for, though arguing from the ways of men with each other, a simple gift might not unnaturally be deemed efficacious to turn away wrath ; it is hard to say, why *the utter destruction* of that gift even in the very act of presenting it should be thought more likely to propitiate the anger of the deity than its *careful preservation*, unless it was additionally supposed, that his anger spent itself upon the slaughtered victim rather than upon the trembling sacrificer. But we are not left to draw *inferences*, the propriety, or at least the certainty, of which might be disputed : there are on record *positive declarations*, which can neither be misunderstood nor explained away. And those declarations are not confined to a single country : we alike meet with them in various regions the most widely separated from each other.

The opinion of the Druids respecting the efficacy of human sacrifices was built entirely, as we learn from Cesar, on their supposed vicariousness. *Unless the life of man were given in exchange for the forfeited life of man, they believed that the deity of the immortal gods could not otherwise be appeased.*[1]

Such also was the doctrine of the Gothic or Scythic Scandinavians. Having *laid it down as a principle, that the effusion of the blood of animals appeased the anger of the gods, and that their justice turned aside upon the victims those strokes which were destined for men ;* they extended the same theory to the shedding of human blood.[2] In honour of the mystical number *three*, a number deemed peculiarly dear to heaven as being the number of the Indo-Scythic Trimurti or great triplicated deity, every ninth month witnessed the groans and dying struggles of nine unfortunate victims. The fatal blow having been struck, the lifeless bodies were consumed in the sacred fire which was kept continually burning ; while the blood was sprinkled, partly upon the surrounding multitude, partly upon the trees of the hallowed grove, and partly upon the images of the gods.[3]

Such likewise was the opinion of the Egyptians in the days of Herodotus. *Having led to the altar the animal destined and marked for the purpose, they kindled a fire. A libation of wine was then poured upon the altar : the god was solemnly invoked : and the victim was killed. Afterwards they cut off his head, and took the skin from the carcase : but upon the head they heaped many imprecations. Such, as had a market-place at hand, carried it*

[1] Cæsar. Comment. lib. vi. c. 16.
[2] Mallet's North. Ant. vol. i. c. 7.
[3] Mallet's North. Ant. vol. i. c. 7. Olai Magni Hist. lib. iii. c. 7.

there, and sold it to the Greek traders: if they had not this opportunity of disposing of it, they threw it into the river. The mode, in which they imprecated the head, was by wishing, that, whatever evil menaced either the sacrificers in particular or Egypt in general, it might fall upon that head. This ceremony respecting the head of the slaughtered animal, and this custom of pouring a libation of wine upon the altar, was indiscriminately observed by all the Egyptians: in consequence of which, none of them would, on any account, eat of the head of a beast; doubtless from a persuasion, that all the evils, which would have fallen upon themselves, were transferred to the head of their substitute the offered victim.[1]

Such again was palpably the sentiment of the Athenians and the Massilians in their remarkable annual sacrifice of a man for the welfare of the state. They loaded him with the most dreadful curses: they prayed, that the wrath of the gods might fall upon his devoted head, and thus be diverted from the rest of the citizens: and they solemnly called upon him to become their ransom, their salvation, and their redemption; life for life, and body for body. After this preliminary ceremony, they cast him into the sea as an offering to Neptune.[2]

An exactly similar opinion prevailed among the Chinese, as may be collected from a circumstance recorded in the history of their emperor Ching-Tang. The country was visited by a drought for the space of seven successive years: and, to avert the calamity, the prayers and subsequent sacrifice of a man were said to be required by heaven. On this the aged monarch offered himself as a victim: and he is described as supplicating the deity, that his life might be accepted as an atonement for the sins of his people, and that the divine wrath might pass by them and descend upon his devoted head. The will however is said to have been accepted for the deed, and the life of the prince was not required: yet both the demand and the offer sufficiently shew, that the essence of sacrifice was believed to be its vicariousness.[3]

---

[1] Herod. lib. ii. c. 39.
[2] Hesych. Lex. et Suid. Lex. voc. περιψημα, καθαρμα.
[3] Martin. Hist. Sin. lib. iii. p. 75.

Such also must have been the opinion of the Phenicians, as we may collect both from the story of their god Cronus or Il, and from the prefatory remarks with which that story is introduced. It seems very evidently to have been founded in the first instance on the intended sacrifice of Isaac : but the whole narrative, as given by Eusebius, proves it to have been an exemplification of the doctrine of vicariousness. We are told by this author, speaking of the Phenicians, that it was an established custom among the ancients, in any calamitous or dangerous emergency, for the rulers of the state to offer up, in prevention of the general ruin, the best beloved of their children, as a ransom paid to the avenging demons. We are further told, that they, who were thus devoted, were devoted mystically. And we are finally presented with an instance of this sacrificial redemption, the one being a ransom for the many, in the case of Il or Cronus ; who, when the nation was endangered by a perilous war, dressed up his son in the emblems of royalty, and offered him as a victim on an altar specially prepared for that purpose.[1] Here the mystic sacrifice of the son was plainly designed to avert the wrath of the gods from the nation at large, and to transfer it to the head of the substituted victim ; who, by suffering in his own person what would otherwise have fallen upon the people, became the price of their redemption from punishment.

There is a closely parallel case recorded in Scripture, which proves that a similar notion must have been familiar to the Moabites. When the king of that nation was endangered by the successful progress of the Israelites, he devoted his eldest son as a burnt offering ; hoping, that the wrath of the gods might descend upon the head of the substituted victim, rather than upon himself and his people.[2]

The same idea must also have prevailed in Peru : for, to say nothing of the two hundred children who were annually sacrificed for the health of the Ynca, we are informed by Acosta, that, in cases of sickness, it was usual for a Peruvian to offer up his son to Virachoca, beseeching him to spare his life and to be satisfied with the blood of his child. We may equally

_____
[1] Euseb. Præp. Evan. lib. i. c. 10. lib. iv. c. 16.
[2] 2 Kings iii. 27.

trace it in the sentiment; which caused the Athenian Codrus, the Theban Meneceus, and the Roman Decii, to devote themselves to the infernal gods for the redemption of their respective countries. And we may finally observe it exemplified, in the most decisive terms, by the remarkable phraseology which pervades the Sanguinary Chapter of the Hindoo Calica Puran. The sacrificer of a human victim is directed to address him, previous to his slaughter, in the following words. *O best of men! O most auspicious! O thou, who art an assemblage of all the deities, and most exquisite! Bestow thy protection on me. Save me, thy devoted. Save my sons, my cattle, and kindred. Preserve the state, the ministers belonging to it, and all friends: and, as death is unavoidable, part with thy life, doing an act of benevolence. Bestow upon me, O most auspicious, the bliss which is obtained by the most austere devotion, by acts of charity, and by performance of religious ceremonies: and, at the same time, O most excellent, attain supreme bliss thyself. May thy auspices, O most auspicious, keep me secure from Racshasas, Pisachos, terrors, serpents, bad princes, enemies, and other evils: and, death being inevitable, charm Bhagavati in thy last moments by copious streams of blood spouting from the arteries of thy fleshy neck.[1]*

In short, the theory of the vicariousness of sacrifice is by various ancient writers so explicitly maintained, that there cannot be a doubt of such being the received doctrine of the pagans. The word *peripsema*, which was used to describe the nature of the annual human sacrifice of the Athenians that I have already noticed, is defined by Hesychius, as meaning *life for life*.[2] The parallel term *piaculum* is used by Plautus in such a manner, as necessarily to involve the idea of *vicarious suffering*.[3] Ovid describes the purport and intention of a sacrifice, by intimating, that the heart of the victim was hoped to serve as a substitute for the heart of the offerer, its fibres for

[1] Asiat. Res. vol. v. p. 379, 380.

[2] His explanatory term is ἀντίψυχον.

[3] Men' piaculum oportet fieri propter stultitiam tuam,
     Ut meum tergum stultitiæ tuæ subdas succedaneum.

                                        Plaut. Epid. p. 412.

his fibres, its life for his life.[1] And Porphyry asserts it to have been the general belief and tradition, deduced from the mythologic or fabulous ages, that animal sacrifices were resorted to in such cases as required life for life.[2]

2. A similar idea pervades every part of the Levitical institutions.

This is not a place to discuss the topic at large; and indeed such a discussion is rendered plainly superfluous by the labours of the author, to whom I have already acknowledged my obligations: I shall content myself therefore with adducing a single proof, that the doctrine of vicariousness was no less decidedly recognized by the law of Moses than in the theory of the pagan sacrificers.

It is presented in the very same light by the Law of Moses.

In the case of the scape-goat, the transfer of the iniquities of the whole congregation to the substituted animal is expressly declared to have been represented by the scenical action of the high-priest laying them, as it were, upon its head : so that, when the ceremony of imposition of hands had been duly performed, the goat was considered as bearing upon him all the transgressions of the Israelites.[3]

Here then we have the rite of *the priest's imposition of hands upon the head of an animal* authoritatively explained to denote *the transfer of sins from the people to their substitute:* consequently, when we find this ceremony used in sacrifice, we can be at no loss to understand its import. Now, to omit other instances, we are told in the description of the sacrifice offered by Hezekiah, that *the object* of it was to make atonement for all Israel, and that *the mode* of offering it was by *the imposition of hands* previous to the slaughter of the animals which were devoted as a sin-offering.[4] Such being the *formula*, there is no room for mistaking the *purport* of the whole ceremony. The sacrifice itself was expiatory or piacular: for, agreeably to the general declaration of the apostle that without shedding of blood there was no remission of sins, we are informed, that it was a sin-offering,

[1] Cor pro corde precor, pro fibris sumite fibras,
      Hanc animam vobis pro meliore damus.
                          Ovid. Fast. lib. vi. ver. 161.

[2] Porph. de Abstin. lib. iv. § 15.

[3] Levit. xvi. 21, 22.   [4] 2 Chron. xxix. 23.

and that the design of it was to make atonement for the people. And the specific manner of its operation was decidedly according to the principles of vicariousness : for the imposition of hands forms a part of the ceremony; and we are positively told, that such imposition represented the transfer of sin from the Israelites to the substituted animal. In short, the whole rite, with its attendant ceremonial, is palpably analogous to those peculiar sacrifices of the Egyptians and Athenians, which have already been noticed. The sins of the community were alike, in each case, supposed to be transferred to the appointed victim : and that victim, thus bearing the iniquities of others, was devoted to death in the room of those whom it represented.

Similar sentiments are entertained of it by the Jews.

.3. Such accordingly is the light, in which the ordinance of sacrifice has justly been understood by the Israelites themselves.

Abarbanel, in the introduction to his Commentary on Leviticus, represents the ceremony of imposition of hands upon the head of the victim, as a symbolical translation of the sins of the offender upon the head of the sacrifice.[1] And, agreeably to this theory, was the ordinary practice of his countrymen. When a person presented his sacrifice, he was directed to say; *O God, I have sinned, I have done perversely, I have trespassed before thee, and have done so and so. Lo! now I repent, and am truly sorry for my misdeeds. Let this victim be my expiation.* The last words were accompanied by the action of laying hands on the head of the victim, and they were considered by the Jews to be equivalent to this : *Let the evils, which in justice should have fallen on my head, light upon the head of this victim.*[2] Thus Baal Aruch says, that, *wherever the expression, Let me be another's expiation, is used, it is the same as if it had been said, Let me be put in his room, that I may bear his guilt : and this again is equivalent to saying, Let this act, whereby I take on me his transgression, obtain for him his pardon.* Thus also Solomon Jarchi says, *Let us be your expiation, signifies, Let us be put in your place, that the evil, which should have fallen upon you, may all light on us.* And in the same manner

[1] Abarb. cited by Magee No. xxxix.
[2] Outram. de Sacr. lib. i. c. 22. § 5, 6, 9. apud Magee No. xxxix.

the formula is explained by Obadias de Bartenora and other learned Jews.[1]

Similar to this is the mode, in which the burnt offerings and sacrifices for sin are understood by the Rabbinical writers. Thus Nachmanides remarks, that *it was right, that the offerer's own blood should be shed and his body burnt : but that the Creator, in his mercy, hath accepted this victim from him, as a vicarious substitute and an atonement ; that its blood should be poured out instead of his blood, and its life stand in place of his life.* Thus also Isaac Ben-Arama observes, that *the offender, when he beholds the victim, on account of his sin, slain, skinned, cut in pieces, and burnt with fire upon the altar, should reflect, that thus he must have been treated, had not God in his clemency accepted this expiation for his life.* Thus again David de Pomis pronounces the victim to be the vicarious substitute for the offerer. And thus Isaac Abarbanel affirms, that *the offerer deserved, that his blood should be poured out and his body burnt for his sins ; but that God, in his clemency, accepted from him the victim as his vicarious substitute and expiation, whose blood was poured out in place of his blood, and whose life was given in lieu of his life.*[2]

To these testimonies may properly be subjoined the remarkable account of the expiatory sacrifice of a cock by the modern Jews, as detailed by Buxtorf. Each father of a family begins the ceremony, by stepping forth into the midst of the assembly with a cock in his hands, and by repeating certain appropriate texts from Scripture. Then he thrice strikes the cock against his head, and at each blow exclaims ; *May this cock be accepted in exchange for me, may he succeed to my place, may he be an expiation for me! On this cock death shall be inflicted, but to me and to all Israel there shall be a fortunate life. Amen.* Afterwards, placing his hands upon the victim, he slays him. Then, drawing the skin tight round the neck, he mentally confesses, that he himself was worthy of strangulation, but that he substituted and offered the cock in his own room. Next he cuts its throat with a knife, silently reflecting, that he was thus worthy of being slain with the sword. Next he violently dashes the carcase on the ground, to denote that he was worthy of being stoned to death. Lastly he roasts it with fire, to intimate that he deserved the punishment of burning. And thus, by these several actions, the idea was conveyed, that the cock underwent four sorts of death in the place of the Jews, being accepted as their representative and substitute.[1]

Such also were the sentiments of the ancient patriarchs.

4. As the very same sentiments respecting the design of sacrifice prevailed both among the Israelites and the pagans, and as the origin of the rite itself may clearly be traced even to the first age of the world, it seems inevitably to follow, that a similar opinion of its purport must have been entertained by the early patriarchs : for, since the rite, whether adopted by the Gentiles or the Israelites, was borrowed from a common source, and since they both attributed precisely the same efficacy to it; it is incredible, that their patriarchal predecessors should yet have thought quite differently on the subject. With this conclusion the history of the first-recorded sacrifice, as illustrated by the inspired author of the Epistle to the Hebrews, will be found exactly to agree.

The divine institution of the rite from the sacrifice of Abel.

(1.) In the traditions of the Gentiles, confirmed by the testimony of Holy Writ itself, we have seen, that the origin of the rite is to be deduced from the two successive great fathers Adam and Noah, each of whom was the earliest sacrificer in his own peculiar world. But, though such was its origin in *practice*, we cannot reasonably stop here and pronounce it to be a mere *human* institution, which was first excogitated by Adam and afterwards revived by Noah. The sacrifice of Abel, when viewed in all its bearings, necessarily, so far as I can judge, presupposes the *divine* institution of the rite. Why should that righteous man have imagined, that he could please the Deity, by slaying a firstling lamb, and by burning it upon an altar? What connection is there between the means and the end? Abel could not but have known, that God, as a merciful God, took no pleasure in the sufferings of the lamb. How then are we to account for his attempting to *please* such a God by what abstractedly is an act of cruelty? Would any man under his circumstances, wholly unauthorized by the Deity and acting solely according to the dictates of his own imagin-

[1] Buxtorf. Synag. Judaic. p. 509—512. apud Magee.

ation, have ever attempted in so unlikely and unpromising a manner to accomplish his purpose? Had he received no previous intimation to the contrary, might he not have naturally concluded, that such an act, instead of being pleasing, would be highly offensive, to God? How then came he to venture upon the commission of an act, in itself so singular and so little likely to be grateful to his beneficent Creator? Are we not almost compelled to suppose, that his oblation was not an unauthorized act of *will-worship;* but that he had previously been *taught,* and consequently that he was *fully assured,* that on some account or other the act *would* please God? Granting however, what scarcely *can* be granted consistently with reason and probability, that the sacrifice of Abel *was* no better than an unauthorized act of will-worship, and that most unaccountably he stumbled upon a mode of *pleasing* God which abstractedly he might have guessed to be much more likely to *displease* him : granting all this, how are we to account for the circumstance, that an act, which when thus considered was manifestly an act of rash and unwarrantable presumption, should after all most strangely prove *acceptable* to the Deity? We can only account for it by the supposition, that one of the most decided acts of will-worship that can well be imagined might yet prove acceptable to God; and might not only prove acceptable to him in a single instance, but that it might even be afterwards adopted by him into the ritual which he appointed for his chosen people. Such a supposition however directly contradicts the positive declaration of Christ, that it is vain to worship God by teaching for doctrines the mere unauthorized commands of erring men.[1] Hence it is evident, that, if the sacrifice of Abel had been an act of will-worship, it could not for that very reason have been pleasing to God. But it *was* pleasing to God : therefore it could not have been an act of will-worship. Consequently, since it was *not* an act of will-worship, it must have been of divine institution.[2]

[1] Mark vii. 7.

[2] This argument is used by Hallet: and he esteems it so conclusive, that he does not hesitate to pronounce it a *demonstration* of the divine institution of sacrifice. *Abel's sacrifice,* says he, *could not have been acceptable, if it had not been of divine appointment, according to that obvious maxim of all true religion, In vain do they worship God, teaching*

Sacrifice being thus in the first instance a divine ordinance, we have to inquire, why the oblation of Abel was acceptable and the oblation of Cain *not* acceptable to God, since they both equally sacrificed. This inquiry will serve to establish the opinion, which has already been advanced, that precisely the same sentiments respecting the nature and efficacy of sacrifice were entertained both by the early patriarchs, the Gentiles, and the Israelites: in other words, that they all equally held the doctrine of vicarious expiation. But, if this doctrine were held from the beginning, then the conclusion seems to be inevitable; that, since sacrifice itself was a divine institution, the accompanying and explanatory doctrine was a divine revelation: that is to say, the Almighty was pleased to declare, that on some account or other man stood in need of vicarious expiation to reconcile him to his Maker.

(2.) It is an established maxim of Scripture, by which alone we are taught the will of God, that *without shedding of blood there is no remission of sins.*[1] Now the sacrifice of Abel consisted of the firstlings of his flock, while the sacrifice of Cain was composed of the produce of the earth: and we are told, that the former was accepted, but that the latter was rejected. This different fate of the two oblations is best explained by the grand sacrificial maxim: the offering of Abel *was* accepted, because blood *was* shed, and because expiation was thus made by a transfer of the sins of the sacrificer to the victim agreeably to the tenor of the divine institution; the offering of Cain was *not* accepted, because blood was *not* shed, because *no* vicarious expiation was made, and because the offering itself *not* being agreeable to the divine institution was in reality a mere act of will-worship.

---

for doctrines the commandments of men. Thus Abel must have worshipped God in vain, had his sacrificing been merely a commandment of his father Adam or an invention of his own. And, to make this matter more evident, why do we not now offer up a bullock, a sheep, or a pigeon, as a thank-offering after any remarkable deliverance, or as an evidence of our apprehensions of the demerit of sin? The true reason is, because we cannot know that God will accept such will-worship, and so conclude that we should herein worship God in vain. As Abel then did not sacrifice in vain, it was not will-worship, but a divine appointment. Hallet on Heb. xi. 4. cited by Magee.

[1] Heb. ix. 22.

The righteousness of Abel, in short, consisted in a steady adherence to the precise mode of sacrifice as it had been first appointed immediately after the fall, and in a firm belief in the accompanying explanatory revelation without any presumptuous questioning of the fitness of such an ordinance : the essential guilt of Cain consisted in a daring departure both from the form of the divine institution and from the doctrine expressively shadowed out by that form. Like not a few in modern days, he could discern no propriety in connecting the forgiveness of sins with the effusion of blood. He argued, he disbelieved, and he disobeyed. He attempted to convert an expiatory sacrifice into one that was purely eucharistic : or perhaps he reasoned, that the wrath of God, granting that man was not *altogether* immaculate, might just as well be appeased by the burning of vegetables as by the burning of a slaughtered lamb. His offering accordingly, being a palpable act of daring will-worship tinged largely with a spirit of unsubmissive infidelity, was rejected : but God nevertheless condescended, both to point out the ground of its rejection, and to lead him to what alone could be deemed a proper sacrifice. *If thou doest well, shalt thou not be accepted? If thou doest not well, a sin-offering coucheth at the door.*[1] That is to say, *If thou canst lay claim to perfect and undeviating innocence, thou shalt surely be accepted on the score of thy own righteousness ; for, in that case, no propitiatory sacrifice is necessary : but, if thy conscience accuse thee of much evil, as it certainly must do, a remedy is still provided. Thou must bring an offering for thine iniquity to appease my wrath : but it must be such an offering as I have myself appointed. Thy bloodless vegetable sacrifice I cannot accept. Bring, like thy brother, a firstling lamb to make expiation for thine offences ; agreeably to the rite, which I instituted after the transgression of thy parents ; and it will in no wise be refused. Lo, the victim*

---

[1] Gen. iv. 7. It is well observed by Mr. Parkhurst, that the word רבץ signifies *to couch* or *lie like a beast ;* and that, in this passage, the verb, although in the masculine form, has the feminine substantive חטאת for its subject. Such a construction shews, that not sin, but a sin-offering, is intended : for the masculine verb agrees with the masculine name of the animal covertly alluded to by the name of *a sin-offering,* which word in the Hebrew is feminine ; a manner of construction not uncommon in that language. See Parkhurst's Heb. Lex. Vox חטא.

is ready! An animal, proper to be a sin-offering, even now coucheth at the door. Thy brother's sacrifice was accepted, because it was the oblation of such an animal. Imitate his example; seek not to be wiser than thy Maker: and then thy sacrifice shall not be rejected with disdain.

This is the natural and consistent mode of understanding the relation of Moses, when a phrase, ill-rendered in our common English version *sin lieth at the door*, is more intelligibly translated, as it certainly ought to be translated, *a sin-offering coucheth at the door:* and it is both confirmed by a brief observation of St. Paul, and receives from it additional illustration. *BY FAITH*, says he, *Abel offered unto God a more excellent sacrifice than Cain.*[1] What constituted the acceptableness of one sacrifice then, and the unacceptableness of the other, was FAITH, and WANT OF FAITH: and the faith of Abel was of such a description as led him to devote a more excellent, or rather (as the original word properly denotes) *a more full or more ample*, sacrifice than his brother. Now faith, in general, must have some definite object proposed to it: and faith, as exemplified in any particular instance, must be so understood as not to contradict the obvious context of the instance so adduced. If then the offering of Abel were merely the invention of unauthorized will-worship; it is difficult to say, wherein his faith consisted: because, in the language of Scripture, faith has always relation to some revealed communication of God. And if, on the other hand, the modes of sacrifice adopted by each brother had been *equally* of divine primeval institution; it is no less hard to determine, why Abel should be said to have *had* faith, and Cain (by necessary implication) *not to* have had faith: because the very act of offering involves a persuasion that the oblation would be accepted. Had not Cain believed in a general way, that *his* sacrifice would be as grateful to God as *Abel's*, he would plainly not have offered it at all: for the mere circumstance of offering it necessarily implies *this* sort of belief. Of *such* faith then, whether well or ill founded, Cain possessed as large a share as Abel. Consequently, this mere general persuasion cannot be the distinctive faith intended by the apostle: because *that* was a faith, which Abel *had*, and which Cain *had not*.

[1] Heb. xi. 4.

Of what nature then was the faith of Abel, which is attributed to him by St. Paul? We find it distinguished by two characteristics: it induced him to offer to God a more full or more ample sacrifice than Cain; and it was analogous, as appears from the general context, to the faith of all the other ancient patriarchs.

With regard to the first, since the sacrifice of Abel was more full than that of Cain, it must have comprehended something which the other did *not* comprehend. But the precise point wherein they differed was this: in the sacrifice of Abel the blood of a victim was shed; in the sacrifice of Cain no blood was shed: consequently, *the effusion of blood*, being the precise thing which the one comprehended and which the other did not comprehend, must have been that which made the one sacrifice more full or more ample than the other. Now it was *by faith* that Abel offered this more full sacrifice than that of Cain. The faith therefore of Abel must have been displayed in the precise point of shedding the blood of a victim; because in this point only was his sacrifice more full than that of his brother.

With regard to the second characteristic, the faith of Abel is spoken of as being analogous to the faith of all the other patriarchs. But *their* faith, as celebrated by the apostle, is clearly a prospective faith in Christ, who in due season should redeem mankind by his one oblation of himself once offered.[1] The faith therefore of Abel was a prospective faith in the sacrifice of the Messiah.

Thus it appears, that the faith of Abel was displayed at once in shedding the blood of an expiatory victim, and in relying upon the efficacy of the yet future expiatory sacrifice of Christ. When these two particulars are viewed, thus palpably in immediate connection with each other, I see not what inference we can draw from them except this: that the bloody sacrifice of Abel's victim, and the bloody sacrifice of Christ, had a common end; that, as the sacrifice of Abel's victim was expiatory (a conclusion, to which we had previously been brought), the sacrifice of Christ was likewise expiatory; and that, as the faith of Abel was both specially displayed in shedding the

---

[1] See particularly Heb. xi. 8, 9, 10, 11, 13, 17, 18, 19, 24, 26, 28, 39, 40. and xii. 1, 2, viewed in connection.

blood of his victim and was likewise exercised on the sufferings of the future redeemer, the slaughter of the victim and the death of Christ stood in some sort of mutual relation.

III. Such a conclusion as this being inevitably drawn, so far as I can judge, from the language of the apostle considered as explanatory of the narrative of Moses, we are next led to inquire into the nature of that mutual relation, which subsists between the two piacular sacrifices of Abel's victim and the promised Messiah.

Now reason itself may teach us, independent of revelation, that the sins of man cannot really be transferred to an animal victim, and that the slaughter of an unintelligent beast can possess no proper inherent efficacy towards the expiating of transgression. But on this point revelation is not silent, either under the Law or under the Gospel. The sacrifices of animals, when rested on as *intrinsically* piacular, are declared to be vain and abominable: and we are expressly assured, that *it is not possible, that the blood of bulls and of goats should take away sin.*[1] Yet, notwithstanding these assertions, we are taught even in Scripture itself, that expiation was the end of animal sacrifices: and we know, that such a belief prevailed alike among the Gentiles, the Israelites, and the ancient patriarchs. This being the case, since animal sacrifices are not intrinsically piacular, since they were nevertheless ordained by God from the beginning, since a piacular virtue has in all ages and countries been attributed to them, and since the opinion has been sanctioned by the voice of revelation itself: we can only conclude, to avoid a palpable contradiction, that their piacular efficacy was not real but figurative; that they were expiatory, solely as shadowing out a proper expiation; and that, since the bloody sacrifice of an animal, and the predicted Messiah, stood (as we collect from the apostle) immediately associated in the faith of Abel, the sacrifice of that animal, and thence all other sacrifices, ought to be deemed (what divines call) *typical* of the sacrifice of Christ. Such in fact is the reasoning, and such the conclusion, of St. Paul in his epistle to the Hebrews: and the result of the whole investigation will be, that the widely-prevailing notion of the expiatory virtue of sacrifice ori-

[1] Isaiah i. 11, 12, 13. Heb. x. 4.

III. EACH SACRIFICE SHADOWED OUT THE FUTURE SACRIFICE OF MESSIAH

ginated from the circumstance of the rite having been first ordained by God to prefigure the mode and intent of the mysterious piacular sacrifice of the redeemer.

1. I think there is reason to believe, that the patriarchs understood, though darkly and imperfectly, that the promised liberator, who was destined to bruise the head of the serpent while the poisonous reptile should bruise his heel, would become a victim to expiate the sins of mankind by bearing in their stead the whole weight of almighty wrath.

Some such idea must have been suggested to the mind of Abraham by the enjoined, though interrupted, sacrifice of his son ; provided only that he was aware, that the whole transaction was what the apostle styles *a figure* or *parable*.[1] That he possessed this degree of insight into the nature of the transaction, cannot indeed be proved from the narrative of Moses independent of the authoritative elucidation of St. Paul: but that elucidation seems clearly to presume, that he *did* understand its nature. He is said to have parabolically devoted his son by that same faith, which he possessed in common with all the other patriarchs. But the faith, of which the apostle is here treating, is faith in a promised Redeemer. Therefore the parabolical sacrifice and recovery of Isaac, being connected with this faith, must also in the mind of Abraham have been connected with the subject of his faith: in other words, they must have been viewed as exhibiting the future sacrifice and recovery of him, in whose advent he believed that all nations of the earth would be blessed.

With the opinion here advanced a remarkable expression, in the Phenician account of the sacrifice of the only son of Cronus, most singularly coincides. That legend bears so close a resemblance to the history of the prevented sacrifice of Isaac, that, with Bochart and other writers who have discussed the subject, I think there can be little doubt of the former having been borrowed from the latter. Now we are told, that the son of Cronus, and all others who were devoted in a similar manner, were sacrificed MYSTI-CALLY.[2] Such, it seems, was the opinion of the Phenicians: and, as they

[1] Heb. xi. 19.

[2] Κατεσφαττοντο δε οἱ διδομενοι ΜΥΣΤΙΚΩΣ. Euseb. Præp. Evan. lib. i. c. 10. lib. iv. c. 16.

borrowed the *legend* from the sacrifice of Isaac, the presumption is, that the *opinion* was derived from the same source. But, if the opinion was derived from the same source (and it is hard to say, from what other source such an opinion *could* have been derived); then Abraham must have believed, that the whole transaction in which he was engaged was of a mystical nature. And, if he believed it to be of a mystical nature, then he must have believed, that it shadowed out something more than met the eye : for such is the only idea, which we can attach to a mystical exhibition. This then being apparently Abraham's view of the matter, I see not how we can suppose him to have beheld the transaction as a *mystical* one ; unless with the eye of faith he looked forward through it to the death and revival of him, who on the present memorable occasion was typified by Isaac. And, that he *did* thus look forward, or in other words that he *did* consider the transaction as a mystical one, is not obscurely intimated by our Lord himself. *Abraham,* says he, *rejoiced to see my day : he saw it, and was glad.* Now, it may be asked, when was it that Abraham saw what is emphatically called *the day of Christ,* except he beheld it scenically in the devoting and recovering of Isaac ? And, if he beheld it at that time, he must have deemed the transaction a mystical one. But this is the very conclusion, to which we had previously been brought, by considering the Phenician legend and the opinion attached to it.

2. The sentiment however itself, I mean the sentiment that *piacular sacrifices only shadowed out the expiatory oblation of a nobler victim,* must have been prior to the days of Abraham, and must have been even familiar to the early patriarchs both antediluvian and postdiluvian. This I gather from a very singular pagan notion ; which cannot easily be accounted for on any other theory, but which on this is very readily explained.

The notion appears with the greatest distinctness in the mythology of Hindostan, but it may likewise be traced in other kindred systems. We have seen, that in more than one instance the predicted characteristic of the Messiah, *his treading on the crushed head of the serpent,* is ascribed to the great father ; although he is a compound of Adam and Noah, and therefore a totally distinct personage from the Messiah. The circumstance doubtless originated from the humour of decorating him with every divine function, when once they elevated a mere mortal to the rank of supreme deity. Agreeably to this humour, I apprehend, the Hindoos represent the great father, under the appellation of *Brahma*, as being solemnly offered up in sacrifice by the assembled gods. He is expressly denominated *a victim*: and, by the immolation of *him*, which is spoken of as a primeval duty, the hero-gods, or deified ancestors of mankind, are said to attain heaven, where former gods and mighty demigods abide. Yet, even while engaged in sacrificing him, such was his dignity, that they worshipped the victim whom they immolated.[1]

This idea, which may readily be accounted for on the supposition that the future expiatory sacrifice of the Messiah was obscurely known to the early patriarchs, enters into the whole theory of Hindoo oblation. The devoted victim, especially if he be a man, is considered as indentified with the god to whom he is offered: and, as such, he is, previous to his immolation, adored by the sacrificer; just as the hero-gods are feigned to have adored their nobler victim Brahma. The worship paid to him is likewise declared to be of a *mysterious* nature.[2] This sentiment exactly corresponds with the

---

[1] *The embodied spirit, which hath a thousand heads, a thousand eyes, a thousand feet, stands in the human breast, while he totally pervades the earth—That three-fold being rose above this world—From him sprang Viraj; from whom the first man was produced: and he, being successively reproduced, peopled the earth—Him the gods, the demigods, named Sadhya; and the holy sages immolated him as a victim on sacred grass, and thus performed a solemn act of religion. Into how many portions did they divide this being, whom they immolated? What did his mouth become? What are his arms, his thighs, and his feet, now called? His mouth became a priest: his arm was made a soldier: his thigh was transformed into a husbandman: from his feet sprang the servile man—In that solemn sacrifice which the gods performed with him as a victim, spring was the butter, summer the fuel, and sultry weather the oblation. Seven were the moats surrounding the altar; thrice seven were the logs of holy fuel; at that sacrifice, which the gods performed, immolating this being as the victim. By that sacrifice the gods worshipped this victim. Such were primeval duties; and thus did they attain heaven, where former gods and mighty demigods abide. Asiat. Research. vol. vii. p. 251, 252.*

[2] *Causing the victim to face the north, let the sacrificer worship the several deities presiding over the different parts of the victim's body: let the worship be then paid to the victim himself by his name—O best of men! O most auspicious! O thou, who art an assemblage of all the deities, and most exquisite! Bestow thy protection upon me; and part with thy organs of life, doing an act of benevolence!—Thus let the sacrificer worship the victim. When this has been*

Phenician doctrine, that piacular oblations of human victims for the safety of the state were to be considered as something *mystical;* and the Hindoo code teaches us, *how* they are mystical: each victim shadows out the victim Brahma, through the offering of whom the hero-gods attain the felicity of heaven; and he is at once worshipped and immolated, as representing what they denominate *the great universal sacrifice.*

A similar notion seems to have prevailed among the ancient Chinese: for their great father Fo-hi, who is the same as Fo or Buddha, and who in character must ultimately be identified with Brahma, is styled by them, as Brahma is by the Hindoos, *the victim* or *oblation.* So appropriate indeed is this title deemed, that it is even incorporated with his name; for the syllable *Hi* in *Fo-hi* denotes (we are told) *a victim:* whence the compound appellation *Fo-hi* will signify *Fo the victim.*[1]

This opinion, unless I am much mistaken, has given rise to the fable of Hercules burning himself on the summit of mount Œta. Hercules may be shewn to be the same as Fohi or Buddha, and like them ultimately the same also as Brahma and Bali. Now his self immolation, disfigured as the legend has been by Hellenic fabulists, bears the closest resemblance in almost every particular to a sacrifice. He burns himself on a pile of wood: this pile is designedly erected on the top of mount Œta: and mount Œta was one of the high places of Jupiter, where sacrifices were wont to be offered up to him. Hence, when the hero mentions his purpose to his son Hyllus, the youth is represented by Sophocles as saying, that he well knew

---

done, O my children! the victim is even as myself, and the guardian deities of the ten quarters take place in him. Then Brahma and all the other deities assemble in the victim: and, be he ever so great a sinner, he becomes pure from sin and his blood changes to ambrosia—On occasions of sacrifices to other deities also, both the deities and victims must be worshipped, previous to the immolation—Having first worshipped the victim, whether human, beast, or bird, as directed, let the sacrificer immolate him, and address the deity with the text laid down before. This worship of the victim is expressly declared to be mysterious. Let the sacrificer say, Mysterious praise to this victim. Asiat. Res. vol. v. p. 379, 380, 381, 382, 386.

[1] Asiat. Res. vol. ii. p. 375. Le Compte's China. p. 310. Le Compte was so struck with the singularity of the title, that he observed upon it, that *it was a name, which the greatest saints of the Old or New Testament would have been proud to have, and which was reserved for him alone who made himself an oblation both for saints and sinners.*

the place having frequently stood there as a sacrificer : and the scholiast aptly remarks, that Œta and every other high hill was styled *the hill of Jupiter*, because to the loftiest of the gods sacrifices ought to be offered on the loftiest eminences.[1] I am the more confirmed in this supposition, both by the general character of Hercules, who is certainly the great father, and who yet like Vishnou is described as treading on the head of the serpent; and likewise by finding, that the Egyptians had actually a story of his being led bound as a victim for the purpose of being sacrificed to Jupiter. He is said indeed to have successfully resisted the attempt to immolate him : but this I take to have been a corruption of the genuine legend made either by the Greeks or the Egyptians themselves.[2]

Among this latter people we may also observe the Hindoo theory, that each victim represented the god to whom it was devoted. We learn from Diodorus, that the Egyptians sacrificed red bulls, because the sacred colour of Typhon was supposed to be red; and that their ancient sovereigns were wont, for the same reason, to immolate on the tomb or high-place of Osiris men of a ruddy complexion.[3] Hence it appears, that a resemblance between the god and the victim, so that the victim might fitly represent the god, was studiously aimed at : and it may be observed, that, by what was termed *the mystic theocrasia*, the character of Typhon finally melts into that of Osiris.

The notion, which is so eminently conspicuous in Hindoo theology, appears again with equal distinctness in the religion of the Mexicans; and was doubtless, with the rest of their superstition, brought by their forefathers out of Asia. We are told by the Spanish historians, that they had a strange kind of idol, which was not an image, but a true man. For, when they took a captive, before they sacrificed him, they gave to him the name of the idol to which he was destined to be offered; and, in order to make the resemblance as complete as possible, they decorated him with the same ornaments. During the time that this mummery continued, they worshipped him precisely as they did the god, whom he represented. When he went through the streets, the people came forth to adore him, and brought their

---

[1] Soph. Trachin. ver. 1208. Schol. in ver. 1207. [2] Herod. lib. ii. c. 45.
[3] Diod. Bibl. lib. i. p. 79.

children and their sick that he might bless and cure them.   In every thing he was suffered to have his pleasure, except only that he was always attended by ten or twelve men lest he should make his escape : and he himself, that he might be duly reverenced when he appeared in public, sometimes sounded a small flute by way of giving notice of his approach.   But, when the feast-day arrived, this victim-god, who had for months been an object of religious veneration, was solemnly devoted in sacrifice.[1]

To the same source may be traced the misdeemed meritorious suicides and rigid macerations of the Hindoos.   It was an established principle of Paganism, that the priests and the mystæ represented the god whom they venerated.   On this account they assumed the titles of the deity; and, in the course of their initiation into his orgies, they exhibited in their own persons all that he was believed to have done and suffered.   Now, since among other matters he was believed to have been offered up as a victim, and since every victim was thought to symbolize him, his frantic votaries were led to imagine, that no service could be more acceptable than self-immolation; by which they should first imitate his sacrificial death, and afterwards be really made one with him by a rapturous absorption into his essence.   Such is the boon held out in the Institutes of Menu to the Brahmen, who, after undergoing every variety of willing torture, should finally procure death by resolute inanition.   *Let him advance in a straight path towards the invincible north-eastern point, feeding on water and air till his mortal frame totally decay, and his soul become united with the supreme.   A Brahmen, having shuffled off his body by any of those modes which great sages practised, and becoming void of sorrow and fear, rises to exaltation in the divine essence.*[2]   The whole of this long-continued meditative austerity, which is most meritorious if it end in a voluntary death, is mystically considered in the light of a sacrifice.   *He, who frequently performs disinterested acts of religion, becomes for ever exempt from a body composed of the five elements.   Equally perceiving the Supreme soul in all beings and all beings in the Supreme soul, he sacrifices his own spirit by*

[1] Purch. Pilg. b. viii. c. 11. 796. 797.
[2] Instit. of Menu. chap. vi. p. 148, 149.

fixing it on the spirit of God, and approaches the nature of that sole divinity who shines by his own effulgence.[1] Such is the principle, that actuates the wretched suicides who cast themselves beneath the wheels of the ponderous car of Jagan-Nath. This deity unites in his own person the triple divinity of the Hindoos; and he is likewise the same as Buddha, in whom that triple divinity is similarly united. Jagan-Nath therefore, being one with Brahma and Fo-hi, is a victim-god; and his imitative votaries seek to propitiate him by themselves becoming willing victims, in hopes of thus being hereafter blissfully swallowed up in his essence.

All these various instances teach us, in what sense the Phenicians esteemed their piacular sacrifices *mystical*. The slaughtered victim represented the victim god, and was worshipped as his proxy: but the idea of a victim-god, whom the erring pagans identified with their great father, was apparently taken from the patriarchal belief, that he, whose heel should be bruised by the infernal serpent, should in fulness of time become a piacular sacrifice for the sins of the whole world.

3. It is obvious, that expiatory oblations necessarily presuppose guilt on the part of the offerer: and accordingly an idea of lost integrity seems to have pervaded nearly the whole world, and to have entered (as we shall hereafter see) into the very essence of the pagan mysteries.

Several ancient writers use very remarkable language concerning this point. According to Hierocles, there is a meadow of destruction and a meadow of truth. The desire of fleeing from the one impels the soul towards the other: but, stripped of her plumage, she is precipitated from it, and enters into an earthly body deprived of her former happy estate.[2] This deplumation of the soul he afterwards styles, in plain terms, *a flight* or *apostasy from God :*[3] and he says, that it is the same as the Platonic descent or lapse of the soul through some great calamity which she has experienced.[4] *Most men,* he observes, *are bad; and are, by the violence of their passions, bowed down to the earth. But this evil they have brought upon themselves*

[1] Instit. of Menu. chap. xii. p. 357.
[2] Hieroc. in Aur. Carm. p. 254.
[3] Ibid. p. 257.   [4] Ibid. p. 254.

*by their voluntary apostasy from God, and by their withdrawing them-
selves from that communion with him which they once in a pure light enjoyed. The reality of such a mental alienation from the Supreme Being is
proved by our strong tendency towards the earth : and our sole deliverance
from this state of spiritual degradation is our return unto him.*[1] Plato, in
a similar manner, speaks of the bondage of the soul; and laments, as its
worst misfortune, that it not only disregarded its captivity, but lent its own
assistance to rivet the chain.[2] He even asserts the doctrine of original sin;
a tenet, which he probably learned from his intercourse with the Jews. *The
cause of our wickedness,* says he, *is derived from our parents and the constitution of our nature, rather than from ourselves ; so that we never relinquish those actions, by which we imitate the primitive fault of our first
ancestors.*[3] And he tells us, that he had been informed by the wise, that
we are now dead, and that the body is no more than the soul's sepulchre.[4]
The era, to which he ascribes the commencement of this depravation, is
the end of the golden age or the age of innocence in Paradise:[5] that is to
say, he ascribes it to the period where Scripture places the fall of man.

---

[1] Ibid. p. 261, 262.

[2] Plut. Phæd. § 33. The following are some of the remarkable expressions employed by
him :—ατεχνως διαδεδεμενην—ως αν μαλιστα αυτος ο δεδεμενος ξυλλγπτωρ ειη τω δεδεσθαι—
ο παντων μεγιστον τε κακων και εσχατον εστι, τουτο πασχει, και ου λογιζεται αυτο.

[3] Plat. Tim. p. 103.   [4] Plat. Gorg. p. 493.

[5] Plat. Polit. p. 251.

END OF VOL. I.

Printed in the United States
65282LVS00003B/6

9 780766 193376